ON DESCARTES' METAPHYSICAL PRISM

ON DESCARTES' METAPHYSICAL PRISM

The Constitution and the Limits of Onto-theo-logy in Cartesian Thought

✴

JEAN-LUC MARION

Translated by Jeffrey L. Kosky

The University of Chicago Press
Chicago and London

JEAN-LUC MARION is professor of philosophy at the Sorbonne.
He has written a number of books on philosophy,
including *God without Being* (1991) and *Cartesian Questions* (1999),
both published in translation by the University of Chicago Press.

The University of Chicago Press, Chicago 60637
The University of Chicago Press, Ltd., London
© 1999 by The University of Chicago
All rights reserved. Published 1999
07 06 05 04 03 02 01 00 99 1 2 3 4 5

ISBN: 0-226-50538-3 (cloth)
ISBN: 0-226-50539-1 (paper)

Originally published as *Sur le prisme métaphysique de Descartes,*
© Presses Universitaires de France, 1986.

Library of Congress Cataloging-in-Publication Data

Marion, Jean-Luc. 1946–
   [Sur le prisme méthaphysique de Descartes. English]
   On Descartes' metaphysical prism : the constitution and the limits of onto-
theology in Cartesian thought / Jean-Luc Marion ; translated by Jeffrey L. Kosky.
      p.   cm.
   Includes bibliographical references and index.
   ISBN 0-226-50538-3 (hardcover : alk. paper).—ISBN 0-226-50539-1 (pbk. : alk.
paper)
   1. Descartes, René, 1596–1650—Contributions in metaphysics.
   2. Metaphysics.   I. Title.
B1878.M5M3713   1999
110′.92—dc21   98-35104
                                                                            CIP

⊗The paper used in this publication meets the minimum requirements
of the American National Standard for Information Sciences—
Permanence of Paper for Printed Library Materials,
ANSI Z39.48-1992.

CONTENTS

Translator's Acknowledgments

If this translation could be held to a prism of its own, one would see in the spectrum of its refracted light the contributions of numerous persons whose care, encouragement, and assistance have lent their color to what I, something of a prism in reverse, have composed here. Since these individual colors are perhaps no longer visible in the work that follows, I want these acknowledgments to serve as just such a prism, letting those who have colored my composition be seen and thanked in their own light.

Above all, thanks are due to Jean-Luc Marion, a friend, for seeing something in me that I did not and inviting me to undertake this project. This translation has benefited greatly from his reading, his comments, and his confidence that I was the man for the job. The time needed to do this work would not have been possible without the support of my parents, Michael and Marsha Kosky, and that time would not have been enough without the patience of David Brent at the University of Chicago Press and of Dan Garber, who waited to read and comment on the whole. I also want to thank Jeffrey Stern for his unflagging care and support; without it, all the time in the world would not have been enough for the work to get done. Thomas Carlson offered indefatigable encouragement as well as invaluable help with difficult passages and always seemed able to find a light at the end of the tunnel. His companionship made the time of this translation far less lonesome. Finally, thanks are due to the people of Redmoon Theater in Chicago—especially Angela Goodrich, Dodie Holderfield, Jim Lasko, Kristi Randall, Tria Smith, and Blair Thomas—who have given me so much more than a place to work.

J. L. K.
Chicago, November 1997

It is always strange for an author to see one of his books live a new life ten years after the first by passing from one language to another. One cannot help wondering how far the second life will differ from the first, possibly improving it or perhaps contradicting it. But when one is dealing with the passage from French to English of a work in the history of philosophy, especially a work whose characteristics, according to the majority of its readers, belong to a typically "continental" style, the author finds himself as surprised as he could possibly be.

How could he not be surprised, seeing a translation of a book dedicated to Descartes? First because, for obvious technical reasons, editors often hesitate, in the United States as everywhere else, to assume the tasks inherent to such a process (not only to have the text translated, but here to translate and retain the Greek and Latin in the notes and the citations). Consequently, I feel obliged to acknowledge the generosity and serious-mindedness of the University of Chicago Press, which in the person of David Brent has not shrunk before the effort and the investment. I am honored to see one of my works, in France reputed to be technical or, worse yet, a commentary on a single author, transported to the other side of the Atlantic. This is something quite unusual, and I am well aware of its cost.

But there is still more that is surprising: at issue is a book dedicated to Descartes. One can, without prejudice, say that American philosophy has never held Descartes to be one of its founding fathers, but has long considered him the a priori and deductive thinker par excellence, condemning experience and empiricism, refuted by Locke and by Newton, too religious for some, almost atheistic for others, and only to be used as a source of "logical flaws," furnishing material for the debates of analytic philosophy (the "self," the inconclusive proofs for the existence of God, and the all-too-famous "Cartesian circle" and "mind-body problem," etc.). This book (in fact, these books, since the English translation of *Questions cartésiennes* is being published almost concurrently with the translation of *Sur le prisme métaphysique de Descartes*) therefore could not have appeared if, first, Descartes' image in the United States had not been profoundly modified.[1] Without this evolution, it would have been impossible to imagine an intellectual interest and a public for such a book.[2] I feel obliged here to acknowledge the remarkable efforts of R. Popkin, G. Sebba, M. Wilson, H. Frankfurt, E. Curley, R. Kennington, R. Watson, and many others, but also, more recently, those of C. Larmore, R. Ariew, S. Nadler, D. Des Chesne, and a host of additional young researchers. Above all, though, I must acknowledge my first friend at the University of Chicago, Daniel Garber. As much by his decisive publications—be they individual (as *The Metaphysical Physics of Descartes*) or collective (recently, with M. Ayers, the monumental *Cambridge History of Seventeenth-Century Philosophy*)—as by his national and international intellectual influence, my esteemed colleague from Hyde Park has contributed powerfully to the development of Cartesian studies, the establishment of real and persistent intellectual connections between the two coasts of the Atlantic, and hence to the production of a new, more exact, and above all more intelligent and complex image of Descartes' thought and the role he plays in the history of philosophy. Thus the present translation reflects, for the most part, a collaboration begun in the mid-1980s when, invited for the first time to give a lecture in the United States (at Columbia University), I met, at my friend and host Charles Larmore's house, an unknown, most kind, and very learned man, Daniel Garber. Since this meeting, not a year has passed without our working together and without my coming to the United States to pursue the advances in philosophy, with the hope of contributing to them. By joint colloquia that became collective works, by exchanges that became translations, a continuum was set up between the two countries and the ways of working. Now, the waters on both sides of the locks have risen to the same level, the gates can open, and the passage can be completed. What is astonishing for me therefore is perhaps that I no longer have to be astonished by what, from the outside or twenty years ago, would have stunned me.

This book, however, could still surprise some readers—not by chance,

---

1. See an outline of this evolution in "Le paradigme cartésien de la métaphysique," Actes du colloque pour le quatrième centenaire de la naissance de Descartes, *Laval théologique et philosophique*, 53/3, Québec, 1997.

2. The same is true for an undertaking as important and significant as the translation of Descartes' writings by J. Cottingham, Robert Stoothof, and Dugald Murdoch for Cambridge University Press.

but for very understandable reasons. I assume certain hermeneutic principles that are not universally acknowledged, either here or in France. I would like briefly to identify and make a case for them.

First of all, I assume that the history of philosophy must remain philosophical. There is nothing more illusory, and therefore dangerous, than claiming or imagining that one can accede to a text (to an author) without any presupposition, without any prior philosophical decision. The viewpoint of "simple common sense," supposing it can ever really be maintained, or even acquired, already refers to a vision of the world in which this "common sense" makes sense. For, in order to interpret a text of philosophy, whether by another author or from the distant past or from another culture, one must always already have come to philosophy itself in one form or another. This hermeneutic circle has nothing vicious about it. On the contrary, it alone ensures the philosophical virtue of the history of philosophy. Here it is important to emphasize that I clearly distinguish the history of philosophy from the history of ideas (at least in its European sense), in that the former implies a philosophical vision while the latter attempts to get by without one (perhaps without ever succeeding). Further, not only does the history of philosophy imply a philosophical experience, but, reciprocally, philosophy always implies, in each moment of its evolution, a reappropriation of its history. Otherwise it risks repeating options and orientations that have already been tried and realized in the past but have partially or totally failed. Above all, in philosophically rereading its own history, philosophy becomes conscious that none of its contemporary positions could have taken shape if they had not responded, more or less directly, to questions posed earlier. In short, we can read Descartes only if we have at least a precomprehension of what the philosophical operations of thought, of doubt, of the *ego,* of representation, of the infinite, etc., mean to say or can say. And today we would not have to respond to the question of the intentionality of thought, or of linguistic acts, or of self-consciousness, if a tradition, born for the most part with Descartes, had not imposed these questions on us.[3]

3. This is what distinguishes philosophy from the exact sciences, which have no need of meditating on their history in order to progress, but perhaps not from the history of those sciences. This history supposes a contemporary normative model (if not one absolutely true) in order to reconstruct or interpret past scientific situations. I fully subscribe to the judgment of Dan Garber: ". . . the history of philosophy can be important not because it leads to philosophical truths, but because it leads to philosophical questions." See Garber, "Does History Have a Future? Some Reflections on Bennett and Doing Philosophy Historically," in Peter Hare, ed., *Doing Philosophy Historically* (Buffalo, N.Y.: Prometheus Press, 1988), p. 40.

Next, I assume that the history of philosophy, the history of any period of philosophy, can and must become a special occasion for resolving or at least posing a question that is essential to contemporary philosophy. Contemporary philosophy has run into—and there is no need to confirm this with many arguments—an investigation of "the end of philosophy," often conveyed and divulged by the goal of "deconstructing" the "metaphysics of presence," which involves tracking down the latter in all figures of philosophy, especially the most eminent. These investigations, which come for the most part from Heidegger (on whom Derrida depends) are not merely fashionable, even though they can sometimes become so. At issue is a debate essential to every philosophical attempt, which asks if it bears on presence, subsistence, in short on Being such as it could (and should), after having triumphed in Hegel, be radically put into question starting with Nietzsche. Heidegger here retrieves a hermeneutic that is, strangely enough, approached by authors as different from him as Etienne Gilson or, in his own way, Carnap and logical positivism (without even broaching the case of Wittgenstein). For they all converge on at least one point: they all put into question the equivalence between the present task of philosophy and the historically completed "metaphysics"; in short, they all put into question the uninvestigated preeminence of its key concepts—"presence," "essence," "being" rather than "Being," "ground," "cause," etc. Today, we should carry on this debate, if only to guarantee for philosophy an authentic, not merely a documentary or ideological, possibility. To conduct this debate properly, without reducing it to ideological confrontations and simplistic slogans, it is necessary to examine, in central but precise cases—in this instance that of Descartes—the following questions: (1) Strictly speaking, is a metaphysics at issue in this philosophy? Thus one must also investigate the meaning or meanings of "metaphysics" appropriate in this case.[4] (2) Does what falls within metaphysics in this philosophy exhaust it entirely, expose it to its overcoming by another thought, itself not metaphysical, or by itself such that it partly removes itself from what remains metaphysical in it?[5] By pursuing these investigations step by step (and by repeating

4. Here I use two distinct meanings: (a) *metaphysica* in the sense that, beginning with the later scholastics, it is constituted in a system (and it is not certain that Descartes is unambiguously inscribed within it; see chapter I); and (b) "metaphysics" in the speculative sense that Heidegger understands it—as onto-theo-logy (and Descartes seems to assume this model, while complicating it; see chapter II).

5. Here the philosophy of Descartes is overcome as metaphysics, at once globally by Pascal (chapter V) and partially by itself (chapter III, §15; chapter IV, §20).

this work in the case of other leading authors of the tradition) it becomes, or will become, possible to reach a precise determination of the nature and the limits of "metaphysics" in general, of onto-theo-logy in particular. Only on this condition could the legitimate but often unreflective and illusory goal of thinking in a nonmetaphysical way find *a contrario* some determination. Once again, in this case particularly (but in others too, no doubt), only the history of philosophy permits a rational confrontation with questions that are decisive for philosophy itself.

I assume finally that there is no contradiction between, on the one hand, a conceptual, speculative, and even (within certain limits) systematic interpretation of an author and, on the other, erudition. The authors who, on the one hand, made and published the first electronic index to Descartes, continued and expanded the bibliography begun by G. Sebba, retranslated and annotated his previously marginalized texts, and finally reconstructed his neo-scholastic environment are the same ones who, on the other, put to use the interpretive models built by Kant, Hegel, Husserl, and Heidegger. Historical ignorance does not suffice for reaching speculative excellence, any more than conceptual weakness guarantees a flawless positivity. In this sense, Hegel, Heidegger, and even Nietzsche have done more for understanding certain of Descartes' most difficult texts than the troops of critics who pride themselves on ignoring the contributions of these philosophers.

I hope that in the following pages these methodological assumptions will become acceptable to the majority of my readers and that the initial surprise will dissipate and simply leave a place for the thing and its question. In any case, readers are always right and in the end understand quite well the intention and the drift of a book. This has been my experience not only in France but even more in the United States. It is therefore with confidence that I leave this book to its second life.

There remain just a few details to add. (1) Since the French edition of this work appeared in 1986, an earlier work of mine, on which it was by and large based, entitled *Sur la théologie blanche de Descartes* (in the series "Philosophie d'aujourd'hui"; Paris: Presses universitaires de France, 1981), went into a second edition in 1991 (in "Quadrige"; Paris: PUF). Expanded and corrected, it validates it. (2) Similarly, one must consider *Questions cartésiennes* (Paris: PUF, 1991; translated as *Cartesian Questions*, University of Chicago Press, 1999) and *Questions cartésiennes II* (Paris: PUF, 1996) as commentaries, confirmations, and sometimes corrections of the theses advanced in the 1986 work, which I still consider the focus of the interpretation. (3) Last but not least, chapter V, "Overcoming," has itself since been overcome, developed, and confirmed by the remarkable work of my former student, now my colleague at the University of Caen, Vincent Carraud, *Pascal et la philosophie* (Paris: PUF, 1992).

I owe a final debt of gratitude, in fact a tribute of my esteem and admiration, to Jeffrey Kosky. He was my student at the University of Chicago; he soon became a friend as well as a skilled translator, to the point and especially intelligent about what was essential. As with Thomas Carlson (University of California at Santa Barbara), I judge myself very fortunate to have been gifted with such translators in the full sense of the word—such interpreters.

J.-L. M.
Chicago, May 1998

PREFACE

We here offer up the conclusion of a double Cartesian triptych. The first, centering on our study *Sur l'ontologie grise de Descartes* (Paris, 1975), consisted of an annotated translation of *Règles utiles et claires pour la direction de l'esprit en la recherche de la vérité* (La Haye, 1977) and an *Index des Regulae ad directionem ingenii* (in collaboration with J.-R. Armogathe, Rome, 1976). By interpreting Descartes' first great text in terms of the question of Being and beings, we were able to establish a Cartesian ontology as the first panel in a second triptych. This was then balanced out by a study *Sur la théologie blanche de Descartes* (Paris, 1981), which zeroed in on the essential ambiguity of the first foundation in what Descartes had established. But the central element still remained. This is what we venture to put forth today, the last really but the first conceptually, since it tries to determine the Cartesian figure of onto-theo-logy. Circumstances as well as a certain novelty to the questions mean that we cannot base ourselves here as much as elsewhere on the works of previous or contemporary interpreters. We are thus exposing ourselves to originalities that we would have preferred to avoid, and we adopt a dispassionate discussion, so that the argument might finish with a decision about what is true and what is false in our results. Having already benefited from this fruitful debate, we hope for it again today.

This work would not have been possible without the amicable assistance of several institutions—the Société française de Philosophie (and its president, Professor Jacques D'Hondt), the University of Tübingen (and Professor L. Œing-Hanhoff)—and of Professor Amélie O. Rorty (University of Rutgers, New Jersey), whom I would like to thank here. I also owe much to the comments of my friends J.-R. Armogathe (EPHE, Paris), J.-M. Beyssade (Université Paris X), J.-F. Courtine (CNRS, Paris), C. Larmore (Columbia University, New York), P. Magnard (Université de Poitiers), and W. Röd (University of Innsbruck).
Finally, I am pleased to acknowledge, with this work, the students

and my colleagues in the department of philosophy at the Université de Poitiers, who accommodated me and are pursuing, despite an environment that is difficult at times, the tradition of real philosophy in a place where Descartes spent the last years of his university life.*

J.-L. M.
Poitiers, 15 September 1985–19 May 1986

*The discovery, by J.-R. Armogathe and V. Carraud, of the doctoral thesis defended by Descartes on 21 December 1616 at Poitiers confirms that he really was "admitted to the ranks of the learned" (AT VI, 4, 27 = PW I, 113). See "Bulletin Cartésien XV," *Archives de Philosophie,* 1982/1, p. 1–4, and *Nouvelles de la République des lettres,* 1988/2, pp. 123–45.

BIBLIOGRAPHICAL NOTE

References to Descartes are cited according to the Adam-Tannery edition, *Œuvres de Descartes* (new edition by P. Costabel and B. Rochot, Paris, Vrin-CNRS, 1966–), which is abbreviated AT. We have indicated the volume number, the page, and the line—except in the case of the *Meditationes et Responsiones,* where we have sometimes omitted the volume number (VII), and in that of the *Discours de la Méthode,* which we have abbreviated DM without including the volume number (VI).[1]

For the other authors, the complete reference is given when they first appear; thereafter, they are referred to with (op. cit.).

In the body of the text, all the citations in foreign languages have been translated; in this case the original appears in a note. There is one exception, however: the Latin texts of Descartes have been kept in their original, without being translated, in accordance with a principle followed in *Sur la théologie blanche de Descartes,* Paris, 1981 (see p. 7).[2]

Finally, may we be excused for citing ourselves more often than good taste will tolerate. This is done only out of a concern for concision: we refer to former analyses, absolutely indispensable to setting forth their present conclusion, so as not to have to repeat them and not to overburden an already long text.

1. All English translations of Descartes' work have been taken from *The Philosophical Writings of Descartes,* ed. John Cottingham, Robert Stoothof, and Dugald Murdoch. (Cambridge: Cambridge University Press, 1985), which is abbreviated PW. References to the English translation are included along with references to AT following a "=." They indicate first the volume number (I, II, or III), then the page number. In certain cases, the text cited has not been included in PW, in which case we have noted as much.—Trans.

2. Though this is true of the French original, it is not so in this English translation—as the reader will soon see. In order to facilitate the reading of this work by its English-speaking audience, the author, the translator, and the editors have added the English translation of Descartes to the body of the text in square brackets.—Trans.

The Closure of a Question

Does Cartesian thought belong to metaphysics? As paradoxical as it seems, this question cannot be avoided. Before attempting to answer it, it is a good idea to construct it. The possibility that Descartes might be foreign to metaphysics is suggested, first and symbolically, by the fact that he did *not* write *Méditations métaphysiques;* for the adjective [*métaphysique,* metaphysical] here comes from a translator's addition to the original title: *Meditationes de prima Philosophia.* Of course, one must not deduce from such a disparity more than it can suggest; but it is the case that current usage constantly attributes to metaphysics an eminent function in a Cartesian title—and even the most important among them—where it does not appear. Without a doubt, this signals a genuine difficulty: if even the most eminent historians continually evoke a "metaphysics" of Descartes, they often do not justify their choice of this term. It is, in effect, one thing to study—masterfully and precisely—the doctrine of the *Meditationes;* it is another to establish that this doctrine carries out what the tradition prior to Descartes understood by the name metaphysics. As much as the first task was and always has been the object of greatest care, the second still remains to be undertaken in an essential way. The same question also holds for those explanations of the doctrine of the *Meditationes* which claims the title of a first philosophy: Does Descartes do justice to what his predecessors understood quite precisely by the title *philosophia prima*? In the present work, we will not attempt to explain the doctrine of the *Meditationes,* contrary to our illustrious forerunners,[1] but to see if and to what extent it constitutes a

---

1. Let us here cite only the title of F. Alquié, *La découverte métaphysique de l'homme chez Descartes* (Paris, 1950 and 1966), in which "metaphysics" is defined only by an indeterminate "passing beyond" ("... Descartes discovered man metaphysically as the power to pass beyond the object towards Being ..." [p. xi]), and that of H. Gouhier (*La pensée métaphysique de Descartes* [Paris, 1962]), who from the outset sets restrictions for his investigation: "This book is not an exposition of Cartesian metaphysics; ... it will even be supposed that this metaphysics is well known ..." (p. 9). It is thus and first of all the very

metaphysics, according to the criteria that used to define it before Descartes and his time.

This undertaking does not seek a forced or artificial originality. Two reasons make it more or less impossible to escape.

(a) First, a historical reason: when Descartes enters the scene, the philosophical tradition has already gained, at the end of a difficult journey going back to the first commentators of Aristotle and traversing all medieval thought, a more or less definite concept of metaphysics. Saint Thomas—who, it might be added, uses the term only infrequently—defines metaphysics in this way: ". . . In metaphysics, the philosopher [Aristotle] at once determines being in general and the first being, which is separate from matter." Suarez—who makes metaphysics a fundamental term—defines it as ". . . the science which contemplates being as being or insofar as it abstracts being from matter."[2] In both cases, metaphysics concerns being, whether it be common and apprehended as such or first and abstracted from matter. But when Kant considers the last scholastic tradition—namely, the philosophy of the German School—what concept of metaphysics does he find? That which is offered to him by, among others, Baumgarten: "Metaphysics is the science which contains the first principles of human knowledge." This is transposed word for word in Kant's precritical writings: "That part of philosophy which contains the first principles of the use of pure intellect is metaphysics."[3] In both these

---

notion of metaphysics that is supposed to be known. Likewise for J. Vuillemin, *Mathématiques et Métaphysique chez Descartes* (Paris, 1960), or for W. Röd, *Descartes' Erste Philosophie* (Bonn, 1971); J.-M. Beyssade, *La philosophie première de Descartes. Le temps et la cohérence de la métaphysique* (Paris, 1979); and L. Beck, *The Metaphysics of Descartes. A Study of the Meditations* (Oxford, 1966), etc. The relevance of these classic studies makes it all the more remarkable that an investigation of the metaphysical essence of Cartesian thought (or the lack thereof) is absent in them.

2. Respectively, Saint Thomas, *In Aristotelis de Generatione et Corruptione, Prooemium 2:* "Et inde est quod Philosophus in Metaphysica simul determinat de ente in communi et de ente primo, quod est a materia separatum" (ed. R. Spiazzi [Rome, 1952], p. 316; see *infra*, chap. I, n. 59); and Suarez, *Disputationes Metaphysicae, I,* s. 3, n. 1: "Sub qua ratione definiri potest metaphysicam esse scientiam quae ens, in quantum ens, seu in quantum a materia abstrahit secundum esse, contemplatur" (*Opera omnia,* ed. C. Berton, vol. 25 [Paris, 1866], p. 22).

3. A. G. Baumgarten, *Metaphysica,* §1: "Metaphysica est scientia prima cognitionis humanae principia continens" (Frankfurt an der Oder, 1739; Halle, 1757; reproduced in *Kants Gesammelte Schriften* [Berlin, 1902–], vol. XVII [Berlin/Leipzig, 1926], p. 23). Then Kant, *De Mundi sensibilis atque intelligibilis forma et principiis,* §8: "Philosophia autem prima continens principia usus intellectus puri est METAPHYSICA" (*Kants Gesammelte Schriften,* vol. II [Berlin, 1902, then 1968 (Akademie-Textausgabe), p. 395] [English trans., p. 157]). See *To Markus Herz,* 21 August 1772, ibid., vol. X, p. 129 [English trans., p. 71]; *Vorle-*

cases, metaphysics no longer concerns being in its various states, but knowledge, which is taken in terms of the human understanding. Accordingly, the *"metaphysics of metaphysics"*[4] will be set forth as a critique of pure reason: metaphysics has already been identified with the principles of the pure understanding, and it is simply repeated by the critique (the critical knowledge) (of the principles) of knowledge. How are we to understand the fact that metaphysics passes so radically from one domain to the other? How is this Copernican revolution in the concept of metaphysics accomplished? Here neither Spinoza nor Malebranche nor even Leibniz seems to be decisive, or, if they are, they owe it to what is Cartesian in them. That is to say, Descartes clearly and consciously marks a reversal in the essence of metaphysics. He suggests it explicitly when commenting on the Latin title that he spells out for the *Meditationes*. In this explanation, he privileges the notion of first philosophy to the detriment of that of metaphysics: "I have not put any title on it, but it seems to me that the most suitable would be *René Descartes' Meditations on First Philosophy* because I do not confine my discussion to God and the soul, but deal in general with all the first things to be known by philosophizing."[5] Here primacy passes decisively from the first being (to be known) to knowledge itself (eventually fixed in a being); inversely, being as such (and even as first) disappears. In the very title of the *Meditationes*, through what is silent in it and equally in its acknowledged intentions, is accomplished the reversal of the definition of metaphysics that opposes the first scholastic to the last, that is, Saint Thomas (and Suarez) to Kant (and the *Schulmetaphysik*). This observation at once calls for confirmation: did Descartes actually and in full knowledge of the facts redefine the previous and contemporary concept of *Metaphysica*? If this is the case, wouldn't the radical modification thus brought to bear on the old concept of metaphysics quite simply forbid one from henceforth maintaining the term and the title? Renouncing the concept of metaphysics, wouldn't Descartes also renounce the very name *Metaphysica* (chapter I)? This line of questioning will

---

sungen über Metaphysik, N. 4360: *"Metaphysica est logica intellectus puri,"* N. 4284: "Metaphysik ist nicht Wissenschaft, nicht Gelehrsamkeit, sondern bloss der sich selbst kennende Verstand, mithin ist es bloss eine Berichtigung des gesunden Verstandes und Vernunft" (op. cit., vol. 17, respectively pp. 518 and 495); N. 5667: "Metaphysik ist das System [der Prinzipien] aller Erkenntnis *a priori* aus Begriffen überhaupt" (ibid., vol. 18 [Berlin, 1928], p. 323; see N. 5674, p. 325).

4. Kant, *To Markus Herz,* 1 May 1781, op. cit., vol. X, p. 269 [English trans., p. 95].

5. Descartes, *To Mersenne,* 11 November 1640 (AT III, 235, 13–18 = PW III, 157).

lead us to exit the historical domain, for the sake of reaching the thing itself.

(b) For conceptual reasons, it is incumbent upon us to ask if the thought of the *Meditationes* can still legitimately lay claim to the title of a *Metaphysica* after having refused the concept of metaphysics elaborated by its predecessors. The answer to this question will also hold the key to granting, or not, the metaphysical authenticity of post-Cartesian philosophies, a matter that, it must be admitted, often remains highly problematic all the way until Kant. To find a satisfactory answer, it is not enough to invoke the authority of Hegel, who draws out a ". . . concept of Descartes' metaphysics."[6] One must have recourse to a concept of metaphysics as such, which can then be used to assess Cartesian thought. Besides the scholastic concept that articulates metaphysics in an ontology (or general metaphysics) and a special metaphysics (divided into rational theology, psychology, and cosmology), we have retained the model proposed by Heidegger, that of an onto-theo-logical constitution of metaphysics. Besides the fact that Schopenhauer had already evoked an ". . . ontotheological proposition of Descartes' . . . ,"[7] this choice is necessary for two reasons, of unequal weight. The most forceful goes without saying: today, the model of an onto-theo-logical constitution appears to be not only the most fruitful, but also one of the only ones available; it is not a question of imposing it on Descartes, but of using it to test in what ways Descartes is constituted according to a figure of onto-theo-logy. Reciprocally, in being applied to Descartes, the onto-theo-logical model will be subject to a new test of its own validity and will undergo some modifications. The confrontation of the one with the other is all the more necessary since, to our knowledge and in the texts published at this time, Heidegger never explicitly attempted an onto-theo-logical hermeneutic of Cartesian thought, while he did venture one in the case of Plato, Aristotle, Leibniz, Kant, Hegel, and Nietzsche. Must we detect in this a new sign of Descartes' problematic metaphysical status? Or, on the contrary, should we see this as evidence that his exceptional metaphysical situation threatens the model of a simple onto-theo-

6. Hegel, *Phänomenologie des Geistes:* ". . . nicht zum Begriffe der Cartesianischen Metaphysik gekommen . . ." (*Gesammelte Werke,* vol. 9, ed. W. Bonsiepen and R. Heede [Hamburg, 1980], p. 313 [English trans., p. 352 (modified)]).

7. Schopenhauer, ". . . den . . . ontotheologischen Satz des Cartesius' ipsa naturae Dei immensitas est causa sive ratio, propter quam nulla causa indiget ad existendum," *Ueber die vierfache Wurzel des Satzes vom zureichenden Grunde,* II, §8. *Sämtliche Werke,* hrg. Deussen (Munich, 1911), Bd. I, 11 [English trans., p. 20].

logy? Their confrontation, at the very least, cannot be avoided.[8] The weaker of the two reasons can now be stated: today, we have recourse to the model of an onto-theo-logical constitution because our previous studies call for it and permit it. In effect, from the beginning, our studies have been organized by reference to onto-theo-logy. *Sur l'ontologie grise de Descartes* attempted to draw out, from behind the appearance (and the reality) of the *Regulae*'s anti-Aristotelian epistemology, the counter-ontology that alone allows the mind to disqualify the οὐσία of beings so that they might be reduced to the rank of objects; an ontology, even one tinted gray and hiding under the cover of a doctrine of certain and evident science, is deployed in what Descartes set forth. *Sur la théologie blanche de Descartes* attempted to identify the place of the first principle and the ambiguity of (the) primordial being. It did so by understanding the 1630 doctrine concerning the creation of the eternal truths as at once a revival of the question of the *analogia entis* and a transition to the problematic of the ground, thus to the principle of reason. Today, we can join these two attempts, both of which aimed to conceive the onto-theological figure of Cartesian thought. Such a project requires much more than an addition, since it implies not only that a single logic harmonize the two beings affected by ontology and theology, but above all that a new term appear, one that is absolutely real though not ontic: metaphysics itself. The gray ontology cannot be articulated with the white theology except in the crucible of a metaphysics, which, older than they are, has been governing them well before it might appear in the daylight of a concept. Thus, we are attempting here to complete the attempt that we have been making for a decade: to constitute Cartesian thought as a fully complete metaphysics (chapter II).[9]

---

8. Here we rely on an attempt outlined previously: "Heidegger et la situation métaphysique de Descartes," *Archives de Philosophie* 38/2 (1975).

9. The formula ". . . constitution of Descartes' metaphysics . . ." is not specifically Heideggerian: for example, it appears at the hand of F. Alquié, "Expérience ontologique et déduction systématique dans la constitution de la métaphysique de Descartes," in *Descartes. Cahiers de Royaumont* (Paris, 1957), p. 10 (reappearing in *Etudes cartésiennes* [Paris, 1982], pp. 31–52). E. Gilson's slow but complete discovery of Cartesian thought's metaphysical status offers a model that is all the more precious in that it remains isolated. On this point, see our study "L'instauration de la rupture: Gilson à la lecture de Descartes," in *Etienne Gilson et nous. La philosophie et son histoire* (Paris, 1980). Inversely, D. Heinrich formulates a result, for which he does not furnish the demonstration: "Man kann also sagen, dass die von Cartesius begründete Ontotheologie die Metaphysik der Neuzeit sowohl auf ihren Höhenpunkt geführt als auch in ihre Krise gebracht hat" (*Der ontologische Gottesbeweis* [Tübingen, 1960], p. 6).

Such constitution—supposing of course that it can be established in the texts—throws a new light on all Cartesian thought. Or more exactly, the onto-theo-logical constitution exercises over Cartesian thought and its evidence something like the effect that a prism has on the light it filters: it causes the metaphysical spectrum of Cartesian thought to appear, since it decomposes it in the way that a prism decomposes natural light. From this spectral decomposition, there has resulted what we already ventured to put forth, with more awkwardness than style, under the titles "gray ontology" and "white theology." Through the prism of onto-theo-logical constitution, even the apparently nonmetaphysical texts of the Cartesian *corpus* display, like so many primary colors, the constituted and constitutive elements of a metaphysics. If, in this third study, there is no longer any color tinting the title, this is because it is no longer a question of one or the other quasi-color of the spectrum, but of the prism itself that produces them and therefore precedes them. Onto-theo-logy remains achromatic precisely because, like a prism, it produces the fundamental metaphysical "colors." Thus, it is incumbent upon us to undertake, from the point of view of onto-theo-logy, a spectral analysis of the fundamental theses of Cartesian thought in order to see if and within what limits they belong to metaphysics. We have retained, for these purposes, two privileged beings, the *ego* (chapter III) and God (chapter IV). In both cases, it is first a question of deciding whether or not these distinguished beings take on the characteristics of onto-theo-logy such as they have been described by the metaphysicians themselves; but it is also a question of testing the coherence and the power of the concept of onto-theo-logy by imposing on it the double burden of interpreting both the primacy of a finite being (the *ego*) and the polysemy of an infinite being (God). The substantiality of the *res cogitans* and the plurality of the divine names thus issue something like two challenges to the onto-theo-logical definition of metaphysics. We are not simply attempting to determine if and how Descartes attains the rank of a metaphysician by being onto-theo-logically constituted; we also intend to put the validity of the onto-theo-logical determination of metaphysics to the test of the Cartesian *corpus*. At the risk of simplifying, for us it is a matter of understanding, verifying, and thus also "falsifying" the thesis, proposed by Heidegger, that there is an essentially onto-theo-logical constitution of metaphysics; we intend to do this by applying it to the philosopher that we know the least poorly, Descartes. By putting an end to this long research, we hope thus to close, at least for ourselves, a twofold question: first, concerning the metaphysical legitimacy of Descartes by analyzing his conceptual spectrum through the prism of onto-theo-logical constitution; next, concerning the validity of onto-theo-logy as the fundamental determination of metaphysics through the test of the Cartesian *corpus*. In both cases, the question will receive a positive answer—up until a certain point only.

For if onto-theo-logical constitution strictly delimits the Cartesian constitution of metaphysics, it fixes its limits; therefore, by closing it, it opens the possibility of its overcoming.

METAPHYSICS

§1. An Undetermined Question

Métaphysique—the term appears neither at the outset nor frequently in Descartes' texts. This fact must be emphasized, and firmly established, before speculating on a possible Cartesian concept of metaphysics. The appearance of the term is belated, insofar as its first occurrence does not appear before the celebrated *Letter to Mersenne* of 15 April 1630, where it still is not yet a matter of the substantive, but of a qualifier: ". . . to prove metaphysical truths . . ." (AT I, 144, 15, see also 144, 4 = PW III, 22). Its appearance remains rare—perhaps in the sense in which Descartes speaks of "a rare body" (AT XI, 23, 5 = PW I, 88): the *Discourse on the Method* will include only two occurrences (there too, just adjectives, DM 31, 15; 38, 3 = PW I, 126; 130), and the *Meditationes* themselves offer only a hapax, still adjectival and disparaging: ". . . valde tenuis et, ut ita dicam, Metaphysica dubitandi ratio [any reason for doubt which . . . is a very slight and, so to speak, metaphysical one] . . ." (AT VII, 36, 24–25 = PW II, 25); or in French: ". . . une opinion bien légère, et pour ainsi dire Métaphysique [a frivolous and, so to speak, metaphysical opinion]" (AT IX-1, 28, 38–39). Would metaphysics be equivalent to the frivolity of a paradoxical behavior, exaggerated and full of sophisms, in short foreign to the sane solidity of authentic knowing? Does Descartes give in to the simplistic and always seductive mockery of the masses, a mockery that disqualifies the very project of metaphysics as such? Before concluding that Descartes indeed closes the question of metaphysics at the very moment of opening it, another fact must be considered. Descartes did not write *Meditationes metaphysicae*, but—as we will see in detail later—*Meditationes de prima Philosophia*, ". . . on first philosophy." This means that the term *metaphysics* owes its reserve to the preeminence of that of first philosophy, which is its double, indeed its replacement. Significant in this regard is the *Letter . . . which may here serve as a preface* to the 1647 French translation of the *Principia*. Here 9 for the first time in a signed work, Descartes officially defines metaphysics, in a famous formulation that reads:

> The first part of [true] philosophy is metaphysics, which contains the principles of knowledge, including the explanation of the principal attributes of God, the non-material nature of our souls and all the clear and distinct notions which are in us.... Thus the whole of philosophy is like a tree. The roots are metaphysics, the trunk is physics, and the branches emerging from the trunk are all the other sciences, which may be reduced to three principle ones, namely medicine, mechanics, and morals. [AT IX-2, 14, 7–28 = PW I, 186.]

This formulation is no doubt too famous, since behind a quite academic clarity it hides several theoretical decisions. It is not self-evident that metaphysics actually does constitute the roots of physics, or anything else, if elsewhere it is admitted that it crowns all the other sciences, as the most "frivolous," abstract, and hyperbolic of them all. Moreover, it is not self-evident that it must be justified in terms of its usefulness by referring to the derived sciences that it would render possible as intermediaries: ". . . just as it is not the roots or the trunk of a tree from which one gathers the fruit, but only the ends of the branches, so the principal use of all philosophy depends on those parts of it which can only be learnt last of all" (15, 1–5 = 186 [modified]). For the indirect usefulness thus accorded to metaphysics would be meaningful only if metaphysics were obliged to be of service to anything else.[1] Above all, this apparently unreserved acknowledgment of metaphysics hides the fact that it does not exert a full and total authority. This is so for a twofold reason. First, because it is inscribed in the larger field of philosophy, and "'philosophy' means the study of wisdom, and by 'wisdom' is meant not only prudence in our everyday affairs but also a perfect knowledge of all things that mankind is capable of knowing, both for the conduct of life and for the preservation of health and the discovery of all manner of skills" (2, 7–13 = 179). Next, because in the philosophical field itself, metaphysics is interchangeable with other denominations—for example, but not by

---

1. The criterion "the usefulness of this philosophy" (AT IX-2, 3, 6–7 = PW I, 180 [modified]) refers to previous decisions: in the *Regulae,* to the *utilitas methodi* (AT X, 373, 3 = PW I, 17); in the *Discourse on the Method,* to the philosophy that went from being "speculative" to being "practical" (AT VI, 62, 1; 61, 30 = PW I, 142; 142), a transition that follows from the criterion of usefulness (DM, 41, 17–18 = 131; see 6, 3 and 17, 29 = 113 and 119) being a synonym for truth (DM, 66, 20–21 = 145). See also *Règles utiles et claires pour la direction de l'esprit en la recherche de la vérité,* p. 134.

chance, with *prima Philosophia*. This interchangeability is seen in the dedicatory *Letter* of the *Principia*:

> ... et fere omnibus in usu venit ut, si versati sint in Metaphysicis, a Geometricis abhorreant; si vero Geometriam excoluerint, quae de prima Philosophia scripsi, non capiant. ... [It generally happens with almost everyone else that if they are accomplished in Metaphysics they hate Geometry, while if they have mastered Geometry they do not grasp what I have written on first philosophy.] [AT VIII-1, 4, 3–6 = PW I, 192.]

The apparent contradiction arises between, on the one hand, geometry, and on the other, metaphysics or first philosophy indifferently. This ambiguous ambivalence is confirmed in the very organization of the *Principia*, which, in the guise of a metaphysics, devote their "part one" solely to the "principiis cognitionis humanae [Principles of Human Knowledge]" (5, 4 = 193), without making even the slightest explicit mention of metaphysics. From now on, we cannot avoid confronting a difficulty: if Descartes grants to metaphysics only the role of a substitute for and qualifier of "first philosophy," can it still be admitted that he thought metaphysics in its most original essence, and that he constituted a particular figure of it? Shouldn't we suppose, on the contrary, that he broached it only in a roundabout way, by chance and tactically more than by a necessity of thought—just like many others? In short, based on the terminological difficulties, shouldn't we conclude that Descartes conceptually avoided all constitution of metaphysics?

Not at all, and for several reasons: *(a)* The absence of homogeneous and recurring occurrences of the term *metaphysics* does not forbid a meditation on the essence of metaphysics itself. Otherwise, Aristotle, being completely ignorant of the neologism that the tradition imposed on the collection of certain of his treatises, would have been the first to have abandoned the question of metaphysics. And the same would be true of Saint Thomas, who employs this term only parsimoniously. Even if Descartes had omitted it totally, one could still maintain that such silence nevertheless offers an avatar of the historical destiny of metaphysics—a destiny made more of disappearances than of retrievals. Perhaps it must be acknowledged that in Descartes' hesitations and uncertainties, a figure of metaphysics—in part only suggested, in part plainly visible—is again being played out, and the continuity of a single destiny of metaphysics is still being attested to. In short, in silencing *metaphysics* almost totally, Descartes could be making a decision about the essence of metaphysics. *(b)* But Descartes was also compelled to confront explicitly the question of a definition of metaphysics. At the moment when he delivers his manuscript of the *Meditationes* to Mersenne, Descartes acknowledges that his "plan is to write a series of theses which will constitute a complete textbook of [his] philosophy . . . [and] in the same volume . . . to have printed a textbook of traditional philosophy . . . with [his own] notes at the end of each proposition," ending with "a comparison between the two philosophies."[2] Now in order to carry out such a project, Descartes had to make reference to his scholastic contemporaries; therefore, he had to have read them:

> . . . I should like to reread some of their philosophy, which I have not looked at for twenty years. I want to see if I like it better now than I did before. For this purpose, I beg you to send me the names of the authors who have written textbooks of philosophy, and to tell me which are the most commonly used, and whether they have any new ones since twenty years ago, I remember only some of Conimbricenses, Toletus and Rubius. I would also like to know if there is in current use any abstract of the whole of scholastic philosophy; this would save me the time it would take to read their huge tomes. There was, I think, a Carthusian or Feuillant who made such an abstract, but I do not remember his name.[3]

In fact, among the possible authors, Descartes will prefer Eustache de Saint-Paul, whose *Summa Philosophiae quadripartita de rebus Dialecticis, Moralibus, Physicis et Metaphysicis* was greeted with success upon its appearance in Paris in 1609.[4] It is very probable that this title (which was quite common) serves as the model for the one that Descartes provisionally formulates for his future *Principia:* "Summa quidem Philosophiae conscribo, et in ea fateor permulta esse ab iis quae in ipsorum [the Jesuits] scholis doceri solent, valde diversa [I am writing a *Summa* of

---

2. *To Mersenne,* 11 November 1640 (AT III, 233, 4–15 = PW III, 156–57). Such a "comparison" would not only have put two incompatible philosophies into relation with each other; but in a still more extraordinary concession, it would also have adopted, in order to establish this relation, the order of the Schools (*Letters to Mersenne and to Charlet (?),* December 1640 [AT III, 259, 19–260, 10 and 270, 1–9 = PW III, 161 and not included]).

3. *To Mersenne,* 30 September 1640 (AT III, 185, 4–18 = PW III, 153–54).

4. Besides Tolet, Rubius, and the Conimbricenses (cited, but rejected as "too long," in AT III, 251, 15–16 = not included in PW), Descartes also mentions Abra de Raconis (or C. F. d'Abra, S.J.), *Totius Philosophiae, hoc est logicae, moralis, physicae et metaphysicae brevis . . . tractatio,* Paris, 1622, whom Mersenne had suggested to him (AT III, 234, 6–10; 251, 13–15 = neither included in PW); but he will opt finally for Eustache de Saint-Paul (AT III, 185, 16–18; 232, 5–8; 259, 23–24; 260, 5–7 = PW III, 154; 156; 161; 161) as the author of "the best book of its kind ever made" (AT III, 232, 6–7; 470, 7–9 = PW III, 156; not included in PW). This is no doubt why Eustache's death will leave Descartes "grieved"

Philosophy, and I confess that in it there is much that is quite different
from what is customarily taught in the schools of the Jesuits]"; or: "... I
shall call it [my *World*] *Summa Philosophiae* to make it more welcome
to the scholastics."[5] But along with the title, it is also the fourfold division
of philosophy to which Descartes is compelled to refer, and all the more
strictly since it is a question of setting himself apart from it in a strict
parallel. Descartes had completed this fourfold course earlier, during his
years studying philosophy at La Flèche. He will recall it during his polemic with Voetius: "... quia dudum scholarum Philosophiam, nomina-
tim Logicam, Metaphysicam, Physicam si non accuratissime, saltem
mediocriter perdidicimus [Not too long ago we learned the philosophy of
the schools—namely, logic, metaphysics, and Physics—if not thoroughly,
then at least with some measure of success]." As for the last, missing,
term of the fourfold division, it shows up in the global opposition between what holds "in Ethicis" and what holds "in Metaphysicis."[6] This
fourfold division, which Abra de Raconis and Scipion Dupleix also adhere to, establishes conceptually as well as tactically that Descartes dealt
with metaphysics as such; its absence would have ruined the didactic
ambition that he never ceased confessing to his correspondents. *(c)* Consequently, if despite these constraints the Cartesian determination of
metaphysics remained clouded by hesitancies or obscurities, these ambiguities would not result from mere ignorance or negligence. Rather, they
would attest, be it only negatively, to the difficulty of the reinterpretation
attempted by Descartes. They would measure *a contrario* a change in
the essence (and not merely the lexicon) of metaphysics in its historical
destiny. This is why, in systematically examining the rare occurrences of

(AT III, 286, 3 = not included in PW). For the comparative study of the acceptations of
métaphysique/metaphysica in Descartes, his contemporaries, and his immediate predecessors, we assume the constituent parts and the method used in *Sur la théologie blanche de
Descartes,* pp. 14–16. Such a "comparison" in a sense suggested itself as early as Descartes'
years at La Flèche (DM, 8, 18–29; 16, 5–7 = PW I, 114–15; 118–19) and would be pursued
well after his death by the Cartesian school. See, for example, R. P. René Le Bossu, *Parallèle des principes de la physique d'Aristote et de celle de René Descartes,* Paris, 1674, who
himself was the successor at Heereboord to J. de Raey or J. du Roure (see our note in
Bulletin Cartésien XII, *Archives de Philosophie* 1983/3: 27).

5. *To Huygens,* 31 January 1642 (AT III, 523, 16–19; ibid. = not included in PW; PW
III, 210).

6. Respectively, *To Regius,* January 1642 (AT III, 500, 21– 23 = not included in PW)
and *To Hyperaspistes,* August 1641 (AT III, 431, 14*ff.* = PW III, 195). On this point, see
Principia Philosophiae III, §3 and the pair "... the discourses of Morality and of
Metaphysics ..." (*To Mersenne,* 27 May 1638 [AT II, 145, 3-4 = not included in PW]).
Concerning the fourfold division, see *infra,* n. 23.

métaphysique or *metaphysica* in the Cartesian *corpus,* we will have to assess the innovations through "comparison" with "the entire body of Philosophy," which had posed the question of metaphysics to Descartes himself. It will therefore be a question of reconstituting, on the basis of Saint Thomas, Pererius, Fonseca, and Suarez, but also Goclenius, Eustache de Saint-Paul, Scipion Dupleix, and Abra de Raconis, the path of thought that, from revisions into displacements, led Descartes to a radically new concept of metaphysics.

§2. Metaphysics as Transgression

Seen in this way, the first occurrences of *métaphysique* become significant, even in the allusive context of the *Letter to Mersenne* of 15 April 1630. This letter responds to a question that Mersenne thought of as being "theological," but which, according to Descartes, "is a metaphysical question which is to be examined by human reason." This is a debate that cannot be resolved, since the debated question has not been transmitted to us.[7] However, its exact terms are less important than the two determinations of the concept of metaphysics that it makes possible. The first: ". . . at least I think that I have found how to prove metaphysical truths in a manner which is more evident than the proofs of geometry" (AT I, 144, 14–17 = PW III, 22). And: ". . . a number of metaphysical topics and especially the following. The mathematical truths which you call eternal have been laid down by God and depend on him entirely no less than the rest of his creatures" (145, 6–10 = 22–23). In other words, "metaphysical truths" or "metaphysical questions" transgress "mathematical truths" as well as the "proofs of Geometry." Simply put, metaphysics surpasses mathematics in certitude as well as in dignity, since it goes so far as to conceive its dependent and created status. The task before us now is to determine the nature and scope of this transgression. At the barest minimum, the gap between mathematics and metaphysics is marked straightaway by the extreme difficulty, if not the impossibility, of each of the two sciences understanding the other. As soon as the metaphysical transgression is suggested, Descartes adds: "in my own opinion that is: I do not know if I shall be able to convince others of it" (144, 17–18 = 22). He thus observes two things: (1) if the mathematicians

---

7. AT I, 143, 25 and 144, 3–5 = PW III, 22 and ibid. We have nevertheless attempted elsewhere to reconstruct the question that Mersenne posed to Descartes (*Sur la théologie blanche de Descartes,* pp. 162–68).

confine themselves strictly to the rationality of their science, they cannot think that "God is a cause whose power surpasses the bounds of human understanding, and [that] the necessity of these [mathematical] truths does not exceed our knowledge." (2) Metaphysics and mathematics are most often mutually exclusive:

> ... quamvis eas [demonstrationes] quibus hîc utor certitudine et evidentia Geometricas aequare vel etiam superare existimem, vereor tamen ne a multis satis percipi non possint ... Nec certe plures in mundo Metaphysicis studiis quam Geometricis apti reperiuntur. [Although the proofs I employ here are in my view as certain and evident as the proofs of geometry, if not more so, it will, I fear, be impossible for many people to achieve an adequate perception of them. ... Moreover, people who have an aptitude for metaphysical studies are certainly not to be found in the world in any greater numbers than those who have an aptitude for geometry.]

And reciprocally,

> ... fere omnibus usu venit, ut, si versati sint in Metaphysicis, a Geometricis abhorreant; si vero Geometriam excoluerint, quae de prima Philosophia scripsi non capiant. [It generally happens with almost everyone else that if they are accomplished in Metaphysics they hate Geometry, while if they have mastered Geometry, they do not grasp what I have written on First Philosophy.][8]

This incompatibility does not depend on an accidental insufficiency in minds that are incapable of two different sciences; rather, it results from a more essential contradiction between their conditions of possibility. For "the imagination, which is the part of the mind that most helps mathematics, is more of a hindrance than a help in metaphysical speculation."[9] In effect, the imagination functions as an auxiliary to the pure understanding, allowing it to grasp geometrical extension as a real object while

8. Respectively, *To Mersenne,* 6 May 1630 (AT I, 150, 17–20 = PW III, 25 [modified]); *Meditations, Letter to the Sorbonne* (AT VII, 4, 24–31 = PW II, 5), and finally *Principia philosophiae, Epistula ...* (AT VIII-1, 4, 3–6 = PW I, 192). See also *To Mersenne,* 27 August 1639: "... metaphysics, a science that hardly anyone understands" (AT II, 570, 18–20 = PW III, 137); or *To Mersenne,* 16 October 1639: "... there are few who are capable of understanding metaphysics" (AT II, 596, 22–23 = PW III, 139). See *infra,* n. 31.

9. *To Mersenne,* 13 November 1639 (AT II, 622, 13–16 = PW III, 141). See *To Elisabeth,* 28 June 1643: "Metaphysical thoughts which exercise the pure intellect help to familiarize us with the notion of the soul; and the study of mathematics, which exercises mainly the imagination ..., accustoms us to form very distinct notions of body" (AT III, 692, 10–16 = PW III, 227).

in fact this extension never appears except by abstraction from particular, physical objects. Thus, metaphysics, according to the *Letter to Mersenne* of 15 April 1630, receives its first characteristic—transgressing mathematics. It passes beyond mathematics by positing it, because it apprehends mathematics as "created," that is to say, at once as dependent on something previously established (on a prior system of axioms) and as instituted by an authority that remains unintelligible to it, since it founds mathematics.

The same text also offers a second determination of the Cartesian concept of metaphysics. While the first advanced the claim that metaphysics transgresses mathematics (by creation), the second claims that it transgresses physics (by foundation). That is, Descartes passes into metaphysics only inasmuch as he seeks a foundation of physics: ". . . I would not have been able to discover the foundations of physics if I had not looked for them along that road" (AT I, 144, 9–11 = PW III, 22). Physics never needs anything but itself, except when one has to reach its "foundations." In that case, it is necessary "in [a] treatise on physics . . . to discuss a number of metaphysical topics" (145, 5–6 = PW III, 22). In itself, sensible experience remains "without foundation" (AT I, 97, 21 = not included in PW), and physics would discover its rationality only by transgressing itself and passing unto metaphysics. *Meta*physics is directly equivalent to the *principle* of physics, as much when it is completed (". . . the little book on metaphysics which I sent you contains all the principles of my physics," ". . . these six meditations contain all the foundations of my physics") as when it is merely intended (". . . a previous demonstration of the principles of physics by metaphysics—which is something I hope to do some day but which has not yet been done.")[10] An excellent example of the functioning of these *principia Metaphysica*[11] is given by the Cartesian formulation of what will later become the principle of inertia. It concerns the "two principles of physics" required in order to answer several questions Mersenne had posed. The first principle is negative: the rejection of real substantial qualities. But the second is positive: "The other principle is that whatever is or exists remains always in the state in which it is, unless some external cause changes it." This principle in turn requires a foundation that is strictly nonphysical,

---

10. *To Mersenne,* respectively, 11 November 1640 (AT III, 233, 24–26); 28 January 1641 (AT III, 298, 1–2); 27 May 1638 (AT II, 141, 25–142, 2) = PW III, 157; 173; 103.

11. *To Regius,* June 1642 (AT III, 566, 29 = PW III, 214), or ". . . the principles of metaphysics . . . ," *To Elisabeth,* 28 June 1643 (AT III, 695, 5–6 = PW III, 228).

literally metaphysical: "I prove this by metaphysics; for God, who is the author of all things, is entirely perfect and unchangeable; and so it seems to me absurd that any simple thing which exists, and so has God for its author, should have in itself the principle of its destruction."[12] Here, then, Descartes is talking about the very God, "author of the essence of created things no less than of their existence . . . author of everything" (AT I, 152, 2–7 = PW III, 25), who, in 1630, also launched metaphysics by setting out from physics. The lucidity of Descartes' procedure should be noted: it is not a question of founding a physical thesis directly on a metaphysical principle, but of assuring what physics *already* considers as a principle—all bodies persist in a state, whatever it might be, provided no exterior force prevents them from doing so—on the basis of a principle that is more fundamental, metaphysical. But why require a principle of the principle, a foundation of the foundation, according to a fantastic demand that would transgress itself indefinitely without ever coming to an end? In fact, the physical principle or foundation is doubled metaphysically only so that it does *not* have to dissipate in an infinite regression, and so that it might find assurance in an ultimate authority—the creator of the eternal truths—by borrowing from it a sort of epistemological eternity that would remove the principle or foundation from the indefinitely regressive causal chain. The principle of inertia implies that any body, even and above all a body in motion, can be considered as remaining, by itself, always in the same state. Physically and empirically, there is an unsustainable paradox in considering a movement as a stable state—whatever might be the theoretical fruitfulness of it. This paradox is discovered again in the second of the "laws of Nature," which supposes that all motion is rectilinear. In fact, according to experience and observation, motion is almost never rectilinear nor indefinitely prolonged. These paradoxes, although or because they are foundational in physical theory, cannot be established in the field of the physics that they make possible. Therefore they must be established beyond, in a transgression that leads to metaphysics: the physical principles are dis-

---

12. *To Mersenne,* 26 April 1643 (AT III, 648, 2; 649, 12–25 = PW III, 216; ibid.). See the parallel in *Principia philosophiae II,* §§36 and 41–42. Whence the fault of Regius, who ". . . changed the order and denied certain truths of metaphysics on which the whole of physics must be based" (*Principles of Philosophy,* preface to the French edition [AT IX-2, 19, 24–26 = PW I, 189]). The dependence is not in any way equal to a straightforwardly metaphysical deduction of the laws of physics, as has been proven clearly by D. M. Clarke, "Physique et métaphysique chez Descartes," *Archives de Philosophie* 1980/3, and *Descartes' Philosophy of Science* (Manchester, 1982). See *infra,* chap. III, §14.

covered, like the mathematical truths and through their intermediacy, to be "eternal truths," thus to be created by God. In the creative act itself, God puts into operation the characteristics of his own divinity. He thus marks creatures with his own immutability, and these creatures include the movements that, in consequence of being marked with the divine immutability, will be enacted as immutable states of rectilinear transport (with the exception of collisions with another body in motion). The metaphysical foundation of physical principles therefore implies neither confusion nor dogmatism: the paradoxes of the theory, insoluble because related to principles, are grounded not through regression to statements about primary experiences or to a system of axioms, but through recourse to a heterogeneous model (here a theological one), which without risk of confusion assures its possibility. In this example, the divine immutability, by way of a metaphysical model, renders intelligible the physical paradox of a motion considered as a state. Thus, in 1630, metaphysics is characterized also by the transgression of physics.

Though it is not evoked very succinctly, the concept of metaphysics thus receives no less than two precise determinations. The metaphysical moment of philosophy transgresses physics (by foundation) on the one hand, and mathematics (by creation) on the other. Metaphysics attests to its relevance only by passing beyond (therefore disqualifying as much as confirming) two other sciences, which are linked by a relation of encoding that joins them definitively.[13] This double transgression suffices for schematizing the relation of the three principal sciences—metaphysics, mathematics, and physics—according to Descartes. But at the same time, another piece of evidence forces itself upon us: this Cartesian schema reproduces the same set of themes found in Aristotle's consideration of the same three sciences. To verify this, it suffices to recall the hierarchy of the theoretical sciences as it is explained by Aristotle in *Book E* of what, since Andronicus, the tradition has called *Metaphysics*. First, natural science considers things in motion (thus affected by "matter," consequently not eternal) and separate (that is to say, distinct and individualized in "actuality"). Second, mathematical science considers

---

13. On the doctrine of the code as the relation between physics and mathematics, we refer to *Sur la théologie blanche de Descartes,* pp. 231–63. On the passage to metaphysics in the *Letter to Mersenne* of 15 April 1630, see ibid., pp. 304–12. The code is put into practice with mechanics as its operative agent: ". . . provided you suppose that in everything nature acts exactly in accordance with the laws of mechanics, and that these laws have been imposed on it by God" (*To Mersenne,* 20 February 1639 [AT II, 525, 9–11 = PW III, 134]).

things that are immobile (since abstracted from their "matter"), but not separate (since abstraction alone distinguishes them from the physical "matter" from which they come). Third, theological science considers things that are separate and immobile, therefore beings free of all "matter," not by abstraction but in reality: "If there is something which is eternal and immobile and separated (εἰ δέ τί ἐστιν ἀΐδιον καὶ ἀκίνητον καὶ χωριστόν) clearly, the knowledge of it belongs to a theoretical science—not, however, to natural science (for natural science deals with certain movable things), nor to mathematics, but to a science prior to both (προτερᾶς ἀμφοῖν)."[14] This theoretical science considers immobile, eternal, and separate things, which "are causes of so much of the divine as appears to us," such that "if the divine resides anywhere (εἴ που τὸ Θεῖον ὑπάρχει), it resides in things of this sort." Consequently, it is appropriate to name this science theological science, and to grant it the status of "first science," or indeed "first philosophy."[15] The similarity between the Aristotelian and Cartesian set of themes is all the more compelling since many details confirm it. *(a)* Aristotle does not submit to theology merely the particular mathematical disciplines (geometry,

14. *Metaphysics E,* 1, 1026 *a* 11–13 [English trans., p. 1620 (modified)]. A capital difference nonetheless remains: for Descartes, mathematics governs physics (through the mediation of mechanics: DM, 54, 26–27 = PW I, 139, and *To Plempius,* 3 October 1637 [AT I, 421, 7–17 = PW III, 64]), while for Aristotle, if, by some impossibility, "theological science" were to be missing, then "natural science [would] be the first science" (E 1, 1026 *a* 29 [English trans., p. 1620]), not mathematics. Descartes thus substitutes a continuous hierarchy physics/mathematics/metaphysics for the parallel and double transgression of both physics and mathematics by a single theology, which Aristotle established. It is nonetheless true that in 1647, Descartes will return to Aristotle's position: "The second part [of true philosophy, after metaphysics] is physics" (AT IX-2, 14, 13 = PW I, 186). That the formula μετὰ τὰ φυσικὰ should not be understood merely as a bibliographical notation, but that, beyond Andronicus, it can be dated much earlier, ". . . und so wäre kein anderer als Aristoteles der Urheber des Namen Metaphysik [and so no one else but Aristotle was the first proponent of the name metaphysics]," and that it can be applied without contradiction to φιλοσοφία πρώτη—this is the position held by H. Reiner, "Die Entstehung und ursprüngliche Bedeutung des Namens Metaphysik," *Zeitschrift für philosophische Forschung,* 8, 1954 (pp. 210–37). See also H. Wagner, "Das Problem des aristotelischen Metaphysiksbegriffs," *Philosophische Rundschau,* 1957, and E. Vollrath, *Die These der Metaphysik. Zur Gestalt der Metaphysik bei Aristoteles, Kant, und Hegel* (Wuppertal, 1969). This entire debate takes place, however, within the horizon of a strictly ontic determination of φύσις and φυσικὰ, which it is eventually a matter of transgressing. But an other (ontological?) interpretation of φύσις would open a radically other retrieval of the essence of metaphysics; thus Heidegger, *Die Grundbegriffe der Metaphysik* (WS 1929–1930), G. A., 29/30, §§8–15 [English trans., pp. 25–57].

15. *Metaphysics E,* 1, respectively 1026 *a* 18; 20; 29; 30 [English trans., p. 1620; 1620 (modified); 1620; 1620].

arithmetic, etc.); he envisages nothing less than a "universal mathematics [applying] alike to all, καθόλου πασῶν κοινή," thus a universal science of quantity and of its measure, which, without being confused with them, precedes and renders possible the sciences commonly called mathematical.[16] Such a metamathematical science, in Aristotle, anticipates the *Mathesis Universalis* of *Regula IV*—at least in terms of the parameter measure, that of order remaining particular to the Cartesian project. Both cases thus concern a transgression of mathematics, taken each time in its most dignified form—that is, in its metamathematical figure of a science of measure in general. What metaphysics transgresses is therefore nothing less than the ultimate (metamathematical) accomplishment of mathematics in its totality. *(b)* Descartes does not introduce theology any less than Aristotle did. This must be emphasized all the more since such an appearance of the theological moment is very rare. That is, Descartes ordinarily refuses "to involve [himself] in theology" (AT I, 150, 24–25 = PW III, 25) because he defines it strictly as revealed theology, not as natural theology: ". . . anything dependent on revelation, which is what I call theology in the strict sense . . ." (AT I, 144, 2–3 = PW III, 22). In 1637, *The Discourse on the Method* posits, even more precisely, that "theology instructs us how to reach heaven" (DM, 6, 7–8 = PW I, 113) and that in order to "succeed, [one] would need to have some extraordinary aid from heaven and to be more than a mere man" (DM, 6, 7–8 = PW I, 114). Likewise, Descartes most often mentions theology only in order to dodge the question: "The . . . last points of your letter are all theological matters, so if you please I will say nothing about them" (AT I, 153, 24–26 = PW III, 26). However, with regard to the creation of the eternal truths, this rule suffers one of its rare exceptions in that Descartes claims for metaphysics a question that Mersenne held to be theological. What was it? We will remain ignorant of it, since we no longer have the letter from Mersenne to which Descartes was responding. Nevertheless, Descartes' pronouncement is unambiguous:

> Your question of theology is beyond my mental capacity, but it does not seem to me outside my province, since it has no concern with anything dependent on revelation, which is what I call theology in the strict sense; it is a metaphysical question which is to be examined by human reason. I

16. *Metaphysics E,* 1, 1026 *a* 27 [English trans., p. 1620]. On the Aristotelian parallels, the identification of this universal mathematics, and its difference from the Cartesian *Mathesis Universalis,* see our analyses in *Sur l'ontologie grise de Descartes,* pp. 62–64, and *René Descartes. Règles utiles et claires pour la direction de l'esprit en la recherche de la vérité,* pp. 155–64, 302–9.

think that all those to whom God has given the use of this reason have an
obligation to employ it principally in the endeavor to know him and to
know themselves. That is the task with which I began my studies; and I
can say that I would not have been able to discover the foundations of
physics if I had not looked for them along that road.[17]

Let us repeat, this is the first Cartesian occurrence of *métaphysique;* it
appears in a striking and rare synonymy with *théologie* [theology]. The
fact that it concerns natural theology does not weaken the rapprochement with Aristotle's "theological science." Quite to the contrary: metaphysics transgresses mathematics (by creation) as well as physics (by
foundation) in such a way as to fill an explicitly theological function; for
it is as theologically occupied with "the greatness of God" (AT I, 145,
21–22 = PW III, 23) that metaphysics here transcends physics and mathematics—as if it were the case that, sustained by a divine φύσις, the
science that will be named *μεταφυσική passed beyond the theoretical
sciences μαθηματική and φυσική. The nomenclature of the three sciences
thus remains unchanged from Aristotle to Descartes: it is always a question of physics, mathematics (the different branches being united beneath the banner of a science of quantity in general, by which Aristotle
anticipates the Cartesian language), and finally a theology (Descartes
here retrieving, alongside *métaphysique* and despite the revealed sense
of the term, the Aristotelian usage). *(c)* The similarity of these two thematics becomes still more striking if one measures Descartes' thesis
against that of the leading figures of his day. Like many others, Kepler,
Mersenne, and Galileo hold the mathematical truths to be uncreated
because they attribute them to divine understanding; accordingly, natural theology transgresses physics only by in turn divinizing mathematics,
since God created the physical world only by obeying the univocal and
singular mathematical rationality.[18] In this schema, mathematics earns
an immediately theological status and thus, along with the uncreated
eternity of God, partakes of transcendence with respect to the physical
universe. As a corollary, it does not appear that a metaphysics is any
longer possible, nor really required, inasmuch as the univocal rationality
of divine mathematics has taken its place. When Descartes, against the
reigning opinion, establishes the creation of "the mathematical truths"
(AT I, 145, 7 = PW III, 23), he acknowledges his own apprehension of
divine, explicitly Christian, transcendence in such a way as to contest the

17. *To Mersenne,* 15 April 1630 (AT I, 143, 25–144, 11 = PW III, 22).
18. See *Sur la théologie blanche de Descartes,* chaps. 9–11.

pagan submission of God, "as if he were Jupiter or Saturn . . . , to the Styx and the Fates" (145, 11–12 = 23). But he is no less acknowledging the Aristotelian thematic of the theoretical sciences, in which, with less "paganism" than many of the moderns, mathematical science in general is lowered from the divine rank, now occupied by the sole theological science, to the point of even being obliged to yield the second rank to physics. In short, if one sticks strictly to the hierarchy of the sciences and does not consider the metamorphoses of their respective objects (passage from φύσις to *monde,* from καθόλου πασῶν κοινή μαθηματικὴ to *Mathesis Universalis,* and finally from τὸ Θεῖον to God the creator), the creation of the eternal truths restores and respects the Aristotelian view of the theoretical sciences. In his *Letter to Mersenne* of 15 April 1630, Descartes retrieves the definition of φιλοσοφία πρώτη that Aristotle established in *Metaphysics E,* 1: there is a first philosophy, assumed conjointly by theology (a natural theology, or at least not a revealed one) and by metaphysics (still literally unknown by Aristotle), and it is established by transgressing mathematics as well as physics.

This result finds confirmation in a second similarity. In 1630, Descartes also reproduces the scholarly and scholastic definition of the notion that is destined for, if not always thought as, metaphysics. In Cartesian terms, the "metaphysical questions," therefore also the "metaphysical truths" (AT I, 144, 15, also 145, 6 = PW III, 22, also 23), become accessible only to a mind capable of conceiving an inconceivable: "God is a cause whose power surpasses the bounds of human understanding" (150, 18–19 = 25). Metaphysics is opened only by surpassing the ordinary conditions of knowing, precisely because the formal object of this new knowing exceeds the scope of ordinary knowing. Metaphysics "surpasses" (ibid.) the other sciences for Descartes just as, for Aristotle, the πρώτη φιλοσοφία "is superior to" the other theoretical sciences.[19] In this way, Descartes also appropriates the etymology, as disputable as it is widespread, of *meta*physics as transgression of the physics *after* which it would come. This commonplace appears in, among other authors, Fonseca: "On account of this, it happens that the science which is treated in these books is customarily named by the Moderns simply Metaphysics, that is to say the science of things post- or super-natural, while Aristotle often names it first philosophy."[20] Suarez, not without competition from

---

19. αἱρετώτεραι, *Metaphysics E,* 1, 1026 *a* 22– 23 [English trans., p. 1620 (modified)].

20. Fonseca: "Hînc factum est ut scientia ipsa, quae his libris traditur, simplici nomine appellari soleat a Recentioribus Metaphysica, quasi Postnaturalium aut Supranaturalium

others, is even more clear about stamping the definition of metaphysics with the sense of a transgression that "surpasses" physics: ". . . On account of which it was named metaphysics, not so much by Aristotle as by his interpreters. This name was taken from the title with which Aristotle prefaced his work of metaphysics, τῶν μετὰ τὰ φυσικὰ, that is to say, on the things that follow the natural sciences and natural things. . . . This is why it was called *metaphysics:* it was instituted after or beyond physics."[21] In the scholarly treatises, to which Descartes does not hesitate to refer, this conventional etymology always serves to justify the fact that πρώτη φιλοσοφία could, without any Aristotelian authority, be abolished in a *metaphysica* that encompasses it or replaces it. Eustache de Saint-Paul cites metaphysics as the fourth meaning of philosophy "because in the theoretical order, it follows physics, or rather comes after it." Abra de Raconis, in setting forth the fifth and final meaning, says that "in the end, it is named metaphysics, that is to say post-natural science or the discipline concerned with the things that follow natural things." Scipion Dupleix, on the contrary, makes it the first sense:

> The first and the most common is the name Metaphysics, which is given to this science for two reasons. First, because it is about supernatural things such as God or the angels. . . . The other is that the Philosopher has titled the books that he wrote about this science τῶν μετὰ τὰ φυσικά, that is to say: *On the things which follow natural things,* or what follows physics and the science of natural things.[22]

Metaphysics [*La métaphysique*] is defined and constituted by the very act of transgressing all other science. In 1630, Descartes had instituted

---

scientia, cum ab Aristotele saepe appellatur prima Philosophia," *In Libros Metaphysicorum Aristotelis, I, proemium,* chap. VIII (Rome, 1577), vol. 1, p. 29.

21. Suarez: ". . . ex quo etiam *metaphysica* nominata est; quod nomen non tam ab Aristotele, quam ab ejus interpretatibus habuit; sumptum vero est ex inscriptione quam Aristoteles suis Metaphysicae libris praescripsit, videlicet τῶν μετὰ τὰ φυσικὰ, id est, de his rebus, quae scientias seu res naturales consequuntur," *Disputationes Metaphysicae, Disp. I,* s. 1, *Prooemium,* vol. 25, p. 2. See also: ". . . hanc scientiam transphysicam seu postphysicam vocavit [Aristotle]," *Disp. I,* s. 1, n. 13, loc. cit., p. 29. The equivalence of *meta*physics and *trans*physics goes back at least to Saint Thomas, *In XII Libros Metaphysicorum Expositio, Prooemium,* ed. Cathala (Rome, 1964), p. 2 [English trans., p. 4].

22. Respectively, Eustache de Saint-Paul: ". . . quia Physicam ordine doctrinae sequitur, sive quia illam praetergreditur," *Summa Philosophiae quadripartita de rebus dialecticis, moralibus, physicis et metaphysicis, Praefatio,* q. 1 (Paris, 1609 [and 1617, 4th ed.]), p. 1; Abra de Raconis: "Tandem appellatur Metaphysica, id est post-naturalis scientia, seu disciplina rerum res naturales consequentium," *Totius Philosophiae, hoc est logicae, moralis, physicae et metaphysicae brevis tractatio* (Paris, 1622), cited here according to the edition

the metaphysical [*la métaphysique*] on the basis of the fact that he had transgressed mathematics as well as physics; but in the very particular context prompted by the exigencies of the method (and of the code), *métaphysique* is in play only as a qualifier, not yet as the denomination of a completed science. But in 1647, when he was composing a preface for the French translation of the *Principia Philosophiae,* Descartes won fully metaphysical positions by his own means: he can therefore grant himself the liberty of taking up pedagogically, but without risk of confusion, the themes and the lexicon of scholastic philosophy. *(a)* From now on, metaphysics will appear officially in and be defined clearly by the transgression of physics: ". . . The first part of philosophy is metaphysics. . . . The second part is physics" (AT IX-2, 14, 7–13 = PW I, 186). Even here, the Aristotelian hierarchy seems to be formally maintained, given that metaphysics transgresses physics and not, directly, mathematics (as was the case in 1630). *(b)* The plan "to write in order a complete textbook of [his] philosophy" (AT III, 233, 4–5 = PW III, 156–57 [modified]) supposed taking up the four parts that, scholastically, organized philosophy: logic (sometimes called dialectic), morals, physics, and metaphysics. This is the way that Abra de Raconis and Eustache de Saint-Paul, authors mentioned many times by Descartes, proceeded.[23] And in fact, Descartes, at least in part, resumes this organization of philosophy, seeing that he is inspired by it, more than by Porphyry, to postulate that "the whole of philosophy is like a tree. The roots are metaphysics, the trunk is physics, and the branches emerging from the trunk are all the other sciences, which may be reduced to three principal ones, namely medicine, mechanics and morals" (AT IX-2, 14, 24–28 = PW I, 186). In this "tree," one can easily recognize three of the ordinary sections of a "complete textbook of philosophy": metaphysics, physics, and morals. It is missing logic or dialectics, which had been rejected ever since the *Re-*

---

of 1651, *Quarta Pars Philosophiae seu Metaphysica* (preceded by the *Tertia Pars Philosophiae seu Physica*), *Praeludium primum, De Nominibus Metaphysicae,* p. 2; Scipion Dupleix, *La Métaphysique ou science surnaturelle,* I, 2, *Des divers noms de la Métaphysique* (Paris, 1610), cited here according to the edition of 1626, p. 19 (see his *Physique,* I, 2 [Paris, 1603 and 1984], p. 36).

23. Eustache de Saint-Paul, *Summa Philosophiae Quadripartita, de rebus dialectis, moralibus, physicis et metaphysicis;* or Abra de Raconis, *Totius Philosophiae, hoc est logicae, moralis, physicae et metaphysicae brevis tractatio* (see *supra,* n. 4). Scipion Dupleix in 1632 gathered into a single collection entitled *Corps entier de philosophie* his previous works: *La logique ou l'art de discourir* (1600), *La Physique ou science naturelle* (1603), *L'Ethique ou philosophie morale* (1617), and *La Métaphysique ou science surnaturelle* (1610).

gulae in conjunction with Descartes' constant effort to distance himself from the formalism that issues from the categories of being.[24] The absence of mathematics does not cause any real difficulty, since the text is here speaking about the parts of "true philosophy" (AT IX-2, 14, 7–8 = PW I, 186), and of them alone; they do not legitimately include mathematics. Descartes thus reproduces, without breaking, the scholastic division of the curriculum, a division which, for that matter, is of Stoic origin. The appearance of mathematics in the thematic of 1630 is explained, on the contrary, by the confrontation with an Aristotelian thematic (*Metaphysics E,* 1). The real difficulty would consist largely in determining why and how Descartes can use two disparate classifications, harmonize them, and make use of the distances between them. It remains the case that, in 1647, mathematics is implicit and presupposed in the physics whose encoding it assures and in the mechanics where it passes into actuality.[25] As for the mention of medicine, it transcribes into Cartesian terms the subset common to morals and mechanics, with a dependency on physics. It is therefore not unreasonable to consider the Cartesian divisions of philosophy in 1647 as a modification of the scholastic fourfold division, consequently also as a confirmation of the commonly held definition of metaphysics.

The two similarities thus drawn out allow us to delimit a Cartesian sense of *métaphysique.* According to the commonly held doctrine, the determination of metaphysics as that part of philosophy which transgresses physics ends up defining an essential characteristic of it—metaphysics abstracts its formal object from all matter. Confirmations of this thesis are not lacking, in particular in the Jesuit authors. *(a)* Pererius points out, from among all the different abstractions, the most complete:

---

24. See *Regulae* (AT X, 36, 5, 7–9; 372, 22–373, 2; 406, 9–26, etc. = PW I, 12; 16; 36 [and the corresponding notes in *Règles utiles et claires . . . ,* pp. 133 and 218]). Concerning the Cartesian "tree," one can consult P. Mesnard, "L'arbre de la sagesse," *Descartes,* Cahiers de Royaumont (Paris, 1957).

25. On the relation between mathematics and physics, see the formula ". . . use mathematical methods in the investigation of physical questions" (*To Mersenne,* 11 October 1638 [AT II, 380, 5–6 = PW III, 124]) or ". . . my entire physics is nothing but geometry" (*To Mersenne,* 27 July 1638 [AT II, 268, 13–14 = PW III, 118]). On the relation between mechanics and physics (*supra,* n. 13), see DM, 54, 26–27: ". . . the laws of mechanics, which are identical with the laws of nature" (or also *To Plempius,* 3 October 1637 [AT I, 420, 21–422, 5 = PW III, 64]); *To Morin,* 13 July 1638: ". . . the laws of mechanics and of true physics" (AT II, 212, 25–26 = not included in PW); *To Florimond de Beaune,* 30 April 1639: ". . . although my entire physics is nothing but mechanics . . ." (AT II, 542, 18–20 = PW III, 135).

". . . the third is the abstraction of the thing with respect to all matter, in terms of reality as well of reason. This abstraction we observe in God and the intelligences." In particular, this abstraction passes beyond the simple mathematical abstraction, which merely proceeds rationally, not in reality. *(b)* Suarez makes it unequivocally clear how abstraction can effectively put into operation the metaphysical transgression:

> For this [last] science makes an abstraction [with respect to] sensible and material things (which are called physical, because they are the ones with which natural philosophy is concerned). It also contemplates divine things and things separate from matter, as well as the common definitions of be-ing [*communes rationes entis*], which can exist apart from matter. It was therefore named metaphysics, as it was instituted after physics or beyond physics.

(c) Abra de Raconis pushes Suarez's thesis to its conclusion in order to complete the abstraction: "It must be established that being abstracted as much from God as from creatures is the adequate object of metaphysics."[26] Such a convergence is all the more weighty as the author that Descartes privileges from among all the scholastics—Eustache de Saint-Paul—repeats it at the conclusion of a discussion, inspired by Suarez, concerning the object of metaphysics: "Hence, one can conclude with the following definition of metaphysics: it is called a theoretical science of real being, complete and *per se,* abstracted from all matter indiffer-ently." Moreover, the metaphysical abstraction leads so necessarily to the consideration of the *ens* as such that the neologism *ontology* (still writ-ten, it is true, in Greek) appeared for the first time in the history of philosophy when Goclenius, in 1613, defines abstraction: "Separation and abstraction from matter occurs not only from singular [matter], but also from universal [matter], and even just rationally, as from a simple

26. Respectively, Pererius: "Tertia est abstractio rei ab omni materia, tam secundum rem, quam secundum rationem, quam abstractionem cernimus in Deo et intelligentiis," *De Communibus omnium rerum naturalium principiis et affectionibus,* I, 5 (Rome, 1576), p. 10. Suarez: "Abstrahit enim haec scientia de sensibilibus seu materialibus rebus (quae physicae dicuntur, quoniam in eis naturalis philosophia versatur) et res divinas et materia separatas et communes rationes entis, quae absque materia existere possunt, contemplatur: et ideo metaphysica dicta est, quasi post physicam seu ultra physicam constituta," *Disputationes Metaphysicae, I, Proemium,* vol. 25, p. 2. (See also: ". . . metaphysicam esse scientiam quae ens, in quantum ens, seu in quantum a materia abstrahit secundum esse, contemplatur," ibid., s. 3, n. 1, vol. 25, p. 22.) Abra de Raconis: "Ens abstractum a Deo et creaturis stat-uendum est adaequatum metaphysicae objectum," *Totius philosophiae . . . brevis tractatio, IV. Metaphysica. Praeludium quartum,* s. 2, post. prop., op. cit., p. 8.

body and a mixed body. Of this last type is the mathematical [abstraction] and therefore the ὀντολογικὴ, that is to say, that of the philosophy which treats being or the transcendentals."[27] The abstraction here transgresses matter, but also the particular essences, and passes unto the ὄν ἣ ὄν, beings in their beingness. Hence, all metaphysics depends on the power of abstraction.

This commonly held thesis clarifies several series of Cartesian texts, which, without being thus collected together, would have remained obscure or insignificant. In the first place, for Descartes too, metaphysics begins when matter disappears, thus when "immaterial or metaphysical things" appear (AT IX-2, 10, 13 = PW I, 184); for it is always opened "by the idea of God, the idea of the soul, and the ideas of imperceptible things."[28] Second, Descartes confirms and passes beyond the commonly held doctrine in that in his eyes, the metaphysical abstraction does not demand merely that the object be empty of all matter, but above all that the mind itself first be abstracted from sensible considerations. The endlessly repeated injunction calling for an *abductio mentis a sensibus* repeats in the case of the mind what the concept of metaphysics already implies:

Quamvis enim jam ante dictum sit a multis, ad res Metaphysicas intelligendas mentem a sensibus esse abducendam, nemo tamen adhuc, quod sciam, qua ratione id fieri possit, ostenderat. [Admittedly many people had previously said that in order to understand metaphysical matters the mind must

27. Respectively, Eustache de Saint-Paul: "Ex his colligi potest haec Metaphysicae definitio ut videlicet dicatur scientia theorica de ente reali per se et completo ab omni materia saltem secundum indifferentiam abstracto," *Summa philosophiae quadripartita, Praefatio,* q. 2, p. 5; Goclenius: "Sejunctio et Abstractio a materia est cum singuli, tum universali, etiam secundum rationem tantum, ut a corpore simplici et mixto. Mathematica haec est et ὀντολογικὴ id est Philosophiae de ente seu Transcendentibus." As an aside, this paragraph is subtitled ὀντολογία *et philosophia de ENTE, Lexicon philosophicum* (Frankfurt, 1613), p. 16. On the determination of the object of metaphysics, in the most strict sense, to the point that it gives rise to the neologism *ontology,* the study of M. Wundt must always be consulted (*Die deutsche Schulmetaphysik des 17. Jahrhundert* [Tübingen, 1939], particularly Hpst. II, S. 1 *a* and *b,* pp. 162–87), as well as that of P. Petersen, *Geschichte der aristotelischen Philosophie im protestantischen Deutschland* (Leipzig, 1921, and Stuttgart, 1962), particularly pp. 259*ff.* See *infra,* chap. II, §1, n. 8.

28. *To Mersenne,* July 1641 (AT III, 392, 12–13 = PW III, 185). See: "... [res] intelligibiles tantum, atque ab omni materia secretas [things which are the object of the intellect alone and are totally separate from matter] ..." (AT VII, 53, 4–5 = PW II, 37), and *To Mersenne,* 25 November 1630: "... a little treatise of Metaphysics ... in which I set out principally to prove *the existence of God and of our souls* when they are separate from the body" (AT I, 182, 18–22 = PW III, 29).

be abstracted from the sensible; but no one, so far as I know, had shown how this could be done.] [AT VII, 131, 6–10 = PW II, 94 (modified).]

Descartes believes that he, better than any of his predecessors, has effectively accomplished the radical abstraction of metaphysics because in the act of the *cogito,* the *mens* is itself perceived for the first time before and without the body (AT VII, 131, 10–133, 16 = PW II, 94–96). More, he will add, it accomplishes this as early as the doubt that, for that reason, is rightly named metaphysical:

> In prima [Meditatione], causae exponuntur propter quas de rebus omnibus, praesertim materialibus, possimus dubitare. . . . Etsi autem istius tantae dubitationis utilitas prima fronte non appareat, est tamen in eo maxima quod ab omnibus praejudiciis nos liberet, viamque facillimam sternat ad mentem a sensibus abducendam. [In the First Meditation reasons are provided which give us possible grounds for doubt about all things, especially material things. . . . Although the usefulness of such extensive doubt is not apparent at first sight, its greatest benefit lies in freeing us from all our preconceived opinions, and providing the easiest route by which the mind may be abstracted from the sensible.] [AT VII, 12, 1–8 = PW II, 9 (modified).][29]

The mind's *abductio* beyond the sensible no doubt marks something like the birth of the *mens;* but the *mens* then emphatically transgresses physics (sensation and the sensible) as well as mathematics (imagination)— that is to say, it transgresses the sensible in its two states, either universal (the second sensibles) or particular (the first sensibles). Doubt does not make possible just the *ego,* being inasmuch as thinking; it first makes it possible to open the entire horizon of metaphysics, in that, through it, the *ego* thinks purely the insensible beings in general. The winning of the *ego cogito* must not hide the fact that, through it, doubt about the sensible permits transgressing physics, just as in return the transgression of mathematics compels one to doubt the imaginable. Doubt alone and as such reaches the nonsensible, whatever it might be. In short, it inaugurates metaphysics in all its splendor. Third, it is necessary to consider

---

29. "Abducere mentem a sensibus"; the formula appears often: AT I, 560, 16; AT VII, 9, 25–27; 12, 7–8; 14, 20–21; 52, 23–24; 131, 8–9, etc. = PW III, 86; PW II, 8; 9; 10; 37; 94. This does not concern a psychological propedeutic to meditation in general (such as, for example, no longer being preoccupied with the affairs of the world, suspending one's passions, struggling against one's prejudices, etc.); rather, it concerns the very act through which the formal object of metaphysics is liberated.

attentively the reservations with which Descartes appears to deal with his own project—for example, in 1637: "I do not know whether I should tell you of the first meditations that I had there, for they are perhaps too metaphysical and uncommon for everyone's taste" (DM 31, 14–17 = PW I, 126). Here the expression "uncommon" does not suggest any extravagance, but the metaphysical abstraction and the passage to the limit that it forces on the mind. Thus in 1641, the "metaphysical certainty" of 1637 (DM 38, 3–4 = PW I, 130) is balanced by a "valde tenuis et, ut ita loquar, Metaphysica dubitandi ratio [a very tenuous and, so to speak, metaphysical reason for doubt]" (AT VII, 36, 24–25 = PW II, 25 [modified]). But to be more exact, *every* metaphysical reason by definition must remain very tenuous, since it is defined by abstraction. If, after the fact, "hyperbolicae ... dubitationes, ut risu dignae, sunt explodendae [The hyperbolic doubts of the last few days should be dismissed as laughable]" (AT VII, 89, 18–20 = PW II, 61 [modified]), this is not because they are laughable insofar as they are metaphysical, but simply because their hyperbole is shown in the end to be false. The tenuity beyond what is common had nothing laughable about it, since by definition and in strict consequence of the metaphysical abstraction, doubt (and the certainty that alone lifts it) can be stated only as an extreme limit, beyond all (sensible and physical) perception and all (mathematical) imagination. Doubt, if it is to put metaphysics into practice and to be put into practice as metaphysical, must be so abstract that it cannot be anything but tenuous and hyperbolic. Consequently, it is not disqualified by its tenuous hyperbole, but in fact it is qualified by such tenuous hyperbole as metaphysical. In short, the metaphysical transgression definitively affects the itinerary and the conclusions of the *Meditationes,* even and especially if "metaphysical certainty" ends up completing hyperbolic doubt. Fourth, Descartes always admitted and even proclaimed that, in its very principle, the transgression defining metaphysics is difficult to access by the thoughts that it transgresses, and thus, first of all, by mathematical thought. Ever since the *Letter to Mersenne* of 15 April 1630, metaphysics joins certainty together with incomprehensibility in the eyes of the other sciences: "... at least I think that I have found how to prove metaphysical truths in a manner which is more evident than the proofs of geometry—in my own opinion that is: I do not know if I shall be able to convince others of it."[30] To be sure, Descartes admits elsewhere that

30. AT I, 144, 14–18 = PW III, 22. See *To Mersenne,* 25 November 1630: "... I do not know whether I would be able to make everyone understand it [the evident proof that

"metaphysics [is] a science that hardly anyone understands" or that "there are few who are capable of understanding metaphysics."[31] But he is not suggesting by this that he has any reservations about the validity and legitimacy of the metaphysical enterprise as such. He is merely observing that in being defined through abstraction from all matter and through independence with respect to the faculties that apprehend matter (the senses and the imagination), access to metaphysics is forbidden to the minds of the majority—better, to the great majority of speculative minds, since the mathematicians can study extension only by apprehending it through the imagination. Metaphysics remains incomprehensible to the mathematicians, not through lack of rigor or formalization, but because of an excess of abstraction; "for the imagination, which is the part of the mind that most helps mathematics, is more of a hindrance than a help in metaphysical speculation." The transition from the inferior sciences to metaphysics is produced only by a discontinuity: to pass from one science to the other, it is necessary to pass from one dominant faculty to another, one that contradicts the conditions for exercising the first: "Metaphysical thoughts, which exercise the pure intellect, help to familiarize us with the notion of the soul; and the study of mathematics, which exercises mainly the imagination in the consideration of shapes and motions, accustoms us to form very distinct notions of the body."[32] Either the mind, as pure intellect, thinks by perfect abstraction and attains "things insensible," thus metaphysical, or the mind is linked to the imagination in order to deal with extension and then attains bodies only, thus mathematical. This exclusive alternative has an unavoidable consequence: "... fere omnibus usu venit ut, si versati sint in Metaphysicis, a Geometricas abhorrent; si vero Geometriam excoluerint, quae de prima Philosophia scripsi non capiant [It generally happens with almost

---

God is] the way I can" (AT I, 182, 4–6 = PW III, 29); *To Mersenne,* July 1640 (AT III, 102, 4–105, 16 = not included in PW); *To Gibieuf,* 11 November 1640: "... I cannot ensure that those of every level of intelligence will be capable of understanding the proofs ..." (AT III, 237, 20–21 = PW III, 158). DM, 37, 1–14 = PW I, 129 connects this difficulty to their failing to credit the metaphysical abstraction.

31. Respectively, *To Mersenne,* 27 August 1639 (AT II, 570, 18–20 = PW III, 137); 16 October 1639 (AT II, 596, 22–23 = PW III, 139). See also: "Nec certe plures in Metaphysicis studiis quam Geometricis apti reperiuntur [People who have an aptitude for metaphysical studies are certainly not to be found in the world in any greater numbers than those who have an aptitude for geometry]" (AT VII, 4, 30–31 = PW II, 5).

32. *To Mersenne,* 13 November 1639 (AT II, 622, 13–16 = PW III, 141); *To Elisabeth,* 28 June 1643 (AT III, 692, 10–16 = PW III, 227). See also *To Henry More,* 5 February 1649 (AT V, 269, 23–270, 31 = PW III, 361–62).

everyone else that if they are accomplished in Metaphysics they hate
Geometry, while if they have mastered Geometry they do not grasp what
I have written on First Philosophy]."[33] Thus, abstraction, precisely because it accomplishes metaphysics and produces it in actuality, renders
metaphysics inaccessible and, literally, incomprehensible to the mathematical imagination. Since it is constituted by transgression of (abstraction from) the sensible, metaphysics is established only by eluding the
grasp of what it overcomes. Metaphysics is confirmed in its very incomprehensibility.

The occurrences of *métaphysique* in the Cartesian corpus, however
rare and dispersed they might be, thus find a real coherence as soon as
they are related to the Aristotelian determinations, but also the scholastic ones, accepted by Descartes' contemporaries. Thus, from 1630 on,
Descartes assumes as his own the goal of Aristotle in *E1:* to constitute a
science that passes beyond physics and mathematics. He also recovers
abstraction as the privileged act for transgressing the two secondary sciences, and he expands its power through the *abductio mentis a sensibus.*
On this henceforth secure basis, the decisive question can be raised:
since *metaphysics* does indeed come up in the Cartesian corpus, how is
the concept of metaphysics properly understood?

§3. Two Decisions in Favor of a First Philosophy

In this way, the occurrences of *métaphysique* scattered throughout the
Cartesian corpus form a system, or at least are organized cohesively in
their relation to the contemporary philosophical lexicon and usage.
What remains is for us to assess, based on these similarities, the differences produced by the decisions particular to Descartes. This amounts
to investigating the identity of the metaphysics established in 1641 by
the *Meditationes.*

It is precisely in this text that the displacement is accomplished most
indisputably, since Descartes expressly denies to the *Meditationes* the
title *metaphysicae.* The originality of the *Meditationes* is found in this:

33. *Principia Philosophiae, Epistula dedicatoria* (AT VIII-1, 4, 3–6 = PW I, 192). To
illustrate this incompatibility of the two sciences existing in a single individual, Descartes
points to Fermat: "Just between us, I hold M. Fermat to be one of the least capable of
raising strong objections. I believe that he knows mathematics, but in philosophy, I have
always thought that he reasons poorly" (*To Mersenne,* 4 March 1641 [AT III, 328, 10–14 =
not included in PW]). See also (in addition to notes 8 and 9 *supra*) *To Mersenne,* 6 May
1630 (AT I, 150, 4–22 = PW III, 24– 25).

they are *not metaphysicae*. This must be emphasized all the more, as it is not visible in the French translation, which, by speaking of *Méditations métaphysiques,* ignores Descartes' repeated warnings to Mersenne on the occasion of the manuscript's final revision. For if he often designates the *Meditationes* as "[his] *Metaphysics*,"[34] Descartes twice presents, quite clearly, the reason that nonetheless forbids their being qualified as *metaphysicae*: "Yesterday I sent my *Metaphysics* to M. de Zuytlichem [Huygens] to post on to you . . . I have not put any title on it, but it seems to me that the most suitable would be *René Descartes' Meditations on First Philosophy* because I do not confine my discussion to God and the soul, but deal in general with all the first things to be known by philosophizing." On the same day and to the same correspondent, in similar terms: "I am finally sending to you my work on metaphysics, which I have not yet put a title to, so that I can make you its godfather and leave the baptism to you. I think, as I wrote to you in my previous letter, that it could be called *Meditationes de Prima Philosophia;* for in the book I deal not just with God and the soul, but in general with all the first things that can be known by philosophizing in an orderly way."[35] In fact, the

34. ". . . my Metaphysics . . . ," *To Mersenne,* 28 October 1640 (AT III, 216, 5 = PW III, 156). The formula often reappears elsewhere: 11 November 1640 (AT III, 234, 17 and 235, 10 = PW III, not included and 157); 18 November 1640 (AT III, 243, 3–4 = not included in PW); 24 December 1640(?) (AT III, 265, 13 = PW III, 163); 31 December 1640 (AT III, 271, 8 = PW III, 165; AT III, 275, 2 and 276, 3 = PW III, 166 and 167); 21 January 1641 (AT III, 284, 27 and 286, 19 = PW III, 169 and not included); 28 January 1641 (AT III, 296, 24 and 297, 1 = neither included in PW); 4 March 1641 (AT III, 328, 2 = not included in PW); 18 March 1641 (AT III, 334, 4 and 340, 7–8 = PW III, 175 and 177); 21 April 1641 (AT III, 359, 7 and 363, 13 = neither included in PW); September 1641 (AT III, 436, 14 and 438, 14 = PW III, 198 and 198). This phrase is not another title for the *Meditationes* (as F. Alquié leads us to believe by systematically using italics in his edition, in contrast with the usage of AT). It is rather an abridged formula for more lengthy designations: ". . . the work on metaphysics . . ." (*To Gibieuf,* 11 November 1640 [AT III, 237, 7 = PW III, 157]), ". . . my work on metaphysics . . ." (*To Mersenne,* 11 November 1640 [AT III, 238, 18 = PW III, 158]), ". . . the little book on metaphysics . . ." (ibid., 233, 24–25 = PW III, 157), ". . . my meditations on metaphysics . . ." (*To Mersenne,* December 1640 [AT III, 260, 9–10 = PW III, 161]), ". . . my thoughts about metaphysics . . ." (*To Gibieuf,* 19 January 1642 [AT III, 472, 7–8 = not included in PW]), ". . . my musings about metaphysics . . ." (*To Huygens,* 12 November 1640 [AT III, 241, 3– 4; see also 763, 2 = neither included in PW)], etc. The parallel with ". . . my *Physics* and *Metaphysics* . . ." (*To Huygens,* March 1638 [AT II, 50, 13–14 = PW III, 92]; *To Vatier,* 22 November 1638 [AT I, 564, 14 = PW III, 88]) confirms our point: since "physics" never constituted a title, or even part of a title, for one of Descartes' works, "metaphysics" also remains a simple, conventional denomination, in accord with the order of the matters being considered.

35. *To Mersenne,* 11 November 1640 (AT III, respectively 235, 10–18 and 239, 2–7 = PW III, 157 [modified] and 158 [modified]). In the public discussions and contrary to the

title of the two Latin editions will remain unchanged ... *de prima Philosophia,* while *animae immortalitas* will be converted to *animae humanae a corpore distinctio* (AT VII, pp. xix, xxi, xxii, vi, and 17). Even the French translation, which illegitimately adds "... métaphysiques," retains an echo of *prima Philosophia* by going on to explain itself with: *Les Méditations métaphysiques de René Descartes touchant la première philosophie.*[36] It is thus a matter of a clear and steadfast decision—a decision against *métaphysique/metaphysica* and in favor of *philosophie première/prima philosophia,* in the strict sense of φιλοσοφία πρώτη and following Aristotle's nomenclature. From this lexical choice, two lines of questioning are born. Without pursuing them, the Cartesian decision, as clear as it might be, will remain meaningless. It is thus first (§3) a matter of assessing its real importance for Descartes himself: what domain is opened for investigation by each of the two opposing terms? What privilege authorizes first philosophy to gain the upper hand over metaphysics? Then (§4) it will be necessary to assess the displacements that the Cartesian choices force upon the thematics of metaphysics, considered in its historiological state as well as its historical evolution.

The declared intention is stated explicitly and clearly, at least at first glance: Descartes prefers to qualify the *Meditationes* with the title *prima Philosophia* rather than that of *metaphysica* because in them he deals "not just with God and the soul, but in general with all the first things" (AT III, 239, 5–7; 235, 15–17 = PW III, 158; 157). This formulation is

---

approximations used in the correspondence, Descartes respects the printed title: "... ut in Meditationibus de prima Philosophia nuper editis [as may be seen in the recently published *Meditations on First Philosophy*] ...," "... meas Meditationes de prima Philosophia edi [curare] ..." (*To Regius,* January 1642 [AT III, 503, 15 and 507, 24–25 = PW III, 208 and not included]). The choice of 1641 bears the trace of a confusion between the two titles: *Meditationes Metaphysicae de prima Philosophia* (AT VII, 448 is equal to AT III, 418 = neither included in PW). Does this echo Mersenne's hesitancy and Descartes' emendations?

36. Title of the editions of 1647, 1661, and 1673 (AT IX-1, pp. xi, xiii, and xv). The adjective *metaphysical* is of so little importance that, even in these editions, it disappears when it is repeated just before the first meditation. One finds there, for the first time, an exact translation of the Latin title: "Meditations on first philosophy in which are demonstrated the existence of God and the distinction between the human soul and the body" (AT IX-1, 13 = AT VII, 17 = PW II, 12). It is regrettable that J.-M. Beyssade's edition of the *Meditationes/Méditations,* irreplaceable in so many other respects, neither mentions this correction nor compares the titles (Jean-Marie Beyssade, *Méditations métaphysiques. Objections et réponses suivies de quatre lettres* [Paris: Garnier-Flammarion, 1979]). One can observe, in addition, that Husserl, resuming Descartes' path, will also come to think "... metaphysics as 'first philosophy'" (*Cartesianische Meditationen,* §60, Husserliana, I, p. 166 [English trans., p. 139]).

surprising in and of itself, but also because it seems immediately contradicted by the developed title of the *Meditationes,* which explicitly mentions the existence of God and the real distinction between the soul and the body—". . . in quibus [= in qua] Dei existentia et animae a corpore distinctio demonstrantur [in which are demonstrated the existence of God and the distinction between the human soul and the body]."[37] For these two "points concerning God and the soul" (AT III, 268, 10–11 = PW III, 164) characterize metaphysics in its most strict sense. Elsewhere Descartes comments on his "work of metaphysics" as follows: "The route which I take to make known the nature of the human soul and to demonstrate the existence of God is the only one which could enable us to reach our destination"; or, "for metaphysics," "I think that I have fully demonstrated the existence of God and the immortality of the soul." In short, "the principles of metaphysics . . . give us the knowledge of God and of our soul."[38] In the same vein, metaphysics can even be partially confused with theology—since it covers two regions proper to it, God and the (immortal or at least immaterial) soul: "Semper existimavi duas quaestiones, de Deo et de anima, praecipuas esse ex iis quae Philosophiae potius quam Theologiae ope demonstrandae [I have always thought that two topics—namely God and the soul—are prime examples of subjects where demonstrative proofs ought to be given with the aid of philosophy rather than theology]" (AT VII, 1, 7–9 = PW II, 3). Hence, two theological questions are found to be in fact straightforwardly metaphysical and thus are to be counted within a metaphysics that has become

37. AT VII, 17 = PW II, 12. The often emphasized variations in how the Latin title is phrased perhaps do not merit so much attention: the passage from *in qua* [*prima philosophia*] to *in quibus* [*Meditationibus*] does not in any way alter the choice in favor of *prima philosophia* and to the detriment of *metaphysica* (in *both* versions). As for the passage from *immortalitas* to *distinctio a corpore,* though appearing only in 1642, it in fact can be found at least as early as 1640: "You say that I have not said a word about the immortality of the soul. You should not be surprised. I could not prove that God could not annihilate the soul, but only that it is by nature entirely distinct from the body, and consequently it is not bound by nature to die with it. This is all that is required as a foundation for religion, and is all that I had any intention of proving" (*To Mersenne,* 24 December 1640 [AT III, 265, 28–266, 8 = PW III, 163]).

38. Respectively, *To Gibieuf,* 11 November 1640 (AT III, 237, 6; 9–12 = PW III, 157; 158); then *To Huygens,* July 1640 (AT III, 103, 6–7; 102, 27–103, 2 = PW III, 150; 150); finally, *To Elisabeth,* 28 June 1643 (AT III, 695, 5–7 = PW III, 228). See also *To Mersenne,* 31 December 1640: ". . . I send you an abstract of my *Metaphysics.* . . . Without wrecking the order, I could not prove that the soul is distinct from the body before proving the existence of God . . ." (AT III, 271, 7–8; 272, 3–6 = PW III, 165); *To Regius,* January 1642 (AT III, 503, 6–17 = PW III, 207–8).

equivalent to rational theology: "... haec a priori Metaphysica sive Theologica [the following *a priori* metaphysical or theological ones]" (AT III, 505, 10–11 = PW III, 208), as Descartes will unhesitatingly state their equivalence from time to time. Nonetheless, this equivalence, however surprising it might be, allows us to see that opposed to metaphysics, which has been narrowly limited to the domain of rational theology, there might be a "first philosophy," which, passing beyond, aims at "... in general ... all the first things" (AT III, 235, 17; 239, 6 = PW III, 157; 158). In Aristotelian terms, one would say that φιλοσοφία πρώτη here concerns *all* really separate and immaterial nature, therefore that it considers not only "... the idea of God [and] the idea of the soul," but "... the ideas of nonsensible things" (AT III, 392, 13, see 18 = PW III, 184 [modified], see 185) "in general." It thus admits other nonsensible natures besides God and the soul. Therefore, given that for Descartes, God and the soul exhaust the field of metaphysics, the enlargement of this field immediately postulates a new discipline—first philosophy, which alone bears on *all* the first things, whatever they might be and whatever might be their primacy. The transition from one discipline to the other is marked quite clearly: "... iterum hîc aggredior easdem de Deo et mente humana quaestiones, *simulque* totius primae Philosophiae initia tractare [I am again tackling the same questions concerning God and the human mind; and *at the same time* I am also going to deal with the foundations of First Philosophy in its entirety]"; or in French: "... j'entreprends derechef de traiter de Dieu et de l'âme humaine, *et ensemble* de jetter les fondements de la philosophie première."[39] No doubt the equivalence remains, which permits him to say from time to time "first philosophy or metaphysics," almost indifferently (AT IX-2, 16, 15–16 = PW I, 187). Two regions in fact remain common to these distinct disciplines. However, first philosophy passes beyond metaphysics by being extended to *all* primacy; hence it is universal as well as first. It is enough for the "things" to be attested to as "first" for "first philosophy" immediately to confirm its universality in them. Such an extension implies a rigorous and powerful determination of primacy such that it can exert itself in a field much more "general" than that to which metaphysics is confined—namely, simple abstraction. First philosophy must practice more primacy than metaphysics practices abstraction. Thus, Des-

---

39. *Meditationes ... , Praefatio ad lectorem* (AT VII, 9, 20–23 = PW II, 8 [modified]), and its French translation by Clerselier, omitted in AT IX-1, but reproduced in *Œuvres philosophiques,* ed. F. Alquié, vol. 2, p. 392.

cartes has made a first decision concerning the essence of metaphysics: first philosophy is more essential to the question of metaphysics than is the metaphysical discipline itself. The former covers the domain of the latter (God and the soul), while also passing beyond it toward "all the first things in general." Before assessing the historical importance of this decision by relating it to the definitions of *metaphysics* and *first philosophy* prior to and contemporaneous with Descartes, it must still be asked how primacy is to be understood here, such that it can be extended "in general" and can exceed God and the soul. Or in other words: by what relation can primacy reach the universal instead of being subtracted from it as a particular region par excellence? In short, according to what parameter does primacy succeed in transgressing the very transgression that is accomplished by metaphysics and that defines it?

Such a conflict of transgressions leads us to consider the second Cartesian decision in favor of the primacy of first philosophy, a decision made in the very same texts that stated the previous one. In order to make the exposition easier to follow, we had refrained from a thorough examination; but now we must comment on them in full: ". . . because I do not confine my discussion to God and the soul, but deal in general with all the first things to be known by philosophizing" (AT III, 235, 15–18 = PW III, 157 [modified]); and ". . . I deal not just with God and the soul, but in general with all the first things that can be known by philosophizing according to the order" (AT III, 239, 5–7 = PW III, 158 [modified]). Primacy—which alone guarantees first philosophy its priority over metaphysics—is to be determined within the order of knowledge, such as it determines the Cartesian way of philosophizing. According to the order of knowledge, knowledge has an absolute priority. Therefore, the first being that knowledge knows will be the one that exerts it, the *ego*, which thus will necessarily precede the knowledge and existence of God. As the *Principia* puts it, ". . . haec cognitio *ego cogito, ergo sum*, est omnium prima et certissima, quae cuilibet ordine philosophanti occurrat [This piece of knowledge—*I am thinking, therefore I exist*—is the first and most certain of all to occur to anyone who philosophizes in an orderly way]." The *Principia* thus confirm in advance the privilege that the *Preface* of 1647 will accord to the same *ego:* ". . . I took the being [*être*] or existence of this thought as my first principle, and from it I deduced very clearly the following: there is a God. . . ."[40] Pri-

---

40. Respectively, *Principia Philosophiae, I,* §7 (AT VIII-1, 7, 7–9 = PW I, 195) (in addition, the heading ". . . atque hoc est primum, quod ordine philosophando cognoscimus

macy, then, does not qualify the *ego* as such (not that Descartes questions its primacy over God, since he affirms it explicitly); rather it is the knowledge of the *ego,* not directly the *ego* in and of itself, that precedes the knowledge of God. Its primacy therefore does not come to the *ego* from its own reserves, but only from thought—which, in turn, it exerts par excellence. Primacy is therefore not stolen from God by the *ego,* nor from God and the soul by some third being; primacy relativizes all beings by attaching itself to the only thought that thinks them all. More exactly, primacy qualifies all thoughts so long as they follow the very order of thought in operation: ". . . direct my thought in an orderly manner" (DM 18, 27 = PW I, 120). These new "first things" reveal themselves only in the order established for making them evident through the series of things to be known; one thing precedes another (and thus confirms the new definition of primacy) when and only when it makes knowledge of it possible. Thus, the classification of the sciences will have to break with every hierarchy of beings as soon as the method requires that

> . . . res omnes per quasdam series posse disponi, non quidem in quantum ad aliquod genus entis referuntur, sicut Philosophi in categorias suas diviserunt, sed in quantum unae ex aliis cognosci possunt, ita ut, quoties aliqua difficultas occurrit, statim advertere possimus, utrum profuturum sit aliquas alias prius, et quasnam et quo ordine perlustrare. [All things can be arranged serially in various groups, not in so far as they can be referred to some genus of beings (such as the categories into which philosophers divide things), but in so far as some things can be known on the basis of others. Thus when a difficulty arises, we can see at once whether it will be worth looking at any others first, and if so which ones and in what order.] [AT X, 381, 9–16 = PW I, 21.]

The classification of the sciences ought to be done in accordance with the order in which the knowledges are engendered each from the other. Applied to the relation between philosophy and the other sciences, this method implies a revolution: from now on, the primacy of philosophy will no longer be exerted according to the likely order of the matters under consideration, nor will it be based on a hierarchy of beings culmi-

---

[This is the first thing we come to know when we philosophize in an orderly way] . . ."); then *Principia, Preface* (AT IX-2, 10, 4–7 = PW I, 184 [modified]). See DM, 32, 15–23 = PW I, 127. See *To Clerselier,* June–July 1646 (AT IV, 444, 23–25 = PW III, 290). For Descartes, it is all a matter of explaining "the whole of philosophy in an orderly way, without having omitted any of the things which ought to precede the topics I wrote about last . . ." (AT IX-2, 16, 30–17, 1 = PW III, 187–88).

nating in a theology and respecting the parameter of beings in their Being (ontology), since the categories and the genuses of beings have been rendered obsolete—as a result of the method. If philosophy claims to have restored its primacy, it will succeed in doing this only by accomplishing it according to the order of thoughts, thus by establishing itself as the first thought (or the first series of thoughts) allowing the other thoughts to be engendered—without any consideration of the relative dignity of the beings involved in each case. In other words, philosophy no longer borrows its primacy from certain regions of being, those supposed to be intrinsically first (God, the soul, the separate intelligences—in short, the domain of rational theology), nor from being considered as such (ontology), since being no longer enters into play and is disqualified as soon as the *ordo cognoscendi* arrives on the scene. Philosophy will reestablish its primacy over the other sciences by producing it itself by means of the order; that is to say, it will do so by installing itself as the unique instance of all the first thoughts that generate other thoughts (sciences), whatever they might be, and whatever might be the corresponding beings.[41] The radicality of such a change in the essence of philosophy (and not only in its role in the classification of the sciences) makes it easier to explain the upheaval and at times the imprecision of its Cartesian titling. For all the previous denominations become obsolete as soon as the order laid out by the method appears. A first decision contested the primacy of metaphysics, as a title and as a science. First philosophy then inherited it. It did so, however, without this phrase of Aristotelian origin being able to keep, in a context inaugurated by the *Regulae,* even the least bit of legitimacy or rigor. How can one still speak of "first philosophy," when reference neither can nor must be made to a first being? A second decision will therefore have to detach the phrase *first philosophy* from its former sense. In this way, under the same name, a new concept of first philosophy might be forged.

This is what is intended by the definitions given in the *Preface* to the *Principles* of 1647: ". . . The first part of philosophy is metaphysics, which contains the principles of knowledge, including the explanation of the principal attributes of God, the non-material nature of our souls and all the clear and distinct notions which are in us" (AT IX-2, 14, 7–12 = PW I, 186). This formulation calls for several remarks. *(a)* Here, *metaphysics* does not suggest that Descartes has in some way changed his mind and

41. On the ontological status of the order of knowledge, one can refer to *Sur l'ontologie grise de Descartes,* §§30–31.

put into question the first decision in favor of *first philosophy*. Rather, these two terms are disqualified (or overinterpreted) indifferently by the new primacy. Hence, their eventual equivalence: ". . . what may be called 'first philosophy' or 'metaphysics'" (16, 15–16 = 187). In themselves, these two terms are seen to be indifferent, indeed equivalent, in the light of a wholly other concept of primacy. *(b)* The fundamental determination of primacy in philosophy was in fact given in the text that immediately precedes this one: ". . . the first part [of true philosophy] is metaphysics, which contains the principles of knowledge . . ." (14, 8–9 = 186); and: ". . . I divided the book [the *Principles of Philosophy*] into four parts. The first contains the principles of knowledge" (16, 12–14 = 187). Primacy befalls philosophy neither from the old title of φιλοσοφία πρώτη, nor from the corresponding ontic region, but from its original function as the science of principles, principles that the other sciences borrow from it (DM, 8, 30–31; 21, 30 = 115; 121). All the other sciences draw their principles from this single primacy—physics, of course; mechanics, as well as medicine and morals; but also (and this is the fundamental point) metaphysics in the narrow and old sense of the term; for this holds also for "the foundations of metaphysics" (16, 3 = 187). Even though it constitutes its "roots" (14, 25 = 186), metaphysics does not coincide with the entire philosophical tree, and especially not with the originary primacy. *(c)* For the principles, inasmuch as they are "principles of knowledge" (14, 9 = 186), are first defined by the epistemological overdetermination of the beings that are commonly called metaphysical or said to belong to first philosophy (in the old sense). Neither God nor the soul, insofar as they are beings, deserve to be called principles of knowledge; only the "explanation" of God and the soul merits such a title (14, 10 = 186). For—secondly—the principles of knowledge are defined as "the first causes and true principles" (5, 22 = 181), as "the cause or principle" (8, 10 = 183). In short, primacy defines the principle solely on the basis of the fact that the latter inaugurates knowledge through causes (the sole certain knowledge): "in order to set about acquiring . . . that to which the term 'to philosophize' strictly refers, we must start with the search for first causes, that is to say principles" (2, 17–18 = 179 [modified]). Hence, finally, these principles can be defined, beyond God and the soul (reduced to their "explanation"), as "all the clear and distinct notions which are in us" (14, 12 = 186). What counts as first principle, and therefore what guarantees for philosophy the function of first philosophy, is any and all evidence that is irreducible to another, more originary evidence; no consideration is given to the ontic status of its possible object. The only condition is that such evidence inaugurate a *series rerum quae-rendarum* (AT X, 392, 10 = PW I, 28)—that is to say, that it make it possible for other evidence to be brought to light. Consequently, between what is called Descartes' method and what is called his metaphysics, we have found relations that are sufficiently complex to forbid confusing them as well as separating them absolutely. To be sure, only evident knowledge attains the dignified rank of first philosophy; but by assuming this rank, evident knowledge enters into a debate with *metaphysica* as it had been previously defined.

§4. Primacy and Universality: The Order and Being [l'étant]

Descartes thinks metaphysics as first philosophy because he thoroughly modifies the essence of primacy, which defines first philosophy in its new sense. This double decision would remain empty, however, if its conceptual import were not assessed. It can be assessed only if one repeats the displacements that the Cartesian decisions imposed on the previous definitions of metaphysics as well as first philosophy.

To confine ourselves at first to an authority acknowledged in his own time and known to Descartes, let us again consider the thematics of Suarez: philosophy at once bears on "the most noble beings and the most universal definitions of being," for "the same [and singular] science which treats these special objects considers at the same time [*simul*] all the predicates which are common to them and other things, and this defines all metaphysical doctrine."[42] Whatever the variations might be,

---

42. Suarez, *Disputationes Metaphysicae,* respectively *I,* s. 4, n. 2: ". . . haec scientia . . . tractat . . . de nobilissimis entibus et de universalissimis rationibus entis et maxime abstractis" (vol. 25, 26). Then *I,* s. 3, n. 10: ". . . eadem ergo scientia, quae de his specialibus objectis tractat, simul considerat omnia praedicta, quae illis sunt cum aliis rebus communia, et haec est tota metaphysica doctrina; est ergo una scientia" (vol. 25, p. 25). See *I,* s. 5, n. 23: "Distinguendae videntur duae partes hujus doctrinae: una est quae de ente ut ens est, ejusque principiis et proprietatibus disserit. Altera est, quae tractat de aliquibus peculiaribus rationibus entium, praesertim de immaterialibus" (vol. 25, 43). On the prior history of the distinctions that end up in Suarez's duality, consult A. Zimmermann, *Ontologie oder Metaphysik? Die Diskussion über den Gegenstand der Metaphysik im 13. und 14. Jahrhundert. Texte und Untersuchungen* (Leiden/Cologne, 1965). On Suarez's doctrine of metaphysics, refer to J.-F. Courtine, "Le projet suarézien de la métaphysique," *Archives de Philosophie* 42/2 (1979), and H. Siegfried, *Wahrheit und Metaphysik bei Suarez* (Bonn, 1967). As for the fundamental meaning of this doctrine, one should refer to M. Heidegger, *Die Grundbegriffe der Metaphysik,* particularly §14, "The concept of metaphysics in Franz Suarez and the fundamental character of modern metaphysics," G. A., 29/30 [English trans., pp. 51–55].

the two domains of the one philosophy represent in Suarez a retrieval of the duality inaugurated, but not resolved, by Aristotle: a definition is given, on the one hand, for a φιλοσοφία πρώτη as the doctrine of the most divine beings, and on the other, for an ἐπιστήμη τις considering τὸ ὄν ᾗ ὄν. Aristotle does not unite them beneath a common title, in contrast to Suarez, who unites them in the neologism *metaphysica*. Far from guaranteeing that Suarez thought the unity of philosophy more radically than did Aristotle, the appearance of this term no doubt signals the contrary: a purely verbal connection masks, by pretending to suppress, the internal tension between the two dimensions of the question about the Being of beings. Nevertheless, one can consider more carefully the way in which Suarez composes the two domains of what thus becomes *the* metaphysics; for his decision exercises a decisive influence over all modern philosophy, through Descartes. Beneath the title *metaphysica*, Suarez gathers two sciences issuing from the Aristotelian duality:

> It is to be affirmed, however, with the commonly held opinion, that metaphysics is purely and simply one single science with a specific unity. For this seems clearly to have been the opinion of Aristotle, . . . who attributes to it, as if to a single and selfsame science, names and attributes which are appropriate to it in part insofar as it deals with God and the intelligences (for this reason it is named theology, divine science, and first philosophy) and in part insofar as it deals with being as being, with its first attributes and principles (for which reason it is called universal science and metaphysics). It is called wisdom [sapientia] in that it encompasses all that and contemplates the first principles and the first causes of things.[43]

Two reasons justify comparing this schematic with the Cartesian choices. First, it culminates in *Sapientia,* science of causes and principles, exactly

---

43. Suarez, *Disputationes Metaphysicae, I,* s. 3, n. 9:

Nihilominus asserendum est cum communi sententia, metaphysicam simpliciter esse unam scientiam specie. Haec enim videtur clara mens Aristotelis in toto prooemio seu c. 1 et 2 lib. 1 Metaphys., ubi semper de hac scientia tanquam de una specie loquitur, eique tanquam uni et eidem attribuit nomina et attributa quae partim illi conveniunt secundum quod versatur circa Deum et intelligentias; sic enim vocatur theologia, seu scientia divina et prima philosophia; partim ut versatur circa ens in quantum ens et prima principia ejus, qua ratione dicitur scientia universalis et metaphysica. Sapientia autem vocatur quatenus haec omnia complectitur, et prima principia primasque rerum causas contemplatur.

(Vol. 25, p. 24.)

as Descartes' own schema opened with wisdom: ". . . the word 'philosophy' means the study of wisdom . . . ; in order to set about acquiring it—and it is this activity to which the term 'to philosophize' strictly refers—we must start with the search for first causes or principles" (AT IX-2, 2, 7–18 = PW I, 179), "a fifth way for reaching wisdom . . . consists in the search for the first causes and the true principles" (5, 19–22 = 181), ". . . the true principles enabling one to reach the highest degree of wisdom" (9, 15–17 = 183). The goal—to reach wisdom, the ultimate accomplishment of philosophy, through the knowledge of principles—is thus as valid for Descartes as it is for Suarez. Next, a second point is common to them: for the one as well as for the other, the task is to assign correctly the diverse titles of philosophy, particularly those of *metaphysica* and *philosophia prima*. It will therefore be here that Descartes' innovation will show itself most clearly.

One difference presents itself at the very outset. For Descartes, the choice in favor of *philosophia prima,* and to the detriment of *metaphysica,* results from the fundamental decision not to "confine [his] discussion to God and the soul in particular but to deal in general with all the first things" (AT III, 235, 16–17 = PW III, 157 [modified]), or not to deal "just with God and the soul, but in general with all the first things" (AT III, 239, 5–6 = PW III, 158). In short, *prima philosophia* covers a more "general," less "particular," domain than that of metaphysics. But for Suarez, the situation is exactly the inverse, since *prima philosophia* concerns only God and the intelligences, far from passing beyond them toward a more vast horizon: ". . . concerning God and the intelligences (*circa Deum et intelligentias*)." According to Suarez's thematic, the two objects mentioned by Descartes in the fully developed title of the *Meditationes* would define precisely *prima philosophia* in its more particular acceptation, thus contradicting the suggestions made to Mersenne. Consequently, if for Descartes it is metaphysics that can sometimes be confused with rational theology (". . . metaphysica sive theologica . . ." [AT III, 505, 10–11]), for Suarez it is *prima philosophia* that is reducible to theology: ". . . sic enim vocatur theologia, seu scientia divina et prima philosophia [It is called theology, or divine science and first philosophy]." And while for Descartes *prima philosophia* alone studies "in general," Suarez accords universality only to metaphysics: ". . . qua ratione dicitur scientia universalis et metaphysica [for which reason it is called universal science and metaphysics]." Everything happens as if Descartes took up the Suarezian couple *prima philosophia/metaphysica* only in order to invert the characteristics of each: the first becomes universal and not theological, the second becomes particular and theological. This reversal deserves all the more attention as it contradicts the usage common among Descartes' contemporaries. For them, the rival terms are distinguished by the more or less exclusive consideration of God and the separate intelligences. Thus Abra de Raconis, detailing the names of metaphysics, mentions "Philosophia simpliciter," then "first philosophy . . . when it speaks of the most noble things, namely God and the angels," next "theologia rationalis," and only in the end "Metaphysica."[44] As for Scipion Dupleix, in a similar discussion, after having observed the recent introduction of the term *metaphysics,* he mentions in the second place "that of Knowledge or Wisdom," in the third, that of "theology or science of God," and finally, in the fifth rank, "first philosophy or first science, inasmuch as it considers the first being among beings."[45] Eustache de Saint-Paul defends the same position: when considering the narrow definition of metaphysics, he immediately objects that its adherents ". . . do not assign to metaphysics a great enough object, as will appear evident," if one supposes that "the ordinary proposition is much more likely: the object of Metaphysics, adequate and *per se* . . . , is real being, *per se,* complete, common to God and creatures."[46] In light of all this, should it be concluded that Descartes' decision is absolutely original and admits no precedent? If a precedent nevertheless must be found, it would have to be discovered in an authority recognized by his contemporaries and likely to be known by Descartes himself (or at least accessible to him). This appears to be the case with Pererius (Bruno Pereira, 1535–1610), the celebrated Spanish Jesuit who taught at the *Collegium Romanum* up until his death in 1610, and published, among other works, *De commu-*

44. Abra de Raconis, *Totius Philosophiae . . . brevis tractatio, Praeludium primum (= Quarta pars . . .):* ". . . nomine primae Philosophiae . . . cum de praestantissimis rebus, Deo nempe et angelis, verba faciat" (op. cit., p. 2).

45. Scipion Dupleix, *La Métaphysique ou science surnaturelle, I, 2, Des divers noms de la Métaphysique,* op. cit., pp. 17–18. See: "Metaphysics considers all things insofar as they are, but principally the sovereign God, author and preserver of those things and the Spirits, Angels and Intelligences, which Plato calls minor deities" (*Logique, I,* 3, op. cit., p. 32; see also *I,* 4, p. 36).

46. Eustache de Saint-Paul, *Summa Philosophiae quadripartita . . . , Praefatio,* q. 2:

> Dissentiunt de re propositia Philosophi; alii enim Deum, alii substantias separatas, alii substantiam in communi, alii ens finitum quod vocant praedicamentale, objectum esse Metaphysicae contendunt: sed hi omnes non satis amplum illud assignant, ut patebit. . . . Est igitur longe verisimilior communis sententia: Objectum per se et adequatum Metaphysicae (de eo enim, non vero de objecto per accidens, aut partiali proposita quaestio intelligenda est) esse *ens reale, per se, completum, commune Deo et rebus creatis.*

(Op. cit., *IV,* p. 3.) See also: ". . . haec Metaphysicae definitio, ut videlicet dicatur theoretica de ente reali per se et completo ab omni materia saltem secundum indifferentiam abstracto" (ibid., p. 5).

nibus omnium rerum naturalium principiis et affectionibus libri quinde-cim in 1576 (which resumed a commentary on the *Physics* that first appeared in 1562). This work was reprinted often until the beginning of the next century, in France and in Germany as well as in Italy. Now we have proof that, in other respects, Descartes was influenced by Pererius on at least one other point: in the *Regulae,* he borrows from him the phrase *Mathesis Universalis.*[47] He was perfectly capable of knowing about it also from other theses in other works. And yet there is only one that was able to make an impression on him: contrary to and before the Suarezian division, Pererius—Jesuit against Jesuit—had accorded to first philosophy a status that anticipates Descartes. To be sure, he sometimes confuses the competing titles, as if to emphasize their difficulty: "It is the shared opinion of all that Metaphysics surpasses the other sciences in dignity because of the supreme nobility of the things it treats. For it deals with God and the intelligences; consequently it is called first philosophy, Metaphysics, Wisdom, Theology, that is to say, science of God, either because God alone properly has such a science or because it alone contains the science of divine things."[48] But the considerations that aim to specify the parts (and therefore the formal objects) of philosophy end up at a clear-cut threefold division, and this threefold division contradicts in advance Suarez's twofold division. It thus anticipates Descartes' terminology:

> I posit that there are three parts of Metaphysics and therefore that it is approached in a threefold way: The first is the principle and the end of all the others (this is why this science receives the name Metaphysics, theology, and the most noble of all); it treats things separate from matter, in reality as much as by reason, such as the intelligences and God. The second is that in which the transcendentals appear, such as being, one, true

47. Editions published in 1579 and 1586 in Paris, 1585 and 1588 in Lyon, 1595, 1603, and 1618 in Cologne, etc. (See C. Sommervogel, *Bibliothèque des Ecrivains de la Compagnie de Jésus,* vol. VI, 499–507). On the role of Pererius in the formation of the Cartesian theory of science, see G. Capulli, *Mathesis Universalis. Genesi di una idea nel XVI secolo* (Rome, 1969), and our annotation of *Règles utiles et claires pour la direction de l'esprit en la recherche de la vérité* (The Hague, 1977), pp. 161*ff.* Pererius' influence (in particular, his influence on Goclenius, the "inventor" of ὀντολογία) was pointed out and highlighted by M. Wundt, *Die deutsche Schulmetaphysik des 17. Jahrhunderts,* pp. 169*ff.*

48. *De Communibus omnium rerum . . . , I,* 16: "Est consors sententia omnium Metaphysicam dignitate antecellere reliquis disciplinis propter summam nobilitatem earum rerum quas tractat; agit enim de Deo et intelligentiis; quapropter vocatur prima Philosophia, Metaphysica, Sapientia, Theologia, hoc est scientia Dei; vel quoniam hanc proprie solus Deus habet, vel quia haec sola continet scientiam rerum divinarum" (1576 ed., p. 31).

good, act, and power; this is why this part of Metaphysics is called the most universal and exercises a power and a prerogative over all the other sciences. The third comprises the ten categories.

Bracketing a consideration of the categories, metaphysics is well and truly divided into, on the one hand, a metaphysics restricted to theology (God and the intelligences), as in Descartes, and, on the other hand, a "pars . . . universalissima," constituted of the transcendentals. The identity, as yet anonymous, of this universality is soon stated more precisely: "There must necessarily be two sciences distinct from one another: one which treats the transcendentals and the most universal things; another which treats [only] the intelligences. The first is called *prima philosophia* and *universal science;* the second properly Metaphysics, Theology, Wisdom, divine science."[49] Thus, first philosophy exchanges characteristics with metaphysics: the region of the divine (God and the separate intelligences) passes from first philosophy to metaphysics; this implies that metaphysics, now *de intelligentiis,* is reduced to theology, and that *prima philosophia* is detached from the φιλοσοφία πρώτη that is attached to the divine alone (τὸ Θεῖον). Accordingly, *prima philosophia* will exercise a primacy of a radically new sort, since it in fact extends to universality: ". . . dicitur universalissima . . . , agat de . . . universalissimis rebus, . . . dicitur prima Philosophia et scientia universalis [It is called the most universal . . . , it treats . . . the most universal things, . . . it is called first philosophy and universal science]." Pererius thus inverts, some thirty years in advance, the thematic of Suarez, and in this way anticipates the position that Descartes will adopt in 1640: *prima Philosophia* is *scientia universalis,* indeed *universalissima,* because *de facto* and *de jure* it deals

49. *De Communibus omnium rerum . . . ,* successively, *I,* 6:

Et sic statuo, tres partes esse Metaphysicae, ac proinde triplicem esse considerationem ejus: una est principalis et quasi finis caeterarum (propter quam talis scientia dicitur Metaphysica, Theologia et omnium nobilissima) in qua tractantur res sejunctae a materia secundum rem et rationem, cujusmodi sunt intelligentiae et Deus. Altera est pars in qua declarantur transcendentia, ut ens, unum, verum, bonum, actus, potentia; propter quam partem Metaphysica dicitur universalissima et habere jus et imperium in caeteras scientias. Tertia pars ejus complectitur decem praedicamenta.

(Op. cit., p. 13.) Then: "Tertia conclusio. Necesse esse duas scientias distinctas inter se. Unam quae agat de transcendentibus et universalissimis rebus. Alteram quae de intelligentiis. Illa dicitur prima Philosophia et scientia universalis, haec vocabitur proprie Metaphysica, Theologia, sapientia, Divina Scientia" (op. cit., p. 14). The originality of Pererius' terminology had been signaled by E. Vollrath, "Die Gliederung der Metaphysik in eine *Metaphysica generalis* und eine *Metaphysica specialis,*" *Zeitschrift für philosophische Forschung* XVI/2 (1962). Nonetheless, its importance must not be magnified so much that

"not just with God and the soul in particular, but in general with all the first things . . ." (AT III, 239, 5–6 = PW III, 158 [modified]). Contrary to the regnant Suarezian terminology, Descartes thus reproduces the original and paradoxical interpretation of *prima philosophia* as *universalis,* not as confined to the divine region of being. The affiliation between Pererius and Descartes cannot be confirmed by an admitted reading or a confessed influence; but, thematically, it cannot be denied in the texts themselves. However, identifying the Cartesian position historically, if it ensures that it is interpreted historically, immediately provokes a new conceptual difficulty: how can Descartes think primacy in tandem with universality? To be sure, this question concerns the definition at stake in the *Meditationes,* but it is already posited in the *Regulae,* which, as early as 1627–28, had arrived at a *universalis[sima] Sapientia* (AT X, 360, 19–20) and a *Mathesis universalis* (AT X, 378, 8–9)—in the second case, it might be added, under the influence of Pererius. Would the pairing of universality and primacy include in 1640 the same universal science as in 1627–28? In other words, if the Cartesian *prima philosophia* is exerted "in general," and so conforms to a *scientia universalis* that becomes the *prima philosophia* of Pererius, will it go so far as to absorb the *Mathesis universalis* of the *Regulae?*

In order really to understand such a question, before even pretending to broach its difficulty—which is great—it is wise to approach it by way of a connected difficulty: how does Pererius himself, the initiator of the Cartesian terminology, explain the fact that primacy can be identified with universality? It is in relation to this answer that those (antagonistic ones) of Suarez and Descartes can be clarified. For Pererius, the three parts of philosophy perform very precise functions. *(a)* The third puts the categories into operation, and deals more with the dialectical or logical part of the fourfold studies of scholastic philosophy. It thus falls under the Cartesian critique of these two disciplines (AT X, 405, 21–406, 26 = PW I, 36–7). In any case, for Aristotle, the categories (even as κατηγορ-

---

certain definitions of Saint Thomas are left out: ". . . philosophia prima, in qua determinatur de iis quae sunt communia enti in quantum est ens [first philosophy, in which those things which are common to being insofar as it is being]" (*In Libros Physicorum, I,* 1, n. 4, ed. P. M. Maggiolo (Rome, 1954), p. 3 [English trans., p. 4 [modified]); or ". . . forma est principium essendi et ens in quantum hujusmodi est subjectum primae philosophiae [Form is a principle of existing, and being as such is the subject of first philosophy]" (op. cit., I, 15, n. 140, p. 69 [English trans., p. 66]); and finally: ". . . ea autem quae pertinent ad considerationem philosophie primi, consequuntur ens in quantum ens est, et non aliquid determinatum genus [That which pertains to the consideration of first philosophy follows upon being insofar as it is being, and not upon some determinate genus of being]" (op. cit., III, 6, n. 327, p. 164 [English trans., p. 153]).

ίαι τοῦ ὄντος) do not depend on what will become metaphysics. *(b)* The first part, here qualified as "Metaphysica, Theologia, Sapientia, Divina Scientia" is restricted to the intelligences separated from all matter (rationally or really). It thus corresponds precisely to the "metaphysica sive theologica" (AT III, 505, 10–11 = PW III, 208) that Descartes mentions at least once and in such a way that it is restricted to demonstrating the existence of God and the real distinction of the soul and the body. *(c)* Only the second part remains, ". . . universalissima . . . ," ". . . prima Philosophia et scientia universalis." Does it in fact correspond with what Descartes will attribute properly to *prima Philosophia,* that is to say "in general . . . all the first things that can be known by philosophizing in accordance with the order"? (AT III 239, 6–7, see 235, 17–18 = PW III, 158 [modified], see 157.) Absolutely not and in no way. For Pererius, the third part of philosophy concerns the transcendental determinations of being, and therefore, besides being itself, the true, the one, and the good (which are interchangeable with it), and the pair act/potentiality. The universality of this science stems from the universality of the determinations of being, and these determinations precede, as principles, the particular rationalities. For Pererius, first philosophy evidently deals with the *ens in quantum ens;* it therefore is a forerunner of what, after Goclenius and with Clauberg, will take the name *ontologia* and will claim to correspond with the science of the ὄν ᾗ ὄν in Aristotle. From the point of view of being as such, the particular genuses (as well as the sciences that they occasion) appear secondary and derivative, partial and particular. All the other sciences (including of course theological philosophy) therefore yield before being as such, universal and consequently first— and of course before it alone. In not limiting first philosophy to the divine genus, Pererius does indeed foreshadow Descartes: ". . . the aforementioned universal science ought not deal with the intelligences *per se* and inasmuch as they form a [particular] genus of being, but only perhaps in relation to their substrate, namely inasmuch as they are general principles and universal causes of all beings."[50] But if the distinction is found

---

50. *De Communibus omnium rerum . . . , I,* 7: "Secunda conclusio, praedicta scientia universalis non debet agere de intelligentiis per se et ut sunt species entis, sed tantum fortasse in ordine ad suum subjectum, nimirum ut sunt generalia principia et universalia causae omnium entium" (op. cit., p. 14). The first conclusion must also be cited: ". . . oportet esse aliquam scientiam universalem diversam a scientiis particularibus quae agat de transcendentibus et iis quae sparsa sunt per omnes disciplinas (cujusmodi sunt decem praedicamenta et generales divisiones entis), ita ut subjectum ejusmodi scientiae sit ens ut ens" (ibid.). *Prima philosophia* therefore concerns being as such, and derives its universality only from the primacy of being considered in its Being. A good approach at

again in Descartes—"I deal not just with God and the soul, but in general" (AT III, 239, 5–6 also 235, 15–17 = PW III, 158 also 157)—this could be for a different reason than that given by Pererius. For metaphysics can yield universality to *prima philosophia* for two opposed reasons: either through consideration of being as such (what Pererius does) or else through consideration of the order of knowledge, better, of knowledge as the principle and setting out of the order (Descartes' choice). In short, the universality of *prima philosophia* attests either to the primacy of ontological considerations or to the primacy of the method as the laying out of the order. In the first case, *prima philosophia,* in opposition to Suarez, takes an extra step in the direction of the classical ontology, while in the other, it succeeds in disqualifying the investigation of ὄν ἦ ὄν, in order to construct only a gray ontology. Pererius and Descartes therefore agree only about the titles of philosophy, in no way about what is at stake in it nor about its conceptual definition. To be sure, both the one and the other subordinate theology (paradoxically identified with metaphysics) to a *prima philosophia* that is the sole keeper of universality. But one is concerned with the universality of a question that investigates all beings as beings (ontology), while the other is concerned with the *Mathesis universalis,* which investigates all beings as knowable according to the order and measure. Descartes therefore has taken up the highly original titles introduced by Pererius only so as to better eliminate the very thing that Pererius wanted to consecrate: the question of being as such. The terminological agreement covers over a radical conceptual discord.

Inversely, it must be emphasized that, if Pererius' *scientia universalis* contradicts Suarez's terminology by being titled *prima philosophia,* it nonetheless recovers the concept perfectly. Between Suarez and his elder in the Society of Jesus, the disagreement about the name does not block a total agreement about the thing itself. Pererius distinguishes as the first part of philosophy a "Metaphysica, Theologia," which deals only with God and the intelligences. Suarez too decides in favor of a "theologia seu scientia divina" attached to the same domain. On this point, Descartes confirms the decision of his predecessors by admitting a "metaphysica sive theologica" (AT III, 505, 9–10 = PW III, 208). The same goes for all his contemporaries.[51] However, the second part of phi-

the position of Pererius is made by J.-F. Courtine, "Ontologie ou métaphysique?" *Giornale di Metafisica,* nuova serie, VII (1985): 3–24.

51. Respectively, Pererius, *De Communibus omnium rerum . . . , I,* 6 (op. cit., pp. 13 and 14); Suarez, *Disputationes Metaphysicae, I,* s. 3, n. 9, vol. 25, p. 24. But also Fonseca: ". . . ab Aristotele saepe appelatur prima Philosophia; . . . alias Theologia . . ." (*In Libros*

losophy still remains to be defined. Here the situation changes completely. In effect, Descartes, and Descartes alone, defines the *scientia universalis* by the criterion of the order of knowledge; all the other authors are inclined toward the same definition—in terms of the *ens in quantum ens.* The conceptual agreement between Pererius and Suarez is all the more striking since their terminologies differ: Pererius attributes to the *scientia universalis* the consideration of the transcendentals ". . . such as being, the one, the true, act, and power"; Suarez acknowledges ". . . being as being, its first attributes and principles, on account of which it is named universal science and metaphysics."[52] Suarez nonetheless does not just repeat an Aristotelian thesis; rather, he understands the *ens in quantum ens* in a precisely determined way. *(a)* He ends up with a thesis concerning "the object of metaphysics" defined in this way: "It must be admitted that being as real being is the adequate object of this science. . . . It has been shown that the adequate object of this science must include God and the other immaterial substances, but also the real accidents, with the exception of rational and purely accidental beings. Such an object can be nothing other than being as such. It is therefore this which is its adequate object." Metaphysics considers the genuses and degrees of being indifferently, because it begins by making an abstraction from the gaps between the different substances, separate and not separate, and also from those between substances and real accidents. From this, there arises the paradox of an object that is extended indifferently (if not univocally) from God to the real accidents, with neither hierarchy nor variation. *(b)* This definition of the object of metaphysics explicitly announces its condition of possibility, the objective concept of being: "To constitute such an adequate object, which would include God within it, it is not necessary that some thing or some reason for being be by nature prior to God; it is enough that it be so by means of the abstraction or consideration of the understanding. This has nothing contradictory about it, as we will show later when we deal with the concept of

---

Metaphysicorum Aristotelis. Proemium, III, loc. cit., vol. 1, p. 29); Scipion Dupleix: ". . . Metaphysics or Theology . . . ," ". . . Metaphysics, that is to say supra-natural Philosophy, in other words, Theology" (*La Logique, I,* 3 and 4, op. cit., pp. 32 and 36); Goclenius: "Universalis itaque sapientia in hominum non cadit, sed in Deum tantum. Et tamen similis est, quam primam Philosophiam et theologiam olim, recentiores Metaphysicam nominaverunt, omnium rerum principia, causasque primas, quantum quidem homini cognoscere fas est, comprehendens" (*Lexicon philosophicum,* loc. cit., p. 1008).

52. Respectively, *De communibus omnium rerum . . . I,* 6 (op. cit., p. 14) and *Disputationes Metaphysicae, I,* s. 3, n. 9: ". . . ut versatur circa ens in quantum ens, et prima attributa et principia ejus, qua ratione dicitur scientia universalis et metaphysica" (vol. 25, p. 24).

being." Now the objective concept is defined as "the object itself, insofar as it is known and apprehended by the formal concept," and ". . . what is objected [*ce qui s'objecte*] immediately and adequately before this formal concept." Therefore, the objective concept of being designates being become abstract from all other determination except for being conceived, and so being common to all that can be represented, indifferent to all other difference except the possibility of being represented or not. The universality of metaphysics comes to it less from being than from the objectivization of being, which itself stems from the primacy tyrannically accorded to the representation of being over being itself. *(c)* In consequence, among the other beings reduced to what the formal concept of being apprehends—therefore to the objective concept of being—God will be an object submitted to metaphysics: ". . . being as being includes God who is without principle or cause . . . but being as being is the most imperfect object because it is the most common and is also included in the lowest level of beings. And it would be much more perfect [by being] a substance, either a spiritual substance or God." God thus no longer holds anything but a particular, though eminent, role in the universality of a science that encompasses all that is real—in accordance with the fact that confusion and abstraction open universality.[53] Suarez, like Descartes, enlarges the scope of philosophy so that it reaches beyond immaterial substances. As is the case with Pererius, however, this enlargement leads him to being itself interpreted as real, not at all to the epistemological protologic of Descartes, nor ". . . in general . . . [to] all the first things

53. Suarez, *Disputationes Metaphysicae,* respectively *I,* s. 1, n. 26:

Dicendum est ergo ens in quantum ens reale esse objectum adaequatum hujus scientiae. . . . Ostensum est enim, objectum adaequatum hujus scientiae debere comprehendere Deum, et alias substantias immateriales, non tamen solas illas. Item debere comprehendere non tantum substantias, sed etiam accidentia realia, non tamen entia rationis, et omnino per accidens; sed hujusmodi objectum nullum aliud esse praeter ens ut sic; ergo illud est objectum adaequatum.

(Vol. 25, p. 11.) Then *I,* s. 1, n. 13: "Neque ad hujusmodi objectum adaequatum constituendum, quod Deum sub se comprehendat, necesse est dari aliquid vel aliquam rationem entis, quae sit prior natura Deo, sed satis est ut detur secundum abstractionem vel considerationem intellectus, quod non repugnat, ut infra ostendemus, tractando de conceptu entis" (op. cit., vol. 25, p. 6; see our commentary in *Sur la théologie blanche de Descartes,* §7, pp. 119–32). Then *II,* s. 2, n. 3: ". . . conceptus objectivus nihil aliud est quam objectum ipsum ut cognitum vel apprehensum per talem conceptum formalem" (op. cit., vol. 25, p. 70), and n. 17: ". . . id quod immediate et adaequate objicitur huic conceptui formali . . ." (ibid., p. 76). Finally, *I,* s. 1, n. 27: ". . . ens in quantum ens complectitur Deum qui est sine principio et sine causa . . . , sed ens in quantum ens, est imperfectissimum objectum, quia est communissimum et in infimis etiam entibus includitur, multosque perfectius esset substantia, vel substantia spiritualis, vel Deus" (op. cit., vol. 25, p. 11), or *I,* s. 1, n. 19: ". . . ergo

that can be known by philosophizing in an orderly way" (AT III, 239, 5–7 = PW III, 158 [modified]). Indeed, it leads to what will shortly assume the name *ontologia*. In this, Descartes is not opposed just to Pererius and Suarez, but to all those who foreshadow or inherit the Suarezian definition of metaphysics. Among those who foreshadow it, Fonseca must be called to mind. In order to define metaphysics as a *generalis scientia,* he refutes four identifications of its object: either God alone (Al Farabi), separate substance (Duns Scotus), substance *in commune* (Buridan), and finally categorical *ens.* Next, he goes on to offer a broader definition: ". . . the being common to God and creatures must be considered the subject of this science"; in other words, ". . . the subject of metaphysics is therefore neither God alone nor separate substance nor only substance in common, but the being common to the substances and the accidents."[54] Among those who inherit the Suarezian definition, the majority of the *minores* must be counted, with clear unanimity. Scipion Dupleix suggests, as the eighth of ". . . the different names of metaphysics," that of "Universal Science, which was attributed to it just as much because it deals universally with all being as because, as I just mentioned, its principles are universally useful to all the sciences." He confirms this choice by stating more precisely that metaphysics, science of being as being, excludes only rational being, in the sense that Suarez excluded from it unreal accidents, as well as the field of revealed theology.[55] Still more significant would appear to be the two authors that Descartes had planned to comment on. Abra de Raconis suggests several theses on the object of metaphysics: God alone, or God and the angels, would be part of it, but not the rational beings or the accidents. As a result of this, one conclusion must be drawn: "Being [*l'étant*] abstracted from [the differences between] God and creatures must be established as the adequate

---

absolute Deus cadit sub objectum hujus scientiae" (op. cit., vol. 25, p. 9). On the fact that metaphysics "includes [*comprenne*]" God for Suarez, and on the opposition of this to the Cartesian doctrine, see *Sur la théologie blanche de Descartes,* §7, pp. 132–39.

54. Fonseca, *In Libros Metaphysicorum Aristotelis, III,* chap. I, q. 1, s. 2: ". . . ens commune Deo et creaturis constituendum est hujus scientiae subjectum . . ." (op. cit., vol. 1, p. 497); ". . . generalis scientia. . . . Non est igitur subjectum Metaphysicae, aut solus Deus, aut substantia seperata, aut substantia in communi dumtaxat, sed ens commune substantiis et accidentibus" (ibid., p. 498). Being [*l'étant*] is of course defined beforehand in the broadest (and most Scotist) acceptation of the term: "Nemini dubium erit, quin id quod est sive ens, qua ratione est ens, sit hujus tractationis subjectum, quippe cum Ens, et suo modo sit unum quippiam, et omnia complectatur, quae sine materia aut omnino existunt, aut certe intelligentur, quorum haec scientia et naturas nosse et affectiones intelligere praecipue studet" (ibid., p. 26).

55. Scipion Dupleix, *La Métaphysique ou science surnaturelle,* respectively *I,* 2 and *I,* 3 (op. cit., p. 18).

object of metaphysics."[56] Metaphysics passes beyond the separate substances (where first philosophy is bound) only to the benefit of a being
so abstract that it excludes only the nonreal. In similar terms, Eustache
de Saint-Paul confirms, finally, the supremacy of Suarez's definition. If
he begins by admitting the limited pertinence of other theses, this is because, in spirit, metaphysics does indeed bear on God, if one considers
its first object; and if it is a question of its object considered purely, it
bears on the first and immaterial substance; if it is a question of the
parameter according to which it is practiced in general, it bears on substance; if it is a matter of its means of proof, it bears on categorical being;
finally, if it is a matter of the parameter that encompasses all that metaphysics deals with, without exception, it bears on being taken in the
broadest sense possible. But each of these theses owes its partial pertinence only to a more essential definition: ". . . not one among all these
objects can be called the object *per se* and adequate, excepting the one
that we have pointed out. Hence, we can conclude with the following
definition of metaphysics: the theoretical science of real and complete
being abstracted from all matter, with indifference."[57] Thus the Suarezian
definition of metaphysics was quite widespread among Descartes' contemporaries.

In summary: from Pererius to Fonseca, from Abra de Raconis to Eustache de Saint-Paul, from Suarez to Scipion Dupleix, the duality constitutive of metaphysics always ends up asserting the primacy of a universal
science over *philosophia prima* itself (as rational theology). But this universality never, except in Descartes, falls under the jurisdiction of the

---

56. Abra de Raconis, *Totius philosophiae . . . brevis tractatio (= Quarta pars . . .) Praeludium quartum*, s. 2, *De objecto Metaphyiscae*:

> Prima propositio. Solus Deus non est adaequatum metaphysicae objectum, est tamen
> principale. Secunda propositio: Angeli pertinent ad objectum metaphysicae; illi tamen
> cum Deo non faciunt adaequatum [objectum]. Tertia propositio: Entia rationis non sunt
> de objecto metaphysicae, seu (quod in idem recessit) ens generalissime sumptum, quod
> abstrahit ab ente rei et rationis, non est constituendum metaphysicae objectum. Quarta
> propositio: entia per accidens, ut sic, non habent locum directe in objecto metaphysicae.
> Extrema propositio: Ens abstractum a Deo et creaturis statuendum est adaequatum
> metaphysicae objectum.

(Op. cit., p. 5.)

57. Eustache de Saint-Paul, *Summa Philosophiae . . . , Praefatio*, q. 2: ". . . nullum tamen ex his omnibus dici potest objectum per se et adaequatum praeter illud quod resigna-
vimus. Ex his colligi potest haec Metaphysicae definitio ut videlicet dicatur scientia theoretica de ente reali per se et completo, ab omni materia saltem secundum indifferentiam
abstracto" (op. cit., pp. 4–5). In fewer terms, Goclenius ends up with a similar result: "Scientia igitur est [Metaphysica] ex consideratione ὄντων. Universalis [est] quae considerat
simpliciter ὄντα, seu ὄν ᾗ ὄν. Prima philosophia" (*Lexicon philosophicum*, p. 1011).

primacy of knowing through the order, evidence, and arrangement. It marks the primacy (to the point of confiscating the title *prima philo-sophia* in Pererius) of the science of common being, abstract and universal within the limits of reality. Accordingly, it foreshadows the coming dominance of *ontologia*—which, with Goclenius, still turns up in Greek. The originality of the Cartesian *prima philosophia* is not indicated so much by its having contested a purely theological definition of metaphysics—all his contemporaries also contested this. Rather, it is indicated by Descartes' invoking, for the sake of such an overcoming, an instance radically different from that which the others mobilize. His contemporaries overcome *prima philosophia* (rational theology) in and through the primacy of considering the *ens in quantum ens* universally. In this consideration, the objective concept of *ens* radically modifies Aristotle's ὄν ᾗ ὄν. This undertaking will lead quite rapidly and inevitably to the institution of an ontology, which together with rational theology (and its allied disciplines) will in turn compose the scholastic concept of metaphysics.[58] Descartes, in contrast, breaks with this current, which was dominant before and after him: for him, the universal instance that surpasses the metaphysics reduced to rational theology is no longer the science of being as such (the *ontologia* of the future), but arranging in the order of knowledge, that is to say, knowledge according to the order in which evidence is brought to light. To be sure, for Descartes too, a universal science passes beyond rational theology; but it is the *Mathesis universalis,* or in any case the *universalis Sapientia,* which opens the *Regulae* and inaugurates its singular plan (AT X, 360, 19–20 = PW I, 9). Once again, Descartes contradicts Suarez, and with him the dominant sentiment among his contemporaries. At the exact moment when metaphysics is being constituted as a science that is articulated—academically but also fundamentally—in a protologic (theology and, appended, rational pneumatology and cosmology) that is surpassed by a universal ontology, Descartes proceeds in the opposite direction: he overcomes the theological object of metaphysics while also contesting its ontological undertaking. In both cases, he will do so by having recourse to the singular primacy of the ordering that proceeds according to the demands of certain knowledge. A *prima philosophia* does indeed appear; it is one in which *prima* indicates neither rational theology nor the science of the objective concept of *ens,* but the science of all things insofar as they are arranged in order by knowledge—first inasmuch as known. Metaphysics is constituted as a universal protologic of making evident. Since it con-

58. See the study by E. Vollrath, cited *supra,* n. 49.

tests the (past) primacy of rational theology as well as the (future) universality of ontology, can such a protologic legitimately lay claim to the title metaphysics, or even that of *prima Philosophia*? In short, does the twofold decision made by Descartes still authorize him to assume a place at the heart of metaphysics?

§5. The First Other

To the question of fact—does Descartes construct a concept of metaphysics?—we have won a positive response. In unambiguously deciding in favor of *prima Philosophia,* Descartes contests the reduction of metaphysics to rational theology, without however accepting its universalization by the objective concept of *ens;* in short, Descartes refuses to think metaphysics in terms of the two principal ways available to him—theology and *ontologia.* What remains for us now is to answer the question of legitimacy: the universal protologic of arranging the order according to evidence coming to light—does it still deserve, in one way or another, the name *metaphysics*?

At the very least, a formal response can be given here: If he wants to grant metaphysical status (if not the title *metaphysica*) to the epistemological protologic, Descartes can call on the authority of Saint Thomas. Saint Thomas clearly admits a bipolarization of what we, more often than he, name metaphysics, and what he restricts himself to designating anonymously as *haec scientia,* "the science in question." He recognizes that "In metaphysics, the philosopher [Aristotle] determines at the same time both common being and the first being—that which is separate from all matter." The very primacy of *prima philosophia* is mixed together with the universality of metaphysics so as to compose "a universal and first science which examines the things which the particular sciences disregard. Now such things seem to be the common attributes which belong to common being . . . and the separate substances which lie outside the scope of every particular science."[59] In this two-termed thematic, which conforms to the Aristotelian tension as well as the Suarezian reconciliation, an epistemological protologic of the Cartesian sort has no

---

59. Saint Thomas, respectively, *In Aristotelis de Generatione et Corruptione, Prooemium,* 2: "Et inde est quod Philosophus in Metaphysica simul determinat de ente in communi et de ente primo, quod est a materia separatum" (ed. R. Spiazzi [Rome, 1952], p. 316). Then, *In XII libros Metaphysicorum Exposito,* XI, 1, n. 2146: ". . . necesse fuit quandam scientiam esse universalem et primam, quae perscrutatur ea, de quibus particulares scientiae non considerant. Hujusmodi autem videntur esse tam communia, quae sequuntur

place, nor even the least bit of legitimacy. But, at times, Saint Thomas also lays out a thematic in three terms, one that makes room for a supplementary metaphysical place. And this must be considered when one is seeking a site for the Cartesian protologic. In effect, the *Commentary on the Metaphysics* of Aristotle posits that ". . . three names arise for this science." "It is called *divine science* or *theology* inasmuch as it considers the aforementioned substances"—namely ". . . those things which are the most separate from matter . . . not only rationally, like the mathematical [idealities], but also in Being, as God and the separate intelligences are." It is called "*metaphysics,* inasmuch as it considers being and the

---

esse commune . . . , quam etiam substantiae separatae, quae excedunt considerationem omnium particularium scientiarum" (op. cit., p. 509 [English trans., p. 775]). The same duality is found in *III,* 4, n. 384:

> . . . ista scientia considerat ens in quantum ens, pertinet considerare de substantia inquantum est substantia. . . . Verumtamen in substantiis est etiam ordo: nam primae substantiae sunt substantiae immateriales. Unde et earum consideratio pertinet proprie ad philosophum primum. [This science considers being as being; the consideration of substance as substance also belongs to it. . . . There is an order among substances: the first substances are immaterial substances. Whence the consideration of them belongs properly to first philosophy.]

(Op. cit., p. 112 [English trans., p. 156 (modified)]); or in *IV,* 4, n. 593: ". . . ad illam scientiam pertinet consideratio entis communis, ad quam pertinet consideratio entis primi [To that science to which the consideration of first being belongs, there also belongs the consideration of common being] . . ." (op. cit., p. 164 [English trans., p. 237]); and also in *VI,* 1, n. 1169:

> . . . aliquis potest dubitare, utrum prima philosophia sit universalis quasi considerans ens universaliter, aut ejus consideratio sit circa aliquod genus determinatum et naturam unam. Et hoc non videtur . . . philosophia prima est universaliter communis omnium. [Someone can inquire whether first philosophy is universal inasmuch as it considers being in general, or whether it investigates some particular genus or a single nature. Now this does not seem to be the case . . . first philosophy is universally common to all.]

(Op. cit., p. 298 [English trans., p. 462]); or finally, n. 1170: ". . . quia est prima, ideo erit universalis [Since it is first, it will be universal]" (op. cit., p. 298 [English trans., p. 463]). The ambiguity of this dual unity is shown in the possibility of naming the science of separate substances sometimes *philosophia prima* (for example in *Contra Gentes, I,* 70; *In Metaphysicorum libri XII, Prooemium,* loc. cit., p. 2; etc.), sometimes *metaphysica* (*Contra Gentes, I,* 4; *Summa Theologiae IIa–IIae,* q. 9, a. 2, obj. 2; *In Physicorum libros VIII, II,* 11, n. 243, op. cit., p. 118; etc.). Perhaps this is the place to remark, with Heidegger, that "what was to be found as an unspoken problem in Aristotle was presented as firm truth in the Middle Ages, so that the unproblematic nature of the situation, which in a certain sense is found in Aristotle, now becomes raised to a principle" (*Die Grundbegriffe der Metaphysik,* §13, G. A., 29/30, p. 76 [English trans., p. 50]). On the Thomistic definition of metaphysics, refer to E. Gilson, *Le Thomisme,* 5th ed. (Paris, 1945), pp. 27*ff.,* and to A. Zimmerman, *Ontologie oder Metaphysik?* §4, B), op. cit., pp. 159–80.

attributes which naturally accompany being. The transphysical things are discovered by the process of analysis, as the more common are discovered after the less common. And it is called *first philosophy* inasmuch as it considers the first causes of things."[60] Here, apart from the *theologia rationalis* and the *metaphysica* devoted to the *ens ut ens,* thus outside the couple that alone will be dominant among the authors that come later, there is a third term (one that is often hidden by Saint Thomas, who tends to include it in *theologia*). All the particular sciences must receive their principles; and yet they cannot—by definition of principle—reach on their own what makes them possible. An autonomous science is therefore required, one that can ground them and, for that reason, precede them, at once by transgression (as first philosophy of the divine transgresses) and by universality (as the science of the *ens ut ens* is deployed). Its originality can thus be deployed, without risk of dissolution, sometimes with the status of first philosophy—"all the other [sciences] depend on it [*prima Philosophia*] in the sense that they take their principles from it, and also the position to be assumed against those who deny the principles"—and sometimes with the status of metaphysics: "The metaphysician deliberates about first principles. . . . An error which pertains to all beings and to all the sciences is not to be disproved by the natural philosopher, but by the metaphysician"; or,

> However, it is to be borne in mind, in regard to the philosophical sciences, that the inferior sciences neither prove their principles nor dispute with those who deny them, but leave this to a higher science. The highest of them, viz., metaphysics, can dispute with one who denies their principles, if only the opponent will make some concession; but if he concede nothing, it can have no dispute with him, though it can answer his objections.

---

60. Saint Thomas, *In Metaphysicorum libros XII, Prooemium:* ". . . hujus scientiae sortitur tria nomina . . ." (op. cit., p. 2 [English trans., p. 2 (modified)]); "Dicitur enim scientia divina sive theologia, inquantum praedictas substantias considerat . . ." (ibid.)—namely ". . . ea quae sunt maxime a materia separata. . . . Et non solum secundum rationem, sicut mathematica, sed etiam secundum esse, sicut Deus et intelligentiae" (op. cit., p. 1 [English trans., p. 2]). Then: "Metaphysica inquantum considerat ens et ea quae consequuntur ipsum. Haec autem transphysica inveniuntur in via resolutionis, sicut magis communia post minus communia. Dicitur autem prima philosophia, inquantum primas rerum causas consideret" (op. cit., p. 2 [English trans., p. 2]). Citing this text, Heidegger draws attention to its incoherence (which results from "the disparate determinations of the transgression, *des Hinübergehens*"). This incoherence renders the Thomistic definition incapable of being put into practice without remaining vague. This justified reproach, however, should not hide the emergence here, in the new acceptation of *prima philosophia,* of the Cartesian concept of metaphysics as philosophy ordered by the primacy of knowledge (*Die Grundbegriffe der Metaphysik,* §13, G. A., 29/30, p. 77 [English trans., p. 50]).

From now on, the "knowledge of causes" takes on the status either of metaphysics or of first philosophy, no doubt at the risk of being reduced to one or the other of them.[61] But in what concerns us, two points are especially important: first, the primacy of knowledge has been granted, as such and in general, a rank that is at least equal to that of the two other branches of philosophy, *theologia* and *metaphysica;* second, and even more importantly, this has happened under the name *prima Philosophia,* which Descartes will take up to the letter in order to designate the epistemological protologic. On the basis of the three Thomistic senses of metaphysics, one can draw up a table that might clarify the debate, at first sight a confused one, which Descartes conducts in the hope of formulating a new definition, or at least a new titling of philosophy.

	Thomas	*Pererius*	*Suarez*	*Descartes*
Scientia divina sive theologia (naturalis)	+	+	+	+
Metaphysica : ens in quantum ens	+	+	+	− reduced to the following term
Prima philosophia as "all the first things that can be known by philosophizing in an orderly way"	+	− reduced to the second	− reduced to the first	+

61. Saint Thomas, respectively, *Contra Gentes III,* 25 [English trans., pp. 100–101]: ". . . ab ipsa [prima Philosophia] omnes alias [scientias] dependent, utpote ab ipsa accipientes sua principia et directionem contra negantes principia . . .""; *In Physicorum libros VIII,* 5, n. 1006: "Metaphysicus autem considerat de primis principiis. . . . Error autem qui pertinet ad omnia entia et ad omnes scientias, non est reprobandus a naturali [philosopho], se a metaphysico" (op. cit., p. 525 [English trans., p. 496]); *Summa Theologiae Ia,* q. 1, a. 8, c. [English trans., p. 5]: "Sed considerandum est in scientiis philosophicis, quod inferiores scientiae, nec probant sua principia, nec contra negantem principia disputant, sed hoc reliquunt superiori scientiae: suprema vero inter eas, sc. Metaphysica, disputat contra negantem sua principia, si adversarius aliquid concedit; si autem nihil concedit, non potest cum eo disputare; potest tamen solvere rationes ipsius" (See also *In Metaphysicorum libros XII, IV,* 17, n. 736, op. cit., p. 203 [English trans., p. 294]); finally, ". . . causarum cognitio" (*In Metaphysicorum libros XII, Prooemium,* ibid., p. 2 [English trans., p. 2]). Concerning the threefold division of the supreme science according to Saint Thomas, see the fine analyses in James C. Doig, *Aquinas on Metaphysics: A Historical-doctrinal Study of the Commentary on the Metaphysics* (The Hague: Martinus Nijhoff, 1972), in particular chaps. III and IV.

This table obviously calls for some more precise remarks. *(a)* The *scientia divina* or *theologia (rationalis)* appears in all the authors, by virtue of the double authority of Aristotle's φιλοσοφία πρώτη and the exigencies of the Christian faith (based above all on Exodus 3:14 and Romans 1:20). This does not imply, however, that *scientia divina* or *theologia (rationalis)* has the same importance in each author. While for St. Thomas it governs the entire structure, in Pererius and Suarez, on the contrary, it is governed by the consideration of the *ens in quantum ens*. *(b)* In Pererius, the exceptional denomination of the latter consideration as *prima philosophia* does not in any way modify the commonly admitted duality. For beneath this title, it is always a question of the science of being in general. Descartes was able to find only a lexical impulse in this evanescent innovation, in no way a theoretical inheritance. *(c)* The real antecedent, supposing that Descartes might have sought such a precedent, would be found in the autonomy that Saint Thomas sometimes accorded to the science of first principles, thus to a protologic that was irreducibly original and, in this sense, metaphysical. *(d)* Descartes' originality is contained fundamentally in a twofold operation: first, the elimination of all consideration of the *ens in quantum ens* (as early as the *Regulae*); next, the substitution, instead of and in the place of the universal science of the *ens,* of a new metaphysical science—that of the first things in general. In this science, primacy (*prima Philosophia,* "... first things ...") and universality (*universalis[sima] Sapientia,* "... all the [first] things ...") should coincide. Descartes will say *Mathesis universalis.* In this way, the *principia metaphysica* (AT III, 566, 29 = PW III, 214) are not equal to the simple *principia omnis philosophiae* (AT VII, 602, 21 = PW II, 397). They must be understood more rigorously: the primacy of principles depends not on an already constituted metaphysics, but on a metaphysics that they inaugurate in being posited as the first things known by the mind that philosophizes in accordance with the order. Metaphysics does not get cashed out in the form of principles; it is the principles that produce metaphysics—by producing a new primacy, the only one that counts from now on: primacy according to and through the order in which evidence is brought to light.

The Cartesian *prima Philosophia* lays claim to metaphysical dignity, not by virtue of privileged beings, but, beyond them, by virtue of the arrangement in order, as the single correct determination of before and after, of the principle and the derivative. It claims that putting in order by and for the sake of making evident is enough to constitute a metaphysics; no recourse to an *ens in quantum ens* is needed. In Cartesian terms, this amounts to a *Mathesis universalis*, in which being as known mimics, without ever being summed up in, being as being. Related each to the other, Descartes' two principal initiatives aim to reproduce (and thus to destroy) in and through the order of knowledge what Aristotle drew together in the paradox of φιλοσοφία πρώτη—namely, that it is universal inasmuch as it is first, καθόλου οὕτως ὅτι πρώτη.[62] That is, the *Mathesis universalis* of 1627–28 establishes the καθόλου dominion of the order (and of the measure that depends on it), while in 1640, *prima Philosophia* aims to reach the absolutely πρώτη primacy "of all the first things that can be known by philosophizing in accordance with the order." These two attempts, provided that they are joined together, repeat the single Aristotelian paradox. Through reference to Aristotle, they establish a figure that is authentically metaphysical—though one that is declined according to the criterion of the order, no longer according to that of the ὄν ᾗ ὄν. All that remains is for us to briefly formulate its characteristics.

First of all the *Mathesis universalis*. Here alone is universality mentioned in the title, to the detriment of primacy. In effect, science (or *mathesis*—for this Greek term certainly does not designate, at least in this case, the mathematics that it is a question of overcoming, but a *generalis quaedam scientia*, AT X, 378, 4–5 = PW I, 19) gives birth to itself by virtue of a certain universality. The *Mathesis* is defined as *universalis* because it operates on whatever might be, independently of what it is: "... aliter spectandas esse res singulares in ordine ad cognitionem nostram, quam si de iisdem loquamur prout revera existunt [When we consider things in the order that corresponds to our knowledge of them, our view of them must be different from what it would be if we were speaking of them in accordance with how they exist in reality]" (AT X, 418, 1–3 = PW I, 44). It is a question of interpreting beings (here *res*) as knowable, no longer as ὄντα. This new interpretation is practiced according to a new criterion—no longer τὸ ὄν, but *aliquis ordo*: "... illa omnia tantum in quibus aliquis ordo vel mensura examinatur ad Mathesim referri ... [All that, only, (illa omnia tantum) in which questions of order or measure are examined is to be referred to mathematics]" (377, 23–378, 2 = PW I, 19 [modified]). *All* the things and *only* these, *illa omnia tantum:* the phrase would be a simple contradiction if it

---

62. *Metaphysics E,* 1, 1026 *a* 30–31 [English trans., p. 1620]; see also *K,* 7, 1064 *b* 12–14 [English trans., p. 1681]: ἐπιστήμην ... καθόλου τῷ προτέραν [the science ... universal because it is prior] (if the doubtful authenticity of *K* is admitted).

claimed to be announcing the delimitation of a region of being. It does not contradict itself, however, seeing that it suggests an interpretation that concerns *all* beings (*illa omnia*) insofar as they are considered according to only one criterion (*tantum*). Each and all are submitted to interpretation not ᾗ ὄντα, ". . . prout revera existunt [in accordance with how they exist in reality] . . ." (418, 3 = 44), but "prout ab intellectu attinguntur [in so far as they are reached by the intellect]" (399, 6 = 32 [modified]), that is to say, insofar as they are ordered in the understanding, then among themselves. The interpretation is deployed all the more universally as it is put into operation abstractly by the criterion of order. Like measure, but preceding it since it renders it possible, the order allows one to investigate all objects through an abstraction from matter that is as profound as the one produced by the interpretation of the ὄν ᾗ ὄν; for it is a matter of retaining from the beings destitute of their beingness only what they have of order and measure—"id omne . . . quod circa ordinem et mensuram, nulli speciali materiae addictam [all the points that can be raised concerning order and measure whatever species of matter might be at hand] . . ." (378, 5–7 = 19 [modified]). The abstraction abstracts from all matter, therefore from all form informing it (". . . *speciali* materiae . . ."). Accordingly, the interpretation in terms of the order is deployed in each case with as much indifference to the encounter with the nature at issue as was the interpretation ᾗ ὄν: ". . . nec interesse utrum in numeris, vel figuris, vel astris, vel sonis, aliove quovis objecto [It is irrelevant whether the measure in question involves numbers, shapes, stars, sounds, or any other object whatsoever] . . ." (378, 2–3 = 19). Universality is ascribed to the *Mathesis (universalis)* on the basis of the unconditioned efficacy of the criterion of order. It can lay claim to all objects since it does not depend on any of them, but only on the relation—by definition always possible—of the object to the knowing mind. The order orders objects among themselves only because it first orders them in the mind ". . . in ordine ad cognitionem nostram [in the order that corresponds to our knowledge] . . ." (418, 2 = 44), ". . . respectu nostri intellectus [with respect to our intellect] . . ." (419, 6–7 = 44; see 418, 9 = 44). No objects can abandon this order, since it befalls them from the outside in such a way as to order them to what they *are* not—the very mind that interprets them as known. As the mind is never abandoned, as likewise ". . . humana sapientia . . . semper una et eadem manet [Human wisdom . . . always remains one and the same] . . ." (360, 8–9 = 9) and indifferent to any variation in its objects (". . . quantumvis differentibus subjectis applicata [however different the subjects to which it is applied] ..." (360, 9–10 = 9))—in short, since this wisdom deserves the title *universalis[sima] Sapientia* (360, 19–20 = 9)—the order that it deploys and according to which it itself is deployed guarantees its universality. But here the universal no longer characterizes the ὄν ᾗ ὄν that can be made visible by means of φιλοσοφία πρώτη; it characterizes the plan "... res omnes in hac universitate contentas cogitatione ... complecti, ut quomodo singulae mentis nostrae examini subjectae sint, agnoscamus [to encompass in the universal all things contained by thought, with a view to learning in what way particular things may be susceptible of investigation by the human mind]" (398, 14–17 = 31 [modified]). That is, it characterizes the universality produced by submitting things to the thought that contains them, inasmuch as it orders them. The *universitas cogitatione* achieves the καθόλου just as the *prout ab intellectu attinguntur* accomplishes the ὄν ᾗ ὄν—by destroying it. From such a universality, there follows a primacy similarly without compare. Two traits characterize it. *(a)* If Descartes construes the first term of καθόλου οὕτως ὅτι πρώτη, namely καθόλου, in terms of what the *universalitas cogitatione* demands, it can be expected that the second term will undergo a similar displacement. That is, primacy is first only in relation to the mind: "... primum voco simplicissimum et facillimum, ut illo utamur in quaestionibus resolvendis [I call that first which is most simple and most facile, such that we can make use of it in solving problems]" (381, 26–382, 2 = PW I, 21 [modified]). Any term counts as first, provided that it attains as much simplicity, that is to say facility, as possible, such that by starting from it other questions can be resolved.[63] Primacy equals simplicity— "operationes ... simplicissimae et primae [the first and simplest of all ... operations] ..." (372, 18–19 = PW I, 16 [modified])—precisely because, like simplicity, it is determined by its relation to the understanding:

... hîc nos de rebus non agentes, nisi quantum ab intellectu percipiuntur, illas tantum simplices vocamus, quorum cognitio tam perspicua et distincta est, ut in plures magis distincte cognitas mente dividi non possint. [That is

---

63. For the equivalence of simplicity and facility, see references in *Règles utiles et claires pour la direction de l'esprit en la recherche de la vérité,* n. 5, ad loc., p. 171. We here correct our indisputable misreading in the translation of AT X, 381, 26*ff.* = PW I, 21 (p. 18): it must be rendered, according to the parallel with the immediately preceding definition of the absolute (381, 22–26 = 21): "... et je nomme pareillement premier le [terme] très simple et très facile...." As for the Cartesian doctrine of simplicity, see our suggestions in *Sur l'ontologie grise de Descartes,* §22, and the *Règles utiles et claires...,* pp. 238–41.

why, since we are concerned here with things only in so far as they are
perceived by the intellect, we term 'simple' only those things which we
know so clearly and distinctly that they cannot be divided by the mind into
others which are more distinctly known.] [418, 13–17 = PW I, 44.]

Facility attests to simplicity: both the one and the other determine primacy by submitting it to the understanding. Primacy does not determine
the order; it depends on it. The principles play the role of principles
because they are known first. It is thus not a question of principles that
govern knowledge, as ὅθεν γνωστὸν τὸ πρᾶγμα πρῶτον [that from which
a thing can first be known] is for Aristotle.[64] Rather, it is a question of
principles that knowledge institutes, principles that the order has arranged in their place. If the *prima principia* can be known only by *intuitus,* this must be understood more radically than as a simple restatement
of Aristotle's νοῦν τῶν ἀρχῶν [comprehension that grasps the first prin-
ciples].[65] It represents a submission of the first principles to the primacy,
alone originary because the sole operator, of the order's arrangement.
The principles themselves are first only insofar as known: ". . . a primis
et per se notis principiis [from first and self-evident principles] . . ." (387,
16 = 25). Primacy, as well as universality, therefore results from the interpretation of being as known. *(b)* The *Mathesis universalis* unambiguously determines universality, since it grants it; but primacy is missing
from it, from its title as well as its definition. Or rather, primacy is introduced only after the fact, by universality itself: primacy of the first criteria of knowing (*Rule II*), of the first faculties (*Rules III* and *XII-1*), of
the first operations of the mind (*Rules IX–XI*), etc. Primacy is multiplied
insofar as a second primacy is found. This paradox forces itself upon us,
given that all the terms owe their first rank to being arranged in the order
in which they are made evident—even here it is a question of the *artis
secretum* (381, 8 = 21), which sums up the entire *Regulae*. In and through
their very multiplicity, the secondary primacies refer to an originary primacy (". . . utpote aliarum omnium fontem [the source of all the
rest] . . ." (374, 11–12)); namely, the *Mathesis universalis* itself, which surpasses all the other sciences in terms of the facility with which it is known
(". . . facilitate antecellat [superior . . . in . . . facility] . . ." (378, 12 = 19
[modified]). Put otherwise: Descartes posits as *regula prima omnium*
(360, 23 = 9) that before all else (*prius,* 360, 24 = 9), it is necessary to

64. *Metaphysics* Δ, 1, 1013 *a* 14–15 [English trans., p. 1599].
65. *Nicomachean Ethics,* VI, 6, 1141 *a* 7–8 [English trans., p. 1801]. See *Règles utiles et
claires . . .* , pp. 127*ff.*

seek a *finis generalis* (360, 25 = 9), namely, the *universalis*[*sima*] *Sapientia* (360, 19–20 = 9). The universality of science sets itself up, and does so immediately, as the originary primacy. From the beginning to the end of the *Regulae,* it and it alone precedes and dominates: it constructs primacy (*Rules I–IV*) so as to then practice it (*Rules V–XXI*), without this primacy ever becoming other than that of a science. Never does its primacy become that of a being; neither God nor the *ego* nor even the *intellectus* here seems to be in existence, still less to be a being, in such a way that it could lay claim to an ontically assured primacy. Only the *general method* (AT I, 370, 10 = PW III, 58) or the *Mathesis universalis* exert a primacy, one that remains strictly epistemological. Primacy simply collapses the universality of science back into itself.

But *prima Philosophia* attempts to pass from the epistemological primacy to an ontic primacy. This aim is visible as early as the definition of its new Cartesian object: ". . . all the first *things* . . ." (AT III, 235, 16; see 239, 6 = PW III, 157; 158). At issue here is an essential division that Descartes quite lucidly points out in the ambivalence of the concept of principle: ". . . the word 'principle' can be taken in several senses. It is one thing to look for a *common notion* so clear and so general that it can serve as a principle for proving the existence of all the Beings, the *Entia,* to be discovered later; and another thing to look for *a Being* whose existence is known to us better than that of any other, so that it can serve as a *principle* for discovering them" (AT IV, 444, 4–12 = PW III, 290). Either the principle designates a common notion—that is to say, one of the simple natures that makes possible the arrangement according to the order—which puts the *Mathesis universalis* into operation; we then enter into the figure of the *Regulae.* Or, it is a question of finding, as principle, and always in accordance with the order of knowledge, entities [*Entia*], "a Being," and an "existence"; we then discover the figure of the *Meditationes,* which seek the ". . . first *things*. . . ." However, universality is not absent from *prima Philosophia,* seeing as it seeks out ". . . *in general all* the first things . . ." (AT III, 239, 6; 235, 17 = PW III, 158; 157), without restricting itself in advance to the only two beings that the fully developed title of the *Meditationes* mentions, God (existing) and the soul (incorporeal). The difficulty thus consists wholly in identifying the type of universality that *prima Philosophia* employs: is it an ontic universality that serves as the primacy here being sought? Would Descartes have taken up the Aristotelian couple φιλοσοφία πρώτη/καθόλου οὕτως ὅτι πρώτη twice, first as *Mathesis universalis* aiming at a strictly epistemological primacy (*Regulae*), then as *prima Philosophia* supposing

an ontic universality in its very aim at an existing "Being" (*Meditationes*)? Would Descartes, in the first example, have deduced the primacy
missing from universality, and in the second, have inferred the universality failing to appear in primacy, with the result that he produced two
homogeneous and distinct couples—one exclusively epistemological
(*Regulae*) in both dimensions, the other exclusively ontic (*Meditationes*)
in the same two dimensions? Such is not the case. Far from each being
collapsed into itself, the two moments of Cartesian thought refer to each
other through the association of their very dissimilarities: the ontic primacy that *prima Philosophia* exerts always depends, through and
through, on the exclusively epistemological universality exerted by the
Mathesis universalis. This direct relationship gives birth to a distortion
that is essential to Cartesian metaphysics—essential because it also constitutes it. This distortion can be established, at least provisionally, by
three arguments. *(a)* Descartes unambiguously emphasizes the continuity between the method, indeed the *Discourse on the Method,* and *prima
Philosophia.* For as early as 1637, the "general method" (AT I, 370, 10 =
PW III, 58) permits passing beyond the diverse positive sciences to reach
what is commonly called metaphysics: ". . . I have also inserted a certain
amount of metaphysics, physics and medicine in the opening *Discourse*
in order to show that my method extends to topics of all kinds" (AT I,
349, 25–28 = PW III, 53). Thus metaphysics falls within the method, in
keeping with the rule common to all the sciences. It cannot be emphasized enough that the future elaboration of the *Meditationes* will not
question this continuity, since, according to the testimony of Burman,
Descartes still thought in 1649 that ". . . ibi in *Methodo* continetur epit-
ome harum *Meditationum,* quae per eas exponi debet [In that part of
the *Discourse* you have a summary of these *Meditations,* and its meaning
must be explicated by reference to the *Meditations* themselves]."[66] This

66. *Conversation with Burman* (AT V, 153, 22–23 = PW III, 338). See, perhaps
in the same sense, *To Huygens,* 31 July 1640 (AT III, 751, 11–22 = PW III, 150) and *To
Mersenne,* 13 November 1639 (AT II, 622, 16–20 = PW III, 141). In both cases, it is a question of "clarifying" the *Discourse* by means of the *Meditationes,* and not the inverse,
as many casual readers often make it out to be. On this point, the most important text
(but not the most clear) is found in the *Praefatio ad lectorem,* which opens the *Meditationes:*

Quaestiones de Deo et mente humana jam ante paucis attigi in *Dissertationes de Methodo
recte agendae rationis et veritatis in scientiis investigendae,* gallice edita anno 1637, non
quidem ut ipsas ibi accurate tractarem, sed tantum ut deliberarem, et ex lectorem judiciis
addiscerem qua ratione postea essent tractandae. [I briefly touched on the topics of God
and the human mind in my *Discourse on the method of rightly conducting reason and*

text no doubt suggests a continuity in the order of the subject matter, thus one that is most foreign to the Cartesian project; it is more of a pedagogical suggestion than a conceptual dependence. *(b)* That the order of reasons nonetheless abides seems difficult to contest. From the introduction of *prima Philosophia* onwards, the universality of the arrangement in order determines the things sought: "... in general ... all the first things to be discovered by philosophizing ..." (AT III, 235, 7–8; see 239, 6–7 = PW III, 157; 158). If these first things remain undetermined and are not immediately identified with God and the soul, this is because their primacy does not rest on any ontic excellence, but depends on being arranged in the order according to which evidence is brought to light; and according to this order, primacy, even for beings actually existing, does not correspond with the customary objects of metaphysics; other primacies are organized, but several disappear. Here the *rationum series et nexus* (AT VII, 9, 29 = PW II, 8) again corroborates what the *Mathesis universalis* establishes as the "... rerum quaerendarum series [series of objects of investigation]" (AT X, 383, 24–25 = PW I, 22), or as "... nexus naturalemque ordinem [the interconnections between them, and their natural order" (382, 13–14 = 22). *Prima Philosophia* progresses toward beings only by observing at each step what "... ordo videtur exigere [considerations of order appear to dictate]" (AT VII, 36, 30 = PW II, 25)—by constituting series of terms, whose organization starts with the most simple (existing or not, of a known essence or not, in itself relative or not, etc.), so as to arrive finally at primacies that are of course ontic, but epistemologically derived. It would be possible to reread all the *Meditationes* as a particular example of the arrangement in methodical order, where the order of reasons would amount to the application in the metaphysical domain of the "... rerum quaerendarum series [series of objects of investigation]." It would be equally possible to establish a parallel between the principal moments of the order followed in the *Regulae* and the steps of the demonstration accomplished in the *Meditationes.* In both cases, the discontinuity between the two undertakings would be neither exaggerated nor hidden, but sharpened.[67] *(c)* The ultimate argument remains, one that will define a difficulty still to come.

---

seeking the truth in the sciences, which was published in French in 1637. My purpose there was not to provide a full treatment, but merely to offer a sample, and learn from the views of my readers how I should handle these topics at a later date.]

(AT VII, 7, 1–6 = PW II, 6.)

67. Which we have suggested in *Sur l'ontologie grise* ... , §30.

According to a primacy that conforms to the order in which evidence is brought to light, the function of first principle does not fall to God, however infinite and perfect he might be, but to the human *mens* in the figure of the *ego cogito.* The violence and the strangeness of this upheaval must be assessed: ". . . I took the being or the existence of this thought as my first principle, and from it I deduced very clearly the following: there is a God who is the author of everything there is in the world. . . ."[68] In this text, the discrepancy is marked with great clarity: in the order of the *Mathesis universalis,* existence can be established, but only by first of all remaining the existence of a thought, which is as thought thought or thinking. Hence its precedence over another primacy, as indisputably first in its own order as it is second according to the order in which evidence is brought to light: namely, the ontic primacy held by God, author and creator. Nothing precedes him, except the very thought that recognizes him as first.

Descartes understands metaphysics in the sense of *prima Philosophia,* in a complex but, in the end, clear debate with his contemporaries. He wins its dominion, at the side of *theologia* (*naturalis,* soon enough *rationalis*), over *metaphysica* as science of the *ens in quantum ens* (soon enough *ontologia*). From this stems the urgency of assigning its exact nature to the primacy thus privileged. That it concerns ". . . in general . . . all the first things that can be known by philosophizing according to the order" (AT III, 239, 6–7 = PW III, 158 [modified]) does not define the essence of it so much as the contradiction in it. For can universality (". . . in general . . .") coincide with primacy (". . . all the first . . .")? If, to reconcile them, one attributes the first to the *Mathesis universalis* and the second to the *prima Philosophia*—as we have done—doesn't one still risk the contradiction, since the demands of the epistemological order bracket all ontic foundation?

Determining the sense of *metaphysica/métaphysique* in the Cartesian lexicon therefore does not close the question about the Cartesian constitution of metaphysics, but, in the end, opens it to the concept.

---

68. *Principles, Preface* (AT IX-2, 10, 4–8 = PW I, 184 [modified]). See DM, 32, 18–23 = PW I, 127, *Letter to Father Dinet* (AT VII, 573, 14–17 = PW II, 387), and *To Clerselier,* June–July 1646: "In the second sense, the first principle is *that our soul exists,* because there is nothing whose existence is better known to us" (AT IV, 444, 23–25 = PW III, 290). This text is discussed at greater length *infra,* chap. II, §§7 and 10.

TWO

ONTO-THEO-LOGY

§6. Nothing Ontological

We have obtained a paradoxical result. In seeking to determine the essence of Cartesian metaphysics by identifying the various senses of the term *metaphysics* (and its semantic constellation), we reached a point where a decision became impossible: without a doubt, Descartes maintains a univocal, or almost univocal, definition of "metaphysics"; but, upon analysis, this definition reveals a conceptual overturning of previous definitions of the same notion that is so radical that it becomes possible to doubt that Descartes refers to metaphysics or constitutes a metaphysics even when he uses the term. In short, examining the occurrences of *métaphysique/metaphysica* does not allow one to decide if, in Cartesian thought, a figure of metaphysics is indeed being accomplished. For that matter, no purely lexical or philological examination could ever succeed, so long as the targeted and sought-out term has not been sufficiently identified. And yet we have been investigating the presence and the meaning of *métaphysique/metaphysica* according to Descartes without having defined the concept of metaphysics here being sought; and we can sense this insufficiency, in that when confronted by occurrences that are textually indisputable, we still doubt that a figure of metaphysics is actually being accomplished. The latter must therefore obey a strictly conceptual definition. Which one? To reach it, the interpreter must have a lead to pursue. But which one? If Descartes broke with previous concepts of metaphysics and, in what is essential, did so definitively, if his own statements are not enough—at least not at first— to define more precisely the original concept of metaphysics that he produced, then the interpreter can resort only to the concepts of metaphysics attributed to Descartes by indisputable metaphysicians—if only for provisional assistance. For (and this is a first piece of supporting evidence) subsequent tradition has never hesitated to recognize a Cartesian figure of metaphysics, however new it might be—or, rather, precisely because it appears to break with the previous figure of metaphysics. Perhaps more than anyone else, Hegel fixed the Cartesian figure of metaphysics—or, better, fixed the figure of Descartes in the domain of metaphysics. We have observed that, according to the letter of the Cartesian texts, metaphysics becomes first philosophy inasmuch as all beings are considered not first as they are, but as known or knowable; accordingly, primacy passes from the supreme being (whichever it might be) to the instance of knowledge (whichever it might be). This quite imprecise and fragile result finds solid backing in Hegel's judgment about Descartes. According to Hegel, it is necessary to speak of a "metaphysics of Descartes," and one must notice that "the unity of Being and thought here constitutes the first [term]." Descartes is the first (thereby making modernity possible) because he is the first to have established thought (*cogitatio*) as first principle of philosophy: "René Descartes is in reality the real initiator (*Anfänger*) of modern philosophy inasmuch as he made thought the principle"; he was able " . . . , for the first time, to go in and through thought to something secure, to win a pure beginning."[1] What is peculiar to Descartes, which establishes him as the metaphysician par excellence of modernity, is found in this: the question of the beginning and of the first term—in short, the question of the primacy at work in *philosophia prima*—passes from Being to thought. This, then, is why Hegel establishes as the second characteristic trait of "Descartes' metaphysics" the identity of thought and Being—obviously understood in such a way that thought is both the basis and the beneficiary of this identity.[2] Despite its arbitrary appearance, the Hegelian determination of such a metaphysical decision by Descartes can be confirmed. It should even be ventured that, in certain cases, Descartes conformed to it in advance (so to speak)—for instance, in a text where he is emphasizing the discovery and the decision in which his innovation, and thus his priority, consists: ". . . primus enim sum, qui cogitationem tanquam praecipuum attributum substantiae incorporae, et extensionem tanquam praecipuum corporeae, consideravi [For I am the first to have regarded

---

1. Hegel, *Vorlesungen über die Geschichte der Philosophie*, III, 2, 1, A, 1, in *Jubiläum Ausgabe, 19;* respectively pp. 345, 331, and 335 [English trans., 233 (modified), 220 (modified), and 224–25 (modified)]. From now on, it is necessary to consult the excellent translation (and critical edition!), for which we are indebted to the careful work of P. Garniron: Hegel, *Leçons sur l'Histoire de la Philosophie*, vol. 6: *La philosophie moderne. Traduction, annotation, reconstitution du cours de 1825–1826* (Paris, 1985) (for the citations in question, see pp. 1404, 1384, and 1390).

2. Hegel, op. cit., p. 345 [English trans. modified]. See *infra,* chap. III, §12.

thought as the principal attribute of an incorporeal substance, and extension as the principal attribute of a corporeal substance]."³ According to
the facts, Descartes is indeed the first who defined *cogitatio* as the principal attribute of incorporeal substance and extension as that of corporeal
substance; better, he is the first who dared to define a substance on the
basis of *cogitatio,* indeed to determine *cogitatio* itself as a substance. But
this priority, indisputable as it is, would itself not have been possible if
the *cogitatio* had not at the very outset adopted the figure of an *ego;* for
the *cogitatio* becomes the attribute of a *res (cogitans)* because an *ego*
puts it into operation by saying and accomplishing the *cogito.* The *cogitatio* is born from a *cogitare,* which itself can be performed only in the
first person—*cogito.*⁴ Consequently, priority falls finally to the *ego.* Without the *ego* to put the *cogitatio* into operation, the latter could never
attain its own existence (*ego sum, ego existo,* AT VII, 25, 12 = PW II,
17), nor for that matter even the lowest level of *substance,* such that, in
the end, it could constitute the principal attribute. Without any paradox
or play on words, it must therefore be said: Descartes would not have
been the first to have established *cogitatio* as the principal attribute of
incorporeal substance if he had not relied on the absolute priority of the
ego. This priority implies in turn a priority of the *ego* over *esse* or, what
amounts to the same thing, an anteriority of the *sum* to all the other
forms of *esse. Primus sum:* here, before and in excess of the thesis that
he actually was the first to have posed, Descartes tells us with which
primacy first philosophy (such as he inaugurates it) affects the question
of Being. *Primus sum,* the verb *to be* [*être*] intervenes first. This must be
understood in two senses. The verb *to be* [*être*] and also the question of
Being [*être*] (in the metaphysical sense) intervene at first, at the outset,
first. But also, the verb *to be* appears in terms of the first person singular.
Put otherwise: the question of Being can be determined at the outset by
the primacy of a first term, the *ego; esse* is said first in the figure of the
ego. Thus, the formula *primus sum* amounts to the developed formula
primum est: ego sum. We are here over-reading the Cartesian text only
in order to let it say what Descartes no doubt never ceased trying to
think: Being, even that of beings that are not the *ego,* is said first under

3. *Comments on a Certain Broadsheet* (AT VIII-2, 348, 15–17 = PW I, 297).

4. A formula such as "Homo cogitat [Man thinks]" (Spinoza, *Ethics* II, ax. 2 [English
trans., p. 64]) is not at all equal to "ego sum, ego cogito" or to "je pense, donc je suis."
The former concerns an ontic and anthropological description, one whose speaker himself
remains indeterminate and uncertain; it does not at all concern the actual performance of
the first principle.

the figure of the *sum;* the Being of beings is declined, before any other determination, in terms of the first person singular; *esse* is declined according to a prioritized inclination toward the *ego*—thus as a *sum.* The point of departure is found in the assimilation of *esse* to the *cogitatio,* which itself is lorded over by the *ego.* Other texts confirm this reduction of *esse,* led back to the *ego* as a result of the new Cartesian definition of primacy—for instance, when *Principia Philosophiae I,* §7 states "the first and most certain knowledge": ". . . haec cognitio, *ego cogito, ergo sum,* est omnium prima et certissima, quae cuilibet ordine philosophanti occurrat [This piece of knowledge—*I am thinking, therefore I exist*—is the first and most certain of all to occur to anyone who philosophizes in an orderly way]." That the *cogitatio* is equivalent to *esse* can be demonstrated only by the mediation of the *ego,* which exerts the one to the point of deserving the other. But the *ego* is in turn accessible, as first and absolutely certain truth, only to him who philosophizes in accordance with the order—that is to say, the order of knowledge. The *ego* is seen as first and certain, but only according to the order that the primacy of knowledge defines: that is first which is the most certain. Here, therefore, *esse* amounts to *cogitatio* because they both amount to the *ego;* but they amount to the *ego* only by virtue of a radically new primacy: that which is established by the order of knowledge, and which provokes the transformation of metaphysics into *prima Philosophia.* In these two texts, the question of the *esse* of beings comes back directly to the figure of the *ego,* passing by way of the *sum* and in conformity with the rules of an order determined exclusively by priority according to knowledge. Descartes leads *esse* back to the *ego* according to *his* order and according to the unique priority of knowledge. Descartes philosophizes in that he makes a decision about Being, *esse;* namely, that it amounts to *sum.* By this, he repeats, without imitating, Aristotle, who—at the precise moment when he interrogates being as being, and earlier in the very statement of the question—decides that τὸ ὄν amounts to οὐσία : τί τὸ ὄν, τοῦτό ἐστι τίς ἡ οὐσία [The question . . . what being is, is just the question what is οὐσία (substance)].[5] Being amounts either to οὐσία, or to *sum* and thus to the *ego*—producing two radically heterogeneous figures of metaphysics (except that, to speak more precisely, neither the one nor the other properly bears such a title). *Esse,* for Descartes, amounts to *sum,* therefore to the *ego.* This means that the question of *esse* has nei-

---

5. Aristotle, *Metaphysics Z,* I, 1028, *b* 1–4 [English trans., p. 1624 (modified)]. Concerning the interpretation of this text, consult R. Brague, *Du temps chez Platon et Aristote* (Paris, 1982), pp. 145–66.

ther the time nor the freedom to undo itself, in Descartes, from the authority of the *ego*. From the moment the *ego* appears, *esse* disappears as a question, engulfed in the evidence of the *sum; esse* amounts to the *ego*, which appropriates it, because it amounts to the *sum*, in which it is sunk. *Esse* amounts to *sum* because it falls short as a question short-circuited by the certitude of the *ego sum, ego existo*. From the moment the *ego* intervenes, *esse* falls short as a question and is reducible to the absolute but restricted evidence of the certain *sum*. Such a reduction is, to be sure, perfectly justified from the Cartesian point of view: for the order of knowledge, anything certain, even if it is unique, is enough to smother the interrogation and authorizes passing on to the next question. The question of *esse* finds its solution as soon as it finds a first being known with certainty, such that it inaugurates a *series* of other knowable beings. That *esse* can admit other meanings besides *sum* and what follows from the knowing *ego* is not important to Descartes; the question no longer bears on *esse*, but on knowledge in and through the order. The question of the Being of beings does not have to be understood as such; it has to be resolved—undone, completed, reduced. This is accomplished perfectly by leading *esse* back to *sum*, in accordance with the requirements of *prima Philosophia*—the order of knowledge. In short, to the question about the Being of beings, Descartes answers: *primus sum* or else *ego sum* is the first knowledge, therefore the most certain. In short, the way of Being of beings is defined—*sum*, Being in conformity with the *ego*.

Several objections will immediately be raised. It is presumed that they are perfectly justified, but that, precisely because of that, they do more to confirm our claim than to damage it. In the first place, it will be objected that we have excessively overvalued partial and "minor" texts removed from their respective contexts, and have done so with more bad faith than respect for the letter of these texts.[6] But besides the fact that once the letter has been respected, an interpreter must never underestimate a text, indeed must overestimate it on principle, we have here retrieved only theses that Descartes established in quite a number of other places and that even his commentators admit: the question of the ὄν ᾗ ὄν disappears, leaving as its beneficiary the arrangement according to the order of knowledge; therefore, *esse* has meaning and validity only according to what the *ego* knows of it, according to the figure that the

6. J.-M. Beyssade, in "Bulletin Cartésien XIII," *Archives de Philosophie* 1984/3: 50, with regard to a first draft of the present study, appearing under the title "Descartes et l'onto-théologie," in *Bulletin de la Société française de Philosophie*, vol. 76, 1982, pp. 117–71 (see also the German translation in *Zeitschrift für philosophische Forschung* 38/3 [1984]).

ego imposes on it—namely, *sum,* where *esse* is known. The priority of the *ego,* such that it reduces *esse* as question to *sum* as answer, results immediately from the primacy of the order of knowledge over the ontic order. We have merely retrieved, in one or another apparently paradoxical exegesis, what previous research had already established: the Cartesian *prima Philosophia* rejects the object of *metaphysica*—the consideration of the concept "being," which will soon give rise to *ontologia.* A second, immeasurably stronger, objection remains: the fact that the *ego* comes at the head of the order, according to knowledge, and even in the case of *esse*—this is a point that is established explicitly in the *Meditationes* (and, no doubt, already in the *Regulae*). But there remains a second point: if, for Descartes, *esse* becomes questionable and thinkable only under the certain figure of the *sum,* such that it is declined by the *ego,* why does he never approach thematically and as such the mode of Being of the *sum,* whereas he lays out the properties of the *ego* in great abundance (*res cogitans, substantia, mens,* affected by passions, etc.)? In other words, if the *ego sum, ego existo* determines each and every meaning of *esse,* why is the wealth of ontic determinations of the *ego* paired with a massive ontological silence concerning the manner of Being of the *sum*—better, concerning the matter of the Being about which *sum* is intended to be the unique paradigm? This line of questioning, in the form of an objection, in fact goes back to Heidegger, who in 1927 asked: "With the *cogito sum,* Descartes had claimed that he was putting philosophy on a new and firm footing. But, what he left undetermined when he began in this 'radical' way was the kind of Being which belongs to the *res cogitans,* or—more precisely—the *meaning of the Being of the 'sum.'"*[7] That is, the fact that the *ego* is and is first of all does not determine anything about the meaning of the Being of this very particular figure of *esse* that appears with *sum.* It seems irrefutable that Descartes did not answer this question because it was not raised (neither by himself nor by any of his contemporaries) and, no doubt, because he could not conceive it. Can we ourselves understand it, even after *Sein und Zeit*? Can we pursue it in the theses and the texts of Descartes? Nothing is less certain. However, a historical fact obliges us to take up this question, even if only at a very basic level: Descartes' silence about what *sum* says about *esse* actually contrasts with the emergence, in his

---

7. Heidegger, *Sein und Zeit,* §6, p. 24, see §10, p. 46 [English trans., p. 46; p. 71]; and *infra,* chap. III, §§12 and 14. Concerning Heidegger's interpretation of Descartes, see our note on "Heidegger et la situation métaphysique de Descartes," in Bulletin cartésien IV, *Archives de Philosophie* 38/2 (1975).

lifetime, of the concept of *ontologia*. This term enters into the history of metaphysics, first in 1613, when Goclenius writes it still in Greek— "ὀντολογία et philosophia de ENTE"[8]—then emphatically with Clauberg, in 1647, in the first edition of his *Elementa Philosophiae sive Ontosophia,* then, still more clearly, in the editions of 1660, 1664, and 1691.[9] It is therefore during the lifetime of Descartes, and in fact from one of his most committed followers, that there appears both the concept and the denomination *ontologia,* whose popularity will last until Kant. How to explain, in such a context, Descartes' abstention? More than of an abstention, one must speak here of a denegation: never did Descartes attempt the definition of *ens* or of *entia,* except to refute its intelligibility or philosophical utility. Formally, Cartesian philosophy is deployed as an explicit and avowed non-ontology. This paradox can be established by several analyses.

This explicit non-ontology is marked by three constantly employed operations: an elimination, a reduction, and a postulation. *(a)* The elimination concerns what the *Regulae* stigmatize with the name *entia philosophica* or *entia abstracta* and what, at the other extreme of Descartes' literary career, the *Recherche de la Vérité* will name *entia scolastica.*[10] For what reason do these beings merit such an exemplary philosophical definition? *Regula VI* makes it clear: because they each belong respectively to one or another *genus entis,* which genuses of being are them-

---

8. Goclenius, *Lexicon philosophicum,* p. 16. See *supra,* chap. I, §2, n. 27. E. Vollrath, "Die Gliederung der Metaphysik in eine Metaphysica Generalis und eine Metaphysica Specialis," loc. cit., makes it clear that the term is also at work in J. Micraelius, *Lexicon philosophicum* (Iéna, 1653), p. 654; A. Calov, *Metaphysica divina* (Rostock, 1636) (*Praecognita II,* p. 4); and J. H. Alsted, *Cursus Philosophiae Encyclopaedia* (Herborn, 1620), p. 149, who cites Goclenius by name. One can also consult the excellent discussion by J. Ecole in his preface to the re-edition of C. Wolff, *Philosophia rationalis sive Logica, Gesammelte Werke,* II, I, 1, 1 (Hildesheim, 1983), pp. 144–47. It is significant, moreover, that for this science, Goclenius sometimes uses the very phrase by which Descartes excludes all science of the *ens in quantum ens:* "Scientia . . . ex consideratione ὄντων-Universalis, quae considerat simpliciter ὄντα seu ὄν ἧ ὄν. Prima philosophia" (op. cit., p. 1011).

9. Clauberg, *Elementa Philosophiae sive Ontosophia* (Groningue, 1647); then *Metaphysica de Ente, quae rectius Ontosophia . . .* (Amsterdam, 1664); finally reprinted under the same title in *Opera Philosophica Omnia* (Amsterdam, 1691; re-ed. Hildesheim, 1968), defined thus: "Sicut autem Θεοσοφία vel Θεολογία dicitur quae circa Deum occupata est scientia: ita haec, quae non circa hoc vel illud ens speciali nomine insignitum vel proprietate quadam ab aliis distinctum, sed circa ens in genere versatur, non incommode *Ontosophia* vel *Ontologia* dici posse videatur" (vol. I, p. 281).

10. ". . . entia philosophica, quae revera sub imaginationem non cadunt [philosophical beings of the sort that do not fall within the domain of the imagination]" (AT X, 442, 27–28 = PW I, 59 [modified]); *Entia abstracta* (AT X, 443, 8 and 444, 23 = PW I, 59 and 60). Finally: ". . . omnia entia Scholastica, quae ignorabam et de quibus nunquam aliquid

selves constituted (as in the tree of Porphyry mentioned elsewhere)[11] according to the categories of the philosophers, therefore according to the κατηγορίαι τοῦ ὄντος. The initial and recurrent decision of the *Regulae*, thus also of all the thought that follows, will consist in not taking into view things that are susceptible of being made into objects of *intuitus* in terms of the categorical figures of *ens*. This decision, about which Descartes solemnly avers that "praecipuum . . . continet artis secretum, nec ulla utilior est in toto hoc Tractatu [It contains . . . the main secret of my method; and there is no more useful Rule in this whole treatise]," consists in the following:

> . . . res omnes per quasdam series posse disponi, non quidem in quantum ad aliquod genus entis referuntur, sicut illas Philosophi in categorias suas diviserunt, sed in quantum unae ex aliis cognosci possunt. [All things can be arranged serially in various groups, not in so far as they can be referred to some ontological genus (such as the categories into which Philosophers divide things) but in so far as some things can be known on the basis of others. . . .] [AT X, 381, 9–13 = PW I, 21.]

A similar operation is repeated often in the *Regulae*, though without always identifying so clearly the categorical *ens* thus eliminated; in contrast, it will emphasize the instance toward which the *res* is diverted—diverted in the precise sense of a diversion in the flow of water, or, better,

---

inaudiveram, quaeque, ut existimo, in sola tantum eorum, qui ea invenerunt, Phantasia subsistunt [all the scholastic beings which I knew nothing about and had never heard of, and which, so far as I am concerned, subsist only in the imagination of those who have invented them] . . ." (AT X, 517, 23–26 = PW II, 411–12). This last reproach contradicts the preceding ones: Descartes excludes the *entia* of the philosophers first because they do not fall within the domain of the imagination (auxiliary of the understanding in the *Regulae*) and then because all their reality resides in the imagination of the philosophers. *Ens* for Descartes neither always nor first designates the abstract concept of *ens commune* (which, to speak precisely, he does not thematize at all, or at least only a little), but the genus, the species, the specific difference, and the definitions that follow (whence, a constant critique of the definition of *homo* as *animal rationale* [AT, VII, 25, 26–31; AT, X, 517, 6–33 = PW II, 17; 411–12]).

11. The *arbor Porphyrii* mentioned by Epistemon incurs, in response, the critique of the *Metaphysici gradus* (AT X, 516, 12, then 517, 13 and 19 = PW II, 410, then 411–12). It could be possible that by positing that "the whole of philosophy is like a tree. The roots are metaphysics" (*Préface* to the French translation of the *Principia* [AT IX-2, 14, 24–25 = PW I, 186]), Descartes wants precisely to retrieve the tree of Porphyry (see *supra*, chap. I, n. 24). Concerning the translation and the meaning of *Regula VI*, and in particular AT X, 381, 7–16 = PW I, 21, may we be permitted to refer to our *René Descartes. Règles utiles et claires pour la direction de l'esprit dans la recherche de la vérité*, pp. 17*ff.* and 169*ff.*, as well as to *Sur l'ontologie grise*, §§12–14.

a diversion of funds. Thus in *Regula XII:* "... aliter spectandas esse res singulas in ordine ad cognitionem nostram, quam si de iisdem loquamur prout <u>revera</u> existunt [When we consider things in the order that corresponds to our knowledge of them, our view of them must be different from what it would be if we were speaking of them in accordance with how they exist in reality]" (418, 1–3 = 44). And,

> ... his est de rebus non agentes nisi quantum ab intellectu percipiuntur, illas tantum simplices vocamus, quarum cognitio tam perspicua et distincta, ut in plures magis distincte cognitas mente dividi non possint. [That is why since we are concerned here with things only in so far as they are perceived by the intellect, we term 'simple' only those things which we know so clearly and distinctly that they cannot be divided by the mind into others which are more distinctly known.] [418, 12–17 = 44.]

From this result the simple natures, which are simple, or better, which are quite simply, only inasmuch as they are diverted from what they are *revera;* they are, in a word, only "<u>respectu intellectus nostri</u> [with respect to our intellect]" (418, 9; 419, 6–7 = 44; 44). This diversion from the *categoriae* that determine the *genera entium* (390, 10 = 26) refers *res* to the *Mathesis Universalis* (378, 1–2 = 19), "nempe ad ordinem vel ad mensuram [*viz.* order or measure]" (451, 8 = 64), without taking into account the differences introduced by even the least bit of "specialis materia" (378, 6 = 19). Knowledge begins when there disappear, as determining authorities, the matter and therefore the form that, each time, "specialize" it, specify it, give it *forma* and *essentia,* εἶδος and therefore οὐσία. <u>Knowledge begins when the *res* loses all its own essence</u>, therefore when the order imposed by the *ens* and its different meanings is effaced. Each time the *Regulae* evoke the *genus entis,*[12] they eliminate it as radically as possible. Why? Because a genus of being implies a new term, the "*novum* genus *entis*" (427, 9–10 = 49), and therefore also a "novum *ens*" that is inscribed and installed in it (413, 12 = 41). This new being then, by virtue of an *essentia* irreducibly imbricated in the categories, demands recognition—therefore, in the first place, a confession of ignorance by the mind that cannot yet reach this new (categorical) region of being. Every *novum ens* exhibits its novelty in the figure of an *aliquod genus entis* [*mihi*] *ignotum* (427, 9–10 = 49). Ten years after the *Regulae,* Descartes will again evoke a "philosophical entity which is

12. *Genus entis* (AT X, 390, 10; 438, 15; 427, 10; 439, 2 = PW I, 26; 56; 49; 57).

unknown to me."[13] Let us understand this clearly: unknown, this being will remain so as long as one insists on viewing it as the philosophers want to, that is, according to the *categoriae entis,* and not as is required by the order, *respectu intellectus nostri.* Clearly, Descartes requires that one quit philosophy, inasmuch as philosophy considers beings according to their *genera entium* and therefore according to the categories of the *ens.* In short, he requires that one renounce philosophy as ontology.

This elimination allows one to reach *(b)* the reduction. Reduction, because the elimination of the *ens philosophicum* is reached only on a tangent and always admits a residue. Two occurrences of *ens* in the *Regulae*—the only ones that are not affected by any disqualification—allow one to define more precisely the status of this residue. The first (*Regula XIV,* 446, 3–10 = PW I, 61) concerns an extended *subjectum,* such as it presents itself in its particular essence as a being; namely, that being appropriate to what geometry requires. Insofar as the mind intends only a figure, it will consider only its aspect of *figuratum;* if the mind intends a body, it will consider the three dimensions of Galilean space; if it intends a surface, two dimensions only; if it intends a line, only one dimension; and finally, if it intends only a point, it will consider it "omisso omni alio, praeterquam quod sit ens [leaving out every other property except that it is a being]" (446, 9–10 = 61 [modified]). *Ens* therefore shows up, finally irreducible, in order to connote pure and simple position, without any measurable extension. It connotes unextended position, but also irreal position (to speak a Husserlian language). No *res* endowed with individuality, existence, or even essence appears here. What then merits the title *ens,* and why, precisely here, does it not suffer any disqualification? This two-pronged question easily receives its single answer: *ens* indicates purely and simply the lowest-level object offered to the imaginative gaze of the mind, and it is enjoined to it all the more perfectly as it results from it. *Ens* retains nothing, here, of essence, *genus* [*entis*], or the categories. It doesn't even appear until the initial *subjectum,* and with it all "unknown . . . philosophical Being," has disappeared. Now let us consider the second occurrence, taken from the same *Regula:* ". . . notorum entium sive naturarum mixturam [that combination of familiar

---

13. *To Morin,* 12 September 1638 (AT II, 364, 4–5 and 367, 19–20 = PW, III, 121 and 122). The best examples of such "philosophical beings [*êtres philosophiques*]," eliminated because seen as unknowable, come from the *Regulae:* disqualification of motion (AT X, 426, 16–25 = 49) and of place (426, 9–16 and 433, 14–434, I = 49 and 53). See *Sur l'ontologie grise . . . ,* §24, pp. 146*ff.,* as well as §28, and *Règles utiles . . . ,* pp. 248–49 (other references).

beings that is natures] ..." (439, 8 = 57 [modified]). The knowledge of every question (here it is that of a magnet) is summed up in the combination of beings already known. Why here speak positively of beings, and call them known, when previously (and subsequently) they will have been called unknown and for that very reason disqualified? Obvious answer: "notorum entium *sive naturarum* [familiar beings *that is natures*]"; in other words, the choice here results from the equivalence of these *entia* with the simple natures, which consist entirely in the knowledge that the constitutive mind has of them. Thus, the *ens* will still be admitted at the terminal point of the elimination only in the exact measure in which it is reduced to precisely what the elimination aimed to extract— a pure, simple, empty, and uniform objectivity. Uniform because absolutely destitute of all *forma*, as well as even the least bit of *essentia*. There remains, in short, an *ens* without any of the four possible acceptations of ὄν according to Aristotle—who described it in terms of the categories, in terms of δύναμις/ἐνέργεια [potentiality/actuality], in terms of οὐσία/συμβεβηκὸς [substance/accidents], and finally in terms of the true and the false.[14] First, Descartes contests the categorical acceptation of the *ens*—"... res omnes per quasdam series posse disponi, non quidem in quantum ad aliquod genus entis referuntur, sicut illas Philosophi in categorias suas diviserunt, sed in quantum unae ex aliis cognosci possunt [All things can be arranged serially in various groups, not in so far as they can be referred to some ontological genus (such as the categories into which philosophers divide things), but in so far as some things can be known on the basis of others]."[15] He then contests the validity of every distinction between *actus* and *potentia*, because the *ens* in potential is in the end simply nothing: "... esse potentiali, quod proprie loquendo nihil est [potential Being that strictly speaking is nothing]."[16] As for the couple *substantia/accidens*, it is rendered obsolete from the epistemological point of view that Descartes definitively adopted—either because accidentality and contingency must disappear in the deduction that al-

---

14. See *Metaphysics E*, 4, 1027 *b* 25–27 [English trans., p. 1623]. As is well known, this text is already in retreat from the position taken in *Metaphysics Θ* 10, 1051 *a* 34*ff.* [English trans., p. 1660]. The latter position alone attains the true as the meaning, and first meaning of the ὄν. The comparison with the *Regulae* is indicated by Heidegger himself in *Wegmarken*, G. A., 9, p. 233.

15. *Regula VI* (AT X, 381, 9–13 = PW I, 21); see *Règles utiles et claires . . .* , p. 171.

16. *Meditatio III* (AT VII, 47, 21–22 = PW II, 32). It is clear that the refusal of this meaning of the Being of beings both provokes and implies the criticism of the Aristotelian definition of motion in *Regula XII* (AT X, 426, 16–22 = PW I, 49).

ways aims for necessity (*Regula XII*), or because substance can be known only through its principal attribute, and all the more so when a great number of attributes is known in addition.[17] There remains a fourth sense of *ens*, which Descartes indisputably privileges and seems to take up from Aristotle: "... veritatem proprie vel falsitatem non nisi in solo intellectu esse posse [There can be no truth or falsity in the strict sense except in the intellect alone]" (AT X, 396, 3–4 = PW I, 30). This rapprochement is confirmed elsewhere when Descartes introduces Being explicitly: "Truth consists in being [*être*] and falsehood only in non-being, so that the idea of the infinite, which includes all being [*être*], includes all that there is of truth in things."[18] The *ens* is thus reduced to a single one of its Aristotelian acceptations: Being in the understanding. But the very rapprochement between ἐν διανοίᾳ and *in solo intellectu* brings to the fore the deep difference that separates the two theses on the Being of beings: for Aristotle, διανοία contributes entirely to revealing the εἶδος, thus the οὐσία, of the thing; for Descartes, in contrast, the *intellectus* can accomplish the representation of an object only by abstracting from its essence, from its actuality and from its categorical definition. Accordingly, in Descartes, Being in the mode of the true is reduced to Being in the mode of represented objectivity. The truth is not merely situated, among other meanings of *ens*, in the understanding; it results from the understanding, as the sole authority that determines the Being of beings. To be [*être*] as true hypertrophies and becomes the sole meaning of *ens*; but most importantly, it is radicalized into to be [*être*] as representation. *Ens non in quantum ens, sed in quantum repraesentatum, ut objectum*—it could be summed up.

representation

The elimination and then the reduction of the *ens* to the lowest level of objectness leads finally to the third stage: *(c)* Descartes postulates that the evidence for the question of the Being of beings is so obvious that the answer never ceases to disqualify, smother, and annihilate the question from which it, so to speak, no longer comes, and of which it no longer has any need. The question about the Being of beings succumbs in advance before the superabundant certainty of the answer: to be [*être*], as an object representable with certainty, amounts to existing; and existence calls for neither definition nor justification. In this way, the question of the Being of beings does not so much fall victim to downsiz-

17. See, for example, AT VII, 222, 1–14; 360, 2–6; *Principia Philosophiae I,* §§52–53 = PW II, 156; 249; PW I, 210–11. See *infra,* chap. III, §13.
18. *To Clerselier,* 23 April 1649 (AT V, 356, 15–18 = PW III, 377).

ing at the hand of Descartes, as it is replaced by an answer, always postulated and yet nowhere thought as such—for existence is self-evident:
"Nota est omnibus essentiae ab existentia distinctio [The distinction
between essence and existence is known to everyone]," an answer to
Hobbes retorts magnificently (AT, VII, 194, 11 = PW II, 136); or: "Nemi-
nem enim unquam tam stupidum existitisse crediderim, qui . . . quid sit
existentia edocendus fuerit [I would never have believed that there has
ever existed anyone so dull that he had to be told what existence is]."
Accordingly, it is useless to speak of it: "I do not remember where I
spoke of the distinction between essence and existence." This is because
the evidence that characterizes them also confuses them:

> . . . non idem [modaliter differre] est de triangulo extra cogitationem exis-
> tente, in quo manifestum mihi videtur, essentiam et existentiam nullo
> modo distingui; et idem de omnibus universalibus. [The case is not the
> same (differing modally) with the triangle existing outside thought, in
> which it seems manifest to me that essence and existence are in no way
> distinct. The same is the case with all universals.]

In short, ". . . existentia nihil aliud [est] quam essentia existens [Exis-
tence (is) nothing other than existing essence]."[19] Essence is reduced to
existence because Being in general is led back to existence, as much in
the case of the *ego*—". . . ego sum, ego existo [I am, I exist] . . ." (AT
VII, 25, 12; see also 27, 9 = PW II, 17; 18)—as in that of God—". . . God,
who is this perfect Being [*être*], is or exists . . ." (DM, 36, 30; see also 38,
19 = PW I, 129 [modified]; 130). But, it will be objected, doesn't our
thesis contradict itself by attributing to Descartes a double presupposition, first of Being as represented, then of Being as existence, by definition located outside thought? Not at all, since Descartes determines the
primacy of existence precisely in its susceptibility to representation. That
is, ever since the *Regulae*, existence has been counted among the simple
natures, which, by definition, are completely and perfectly knowable—
". . . uniusquisque animo potest intueri se existere [everyone can mentally intuit that he exists] . . ." (AT X, 368, 21–22; see 419, 22 and 420,
7–8 = PW I, 14; 45; 45). And, in this way, existence can be known not
despite but indeed in virtue of its exteriority to the mind, because it

---

19. Respectively, *Recherche de la Vérité* (AT X, 524, 10–11 = PW II, 417); *A X*, 1645
or 1646 (AT IV, 348, 7–9 = PW III, 279; then [in Latin] 350, 7–10 = PW III, 280); finally
Conversation with Burman (AT V, 164, 29–30 = ed. J.-M. Beyssade, §28, op. cit., p. 79 =
not included in PW). See *To Hyperaspistes,* August 1641 (AT III, 435, 1–13 = PW III, 197).

better accomplishes the objectness [*objectité*] of an *objectum* set in front of and thus for the *ego*. Accordingly, existence permits conceiving all things as objects, in consequence of their own conceivability:

> In omnis rei idea sive conceptu continetur existentia, quia nihil possumus concipere nisi sub ratione existentis; nempe continetur existentia possibilis sive contingens in conceptu rei limitatae, sed necessaria et perfecta in conceptu entis summe perfecti. [Existence is contained in the idea or concept of every single thing, since we cannot conceive of anything except as existing. Possible or contingent existence is contained in the concept of a limited thing, whereas necessary and perfect existence is contained in the concept of a supremely perfect being.] [AT VII, 166, 14–18 = PW II, 117.]

At issue here is one of the "axiomata sive communes notiones" of the appendix in geometrical order to the *Secundae Responsiones*. Descartes postulates that every thing, thus every being, can be reduced to existence straightaway, because existence conceives (*in conceptu*) in every case that beings be finite or infinite, contingent or necessary. The entire lexicon of the Being of beings is led back to representation, by the very movement that brings it back to existence:

> . . . quis enim nescit per *rem* intelligi *ens reale,* atque *ens* dici ab *essendo* sive existendo, atque ipsas rerum naturas dici a Philosophis *essentias,* propterea quod illas non nisi ut *essentes* sive existentes concipere possumus? [Who does not know that by *thing* one understands *real being,* and that *ens* is said by *essence* or *existence,* on account of which we cannot conceive these things except as *essences* or existences?] [AT VIII-2, 60, 12–16 = not included in PW.]

The postulation of existence, as the accomplishment of the objectness [*objectité*] of the Being of beings, is here declared all the more bluntly, since the polemical spirit of the confrontation with Voëtius frees Descartes from his habitual prudence. Beings must be conceived and, in order to succeed in that, must be reduced to existence, the sole acceptation of the Being of beings. But since existence works to produce evidence as an axiom of experience, since it itself is produced in evidence as the object par excellence, when the sense of the Being of beings is taken to be existence, it succumbs to its own evidence and disappears in it. Existence accomplishes and produces so much evidence that it is dissolved in it. About the Being of beings as existence evident for representation, there is nothing more that can be said. It even seems to us that Descartes drew this consequence explicitly, or that, at the very least, an enigmatic text from his *Conversation with Burman* lets it be divined: "V. in Meta-physica nihil intelligitur per ens." No doubt, one could understand this text, as does a recent translator, to be saying "A voir en métaphysique: le néant ne s'entend que par l'être [In metaphysics: nothingness is under-stood only by means of Being]."[20] But it also seems permissible to under-stand it literally: nothing is understood, nor to be understood, by *being;* or again: when one says *being,* in the sense of existence, one says noth-ing—not because existence is abolished in a nothing, nor because inde-terminate Being is confused with indeterminate nothing (Hegel), but be-cause in the supreme evidence of existence nothing can any longer be said about Being. In this way, Descartes appears to be the first of the metaphysicians—"nemo ante me [no one before me]" (AT, VIII-2, 347, 13 = PW I, 296)—who believed that he was able to dispense with think-ing the Being of beings as such, except to disqualify it as "novum ens inutiliter [admittendum] [The useless assumption . . . of some new en-tity]" (AT X, 413, 12 = PW I, 41). The question of the Being of beings is not posed, since the answer precedes it—beings are evidently in terms of existence, about which there is nothing to be understood, nor ex-pected. The very absence of a thought of the nothing confirms that there is no longer a place here for questioning the Being of beings, and that nothing ontological is established.

§7. Principle and *Causa Sui*

In sticking to his concept of *prima Philosophia,* Descartes therefore ar-rives at nothing ontological. And yet, postulates Heidegger, "any meta-

---

20. AT V, 153, 32. J.-M. Beyssade, op. cit., §13, pp. 44–45, bases his translation on *To Hyperaspistes,* August 1641, n. 6 (AT III, 426, 27–427, 20 = PW III, 191–92)—to which there can also be added: "Ego enim, qui per falsum nihil aliud intelligo quam veri priva-tionem [I understand falsity to be merely a privation of the truth]" (AT VII, 378, 21 = PW II, 260), and other texts. [The English translation of the text from the *Conversation with Burman* understands it as does Beyssade. PW III, 339 reads, "In metaphysics our under-standing of nothingness derives from that of Being."—Trans.] Nothing ontological is also found in Pascal: "We cannot define a word without beginning with the words *it is,* whether expressed or understood. Therefore, to define being [*être*] we should have to say *it is,* and thus we should use the word to be defined in the definition" (*De l'esprit géométrique,* in *Œuvres complètes* (Paris: L. Lafuma, 1963), p. 350 [English trans., p. 192]). This same text criticizes the Aristotelian definitions of *man,* of light, and of time—exactly as Descartes did (see n. 10). A parallel text authenticates this: "Who can even know what Being is, which cannot be defined since there is nothing more general, and since to explain it one would have to use the same word by saying: It is . . . ?" (*Entretien avec M. de Saci,* ibid., p. 294 [English trans., p. 126]). Despite our disparate intentions, we are pleased to put the

physical thinking is onto-logy or it is nothing at all."[21] Shouldn't it therefore be admitted, once and for all, that the Cartesian enterprise decidedly does *not* belong to metaphysics? As provocative and paradoxical as this seems, such a conclusion is by no means untenable. Better, it would even do justice to the claim to absolute originality that Descartes never ceased to make; and, for that matter, it would join up with the opinions of certain celebrated commentators who insist on emphasizing in Descartes the end of all "realism" and the commencement of a pure reign of "consciousness," or who deplore in him a "degradation" of ancient philosophy.[22] With the exception of resting content with an imprecise and hazy acceptation of the concept of metaphysics, wouldn't it be most expedient and most clear to renounce using this term in regard to Descartes? The inquiries into terminology (chapter I), as well as into the role of the question of the Being of beings (chapter II, §6), seem to point definitively toward this conclusion.

However, it is not acceptable to give in to this all too simple conclusion, for several reasons: *(a)* We have ended up with nothing ontological in Cartesian thought as a result of the primacy of the question of repre-

---

expression "nothing ontological" beneath the banner of F. Alquié, "Descartes et l'ontologie négative," *Revue internationale de Philosophie* (1950), reappearing in *Etudes cartésiennes* (Paris, 1982).

21. Heidegger, *Holzwege,* G. A., 5, p. 210, 1950 ed., p. 194 [English trans., "The Word of Nietzsche: God Is Dead," p. 55].

22. Consider here L. Liard: "What characterizes his [Descartes'] physics and is in fact an entirely novel and unprecedented thing is the absence of any metaphysical idea." Consequently: "In the entire work of Descartes, the method and the sciences constitute a distinct and independent work. What has been inserted into the method from metaphysics can be detached from it without harm" (*Descartes* [Paris, 1882], pp. 69 and 14). The same analysis, played out in a reverse sense, can be found in J. Maritain: "Descartes is a metaphysician who is unfaithful to metaphysics—and one who voluntarily strays in the direction of the plains, towards the vast flat country watered by the river Mathematics"; therefore "it seems to us that Descartes has, properly speaking, *degraded* metaphysics" (*Le songe de Descartes et autres essais* [Paris, n.d.], pp. 132–33). It falls to L. Brunschvicg to formulate the motive for this supposed desertion of metaphysics; namely, indifference to or even rejection of Being: "Descartes rejects [. . .] the *universals of the dialecticians* and he abandons to its illusory destiny the entirety of the concept of Being," that is to say, "the illusory preoccupation with principles of Being" (*Les progrès de la conscience dans la philosophie occidentale* [Paris, 1927], vol. 1, p. 138; *Ecrits philosophiques* [Paris, 1950], vol. 1, p. 7). This was also the position of E. Gilson, at least at first (up until 1925); see our study "L'instauration de la rupture. Gilson à la lecture de Descartes," in *Etienne Gilson et nous: la philosophie et son histoire* (Paris, 1980). See, more recently, the summary of this question by V. Carraud, "Descartes appartiene alla storia della metaphysica?" in *Descartes metafisico, Interpretazioni del Novecento,* ed. J.-R. Armogathe and G. Belgioioso (Rome: Istituto dell'Enciclopedia Italiana, 1994), pp. 165–70.

sentation over that of beings as such. Descartes abandons ontology—science of the *ens in quantum ens*—because he tries first to fix the conditions for the representation of beings—*ens in quantum cognitum.* This result will not be put into question, and will find still more evidence to back it up (chapter II, §8). But perhaps it does not lead to nothing ontological; or rather, it would lead to nothing ontological only if *ontologia,* such as it has been deployed historically from Clauberg to Wolff, contradicted the primacy of consciousness over the interrogation of the *ens* as such—in short, if ontology itself, as a historically dated philosophical discipline (and one historically contemporaneous with Descartes), reached the *ens in quantum ens* only by some means besides the presupposition of its representability—*ut cognitum.* Now, this does indeed seem to be the case. We will confine ourselves to a single, privileged example, that of Clauberg, a Cartesian who was the first to appoint, as early as 1647, an entirely separate discipline called *ontologia* to the rank of fundamental science. What definition of *ens* does he use? With an admirable clarity and a similar sense of straightforwardness, Clauberg defines it from the opening pages of his *Ontosophia* (titled "... *Metaphysica,* sed aptius *Ontologia* vel scientia Catholica, eine allgemeine Wissenschaft et Philosophia universalis ..."). Three meanings of *ens* can be distinguished: the third defines it as substance to which accidents are opposed; the second defines it as *aliquid,* really being, even without being thought ("... nemine etiam cogitante ..."), which is opposed only to pure *nihil;* finally, the first meaning defines it in terms of the *cogitatio,* and consequently without anything being contrary to it: "... denotat omne quod cogitari potest (distinctionis causa vocatur *intelligibile*) [it denotes all that can be thought (on account of which it is called *intelligibile*)]." Of course, Clauberg recognizes that the third acceptation of *ens*—substance—remains the most powerful ("... potissimum illud ..."). However, aiming for a better understanding of the question ("... ad meliorem hujus notitiam ..."), he privileges the first two acceptations; in fact, he privileges the first above all, seeing that he begins "... universal science by starting with thinkable being, just as first philosophy, beginning with the singular, considers nothing before the mind thinking itself [inchoaturi universalem philosophiam ab *Ente cogitabili,* quemadmodum a singulari incipiens prima philosophia nihil prius considerat *Mente cogitante*]."[23] In other words, *ontologia* does not consider being in terms

23. J. Clauberg, *Metaphysica de ente, quae rectius Ontosophia ...,* in *Opera omnia philosophica* (Amsterdam, 1691; re-ed. Hildesheim, 1968), respectively §§2, 4, and 5, p. 283.

of itself—since in this case, it would be acceptable to see it in the way Aristotle did, as substance, οὐσία, where it is deployed *potissimum.* Rather, it considers being truly and first on the basis of the *cogitatio,* therefore in the role of *ens cogitabile,* of beings inasmuch as they are thinkable, conceived, and represented, not inasmuch as they are beings. Hence a canonic definition: "Being is, in whatever way it might be whatever it might be, that which can be thought and uttered [Ens est quicquid quovis modo est, cogitari ac dici potest]." This definition goes so far that even *nihil* becomes a being, provided that I think it. Concerning being, *ontologia* says first and above all that it is thinkable and thought: "Cogitatur autem Ens, cum animo percipitur [being is thought when it is perceived by the mind]."[24] Does Clauberg, at the very moment of determining *ontologia* and precisely *in order to* establish it, reproduce the "nothing ontological" that we had stigmatized in Descartes—namely, that the science of being is first of all a science of the science of being, a science of being seen from the point of view of its representation? This question finds an explicit answer in a note that Clauberg adds to the text that deduces the primacy of the *ens cogitabile* from the primacy of the *Mens cogitans: "Prima Philosophia:* it is not named thus on account of the universality of the object which it treats, but because whoever philosophizes seriously must begin with it. That is, starting from the knowledge

24. Op. cit., §§6 and 9 (ibid.). See §10: "Nam eo ipso quo quid apprehendimus, jam est intelligibile, et per consequens Ens in prima significatione" (op. cit., p. 294). Naturally, Clauberg retrieves the objective concept of beings (used in §16, ibid.), following an obvious affiliation with Suarez: the objective concept objectivizes beings by means of the formal concept, act of the understanding, ". . . conceptui formali enti respondere unum conceptum objectivum adaequatum et immediatum. . . . Necesse est conceptum formalem entis habere aliquod adaequatum conceptum objectum . . . quia ille conceptus formalis est actus intellectus; omnis autem actus intellectus, sicut et omnis actus, quatenus unus est, habere debet aliquod objectum adaequatum, a quo habeat unitatem" (*Disputationes Metaphysicae, II,* s. 2, n. 8, op. cit., vol. 25, p. 72. See our analyses in *Sur la théologie blanche de Descartes,* §7, pp. 123–35). This determination of *ens* in terms of the essence of representation is then deployed explicitly in Leibniz, who locates what he also names *ontologia seu scientia de Aliquo et Nihilo* in the field of the ". . . scientia de cogitabili in universum quatenus tale est [science of what is universally thinkable insofar as it is such]" (*Fragments inédits,* ed. L. Couturat (Paris, 1903), pp. 511*ff.* [English trans., p. 5]). Wolff will also uphold this decision when he defines beings in terms of possibility—"Ens dicitur, quod existere potest, consequenter cui existentia non repugnat"— and possibility in terms of representation—"*Possibile* semper *est* aliquid, *eidem* semper *notio respondet . . . ," ". . . Id, cui aliqua respondet notio, possibile est. . . .*" This notion is determined in explicit agreement with Clauberg and, above all, with Descartes, *Principia Philosophiae I,* §45 (*Ontologia,* respectively §§134, 102, and 103, finally note to §103 [Leipzig, 1729]; *Gessamelte Werke,* II, 3 [Hildesheim, 1962], pp. 135*ff.,* 84 and 85). See F. L. Marcolungo, *Wolff e il possibile* (Padua, 1982).

of his own mind and of that of God, etc. This *prima philosophia* is contained in the six *Meditationes* of Descartes."[25] The reference does not suffer any restrictions: in order to specify the reasons that cause him to prefer as the first meaning of being precisely that in which being does not intervene as itself but as thinkable—*ens cogitabile*—and thus in order to justify the paradoxical acceptation of the primacy that is opposed to the traditional priority of οὐσία, Clauberg refers to the Cartesian determination of *prima Philosophia*. In this determination, *prima* is applied to the order of knowledge, not to the order of being in its Being. If *ontologia* establishes its dominion by transposing being from οὐσία to *ens cogitabile,* as Clauberg explicitly claims, then it presupposes that being can, in the first place, be submitted *a priori* to the yoke of the *cogitatio.* That is to say, *ontologia* rests on the Cartesian decisions about *prima Philosophia,* a fact that Clauberg also recognizes expressly. It must therefore be concluded that, as a discipline, *ontologia* depends so radically on the fact of there being nothing ontological in Descartes that, actually, it could have appeared historically only after, and thanks to, what Descartes instituted. Clauberg could have deployed the *Defensio cartesiana* only insofar as he was himself, more essentially, defended by what Descartes inaugurated. We do not have to develop here the arguments in favor of such a line of descent connecting the Cartesian nothing ontological to the appearance of *ontologia* as a discipline. On the other hand, we do have to envision a revision in the status of the nothing ontological attributed to Descartes: if it actually does make possible the appearance of *ontologia,* then, on the one hand, the latter perhaps accomplishes a new and decisive step in the mis-taking (not the taking up) of the question of being as such, and on the other hand, nothing ontological itself undoubtedly harbors a radical decision concerning the Being of beings, precisely in that it lowers it to the rank of represented being. From this perspective, nothing ontological would therefore become less an indication of Descartes' having abandoned the question of the Being of beings than a paradoxical sign that he is profoundly invested in it—voluntarily or not, it matters little. "All metaphysical thought is onto-logy or else it is absolutely nothing": it could be possible that Cartesian thought is an

25. "... sic dicta non propter universalitatem objecti, de quo agit; sed quo serio philosophaturus ab ea debeat incipere. Nempe a cogitatione suae mentis et Dei, etc. Haec prima philosophia sex Meditationibus cartesii continetur ..." Op. cit., p. 283, note to §5. This reference alone suffices to render problematic M. Wundt's claim that, throughout the progress of his career, Clauberg had not been "... in keiner Weise [von Descartes] beeinflusst [influenced by Descartes in any way at all]" (*Die deutsche Schulmetaphysik des 17. Jahrhunderts,* p. 94).

ontology—the one that permits *ontologia* to be constituted as the thought of beings as thinkable—and therefore that it belongs to metaphysics, and is not nothing.

A second reason to inscribe Descartes within the horizon of metaphysics can be found, once again, in Heidegger. *(b)* Heidegger does not say simply that all metaphysics is ontology, in the sense of *ontologia* as a historically determined discipline; he evokes an onto-logy. The dash here indicates a joint where logic and being is connected, or more exactly the λόγος (of which logic offers only one of the avatars) and the ὄν (of which *ens* undoubtedly does not contain all). In the course of the development of metaphysics, the λόγος assumes the more and more weighty and powerful function of a foundation. This foundation is finally manifest in a clear-cut figure, whose blueprint Heidegger sketches under the title "the onto-theo-logical constitution of metaphysics." According to this constitution, the "logical" foundation, the λόγος, states being in an onto-logy only by duplicating its own anteriority to being in a theo-logy, where, still in the role of ground, it also precedes the divine. The λόγος, which says (and grounds) being in Being also, in a profound and confused unity, says it (and grounds it) in the supreme being, τὸ Θεῖον. If metaphysics must be identified as essentially onto-logy, this is because, for that very reason, ". . . more rigorously and clearly thought out, metaphysics is onto-theo-logic."[26] Onto-theo-logy provides the "fundamental trait" of all metaphysics, because it marks not only the tension between two dimensions of being (being as such, τὸ ὄν ᾗ ὄν, and being at its most excellent, τὸ θεῖον), but also because it marks the foundation that unites them reciprocally and governs them from the ground up: "Being grounds beings, and beings, as what *is* most of all, account for Being [*gründet Sein das Seiende, begründet das Seiende als das Seiendste das Sein*]."[27] The being par excellence finds its ground insofar as it accomplishes beings in their Being and exemplifies the way of Being of beings. Reciprocally, beings in their Being can be grounded in their mode of production by the being that excels at accomplishing the Being of all beings. In this way, the doubling of the foundation assures the specificity of onto-logy as well as of theo-logy, by the sole condition of condition itself—logical conditioning, i.e., λόγος, *ratio, causa,* sufficient reason, concept, etc. Let us accept, as a working hypothesis, this definition of the essence of metaphysics and ask if Descartes can live up to it. Without prejudicing analy-

"Grund"

---

26. Heidegger, *Identität und Differenz* (Pfullingen, 1957), p. 50 [English trans., p. 59].
27. Ibid., p. 62 [English trans., p. 69].

ses that are still to be conducted, we can right away put forth two arguments in favor of an at least provisionally positive response. First a fact: Descartes seems to have foreseen that metaphysics is constituted according to the tension between two foundations, an onto-logical one and a theo-logical one. Here one must reflect on the ambiguity, which he recognized, of the concept "principle," an ambiguity that renders possible the transformation of primacy: ". . . the word principle can be taken in several senses. It is one thing to look for a *common notion* so clear and general that it can serve as a principle for proving the existence of all the beings [*les êtres*], or entities [*les entia*], to be discovered later; and another thing to look for a *being* [*un être*], whose existence is known to us better than that of any other so that it can serve as a principle for knowing them." The duality of principles leads, on the one hand, to a principle that is useful when we try to arrive at the existence of beings: "In the first sense, it can be said that 'It is impossible for the same thing both to be and not to be at the same time' is a principle." On the other hand, this duality leads to a principle that makes a being known directly: "In the second sense, the first principle is *that our soul exists,* because there is nothing whose existence is better known to us."[28] Either the principle directly concerns a "Being" (read: a "being") that is first and par excellence because it exemplifies the way of Being of all beings—in which case, it is precisely a matter of the *ego cogito,* being inasmuch as it thinks first—or the principle concerns all possible beings, excluding the impossible ones (and defining them as such), because it states their way of Being beings. The first sense of principle refers to theo-logy, with the aporia that the being par excellence is identified with the *ego* and not with God. The second refers to onto-logy, with the aporia that it does not refer—at least not explicitly—to a principle that Descartes actually used, but to a statement of the principle of noncontradiction, such as it defines the ὄν ᾗ ὄν according to Aristotle. At the very least, it appears clear that the duality in the concept "principle" opens the possibility of looking for the eventual duality of an onto-logy in tension with a theo-logy within the Cartesian project. But a second argument is at once added to the first: metaphysics is constituted as an onto-theo-logy, or more exactly, as an onto-theo-*logy*. In fact, the two approaches to being depend on the λόγος—first because they both say it, then and above all, because in saying being, they ground it and also ground their own dis-

---

28. *To Clerselier,* June–July 1646 (AT IV, 444, 4–12; 13–14; 23–25 = PW III, 290 [modified]; 290; 290).

course in return. In all sorts of ways, the λόγος precedes the ὄν and the θεῖον. Now, haven't we emphasized over and over again that for Descartes the *cogitatio* precedes the *ens in quantum ens* precisely in order to ground it in terms of the criteria of certainty? Doesn't the *cogitatio* as *a priori* condition, but also as certain foundation, fulfill the duties of the λόγος of onto-theo-*logy*? At the very least, this hypothesis cannot be ruled out right away—provided one can show that the *cogitatio* determines and also grounds the thought of the being par excellence—in short, that it determines God. We ask at last: can Cartesian thought accede to an authentically metaphysical status, if we accept the hypothesis according to which metaphysics would be defined conceptually as onto-theo-logy?

By referring to the onto-theo-logical constitution of metaphysics, which we have assumed as a working hypothesis yet to be confirmed, a third argument in favor of according a rigorously metaphysical status to Cartesian thought could be made. As a consequence of the claim that "more rigorously and clearly thought out, metaphysics is an onto-theology," Heidegger observes that Being can be accomplished only as ground. The ground requires not simply a *causa prima,* but also that the latter be deployed with an *ultima ratio,* to the point that both coincide in a unique being par excellence, *causa sive ratio* of all other beings. When this internal requirement of metaphysics comes to be met, the being par excellence assumes a name and a definition, *causa sui:* "The Being of beings, in the sense of ground [*Grund*] can fundamentally [*gründlich*] be represented only as *causa sui.* This is the metaphysical concept of God." In other words, ". . . the conciliation (*Austrag*) results in and gives Being as the generative ground. This ground itself needs to be properly accounted for by that for which it accounts, that is, by causation (*Verursachung*) through the most original of things (*ursprünglichste Sache*). This thing is the cause (*Ursache*) as *causa sui.* This is the right name for God in philosophy. Man can neither pray nor sacrifice to this god."[29] Our task here cannot be to verify or annul the theological repercussions of the *causa sui* or its importance in the history of philosophy.[30] But one question can no longer be avoided: is it really possible for Descartes not to belong officially to metaphysics as we have discussed it, when he was the first to have forged and put in place the phrase *causa*

29. Heidegger, op. cit., p. 64 [English trans., p. 60; p. 72 (modified)].
30. See, however, several suggestions *infra,* chap. IV, §19, and in *Sur la théologie blanche de Descartes . . . ,* §17.

sui? This textual evidence must be emphasized: Spinoza is no more the creator than the thinker of the *causa sui.* He is *not* its creator, as he himself indicates when he employs this phrase for the first time: ". . . si res sit in se sive, ut vulgo dicitur, causa sui, tum per solam suam essentiam debebit intelligi [if the thing is in itself, or, as is commonly said, self-caused, *causa sui,* then it will have to be understood solely through its essence]."[31] His hesitation ". . . *ut vulgo dicitur,* as is commonly said . . ." in effect supposes at least one precedent; and it is difficult to imagine that Spinoza is not thinking first of Descartes, whose theses he is constantly assuming and disputing in the same treatise. Spinoza does *not* think the *causa sui* in an original way, seeing as he is limited either to identifying it with the ontological argument—"By *causa sui* I mean that whose essence involves existence; or that whose nature can be conceived only as existing"—or to extending it to the production of finite modes: "In the same sense that God is said to be self-caused he must also be said to be the cause of all things."[32] The noticeable absence of any real discussion about the coherence and the repercussions of a *causa sui* can be explained (unless one wants to accuse Spinoza of theoretical negligence) only if Spinoza has supposed the notion to be already established and justified by others—in fact by Descartes in the *Iae* and *IVae Responsiones.* The charge of introducing this apparently contradictory concept falls to Descartes, who himself recognized that "[it] was too crude."[33] Therefore, if *causa sui* does indeed characterize the completed concept of metaphysics understood as onto-theo-logy, how could Descartes, who was historically the first to have introduced the phrase *causa sui* into the lexicon of metaphysics, not himself belong to metaphysics—or better, not mark an essential figure of it?

For these reasons—nothing ontological as the presupposition of *ontologia;* the onto-theo-logical constitution suggested by the duality of the concept *principle* and by the priority of the *cogitatio;* finally the introduction of the *causa sui*—we cannot abandon the task of drawing out the rigorously metaphysical status of Cartesian thought, despite the denials and paradoxes with which its lexicon afflicts previous usage. But the at-

31. Spinoza, *De Intellectus Emendatione,* §92 [English trans., p. 257].
32. Spinoza, *Ethics* I, respectively *definition* I and §25, scholium [English trans., pp. 31; 49].
33. *To Mersenne,* 4 March 1641 (AT III, 330, 18–19 = PW III, 174). See the reaction of Arnauld when faced with the *causa efficiens respectu sui* (mentioned in the *Iae Responsiones* [AT VII, 111, 5–7 = PW II, 80]): ". . . sane durum mihi videtur, et falsum [This seems to me to be a hard saying, and indeed to be false]" (208, 16 = 146).

tempt can no longer succeed in reaching its goal if it limits itself to a strictly lexical investigation; the metaphysical authenticity of Cartesian thought can be established only by pursuing a conceptual hermeneutic. We choose, as theoretical model and in the role of a working hypothesis, the definition of metaphysics by onto-theo-logical constitution. Henceforth, the question becomes: does Cartesian thought satisfy onto-theology, and if so, what figure of it does it produce?

§8. The First Pronouncement about the Being of Beings: *Cogitatio*

Our endeavor to extract a Cartesian ontology (therefore a metaphysics) foundered on its first try when confronted with the disqualification of all *novum ens,* in fact of all *ens* as such, to the benefit of that which, whatever it might be, is offered to knowledge, its laws, and its requirements. Our attempt must therefore be resumed at this point. We have available to us at least one positive lead: in one place, Descartes names the fully knowable residue *ens notum* (AT X, 439, 8). In this way, he anticipates what Clauberg will name *ens cogitabile,* and what allows an *ontologia* to be established. Consequently, the Cartesian *ens notum* does not exclude a determination of the *ens* as such in its—represented—universality. This *ens notum,* then, we understand in the obvious sense of being known. But just as well and above all, we understand it in the precise sense that the known, inasmuch as purely and only known, is still a being. To remain as known amounts to remaining as a being: the epistemological reduction of every occurrence (*ea omnia quae occurrunt,* the *Regulae* say in their very first heading, AT X, 359, 6) to what can be known repeats, while displacing, the reduction that, according to Aristotle, "a certain science" effects when it reduces, or better, reconducts, the ὄν to itself inasmuch as it is, and nothing else. Here is the decisive point about which everything else revolves: the Cartesian reduction of the world to its reduced and conditional status as object does not totally abandon reconducting the world to the status of being; it repeats it, with a slight displacement. Or rather, in its very violence, this displacement tries to resume in a novel way the Aristotelian move, the move from which all subsequent metaphysical ontology comes. From the moment that "[things] can be the objects of true thoughts" (AT II, 597, 15–16 = PW III, 139), when therefore the thing is exhausted in the operation that makes of it a "res repraesentata" (AT VII, 8, 23), when the world must run the gauntlet, or rather prostrate itself before the rostrum of the *objectum purae Matheseos,* which constitutes what is essential in the legacy passed on to the *Meditationes* from the *Regulae* (a point that cannot be emphasized too much)[34]—when this is so, the *ens in quantum ens* is, again and finally, at issue. In other words, Being known always conveys a way, exactly, of Being. The way of Being that leads beings back to their status as pure beings is put forth in what Descartes inaugurated—Being in the mode of *objectum*. Descartes declares it explicitly: ". . . quantumvis imperfectus sit iste essendi modus, quo res est objective in intellectu per ideam, non tamen profecto plane nihil est, nec proinde a nihilo esse potest [the mode of Being by which a thing exists objectively in the intellect by way of an idea, imperfect though it may be, is certainly not nothing, and so it cannot come from nothing]" (AT VII, 41, 26–29 = PW II, 29); or, as the French translation develops it, excellently for once: ". . . pour imparfaite que soit cette façon d'être, par laquelle une chose est objectivement ou par représentation dans l'entendement par son idée, certes on ne peut néanmoins dire que cette façon et manière-là ne soit rien, ni par conséquent que cette idée tire son origine du néant" (AT IX-I, 33, 5–10); and also: ". . . qui sane essendi modus longe imperfectior est quam ille quo res extra intellectum existunt, sed non idcirco plane nihil est, ut jam ante scripsi [Now this mode of being is of course much less perfect than that possessed by things which exist outside the intellect; but as I did explain, it is not therefore simply nothing]" (AT VII, 103, 1–4 = PW II, 75). Objective reality remains—officially, for without doing so it would not have a case to argue—an *esse objectivum*.[35] There-

---

34. *Objectum purae Matheseos* (AT VII, 71, 8 and 15; 74, 2; 80, 9–10 = PW II, 49 and 50; 51; 55) refers, more so than to the "object studied by the geometers" (DM, AT VI, 36, 5 = PW I, 129), to what *Regula IV* names a *Mathesis valde diversa a vulgari* [a kind of mathematics quite different from the one which prevails today] (AT X, 376, 4 = 18)—namely, the *Mathesis universalis,* which has as *objectum* (378, 3 = 19) ". . . illa omnia tantum in quibus aliquis ordo vel mensura examinatur [only all that in which questions of order and measure are being considered]" (377, 23–378, 1 = 19). When the course of the *Meditationes* recovers the *verae et immutabiles naturae* (AT VII, 64, 11 = PW II, 44) that had been revoked by doubt ("simplicia et universalia vera," 20, 11 = 14), it in fact recovers the entire inheritance of the simple natures, therefore of the *Regulae.* See chap. I, §5, n. 66.

35. *Esse objectivum ideae* [objective (B)eing of an idea] (AT VII, 47, 20–21= PW II, 42); see also the Latin translation of DM, VI, 559. This should not be confused with the much more current locution *realitas objectiva,* which leaves out precisely the intervention of *esse.* Access to existence passes through the *cogitatio,* therefore through the *ens cogitatum:* ". . . prius quam inquiram an aliquae tales res extra me existant, considerare debeo illarum ideas, quatenus sunt in mea cogitatione [Before I inquire whether any such things exist outside me, I must consider the ideas of these things, in so far as they exist in my thought]" (AT VII, 63, 12–14 = PW II, 44); or: ". . . jam ad minimum scio illas [res materiales], quatenus sunt purae Matheseos objectum, posse existere, quandoquidem ipsas clare

fore, when Descartes, in response to Burman, once again defines the
"totum et universum Matheseos objectum [the complete and entire object of mathematics]," he can legitimately assimilate it to a "verum et
reale ens [true and real being]" in the same sense in which he accords to
physics an "objectum suum verum et reale ens [object that is a true and
real being]."[36] For Descartes and in contrast with an Aristotelian conception, physics does not reach the *ens* any more than *Mathesis* does, because for Descartes the *ens* is not defined in its relationship with Φύσις,
but uniquely and sufficiently according to objectivity. Accordingly, the
objectum purae Matheseos does not remain a true *ens despite* its distance
from the object of physics (in the sense, for example, of the Scotist *ens
diminutum*), but indeed *because of* this distance. It has to be said that
the most perfect purity of its objectivity qualifies it as an *ens* of the highest degree; all the other objects, however less imperfect they might appear to the readers, remain *de facto* and *de jure* more imperfect beings
because less certain objects. Proof: in order to arrive at them, one will
first have to pass through the *objectum purae Matheseos*. The mind is
known better than and before the body, the mathematical essence of
material things (their theoretical models in the code) before these same
things. Objects are, just inasmuch as they are objects.

Therefore, reaching objectivity, each thing is led back to what it is
inasmuch as it is. But this leading back that stands in the place of ontology (and which can therefore be named gray ontology) would remain
impossible without the intervention of another authority—one that is
other than the thing, but not foreign to the way of Being to which it
accedes as an object. In effect, the thing does not become simply an
object, but the object of an understanding: ". . . intellectum a nullo unquam experimento decipi posse, si praecise tantum intueatur rem sibi
objectam [The intellect can never be deceived by any experience, provided that it intuits the thing objected to it]" (AT X, 423, 1–3 = PW I,
47 [modified]). *Res objecta* because *objecta intellectui:* objectivity implies

---

et distincte percipio [I now know at least that they (material things) are capable of existing,
in so far as they are the object of pure mathematics, since I perceive them clearly and
distinctly]" (AT VII, 71, 14–16 = PW II, 50 [modified]); or finally: "Quippe per ens extensum communiter omnes intelligunt aliquid imaginabile (sive sit ens rationis, sive reale, hoc
enim in medium relinquo) [Commonly when people talk of an extended being, they mean
something imaginable—I leave aside the question whether it is a real being or a rational
being]" (*To H. More,* 5 February 1649 [AT V, 270, 1–3 = PW III, 361 (modified)]).

36. *Conversation with Burman* (AT V, 160, 17–19 = PW III, 343 [modified]). Concerning this text, see G. Brown, "*Vera entia.* The nature of mathematical objects in Descartes,"
Journal of the History of Philosophy 1980/18.

the objectness that objects the thing to the understanding. Or, according to another lexicon: "... semper quidem aliquam rem ut subjectum meae cogitationis apprehendo [There is always a particular thing which I take as the object of my thought]" (AT VII, 37, 8–9 = PW II, 26). The thing accedes to objectivity, which alone can establish it as a being, strictly in the degree to which it is submitted to the requirements of the *cogitatio.* The *Regulae* are still very much at work in the *Meditationes,* and the gray ontology does not disappear in the white theology, which, on the contrary, presupposes it. However, the second formulation marks a new step forward: the thing is submitted not simply to the *cogitatio* in general—in the sense that the *Regulae* would here say *intellectus*—but, more precisely, to "*meae* cogitationis." Such a mention of the possessive does not betray some unfortunate precritical naïveté confusing the "empirical subject" with pure and constitutive thought. The possessive here defines the very essence of the pure *cogitatio.* The *cogitatio,* as such, implies this possessive, exactly in the sense that, as such, it implies its reflexive: *cogitatio* means *cogitatio sui;* and if Descartes does not use this formula literally, he does speak of the *perceptio ... mei ipsius* (45, 28–29 = 31), of the *idea mei ipsius* (51, 14 = 35), of *sui idea* (375, 21 = 258). On this point, Heidegger ventured to put forth, as a developed formulation of the *ego cogito,* the astonishing clause *cogito me cogitare.* What counts in the present work is not to be found in a debate with Heidegger, where one would contest this formulation as inauthentic (something Heidegger was the first to know) or as quasi-authentic ("... cum videam, sive ... cum cogitem me videre [When I see, that is when I think I see] ..." or "... concipiam me esse rem cogitantem [I conceive that I am a thinking thing] ..." [33, 12–14; 44, 24 = 22 (modified); 30 (modified)]).[37] Rather, what counts resides in the *cogitatio*'s ownmost characteristic: it comes back to itself. It comes down to coming back to itself, to the point of knowing itself first (... *me cogitare*), to the point of constituting itself as a being (*ego*), because, more originally, it bends back over itself. The *cogitatio,* in contrast to thought,[38] does not reproduce what it cognizes, nor does it purely and simply represent it. Or, if it does represent what it cognizes, it does so by reflecting it, like a converging mirror that reflects its rays by focusing them on a single point so as to render its object

37. Concerning this formula introduced by Heidegger and his relation to the Cartesian texts, see our analysis in *Sur la théologie blanche de Descartes,* pp. 388–92. References to some of the relevant passages in Heidegger are given in n. 32.

38. See *Règles utiles et claires ... ,* pp. 93–95.

perfectly visible and at the same time appropriate it—as in the classical view. And in fact, Descartes sometimes emphasizes that the *cogitatio* turns what it sees into itself: "... *operatio mentis imaginantis, sive ad istas species se convertentis est cogitatio* [When the mind imagines or turns towards those impressions, its operation is a thought]" (AT III, 361, 13–15 = PW III, 180). The single point that the *cogitatio* at once aims at and produces is named the object—at first, in the sense of the objective, at which it takes aim by turning itself toward it and finally returning it toward itself. The concentration of the gaze (*intuitus*) that assures its object the intense luminosity of rationality, by exposing it in full light, depends on the curve of the mirror. If the objectivity of knowing depends on the object, the object depends on the objectness of its being made evident, which in turn depends on the curve of cognitive thought. Curve of thought, the *cogitatio* implies a reflecting appropriation, the ultimate implication of which is named—*ego*. The *ego* is not added to the *cogitatio* as an adjoining specification, one that is eventually superfluous because it is too mixed up with psychology or "subjectivity." The *ego* conveys the proper name of the *cogitatio* by manifesting its reflecting and appropriating essence—curve of thought. Just as an *objectum* cannot be without a *cogitatio* that assures it of its objectivity, a *cogitatio* could not assure the certitude of its object without a curve, which is named—*ego*. A *cogitatio* without *ego* would again become simple thought, therefore thought becalmed and powerless to produce an object. What is currently named "the Cartesian *cogito*"—that is, what Descartes more often calls "the first principle [which] is *that our soul exists,* because there is nothing whose existence is better known to us," or "*haec cognitio, ego cogito, ergo sum,* [...] *omnium prima et certissima* [This piece of knowledge—*I am thinking, therefore I exist*—is the first and most certain of all]"— appears directly in the exercise of every *cogitatio,* or better, in the leading back of each thing to the status of an *objectum.*[39] This principle does not necessitate any new operation of thought, since it itself and it alone makes thought possible as a *cogitatio* effecting an *objectum.* If this connection is admitted (and we will confirm it soon enough), one consequence stands out. We have established that beings are as objects; the object thus becomes *ens* only as *cogitatum,* and with the *cogitatum,* a way of Being is at issue. Likewise, the *cogitatum* in turn implies the *ego* [*cogitans*]. Therefore, the *ego* shows up in the meaning of Being that

---

39. Respectively, *To Clerselier,* June–July 1646 (AT IV, 444, 23–25 = PW III, 290), and *Principia Philosophiae I,* §7.

allows the *cogitatum* to be as a being in its Being. The thesis that every object as such, therefore as *cogitatum,* is, implies in turn that the *ego,* before and more essentially than every other being, and as long as it is cognizing, exists. The *ego* exists before and more certainly than all other beings because, and solely because, every being is only as *objectum,* therefore as *cogitatum.* Inversely, the *ego* exists par excellence and with priority, because, and solely because, all the other beings are only as objects of a *cogitatio,* are only as *cogitata:* "Nihil prius cognosci posse quam intellectum, cum ab hoc caeterorum omnium cognitio dependeat, et non contra [Nothing can be known prior to the intellect, since knowledge of everything else depends on the intellect, and not *vice versa*]" (AT X, 395, 22–24 = PW I, 30). A declaration about the way of Being of beings (onto-logy) and a proposition concerning the singular existence of a being par excellence (theo-logy) thus maintain a reciprocal relation of grounding. The existence of the *ego* accounts for (*begründet*) the way of Being of the *cogitata;* the way of Being that is manifest in the *cogitata,* by revealing them as beings, grounds (*gründet*) the *ego* in its privileged existence. Such grounding, double and crossed, satisfies to the letter the characteristics of what Heidegger unveiled with the name "onto-theo-logical constitution of metaphysics." It is even easy for us to specify the nature of the "logic" in Cartesian thought. The λόγος is here put into operation as *cogitatio,* curve of thought. As a result of the "logical" decision that is accomplished by the *cogitatio,* onto-logy envisages beings as such as *cogitata,* and theo-logy sets forth the being par excellence in the *cogitans,* the *ego.* It must therefore be concluded that Cartesian thought fully belongs to metaphysics, at least if metaphysics admits of an onto-theo-logical constitution.

However, from a strictly Cartesian point of view, this conclusion gives rise to at least two objections that cannot be bypassed. First, our analysis of the relation (implication) that holds between the object and the *ego* seems, as it were, to deduce the existence of the *ego* from the nature of the objects. It would thus be in contradiction with the fundamental order of the Cartesian way of thinking, a way of thought in which only "... minimum quid ... quod certum sit et inconcussum [one thing, however slight, that is certain and unshakable] ..." (AT VII, 24, 12–13 = PW II, 16) allows one subsequently to recover other beings. What is more, this analysis arrives at the existence of the *ego* without passing through doubt, or—openly!— admitting that a new operation of thought—that is, a particular reasoning—is required for this effect. And yet, the existence of the *ego* requires a reasoning like no other, since it is discursive without deriving from a syllogism. To this a second objection is added: such an onto-theo-logical rendering of Cartesian thought leads one to identify the being par excellence with the *ego*, thus with a finite being and not with God. Besides the fact that this discrepancy makes nothing of an entire dimension of the explicitly theistic intention of Descartes, it is also a massive contradiction of the textual evidence: the phrase *summum ens* appears often in the *Meditationes*, yet it always designates God, never the *ego*.[40] Let us try to respond. *(a)* As for the way of thinking that leads objects directly back to the *ego*, it should not be so surprising, since it concerns the deployment of beings, as *cogitata*, including also the *cogitans*, whose existence alone renders them thought, therefore renders their Being possible. A classic text quite obviously confirms this: the analysis of the piece of wax. Apparently, the thing is "with much more distinctness" (29, 23 = PW II, 20) than the *cogitans*, which remains something about which a decision cannot be made, ". . . nescio quid mei, quod sub imaginationem non venit [this puzzling 'I' which cannot be pictured in the imagination] . . ." (29, 23–24 = 20). In reality and at the end of the analysis, indetermination will, inversely, characterize the wax ". . . extensum quid, flexibile, mutabile [something extended, flexible, and changeable]" (31, 2–3 = 20). Whence comes this reversal? From the reduction, as if by degrees, of the wax, thus of each and every thing, first to the status of *objectum*, then and indissolubly to the status of *cogitatum*— ". . . illud quod nunc cogito [that which I am now thinking] . . ." (30, 26 = PW II, 25 [modified])—which is found beyond but also thanks to sensible perception and the imagination, and which results from *solius mentis inspectio* (31, 25 = 21). *Inspectio* here counts as *cogitatio*, just as *mens* counts as the *ego* (*cogitans*). This analysis, like its parallels in the *Regulae* and the *Principia Philosophiae*,[41] extracts the *ego* (*cogitans*) directly

---

40. *Summum ens:* AT VII, 54, 18–19, 22; 67, 21, 27; 135, 4– 5; 144, 3; 374, 13; 428, 12, etc. = PW II, 38, 38; 46, 47; 97; 103; 257; 289. In each of these examples, it is a question of one of the Cartesian divine names; see *infra,* chap. IV, §18, n. 50.

41. In the *Regulae:*

> Si vero eadem via ostendere velim, animam rationalem non esse corpoream, non opus erit enumerationem esse completam, sed sufficiet, si omnia simul corpora aliquot collectionibus ita complectar, ut animam rationalem ad nullam ex his referri posse demonstrem. [If I wish to show in the same way that the rational soul is not corporeal, there is no need for the enumeration to be complete; it will be sufficient if I group all bodies together into several classes so as to demonstrate that the rational soul cannot be assigned to any of these.]

(AT X, 390, 13–18 = PW I, 26–27); or

> Neque immensum est opus, res omnes in hac universitate contentas cogitatione velle complecti, ut, quomodo singulae mentis nostrae examini subjectae sint, agnoscamus; nihil

from the *cogitatum,* or rather from the interpretation of the *objectum* as a *cogitatum*—in this case the interpretation of the wax as ". . . nihil aliud quam . . . quid [nothing other than that] . . ." (31, 3 = 20 [modified]). The *cogito* is extracted from the analysis of the *objectum* as a piece of *cogitatio,* as *cogitatum quid,* as an objective aimed at by an intention— ". . . id quod . . . sola judicandi facultate, quae in mente mea est, comprehendo [something which . . . I comprehend solely by the faculty of judgment which is in my mind]" (32, 11–12 = 21 [modified]). Now, it must immediately be made clear that this strict implication of the *cogito* in every *cogitatum* does not in any way contradict the specific instance that, just before the analysis of the piece of wax, is given as a demonstration of the existence of the *ego.* In fact, the texts remain strictly parallel. Just as the analysis of the so-called piece of wax in fact carries out an analysis of the wax as *cogitatum,* next of the *cogitatum* as supposing more essentially a *cogito* to cognize it, so too does the demonstration of the existence of the *ego* remain indifferent to the random identity of the *cogitatum* that serves as the occasion for the *cogitans* to discover itself as *ego.* To be sure, this demonstration calls on a particular utterance, "*Ego sum, ego existo*" (25, 12 = 17); but this particular utterance owes its privilege more to the anticipation of the result—what exists has a name: *ego*— than to any particular relevance it might have. The proof of this is that every operation of the *cogitatio* (doubting, understanding, affirming, denying, willing, not willing, imagining, and sensing) (28, 20–23 = 19), and even every operation of the still doubtful body (walking, etc.), allows one to reach the existence of the *ego*—on just one condition: namely, that this operation or this action be brought back, as *objectum,* to the status of *cogitatum,* so that in this way it makes the cognizing *ego* appear in it. To be sure, if I walk, I am, but only ". . . quatenus ambulandi conscientia cogitatio est [in so far as the awareness of walking is a thought]" (352, 12–13 = 244). Therefore, the meaning of the cognized statement matters little; what alone matters is the analysis of any statement whatsoever as *cogitatum,* then the reduction of this *cogitatum* to the *ego cogito.*

Moreover, the classic texts of *Meditatio II* do not make the existence

---

enim tam multiplex esse potest aut dispersum, quod per illum, de qua egimus, enumerationem certis limitibus circumscribi atque in aliquot capita non possit. [Nor is it an immeasurable task to seek to encompass in thought everything in the universe, with a view to learning in what way particular things may be susceptible of investigation by the human mind. For nothing can be so many-sided or diffuse that it cannot be encompassed within definite limits or arranged under a few headings by means of the method of enumeration we have been discussing.]

(398, 14–20 = 31.) In the *Principia,* not only *I,* §11, but also *II,* §§4, 9, and 11.

of the *ego* appear by means of the particular utterance "*Ego sum, ego existo*," but by means of the thought that actually cognizes this statement. Moreover, in order to emphasize that winning the *ego* depends on the *cogitatio* being in operation (and not on a specific *cogitatum*), these texts go so far as to introduce the cognitive performative "... hoc pronuntia-tum ... quoties a me profertur vel mente concipitur, necessario esse verum [This proposition ... is necessarily true whenever it is put forward by me or conceived in my mind]" (25, 11–13).[42] The meaning of the *cogi-tatum*, even here, decides nothing; the reduction of any *cogitatum*, no matter what, to the actually operative *cogitatio* decides everything. Therefore, since the two *cogitata*—"piece of wax" and "*Ego sum, ego existo*"—differ only in meaning, and since what is essential is played out in the *cogitatio* that is being enacted and manifested in both, the two analyses amount to the same—seeing as they lead two *cogitata* back to the single *ego*, the being par excellence whose primacy grounds them as real and true objects.

A second difficulty remains: *(b)* in the onto-theo-logical constitution whose Cartesian figure we are trying to draw out, we did not identify God as the being par excellence, but the *ego*—under the reconstructed title *cogitatio sui*. This being the case, isn't our project immediately dis-qualified by its discrepancy with Descartes' personal conviction, his con-tinued use of *summum ens,* and finally the role of the proofs for the existence of God? But the simple fact that a discrepancy shows up is not enough to disqualify our project. For that matter, we will not even seek to reduce or to hide this discrepancy, since it seems to us that it helps pin down at least one of the most decisive of Descartes' initiatives. We will attempt only to define it more precisely, so that the real difficulty does not disappear in misunderstandings. Hence, a few points to note. First of all, it must be repeated that the theo-logy of metaphysics remains essentially a the*io*-logy that concerns the being par excellence (the di-vine), without making any prejudicial judgments as to the ontic region where it appears—mortals, the demons and the angels, the gods, God. Ancient thought provides enough illustrations of this uncertainty, and Descartes is reminded of it when he evokes certain ontic instances that would stand above or substitute themselves for the God of Christians. In the first case, he has only to think of "... Styx and the fates ..." (AT I, 145, 11–12 = 23), from whom God will be delivered by the creation of the eternal truths in 1630; in the second, of *fatum,* of *casus* (τύχη,

---

chance), and of the *continuata rerum series* [continuous chain of events] that, before the "evil genius," replace the hypothesis of an all-powerful God during the hyperbolic doubt of *Meditatio I* (AT VII, 21, 20–21 = 14). In this limited sense, a discrepancy between God and the supreme being would not be unprecedented. Second, if Descartes defines the being par excellence of the *cogitatio* (which we designate by *cogitatio sui*) as the *ego* (*cogito*), perhaps he does so for a fundamental reason concerning the essence of the divine. God is defined neither by the understanding, nor by the *cogitatio,* but by ". . . incomprehensible power . . ." (in 1630), by the *immensa et incomprehensibilis potentia* (in 1641).[43] God is not defined by the *cogitatio,* or rather, his eventual rank as the being par excellence cannot be reached by an instance such as the *cogitatio,* which would be too little elevated, so to speak, to be able to utter the infinite. To be sure, God can be cognized: the *idea Dei,* though incomprehensible, remains intelligible, to the very point of offering the ". . . truest and most clear and distinct . . ." idea (AT VII, 46, 28 = 32). But, and this is precisely the point, God here remains a *cogitatum;* he must, as its object, be submitted to the *ego* that, cognizingly, intends him; the more it is emphasized that God falls within the domain of the *cogitatio* as *cogitatum* par excellence (something that still remains to be established), the more strongly will it be confirmed that he is subject to and does not exert the *cogitatio,* still less the *cogitatio sui.* However, it will be objected anew, doesn't Descartes sometimes acknowledge a *cogitatio* in God, who, in this case, far from enduring its gaze, actually carries it out? It is important to cite the principal texts. In *Principia Philosophiae I,* §54, Descartes admits that we have ". . . duas claras et distinctas . . . notiones, sive ideas, unam substantiae cogitantis creatae, aliam substantiae corporae [two clear and distinct notions or ideas, one of created thinking substance, and the other of corporeal substance] . . ." On the basis of the strict distinction separating them, he then infers that we can also have ". . . ideam claram et distinctam substantiae cogitantis increatae et independentis, id est Dei [a clear and distinct idea of uncreated and independent thinking substance, that is of God]. . . ." And yet, appearances to the contrary notwithstanding, it need not be concluded that here God is characterized essentially by the *cogitatio.* For Descartes immediately adds a restriction:

---

43. Respectively AT I, 146, 4–5 and 150, 22 = PW III, 23 [modified] and 25, completed by *immensa et incomprehensibilis potentia* (AT VII, 110, 27 = PW II, 79); then AT VII, 237, 8–9; 110, 27; and 112, 10; 109, 4 and 236, 9 = PW II, 165; 79, and 80; 78 and 165. See *infra,* chap. IV, §§19 and following.

this idea remains correct provided that we do not suppose it to give us an adequate knowledge of the divine properties, ". . . modo ne illam adaequate omnia quae in Deo sunt exhibere supponamus [We must simply avoid supposing that the idea adequately represents everything which is found in God]." The determination of God as *substantia cogitans* is legitimate, on condition that it not be held as adequate. There is nothing surprising in this: like the concept of substance, that of *cogitatio* is subject to the general caution posted in §51: ". . . nomen substantiae non convenit Deo et illis [creaturis] *univoce* [The term substance does not apply univocally . . . to God and to (creatures)] . . ." Just as in God substance must be reinterpreted in terms of the infinity which means that it is not said in a univocal way when applied to finite substance, so too does the *cogitatio,* applied to God, become inadequate to the finite *cogitatio.*[44] Accordingly, one could venture to say that, in Cartesian terms, the *cogitatio*—precisely because it reflects itself in a convex mirror—can be only finite. But there are other texts that do state a *cogitatio* common to God and the *ego,* to the infinite and the finite. For example, in 1637: ". . . You acquire by degrees a very clear, dare I say intuitive, notion of intellectual nature in general. This is the idea which, if considered without limitation, represents God, and if limited, is the idea of an angel or a human soul." To which there corresponds in 1641: ". . . et perspicuum est perfectissimam illam vim cogitandi, quam in Deo esse intelligimus, per illam minus perfectam, quae in nobis est, repraesentari [And it is quite clear that the wholly perfect power of thought which we understand to be in God is

44. The restriction ". . . ne illam adaequate . . . supponamus [We must simply avoid supposing that the idea adequately represents] . . ." in §54 consequently must be understood in at least two ways: (a) In relation to the title of this same §54—instead of mentioning a cognizing uncreated substance, it opposes the notion of God to the finite cognizing substance as well as to the body: "quomodo claras et distinctas notiones habere possimus, substantiae cogitantis, et corporeae, item Dei [how we can have clear and distinct notions of thinking substance and of corporeal substance, and also of God]." (b) In relation to the title of §51: "Quid sit substantia, et quod istud nomen Deo et creaturis non conveniat univoce [What is meant by 'substance'—a term which does not apply univocally to God and his creatures]." This becomes illuminating when contrasted with that of §52: "Quod menti et corpori univoce conveniat [The term 'substance' applies univocally to mind and to body]." The univocity of substance (and of the attributes that are attached to it in order to make it knowable) is limited to creatures. Consequently if an attribute (the *cogitatio,* for example) is added to the infinite substance of God, it will be said in an equivocal way of created substances. On this equivocalness, see *Sur la théologie blanche de Descartes,* §5, pp. 72*ff.,* §7, 110–13, and *infra,* chap. IV, §17. We here thank J.-M. Beyssade for having drawn our attention to §54 (loc. cit., p. 47) and for thus having given us the occasion to strengthen our analysis by discussing his.

represented by means of that less perfect faculty which we possess]."[45] Nevertheless, these same texts in fact work to exclude God from the *cogitatio*. First, because the continuity, in the *intellectual nature in general* as well as the *vis cogitandi*, always holds in a relation of the finite to the infinite, which affects all that it concerns with equivocity. Next, because both are being attributed to God, not in that he exerts them, but because they permit the *ego* to know him as a *cogitatum:* ". . . the idea . . . which represents God to us . . . ," and ". . . vim cogitandi, quam in Deo esse intelligimus, . . . repraesentari [the power of thought which we understand to be in God . . . is represented]." Marvelously, the *cogitatio* is granted to God only so that we might again make it our *cogitatum*. In no way then is this *cogitatio* imposed on the *ego*, nor does it rob the *ego* of the *cogitatio sui* or define it as an *objectum* of God. Finally, it is especially appropriate to emphasize that God is never defined in the strict sense by the *cogitatio*—neither here nor, to our knowledge, elsewhere. It is beside the point to object that God also possesses *cogitationes* (for example AT V, 193, 17 = PW III, 355)—this is self-evident. Instead, the point is to understand why God is never defined radically as *cogitans*, to such a degree that he would assume the *cogitatio sui*—in the sense that, elsewhere, Descartes maintains the definition "Deus est suum esse."[46] To be sure, the *cogitatio* is relevant when speaking of God as eminent; but it does not define him in the way a principal attribute makes a finite substance known, nor does it name him as would a privileged divine name. It remains merely a perfection by which we represent him to ourselves—inadequately to be sure—in agreement with the non-univocity that the infinite imposes on the representations of it that the finite forges for itself. Finally, a third piece of evidence can confirm *a contrario* that Descartes consciously chose to think God without recourse to a definition by the *cogitatio*. He was not at all ignorant of the way that he refused to adopt, seeing as he describes it precisely in a singular text:

45. Respectively, *To X**, March 1637 (AT I, 353, 21–26 = PW III, 55 [commentary in *Règles utiles et claires . . .* , p. 296]), and *Vae Responsiones* (AT VII, 373, 3–6 = PW II, 257). Concerning the (rare) occurrences of *intellectus divinus* (for example in AT VII, 432, 3–4 = PW II, 291) and their limits, see *Sur la théologie blanche de Descartes*, §13, pp. 294*ff.*

46. *Vae Responsiones* (AT VII, 383, 15 = PW II, 263), or *To Hyperaspistes*, August 1641, n. 13. The latter refers explicitly to the theological (in fact Thomist) definition of the essence of God: "Ubi dixi Deum esse *suum esse* [in the preceding text], usus sum modo loquendi Theologis usitatissimo, quo intelligitur ad Dei essentiam pertinere ut existat [When I said that God is his own existence, I was using the regular theological idiom, which means that it belongs to God's essence to exist]" (AT III, 433, 9–11 = PW III, 196).

Neque enim magis urget, quod ideam Dei, quae in nobis est, ens rationis appelletis. Neque enim hoc eo sensu verum est, quo per *ens rationis* intelligitur id quod non est, sed tantum quo omnis operatio intellectus *ens rationis,* hoc est a ratione profectum; atque etiam totus hic mundus ens rationis divinae, hoc est ens per simplicem actum mentis divinae creatum, dici potest. [As for your calling the idea of God which is in us a "conceptual entity," this is not a compelling objection. If by "conceptual entity" is meant something which does not exist, it is not true that the idea of God is a conceptual entity in this sense. It is true only in the sense in which every operation of the intellect is a conceptual entity, that is, an entity which has its origin in thought; and indeed this entire universe can be said to be an entity originating in God's thought.][47]

Here Descartes is clearly recounting the positions of Suarez: *ens rationis* can be understood as a nothing excluded from the objects of metaphysics, but also as an instrument of reason, admitted out of consideration for its analogy with *ens reale.* Accordingly, it can also be said that "God has a most perfect knowledge of the *entia rationis.* . . ."[48] If this position had been set out, it would certainly have made it possible to dismiss the discrepancy between God and the (cognizing) being par excellence; but this would have been accomplished at the cost—unacceptable to Descartes—of a real univocity between cognizing consciousness (representing an object) and infinity: through the understanding that would have been attributed to God in a real distinction from the will, God would have become a simple *res cogitans* carried to perfection, which would be immediately susceptible of contradicting itself as a "field of what is possible" and an irrational power. Malebranche, indeed Leibniz, yielded to this simple solution. Descartes refused it from the time he proposed the creation of the eternal truths. Thus one need not be surprised that, from the Cartesian point of view, the *cogitatio sui* of a being par excellence does not fall to God, but to the *ego* alone. God does not remain on the hither side of the *cogitatio (sui);* he transgresses it, as the infinite transgresses the finite. The *cogitatio sui* offers too little to be able to designate God. A finite *res cogitans* is enough to accomplish the gaze focused on objectness.

It is therefore not appropriate to diminish the discrepancy or to avoid

47. *IIae Responsiones* (AT VII, 134, 21–26 = PW II, 96–97).
48. Suarez, an allusion first to *Disputationes Metaphysicae,* I, s. 1, n. 6, vol. 25, pp. 3–4; then a citation of "Deus perfectissime cognoscit entia rationis . . . ," ibid., *LIV,* s. 2, n. 23, vol. 26, p. 1025. One can compare this with *De divina substantia, XIII,* n. 7, vol. 1, p. 40, and *De Anima, IV,* 1, n. 3, vol. 3, pp. 713*ff.*

the difficulty; they rest on solid reasons. Rather, if we want to conceive the essence of Cartesian metaphysics, it is more prudent to measure the extent to which they exercise a determinative influence. Starting from the *cogitatio,* we obtained a result: the *ens ut cogitatum* reveals an ontology of the *cogitatio* that is applied to all being as such (therefore as known, no longer as being); the reflection of the gaze that carries out the *cogitatio* subsequently designates a being par excellence, one having the function of *causa sui,* which the *ego* alone can and must claim. A complete figure of onto-theo-logy thus follows: being as *cogitatum* grounds the being par excellence, which in return produces, as *cogitatio (sui),* all *cogitatum.* The "logical" moment unites the two terms all the more readily since it coincides with the very *cogitatio* that is also manifest in them, sometimes as object (*ens ut cogitatum*), sometimes as reflexive gaze (*cogitatio sui*). Thus is stated Descartes' first pronouncement about the Being of beings: the onto-theo-logical constitution of the *cogitatio.* This result, as solidly confirmed as it might be, nonetheless lets a difficulty remain: the discrepancy between the being par excellence and God. It forbids Descartes from conceptually doing justice to the God that he never ceases claiming, clearly and sincerely, to celebrate. It therefore could not have forced itself on him if powerful conceptual reasons had not constrained him to it: the fact that, from the point of view of an onto-theo-logy of the *cogitatio,* God no longer coincides with the being par excellence (and, in a bizarre retreat, relinquishes it to the *mens humana*) suggests first an intrinsic limitation of the *cogitatio* itself. This fundamental trait of being leaves out at least one region of being—not the least but the first: God, bearing the name of the infinite. The infinite, otherwise named *incomprehensible power,* exceeds the onto-theo-logy of the *cogitatio.* This exceeding thus puts us on the way to a new question, provided we do not try to reduce it too quickly: can the first fundamental trait of beings, the *cogitatio,* be overcome by a still *more* fundamental trait? To pass beyond the *cogitatio,* toward a second authority exerting still more power over all beings—would this then lead to an even more radical identification of the Cartesian figure of metaphysics?

§9. The Second Pronouncement about the Being of Beings: *Causa*

Beings can also and, in fact, can more fundamentally be said as such and without exception in terms of causality. At this point, then, it is necessary to draw out, with as much precision as possible, the multiform and unchanging declaration that, without flinching even once from 1641 on, submits all existence (therefore all beings inasmuch as they are) to a causality raised to the rank of onto-logical reason and principle. Let us recall the chief statements of the second Cartesian pronouncement about the most fundamental trait of beings:

> Dictat autem profecto lumen naturae nullam rem existere, de qua non liceat petere cur existat, sive in ejus causam efficientem inquirere, aut si non habet, cur illa non indigeat, postulare. [The light of nature established (Dictat autem profecto lumen naturae) that if anything exists we may always ask why it exists; that is, we may inquire into its efficient cause, or, if it does not have one, we may demand why it does not need one.] [AT VII, 108, 18–22 = PW II, 78.]

Or:

> Nulla res existit de qua non possit quaeri quaenam sit causa cur existat. Hoc enim de ipso Deo quaeri potest, non quod indigeat ulla causa ut existat, sed quia ipsa ejus naturae immensitas est causa sive ratio, propter quam nulla causa indiget ad existendum. [Concerning every existing thing it is possible to ask what is the cause of its existence. This question may even be asked concerning God, not because he needs any cause in order to exist, but because the immensity of his nature is the cause or reason why he needs no cause in order to exist.] [164, 28–165, 3 = 116.]

And finally:

> Atqui considerationem causae efficientis esse primum et praecipuum medium, ne dicam unicum, quod habeamus ad existentiam Dei probandam, puto omnibus esse manifestum. Illud autem accurate persequi non possumus, nisi licentiam demus animo nostro in rerum omnium, etiam ipsius Dei, causas efficientes inquirendi: quo enim jure Deum inde exciperemus, priusquam illum existere sit probatum? [But I think it is clear to everyone (omnibus esse manifestum) that a consideration of efficient causes is the primary and principal way, if not the only way, that we have of proving the existence of God. We cannot develop this proof with precision unless we grant our minds the freedom to inquire into the efficient causes of all things, even God himself. For what right do we have to make God an exception, if we have not yet proved that he exists?] [238, 11–18 = 166.]

These three classic texts, put forth in *Responsiones I, II, and IV* respectively, agree almost exactly to the letter.[49] Let it suffice here if we empha-

---

49. See also:

Per se autem notum mihi videtur, omne id quod est, vel esse a causa, vel a se tanquam a causa; nam cum non modo existentiam, sed etiam existentiae negationem intelligamus, nihil possumus fingere ita esse a se, ut nulla danda sit ratio cur potius existat quam non

size the prominent points overlapping in their superimposed profiles: *(a)* *Causa* here does not govern merely the rigor of intelligibility, but above all the proof for *existentia*. It is not limited to its already regnant epistemological function (to know implies to know by causes), but takes into account, sufficiently and exclusively, all *existentia;* and *existentia* marks, in Cartesian terms, the meaning—that is self-evident and par excellence—of the Being of beings. Thus, through *causa,* beings play out their very Being, thereby appear as beings. Existing as caused, beings are manifest as beings strictly in the degree to which they appear in the light—or rather the shadow—of the cause of their existence. More essentially than as *ens qua cogitatum, ens* is stated in its Being *qua causatum.* The advance of the *ens causatum* over the *ens qua cogitatum* is marked precisely in that the one remains confined within the realm of possibility or *ens rationis* (which, for Descartes, is nearly confused with *nihil*), while only the other opens access to existence, the royal meaning of Being. The necessity to which the dominion of *cogitatio* constrained us disappears here; that is to say, it is no longer necessary to carefully and sometimes subtly reinterpret every *cogitatum* as an *ens cogitatum,* every object of cognition as still and always a being viewed as such under the mode of cognition itself (gray ontology). Here causality manifests the *ens in quantum ens* directly, since its sole and explicit stake has the name *existentia. (b)* This direct advance in the question of the meanings of the Being of beings is reinforced by a second breakthrough: *causa* here decides the existence of *all* beings, without any exception. The dignity of existence among the other ways of Being (and indeed of not Being) appears such that none of the beings can or should be exempt from recognizing the *causae dignitas* (242, 5 = 168). No more than a being could dispense with existing could it dispense with *causa,* whether it be to exert *causa* or be subject to it in such a way that, by this subjection, it receives from *causa* the right to exist. Better, if by some extraordinary chance a being could dispense with its cause, it would still be necessary to give

---

existat, hoc est ut illud *a se* non debeamus interpretari tanquam a causa, propter exuperantiam potestatis, quam in uno Deo esse posse facillime demonstratur. [What does seem to me self-evident is that whatever exists either derives its existence from a cause or derives its existence from itself as from a cause. For since we understand not only what is meant by existence but also what is meant by its negation, it is impossible for us to imagine anything deriving existence from itself without there being some reason why it should exist rather than not exist. So in such a case, we are bound to interpret "from itself" in a causal sense, because of the superabundance of power involved—a superabundance which, as is very easily demonstrated, can exist in God alone.]

(*Iae Responsiones* [AT VII, 112, 3–11 = PW II, 80].) In fact, the first formulation shows up as early as AT VII, 40, 21–23 = PW II, 28 (see *infra,* §10).

the reason for this. Hence an unavoidable consequence: God himself, if he exists and if his existence can and must be proven, depends on *causa*. God does not make an exception to the pronouncement about the *ens in quantum causatum:* "Hoc enim de ipso Deo quaeri potest [This question may even be asked concerning God] . . .,"

> Illud [existentia Dei] autem accurate persequi non possumus, nisi licentiam demus animo nostro in rerum omnium, etiam ipsius Dei, causas efficientes inquirendi: quo enim jure Deum inde exciperemus, priusquam illum existere sit probatum? [We cannot develop this (the existence of God) with precision unless we grant to our minds the freedom to inquire into the efficient causes of all things, even God himself. For what right do we have to make God an exception, if we have not yet proved that he exists?]

> Quomodo enim ii qui Deum nondum norunt, in causam aliarum rerum efficientem inquirerent, ut hoc pacto ad Dei cognitionem denirent, nisi putarent cujusque rei causam efficientem posse inquiriri? [How would those who do not yet know that God exists be able to inquire into the efficient cause of other things, with the aim of eventually arriving at knowledge of God, unless they thought it possible to inquire into the efficient cause of all things?][50]

God does not make an exception to the pronouncement about the Being of beings as *causa,* though he did make an exception to the first pronouncement about the Being of beings in terms of the *cogitatio.* God appears here as a being subject to common law, and no longer outside this law. This situation can be described perfectly as a formal univocity. This formal univocity is in no way changed by the fact that the causality here invoked with regard to God oscillates between several determinations—namely, between strictly efficient causality and formal causality—by way of a quite strange *conceptus quidam causae efficienti et formali communis* [concept of cause that is common to both an efficient and a formal cause] (238, 24–25 = 166) whose *intermedium* (239, 17 = 167) plays only a brief intermission. This oscillation does not contradict our thesis of a formal univocity because, first of all, when Descartes is speaking most unreservedly, especially at the beginning of the debate with Caterus, he imposes on God not merely undifferentiated causality, but efficient causality—in all its brutality: ". . . non dixi impossibile esse

---

50. Respectively AT VII, 164, 29–165, 1; 238, 14–18, and 244, 21–25 = PW II, 116; 166; 170. See also *Sur la théologie blanche de Descartes,* §18, in particular pp. 429*ff.*

ut aliquid sit causa efficiens sui ipsius [I did not say that it was impossible for something to be the efficient cause of itself] . . ." (108, 7–8 = 78).[51] When confronting Arnauld, Descartes again takes as principle the *consideratio causae efficientis* [consideration of efficient causes] (238, 11 = 167) and constructs his new concept of *causa sui* precisely through an analogy with efficient causality, and it alone: ". . . per analogiam ad efficientem [analogous to an efficient cause] . . ." (240, 12 = 167) ". . . analogia causae efficientis usus sim [I use the analogy of an efficient cause] . . ." (241, 25 = 168 [modified]), ". . . magnam analogiam cum efficiente, ideoque quasi causa efficiens vocari potest [strongly analogous to an efficient cause, and hence can be called something close to an efficient cause]" (243, 25–26 = 170). In short, it is obvious that the causality that underlies the *causa sui* is not confused with the efficient causality ordinarily associated with finite beings; but it is indeed by reference to efficiency that the causality of the *causa sui* is constituted, without ever being definitively detached from it. This first debate, whatever might be its outcome, remains unimportant; for the formal univocity does not concern efficient causality, but causality as such. What is important here is that God exists insofar as he satisfies the demand for a cause, whatever it might be, and even if it is reduced to a *ratio* that merely offers an account of the absence of a *causa* in God. For even and especially in this case, it is clear that God is submitted not only to the requirement of a cause in order to exist, but to the requirement of a *causa sive ratio:* ". . . quia ipsa ejus naturae immensitas est causa sive ratio, propter quam nulla causa indiget ad existendum [The immensity of his nature is the

---

51. J.-M. Beyssade's critical remark—namely, that ". . . every affirmation of univocity made for the benefit of the efficient cause is in flagrant contradiction with the Cartesian text" (op. cit., p. 49)—thus itself appears to be in flagrant contradiction with certain Cartesian texts. To be sure, in the course of a delayed and sometimes ambiguous polemic, Descartes was led to markedly soften his initial positions:

> . . . me nunquam scripsisse, *Deum non modo negative, sed et positive, sui causam efficientem dici debere,* . . . . Quaerat, legat, evolvat mea scripta: nihil unquam simile in illis reperiet, sed omnino contrarium. Me vero a talibus opinionum portentis quam maxime esse remotum, notissimum est iis omnibus, qui vel scripta mea legerunt, vel aliquam mei notitiam habent, vel saltem omnino fatuum esse non putant. [I have never written that God should be called "the efficient cause of himself not just in a negative sense but also in a positive sense," . . . . However carefully he sifts, scans, and pores over my writings, he will not find in them anything like this—quite the reverse in fact. Anyone who has read my writings, or has any knowledge of me, or at least does not think me utterly silly, knows that I am totally opposed to such extravagant views.]

(*Notae in programma quoddam* . . . [AT VIII-2, 368, 28–369, 5 = PW I, 310].) But the fact remains that he actually did, from time to time, think God as efficient cause of himself. In

cause or reason why he needs no cause in order to exist]" (165, 2–3 = 116), ". . . ubi verbum *sui causa,* nullo modo de efficiente potest intelligi, sed tantum quod inexhausta Dei potentia si causa sive ratio, propter quam causa non indiget [The phrase *causa sui* cannot possibly be taken to mean an efficient cause; it simply means that the inexhaustible power of God is the cause or reason for his not needing a cause]" (236, 7–10 = 165). Even if God does not have an efficient cause, indeed even if he has dispensed with the need for any other cause except for the immensity of his own essence (positions that Descartes does not in fact clearly affirm), he will nonetheless be submitted to the requirement of a *causa sive ratio.* And it is difficult not to recognize in this formula what Leibniz soon after will name "the great principle"—the principle of sufficient reason, which alone determines existence and whose formal univocity is imposed on God himself.[52] God does not have any other cause except for his own essence; but far from marking some sort of diminishment in the sway of *causa,* this particular case gives Descartes an occasion to extend it further by deepening *causa* to include *ratio.* Causality, and particularly efficient causality, henceforth serves a more essential and universal rationality, one that takes charge of the ways of Being of all beings, without any exception. The first two advances made by the interpretation of the *ens ut causatum* split off in two compatible directions: on the one hand, direct access to the question of the meaning of the Being of beings; on the other hand, the recovery of the divine being, until now unattainable

---

addition to AT VII, 108, 7–8 = PW II, 78, see

> Quamvis enim dicere non opus sit illum esse causam efficientem sui ipsius, ne forte de verbis disputetur . . . omnino licet cogitare illum quoddammodo idem praestare respectu sui ipsius quod causa efficiens respectu sui effectus. [There is no need to say that God is the efficient cause of himself, for this might give rise to a verbal dispute. . . . We are quite entitled to think that in a sense he stands in the same relation to himself as an efficient cause does to its effect.]

(110, 31 = 80.) This text will be cited and disputed by Arnauld (208, 14–16 = 146) and then explained again by Descartes (235, 17–19 = 164–65). In this text, the objection is reduced to a simple dispute about words and the qualification *quodammodo* [in a sense] poses no obstacle to the *causa sui* being understood with reference to efficiency. Often the corrective measures that introduce the *causa sui* when it is thought in terms of efficiency count less as retractions than as confirmations exercising prudence (for example, in 109, 6; 111, 5; 242, 10; 243, 25 = 78; 80; 169; 170).

52. Leibniz: "We must rise to metaphysics, making use of the *great principle,* commonly but little employed, which holds that nothing takes place without sufficient reason, that is to say nothing happens without its being possible for one who has enough knowledge of things to give a reason sufficient to determine why it is thus and not otherwise" (*Principes de la Nature et de la Grâce,* §7, ed. Gerhardt *Ph. S.,* VI, 602 [English trans., p. 199]).

by the interpretation of the *ens ut cogitatum.* *(c)* The dignified rank of the most fundamental trait of beings is accorded to the *causa (sive ratio)* as a tyrannical evidence ("Dictat autem ... [It is said]," "... omnibus esse manifestum [It is clear to everyone]") (108, 18 and 238, 13–14 = 78 and 166). Elsewhere, it is an axiom (164, 25 = 116). In effect, Descartes can only practice what we above called a postulation of evidence: putting *causa (sive ratio)* in the place of principle remains a principle only to the degree that precisely no other cause can come and offer a reason for it. Only this unreasonableness makes *ratio*'s cause into a principle. Or in other words: that all existence must offer a reason for its cause, this becomes a principle only by imposing itself without reason or cause. We will therefore let the Latin speak the other registers of its meaning and understand the formula "Dictat autem lumen naturae ..." as a *dictat* of reason, one that dictates to the *ens in quantum ens* that it will be only insofar as it is caused: *ens ut causatum.*

We just observed that the sway that *causa* holds over beings exceeds that of the *cogitatio.* Now it is important to define more precisely the steps by which it comes to assume this dominant position. Only by following such a course will it be possible for us to think, at least in outline, about the decisive import of the ultimate Cartesian pronouncement about being in its Being. At first, one notices that beginning with the *Regulae, causa,* among all the so-called absolute notions, enjoys an exceptional privilege. That is, according to *Regula VI,* the *ordo rerum cognoscendarum* overturns chiefly, but not exclusively, the order that issues from the Aristotelian categories. It does this by separating the couple cause and effect, a couple that was until this time held to be strictly correlative: "... apud Philosophos quidem causa et effectus sunt correlativa; hic vero si quaeramus qualis sit effectus, oportet prius causam cognoscere, et non contra [Philosophers of course recognize that cause and effect are correlatives; but in the present case, if we want to know what the effect is, we must know the cause first, and not *vice versa*]" (AT X, 383, 5–8 = PW I, 22). In other words, if it is a matter of knowing— and on principle, here it is never a matter of anything but knowing—the correlation is undone, and *causa* gains an indisputable priority: it renders a reason for its effect in that it renders it knowable.[53] This primacy is

53. *Sur l'ontologie grise ...* , §14. This privilege of *causa* alone gives weight to the formula of Spinoza: "Cognitio effectus nihil aliud est, quam perfectiorem causae cognitionem acquirere [The knowledge of the effect is nothing other than to acquire a more perfect knowledge of the cause]" (*De Intellectus Emendatione,* §92; see *Tractatus theologico-politicus,* chap. IV).

set up quite conscientiously, "de industria" (383, 3 = 22), following the example of just one other priority—that of equality over inequality. These two priorities are enough to fix the two parameters of *Mathesis Universalis,* order and measure. In other words, they suffice for the functioning of the only two operators of evidence that are essential to Cartesian science, *series* (or succession) and equality. The *Meditationes* will assume this point to be established: they ask, ". . . undenam posset assumere realitatem suam effectus, nisi a causa [where . . . could the effect gets its reality from, if not from the cause]?" (AT VII, 40, 24–25 = PW II, 28) when they want to illustrate the *causae dignitas,* as opposed to the *effectus indignitas* (242, 5 and 6 = 168 and 169). Nevertheless, a difference stops us from pushing the assimilation further: in 1627, the anteriority of *causa* pertains to the intention to know (*cognosci*), while in 1641 this anteriority also bears on *realitas* (thus, in fact, on existence). This difference confirms the hypothesis that the ontic pertinence of *causa* is not acquired all at once. Why this gap, it will perhaps be objected, seeing that in the *Regulae, causa* already precedes, as an absolute term, all the other notions and simple natures? Answer: It precedes only other *notions,* and limits its priority to the domain that is defined and invested by a term still more absolute than every absolute notion; namely, the understanding itself, which refers to all things ". . . eo sensu quo ad nostrum propositum utiles esse possunt [with regard to their possible usefulness to our project]" (AT X, 381, 18–19 = 21), thus including in advance "quomodo singulae mentis nostrae examini subjectae sint [in what way particular things may be susceptible of investigation by the human mind]" (398, 16–17 = 31). To be sure, *causa* no longer depends on *effectus;* but it does depend even more on the *mens,* which assures it of its unique but conditional priority. One term at least does not fall under the absolute *causa,* the *mens* that exerts it, or else the *cogitatio* that alone comprehends *res omnes* in their *universitas* (398, 15 = 31). We have again verified our interpretation: the priority of *causa* stumbles over the *cogitatio,* the sole absolute term in the *Regulae;* it is therefore subordinated to the onto-theo-logy of the *ens qua cogitatum,* whose limits it, a distinguished and dutiful servant, does not contest.

Cause therefore can become the principle and *dictat* of reason only by going beyond the very priority that the *cogitatio* accorded to it. How far? As far as inverting the relation of comprehender and comprehended that holds between the *cogitatio* and *causa:* that is, to the point that the priority of *causa* is no longer secured by the *cogitatio,* thus under its protection, but the *cogitatio* is submitted to *causa,* eventually owing to the *cogitatio* itself. Logically, it seems possible and thinkable to submit God too to the *causa sive ratio* only from the moment when the *cogitatio* in all its dimensions (thus also the *ego cogito*) first confesses the *causa* as *ultima ratio*. On the path of this reversal, the three *Letters to Mersenne* of 1630, in which Descartes declares the creation of the eternal truths by God, mark a decisive step. A single example will suffice for our purposes:

> You ask me by what kind of causality God established the eternal truths [*in quo genere causae Deus disposuit aeternas veritates*]. I reply: by the same kind of causality [*in eodem genere causae*] as he created all things, that is to say, as their efficient and total cause [*ut efficiens et totalis causa*]. For it is certain that he is the author of the essence of created things no less than of their existence; and this essence is nothing other than the eternal truths. [AT I, 151, 1–152, 5 = PW III, 25.]

Existences are created by the efficient causality of God—this is nothing but banal. Nothing, by contrast, of the banal belongs to the thesis of the creation of the eternal essences of things by efficient causality—and these essences, by the way, include mathematical truths as well as logical principles, ethical values, etc. Therefore, though truths, thoughts, *cogitationes* are imposed on our understanding with necessary and unconditional evidence, they are still created according to efficient causality. The *cogitatio,* taken in its most essential characteristics, is bypassed by the cause. The latter, according to an inevitable consequence, therefore escapes the *cogitatio,* which henceforth can no longer apprehend it except as ". . . incomprehensible power" (AT I, 150, 22; 146, 4–5 = PW III, 25; 23). Independent of its overall significance for Cartesian thought, the novelty of 1630 marks the first and definitive subversion of the *cogitatio* by *causa*. By referring to it, the sometimes underground work of the *Meditationes* becomes all the more easy to spot. At a precise theoretical moment, Descartes explicitly posits as a principle—better, as a principle without reason precisely in that it claims to offer a reason for all, universally—the following: "Jam vero lumine naturali manifestum est tantumdem ad minimum esse debere in causa efficiente et totali, quantum in ejusdem causae effectu [It is manifest by the natural light that there must be at least as much <reality> in the efficient and total cause as in the effect of that cause] . . ." (AT VII, 40, 21–23 = PW II, 28). Once again it is a question of causality in all its splendor, total just as much as efficient, as when in 1630 it subverted the *cogitatio* for the first time (AT I, 152, 1–2 = PW III, 25). Why therefore does it come up only in the midst of

Meditatio III, if it has already been said not to suffer any exception? Why not introduce the principle from the very beginning? The answer forces itself upon us: because in the beginning is the *cogitatio,* whose proper role is to lead from doubt to the *ego (cogito).* Causality, efficient as well as total, ought to come up only at the precise moment when the *ego* itself sets out in quest of the ground of its own cognitive existence. And in order to cross from existence as a cognitive being to an absolutely grounded existence, the *ego* must stop defining itself in terms of the essence of the *ens ut cogitatum* and appeal to a more essential pronouncement about being in its Being: *ens ut causatum,* which then and only then comes up as an evidence that cannot be gotten around. Posed as a new principle, indeed as the second beginning of the *Meditationes, causa* immediately and directly deploys its authority over that which is to be surpassed, the *cogitatio* itself. Hence this audacious statement, which Descartes was without a doubt the first to have ventured: ". . . hoc non modo perspicue verum est de iis effectibus, quorum realitas est actualis sive formalis, sed etiam de ideis, in quibus consideratur tantum realitas objectiva [This is transparently true not only in the case of effects which possess . . . actual or formal reality, but also in the case of ideas where one is considering only . . . objective reality]" (41, 1–4 = 28). All beings are as *cogitatum, Meditatio II* had established. *Meditatio III* confirms this, but also completes it: all *cogitata* depend on a *cogitatio,* which itself is only as caused, as a *causatum.* More essential to beings than their status as *cogitatum* is their rank as *causatum*—the dignified rank of *causatum* is more profound than the *effectus indignitas* (242, 6), for it is produced directly by the *causa* as such. This redoubling leads in an exemplary way to the so-called proof for the existence of God by effects. This proof should be defined more precisely: proof by the *idea Dei* having the status of *causatum,* an idea that ". . . nec comprehendere, nec forte etiam attingere cogitatione ullo modo possum [I cannot in any way grasp and perhaps cannot even reach in my thought]."[54]

The highest *cogitatio,* the one that conveys the idea of God, cannot deliver the existence of God, unless it admits of being reconsidered in terms of the efficient and total *causa, ut causatum.* If even this *cogitatio*

---

54. AT VII, 46, 20–21 = PW II, 32. The text here speaks about other properties of the divine essence—". . . alia innumera in Deo [countless additional attributes of God] . . ."; but they only cause the redoubling of the incomprehensibility that characterizes the infinity of God in the first place: "Nec obstat quod non comprehendam infinitum [This does not run contrary to the fact that I do not grasp the infinite] . . ." (46, 18–19 = 32 [modified]). This is confirmed by 52, 2–6 = 35.

can be interpreted *ut causata,* how much more so can all the others ("Caetera autem omnia . . . ," 45, 1 = 31), seeing as they claim only the *ego,* finite substance, as their sufficient cause. There is then no *cogitatio* that should not first be understood as caused, therefore included in the interpretation of being as such *ut causatum.* Nevertheless, despite this point being established, a final obstacle still remains to be crossed. The fact that the *cogitationes* are submitted to causality does indeed represent a considerable point, but it is one that decides nothing about the *cogito* itself. Couldn't it be said that so long as the *ego cogito* remains an autonomous and sufficient principle, its *cogitatio* is removed from the sway of the *causa sive ratio*—in how it functions, if not in what it produces? As seductive as it appears, this position does not offer any security. For the *ego* itself is inscribed in a *causa* that bears the name God: "Deus mei causa est, ego ejus effectus [God is the cause of me, and I am an effect of him]."[55] The *ego* makes no exception to the universality of the divine creative cause, since the very idea of God as *summe potens* implies that ". . . tum ego ipse, tum aliud omne . . . est creatum [both myself and everything else is created] . . ." by him (45, 13–14 = 31). Essences, but also the *ego,* have God for their cause, just as much as existences do. One must push the point even farther: the *idea Dei* shows up as an *ens causatum* without any possible cause besides God; and, Descartes states precisely, the likeness of God ". . . in qua Dei idea continetur, a me percipi per eandem facultatem, per quam ego ipse a me percipior [which includes the idea of God, is perceived by me with the same faculty that enables me to perceive myself]" (51, 21–23 = 35 [modified]). The same faculty allows me to perceive myself and to perceive the *idea Dei.* This faculty is named *cogitatio.* Through it, at one and the same time, I perceive myself and I perceive the *idea Dei.* We propose understanding this ambivalence by referring to the duality of the pronouncements about the Being of all beings: the *cogitatio* can either be understood in terms of the *ens ut cogitatum,* whereby it delivers the *ego;* or the very same *cogitatio* can be taken in terms of the *ens ut causatum,* whereby it brings us to the existence of God. The discrepancy between

---

55. *Conversation with Burman* (AT V, 156, 8 = PW III, 340) (which subsequently concludes that God is *causa totalis*!). God appears as *causa ultima* (AT VII, 50, 6 = 34), *Author* (48, 27; 62, 17, etc. = 33; 43; etc.) who produces me (50, 9 = 34), or makes me (61, 19 = 42). Undoubtedly, the *ego* acknowledges itself to be *creatus* (AT VII, 45, 14; 51, 19; 54, 19; 55, 11, etc. = 31; 35; 38; 38; etc.), but no less also *effectus.* In this precise sense, Descartes does not so much deploy the *ens* as *creatum* as he reduces (and abolishes) the thought of creation to that of efficiency, which has become the single cause.

the two points of arrival results only from the subversion of the *cogitatio* by the *causa*.

For the non-published part of *Sein und Zeit,* Heidegger promised a "phenomenological destruction of the 'cogito sum.'"[56]We gladly venture to suggest that Descartes himself accomplished this destruction: the *cogitatio,* as principal attribute of an *ego (res) cogitans,* can be brought from an onto-logy of the *ens ut cogitatum (cogitatio sui)* back to an onto-logy of the *ens ut causatum.* The critique of the absolute rule of cognitive representation and the transcendental egology that it implies does not in any way transgress Cartesian thought; it occupies a central place in it. The destruction of the *ego cogito* was first of all the task of Descartes. Once this point is established, one is not prevented from asking about the nature of such a self-destruction. To be sure, there is nothing phenomenological about it since it oversteps the *cogitatio* in view of the *causa sive ratio,* therefore in view of the principle of reason in which the metaphysics of subsistent presence is accomplished. The Cartesian destruction of the "cogito sum" thus reinforces the metaphysics of presence, far from putting it into question. In opposition to the "phenomenological destruction" projected (but not accomplished) by *Sein und Zeit, Meditatio III,* at its decisive moment (AT VII, 40, 5–25 = PW II, 27–28), carries out only a metaphysical destruction of the *ego cogito,* with the *ego ut ens causatum* as its beneficiary.

All exceptions and obstacles having been reduced, it is legitimate to cite *causa* as the most fundamental trait of being— of being taken in view as such, according to the formula of 1641: "Per se autem notum mihi videtur, omne id quod est, vel esse a causa, vel a se tanquam a causa [What does seem to me self-evident is that all that exists either derives its existence from a cause or derives its existence from itself as from a cause]" (112, 3–5 = 80 [modified]). In this *omne id quod est,* we can read nothing other than being taken universally as such. It must therefore be translated: being as such and universally is only through a cause—differ-

---

56. Heidegger, *Sein und Zeit,* §18, op. cit., p. 89 [English trans., p. 123]. From §6 on, Descartes is subsumed within the project of "destroying the history of ontology" (op. cit., p. 19 [English trans., p. 41]). On Descartes' place in this history and its destruction, see in particular pp. 24–25 [English trans., pp. 45–47]. Subsequently §75 will call this project "destroying the history of philosophy historiologically" (p. 392 [English trans., p. 444]). In this sense, and in this sense only, we would hope that the present work will be counted as a contribution to such a destructive task—in the sense of making manifest a thought that is equal to the question of Being, which it mistakes in the very moment that it responds to it.

ent from or identical to itself, it does not matter. The *causa* becomes the principle of an onto-logy grounded strictly rationally. Whatever it might be, it will be grounded in its Being inasmuch as it is caused, "... omne id quod est esse a causa [All that exists derives its existence from a cause]...." In light of the fact that this rational grounding is deployed universally, why does Descartes add "... vel a se tanquam a causa [or from itself as from a cause]?" Before every other factual and doctrinal explanation, let us again consider the onto-theo-logical constitution of (all thought that intends to be constituted as) metaphysical thought: the Being of beings as such grounds all beings (onto-logy) and, inseparably, the being par excellence grounds and supports the Being of beings (theo-logy). The Being of beings as such maintains a relation of reciprocal grounding with the being par excellence—though, in each case, the modes of grounding differ (*gründen/begründen*). In terms of this figure, it becomes perfectly understandable that Descartes would state the connection joining *omne id quod est* to *causa* twice. For, despite stylistic appearances, the two formulae are not in fact parallel. The first, which links *omne id quod est* to "... esse a causa ... ," puts forth an onto-logy that brings to light the way of Being of all beings, grounded by it through rules common (in Cartesian terms) to all finite beings, and therefore *ab alio*. In contrast, the second, which bases *omne id quod est* on "... esse a se tanquam a causa," concerns only a single being, the only one who is *a se*—namely, the being par excellence. This formulation puts into play a reversed (not inverted) grounding of all other (finite) beings by the excellence of an exceptional being. In fact, the second formulation is a pronouncement concerning the theo-logy that completes the onto-theo-logy of the *causa*.

Proving this does not pose any insurmountable difficulty. By hypothesis, if the onto-theo-logy of *causa* oversteps that of the *cogitatio*, the corresponding being par excellence must be displaced from the *ego* to God—or, more exactly, from the cognitive ground of the *ens ut cogitatum* to the causal ground of the *ens ut causatum*, therefore from the *ego (cogito)* to a causal God who first causes himself just as the *ego* first cognizes itself: *causa sui* after the fashion of and like *cogitatio sui*.[57] Not only did Descartes explicitly try to bring about this displacement in *Meditatio III*, but he accomplishes it in a text that, for the first time, an-

---

57. We risk this formula first because it is not shocking to Latin-speaking peoples, next because it is not without parallels from the hand of Descartes—be this only *idea mei ipsius* (AT VII, 51, 14 = 35). See *supra*, §8.

nounces the hypothesis of a positive aseity. Caterus and Arnauld will even point to this fact when they try to compel Descartes to make public his decision to name and define God as *causa sui*.[58] This text goes as follows: "Atqui, si a me essem, nec dubitarem, nec optarem, nec omnino quicquam mihi deesset; omnes enim perfectiones quarum idea aliqua in me est, mihi dedissem, atque ipsemet Deus essem [Yet if I derived my existence from myself, then I should neither doubt nor want, nor lack anything at all; for I should have given myself all the perfections of which I have any idea, and thus I should myself be God]" (48, 7–10 = 33). An astonishing text for more than just one reason: *(a)* It speaks of searching for a being par excellence by means of the onto-logy of *causa,* which was just hypothesized several pages earlier (40, 21–25 = 28). This onto-logy can be said to bear implicitly within it the phrase ". . . a se tanquam a causa . . . ," since this formula appears in the *Primae Responsiones* as a commentary on this very text (95, 1–27 then 111, 20–112, 16 = 68–69 then 80). It must therefore be said that here the onto-logy of the *ens ut causatum* tries for the first time to accomplish itself in a being par excellence. *(b)* It speaks of the *ego.* That is, the thought of the *causa* intervenes only on the basis of what the thought of the *cogitatio* has already gained. Just as, after completing the *cogitatio* in the *ego,* Descartes submits both to the more fundamental consideration of the *causa,* so too does he begin here by considering the ultimate point at which the onto-theo-logy of *cogitatio* culminated: the *ego,* being par excellence as *cogito.* To this *ego,* considered to be this being, he applies the onto-theo-logical hypothesis that is imposed by the second pronouncement about the Being of beings. He tests whether or not the *ego* can satisfy the *causa* par excellence. Conceptually, this crucial question is put as follows: can the *ego* be conceived and thus be *a se,* when *a se* implies *a se* positively, *tanquam a causa? (c)* The retreat of the onto-theo-logy of the *cogitatio* before that of the *causa* is accomplished on the basis of the *ego,* which, examining itself, notices that, while it can always illustrate cognitive excellence, it

58. Caterus' point of departure is located precisely in this text, which he cites, from the *Meditationes* (AT VII, 48, 7–10 = 94, 8–13). Arnauld too will discuss it, making express reference to its first citation by Caterus (207, 25–208 = 94, 8–13). The debate about the *causa sui* is thus broached by the hypothesis of the ego's positive aseity (a hypothesis that, to be sure, Descartes will immediately contest), and not by the aseity of God. Therefore when *causa sui* is first considered, the *ego* is its beneficiary. This gives reason to suppose that, conceptually if not lexically, the formula *causa sui* is an imitation of the *cogitatio sui* transposed into the order of cause—in short, that it is *causa sui* that imitates the *cogitatio sui* and not the inverse. It must not be forgotten that in the sense in which Descartes understands it, *causa sui* is a neologism.

cannot suffice for causal excellence. This confession of powerlessness (*powerlessness* in the strict sense, which by contrast will determine the real being par excellence as ". . . incomprehensible power . . .") is made in the recognition that I doubt. That is, *dubitatio* can be understood in two ways, with two opposed consequences: as *cogitatio,* it assures the certainty of the *cogito* and the ontic excellence of the *ego,* despite the uncertainty about its modality; but insofar as it requires a cause, the same *dubitatio* tells us that the *ego* does not maintain a relation of cause and effect with all its thoughts, thus that, in certain cases, it does not exert the totality of the *causa efficiens* that is nonetheless required *etiam de ideis* [also in the case of ideas] (41, 3 = 28). In doubting, the *ego* confirms its ontic primacy as *cogitatio,* but it weakens any pretense that it might have to ontic excellence as *causa.* In short, it notices by itself that ". . . nihil aliud sim quam res cogitans [I am nothing but a thinking thing] . . ." (49, 15 = 33). Confessing this reduction indicates that the *ego* has renounced, in this second moment, accomplishing the excellence of being.[59] The onto-theo-logy of the *ens ut causatum* will therefore be achieved in God conceived as *causa sui.* The daring represented by this ultimate name of God must not hide another and first daring move on the part of Descartes: God must admit positive aseity (in contrast with Saint Thomas and his disciples) and accept over himself the imperative of *causa sive ratio* only insofar as the being par excellence, whatever it might have been, was obliged to satisfy the *causa sui.* If the *ego* had been able to play the role of this being par excellence, it would also have taken on the name *causa sui*—for there would be no others, in heaven and on earth, nor in Hell. After the insufficiency of the *ego,* God comes along and fills the function of *causa sui.* This function is thus imposed on him only insofar as it precedes him in terms of the necessities proper to the

59. In fact, it is in an indisputably late text that the existence of the *ego* is deduced from doubt, as if the *cogito* were being repeated in the light shed by another principle (God in terms of the cause): ". . . nas non posse dubitare, quin mens nostra existat, . . . sequitur, illam existere [We cannot doubt that our mind exists . . . it follows that our mind exists]" (*Notae in programma quod-dam . . . ,* 1647 [AT VIII-2, 354, 19–21 = PW I, 301]). This would lead one to give an equally late date to the parallel text: ". . . ita ut possimus affirmare simul ac dubitare sum adgressus, etiam cum certitudine me cognoscere experire [Thus I can state that as soon as I began to doubt, I began to have knowledge which was certain]" (*Recherche de la Vérité* [AT X, 525, 4–5 = PW II, 418]). It is well known that these texts, together with *Regulae XII,* "Sum, ergo Deus est [I am, therefore God exists]" (X, 421, 29 = 46), have given some ground for the catchphrase *Dubito, ergo Deus est* to be forged. This allows one to mark the decentering of the *cogito* when it passes under the jurisdiction of the second Cartesian word about the *ens in quantum ens.*

onto-theo-logy of *causa*. Descartes decides on and designs the figure of
the *causa sui,* model for every being par excellence, grounded on and
grounding the *ens ut causatum,* before he determines the identity of the
being (*ego* or else God) who, subsequently and consequently, puts it into
effect.[60] Only in this sense will it be possible to grasp the fact that, after
1641, the *ego* still tries to imitate, tangentially, that which made God a
being par excellence, the *causa sui.* This imitation leads to the reinterpretation of morality and freedom as a way of enacting independence, in a
limited field, by the perfect self-mastery that free will assures to the *ego.*
For ". . . independence, conceived distinctly, includes within it infinity"
(AT III, 191, 15–16 = not included in PW).[61] Thus is completed Descartes' second pronouncement about the most fundamental trait of being: being is as such inasmuch as caused; this way of Being grounds beings by deploying them as *causata* and, inseparably, is itself grounded in
a being par excellence, which is marked as *causa sui.* The onto-theo-
logical constitution deploys the Being of beings in terms of *causa,* and
thus identifies the properly and definitively metaphysical dignity of
Cartesian thought.

§10. A Redoubled Onto-theo-logy

Our task has not yet been completed, however. Quite to the contrary,
we here encounter what is undoubtedly the greatest difficulty. We intended to establish the strictly metaphysical character of Cartesian
thought by recognizing in it a figure of the onto-theo-logical constitution
of all metaphysics. And yet, in wanting to prove this, we could indeed
have proved too much: we discovered not only one but two figures of
this constitution—one according to the *cogitatio,* the other according to
causa. What relation do they have? Do they contradict each other?
Faced with such a proliferation, shouldn't we doubt the operative rigor of

---

60. See *Sur la théologie blanche de Descartes,* §18. It will be observed, nonetheless, that
among the senses of *causa/cause* applied to God, another register subsists: ". . . haec Chari-
tas, hoc est, sancta amicitia, qua Deum prosequimur, et Dei causa etiam omnes homines,
quatenus scimus ipsos a Deo amari [this Charity, that is sacred friendship, with which we
honor God and all men for the sake of God (*Dei causa*) insofar as we know them to be
loved by God.] . . ." (AT VIII-2, 112, 22–24 = not included in PW); ". . . above all since it
is the cause of God that I have undertaken to defend . . ." (AT III, 238, 5–7 = PW III, 158);
". . . to be my protectors in God's cause . . ." (184, 19–20 = 153); ". . . I am championing
the cause of God . . ." (240, 16 = 159).
61. Concerning this reversal of the *similitudo Dei* turning into independence from
God, see *Sur la théologie blanche de Descartes,* §17, pp. 141*ff.*

the very concept of onto-theo-logical constitution, indeed of the notion, imprudently supposed to be univocal, of a single metaphysics?

These questions are not at all rhetorical and cannot receive definitive answers here; we can't even begin to outline them. Nonetheless, we can try to formulate the questions with greater precision. We concede first of all that Heidegger introduces the thesis of an onto-theo-logical constitution of metaphysics only at the end of a reflection on Hegel. A seminar studying Hegel's *Logic* (WS 1956–57) precedes the lecture given on 24 February 1957 at Todtnauberg. No doubt, we must add to this background the courses given during the preceding semester (WS 1955–56) at the University of Freiburg on Leibniz and the *Satz vom Grund*. In this sense, and without wanting to prejudice a more precise textual examination (which only the *Gesamtausgabe* will make possible), we posit that the onto-theo-logical constitution takes form in Heidegger's thought only on the basis of the two figures of metaphysics who make it most overwhelmingly evident and operative, Leibniz and Hegel. However, just as one has to admit "an incubation period of the principle of reason," which itself stems from "an incubation of Being,"[62] it seems to us that one has to admit an incubation period for onto-theo-logical constitution: less an effect in reverse allowing for a retroactive hermeneutic (a reflecting judgment of some sort) in the sense that from Plato and Aristotle metaphysics gives itself to be read as an onto-theo-logy, than a slow emergence, in often quite complex figures, of what, in its Leibnizian and Hegelian achievements, suddenly stands forth with a constitution that is simple because definitively accomplished. Hegel himself, for that matter, was perfectly conscious of a decisive lineage going back to Descartes. From 1807, he puts the moment of absolute freedom under the aegis of the "concept of Cartesian metaphysics . . . namely, that Being and thought are, in themselves, the same."[63] This equivalence, which goes so far as to require the Same between Being and thought, characterizes not only Hegelian (and Leibnizian) onto-theo-logy, but also, if one under-

62. "Aus der Incubation des Seins und ihrer Epochen stammt die Incubationszeit des Satzes vom Grund," *Der Satz vom Grund* (Pfullingen, 1957), S. 114 [English trans., p. 65]. From a historiographical perspective, E. Vollrath draws the same conclusion when he comments on AT VII, 164, 25*ff.*: "Dies ist geradezu eine Vorform des Satz vom Grunde bei Leibniz" (loc. cit., S. 281). But this judgment loses its validity when its author supposes elsewhere that it is the *Mathesis Universalis* that, here, receives a ground. It itself already foreshadows a principle, the *cogitatio*, within a first completed onto-theo-logy, which the passage to *causa* does not complete, but overwhelms and overdetermines.

63. G. W. F. Hegel, *Phänomenologie des Geistes, GW,* vol. 9, op. cit., p. 313 [English trans, p. 352 (modified)]. (See *supra*, n. 6.)

stands thought as *cogitatio,* the first figure of Cartesian onto-theo-logy. Far from preventing us from reaching the properly metaphysical approach to Cartesian thought, the Hegelian rendering of onto-theo-logy would lead us back to it with great urgency. A similar confirmation could easily be found in Leibniz: his "great principle"—which alone permits one to "rise to metaphysics"—namely, "Ratio est in Natura, cur aliquid potius existat quam nihil [There is a reason in Nature why something should exist rather than nothing],"[64] refers literally, if not expressly, to what in the *Responsiones* we recognized as the *dictat* of reason. To historically establish a line of descent connecting the two Cartesian figures of onto-theo-logy to the more completed subsequent figures does not present an insurmountable difficulty: the metaphysics of the *ens ut cogitatum* refers to Hegel, the metaphysics of the *ens ut causatum* to Leibniz. The differences between the two, which remain no less weighty, merely indicate the path that, departing from Descartes, leads to the eventual accomplishments of the destiny of metaphysics. The difficulty is thus transformed: it is not so much a matter of determining *if* the onto-theological constitution pertains to Cartesian thought (and is not limited to the moments eventually reached by Leibniz and Hegel) as it is one of understanding *which* destiny affects, with Descartes, the constitution of metaphysics. In these two figures is there a contradiction, a competition or an incoherence due to something unconscious in metaphysics? Without a doubt, none of these answers is suitable, for, in great thinkers, nothing lurks in the shadows of the nonthought. Perhaps the question should be reversed, then, and we are to ask: the complexity of the figures of onto-theo-logy—can it, before all else, be thematized in a single structure, and, if so, what does Descartes teach us about onto-theo-logical constitution? The simple figure by which Heidegger thematizes it, with regard to Hegel (and Leibniz), might offer only a single example of onto-theo-logical constitution—privileged to be sure, but neither normative nor unique. In contrast, the complication that Descartes imposes on this simple figure might become the rule, or at least the most probable hypothesis, when the metaphysical character of each philosophical thought in general is to be examined. In other words, the onto-theo-logical complexity of Cartesian metaphysics would be less of an exception to the primordial but simple figure of onto-theo-logy that Heidegger lays bare

---

64. Respectively, *Theodicy,* §44, ed. Gehrhardt, *Ph S.,* VI, 127 [English trans., p. 147]; *Principes de la Nature et de la Grâce,* §7, ibid., p. 602 [English trans., p. 199]; and *24 Propositions,* ed. Gehrhardt, *Ph. S.,* VII, p. 289 (= *Opuscules et fragments inédits,* ed. L. Couturat, p. 533 [English trans., p. 145]). See *supra,* n. 42.

in Hegel (and Leibniz) than, on the contrary, Heidegger's simple figure would offer an exceptional rendition of a more complex and eventually infinitely varied game, but one that is no less onto-theo-logical. The Cartesian exception to the simple figure might, in fact, indicate a rule: without exception, onto-theo-logical constitution assumes in metaphysics a far greater complexity than that of its Hegelian achievement. This hypothesis can be verified, and therefore disproved, only by works that seek out such a constitution in this or that thinker of metaphysics (precisely what we have been attempting here, and earlier, with regard to Descartes), or else by ones seeking out the very history of the concept of metaphysics. Let it suffice here to mark the inversion of the question, without expecting the difficult elements that would make up a response.[65]

We can now return to Descartes and attempt to pin down the structure in which the two figures assumed by the onto-theo-logical constitution are joined. We postulate that they are no more opposed than they are contradictory; rather, they are subordinated in a form of onto-theo-logy that is not internally divided, but doubled. We portray this schema in a figure, since, Descartes says, the figure suits the imagination, and since the *imaginationis adjumentum* [aid of the imagination] (AT X, 438, 12 = 58) allows the question "... longe distinctius ab intellectu percipietur [to be perceived much more distinctly by our intellect]" (438, 11 = 58).

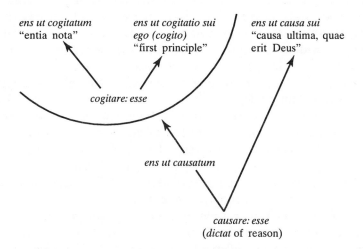

ens ut cogitatum
"entia nota"

ens ut cogitatio sui
ego (cogito)
"first principle"

ens ut causa sui
"causa ultima, quae
erit Deus"

cogitare: esse

ens ut causatum

causare: esse
(*dictat* of reason)

65. See our draft, "Du pareil au même. Ou: comment Heidegger permet de refaire de 'l'histoire de la philosophie,'" in *Martin Heidegger, L'Herne,* ed. Michel Haar (Paris, 1983).

We are not just juxtaposing two onto-theo-logical constitutions; we strengthen the first with a second constitution. Both of them deploy separately, but completely, a thesis concerning the *ens in quantum ens* (either *ens ut cogitatum* or *ens ut causatum*) and a thesis concerning the being par excellence (respectively, *cogitatio sui* and *causa sui*). It is thus a case of a doubling that strengthens, and not of an incoherent or conflictual division: the entire first constitution, in addition to having its own proper articulation, is subsumed within the second constitution and plays the role of the region of being in general. The onto-theo-logical constitution imposed by the *dictat* of reason thinks as *ens causatum* (thus according to an ontology) the totality of the onto-theo-logical constitution deployed in the first pronouncement about beings (*cogitare*), thus the *ens ut cogitatio sui* (*ego,* theology) as well as the *ens ut cogitatum* (ontology). Descartes doubles and strengthens onto-theo-logy by reinterpreting the first acceptation of *esse*—*esse: cogitare*—by means of a second, *esse: causare.*

Far from weakening it, this doubling strengthens the onto-theo-logical constitution that qualifies Cartesian thought as metaphysics. What now remains is for us to offer some clarification in the form of a commentary on this doubling, lest it remain sunk in a trivial contradiction. *(a)* The onto-theo-logy deployed in terms of the *cogitare,* having at stake the pair *ens ut cogitatum* and an *ens* par excellence *ut cogitatio sui,* is thus accomplished *before* the explicit project of *prima Philosophia* that the *Meditationes* represent. In fact, this first figure is put in place as early as the *Regulae;* and if *Mediationes I* and *II* are more closely linked to it, this is because they succeed in formulating, finally, what the *Regulae* cause to be in play without thinking explicitly: namely, the *cogitatio*'s reflection on itself, which is finally witnessed in the *ego.* The hints at the *ego cogito* in 1627 and 1637 must be neither overestimated (the onto-theo-logy of the *cogitatio* is not yet deployed in it) nor underestimated. The structural homology between the *cogitatio* being reflected into an *ego* and the *Mathesis universalis* implying a first *Sapientia universalis* answers to the same exigency: namely, the necessity of grounding the interpretation of *entia* as *cogitata* on a being, a being par excellence, itself conceived as a cognizing par excellence, thus first of itself. *(b)* Reciprocally, the second figure of onto-theo-logy, deployed in terms of *causare* and with the pair *ens ut causatum* and the *ens* par excellence *ut causa sui* being at stake, does not coincide with the domain of the *Meditationes.* This work reaches the being par excellence by name only in *Responsiones I* and *IV,* and determines being as *causatum* only on the basis of *Meditatio III.*

Furthermore, a double lexical fact must detain us here, one that confirms our hypothesis of a doubling and finds a meaning in it. *Substantia* never comes up in the order of reasons before *Meditatio III* (precisely AT VII, 40, 12 = PW II, 28).[66] By chance, a chance that bears a conceptual necessity that is only somewhat hidden, the same page also offers the first theoretically significant occurrence of *causa* in the *Meditationes.* This occurrence is found at the heart of nothing less than the first formulation of the *dictat* of reason: "Jam vero lumine naturali manifestum est tantumdem ad minimum esse debere in *causa* efficiente et totali, quantum in ejusdem *causae* effectu [Now it is manifest by the natural light that there must be at least as much <reality> in the efficient and total cause as in the effect of that cause]" (40, 21–23 = 28).[67] Thus the transition from one onto-theo-logy to another is inscribed in the very text of the *Meditationes,* and could be pinpointed exactly at AT VII, 40, a text that appears as a decisive new beginning of speculative vigor. Moreover, this just recently established double textual fact can be read in the context of a conceptual difficulty that the most authoritative critics have noticed and discussed for a long time: the eventual solution to the continuity of the order of reasons, which alone would allow for overcoming the solipsism of the *ego* for the sake of attaining the existence of God.[68] As with the textual fact, the conceptual difficulty can be clarified by juxtaposing

66. See A. Becco, "Première apparition du terme de substance dans la *Méditation III* de Descartes," *Annales de l'Institut de Philosophie* (Bruxelles: ULB, 1976), and our remarks in Bulletin cartésien VII, *Archives de Philosophie* 1978/4, and in *Sur la théologie blanche de Descartes,* §16, pp. 395*ff.*

67. To our knowledge and in the expectation of a computerized index to the Latin text of the *Meditationes,* before AT VII, 40, 21–23 = 28, *causa* appears only in 33, 16–17 = 22 (". . . vel quavis alia ex causa . . ."), and 33, 21 = 22 (". . . pluribus ex causis innotuit . . ."). In these texts, the cause is never clearly identified, neither with a being nor with a *ratio.* As for 39, 18 = 27 ("exempli causa"), in addition to being beside the point, it does not belong to the register of cause strictly understood, still less to that of efficiency. The two occurrences in the *Synopsis* (14, 27 = 11: ". . . a causa summe perfecta . . ."; and 15, 1–2 = 11: ". . . habere Deum ipsum pro causa") themselves belong precisely to the summary of *Meditatio III.* Finally, it will be observed that DM never employs *cause(s)* in its fourth, nonetheless metaphysical, part (*à cause que,* in DM, 38, 27 and 39, 22, does not constitute a real objection). See P.-A. Cahné, *Index du Discours de la Méthode de René Descartes* (Rome, 1976).

68. F. Alquié, *La découverte métaphysique de l'homme chez Descartes* (Paris, 1960), p. 226; M. Gueroult, *Descartes selon l'ordre des raisons* (Paris, 1953), vol. 1, 229; W. Halbfass, *Descartes' Frage nach der Existenz der Welt* (Munich, 1968), S. 72. This experimental quasi-proof of the articulation and transition between the two onto-theo-logies seems to us to exclude seeing it as ". . . fewer really Cartesian words than artifacts of the commentator" (J.-M. Beyssade, loc. cit., p. 50).

the two onto-theo-logies that overlap at the heart of *Meditatio III*. It seems to us that here the redoubling of onto-theo-logy is verified experimentally, so to speak. *(c)* The fact that the onto- theo-logical domain of *causare* does not coincide with the entire *Meditationes* allows us to address another particular difficulty. That is, it could be objected that all properly and purely ontological consideration abstracts being, by definition, from all determination—*ens in quantum ens*—and in particular from determination by transcendence and creation; *ens creatum* excludes right away *ens in quantum ens*. Duns Scotus and Suarez, among many others, have emphasized this.[69] Therefore, if *causare* appeared only in the first philosophy that is dedicated to God and thus became the synonym of *creare*, no ontology would any longer be possible. But *causare* does not exactly equal *creare* (though it includes it). As early as the *Regulae*, the primacy of *causa* extends itself between two finite terms, and it sustains the physics of the *Discourse on the Method* as well as that of the *Essais*. In all cases, it is put into play without referring to creation or a transcendent causality. From the outset, then, *causa* determines the science of common being, without, however, reducing this being to an *ens creatum*. As proof, recall the submission of God the creator to the requirements of causality: *causa sui,* by the doubling of *causa,* attests to the fact that even the creator must be submitted to *causa;* and if God can be thought as *causa sui,* he could not, even for Descartes, be understood as *creator sui*. Thus *ens ut causatum* is not reducible to *ens creatum*. *(d)* The most considerable difficulty comes from the status of the *ego (cogito)*. In the present schema, it shows up with two opposed meanings. From the point of view of *esse: cogitare,* it fulfills the function of being par excellence, while from the point of view of *esse: causare,* it belongs to the *ens in quantum ens, ut causatum*. This real duplicity, however, allows one to resolve another difficulty, once again one that is purely textual. That is, the *ego cogito* often receives the title "first principle": "... Observing that this truth *'I am thinking, therefore I exist'* was so firm and sure that all the most extravagant suppositions of the sceptics were

---

69. *Sur la théologie blanche de Descartes,* §§6–7. Let us cite, from among others, Duns Scotus: "Intellectus viatoris potest esse certus de Deo, quod sit ens, dubitando de ente finito vel infinito, creato vel increato" (*Ordinatio I,* d. 3, p. 1, q. 1–2, n. 27, ed. Balič, vol. 3, p. 18), or: "Deus non est cognoscibilis a nobis naturaliter nisi ens sit univocum creato et increato" (*Ordinatio I,* d. 3, p. 1, q. 3, n. 139, loc. cit., p. 87). Likewise Suarez: "Per conceptum formalem entis, neque Deus, neque substantia creata, neque accidens repraesentantur, secundum modum quo in re sunt, neque prout inter se differunt, sed solum prout aliquo modo inter se conveniunt, ac similia sunt" (*Disputationes Metaphysicae, II,* s. 2, n. 17, vol. 25, p. 76); or: "nam *ens* in vi nominis sumptum commune est Deo et creaturis, et de Deo affirmari vere potest" (*Disp. II,* s. 4, 11, loc. cit., p. 91).

incapable of shaking it, I decided that I could accept it without scruple as the first principle of the philosophy I was seeking"; "In the second sense, the first principle is that our soul exists, because there is nothing whose existence is better known to us"; and

> . . . I considered that someone who wishes to doubt everything cannot, for all that, doubt that he exists while he is doubting; and that what reasons in this way, being unable to doubt itself while doubting everything else, is not what we call our body but what we call our soul or our thought. Accordingly I took the being or existence of this thought as my first principle, and from it I deduced very clearly the following: there is a God who is the author of everything there is in the world.[70]

How can this "first principle," which submits to itself the very existence of God, be seen elsewhere as [*ens*] *creatum* (AT VII, 45, 14 = PW II, 31), thus consequently as *res incompleta et ab alio dependens* [*a thing which is incomplete and dependent on another*] (51, 24–25; 53, 10–11 = 35; 37). In short, how can this "first principle" admit not deserving the title *summum ens*—". . . nos non esse summum ens et nobis deesse quamplurima* [that we are not the supreme being and that we lack very many things] . . ." (374, 13–14 = 257)? This discrepancy does not in fact entail any contradiction; it merely shows that the *ego* can be read in terms of two Cartesian pronouncements on being as such. In terms of the *cogitatio,* the *ego* counts as a ". . . first principle . . ." precisely because it shows itself as ". . . the most known . . . ," as ". . . firm and assured truth . . . ," in short as ". . . the Being or existence . . ." of a *thought,* thus of a first *cogitatio* that exists as *causa (sui)*. This does not prevent the same *ego* from becoming, by means of the *causa* that the new beginning of *Meditatio III* introduces, an *ens causatum* subject to the law that holds for all beings. The doubling of onto-theo-logy forces upon the *ego* a second metaphysical site, and at the same time, it establishes God, for the first time, in the position of being par excellence—of *summum ens*.[71] The double status of the *ego*—a major difficulty for modern as well as past

70. Respectively DM, AT VI, 32, 18–23 = PW I, 127 (in which ". . . that I was seeking . . ." displaces the Aristotelian ζητούμενον from the ὄν ἦ ὄν to the *ego*); *To Clerselier,* June–July 1646 (AT IV, 444, 23–25 = PW III, 290); and the preface to the French translation of *Principia Philosophiae* (AT IX-2, 9, 29–10, 8 = PW I, 183–84 [modified]). In contrast, *fundamentum* is only rarely and indirectly applied to the *ego cogito* (AT VII, 24, 13–14 = PW II, 16 in relation to 145, 24–27 = 104; DM, Latin translation, AT VI, 558, 28, translating ". . . premier principe . . ." from DM, 32, 23 = PW I, 127).

71. See *supra,* n. 40, and *infra,* chap. IV, §18, n. 50.

interpreters[72]— reflects merely, though to be sure in an exemplary mode, the doubling within the onto-theo-logical constitution of Cartesian metaphysics. *(e)* In the end, *causa sui* is meaningful only in response to the exigencies of the thought that searches out, in accord with the *dictat* of reason, the cause of all beings, ". . . ad causam ultimam deveniatur, quae erit Deus [until eventually the ultimate cause is reached, and this will be God]" (50, 6 = 34). This formula anticipates Leibniz, more so than Spinoza, who takes up the *causa sui* without putting it into question or thinking it radically. Leibniz's principle of sufficient reason also seeks out God in the figure of the ultimate cause: "This is why the ultimate reason of things must lie in a necessary substance. . . . This is what we call God."[73] Here, to be sure, *reason* is substituted for *causa* when it is time to designate the ultimate term; but besides the fact that Descartes had already posited the equivalence of *causa* and *(sive) ratio,* reason merely achieves for Leibniz a sufficiency that is still limited by cause. The onto-theo-logy of *causa* thus points toward Leibniz, through Spinoza, and beyond him. As for the onto-theo-logy of the *cogitatio,* it certainly would not be imprudent to suggest that it clears the way for Malebranche, Locke, and Berkeley, who think being as *cogito* or *cogitatum* (*esse est percipi aut percipere*) and the supreme being as the thought that thinks itself. We have only to point to the fact that they interpret God as Word, or disqualify him as incomprehensible, if we want to develop such a suggestion. In a word, the Cartesian doubling of the onto-theo-logical constitution could find a second quasi-experimental verification in the divergent paths that it makes possible. In any case, the hypotheses await discussion. *(f)* The operation of two distinct onto-theo-logies finds, within the Cartesian text, two more verifications. (1) *Causa* can surpass the *cogitatio:* in fact, God could have created (thus: instituted) truths totally different from those which, in the actual and definitive state of affairs, are established. And, (2) when discussing the status of contradictories, Descartes imagines the possibility—impossible in fact, since not

72. Among the commentators from the past, we cite the clairvoyance of Father René Le Bossu, *Parallèle des Principes de la Physique d'Aristote et de celle de Descartes,* op. cit. He examines the in fact quite problematic compatibility between the primacy of the *ego* as *cogito* in *Principia Philosophiae I,* §7, and that of God as *causa* in §24 (pp. 305–8). Among the moderns, we refer to the lucidity of Maurice Merleau-Ponty: "In Descartes, for example, the two meanings of the word 'nature' (nature in the sense of 'natural light' and in the sense of 'natural inclination') adumbrate two ontologies (an ontology of the object and an ontology of the existent)," *Annuaire du Collège de France,* 1958, appearing in *Le visible et l'invisible* (Paris, 1964), pp. 219–20. [The English translation appears in an editor's note, p. 166, n. 3.—Trans.]

73. Leibniz, *Monadologie* §38, *Ph. S.,* ed. Gerhardt, VI, 613 [English trans., p. 185].

effectively realized—of another group of axioms. In opposition, the *cogitatio* can think what the *causa* can neither produce nor allow to be produced: in this way, the ego can experience its freedom and in this sense think it, even though it cannot understand its compatibility with the all-powerfulness and omniscience of God. But far from reducing freedom to the all-powerful causality of God—as Spinoza, Malebranche, and Leibniz will persistently (and successfully) try to do—Descartes will keep the two antagonists juxtaposed and irreducible. In these two conflicts, why doesn't Descartes attempt the reconciliation that, for better or worse, all his successors will obtain by triumphantly criticizing him? Without a doubt, because in both cases, the creation of the eternal truths is at issue;[74] but above all because in this paradoxical thesis, it is in fact the separation of the two onto-theo-logies that is at issue. That is, the cognizable truths here still admit a cause, ". . . incomprehensible power . . ."

Can the irreducible duality nonetheless be overcome, such that the rationality of the *cogitatio* would be confused with the dominion of the *causa sive ratio*? Descartes' successors had, fundamentally, no other ambition than to establish this. And in fact, at least formally, it appears possible to reduce the one to the other. *Causa sive ratio:* this formula could itself already be understood as the reconciliation of the two onto-theo-logies. For the *cogitatio* has the function of *rationem reddere;* it thereby puts *ratio* into operation. And the *causa (efficiens) sui* is immediately found in the *causa*. This formal reconciliation does not however permit the duality of the onto-theo-logies to be effaced. They reappear in the separation, which Leibniz and Wolff never abolished, between the principle of sufficient reason and the principle of identity. Kant, by consecrating the irreducibility of synthetic judgments to analytic judgments, will confirm, perhaps without knowing it, the irreversible duality of the Cartesian onto-theo-logies. Descartes' metaphysical greatness is no doubt to be found in his having distinguished them, but above all in his having refused to then confuse them too easily.

The precisely metaphysical dignity of Cartesian thought being from now on something firmly established, what remains is for us to confirm what is at stake in these two onto-theo-logies by the successive examination of the two privileged beings put into play in each of them—the *ego* and God.

74. See "De la création des vérités éternelles au principe de raison. Remarques sur l'anti-cartésianisme de Spinoza, Malebranche, et Leibniz," *XVIIeme siècle* (147), 1985/2, and a modified version of this essay in our *Questions cartésiennes II,* Paris: Presses Universitaires de France, 1996.

T H R E E

E G O

§11. On the "Cogito, Sum" as a Primal Utterance

Instituting the *ego,* as *cogito* at the origin of all science, does not confine it to a pure and simple theory of knowledge, however secure it might be. Along with the role it plays in knowledge, it also pertains to the first principle of a metaphysics. We have already seen how the title *metaphysics* (chapter I) and also the concept of onto-theo-logy (chapter II) imply such a rank for the *ego.* This rank is accorded to it as a result of applying to Cartesian theses the unique architectonic requirements of an onto-theo-logical constitution of metaphysics. But such an architecture organizes, not without exerting a little force, statements that inevitably tend to exceed or complicate the elementary schema of onto-theo-logy. Several questions about the *ego* must therefore be posed. Does it play one or several roles? Do all these roles belong to an onto-theo-logy, therefore to a metaphysics? Can one can conceive a sense in which the *ego* would be excepted from metaphysics? But to pass beyond a metaphysics, one must first accede to it. In the case of the *ego,* which exists insofar as it thinks, the difficulty comes from the fact that at first glance it does not exactly merit the rank of metaphysical principle. Descartes himself clearly admits as much: when Father Bourdin objects to him that the *cogito, sum* ends up only at a cliché (*hoc tritum,* AT VII, 531, 15 = PW II, 362) that anyone knows by heart (". . . vel plebeculae familiare [familiar even to the mass of mankind] . . . ," 531, 16 = 362), Descartes does not contest the banality of what he has uttered; he admits it all the more unreservedly as he justifies it by its consequences, which are far less banal: "quia nempe pro nihilo ducit, quod ex his [hoc tritum *Cogito, sum*] et Dei existentiam et reliqua multa demonstrarim [Presumably he regards it as nothing that I demonstrated the existence of God and many other things from this (the cliché 'I am thinking, I exist')]" (551, 9–12 = PW II, 376). From the cliché follows the existence of God and many

128 other results, items that are far less ordinary. The banality of the premises does not disappear with the extraordinary character of the conclusions; it is justified by it. How then can Descartes have built into a metaphysical "first principle" (DM, 32, 23 = AT IX-2, 10, 5–6, etc.) and *fundamentum* (AT VII, 107, 2 = PW II, 77) what he himself recognizes as *tritum*? The elevation of the *cogito, sum* from the rank of something banal to that of a principle attests to the eventual metaphysical coronation of the *ego*. That Descartes saw the difficulty and that he worked a long time to overcome it is confirmed by the texts.

The banality of "cogito sum" stems from the fact, recognized since 1637, that Saint Augustine had already formulated it clearly and on several occasions. Descartes is seen to have proposed, among other texts, the following passage:

> I have no fear of the arguments of the Academics. They say, "Suppose you are mistaken?" I reply, "If I am mistaken, I exist [*si fallor, sum*]." A nonexistent being cannot be mistaken; therefore I must exist, if I am mistaken [*ac per hoc sum, si fallor*]. Then since my being mistaken proves that I exist, how can I be mistaken in thinking that I exist, seeing that my mistake establishes my existence [*quando certum me esse, si fallor*]?[1]

The similarities with the way of thinking developed in *Meditatio II* cannot be disputed. An agreement with the authority of Saint Augustine, in those days enormous, could not hurt; and Descartes takes advantage of it in several places.[2] However, he is forever widening the gap between his argument and Augustinian reasoning. Is this a simple vanity of the

---

1. Saint Augustine, *De Civitate Dei*, XI, 26, *Œuvres de saint Augustin*, vol. 35, ed. G. Bardy and G. Combès (Paris, 1959), pp. 114–15 [English trans., p. 460]. See the note "Saint Augustin et Descartes," pp. 486–87. The other important Augustinian texts are found in *Soliliquia* II, I, 1, *De Libero arbitrio* II, 3, 7, and especially *De Trinitate* X, 10, 15–16. On these three texts, see, in addition to the note by F. J. Thonnard, in *Œuvres de saint Augustin*, vol. 6, Paris, 1952, pp. 517–18, the study by P. Cahné, "Saint Augustin et les philosophes du XVIIeme siècle: ontologie et autobiographie," in *XVIIeme siècle* 135 (1982). On the question as a whole, see the works of L. Blanchet, *Les antécédents historiques du "Je pense donc je suis"* (Paris, 1st ed. 1920, 2d ed. 1985), and E. Gilson, *La liberté chez Descartes et la théologie* (Paris, 1913 and 1982) (especially I, chap. V), and *Etudes sur le rôle de la pensée médiévale dans la formation du système cartésien* (Paris, 1930). One should also consult the more recent studies by G. Rodis-Lewis, "Augustinianisme et cartésianisme," *Augustinus Magister*, Congrès international augustinien (Paris, 1954), vol. 2, pp. 1087–1104; H. Gouhier, *Cartésianisme et Augustinianisme au XVIIeme siècle* (Paris, 1978) (especially chaps. I and II); and John A. Mourant, "The Cogitos: Augustinian and Cartesian," *Augustinian Studies* 10 (1979).

2. For example, *To X,* November 1640: "In itself it is such a simple and natural thing to infer that one exists from the fact that one is doubting that it could have occurred to

author, careful to preserve his originality by hiding his sources or spurn-
ing his predecessors? Such an attitude would be simple-minded, seeing
as the Augustinian tradition gathered genuine thinkers around this argument without interruption all the way until the seventeenth century.[3]
And more important, it would contradict an explicit declaration of Descartes' intentions:

> Addo etiam, quod forte videbitur esse paradoxum, nihil in ea Philosophia
> esse, quatenus censetur Peripatetica, et ab aliis diversa, quod non sit no-
> vum; nihilque in mea, quod non sit vetus. Nam, quantum ad principia, ea
> tantum admitto, quae omnibus omnino Philosophia hactenus communia
> fuere, suntque idcirco omnium antiquissima; et quae deinde ex iis deduco,
> jam ante in ipsis contenta et implicita fuisse tam clare ostendo, ut etiam
> antiquissima, utpote humanis mentibus a natura indita, esse appareat. [I
> shall add something that may seem paradoxical. Everything in peripatetic
> philosophy, regarded as a distinctive school that is different from others,
> is quite new, whereas everything in my philosophy is old. For as far as
> principles are concerned, I only accept those which in the past have always
> been common ground among all philosophers without exception, and
> which are therefore the most ancient of all. Moreover, the conclusions I
> go on to deduce are already contained and implicit in these principles, and
> I show this so clearly as to make it apparent that they too are very ancient,
> in so far as they are naturally implanted in the human mind.][4]

---

any writer. But I am very glad to find myself in agreement with Saint Augustine, if only to
hush the little minds who have tried to find fault with the principle" (AT III, 248, 1–7 =
PW III, 159). And to Arnauld:

> Non hîc morabor in gratiis Viro Clarissimo agendis, quod me divi Augustini authoritate
> adjuvarit, rationesque meas ita proposuerit, ut timere videretur ne non satis fortes aliis
> apparerent. [I shall not waste time here by thanking my distinguished critic for bringing
> in the authority of St. Augustine to support me, and for setting out my arguments so
> vigorously that he seems to fear that their strength may not be sufficiently apparent to
> anyone else.]

(AT VII, 219, 6–9 = PW II, 154.)

3. See the texts collected by E. Gilson in *René Descartes, Discours de la Méthode. Texte
et commentaire* (Paris, 1925), pp. 296*ff.* (based on the study by L. Blanchet, *Les antécédents . . .* , 1st part).

4. *Epistola ad P. Dinet* (AT VII, 580, 16–25 = PW II, 391– 92). See 596, 12–15 = 393:
"Hîc repeto quod supra dixi, meam Philosophiam esse omnium antiquissimam, nihilque
ab ea diversum esse in vulgari, quod non sit novum [Here I will not repeat what I said
about my philosophy being the oldest of all, and about there being nothing in the ordinary
philosophy, in so far as it differs from mine, that is not quite new]." There is no real reason
to doubt the sincerity of this declaration, though there is one for questioning its exactness.
See *supra,* chap. II, §6, and AT X, 204, 2–5 = not included in PW.

The (peripatetic) philosophy that Aristotle inspired is a novelty—and a risky novelty at that—while Cartesian philosophy goes back to the "natural" evidence of incontestable principles, which is, for that very reason, an evidence of the highest antiquity: ". . . nihil est veritate antiquius [nothing is older than the truth]" (AT VII, 3, 25 = PW II, 4). Descartes then did not have any reason to spurn the authority of Saint Augustine; on the contrary, he had very good reasons to invoke it. Why then didn't he do so? Answer: ". . . because he [Saint Augustine] does not seem to me to make use of it in the same way as I do." The *antiquissima* Cartesian philosophy is concerned with establishing the "principia . . . omnibus . . . communia," and in this philosophy, the *ego cogito sum* in fact holds the rank of a principle. But doesn't Saint Augustine, by this same argument, also aim at a first principle? Not at all, thinks Descartes, and with good reason:

> . . . I do indeed find that he does use it to prove the certainty of our existence. He goes on to show that there is a certain likeness of the Trinity in us, in that we exist, we know that we exist, and we love the existence and the knowledge we have. I, on the other hand, use the argument to show that this *I* that is thinking is *an immaterial substance* with no bodily element. These are two very different things.[5]

The opposition stands out all the more clearly when one considers the entire context of the Augustinian argument, as Descartes says he has done. What does *De Civitate Dei XI* aim to accomplish? Against the Manicheans and Origen, it aims to establish that the world, even in the economy of the fall, remains intrinsically good and that it keeps an image of the Trinity. This image is also recognized in man, even in the state of sin: "We do indeed recognize in ourselves (*nos quidem in nobis . . . agnoscimus*) an image of God, that is of the Supreme trinity. It is not an adequate image, but a very distant parallel. It is not co-eternal and, in brief, it is not of the same substance as God. For all that there is nothing in the whole of God's creation so near to him in nature." To this prologue, there corresponds the conclusion: "Now we are human beings, created in our Creator's image."[6] Between these two texts, the argumen-

---

5. Respectively *To Mersenne,* 25 May 1637 (AT I, 376, 20–21 = not included in PW), and *To Colvius,* 14 November 1640 (AT III, 247, 4–248, 1 = PW III, 159 [Descartes' italics]).

6. *De Civitate Dei* XI, 26 then 28; pp. 112–13 and 122–23 [English trans., p. 459 then 463]. The other important Augustinian reference proposed to Descartes, *De Trinitate* X, 10, 14–16, also organizes its demonstration around the constitution of a triad (memory,

tation intends to construct in man three terms liable to be recognized *ad imaginem Dei:* Being, knowing that one is, loving that one is. Self-certainty thus leads self-consciousness back to the inner consciousness of God, which is found to be more essential to consciousness than itself. For the *si fallor, sum* does not aim at the *ego,* nor does it come to a halt in the *res cogitans,* seeing as the *interior intimo meo* transports it, as a derived image, toward the original *exemplar.* The *si fallor, sum* remains the simple, though first, moment of a path that, in two other *more* rich moments (knowing one's Being and loving it), disappropriates the mind from itself by the movement of reappropriating it to its original, God. The *si fallor, sum* does not assure the mind of having its principle in itself, since it does not grant it Being in itself nor saying itself by itself (like substance). On the contrary, *si fallor sum* forbids the mind to remain in itself, exiled from its truth, in order to send it back to the infinite original. The mind is retrieved only insofar as it is exceeded. Saint Augustine does not use the certainty of Being that thought assures in order to set up the mind as a ground, but to convince it that it bears the traces of a prior image, the sole ground, one that is intimately other than it. Certainty refers the mind to a distant ground, far from setting it up as a principle subsisting in itself. Descartes can therefore rightly judge that Saint Augustine's intention and his own "are two very different things." In effect, by means of the certainty of Being that thought secures for what from now on has become an ego, Descartes aims "to show that this *I* which is thinking is an *immaterial subsistence.*" What is at stake, then, is not found simply in the connection of thought and existence, however certain this connection might be. That the mind thinks, therefore that it is insofar as it thinks—this belongs to an inference that is if not banal (*hoc tritum*), at least quite commonplace. What is peculiar to Descartes consists, as he so lucidly indicates, in interpreting the certain and necessary connection of the *cogitatio* and existence as establishing a substance, and moreover a substance that plays the role of first principle. Just as the connection between the two notions is "in itself . . . such a simple and natural thing that it could have occurred to any writer," its interpretation as knowledge *omnium certissima et evidentissima* (AT VII, 25, 18 = PW II, 17) requires a daring and resolute theoretical operation. Pascal, however often he might be polemical in his opposition to Descartes, does not condemn him for this:

---

intelligence, will; ibid., n. 18, op. cit., pp. 154–55), which establishes the soul in ". . . impar imago . . . sed tamen imago [an inadequate image, . . . yet an image]" of the divine essence (ibid., n. 19, loc. cit., pp. 156–57 [English trans., p. 143]).

I should like to ask fair-minded people whether . . . *I think therefore I am*
[is] in effect the same in the mind of Descartes and in the mind of Saint
Augustine[,] who said the same thing twelve hundred years earlier. Indeed,
I am far from saying that Descartes was not [the] real author, even if he
learned [it] only by reading this great saint; for I know what a difference
there is between writing a word by chance, without longer and extended
reflection on it, and noting in this word an admirable chain of consequences that prove the distinction between material and spiritual nature,
and make of it a firm principle supported by an entire system of physics,
as Descartes claimed he was doing.[7]

According to Pascal, Descartes' original contribution does *not* consist in
advancing the proposition "I think, therefore I am," or "cogito, sum,"
but in interpreting it as the discovery of a first principle—Descartes will
even say, of a substance. The search for precursors remains legitimate
and fruitful, but, concerning what is essentially at stake, empty. What is
important does not reside in the statement itself, but in the dignity of
principle that the metaphysical interpretation accords to it for the first
time with Descartes. With the methodological assurance of an experimental scientist, Pascal indicates the decisive distinction: one must not
confuse the primal utterance, which registers the intellectual effect "I
think, therefore I am," "cogito sum," with the theoretical interpretation
that eventually sets it up as a first principle in a substance. The first belongs to empirical experience (here, that of thought), the second to theory—here metaphysics.

This distinction sheds light on the various attempts to attribute precursors to the *cogito*. It is as easy to spot approximations of the primal
utterance, as it is difficult, indeed unwise, to interpret it in the same way
each time. In several cases, the primal utterance can be seen to explicitly
refuse the (metaphysical) interpretation that would set it up as first principle. This is the—exemplary—case with Aristotle. In order to show that
a friend's life is as precious to us as is our own, Aristotle mentions as if in
passing, while following a complex line of argumentation, the following
primal utterance: "if he who sees perceives (αἰσθάνεται) that he sees,
the one who hears, that he hears, and he who walks, that he walks, and

---

7. Pascal, *De l'art de persuader,* in *Œuvres complètes,* ed. L. Lafuma, p. 358 [English
trans., p. 209] (see *Pensées,* L. 696/B. 22). Descartes advanced this argument in a fragment
of his early writings (AT X, 204, 6–15 = not included in PW) without however referring
to "cogito ergo sum." Interpreting it as a *principle* does indeed date from Descartes (AT
IV, 444, 23–25 = PW III, 290: "The first principle is *that our soul exists* because there is
nothing whose existence is better known to us"; AT IX-2, 10, 4–5; AT VI, 32, 18–23; etc. =
PW I, 184; PW I, 127; etc.), and Pascal here cites him to the letter.

in the case of all other activities similarly there is something which perceives (αἰσθανόμενον) that we are active, then accordingly, we perceive
that we perceive, and we think that we think (νοῶμεν, ὅτι νοοῦμεν); and
this is what it is to perceive or to think that we exist (τὸ δ᾽ ὅτι αἰσθανό-
μεθα ἢ νοοῦμεν, ὅτι ἐσμέν) for existence was defined as perceiving or
thinking (τὸ γὰρ εἶναι ἦν αἰσθάνεσθαι)."[8] Thinking that one thinks
amounts to thinking that one is; for in order to think one must be. Aristotle here speaks almost word for word as does Descartes. Why doesn't
the Aristotelian version of the primal utterance lead to a metaphysical
interpretation of the *ego*? Would the self-reflection of thought be forbidden? Not at all. Its truth is well and truly acknowledged:

> For the thinkable implies that there is thought of it, but the thought is not
> relative to that of which it is the thought; for we should then have said the
> same thing twice. Similarly, sight is the sight of something, not of that of
> which it is the sight (though of course it is true to say this, καίτοι γ᾽ ἀληθὲς
> τοῦτο εἰπεῖν); in fact, it is relative to color.[9]

For Aristotle, the vision of vision—which Descartes will record by interpreting it radically as *cogitatio*: ". . . cum videam, sive (quod jam non
distinguo) cum cogitem me videre [when I see, or think I see (I am not
here distinguishing the two)] . . ." (AT VII, 33, 12–13 = PW II, 22)—is
neither illusory nor false, ἀληθές. Aristotle neither ignores nor contests
a thought of thought that leads reflective and redoubled thought to think
itself as a being. Why, once again, doesn't he pursue this thought all the
way to the metaphysical interpretation of an *ego*? For precisely a metaphysical reason: thought (just like sensation) falls into the category of
relation (πρός τι), without however involving one of its characteristic
properties, correlation. Relative terms are, in general, relative reciprocally and each to the other. But if thought, like sensation, is relative to
things known and sensed, the inverse is not true: the known or the sensed
precedes knowledge and sensation; better, the former remain without

---

8. *Nicomachean Ethics* IX, 9, 1170 *a* 29–1170 *b* 1 [English trans., p. 1849]. It does not
seem out of hand to suppose that this text gave birth to and supported Gassendi's objection, an objection that has until now been as misunderstood as its reputation is famous:
AT VII, 258, 23*ff.* and 352, 1–18 = PW II, 180 and 244 (examined again in *Principia Philosophiae* I, §9).

9. *Metaphysics* Δ, 15, 1021 *a* 31–*b* 2 [English trans., p. 1613]. For other antecedents of
the Cartesian form of the conventional statement, see E. Bréhier, "Une forme archaïque
du 'Cogito ergo sum,'" *Revue philosophique* 1943/2; P.-M. Schul, "Y a-t-il une source aris-
totélicienne du 'Cogito'?" *Revue philosophique* 1948/1.

the latter, but not the latter without the former. In short, knowledge in all its states can and must be put into operation only in relation to prior things: "as a rule it is of actual things already existing that we acquire knowledge, προϋπαρχόντων τῶν πραγμάτων."[10] Or also: "The view that neither the objects of sensation nor the sensations would exist is doubtless true ... but that the ὑποκείμενα which cause the sensation should not exist even apart from sensation is impossible."[11] Thought cannot intend itself any more than sensation can, because, not existing in terms of the category οὐσία but in terms of the nonreciprocal πρός τι, it depends on other πράγματα, which are fully (ὑπάρχειν), in advance, as ὑποκείμενα, thus in the mode of οὐσία. Thought can think only an οὐσία; therefore, it cannot think itself, since it remains a simple relation and since οὐσία is defined by, among other characteristics, its absolute difference from relation. "Evidently knowledge and perception and opinion and understanding have always something else as their object, and themselves only by the way (αὐτῆς δ᾽ ἐν παρέργῳ)."[12] According to its Aristotelian interpretation, the primal utterance, whose Cartesian interpretation results in a substance, enables one to reach only a παρέργον—an appendix, an aside, an affair in the margins of the main business, a second degree ἔργον to one side of the ἐνέργεια. For according to Aristotle what is essential answers to the most ancient and most often missing question, τις ἡ οὐσία. But thought does not constitute an οὐσία; on the contrary, it is constituted by the οὐσία that it intends. Committed to the search for οὐσία, it does not have to be thought, much less interpreted, as an οὐσία. Descartes, in contrast, transgresses the Aristotelian interdiction—certainly not when he records a primal utterance that Aristotle had already broached, but when, in reading it, he endeavors to interpret thought as an οὐσία. Aristotle and Descartes are not divided over the primal utterance; they are divided only over whether or not to accord the dignity of οὐσία to thought. Does thought depend on an οὐσία other than it, or is it by itself accomplished in an οὐσία? The answer puts into question the general doctrine of all knowing. Either knowing is governed by the essence of the beings under consideration in each case (to each genus there would therefore correspond a different science) precisely because, in the relation between thought and the thing thought, there is only a single

---

10. *Categories* 7, 7 *b*, 24–25 [English trans., p. 12] (see our analysis of this text and its relation to the *Regulae* in *Sur l'ontologie grise . . .* , §14, 90–92).

11. *Metaphysics* Γ, 5, 1010 *b* 32–35 [English trans., p. 1596].

12. *Metaphysics* Λ, 9, 1074 *b* 35–37 [English trans., p. 1698].

οὐσία, that of the thing; accordingly, thought can be only by borrowing from the thing. Or else, knowing governs all beings as its object, because thought maintains priority in terms of Being as well as in terms of knowing; accordingly, the thing can be only by borrowing from the *mens,* which alone is assured of its beingness. Confronted with the same (or almost the same) primal utterance, Descartes and Aristotle stand apart in terms of their properly metaphysical doctrines of the beingness of beings. The question of the *ego cogito* is not played out in the observation of the experiential fact recorded in "cogito, sum," but in the possibility of reading in the "cogito sum" the emergence of an οὐσία. We discover here, with Aristotle, the same difference that arose between Descartes and Saint Augustine, where what was at stake was to be found in the act of interpreting the primal utterance either in view of a *mens* that is substantial or in view of one that is the image of the Trinity.

There is more: the two precursors can be seen as joining forces in opposing their common adversary. That is, if one considers the most common of the Aristotelian definitions of οὐσία, it will be noticed that this definition could not be applied to the human mind without resulting in a contradiction not only with the Aristotelian interpretation of the primal utterance, but also with its Augustinian interpretation. According to the treatise *Categories,* οὐσία (*substantia*) is defined by a twofold character:[13] remaining in itself and in nothing other (μὴ ἐν ὑποκειμένῳ τινί ἐστιν, *in se esse*), and being spoken about only in terms of itself and not in terms of an other (μὴ καθ᾽ ὑποκειμένου τινὸς λέγεται, *per se dici*). οὐσία is therefore determined by perfect autarky, in terms both of Being and of predication. In order to remain, which will always *stay* its duty and its ownmost trait, it has only to stay in itself and by itself. Descartes, in this a member of the Aristotelian tradition, appropriates the determination of *substantia* in terms of the autarky of subsistence. He defines it ". . . rem quae ita existit, ut nulla alia re indigeat ad existendum [a thing which exists in such a way as to depend on no other thing for its existence]" (*Principia I,* §51). Consequently, to interpret the primal utterance "cogito, sum" as the emergence of a substantial *ego* demands that this *ego* be thought as autarkic. It thus excludes the *ego* from the referential structure that is required by the Augustinian doctrine of the *imago Dei.* The only image that could be acceptable to the substantial *ego* would come from the gaze that it cognitively bears on itself for the purpose of leading the *cogitatio sui* back to the original (divine) gaze that is reflected in it. In this light, the two occurrences in the *Meditationes* of

13. *Categories* 5, 2 *a* 11–12.

the theme *imago Dei* seem well worth mentioning. *(a)* In the conclusion of *Meditatio III,* the theme is put forth quite clearly, and apparently in an Augustinian way: ". . . ex hoc uno quod Deus me creavit, valde credibile est me quodammodo ad imaginem et similitudinem ejus factum esse [The mere fact that God created me is a very strong basis for believing that I am somehow made in his image and likeness] . . ." (AT VII, 51, 18–20 = PW II, 35). But in what way and by what means is the image of God that, so to speak, absorbs the *ego* constituted? Answer: ". . . illamque similitudinem, in qua Dei idea continetur, a me percipi per eandem facultatem, per quam ego ipse a me percipior [That likeness, which includes the idea of God, is perceived by me through the same faculty by which I am perceived by myself]" (51, 21–23 = 35 [modified]). This means: the idea of God, to which the *imago Dei* amounts, is far from constituting the *ego* as its prior, immeasurable, and unrepresentable horizon; rather, the *imago Dei* is itself also constituted by the *cogitatio,* which, in "cogito, sum," reflexively secures its autarkic existence for itself. By a prodigious reversal, the *imago Dei* follows from the *ego,* far from transporting it outside itself into God. *(b)* In the conclusion of *Meditatio IV,* the theme reappears: ". . . adeo ut illa [voluntas, sive arbitrii libertas] praecipue sit, ratione cujus imaginem quandam et similitudinem Dei referre me intelligo [It is above all in virtue of the will (that is, free choice) that I understand myself to bear in some way the image and likeness of God]" (57, 13–14 = 40). The *ego* therefore bears the image of God's likeness in it, or more exactly in a faculty, the will. Wouldn't the will owe this privilege to its referring to the corresponding perfection of God? On the contrary, it is because I already experience the will to be "tantam in me . . . ut nullius majoris ideam apprehendam [in me . . . that I apprehend the idea which has nothing greater than it]" (57, 12–13 = 40 [modified]). Thus it is because the will is already seen to be perfect in me, that I find the image of God in the *ego.* The will signifies the image of God in the *ego* not because it would transport it toward the infinite, but, on the contrary, because it already attests an actual infinite. It therefore confirms the autarky of the *ego.* In both cases, far from making the *ego* depend on God to the point that it would be denied the status of substance, the *imago Dei* serves rather to reinforce the autarky of the *ego.*[14] Aristotle and Saint Augustine, either by refusing to grant thought

14. For a more complete examination of this theme, see *Sur la théologie blanche . . . ,* §17, pp. 396ff. Some of the conclusions drawn by these analyses should be revised, since they do not give a good enough indication of the *ego*'s autarky. The discontinuity, even here, between God and the *ego* was forcefully indicated by H. U. von Balthasar, *Herrlichkeit,* III/1, *Im Raum der Metaphysik* (Einsiedeln, 1965), p. 797.

the status of οὐσία, or by transporting it toward the *imago Dei,* offer in advance a sort of common front opposing Descartes. For all that, however, they do not contest the primal utterance, but assume it and interpret it. Their opposition is addressed only, and in advance, to the Cartesian interpretation of the statement as the emergence, in the *ego,* of a first principle.

Descartes establishes his originality, and above all his point of origin, only by interpreting the "cogito, sum" as the "first principle of the philosophy I was seeking" (AT VI, 32, 23 = PW I, 127). What is proper to principles is found in their many-faceted primacy—in terms of beings, in terms of time, and above all, for Descartes, in terms of knowledge, since "the knowledge of other things must depend on them, in the sense that the principles must be capable of being known without knowledge of these other matters, but not *vice versa*" (AT IX-2, 2, 23–25 = PW I, 179–80). The *ego* therefore can be known—then be—without the οὐσία of the things to be known, and without God, "unica tantum [substantia]" (*Principia I,* §51), whose image it nonetheless bears. All Cartesian interpretation of the primal utterance tends toward a single end: how to pass from "cogito, sum" to the *ego,* first principle and fully constituted substance? The difficulty of such a theoretical leap can be spotted through the opposed interpretations of the same statement. It is also witnessed in the long delay during which Descartes, though he had approached the primal utterance quite early, hesitated to see in it the interpretation that it could support. In short, Descartes was late in recognizing the metaphysical dignity of "cogito, sum" because it depends not on an observation but on a hermeneutic. Let us consider, quickly, the steps in this delay to interpretation. If the *Discourse on the Method* has already won what is essential to the metaphysical position of the *ego* (if not the farthest possible extension of doubt) when it concedes to it the titles "first principle" (AT VI, 32, 23 = PW I, 127) and "substance" (AT VI 33, 4 = PW I, 127), a delay of ten years was nevertheless necessary in order to fully arrive there. The *Regulae,* dating from the winter of 1627, bear witness to a strange and instructive predicament: they constantly mobilize—as simple (and therefore primal) natures—existence, doubt, and thought, without ever arriving at the decisive metaphysical utterance. Four occurrences bear witness to three occasions missed. *(a)* Doubt does indeed inaugurate a necessary connection, but, far from ending up at the existence of what enacts this doubt, it arrives only at the certainty of doubt itself. *Ego* barren of a literally nonexistent *cogito,* Socrates collapses thought into the certainty of itself, without passing beyond the certainty of thought and heading toward the certainty of existence: ". . . si Socrates dicit se dubitare de omnibus, hinc necessario sequitur: ergo hoc saltem intelligit, quod dubitat [If, for example, Socrates says that he doubts everything, it necessarily follows that he understands at least that he is doubting]" (AT X, 421, 19–21 = PW I, 46); and again:

> . . . de ipsa ignorantia, sive potius dubitatione Socratis quaestio fuit, cum primum ad illam conversus Socrates coepit inquirere, an verum esset se de omnibus dubitare, atque hoc ipsum asseruit. [Socrates posed a problem about his own ignorance, or rather doubt: when he became aware of his doubt, he began to ask whether it was true that he was in doubt about everything, and his answer was affirmative.] [432, 24–27 = PW I, 53.]

Thought enters into a necessary connection with certainty, but without attaining existence. *(b)* By contrast, in other places, a necessity can be accorded to existence, draw its origin from thought—however, from thought in the aspect of doubt, not of another existence already presupposed. Thought functions only as a middle term between two existences. The necessity of the connection therefore remains partial, precisely because it rests on the existences thus brought together, and not on thought: ". . . ut quamvis ex eo quod sim, certo concludam Deum esse, non tamen ex eo quod Deus sit, me etiam existere licet affirmare [Thus from the fact that I exist I may conclude with certainty that God exists, but from the fact that God exists I cannot legitimately assert that I too exist]" (422, 3–6 = 46). From the point of view of the *Meditationes,* this conclusion would appear totally erroneous: if I think that God is, I must also conclude that I am, since, if I am not, it is still I who thinks it; therefore, in order to think that I am not (and that God is), it is necessary that I think, thus that I be as thought thinking my own nonexistence. But at the time of the *Regulae,* thought remains a simple means of access to existence, without itself existing as thought—it lacks the status of substance. *(c)* Existence and thought can encounter one another, however, and even in conjunction with the *intuitus.* Nevertheless, this encounter is never accomplished in a *sum* because its terms still remain simply juxtaposed, without being structured logically: ". . . uniusquisque animo potest intueri, se existere, se cogitare, triangulum terminari tribus lineis tantum [Anyone can mentally intuit that he exists, that he is thinking, that a triangle is bounded by just three lines] . . ." (368, 21–23 = PW I, 14). A remarkable text in many ways. First of all, in it, the component parts of the future demonstration of the mind's irreducibility to extension appear exactly on the same footing as extension. Instead of distinguishing the substances, the indifferent enumeration confuses them. Second, the lack of a distinction of the enumerated terms does not call for a particular gaze, but any gaze whatsoever (". . . uniusquisque animo potest intueri [anyone can intuit] . . . ," 368, 21–22 = 14). In 1640, this will still characterize the Augustinian formula (". . . which could have occurred to any writer . . ." AT III, 248, 4 = PW III, 159). In effect, the simple juxtaposition of some simple natures, without arranging them according to the order, does not require any particular speculative attention. Third, it seems that the terms juxtaposed here could just as easily have reached the metaphysical formulation, since what will assume the title *ego/Je* already governs them explicitly. The *Regulae* do not see thought as merely lying alongside existence, but indeed ". . . *se* existere, *se* cogitare . . . ," where the reflexive refers to the remarkable priority of ". . . animo intueri [intuiting with the mind] . . ." (368, 22 = 14 [modified]). In other words, the *cogitatio* does not show up here as just one simple nature among others; it is already at work as the essential reflexive operator in which the *ego*'s primacy over the *cogitatio,* as well as over existence, is fixed. *Uniusquisque animo potest intueri . . . se cogitare* confirms in advance the celebrated and wrongly contested formalization of the *cogito, sum* as, at base, a *cogito me cogitare.*[15] Literally, the *cogitatio* as thinking thought first thinks thought thought in a reflex arc whose reflection designates precisely the *ego.* The arc of reflection is not closed, however, since it does not connect existence to the *cogitatio* in the nodal singularity of an *ego.* The *ego* does not conclude the first stages of an inference because it is not set up on its own at the origin of such an inference. It lacks the status of a principle. In this way, the two criteria that, in his own eyes, distinguish Descartes' undertaking from that of Saint Augustine (and of Aristotle), namely that *cogito, sum* qualifies the *ego/I* as a principle and as a substance, also mark the stages in Descartes' own thought (or nonthought) of the *ego* of the "cogito, sum." The debates about the development of Cartesian doubt and its domain, for example between 1637 and 1641, as well as about its diverse logical and textual formulations, are certainly important. But they should not hide an incomparably more essential divide—that between, on the one hand, the epistemological use of the simple natures *cogitatio, intuitus, existentia* without a fundamental coordination because without fixity by and for

---

15. Heidegger, *Nietzsche II,* pp. 148–68 [English trans., pp. 102–18]. For other references, see our note on "Heidegger et la situation métaphysique de Descartes," *Bulletin cartésien* IV, *Archives de Philosophie* 38/2 (1975).

the *ego* (in the *Regulae*), and, on the other hand, winning the *ego*, according to the joining of existence and the reflexive arc of the *cogitatio*, as absolutely autarkic substance and as radically first principle (1641, but also 1637). This divide reveals a trench that is all the deeper and therefore all the more hidden from the eyes of the critic, since it separates not only Descartes from his predecessors, but also Descartes from Descartes himself.

Thus the *ego's* attainment of an authentic, metaphysical status does not depend on spotting this or that primal utterance, such as "I think therefore I am" or "cogito, sum." It depends on an interpretation that is itself metaphysical, and whose terms can be suggested by the debate between Aristotle, Saint Augustine, and Descartes: does the *ego*, as thinking, reach the rank of substance or that of first principle, both determinations agreeing in that they ascribe to it a unique autarky? The gap, which Pascal indicates quite clearly, between primal utterance and interpretation, between *hoc tritum* and something established metaphysically—can this gap be crossed, and if so, how is this interpretation to be legitimated? This line of questioning is itself subdivided into two questions. *(a)* Which criteria will govern the interpretation of the primal utterance? Saint Augustine adopts a Trinitarian, therefore a theological, criterion. Descartes indicates clearly enough that he rejects this, by invoking a substance for the *ego*. Does he in that way rejoin Aristotle, who interprets the primal utterance in terms of οὐσία? No, since οὐσία is forbidden to the mind that merely relates to it without reaching it. It remains then that the *ego* decides its own identity, for Descartes, according to οὐσία understood as substance. This would imply that its metaphysical status is played out in the possible or impossible equivalence of *ego* and substantiality, according to the mediation of the *cogitatio*. This equivalence, only presumed up until now—can it be enacted? In other words, can we actually produce, starting from the lead it provides, the event that is recorded in the primal utterance? And in this case, by what right can we privilege this unique interpretation? *(b)* The conventional statement uses two verbs, and implies a single subject, *ego*. In the metaphysical interpretation, it is a question of giving a purely metaphysical status to this *ego*. But does it accede to it? And if it does, does it do so totally? This means not only: can the *ego* become totally metaphysical? but also: he who thinks and exists in the guise of the *ego*, namely this man—is he exhausted in such a metaphysical role? In short, between the individual, who is nothing but human, and the *ego*, which aims to be nothing but metaphysical, is there a perfect overlap? These two questions are directed toward a single point: namely, the transition from thought to being, as the manifestation of the ownmost beingness (essence) of this being who is only in thinking, and therefore who, in thinking, uncovers a way of Being of beings.

§12. The Undetermined Equivalence of Being and Thought

The metaphysical interpretation of the primal utterance "cogito, sum," an interpretation demonstrating that the *ego* holds the rank of substance and first principle, is not self-evident, first because Descartes never produced it: either on account of its difficulty being too great (it supposes a concept of metaphysics, its essence and its limits, something a metaphysics cannot attain), or by virtue of its evidence being too great (it is self-evident that every first certainty would have a metaphysical validity). But the demonstration is missing above all because Descartes' general metaphysical intention is hedged about with cautions. Even if the titles (chapter I) and the constitution (chapter II) attest to a metaphysical enterprise, the status of the *ego* of the "cogito, sum" is still susceptible of being withdrawn from metaphysics, in favor of an epistemological or theological function. Moreover, it could happen that the primal utterance never attains the rank of a principle and records only an empirical assertion—this is what Kant reduces it to: ". . . the problematic idealism of Descartes, which holds that there is only one empirical assertion that is indubitably certain, namely that 'I am.'"[16] If the ego assured only its own existence, empirically or even *a priori,* it would in no way attain the dignified rank of a principle, since a principle has as its function to determine other existences made possible by its own. What is more, if the *ego* assured only its own existence, it would still leave its essence undetermined, as in the reproach that Heidegger has leveled against Descartes: "With the '*cogito sum*' Descartes had claimed that he was putting philosophy on a new and firm footing. But what he left undetermined when he began in this 'radical' way, was the kind of Being which belongs to the *res cogitans,* or—more precisely—the *meaning of the Being of the 'sum.'*"[17] If the *ego* does not attain an essence, it cannot be posed as a substance and thereby exhibit the ontology that a metaphysics requires. In order to succeed in attaining a metaphysical status, the *ego* must satisfy requirements that are so strict that it appears problematic

---

16. Kant, *Kritik der reinen Vernunft,* B 274 [English trans., p. 244].
17. Heidegger, *Sein und Zeit,* §6, pp. 24, 19–22 [English trans., p. 46].

that it could ever succeed in doing so. If Kant and Heidegger have contested it, can one still reasonably expect to make a case for it?

But the *ego* that is at play in the primal utterance "cogito, sum" could not shirk its metaphysical functions unless they already characterized it as intrinsic requirements. In short, the *ego* could not be missing from metaphysics if, by right, it did not already belong to it. Consequently, Kant and Heidegger still stigmatize its insufficiencies from a metaphysical point of view. As for the task of positively stating the metaphysical status of the *ego,* it again falls to the thinkers of metaphysics—they alone have good enough access to the essence of metaphysics to recognize its authentic figures among their predecessors. And in fact, metaphysicians have not hesitated to accord a metaphysical status to the *ego* by drawing out the significance of its primal utterance. "Cogito sum" records the experience of the equivalence between thought and Being in a *subjectum,* the *ego.* On this point, one must call to mind the agreement of three philosophers who, in everything else, are divided over what is essential. *(a)* First, Hegel. As early as the *Phenomenology of Spirit,* when he intends to overcome the conflict between materialism and idealism in the *Aufklärung,* Hegel fixes the terms of what will be his abiding interpretation of the Cartesian *ego:*

> They [the two parties to the conflict] have not arrived at the Cartesian concept of metaphysics (*zum Begriffe der Cartesianischen Metaphysik*), that Being and thought are, *in themselves,* the same; they have not arrived at the thought that Being, *pure* Being is not something *concretely real* but a *pure abstraction,* and conversely, pure thought, self-identity or essence, partly is the *negative* of self-consciousness (*Selbstbewusstseyn*) and therefore *Being (Seyn)* partly, as immediately simple, is likewise nothing else but *Being (Seyn); thought* is *thinghood (Dingheit)* or *thinghood* is *thought* (*Dingheit ist Denken*).[18]

In the long exposition that the *Lectures on the History of Philosophy* will devote to Descartes some twenty years later, when Hegel wants to illustrate the definition that "metaphysics is what reaches after substance," he will retrieve the same interpretation of the conventional statement: "The determination of Being is in my 'I'; this connection is itself the first matter. Thought as Being and Being as thought—that is my certainty, 'I'; [this is] the celebrated *cogito ergo sum.*" The utterance must be inter-

---

18. Hegel, *Phänomenologie des Geistes,* GW, vol. 9, op. cit., p. 313 [English trans., p. 352 (modified)].

preted as recording the experience, concerned with a particular fact, of the universal principle of the "unity of Being and thought," a principle with which "we for the first time begin to consider his metaphysics."[19] Cartesian thought becomes metaphysical when the "cogito sum" reveals the identity of Being and thought. *(b)* On this point at least, Schelling agrees with Hegel: "Descartes wanted therefore to find a point where thought or representation (for he does not distinguish the two) and Being immediately coincide—and this he thought he had found through his *cogito ergo sum.* . . . In the *cogito ergo sum,* Descartes thought he had recognized thought and Being as immediately identical."[20] To be sure, as for Hegel, for Schelling the fundamental principle of all metaphysical modernity—the identity of Being and thought—will find its Cartesian accomplishment only in the ontological argument, where the two terms are in play under the sign of the absolute. Nevertheless, the fundamental principle is laid bare as soon as the primal utterance of the *ego* is put forth, and the *ego* thus accedes to a metaphysical rank. *(c)* Feuerbach, several years later and in an entirely different context, offers a quite similar interpretation. In 1833, putting the concept of spirit to the fore, he posits that *"the essence of the mind* is *consciousness (Bewusstsein),* the mind is nothing but consciousness *(Bewusstsein),* nothing but the 'cogito ergo sum,' that is to say the *immediate unity of my thought and my Being,* the essence of my self as mind, or my essence, and in that way

19. Hegel, *Vorlesungen über die Geschichte der Philosophie,* Jubileum Ausgabe, Bd. 19, respectively pp. 331, 339, and 345 [English trans., pp. 220, 228, and 233]. See *Enzyklopädie* (1830), §76 [English trans., p. 122], concerning "the beginning which this philosophy made in modern times as the Cartesian philosophy" with "the simple inseparability of the thought and Being of the thinker—*cogito ergo sum.*" In a supplement to §64, Hegel cites the dissertation of his student H. G. Hotho, *De Philosophia Cartesiana* (Berlin, 1826), a work that is mediocre enough. Hegel mentions in particular the discussion of the "cogito, sum," which retains nothing from the teachings of the master. Concerning the Hegelian reading of Descartes, see J.-L. Marion, "Hegel et le concept de la métaphysique cartésienne," in *Recherches hégéliennes* (CRDHM, Université de Poitiers) 16 (1982): 10*ff*, and B. Bourgeois, "Hegel et Descartes," in *Etudes philosophiques* 2 (1985): 225*ff.*

20. *Zur Geschichte der neueren Philosophie (Münchener Vorlesungen), Sämtliche Werke,* ed. Cotta/Schröter, Bd. X, p. 9 [English trans., p. 46]. This acknowledgment of the fundamental utterance has all the more weight when one notices, with J.-F. Marquet, that "Schelling here attributes to Descartes the formulae of his own System of transcendental idealism: 'Find a point where the object (*Objekt*) and its concept, the object (*Gegenstand*) and its representation are originally . . . one' (*SW,* vol. III, p. 20)." Is this the reason for the strange note claiming that ". . . Cartesius in Bayern zu philosophieren augefangen [hat]," and that "dieser Anfang der völlig freien Philosophie allem Ansehen nach in Bayern gemacht, hier als der Grund der neueren Philosophie gelegt worden" (ibid.)? See J.-F. Marquet, "Schelling et Descartes," *Etudes philosophiques* 1985/2: 237*ff.*

thought itself[,] which is at the same time unmediated, my self-certainty, the immediate affirmation of myself." The Erlangen courses, in 1835–36, will further extend the interpretation:

> I think—for distinguishing is thinking (*Denken*)—(thinking is my *essence*—for I cannot abstract myself from it without ceasing to be), I am mind and this *Being-mind* is my indubitably certain Being. The indubitable reality (*Realität*) of the mind— but not as proclamation, as dogma, in contrast as an actual act, as this *act* of thinking by which I am different from everything sensible and grasp myself in this difference and am certain of myself, conscious of myself—, this is the *principle of philosophy.*[21]

Metaphysics comes to possess its principle only when thought is immediately accomplished as Being. This interpretation of the statement "cogito sum" remains valid and is held in common with Schelling and Hegel, even though it no longer rests on a system of identity or a science of absolute spirit. At issue then is the principle presupposed by *all* the metaphysics of modernity. *(d)* Nietzsche confirms it *a contrario* by deconstructing the metaphysical interpretation of the Cartesian statement. In his view, it does not ground the existence of the *ego* but presupposes it:

> "There is thinking; therefore there is something that thinks (*ein Denkendes*)": this is the upshot of all Descartes' argumentation. But that means positing as "true *a priori*" our belief in the concept of substance—that when there is thought there has to be something "that thinks" is simply a formulation of our grammatical custom that adds a doer to every deed. In short, this is not merely the substantiation of a fact but a logical-metaphysical postulate. —Along the lines followed by Descartes one does not come upon something absolutely certain but only upon the fact of a very strong belief.[22]

The criticism, admirably to the point, confirms our investigation on several levels. It shows first of all that "cogito, sum" remains a simple primal utterance, one that does not affirm any thesis and does not state any

21. Feuerbach, respectively *Geschichte der neueren Philosophie von Bacon von Verulam bis Benedikt Spinoza,* ed. W. Schuffenhauer, *Gesammelte Werke,* Bd. 2 (Berlin, 1968), p. 263, and *Vorlesungen über die Geschichte der neueren Philosophie,* ed. C. Ascheri and E. Ties (Darmstadt, 1974), p. 59.

22. Nietzsche, *Wille zur Macht,* §484 [English trans., p. 268]. The text closes by denouncing the very equivalence that Hegel, Schelling, and Feuerbach hailed between Being and thought: "What Descartes desired was that thought (*Gedanke*) should have, not an *apparent* reality (*Realität*), but a reality *in itself*" [English trans., p. 268].

principle. Next, it indicates that the transition to the concept of substance requires an interpretation, here qualified as a "grammatical cus-
tom," which is no minor thing for Nietzsche. Finally, it shows that the
Cartesian interpretation mobilizes nothing less than the concept of substance, which—a remarkable coincidence!—is equivalent to a metaphysical postulate. Nietzsche therefore confirms the terms of the debate
at the very moment when he challenges its most widely accepted solution: the *ego* accedes to the metaphysical status of a first principle in the
exact degree to which the primal utterance "cogito, sum" is interpreted
as the identification of thought and Being, or as the deduction of substance by thought, or as the reconduction of substance to thought. Substance here does not allude to the classical debate about the "substantia-
tion" of the subject in Descartes. In this polemic, substance arises from
a trivial interpretation of οὐσία as ὑποκείμενον, *substratum,* suppositum,
thus ultimately matter. In contrast, here, substance is understood as οὐσία in the sense of *Wesen, Seiendheit,* beingness of beings. From now on,
the question is formulated as follows: how, on the basis of the thought
operative in the figure of the *ego* in "cogito sum," can a doctrine of substance be formulated? In other words, how can the *ego* constitute an ontology?

The *ego* affirms its claims to Being right away, if one admits the letter
of the formula that replaces the primal utterance in the *Meditationes*—
namely "Ego sum, ego existo [I am, I exist]" (AT VII, 25, 12 = PW II,
17). This new primal utterance is surprising for three reasons of increas-
ing importance. *(a)* Being is understood immediately as existence. *(b)*
The *ego* is established in an immediate relation with Being understood
as existence, without any apparent middle term. *(c)* In contrast to the
ordinary version of the primal utterance "cogito sum," the third part, the
cogitatio, is missing, and this marks an exception unique to the *Meditationes.* From these three characteristics, one conclusion in particular
seems to follow: the *ego* constitutes an ontology immediately, without
the assistance of the *cogitatio.* This conclusion, as natural as it seems,
nonetheless leads to a misreading of the text. To understand why, it is
necessary to reconsider the three characteristics in inverse order. *(c)* It
seems that, in the new conventional statement, "Ego sum, ego existo,"
the mediation of the *cogitatio* does not intervene. In fact, the inverse is
true: thought plays a more essential role in the statement that does not
mention it than it does in that which does mention it. In the second case,
thought is registered in the statement, thus represented as a thought
thought (*cogitatio cogitata*). I think the conventional statement "cogito

sum," which, by including thought among what it observes, transforms it into a thought object, one at the same rank as the other objects of the observation (*sum, ergo,* indeed *ego*). Paradoxically, mentioning thought in the statement amounts to devaluing it; but mentioning it is possible only in a statement. Therefore, if it is not to be devalued, it must be excluded from the statement. This aporia is at once transformed into an opening: if thought is not to be mentioned as a thought thought (*cogitatio cogitata*), this is because it must actually be practiced as a thinking thought (*cogitatio cogitans*). The *ego* accomplishes nothing else but this: its thought, in the act of putting forth (*profertur,* 25, 12 = 17) the performative statement (*pronuntiatum,* 25, 11–12 = 17), sets itself to work as thinking (*mente concipitur,* 25, 13). And in the very act of thinking the statement that excludes it, thought is accomplished by accomplishing its own existence. Thought, when it in fact thinks and thereby doubles its thoughts without including itself in them, attests to itself that it is: ". . . fieri plane non potest, cum videam, sive (quod jam non distinguo) cum cogitem me videre, ut ego ipse cogitans non aliquid sim [When I see, or think I see (I am not here distinguishing the two), it is simply not possible that I who am now thinking am not something]" (33, 11–14 = 22). *Ego ipse cogitans* ends up as *aliquid sum:* myself, I am something insofar as I am thinking. The *ego cogitans* must not be understood as a subject, endowed in addition with the property of thinking, in short as a *res per se apta ad cogitandum* (according to the model of 44, 22–23 = 30), but as a *res* whose *esse* is accomplished and exhausted in the act of thinking. *Ego cogitans* must be understood verbally, in the present participle thus the active of the frequentative *cogitare:* the *ego* in the process of thinking and which, in this sense only, is. The *ego* comes into existence only by the mediation of the *cogitatio* (". . . haec sola a me divelli nequit [This alone is inseparable from me]," 27, 8 = 18), but this *cogitatio* is void of the representation of the *ego* and existence, since it guarantees it. The *cogitatio* does not reach existence as *ego* by thinking itself, but by thinking the very act that it is thinking, and then only by thinking that this act implies a subject, the *ego,* which is. *(b)* Second, it seems that in the statement "Ego sum, ego existo," the *ego* enters into an immediate relation with Being understood as existence without the *cogitatio* securing even the least degree of mediation. In fact, the inverse is true: the *cogitatio* mediates this relation, since the *ego* is and exists only in the exact degree to which it is in fact thinking. The *cogitatio* mediates the relation of the *ego* to existence because it secures it conditionally. The conditionality of the *ego*'s existence is attested to first in terms of time: the *ego* is only as long as (*quamdiu,* 27, 10) and as often as (*quoties,* 25, 12) it is actually thinking (in short, ". . . ego, dum cogito, existam [I exist so long as I am thinking]" (145, 24–25 = 104). Negatively, the same limitation suspends the existence of the *ego* as soon as it stops thinking—in short ". . . si cessarem ab omni cogitatione, . . . illico totus esse desinem [Were I totally to cease from thinking, I should totally cease to exist]" (27, 11–12 = 18). Time, ever to be regained as presence, renders the *ego* contingent through and through, and demands that, at each instant, it use thought to lay hold of an existence that is strictly instantaneous. No doubt the *ego,* thinking thought, is assured of an existence, but an existence that time has eaten away, fragmented, and reduced to the point of rendering it contingent and caducous. Existing in accord with the temporal condition of thought, the *ego* thus exists only as thinking thought. The *ego* does not merely accede to existence *by* thought, but above all *as* thought, and nothing else. Its sole title to existing consists in thought. The *ego* is only insofar as it is thinking ". . . scio me, quatenus sum res quaedam cogitans, existere [I know that I exist in so far as I am a thinking thing]."[23] If thought alone cannot be "separated" (*divelli,* 27, 8 = 18) from the *ego,* the *ego* is by means of thought; better, it is as thought—to be sure not because it is in thought (*ens rationis*), but because it is through thought to the point of becoming identical with its own mode of Being: ". . . natura cogitans quae in me est, vel potius quae ego ipse sum [the thinking nature which is in me, or rather which I am] . . ." (59, 8–9 = 41). Outside of actual thought, no Being for the *ego.* In this way, the *cogitatio* does not merely offer a provisional mediation between the *ego* and existence, but in fact constitutes the definitive horizon of all existence attainable by the *ego.* (*a*) It could seem that Being is equivalent to existence straightaway. And lexically, this is the case—here for the *ego* ("Ego sum, ego existo" 25, 12; 27, 9 = 17; 18), elsewhere for God, who "is or exists" (DM 36, 30; 38, 19 = PW I, 129; 130).[24] So clear

---

23. *Meditatio IV,* 59, 5–6 = PW II, 41 [modified]. The term *quatenus* often qualifies the *res cogitans,* precisely because it sets the limits and conditions of its validity; see also 50, 28; 53, 7; 78, 16–17; 86, 2 = 35; 37; 54; 59. The same act of delimitation is performed by the phrase *nihil aliud quam,* which describes not only the piece of wax (31, 2 = 20), but also the *ego:* ". . . cum nihil aliud sim quam res cogitans [since I am nothing but a thinking thing] . . ." (49, 14–15 = 33), ". . . ego, qui nihil aliud sum quam res cogitans [I, who am nothing but a thinking thing] . . ." (81, 5–6 = 56). Likewise, "sum praecise tantum res cogitans [I am then in the strict sense only a thing that thinks]" (27, 13, see 29, 17–19 = 18 see 19) means: in delimiting exactly what I am to the exclusion of everything else (see 25, 22–24 = 17), there remains (*remanet*) only: *res cogitans.*

24. See above, chap. II, §6.

an equivalence, however, does not indicate that the meaning of "Being" is determined sufficiently. Quite to the contrary, the indetermination of "Being" here reaches its apex. First because the mere fact of setting up, with neither justification nor preparation, an equivalence between a notion as narrow as *existentia* and a concept as imprecise and as enigmatic as Being displays a profound unawareness of the very question of the meaning of Being. Next, the indetermination of "Being" is attested by the interrogation that the *ego,* henceforth being as existing, immediately provokes: "Sum autem res vera et vere existens; sed qualis res [I am a thing which is real and truly exists. But what kind of thing]? " (27, 15–16 = 18). Taken literally, this question amounts to asking τὶ ἔστιν, *quid sit*? after having answered εἰ ἔστιν, *an sit*? But through the mediation of a list of banal questions, it also asks what *res* can mean when it is reachable only within the limits of cognitive thought. The interrogation bears on the essence of the *res*—whose existence just now resulted from the *cogitatio*—but also, inseparably, on the meaning that "Being" or "Existing" can have now that they are no longer broached except by passing through the *cogitatio*. To such a radicalization of Descartes' explicit interrogation, it will be objected that the answer arrives at once: ". . . sed qualis res? Dixi, cogitans [But what kind of thing? As I have just said—a thinking thing]" (27, 16–17 = 18). But this answer only reinforces the question, far from annulling it; for to determine the *res* as *cogitans* redoubles the riddle of the meaning of its Being and its existence: if it is only as thinking, to qualify it as thinking does not add any determination to its mode of existence, nor does it clarify the meaning of its Being. Moreover, to qualify the *res* as *cogitans* amounts to redoubling the indetermination of the cognitive *an sit*? with the indetermination of the cognitive *quid sit*?—by which the original indetermination is raised to the next level. What does "Being" mean when Being is broached only by passing through, only on the basis of, and only within the horizon of the *cogitatio*? The slogan *esse est cogitari aut cogitare* solves nothing; it merely states the riddle, no doubt without even understanding it as a question.

Thus the equivalence of Being and thought that Hegel, Schelling, and Feuerbach attributed to Descartes and that Nietzsche's critique confirmed, can be verified so long as one sticks to the simple interpretation of the primal utterance "Ego sum, ego cogito." In other words, what is called the *cogito* receives its metaphysical interpretation as the equivalence of Being and thought only with the intervention of a third term that mediates it. This term has always been in play, though behind the scenes. It must henceforth be put to the fore. It is called: *ego.* The meaning of Being required by an authentic metaphysical interpretation of the primal utterance "cogito, sum" is determined only by means of the *ego.* The *ego* is given as being a being: ". . . ego aliquid sum [I am . . . something]" (27, 23 = 18), "ego ipse sum qui [I myself am the one who] . . ." (28, 25; see also 29, 5, 7, 11 = 19; see also 19); but as a being that asks itself about what it is: ". . . quaero quis sim ego ille quem novi [I ask what is this 'I' that I know]" (27, 28–29, see 25, 14 = 18 [modified], see 17). No doubt, it interrogates only its own way of Being; but as it by definition determines all other beings, it does not seem unthinkable to suppose that, through it, the meaning of Being in general might become accessible.

§13. The Egological Deduction of Substance

It falls to the *ego* to mediate the equivalence between thought and Being metaphysically, in that, on the one hand, it thinks, and on the other, it is; but above all, it accomplishes this mediation because it introduces a third term: itself, no longer as undetermined *res cogitans,* but as substance residing in itself, spoken of in terms of itself. What is identified vaguely in *Meditatio II* as "ego aliquid sum" (27, 23) is stated exactly as "ego autem substantia [sum]" (45, 7) in *Meditatio III.* The concept of substance's belated appearance in the order of reasons once again marks a decisive step. On our first reading, it relaunched, as if in a second beginning, the order of reasons, and contributed to making the transition from one figure of onto-theo-logy to the other.[25] But also at issue, alongside these ontic stakes, are stakes that one could call ontological. If, on the one hand, the primal utterance "cogito, sum" must be interpreted in view of the equivalence between thought and Being, and if, on the other hand, this equivalence remains undetermined so long as the mediating *ego* is not defined more precisely as a substance, then it must be inferred that with "ego autem substantia," there is at issue the general equivalence between thought and Being, thus the meaning of Being according to Descartes. The arising of *substantia* does not put into play merely the ontic status of the *ego,* but the meaning of Being in general for Cartesian onto-logy. Such an identification of what is at stake can be backed up only if one can establish that the Cartesian concept of substance is equivalent to the *ego,* both in privilege and in principality. Only on this condi-

25. See above, chap. II, §10.

tion will substance be able to take up as its own the mediation that the *ego* assures between thought and Being. Substance can be accorded to the *ego* intrinsically only by coming from it; the ontological pertinence of the concept of substance implies that it is deduced from the *ego,* and from it alone. Before being astonished by this still to be proven thesis— the egological deduction of substance—it must be noted that two authorities back it up. In the first place, Heidegger, who posits that "[Leibniz] like Descartes before him sees in the I, in the *ego cogito,* the dimension from which all the metaphysical concepts must be drawn." In particular if "in working out the problem [of substance] ontologically, Descartes is always far behind the schoolmen," to such a degree that he "[fails] to discuss the meaning of Being which the idea of substantiality embraces," this is because, more fundamentally, "he leaves the '*sum*' completely undiscussed."[26] In short, in claiming to think substance on the basis of the *ego,* Descartes would have transferred to substance as such the ontological indetermination of the meaning of the Being of the *sum,* thus of the *ego.* In the second place, Nietzsche, who, on this matter, anticipates Heidegger: "The concept of substance is a consequence of the concept of the subject: not the reverse!"[27] In effect, the all too classical debate about Descartes' substantialization of thought suffers from a radical indetermination: the concept of substance could indeed, for Descartes, borrow all its characteristics from the *ego,* which even before its own substantialization as *substantia cogitans* thoroughly governs the substantiality of *all* substances and imposes on them its own way of Being. Before the *ego* is substantialized, substance must be deduced from the *ego.* These two interpretations are confirmed by Descartes' text. If *substantia* first occurs in *Meditatio III* for the sake of constructing a proof for the existence of God, this text nevertheless mentions the "finitae substantiae" first (40, 20 = 28). For *substantia* is counted among the number of simple natures available to the *ego,* like shape, number, duration, etc. (43, 20 = 30). In this role, substance belongs among the notions that, in the first place, ". . . ab ipsa mei idea ipsius videor mutuari potuisse [it seems that I could have borrowed . . . from my idea of myself]" (44, 19–20 = 30). Substance is extracted as a loan that the *ego* makes to itself: As I am a substance, I can transfer (*transferre,* 45, 2) substance to other things—despite the difference in attributes (thought in my case,

26. Heidegger, respectively, *Aus der letzter Marburger Vorlesung, Wegmarken,* G. A., 9, p. 89; *Sein und Zeit,* §20, p. 93; §20, p. 93; §10, p. 46 [English trans., p. 126; p. 126; p. 72].
27. Nietzsche, *Wille zur Macht,* §485 [English trans., p. 268].

extension in the other) and in the name of a *ratio substantiae* intelligible to me because deduced from me. This transfer testifies that finite substance is first borrowed from the *ego,* the first substance, origin of all cognition and all recognition of other finite substances. It must not be objected that God alone offers substance par excellence, because infinite (*substantia infinita* 45, 21 = 31), and consequently that he should constitute this origin. For if the ontic argument concludes with the independent existence of the infinite substance (God) when it observes that a finite substance could not produce an infinite objective reality, it implies just as clearly that the *ego* remains ontologically the origin of all substantiality. The proof supposes, far from excluding, that the substantiality of all substance is measured by and deduced from the ego. It is precisely the exception to this principle that compels the *ego* to acknowledge, despite its ontological inclinations (so to speak), the existence of a substance that, instead of being included in the *ratio substantiae* (44, 27 = 30), is in fact understood on the basis of the infinite. The *a posteriori* proof for the existence of God does indeed end up at the ontic primacy of an infinite substance; but this substance is established only by contradicting the deduction of the notion of substance from the *ego;* thus it is established as an exception to the ontological characteristic of substantiality—its debt to the *ego.* Infinite substance's ontic independence from finite substance presupposes, thus confirms, the ontological deduction of substance from the *ego.* This is why substance, as soon as it has become infinite, loses all definition that it might have had in common with all the other substances. In fact, it no longer derives, univocally, from the *ratio substantiae* deduced from the *ego.* This will confirm the irreparable equivocality that affects every definition of substance in general:

> ... nomen substantiae non convenit Deo et illis [res finis] univoce, ut dici solet in Scholis, hoc est nulla ejus nominis significatio potest distincte intelligi, quae Deo et creaturis sit communis. [Hence the term 'substance' does not apply *univocally,* as they in the Schools, to God and to other (finite) things; that is, there is no distinctly intelligible meaning of the term which is common to God and his creatures.] [*Principia Philosophiae I,* §51.]

The substantiality of the finite is deduced and transferred from the *ego,* while in God it is understood on the basis of the infinite, where it is done away with and completed. Therefore, the substances of the world owe their qualification and their way of Being to the *ego, substantia creata* (AT III, 429, 15 = PW III, 193). One point, formally, has thus been established: the *ratio substantiae* is deduced from the *ego,* and the other substances (excepting the infinite substance, which counts as an exception to substantiality) borrow the notion from it. Either substance comes down to the *ego,* or it comes from it.

This result is not enough, however. It shows the egological deduction of substance formally without accomplishing it concretely. The task before us now is to draw out, determination by determination, what substance borrows from the *ego,* besides the Aristotelian determinations of οὐσία. Only then will the egological deduction of substance be completed—which is important to our task (metaphysically interpreting the conventional statement "cogito sum") only insofar as it contributes to drawing out the Cartesian meaning of Being. We will examine the three egological determinations of substance: *(a)* the autonomy of existence, *(b)* the mediation of the attribute, and finally *(c)* the reality of the distinction. *(a)* The autonomy of existence characterizes, par excellence, substance. Descartes here follows Aristotle to the letter: "omne id quod naturaliter sine subjecto esse *potest,* [est] substantia [Everything which can be naturally without a subject is a substance]" (AT VII, 435, 5–6 = PW II, 293 [modified]), ἐν ὑποκειμένῳ οὐδενί ἐστιν. Substance has no substrate, except itself, substrate for the existence and attribution of all other terms; it can be without a substrate, thus without ground or condition: *esse potest.* The ability to be without condition defines the substantiality of substance: ". . . haec est ipsa notio *substantiae,* quod per se, hoc est absque ope ullius alterius substantiae possit existere [The notion of a *substance* is just this—that it can exist by itself, that is without the aid of any other substance]" (AT VII, 226, 3–5 = PW II, 159), ". . . substantiam, sive . . . rem quae per se apta est existere [substance, that is a thing capable of existing by itself]" (44, 22–23 = 30 [modified]), "Per substantiam nihil aliud intelligere possumus, quam rem quae ita existit, ut nulla alia re indigeat ad existendum [By *substance* we can understand nothing other than a thing which exists in such a way as to depend on no other thing for its existence]" (*Principia I,* §51). But as soon as it is posited, this definition, Aristotelian to the letter, appears inadequate: excepting God, infinite substance, all other substance—because finite and created—will possess an equivocal substantiality, placed as it is under the double condition of its creation and its conservation by God. The ability to exist is at once inverted into a dependence for existence, except by the ordinary concurrence of God. The *ratio substantia* (44, 27 = 30) becomes the *communis conceptus* of "res quae solo Dei concursu egent ad existendum [things that need only the concurrence of God to exist]" (*Principia I,* §52). In this new schema, the dependency for existence is doubled: it is found first between the attribute (or the accident) and the substance, then especially between the created substance and God the creator. From this, a difficulty logically arises: instead of putting out of play the (supposedly permanent because ordinary) concurrence of God in such a way that the customary relation of attributes to substance is maintained, why not dispense with a substance that is conditional and allied with accidents? The difficulty is particularly strong in the case of bodies, where, twice, the very notion of a created, extended substance comes up briefly. In the first place, during the debate about the eucharistic transubstantiation, a debate in which Descartes acknowledges that all that which can, through the power of God, dispense with the necessity of a *subjectum* (other than itself) literally becomes a substance, even if it is in fact a matter of accidents: "... quicquid etiam per quantumvis extraordinariam Dei potentiam potest esse sine subjecto, substantia est dicendum [Anything that can exist without a subject even through the power of God, however extraordinary, should also be termed a substance]." The hypothesis of real accidents can disappear, seeing as these accidents without *subjectum* would already count as substances— whence, inversely, substances count only as accidents rid of a *subjectum*.[28] But if the substance changes and only the accidents remain, if both depend equally on the divine concurrence, why still privilege the henceforth accidental substance? An argument stops this line of questioning dead in its tracks: what counts in the physical explanation of the eucharistic transubstantiation cannot be extended to the entire doctrine of substance. Let us accept this argument, despite its weakness (Des-

28. *Responsiones VI* (AT VII, 435, 6–8 = 293 [Correcting the typographical error in the English translation—Trans.]), citing *Categories* 2, 1 *a* 21. Similarly, in response to Arnauld, Descartes emphasizes that the accidents remain when the substances change:

> Praetera nihil est incomprehensibile aut difficile in eo quod Deus creator omnium possit unam substantiam in aliam mutare, quodque haec posterior substantia sub eadem plane superficie remaneat, sub qua prior continebatur ... unde sequitur evidenter, eandem superficiem, quantumvis substantia quae sub ea est mutetur, eodem semper modo agere ac pati debere. [Moreover, there is nothing incomprehensible or difficult in the supposition that God, the creator of all things, is able to change one substance into another, or in the supposition that the latter substance remains within the same surface that contained the former one.... It clearly follows from this that any given surface must always act and react in the same way, even though the substance which is beneath it is changed.]

(AT VII, 255, 9–20 = PW II, 177.) Let us emphasize that transubstantiation does not make an exception to the common theory of substance, for the *potentia Dei ordinaria* "nullo modo differt ab ejus potentia extraordinaria [in no way differs from his extraordinary power]" (435, 3–4 = 293). On this question, see J.-R. Armogathe, *Theologia cartesiana. L'explication physique de l'eucharistie chez Descartes et dom Desgabets* (The Hague, 1977).

cartes forever emphasizing that his theory appeals to miracles far less than every other does, indeed that it dispenses with such an appeal entirely). In the second place, however, the difficulty concerns the entire doctrine of substance. When *Meditatio VI* tries to demonstrate that corporeal things exist, it appeals to substantiality in general: just as the cognitive faculties are found in me, a thinking thing, like modes in a substance (AT VII, 78, 21–28 = PW II, 54), so too can I see that the faculties pertaining to extension can neither be conceived nor remain "absque aliqua substantia cui insint [apart from some substance for them to adhere in]" (79, 1 = 54–55). This hypothesis sanctions the possibility of a finite and created corporeal substance situated between the accidents of extension and the omnipotence of God. Descartes raises two competing objections to it. According to the first, ideas concerning extension would come directly from a *facultas ideas producendi* located in me; as thought modes, ideas pertaining to extension would result from a thinking substance and not, as extended modes, from an extended substance, useless from now on. But I sense the sensible involuntarily, which rules out the possibility that I myself produced the ideas of it. The first hypothesis thus dissolves. The second remains: it could be possible that God directly exerts the *facultas ideas producendi.* In this case, infinite substance would no longer need an extended finite substance in order to affect me with ideas of the sensible. The counter-objection of my receptive passivity no longer counts here; for God would act and I would remain passive. The reason for ruling out this second hypothesis (God would become *fallax*, if he did not act in accordance with the conviction that he put in me) remains quite weak, since it presupposes what must be demonstrated: the homogeneity (the *similitudo*) of the effect with the cause, of the mode and the accident with a substance.[29] Descartes nonetheless is satisfied with it. Why? Because the existence of an extended finite substance is demonstrated not by itself but by virtue of its supposed parallelism with a thinking finite substance: just as the cognitive acts that are grouped together *sub ratione communi cogitationis* directly imply a substantial *res cogitans,* so too do the corporeal acts that are grouped to-

29. See *Sur la théologie blanche de Descartes,* §15, pp. 365–70. Not only is the *similitudo* between the (sensible) effect and the cause (extended substance) not demonstrated, but the Cartesian theory of perception established the impossibility of doing so: the extended cause operates according to mechanical models that do not have any resemblance to their (sensible) effects on us. On this point, Spinoza and Berkeley have reached more Cartesian conclusions than Descartes himself: neither extension nor the extended are to be understood as substances.

gether *sub una communi ratione extensionis* necessarily suppose an extended substance. *Meditatio VI* would demonstrate nothing without this parallelism: "Postquam vero duos distinctos conceptus istarum duarum substantiarum formavimus, facile est, ex dictis in sexta Meditatione, cognoscere an una et eadem sint, an diversae [Once we have formed two distinct concepts of these two substances, it is easy, on the basis of what is said in the Sixth Meditation, to establish whether they are one and the same or different]" (176, 26–29 = 124). The parallelism transfers the finite substantiality that is in thought onto extension and forgoes establishing the substantiality of extension on its own terms. Hence, a new question: how does Descartes establish the parallelism? The text that put forth the *ratio substantiae* by deducing it "ab idea mei ipsius [from my idea of myself]" (44, 19 = 30) also established the parallelism of the two substances straightaway; but in this very same moment, it distorted it. For of the two substances, one has the upper hand—in terms of the order of reasons as well as in itself:

> . . . nam cum cogito lapidem esse substantiam sive esse rem quae apta est existere, itemque me esse substantiam, quamvis concipiam me esse rem cogitantem et non extensam, lapidem vero esse rem extensam et non cogitantem, ac proinde valde diversam, in ratione tamen substantiae videntur convenire. [For example, I think that a stone is a substance, or is a thing capable of existing independently, and I also think that I am a substance. Admittedly I conceive of myself as a thing that thinks and is not extended, whereas I conceive of the stone as a thing that is extended and does not think, so that the two conceptions differ enormously, but they seem to agree with respect to the classification "substance."] [44, 21–28 = 30.]

Substance is *not* distributed evenly, despite what Descartes might say, between thinking substance and extended substance. The reason for this is obvious: to the pair extension/substance, there does not correspond a pair *cogitatio*/substance but a triad: *cogito (concipio)/cogitatio*/substance. That is, the ego does indeed think extended substance, but it also thinks thinking substance. In contrast, extension can never concern anything but extended substance. Moreover, for it to have the possibility of relating to a substance, extension needs a *cogitatio* that thinks it (as simple nature) and interprets it (as principal attribute). The apparent parallelism of substances immediately submits the pair of the first case to the triad of the second. But one must speak of more than just a submission: only the *cogitatio* attains substantiality, on account of the privilege of its double intervention. While extension is not directly assured of its own substance, the *cogitatio* can be; for it alone is substantiality verified, because, if I think the attribute (*cogitatio*), I immediately accomplish it absolutely, without remainder, without condition or exterior concurrence. Therefore, the *cogitatio* becomes a substance based on the simple fact that I think it. *Cogitatio* of the *cogitatio,* which ends up as substance—this schema only repeats in terms of substance what the primal utterance "cogito, sum" formulates in terms of *res (cogitans).* If substance ". . . nulla alia re indige[a]t ad existendum [depend(s) on no other thing for its existence] . . ." (*Principia I,* §51), then only the *ego,* insofar as it cognizes its own *cogitatio,* deserves the name. It needs nothing other than its thinking thought in order to be made to exist as thought thought. This then is why Husserl, at the very moment of separating the region of pure consciousness from the world, will apply the Cartesian definition of substance, neutral in principle, to consciousness alone: "Immanent Being is therefore indubitably absolute Being in the sense that by essential necessity immanental being *nulla 're' indiget ad existendum.* In contradistinction, the world of transcendent *'res'* is entirely referred to consciousness and, more particularly, not to some logically conceived consciousness but to actual consciousness."[30] In this way, he explicitly renews a revolution already implicit in Descartes. If the *cogitatio* was not incessantly assured of itself as thinking thought reduced to "illud . . . quod certum est et inconcussum [what is certain and unshakable]" (25, 23–24 = 17), the general concept of a finite substance, created and dependent on God, would have remained empty, contradictory, and useless. If Descartes retained this concept despite the aporiae that render it almost unthinkable, it is in virtue of the *ego* that thinks substantiality by cognizing itself, and in spite of extension, which, by itself alone, does not reach substantiality. In short, the autonomy of existence, the first characteristic of substance, belongs only to the *ego*— because for Descartes, in contrast to Aristotle, substance comes from it.

The substantiality of substance is defined by a second characteristic: *(b)* the mediation of the attribute. That is, substance as such does not affect us, except by way of an attribute: "Verumtamen non potest substantia primum animadverti ex hoc solo, quod sit res existens, quia hoc solum per se nos non afficit; sed facile ipsam agnoscimus ex quolibet ejus attributo [However we cannot initially become aware of a substance

30. Husserl, *Ideen* I, §49 [English trans., p. 109]. The critical use that Heidegger will make of Husserl's relationship to Descartes is well known, *Prolegomena zur Geschichte des Zeitbegriffs,* §11, G. A., 20, pp. 140–48 [English trans., pp. 102–7].

merely through its being an existing thing, since this alone does not of itself have any effect on us. We can however come to know a substance by one of its attributes] . . ." (*Principia I*, §52). Consequently, it no longer manifests itself immediately: ". . . nihil nunquam aliud requiri putavi ad manifestandam substantiam, praeter varia ejus attributa [I have never thought that anything more is required to reveal a substance than its various attributes]" (AT VII, 360, 3–4 = PW II, 249). From this it follows that we know a substance only through the mediation of an attribute: ". . . ipsam substantiam non immediate per ipsam cognoscamus, sed per hoc tantum quod sit subjectum quorumdam actuum [We do not come to know a substance immediately, through being aware of the substance itself; we come to know it only through its being the subject of certain acts] . . ." (176, 1–3 = 124), "Neque enim substantias immediate cognoscimus, ut alibi notarum est, sed tantum ex eo quod percipiamus quasdam formas sive attributa [We do not have immediate knowledge of substances, as I have noted elsewhere. We know them only by perceiving certain forms or attributes] . . ." (222, 5–7 = 158). Immediacy is forbidden to substance—this point of Descartes' doctrine is formulated as clearly and constantly as possible.[31] However, another Cartesian thesis invalidates it, at least partially. More specifically, in the appendix *more geometrico* to the *Secondae Responsiones*, Descartes defines substance as follows:

> Omnis res cui inest immediate, ut in subjecto, sive per quam existit aliquid quod percipimus, hoc est aliqua proprietas, sive qualitas, sive attributam, cujus realis idea in nobis est, vocatur *Substantia*. [*Substance*. This term applies to every thing in which whatever we perceive immediately resides, as in a subject, or to every thing by means of which whatever we perceive exists. By "whatever we perceive" is meant any property, quality or attribute of which we have a real idea.] [161, 14–17 = 114.]

Such a definition is quite surprising: if the attribute is in the substance immediately, then it can only make it known in an immediate way. An alternative is forced upon us: either the attribute makes the substance known to us mediately because it is neither in it immediately nor it itself; or else the attribute is in the substance immediately, and, even if it is not immediately the substance itself (174, 14–15 = 123), the attribute can

---

31. Whence the commentary offered by Heidegger, who sees in this an anticipation of the Kantian theses, "Sein ist kein reales Prädikat [Being is not a real predicate]," *Sein und Zeit*, §20, p. 94 [English trans., pp. 126–27].

still make substance known immediately; for in this case mediation is inscribed immediately in substance, and is nullified in immediate mediation. Descartes, nevertheless, does not even begin to echo our surprise. On the contrary, he repeats the immediate inherence of the attributes, according to the customary parallel between substances: "Substantia, cui inest immediate cogitatio, vocatur *Mens.* ... Substantia, quae est subjectum immediatum extensionis localis et accidentium quae extensionem praesupponunt ... vocatur *Corpus* [The substance in which thought immediately resides is called *mind.* ... The substance which is the immediate subject of local extension and of the accidents which presuppose extension ... is called *body*" (161, 24–162, 1 = 114). How can he not notice the obvious difficulty here? If the *cogitatio* is found in substance immediately, how would it not also manifest substance immediately as such? But is immediacy, which would authorize a manifestation, found in the second type of substance—extension? Our sense is that this does not turn out to be the case, despite the obvious parallel in the definitions, more rhetorical than conceptual. Between extension and the substance named body, the relation, though qualified as immediate, is concretized in a new term, *subjectum immediatum* (161, 28 = 114). If the general definition mentioned this term (161, 14 = 114), it is remarkable that the definition of thinking substance ignores it.[32] Therefore, in this case, the immediacy of substance to its attributes implies the immediacy of a substrate, *subjectum,* ὑποκείμενον. Extension is in the thing (called extended) as an accident is in a ὑποκείμενον, that is to say as *in alio.* Extension resides immediately in the substance as in its other. Substance alienates extension in welcoming it immediately. The immediacy of substance does not contradict the alienation of the attribute, but accomplishes it. In short, immediacy amounts to mediation—at least here, in the case of extension, where, despite these exceptional occurrences of immediacy, the customary doctrine of the mediated knowledge of substance is confirmed. But how do things stand with the *cogitatio*? Does immediacy also lead it back to a mediation? In the definition of *mens,* as we have already observed, the *subjectum,* which would burden immediacy with mediation, does not come up. Is this a case of simple forgetful-

32. Similarly, *subjectum* disappears in *Responsiones III.* Both the general definition of all substance and that of extended substance mention respectively "subjectum ... actuum [subject of ... acts]" (176, 3 = 124) and "subjectum figurae [subject of shape]" (176, 13 = 124) or "subjectum motus localis [subject of local motion]" (176, 14 = 124); but that of thinking substance omits it: "... substantiam cui insunt, dicimus esse rem cogitantem [We call the substance in which they inhere a 'thinking thing'] ..." (176, 19–20 = 124).

ness, or, on the contrary, of a more primordial grasp of an immediacy that no longer has recourse, as extension did, to a *subjectum,* ὑποκείμε-νον? The answer depends on the meaning of the adverb *immediate.* With regard to the *mens, immediate* (161, 24 = 114) must be understood in terms of the two occurrences of *immediate* that, in definitions I and II, introduce *cogitatio* and *idea.* Consider in the first place: "*Cogitationis* nomine complector illud omne quod sic in nobis est ut ejus immediate conscii simus [*Thought.* I use this term to include everything that is within us in such a way that we are immediately aware of it]" (160, 7–8 = 113). Between the *ego* and the *cogitatio,* there is a relation of radical immediacy—I am conscious of it; it is found without mediation *in nobis.* The *cogitationes* are in the *ego,* as they would be in their subject; but such a subject (and this is why the word *subjectum* does not appear) is not fixed in an other substrate because it is the *ego,* and also because the *ego* is enacted as the coming to consciousness in it of thoughts other than it but that nevertheless can only remain in it since they themselves are only through it. Immediacy is not devalued into a concealed ὑπο-κείμενον and that which conceals it; it is accomplished in an already in-tentional consciousness. What counts for thoughts (*cogitationes*) counts also for ideas. Hence the second definition: "*Ideae* nomine intelligo cu-juslibet formam, per cujus immediatam perceptionem ipsius ejusdem cogitationis conscius sum [*Idea.* I understand this term to mean the form of any given thought, immediate perception of which makes me aware of the thought]" (160, 14–16 = 113). The idea does not weaken cognitive immediacy, but reinforces it: if the *ego* is conscious of any *cogitatio* what-soever, and if the *cogitatio* is already characterized by immediacy, then the idea raises immediacy to the next level—it would be the *forma* of each thing that renders it immediately available to the conscious as pure immediacy. But, it will rightly be objected, can this cognitive and ideal immediacy be applied to the relation between substance and attribute in general? The answer involves several remarks. *(α)* It is no longer a mat-ter of explaining the general relation between substance and attribute, but solely of explaining the immediacy proper to the *mens,* which, in-verting the immediate relation proper to corporeal substance, does not mobilize any *subjectum immediatum. (β)* The general definition of sub-stance, while mentioning the possible use of a *subjectum* (161, 14 = 114), also has recourse to a determination that has done away with it, and understands substance on the basis of perception, of the *idea* and there-fore of the *cogitatio:* "Neque enim ipsius substantiae praecise sumptum aliam habemus ideam, quam quod sit res, in qua formaliter vel eminenter

existit illud aliquid quod percipimus [The only idea we have of a substance itself, in the strict sense, is that it is the thing in which whatever
we perceive . . . exists, either formally or eminently]" (161, 17–20 = 114).
Of substance, we therefore have an *idea,* connected directly to what we
perceive: it is that in which what we perceive exists. If we are not to
conclude from this that we perceive it immediately, we must at least
admit that it is that in which what we immediately perceive exists. But
then, doesn't it constitute, without using the word, a *subjectum?* (γ) This
is not the case, for a fundamental reason: if for corporeal substance, the
cogitatio knows extension immediately, but the *subjectum immediatum*
mediately, this is because to the dyad making up clear and distinct
knowledge (thought/object), a third term is added, designated *subjectum,* distant and opaque residue. In the case of thinking substance,
there are, on the contrary, not three but two terms: the *ego* first enters
into an immediate relation with its *cogitationes* and its *ideas* (thought/
object), then these are related to the thing in which they are (substance);
but as they are never in it except as *ideae* and *cogitationes,* this thing will
still remain the *ego.* The *ego,* as *cogitans,* relates at first immediately to its
cogitationes (*cogitata,* objects), but when, as attributes, these *cogitationes*
must be related to a thing in which they subsist, they have no need of a
third term; it is enough if they are related in the second moment, as
immediately as in the first, to the *ego,* then interpreted as a substance—
but an immediate substance, in contrast with the *subjectum* of extension.
In short, if two relations are indeed found here, as for extended substance, they mobilize only two terms: from the *ego* to the *cogitationes,*
an immediate epistemological relation is laid out; from the *cogitationes*
(attributes) to the *ego* (substance: *res cogitans*), a substantial relation—
always immediate—is laid out. Thus, solely in the case of thinking substance does the reversal of the epistemological relation into a substantial
relation assure the immediacy forbidden to every other substance. Only
the *ego* constitutes an immediately knowable substance. What we noticed above as a contradiction between the immediacy of the substance
described in the appendix to the *Responsiones II* and the mediation of
the attribute affirmed everywhere else is therefore neither illusory nor
unresolvable. In the majority of the texts, Descartes attempts to define
substance on the basis of the most common example: corporeal substance. In this case, he must think it as a final ὑποκείμενον, *subjectum*
eventually *immediatum,* but in fact inaccessible to the *cogitatio* except
through the mediation of the only truly immediate object of the latter,
extension (and the other material simple natures). In other, less numer-

ous cases, Descartes thinks his own concept of substance, by reformulating it in terms of the wholly immediate relation of the *ego* to its *cogitationes:* instead of this relation leading the *ego* to its objects epistemologically, the *cogitationes* are turned back toward the *ego* as attributes are referred to their substance. The immediacy of the first relation (160, 8, 10–11, 15 = 113) plays itself out to the detriment of the second (161, 14–24 = 114). It must therefore be concluded, for the second time, that the substantiality of substance is defined, basically, in terms of the *ego.*

The egological deduction of substance can be confirmed finally by consideration of *(c)* the reality of the distinction between substances. Really distinguishing substances from each other bears on their essential definition, since every substance must be able to exist by itself, thus apart from other substances. How does Descartes assure their distinction? His usual doctrine is put forth with regard to the most exemplary case of the relation between substances, the union of the soul and the body. On the one hand, I have ". . . ideam meî ipsius, quatenus sum tantum res cogitans et non extensa [a clear and distinct idea of myself, in so far as I am a thinking, non-extended thing]"; on the other hand, I have ". . . ideam corporis, quatenus est tantum res extensa, non cogitans [a distinct idea of body, in so far as this is simply an extended, non-thinking thing]" (78, 16–19 = 54). This intelligible distinction counts as a real one because ". . . scio omnia quae clare et distincte intelligo, talia a Deo fieri posse qualia illa intelligo [I know that everything which I clearly and distinctly understand is capable of being created by God so as to correspond exactly with my understanding of it]" (78, 2–3 = 54). On the basis of the separate intelligibility of these two ideas, I can end up at a real distinction between two *res.* Three times at least, Descartes' commentaries on this text apply it to the distinction of each and every substance. The *Responsiones III* conclude: "Postquam vero duos distinctos conceptus istarum duarum substantiarum formavimus, facile est, ex dictis in sexta Meditatione, cognoscere an una et eadem sint, an diversae [Once we have formed two distinct concepts of these two substances, it is easy, on the basis of what is said in the Sixth Meditation, to establish whether they are one and the same or different]" (176, 26–28 = 124)—real *distinction on the basis of distinct concepts of substances. *Responsione IV* continues: ". . . nec ullus unquam qui duas substantias per duos diversos conceptus percipit, non judicavit illas esse realiter distinctas [There is no one who has ever perceived two substances by means of two different concepts without judging that they are really distinct]" (226, 5–7 = 159), and it refers "ad conclusionem de reali *mentis* a *corpore* distinctione, quam demum in sexta Meditatione perfeci [to the conclusion that there is a real distinction between the mind and the body, which I finally established in the Sixth Meditation]" (226, 25–26 = 159). Citing the same text (78, 2*ff.* = 54), the *Conversation with Burman* emphasizes:

> ... ageres certe contra tuam intellectionem et perquam absurde, si illa duo diceres esse eandem substantiam quae tanquam duas substantias, quarum una non solum non involvit alteram, sed etiam negat, clare concipis. [You would be going against your own powers of reasoning in the most absurd fashion if you said the two were one and the same substance. For you have a clear conception of them as two substances which not only do not entail one another but are actually incompatible.][33]

The reasoning is set out with an unyielding clarity: substances are distinguished really if, and only if, their concepts are rationally exclusive. It is not surprising that the role of decoupling substances should be accorded to concepts: concepts pertain to the principal attributes, whose first characteristic is clear and distinct intelligibility. The attributes reproduce the strict parallel of the substances in order to assure their real distinction. A question immediately arises: we just emphasized, in *(a)* and *(b)*, not a parallelism but a hierarchy of the two substances; shouldn't we therefore put back into question the primacy that the *res cogitans* holds within substantiality in general? No, since according to the evidence, it is confirmed here once again. That is, if the distinction of substances is determined by that of their concepts, the distinction of concepts is in turn determined by recourse to the *ego cogito;* therefore, one of the two substances is fundamentally distinguished from the other only by defining it, determining it, and regulating it. The *ego cogito* is not attested to first or only as one of the two distinguished substances (as thinking substance *thought*), but as thinking substance *thinking* the real distinction of substances through the difference of attributes. The claim that thinking substance thinks the distinction of substances even before all substance (extended or *cogitans*) thought is supported by textual occurrences in which the *ego* thinks first: it understands the distinction (*intelligere* 78, 5 = 54), for "... has [substantias] percipimus a se mutuo realiter esse distinctas, ex hoc solo quod unam absque altera clare et distincte intelligimus [We can perceive that two substances are really distinct simply from the fact that we can clearly and distinctly understand one apart from the

---

33. *Conversation with Burman* (AT V, 163, 16–19 = PW III, 345).

other]";[34] it has the idea of each of the substances (*habeo ideam,* 78, 16 = 54, "... the idea which I have of a thinking substance");[35] it apprehends them (*deprehendere,* 227, 19; 355, 1 = 160; 245) and forms the concept of them: "... formoque clarum et distinctum istius substantiae cogitantis conceptum [(I) form a clear and distinct concept of this thinking substance]" (355, 1–3 = 245). The primacy of the *ego* is confirmed not because thinking substance would benefit from some privilege over extended substance, but because both are thought by the anterior thinking *ego.* Such an anteriority of thinking thought, even with respect to the substantiality of substance in general, could be surprising. This happens when one takes shelter in the banality of a common opinion: "... vulgo res omnes eodem modo se habere judicamus in ordine ad ipsam veritatem, quo se habent ad nostram perceptionem [We commonly judge that the order in which things are mutually related in our perception of them corresponds to the order in which they are related in actual reality]" (*Responsiones IV,* 226, 15–18 = 159). But this supposedly banal opinion contradicts a fundamental thesis of the method and the gray ontology: "... aliter spectandas esse res singulas in ordine ad cognitionem nostram, quam si se iisdem loquamur prout revera existunt [When we consider things in the order that corresponds to our knowledge of them, our view of them must be different from what it would be if we were speak-

---

34. *Principia Philosophiae I,* §60 = PW I, 213. See *Responsiones IV* (AT VII, 226, 10, 12, and 21 = PW II, 159). See *To Regius,* June 1642:

> Et sane potest Deus efficere quidquid possumus clare intelligere; nec alia sunt quae a Deo fieri non posse, quam quod repugnantiam involvunt in conceptu, hoc est quae non sunt intelligibilia; possumus autem clare intelligere substantiam cogitantem non extensam, et extensam non cogitantem, ut fateris. [God can surely bring about whatever we can clearly understand; the only things that are said to be impossible for God to do are those which involve a conceptual contradiction, that is, which are not intelligible. But we can clearly understand a thinking substance that is not extended, and an extended substance that does not think, as you agree.]

(AT III, 567, 17–23 = PW III, 214.) The distinction between substances is determined straightaway and essentially *in (meo) conceptu,* just like logical contradiction (see *Sur la théologie blanche de Descartes,* §13, pp. 299–301).

35. *To Gibieuf,* 19 January 1642 (AT III, 475, 23 = PW III, 202). A formulation worthy of admiration, for it unambiguously detaches thinking thought—the operator of the distinction (*the idea that I have*)—from thought thought—the object of the distinction at the same level as thought extension (*of a substance that thinks*). In this light, the apparently monolithic formula "... the idea of an extended substance [*l'idée d'une substance étendue*] ..." is shown to be dual and composed (ibid., 475, 19 = 202 [modified]). [Note: The English translators have already understood the formula as dual and composed, rendering it "the idea of a substance with extension."—Trans.] The same observation can be made with regard to *Responsiones V,* 335, 1–4 = PW II, 232.

ing of them in accordance with how they exist in reality]" (*Regula XII,* AT X 418, 1–3 = PW I, 44). The distinction of substances is, in fact, conferred in our knowledge; their completeness is understood on the basis of their simplicity; and this simplicity is delimited insofar as it is understood. In short, the *ego* operative in the thinking *cogitatio* deduces the real distinction of substances from itself. Thus, by examining *(a)* the autonomy of its existence, *(b)* the mediation of its principal attribute, and *(c)* the reality of its distinction, we have established that, for Descartes, substance is deduced from the *ego.*

To deduce substance from the *ego* means, if we keep to the Kantian signification of deduction, justifying the application of the *ego* to substance. A final task remains for us, then: producing the egological model of substance, which would justify making the transition from the *ego* to substance. This transition was pointed out and denounced by Nietzsche: "The concept of substance is a consequence of the concept of the subject: not the reverse!" It was also confirmed and approved of by Leibniz: "Substantiam ipsam potentia activa et passiva praeditam, veluto τὸ Ego vel simile, pro indivisibili seu perfecta monade habeo [In regard to substance itself being endowed with active and passive power, as an indivisible or perfect monad—like the ego or something similar to it]"; or better: "Further[,] it is by the knowledge of necessary truths and by their abstractions that we are raised to *acts of reflection,* which make us think of what is called the *self,* and consider that this or that is within *us.* And it is thus that in thinking of ourselves, we think of being [*l'Etre*], of substance. . . ."[36] With these two authorities, who agree in recognizing the same deduction only in order to oppose each other in interpreting it, it becomes possible to sketch an egological model of substance. This model is composed of the following moments: *ego*/reflection of thinking thought on thought thought (*cogito me cogitare*)/unity/equality of the one and Being/substance. It is made more explicit by the following transitions. *(a)* The *ego* does not think the thinkable so much as it thinks thought thought. *Videre* is equivalent to *videre videor* (29, 14–15 = 19) because ". . . fieri plane non potest, cum videam, sive (quod jam non distinguo) cum cogitem me videre, ut ego ipse cogitans non aliquid sim [When I see, or think I see (I am not here distinguishing the two), it is simply not possible that I who am now thinking am not something]" (33,

36. Respectively, Nietzsche, *Wille zur Macht,* §485 [English trans., p. 268]; Leibniz, *A de Volder,* 20 June 1703, *Ph. S.,* II, p. 251 [English trans., p. 530], and *Monadologie,* §30, *Ph. S.,* VI, p. 612 [English trans., pp. 183–84].

11–14 = 22). In short, the *ego* does not reach existence by thinking, but by thinking that it thinks—that is to say, by the reflection of thought as thinking on thought as thought. *(b)* From reflection, there is a transition to the only authentic unity, one that is lacking from every being that is not "able to say this 'I' which says so much"; that is, "The true unity is in some way analogous to the soul" and "There is a true unity which corresponds to what is called the 'I' in us."[37] The *animae analogon* alone assures true unity because it culminates in self-identity, which is perfectly accomplished only in the (thinking) thought of thought. Nietzsche confirms this second step by denouncing it: "We have borrowed the concept of unity from our 'ego' concept—our oldest article of faith."[38] *(c)* From unity to Being, the transition dates at least from Aristotle: τὸ ὄν καὶ τὸ ἕν ταὐτὸν καὶ μία φύσις (. . .) ταὐτὸ γὰρ εἷς ἄνθρωπος καὶ ὢν ἄνθρωπος καὶ ἄνθρωπος [if now being and unity are the same and are one thing for one man and a man are the same thing and existent man and a man are the same thing].[39] Leibniz will refer to the Aristotelian thesis almost to the letter: "I maintain as axiomatic this identical proposition, whose differentiation can only be marked by the accentuation—namely, that that which is not truly *one* entity is not truly one *entity* either."[40] Unity is not attributed to Being so much as it is equal to *what* is. For something to be, it must be itself, thus one. *(d)* As for the transition from Being to substance, it does not cause any difficulty, first because Descartes often uses them synonymously (". . . the soul is a being or substance"),[41] next because Aristotle first brought the question τί τὸ ὄν back to the question τις ἡ οὐσία. In this way, an egological model of substance is designed, one that achieves the deduction of substance on the basis of the *ego*. The essence of substance must be said on the basis of the *ego*, which, far from suffering the indetermination of substance, imposes its own determina-

37. Leibniz, respectively *Discours de la Métaphysique*, §34, *Ph. S.,* IV, 459; *Système nouveau . . .* , op. cit., 473 and 482 [English trans., p. 44; 117 (modified); 120] (Heidegger comments on the last of these texts in "Aus der letzten Marburger Vorlesung," *Wegmarken*, G. A., 9, 85).

38. Nietzsche, *Wille zur Macht*, §635 [English trans., p. 338]. We have tried to show that the *I* is not really our oldest article of faith, but an event that has arrived only recently and with difficulty.

39. *Metaphysics* Γ 2, 1003 *b* 22–23, 26–27 [English trans., p. 1585, 1585]. Similarly: τὸ δ' ἕν λέγεται ὥσπερ τὸ ὄν [one of the main senses of 'one' which answer to the senses of 'is']: Z, 4, 1030 *b* 10 [English trans., p. 1627] (or I, 2, 1053 *b* 25 [English trans., p. 1664]).

40. Leibniz, *To Arnauld*, 30 April 1687, *Ph. S.,* II, p. 97 [English trans., p. 67]. See *Discourse on Metaphysics* §8, *Ph. S.,* IV, p. 433 and *Theodicy*, §400, *Ph. S.,* VI, p. 354.

41. *To X*, March 1637 (AT I, 353, 17 = PW III, 55).

tions on it. Not only am I a substance, but substance has first of all the essence of an *I*, because it is deduced from an *ego.*

The thesis that Heidegger argues in *Sein und Zeit* must therefore be challenged. In the first place, it does not appear quite right to say that "the kind of Being which belongs to the *res cogitans*, or—more precisely—the *meaning of the Being of the 'sum'*" remains undetermined, or that "the cogitationes are left ontologically undetermined." Next, it seems highly doubtful that "the *sum* [is] completely undiscussed [*unerörtet*]," for the simple reason that it is difficult to claim that Descartes "[fails] to discuss [*unerörtet*] the meaning of Being which the idea of substantiality embraces, or the character of the 'universality' which belongs to this signification." [42] Or more exactly, if the universality of substantiality never ceases to cause serious difficulties for the Cartesian project, these difficulties result neither from an indetermination of substantiality, nor from a failure to discuss it; on the contrary, they are the result of substance being determined and discussed in terms that are deduced too precisely from the ego alone. For strictly thinking, the characteristics of substance are verified only for and by the *ego;* they give rise to aporiae as soon as Descartes tries to apply them either to extension or to God. Concerning extension, the aporiae are born as soon as one tries to force onto substantiality the autonomy of existence, the mediation of a principal attribute different from it, and finally its distinction from other substances. Concerning God, if autonomy does not cause any difficulty, this is because his eminent substantiality puts into question the self-sufficiency of all other creatures; if his real distinction from other substances does not give rise to any obstacles (it is equivalent to the gap between creator and created), this is because it could just as well forbid the possibility of other substances besides God. As for the mediation of a principal attribute, it is not yet something about which anything decisive can be said: neither extension nor the *cogitatio* are invoked, any more than any other determination—excepting infinity, perfection, and power—as one or several principal attributes of a single substance. [43]

42. Heidegger, *Sein und Zeit,* respectively §6, p. 24; §10, p. 49 (*unbestimmt*); §10, p. 46; §20, p. 93 [English trans., p. 46; p. 75; p. 71; p. 126]. This interpretation in fact dates from 1921–22, as has been established by the recent publication of *Phänomenologische Interpretationen zu Aristoteles. Einführung in die phänomenologische Forschung,* in G. A., 61, Frankfurt am Main, 1985, pp. 175*ff.*

43. On the difficulty involved in treating God as a substance and, *a fortiori,* of assigning a principal attribute to him, see *infra,* chap. IV, §17. The egological deduction of substance poses so great a difficulty for Descartes' thought that his successors will, without fail, at-

None of these aporiae would appear if the *ego* did not determine the substantiality of substance. Don't we now have to take one step further in our critique of the Heideggerian interpretation? Not only does substance determine the Being of the *ego sum* and that of its *cogitationes,* but more important, substance is extended to other beings only after the fact, and perhaps illegitimately. And yet Heidegger clearly emphasizes an inverse movement: Descartes would have thought substance first on the basis of extension, itself interpreted as the certain and permanent object of objectifying knowledge; he would then have tried to fob off the certain knowledge of permanent and subsistent beings onto the *sum* of the *ego,* imposing on it the way of Being of subsistence (*Vorhandenheit* [presence at hand])—in short, giving birth to what metaphysics, ever since, has called consciousness. "[Descartes] takes the Being of 'Dasein' (to whose basic constitution Being-in-the-world belongs) in the very same way as he takes the Being of the *res extensa.*" In this way, the attribution of substantiality to the *ego* would result from two factors: first of all from an indetermination of the Being of this *ego,* ontologically unthought because ontically too well known; then from a "retrospective illumination" or a "retrospective interpretation"[44] of the *cogitatio* in terms of *extensio*—more exactly, of the way of Being of *Dasein* (written as *ego*) in terms of the way of Being of beings within-the-world, themselves reduced to pure and simple subsistence. Both these misunderstandings would be accomplished within the horizon of a complete and general failure to recognize what "world" could signify. Without here challenging the unquestioned privilege that Descartes accords to subsisting presence (*Vorhandenheit* [presence at hand]), we must at least contest the claim that he first thinks substance in terms of *res extensa* and then extends it to the *res cogitans,* which previously had been undiscussed as such. Not only is the meaning of the *ego*'s Being in fact thought—it is thought as substance—but substance is in fact located in and determined by the *ego.* As for the "retrospective interpretation," it concerns only extension and God. For when the simple existence of the *ego* has been established, and when its own essence has been investigated—". . . I examined attentively what I was" (AT VI, 32, 24 = PW I, 127)—the response is advanced without even the least bit of ambiguity: ". . . I knew I was a substance whose whole essence or nature is simply

---

tempt to define substance without a privileged reference to the *ego.* Instead they will refer to God (Spinoza), to extension (Malebranche), and indeed to all beings (Leibniz).

44. *Sein und Zeit,* §21, p. 98 [English trans., p. 131]. *Rückstrahlung,* §5, p. 16, 1 [English trans., p. 37—"reflected back"] and *Rückdeutung,* handwritten note to §12, p. 58.

to think" (AT VI, 33, 3–5 = PW I, 127). This formulation deserves even more attention since here, in contrast to the *Meditationes*, the term *substance* comes up as early as the demonstration of the *ego*, before any mention of God; better, it will no longer reappear in order to qualify God or extension as such.[45] I am a substance—therefore ". . . mentem vero humanum . . . puram esse substantiam [the human mind . . . is a pure substance]" (AT VII, 14, 9–11 = 10)—". . . me esse substantiam [I am a substance] . . ." (44, 23 = 30), ". . . ego autem substantia [I am a substance] . . ." (45, 7 = 31). Not only does substantiality determine the Being of the *ego*, but more radically the *ego* fixes the place of substantiality by rendering it thinkable in terms of its own thought. The *ego* offers a place and offers its place (*erörtet*) to substance. The latter determines its own essence in that henceforth the characteristics of οὐσία, subsisting in itself and being said by itself, must be understood on the basis of the *cogitatio*. The *cogitatio* subsists in each instant without any other condition or substrate but itself; it can be said from itself, since, in the role of thinking thought, it says all other beings that it reduces to thought thought. The *ego*, determined by the operative *cogitatio*, offers its place to all substance. Just like the metaphysicians whose possibility he created intended to do, Descartes too establishes the equivalence of Being and thought by constructing a substantiality that owes everything to the *ego* since it is deduced from it: *ego autem substantia*. This could be understood to mean "la substance, c'est moi," on condition that this equivalence be reversed and turned into this other: "The *ego* alone because it determines its way of Being according to substance, offers a place to substance—in short, substance is *ego*, or is not." If substance is *ego* or is not, the Heideggerian interpretation must be radically contested: what is problematic in the Cartesian doctrine of substance does not stem from an insufficient consideration of the specificity of the *ego* but, inversely, from the determination of substance exclusively in terms of the *ego*, a determination that then runs the risk of not being appropriate to any of the beings that cannot be reduced to the *ego*.

§14. The Subsistent Temporality of the *Ego*

We should therefore contest one of the major conclusions in Heidegger's interpretation: when discussing Descartes' elaboration of substance, it

45. One occurrence, it is true, has an indirect relevance to extension, though the reference is very oblique: "To this, I added many points about the substance, position, motions and all the various qualities of these heavens and stars" (AT VI, 43, 25–28 = PW I, 133).

does not appear tenable to maintain the primacy of beings in the world, understood as *res extensa*. Quite to the contrary, substantiality comes to the *res extensa* from the *ego*, the first substance. The difficulties encountered by the doctrine of material substance are the direct result of the more original difficulty of extending a concept originally elaborated for and through the *ego*. However, pointing out a weakness in Heidegger's interpretation is not enough to disqualify its entire relevance. For what is essentially at stake in it is not to be found in the (erroneous) thesis of an innerworldly origin of substance, since this same thesis will in the end phenomenologically designate all substantiality, in Descartes, as subsistence and permanence. Whatever its origin might be, Cartesian substance manifests its substantiality as the permanence of a subsisting being—this is the sole decisive point according to Heidegger's project in *Sein und Zeit*. That subsistence finally concerns *all* substance, that Descartes does indeed confirm, in *this* sense, the ontological thesis that Hegel (and others) attribute to him, that in the end Cartesian substance does indeed pose the question of the *ego*—all this is from time to time recognized explicitly by Heidegger himself, as when he suggests "how ontologically groundless are the problematics of the Self from Descartes' *res cogitans* right up to Hegel's concept of spirit."[46] Whether one comes to this line of questioning indirectly by starting from the substantiality of the *res extensa,* as happens most often in *Sein und Zeit* (and first in §§19–21), or directly as in the present study, it seems clear that the brunt of Heidegger's interpretation is directed against the mode of Being of the *ego* that thinks. In this, it is not limited to proposing just one more interpretation among the many others already put forth; rather, it poses a question that should be unavoidable in every reading of Descartes. More precisely, Heidegger asks if the *ego,* insofar as it accomplishes the equivalence of Being and thought (*Sein = Denken*), does not mark the apex of the interpretation of the Being of beings as pure and simple persistence in subsistence—and thus does not inaugurate the royal road of erring which, through Kant, ends up at Husserl. Husserl's failure to make a distinction between the ways of Being of two ontically distinguished regions, the world and consciousness, in fact goes back to something left unthought previously and, through Kant, to Descartes: "'Consciousness of my Dasein' means for Kant a consciousness of my Being-present-at-hand [*mon être subsistant*] in the sense of Descartes. When Kant uses the term 'Dasein,' he has in mind the Being-present-at-

---

46. *Sein und Zeit,* §64, n. 1, p. 320 [English trans., p. 497, n. xix]. See *supra,* chap. II, §6.

hand of consciousness [*l'être subsistant de la conscience*] just as much as the Being-present-at-hand of Things [*l'être subsistant de la chose*]."[47] With Descartes, and starting from the *ego* interrogated in its way of Being, it is a matter of subverting the Being of beings as such and universally, through permanent subsistence (*Vorhandenheit*). Consequently, to take Heidegger seriously when he himself undertakes thinking through the Cartesian event in the history of Being amounts to attempting to answer this one question: did Descartes really elaborate a thought of "Being as *Vorhandenheit* [presence-at-hand], as subsistence?" Did he really adhere to the idea of "Being as constant presence-at-hand, *ständiger Vorhandenheit* [*subsistance permanente*]," such that the equation explicitly recognized by his metaphysical descendants (*Sein = Denken*) rests, more fundamentally, on another equality, one that is implicit and visible only through the "destruction of the history of ontology": namely, "Being = constant presence-at-hand, permanent subsistence; *Sein = ständiger Vorhandenheit*"?[48] Or in other words, does not the indetermination that initially stood as a reproach against the way of Being of the *sum* in fact receive its determination, one that is all the more radical insofar as it is hidden (from the eyes of Descartes himself), as pure and simple subsistence? The formula *ego autem substantia* would no longer mean only: "I am substance, because substance is *ego* or is not" (see above, §13); it would also mean: "All substance must, as a result of its origin in the *ego*, subsist in the mode of subsistence of the *ego*." In this way, the *ego* would determine nothing less than the way of Being of beings in general. Through a significant paradox, Heidegger himself puts us on the

47. *Sein und Zeit*, §43, p. 203 [English trans., p. 247]. See *Prolegomena zur Geschichte des Zeitbegriffs*, §22, G. A., 20, especially p. 239 [English trans., p. 177]. [Marion here uses the French term *subsistance* to render Heidegger's *Vorhandenheit*, which the English translators of Heidegger translate as "presence-at-hand." In the present work, these terms, therefore, need to be seen as more or less interchangeable.—Trans.]

48. Respectively, *Prolegomena . . .* , §22, p. 233 [English trans., p. 172 (modified)]; *Sein und Zeit*, §21, p. 96; p. 96 [English trans., p. 129; p. 129]. When commenting on the definition of *substantia* in *Principia Philosophia I*, §51, the *Prolegomena* claim more clearly that

Substantialität meint *Vorhandenheit*, die als solche eines anderen Seienden unbedürftig ist. Die Realität einer *res*, die Substanzialität einer Substanz, das Sein eines Seienden, in strengen Sinn gennomen, besagt: Vorhandenheit im Sinne der Unbedürftigkeit. [Substantiality means *presence-at-hand* (*Vorhandenheit, subsistance*) which as such is in need of no other being. The reality of a *res*, the substantiality of a substance, the Being of a being, taken in a strict sense means presence-at-hand (*Vorhandenheit, subsistance*) in the sense of non-indigence.]

(Pp. 232–33 = p. 172 [modified].) *Sein und Zeit*, §20, is content to summarize this discussion.

road to refuting his secondary thesis when he states his principal thesis. The principal thesis ends up extracting "remaining constant (*ständiger Verbleib*)" as the characteristic trait of beings.[49] But—and with this we see an indication of the secondary thesis—Heidegger here acknowledges only a characteristic of innerworldly being, which he will then be led, wrongly, to identify as the first depository of permanent subsistence. That is, he succeeds in extracting permanent subsistence by considering the celebrated analysis of innerworldly being that Descartes, in *Principia Philosophiae II, §4*, abstracts from all sensible qualities and thereby reduces to extension alone—for it alone is left, persists, remains, "... omnes ejusmodi qualitates, quae in materia corporea sentiuntur, ex ea tolli posse, ipsa integra remanente [All other such qualities that are perceived by the senses as being in corporeal matter can be removed from it, while the matter itself remains intact (ipsa integra remanente)]." *Remanere* can be rendered perfectly by "remaining constant (*ständiger Verbleib*)," which Heidegger uses to translate it. It would have been even more expedient to conduct the same demonstration by considering the analysis of the piece of wax in *Meditatio II*. In this analysis, for the first time, the disappearance of all the sensible qualities of the being called "wax" lets an abstract residue subsist, one that bears the name "wax" only in that it still subsists, though without the characteristics that previously specified it: "Remanetne adhuc eadem cera? Remanere fatendum est; nemo negat, nemo aliter putat ... remanet cera [Does the same wax remain? It must be admitted that it does; no one denies it, no one thinks otherwise ... the wax remains" (AT VII, 30, 19–20, 25 = PW II, 20). The wax remains as such, despite its total sensible disappearance,

49. The formula *ständiger Verbleib* translates *remanere* in Descartes; for example in *Sein und Zeit, §22*, p. 96 and §19, p. 92 [English trans., p. 128 and p. 125]. It is all the more felicitous as a translation since the German *verbleiben* can correspond to *persévérer*. In this light, *remanere* takes on its full meaning: despite the total abstraction from all its sensible qualities, the wax perseveres in its existence; it does not just stay there, but it is obstinate about remaining, thus showing that Being amounts precisely to persisting in subsistence in the present. It will be observed that the *Discourse on the Method* does not think twice about applying the reduction to persistence as soon as doubt is at work (without attaining the certainty of the *ego* as in the *Meditationes* or the certainty of the *res extensa* as in the *Principia*): "... I thought it was necessary to do the very opposite and reject as absolutely false everything in which I could imagine the least doubt, in order to see if I was left believing anything that was entirely indubitable" (DM, 31, 25–30 = PW I, 126–27). The parallel with AT VII, 25, 19–24 = PW II, 17 is all the more striking when one sees in the "entirely indubitable" "... illud tantum quod certum est et inconcussum [exactly and only what is certain and unshakable]." The analysis of the piece of wax, strangely left out of *Sein und Zeit*, had been studied in the *Prolegomena, §22*, pp. 246–47 [English trans., p. 182].

only insofar as—for the *cogitatio* at least—it remains. To remain, *remanere* with constant permanence (*ständiger Verbleib*), constitutes its sole definition. This text confirms Heidegger's principal thesis even better than the one he invokes because subsisting persistence appears in the *Meditationes* before any elaboration of substance (which comes up only in AT VII, 40, 12); accordingly, far from being a result of substance, persistence could, on the contrary, make it possible. In this way, the decision to interpret the Being of beings as permanent subsistence paves the way for and decides in advance the subsequent meaning of substantiality. But this confirmation of Heidegger's principal thesis already gives birth to a suspicion about his secondary thesis: here the persistence of constant permanence (*Ständiger Verbleib*) results less from innerworldly being as such—it cannot yet be defined as *res extensa* grounded with certainty, still less as substance—than it does from the *ego cogito,* which analyzes and reduces them, "solius mentis inspectio" (31, 25 = 21). In this case, how can we not pose the following question: could the *ego cogito* ascertain a permanent persistence in the case of the piece of wax if it itself did not first remain in the mode of subsisting permanence? Shouldn't it, more than each *cogitatum,* persist in order to *see* persistence? In order for such innerworldly being to remain, it is first and radically necessary that the *ego* remain. And if all that remains remains through the *ego,* then the *ego* alone and first remains. A textual confirmation of this conceptual requirement is not absent: *remanere* does not appear for the first time when it is a matter of designating the piece of wax or innerworldly being in general, but when it is a matter of qualifying the *ego* in person in its first appearance and its new certainty:

> Quare jam denuo meditabor quidnam me olim esse crediderim, priusquam in has cogitationes incidissem; ex quo deinde subducam quidquid allatis rationibus vel minimum potuit infirmari, ut ita tandem praecise remaneat illud tantum quod certum est et inconcussum. [I will therefore go back and meditate on what I once believed myself to be, before I embarked on this present train of thought. I will then subtract anything capable of being weakened, even minimally, by the arguments now introduced, so that what remains at the end may be exactly and only what is certain and unshakable.] [25, 19–24 = 17 (modified).]

Before the analysis that abstracts the piece of wax from all that is not reducible to remaining, the same process is applied in an exemplary way to the *ego* itself. What the *ego* once was (*me olim*), that is, prior to thinking thought (*cogitationes*), is reduced, by subtracting (*subducam*) what is uncertain in it, to the unshakable (*certum et inconcussum*), which is all that is left. *Remanere* can and must be understood in the sense of a residue, but also of a persistence in permanence. This determination of the *ego* by persisting permanence has nothing provisional or approximate about it, since it reappears in the last of the *Meditationes,* for the sake of abstracting the *ego* as pure understanding from its adjoining faculty of imagining: "... nam quamvis illa a me abesset, procul dubio manerem nihilominus ille idem qui nunc sum [For if I lacked it, I should undoubtedly remain the same individual as I am now]" (73, 7–9 = 51). The French translation is quick to render this clause as "... je demeurerais toujours le même [I always remain the same] ..." (AT IX-1, 58, 17). It is even less appropriate to play down such an attribution of permanence to the *ego,* since it coincides with the formula *certum et inconcussum,* which—it is well known—is the formula that Heidegger will privilege to the point of adding *fundamentum* to it, and then forging a formula— *fundamentum certum et inconcussum*—which, literally, never appears in the Cartesian texts.[50] Thus, it should be considered as firmly established that "constantly remaining, *ständiger Verbleib*" concerns first and above all the *ego,* which, before all innerworldly being and in order that it might be attributed to them, must itself establish it. More exactly, the *ego* is established in terms of constant permanence; its ontic primacy over other beings depends ontologically on the understanding of the Being of beings as subsisting, thus as persisting in remaining itself, in such a way that it can satisfy the unconditional requirement of certainty. Certainty counts first as an ontological, not an epistemological, determination that compels beings to be in the mode of subsistence (*Vorhandenheit*). The *ego,* precisely because it furnishes the first and most certain of beings, must, more than any other, meet the requirements of subsistence and make visible in itself the constant permanence of beings in general. From this point on, our task is clear, even if it looks difficult. It is a matter of answering the following questions: *(a)* Does the *ego* really exist in the mode of subsistence; indeed—seeing as subsistence is defined by persistence and staying in presence—does it exist only insofar as it remains present in presence? *(b)* On the basis of the mode of Being proper to the *ego,* can we determine a mode of Being persisting in the present that concerns beings in general, such that the temporality of Being according

50. Heidegger uses this formula in *Satz vom Grund* (Pfullingen, 1957), p. 29 [English trans., p. 12]. On its having no basis in the texts of Descartes, see our remarks in *Sur la théologie blanche de Descartes,* pp. 20–23.

to subsistence (*Vorhandenheit*) is attested? *(c)* Inversely, can we confirm the Cartesian temporality of the Being of beings by starting from dimensions of time irreducible to the present? In other words, is the *ego* (and with it, the Being of beings in general) temporalized exclusively and primordially in the present? In short, what Being could be accorded to the past and future by the subsistence of the *ego,* if Being is exactly equal to subsisting in terms of constant persistence? Only an answer to these three questions can draw out the temporality of being in the Cartesian sense, or, what amounts to the same thing, the Being of beings in the Cartesian project.

We must therefore first decide *(a)* if the *ego* exists in the mode of subsistence, that is to say, if it exists insofar as it persists in presence, itself reduced to the narrowest present. That this question must be answered positively seems to result from the way in which the *ego* ascertains its own existence: in many statements always tending to the same point, its existence is stated in terms of time and in view of presence in the present. First characterization: the *ego* is each time it thinks, thus "... statuendum sit hoc pronuntiatum, *Ego sum, ego existo,* quoties a me profertur, vel mente concipitur, necessario esse verum [This proposition, *I am, I exist,* is necessarily true whenever it is put forward by me or conceived by my mind]" (AT VII, 25, 11–13). To be sure, one encounters a similar *quoties* being used to mark an actual thought from other thinkable thoughts (thus, "... quoties tamen de ente primo et summo libet cogitare ... , necesse est ut illi omnes perfectiones attribuam [Whenever I do choose to think of the first and supreme being ... , it is necessary that I attribute all perfections to him] ..." (67, 21–24 = 46–47). But here merely the occurrence of thinking draws out and provokes the occurrence of Being, or rather Being as an occurrence that arrives in the present instant. In the case when the *cogitatio* thinks thought itself, the instant of the *cogitatio* becomes the instant of existing an instantaneous existence, one linked strictly to the instantaneousness of a performance of the *cogitatio.* Following this path, then, we reach the second temporal characterization of the existence assigned to the *ego:* it is as long as it actually cognizes its own thought and doubles its thought thought (its doubts) by its thinking thought; thus "... et fallat quantum potest, nunquam tamen efficiet, ut nihil sim quamdiu me aliquid esse cogitabo [Let him deceive me as much as he can, he will never bring it about that I am nothing so long as I think that I am something]" (25, 8–10 = 17); and "Ego sum, ego existo; certum est. Quamdiu autem? Nempe quamdiu cogito; nam forte etiam fieri posset, si cessarem ab omni cogitatione, ut illico totus esse desinem [I am, I exist—that is certain. But for how long? For as long as I am thinking. For it could be that were I totally to cease from thinking, I should totally cease to exist]" (27, 8–12 = 18). The mention of *praecise* that immediately follows ("... sum igitur praecise tantum res cogitans [I am, then, precisely, only a thinking thing]" 27, 13 = 18), can signify not only a distinction of faculties—I am only insofar as understanding, mind, and reason think in me—but also and especially of temporality: I am only precisely as long as I am thinking. Other examples of this characterization are not absent: "... fallat me quisquis potest, nunquam tamen efficiet ut nihil sim, quamdiu me aliquid esse cogitabo [Let whoever can do so deceive me, he will never bring it about that I am nothing, so long as I continue to think I am something]" (36, 15–17 = 25). Or, "... quamdiu de Deo tantum cogito, totusque in eum me converto, nullam erroris aut falsitatis causam deprehendo [So long as I think only of God, and turn my whole attention to him, I can find no cause of error or falsity]" (54, 8–10 = 38). Or, "... nihilominus non possem iis [quae clare cognosco esse vera] non assentiri, saltem quamdiu ea clare percipio [I cannot but assent to these things (everything which I clearly know to be true) at least so long as I clearly perceive them]" (65, 8–9 = 45). Under the gaze of thinking thought, the evidence of thought thought thus anticipates the temporal characterization of all thought thinking in the light of evidence: the evidence itself exercises a constraint over it only as long as it is actually thinking. The time of evidence, that is to say, the time of thinking thought's presence to an evident object, determines the time of existence when existence itself is only by being thought. In other words, "... ego, dum cogito, existam [I exist so long as I am thinking]" (145, 24 = 104), "Is qui cogitat, non potest non existere dum cogitat [He who thinks cannot but exist while he thinks]" (*Principia Philosophiae I,* §49). From this, the third temporal characterization follows: that the *ego* can exist only as long as (*quamdiu/dum*) and each time (*quoties*) it actually thinks does not however imply that its certain existence endures only for an instant or for several juxtaposed and heterogeneous instants. What is at stake is not to be found in the instantaneousness of existence, but in the submission of its duration to the duration of the *cogitatio*—in short, in its finite and contingent temporality, measured by the temporality of the *cogitatio.* This is why Descartes here admits a moment— "... perspicue intelligimus fieri posse ut existam hoc momento, quo unum quid cogito [We clearly understand that it is possible for me to exist at this moment, while I am thinking of one

thing] . . ."⁵¹—that can have a duration in time: ". . . repugnat enim, ut
putemus id quod cogitat, eo ipso tempore quo cogitat, non existere [For
it is a contradiction to suppose that what thinks does not, at the very
time when it is thinking, exist]" (*Principia Philosophiae I,* §7). The existence of the *ego* is deployed temporally, but according to a temporality
that is first and radically determined by the *cogitatio.* Inversely, if the *ego*
exists only as often and as long as the present moment of the *cogitatio*
endures, this is because the *cogitatio* itself privileges presence in the present in its own temporality. Thus, the threefold temporal characterization
of the *ego*'s existence requires a more rigorous determination of the temporality that originally governs it—the temporality of the *cogitatio.* It is
here that the privilege accorded to presence in the present will become
intelligible.

In what is essential, Descartes has, as early as the *Regulae,* already
reached his definitive determination of the original temporality of the
cogitatio, such as it will be duplicated in the temporality of the *ego.* From
the outset, this *cogitatio* is temporalized in the present because the evidence it wants to attain requires presence—first of all, the presence of
the object, ". . . ne scilicet aliquam ingenii nostri partem objecti praesen-
tis supervacua recordatio surripiat [lest a part of our mind be distracted
by needless recollection from its awareness of the object before it]" (AT
X, 458, 12–13 = PW I, 69 [modified]), such that the memory of a past
object should always be shut out, for it carries the mind outside the experience of a certain thought. Next, presence determines the faculties of
the knowing mind, requiring the *praesens attentio* (417, 7; 454, 10 = 43;
66) of an *intellectus in praesenti* (445, 25 = 61). Only when there is a
perfect *intuitus* will evidence be drawn out, ". . . praesens evidentia,
qualis ad intuitum [necessaria est] [Present evidence is necessary for in-
tuition]" (370, 7–8 = 15 [modified]). In this way, *praesentes ideae* (455,
2 = 67) can appear, and through a perfect synchrony of presences (ob-

---

51. *To Arnauld,* 4 June 1648 (AT V, 193, 18–19 = PW III, 355). No one has done a
better job establishing that the *cogitatio* endures and that a time of thought must be admitted than J.-M. Beyssade, *La philosophie première de Descartes* (Paris, 1979), particularly
pp. 129–76. In any case, the already quite old analyses of Jean Wahl, *Du rôle de l'idée
d'instant dans la philosophie de Descartes* (Paris, 1920 1st ed., 1953 2d ed.), should no
longer be considered definitive, be this only in light of a remark reported by Burman:
". . . quod cogitatio etiam fiat in instanti falsum est, cum omnis actio mea fiat in tempore
[It is false that my thoughts occur instantaneously; for all my acts take up time]" (*Conversation with Burman* [AT V, 148, 22–23 = PW III, 335]).

ject, attention, evidence, and ideas), the *cogitatio* can gaze upon (re-garder, *intueri*) these *ideae* as its *cogitatum*. To gaze upon [*regarder*] here means, according to the same duality found in *intueri,* first to take into view, but also to guard [*garder*] and protect (*tueri*). In short, to gaze upon implies to keep under one's eyes [*garder sous les yeux*], to watch over [*garder du regard*], "to have an eye on [*avoir à l'oeil*]." Such a gaze that keeps watch cannot be carried out if its object does not stay present to its sight; better, it can keep watch over it only if it does not lose it from view at any instant, only if it makes it remain present by a permanent keeping, which makes it persist in presence. From the moment it intends *praesens evidentia,* the *cogitatio* requires of its object that it be precisely (*praecise tantum*) in the mode of persisting presence. This fundamental decision governs the entire development of Cartesian thought. As proof, take only the definition of a clear idea that was set down in 1644:

> Claram voco ideam, quae menti attendenti praesens et aperta est: sicut ea clare a nobis videri dicimus, quae, oculo intuenti praesentia, satis fortiter et aperte illum movent. [I call a perception "clear" when it is present and accessible to the attentive mind—just as we say that we see something clearly when it is present to the eye's gaze and stimulates it with a sufficient degree of strength and accessibility.] [*Principia Philosophiae I,* §45.]

The gaze (of the mind as well as of the eye) is "stimulated" only by an idea that is as present—thus "open," that is to say available and acces-sible to its attention—as it itself has become, by this same attention, present. The evidence arrives when these two presences, the "presence of mind" and the present thing, coincide. They determine presence in terms of this coincidence—unless inversely it is presence that makes it possible for the two present terms to coincide insofar as it alone can put them in the presence of each other.[52] In the *Meditationes* as in the *Regu-*

---

52. On the status and the translation of *intuitus* by "gaze [*regard*]," see our remarks in *Règles utiles et claires . . . ,* pp. 106–7, 119–27, 186–87, 209, and 296–302. The highest point of presence to the thought that keeps watch and gazes over [*garde et regarde*] is of course reached in the idea of God: ". . . ut ad ideam, quam habere possumus de Deo, attendamus, illamque cogitationi nostrae praesenten exhibeamus [give some attention to the idea which we can have of God, and make it directly present to our thought]" (AT VIII-2, 360, 15–17 = PW I, 305 [modified]). In this sense, the end of *Meditatio III* should be read as an example of theological contemplation transposed into metaphysical territory, and also as the apex of the gaze that keeps watch over its object [*le regard qui garde son objet*]—here God—in presence in the present: it is a matter of *intueri* (52, 15) for the longest time possible (*aliquandiu in ipsius Dei contemplatione immorari*). On the ambiguity of this pas-

lae, presence characterizes the object that can most easily be made evident in knowledge, the (mathematical) object of the imagination: ". . . istas tres lineas tanquam praesentes acie mentis intueor [I see the three lines with my mind's eye as if they were present before me]" (AT VII, 72, 8–9 = PW II, 50); but it can also concern the object of sensation: ". . . neque possem objectum ullum sentire, quamvis vellem, nisi illud sensus organo esset praesens, nec possem non sentire cum erat praesens [I could not have sensory awareness of any object, even if I wanted to, unless it was present to my sense organs; and I could not avoid having sensory awareness of it when it was present]" (75, 11–14 = 52). Moreover, the presence of the object to the *cogitatio* can reach such an intensity (such a "presence," the more familiar language says), that it might appear possible to infer its existence directly: ". . . attentius consideranti quidnam sit imaginatio, nihil aliud esse apparet quam quaedam applicatio facultatis cognoscitivae ad corpus ipsi intime praesens, ac proinde existens [When I give more attentive consideration to what imagination is, it seems to be nothing else but an application of the cognitive faculty to a body which is intimately present to it, and which therefore exists]" (71, 23–72, 3 = 50). Without claiming to widen the scope of a formula that concerns only the body proper, it is still legitimate to contemplate the equivalence that quite clearly appears in it, *praesens ac proinde existens.* If existence does not always actually follow from presence, it nonetheless always presupposes it; nothing existing is known or knowable except in the mode of presence. The *cogitatio* gazes only on presence, and therefore keeps watch over existence as a certain object only insofar as existence is presented in the mode of presence in the present. In short, by dint of regarding only presence, the *cogitatio* admits as possible objects only beings that exist in the present. The *cogitatio* temporalizes its *cogitatum* exclusively in the present because it first temporalizes itself exclusively in presence.

But there is more: the *cogitatio* limits neither its own temporalization nor that of its object to a presence reduced to the instant, an atomic and imperceptible point. Present evidence must have a duration in order that the science of objects arranged according to the order might be constituted. Consequently, in order to expand the field of present evidence to include the discursivity of the *series rerum,* the *Regulae* admit, in addi-

---

sage, see our study "De la divinisation à la domination. Etude sur la sémantique de *capable/capax* chez Descartes," *Revue philosophique de Louvain* 1975/2.

tion to the punctual evidence of the *intuitus*, a *motus cogitationis*, which
has as its function to run through the deductions that the punctual *intuitus* cannot treat; but it does this only in view of reaching present evidence, and it succeeds in reaching this evidence only by reproducing, in
temporal succession, the present of the gaze of *intuitus*—through a twofold peculiarity. First, the movement of the *cogitatio* remains continuous
and is never interrupted; accordingly, it keeps watch over the consistency
of the presence lying at the heart of the long chain of consecutive links:

> ... plurimae res certo sciuntur, quamvis ipsae non sint evidentes, modo
> tantum a veris cognitisque principiis deducantur per continuum et nullibi
> interruptum cogitationis motum singula perspicue intuentis. [Very many
> facts which are not self-evident are known with certainty, provided they
> are inferred from true and known principles through a continuous and
> uninterrupted movement of thought in which each individual proposition
> is clearly intuited.] [AT X, 369, 22–26 = PW I, 15.][53]

The *motus cogitationis* is *continuus* only for the sake of continuing, by
displacing without undoing, the gaze of the *intuitus*, which, passing beyond the present instant, nonetheless does not renounce the epistemological primacy of presence, but rather extends it and completes it. From
this comes the second peculiarity: the movement of thought does not
allow for several objects merely to be seen in succession, but above all
for them to be run through so rapidly that the gaze can, in the end,
know their plurality and at the same time (*simul*) apprehend it as strictly
present: "... continuo quodam imaginationis motu singula intuentis
simul et ad alia transeuntis [a continuous movement of the imagination,
simultaneously (*simul*) intuiting one relation and passing on to the
next] ..." (388, 2–4 = 25), "... per motum quemdam cogitationis singula
attente intuentis simul et ad alia transeuntis [a movement of thought, as
it were, which involves attentively intuiting one thing and simultaneously
(*simul*) passing on to the others]" (408, 16–17 = 38 [modified]), "... omnia celerrimo cogitationis motu percurrere et quamplurima simul intueri
[run through all of them with the swiftest sweep of thought and intuit as
many as possible at the same time (*simul*)]" (455, 6–7 = 67). In this way,
presence can be applied to a field much larger than an instantaneous

---

53. In the *Regulae*, the *cogitatio* is quite often defined by such a *motus continuus:* AT
X, 369, 24–25; 387, 11–12 and 21; 388, 2–3; 407, 3; 408, 24–25 = PW I, 15; 25 and 25; 25;
37; 38.

presence.[54] The *motus cogitationis* collapses the far reaches of past discursivity into the present instant—the chosen temporality of the evidence present to the gaze. The horizon of presence exceeds the present because the *cogitatio*, being redoubled by a *motus cogitationis*, leads back to the present what appeared to have escaped it definitively. Since the *cogitatio* has been put into motion, the sway that presence exerts over temporality will exceed the present and prolong it into the fields of the past. But, it will be objected, what does it matter if a temporality of the present dominates, if it is limited to the time of thought and does not determine that of things? But, to speak precisely, in Cartesian terms, there is only one single and unique concept of time, one that is dominant within the entire horizon of beings. And Descartes explicitly repeats the time of being in general on the basis of the time of the *mens*, understood as a *cogitatio*. To prove this, one has only to consider the steps making up the Cartesian determination of time in terms of the *cogitatio*. Descartes first refuses to distinguish between the duration of movable (therefore extended) beings and the duration of beings that are immovable. Despite the cardinal difference between thought and extension, duration remains common to them. Already in the *Regulae, duratio* counts among the common simple natures (AT X, 419, 20–22 = PW I, 45). In the *Principia*, it keeps the same universality and is opposed to time, which follows from it without duplicating it or limiting it:

> Cum tempus a duratione generaliter sumpta distinguimus, dicimusque esse numerum motus, est tantum modus cogitationis; neque enim profecto intelligimus in motu aliam durationem quam in rebus non motis. [When time is distinguished from duration taken in the general sense and called the measure of movement, it is simply a mode of thought. For the duration which we understand to be involved in movement is certainly no different from the duration involved in things which do not move.] [*Principia Philosophiae I,* §57.]

What endures is not first of all the extended thing in motion, but the *cogitatio* itself. Burman's account holds nothing surprising here, since it too allows that what endures par excellence is thinking thought: ". . . omnis actio mea natura fiat in tempore, et ego possum dici in eadem cogitatione continuare et perseverare per aliquod tempus [All my acts

---

54. The reduction of deduction to *intuitus* by the *motus cogitationis* in an explicit temporality of knowledge in the present makes up the expressed aim of *Regula XI* (See *Règles utiles et claires . . .* , pp. 220–23).

take up time, and I can be said to be continuing and carrying on with the same thought during a period of time]."[55] In this, we discover only an explanation of the *quamdiu/momentum* analyzed above as the *ego's* proper way of Being present in presence. And not only does the *mens* (or the *ego*) endure also, but it endures above all. It endures originally, inasmuch as it allocates all duration like an origin. The *mens* endures because duration comes from it, mentally as it were. Descartes does not hesitate to put forth, in the same passage in which he advances the ego-logical deduction of substance, an egological deduction of duration: "... quaedam ad idea mei ipsius videor mutuari potuisse, nempe substantiam, durationem, numerum, et si quae alia sint ejusmodi [It appears that I could have borrowed some of these from my idea of myself, namely substance, duration, number and anything else of this kind]" (AT VII, 44, 19–21 = 30). And, in fact, the two deductions are combined in a single explication (44, 17–45, 8 = 30–31). We discover, here applied to *duratio,* the same reasoning that we saw being used to deal with *substantia* (above, §13)—the *ego* engenders temporality on the basis of its own duration:

> ... itemque, cum percipio me nunc esse, et prius etiam aliquamdiu fuisse recordor, cumque varias habeo cogitationes quarum numerum intelligo, acquiro ideas durationis et numeri, quas deinde ad quascunque alias res possum transferre. [I perceive that I now exist, and remember that I have existed for some time; moreover, I have various thoughts which I can count; it is in these ways that I acquire the ideas of duration and number which I can then transfer to other things.] [44, 28–45, 2 = 30–31.]

This remarkable text demands a precise analysis. First of all, the *ego* perceives, before all duration, its Being in the strict present: *nunc esse* indicates ontically its present existence; but above all it indicates that, ontologically, Being is said in terms of presence. *Nunc esse* ascertains the present existence of the *ego,* but marks essentially the fundamental equivalence of *esse* and *nunc,* of Being and presence—as such. The second step consists in the *ego* becoming conscious of its *cogitationes,* and also that it is a matter of *cogitationes* already passed, therefore that perceiving them amounts to remembering them (*recordari*).[56] In this way,

---

55. *Conversation with Burman* (AT V, 148, 22–25 = PW III, 335). See above, n. 51.

56. This is confirmed by the two *Letters to Arnauld,* 4 June 1648: "... successio in cogitationibus nostris [Our thoughts display a successiveness] ..." (AT V, 193, 16–17 = PW III, 355) and: "... durationis successivae, quam in cogitatione mea ... deprehendo

Descartes anticipates Kant (and the synthesis of the reproduction in the imagination) as well as Husserl (and retention). In the third step, duration is laid bare—which issues in the practice of thinking about the past as well as the present, or rather to the consciousness, which, in order to think thoughts in the present, has to be able to reconduct to this unique present even thoughts already past. The genesis of duration on the basis of the present Being of the *ego* is accomplished through the consciousness of the succession of *cogitationes.* This conscious succession also furnishes the origin of number, which measures and orders them. What now remains is for us to understand how two notions so strictly connected to the *ego* can be transferred to other things so easily that Descartes does not even offer an explanation for it. In short, does *transferre* suggest only an imprecise metaphorization of the duration of consciousness, or does it imply a rigorous process of transposition? The second hypothesis forces itself upon us if we observe the relation, here as yet uninvestigated, connecting number to duration. It is all the more necessary that we notice this relation as Descartes defines time as a number—the number of movement, "... tempus ... dicimusque esse numerum motus [Time is ... called the number of movement] ..." (*Principia Philosophiae I,* §57 [modified]). Such a formula refers explicitly to Aristotle's definition of time, which it cites word for word, to some extent: τοῦτο γάρ ἐστιν ὁ χρόνος, ἀριθμὸς κινήσεως κατὰ τὸ πρότερον καὶ ὕστερον [For time is just this—number of motion in respect of 'before' and 'after'].[57] Another Cartesian text completes the literal citation:

> Non aliter intelligo durationem successivam rerum quae moventur, vel etiam ipsius motus, quam rerum non motarum; prius enim et posterius durationis cujuscunque mihi innotescit per prius et posterius durationis successivae, quam in cogitatione mea, cui res aliae coexistunt, deprehendo.
> [I understand the successive duration of things in motion, and of the motion itself, no differently from that of things that are not in motion; for earlier and later in any duration are known to me by the earlier and later

[the successive duration which I detect in my own thought] ..." (AT V 223, 18–19 = PW III, 358).

57. Aristotle, *Physics IV,* 11, 219, *b* 1–2 [English trans., p. 372]. This celebrated definition could make its way to Descartes by passing through the Conimbricences (so thinks Etienne Gilson, *Index scolastico-cartésien* [Paris, 1913], pp. 284–86). It is not out of the question to consider Suarez, and it is simpler to do so. See *Disputationes Metaphysicae L,* s. 10, nn. 8–10, vol. 26, 960–61.

of the successive duration which I detect in my own thought, with which the other things co-exist.][58]

The successive duration (in terms of before and after) of things in motion, whatever they might be, is understood through the before and after of the successive duration of the *cogitatio.* Time is indeed the number of movement for Descartes as for Aristotle. Descartes here retrieves, to the letter, the Aristotelian definition of time such as it had been transmitted to him by the medievals. This retrieval is accomplished without his making any criticism, unlike his retrievals of the definitions, however comparable, of movement and place.[59] The agreement between Descartes and Aristotle gives cause for a twofold observation. If, following Heidegger, it is admitted that a single and unique "ordinary concept of time" governs and traverses the metaphysical tradition from Aristotle to Hegel, it seems likely that Descartes is inscribed within it; and, in fact, our previous analyses have already drawn out one of its fundamental traits: Descartes too thinks time in terms of presence in the present, a determination that dominates all other temporalization because it renders possible the interpretation of the Being of beings as insistent persistence.[60] We

58. *To Arnauld,* 29 July 1648 (AT V, 223, 14–19 = PW III, 358).

59. The Aristotelian definition of place is criticized explicitly by *Regula XII* (AT X, 426, 9–16), then by *Regula XIII* (433, 14–434, 1 = PW I, 49; 53). As for the Aristotelian definition of time, it suffers the assault of *Regula XII* (426, 16–427, 2 = 49), of *The World or Treatise on Light, VII* (AT XI, 39, 4–22 = 93–94), and of several letters (*To Mersenne,* 16 October 1639 [AT II, 597, 18–27]; *To Boswell?* 1646? [AT IV, 697, 26–698, 2 = PW III, 139; not included in PW]). See our notes in *Règles utiles et claires . . . ,* pp. 248–49 and 254–56. The customary polemic against Aristotle therefore seems, in the definition of time, to undergo a noteworthy cease-fire. This is not a subjective variation on the part of Descartes, but the tacit acknowledgment of his inescapable determination, on this decisive point, by previous metaphysics.

60. *Sein und Zeit,* §§81–82. The "ordinary concept of time" is defined as a "sequence of 'nows' persisting in subsistance (*ständig 'vorhanden'*), at once arising and disappearing" (423 [English trans., p. 475 (modified)]). The terms in which it is defined therefore agree with the Cartesian determination of time. It will also be observed that it is on the occasion of this, the final analysis in *Sein und Zeit,* that Heidegger introduces for the first time (in the texts published to this date, and without making any advance judgments about the 1923–24 course dedicated to *Der Beginn der neuzeitlichen Philosophie*) "the Interpretation of Descartes' 'cogito me cogitare rem'" (433 [English trans., p. 484]). It is therefore not entirely out of place to suppose that Descartes is at issue in the final pages of *Sein und Zeit.* This thesis was formulated by J. Laporte, through entirely different means: "'a thinking thing,' 'an extended thing': what do these terms give us to understand that is not found in the terms 'extension' or 'thought'? Do they signify *permanence?* Permanence always was, for the philosophers who admitted substance, in whatever form, one of its distinctive

will have to return to this new argument in favor of an authentically
metaphysical constitution of Cartesian thought, so decisive is it. But nevertheless, the literal agreement in the two definitions must not be al-
lowed to hide a difference of great consequence. That is to say, if Descartes, defining time as *numerus motus,* does indeed retrieve the Aristotelian position, determining time as ἀριθμὸς κινήσεως, the identity of
the two formulae still does not decide whether the meanings of κίνησις
and *motus* agree or disagree. What, then, is being enumerated in each
case? For Aristotle, the enumerated movement is unfolded, as for Descartes, in terms of before and after, but these latter criteria immediately
imply place, τόπος : τὸ δὴ πρότερον καὶ ὕστερον ἐν τόπῳ πρῶτόν ἐστιν;
place offers the only frame in which a before and an after could *take
place.* Two corollaries are implied. First of all, movement unfolds within
the categories of being considered in Being, and among these categories,
place is included, on a secondary level; movement cannot be produced
apart from the things themselves, and therefore it also cannot be produced apart from the categories that govern them: οὐκ ἔστι δὲ κίνησις
παρὰ τὰ πράγματα· μεταβάλλει γὰρ ἀεὶ τὸ μεταβάλλον ἢ κατ' οὐσίαν, ἢ
κατὰ ποσὸν, ἢ κατὰ ποιὸν ἢ κατὰ τόπον. [There is no such thing as motion
over and above things. It is always with respect to substance or to quantity or to quality or to place that what changes changes]. The second
corollary follows from this: as enumerated number, movement can affect
only a countable being; in short, it is in play between an ὑποκείμενον
and another ὑποκείμενον, or between states of these ὑποκείμενα.[61] No
doubt, ψυχή intervenes for the purpose of enumerating, but it does so
without itself offering the enumerated number, precisely because it is
put into practice as an enumerating number; or to state it more simply,
it carries out the enumeration, namely time. In short, for Aristotle,

characteristics (it is even the only one that Kant will retain in the *First Analogy of Experi-
ence*)." *Le rationalisme de Descartes* (Paris, 1945, 1950), p. 185, see also pp. 189 and 463.
More recently and not without its difficulties, this interpretation reappears in David J.
Marshall, Jr., *Prinzipien der Descartes-Exegese* (Fribourg/Munich, 1979).

61. Aristotle, respectively *Physics IV,* 11, 219 *a* 14–15; *III,* 1, 200 *b* 32–34 [English trans.,
p. 342]; and (by allusion) *V,* 1, 224 *b* 1–10. That time, like movement, is for the most part
concerned with innerworldly beings was clearly demonstrated by W. Wieland, *Die aristotel-
ische Physik* (Göttingen, 1962 1st ed., 1972 2d ed.), §18, pp. 316–34. Even with respect to
the formula κίνησις δέ τις ἐν τῇ ψυχῇ [Movement takes place within the mind] (*Physics IV,*
11, 219, *a* 5–6 [English trans., p. 371]), he maintains that "doch das ist für Aristoteles der
Ausnahmefall; der Normalfall, an dem sich die Zeitlehre durchgehend orientiert, bleibt der
der äusseren Bewegung der Dinge" (pp. 322–23).

movement bears on the beings that are offered to the ψυχή, in no way on the ψυχή itself. This does not seem to be the case for Descartes, be this only for a prohibitive reason: time, or rather the duration that renders it possible, comes up in *Meditatio III* before the existence or even essence of a *res* outside of thought has been established. Duration is already completely determined, to the point that it is able to take up Aristotle's definition of time word for word, before the appearance of beings. In effect, the successive duration of any thing whatsoever (*cujuscunque*) becomes known to me (*mihi innotescit*) only on the basis of a more original duration, one that is defined by the succession of my *cogitationes:* ". . . per prius et posterius durationis successivae, quam in cogitatione mea . . . deprehendo [Earlier and later in any duration are known to me by the earlier and later of the successive duration which I detect in my own thought]."[62] The initial movement, which time (or the duration that produces it) determines and measures, does not unfold in the thing as it passes from one of its states to another by the ἐντελέχεια of its δύναμις; rather, it unfolds in thought, or, more exactly, between the *cogitationes*—here, we again come upon the *motus cogitationis.* Duration is indeed defined as the number of movement, but more specifically as the number of the first movement that the *ego* can ascertain: the *motus cogitationis.* Does this radical disagreement with Aristotle give us cause to doubt that Descartes repeated the "ordinary concept of time," and in it the primacy of presence in the present? On the contrary, it strengthens our view and takes it to the next level; for the *motus cogitationis* attempts to reproduce the *praesens evidentia,* even and especially there where discursivity, thus the realm of the past, seems to forbid it. The *motus cogitationis* helps stretch presence beyond the present, to which it tries to reconduct the past of evidence. Better, the *motus,* if it is unfolded in the *cogitatio,* can attain a present that is still more immediate (still more present—if one can speak this way) than the movement in the things themselves; for, in the moment of their presence, these things are obviously not conscious of it, seeing as they do not have any consciousness. From this it follows that, even when present, they are neither present to themselves nor present to the presence that consciousness bestows. Consciousness (therefore also the *motus cogitationis* that it governs) is found, and it alone, in the absolute present that it produces absolutely as presence to self. Cartesian time thus does not privilege merely presence in the present (as Aristotelian time already had), but the self-

62. *To Arnauld,* 29 July 1648 (AT V, 223, 17–19 = PW III, 358).

presence of the present—time becomes the ego's presence to itself. This is why, when the *ego* perdures in presence (understood as insistent persistence, *ständiger Verbleib*), it perdures in and through the *cogitatio* as the ultimate figure of presence: ". . . ego possum dici in eadem cogitatione continuare et perseverare per aliquod tempus [I can be said to continue and persevere in the same thought during a period of time]."[63] To the first of the three questions that arose from Descartes' understanding temporality on the basis of the *ego*, we can now answer: the *ego*, as much by its presence to itself as by its *motus cogitationis*, reinterprets the Aristotelian definition of time in such a way as to accentuate the "ordinary concept of time" to the point that it passes from presence in the present to the self-presence of presence in the present. It is therefore appropriate to speak of an egological deduction of time in which time is interpreted through and through as subsisting presence.

The second question can now be broached: on the basis of the mode of Being actually persisting in the *ego's* presence in the present, can we determine a mode of temporality and of presence for beings in general? We have established that for Descartes the determinations of substance and duration go hand in hand. First, because they have a common origin: both are deduced from the *ego*, before all other existence (AT VII, 44, 20), in a parallel set of deductions (44, 21–28 is parallel to 44, 28–45, 2). Next because, more generally, "existentia et duratio" (*Principia Philosophiae I,* §56) or "existentia . . . duratio" (AT X, 419, 22 = PW I, 45) offer themselves to be contemplated together. But these suggestions take on their full importance only with a universal principle, which closely connects each to the other: ". . . quia substantia quaevis, si cessat durare, cessat etiam esse, ratione tantum a duratione sua distinguitur [Since a substance cannot cease to endure without also ceasing to be, the distinction between the substance and its duration is merely a conceptual one]" (*Principia Philosophiae I,* §62). In other words, a substance that does not endure ceases in this way even to be a substance, because a substance has Being as its ownmost characteristic. Two consequences follow from this: the first, which Descartes explicitly formulated, is that substance is only conceptually distinguished from duration; the other, left implicit but which is nonetheless decisive, says that Being is equivalent to enduring. And enduring has meaning only in the present, or rather, in a presence that forever brings the other periods of time back into the present. The equivalence of substance and duration thus directly implies that

---

63. *Conversation with Burman* (AT V, 148, 22–25 = PW III, 335 [modified]).

presence in the present governs substance. Several pieces of evidence confirm this—first of all, substance subsists: "... substantiae, hoc est, res per se subsistentes [substances, that is, things which subsist on their own]..." (AT VII, 222, 18 = PW II, 157), "... vera substantia, sive res per se subsistens [a true substance, or self-subsistent thing]...."[64] *Subsistere* and *to subsist* are not exactly the same as *substare*. The last term simply refers to a vertical stance (*stare, se dresser,* to stand upright), while the first ones refer to *sistere, se tenir,* to stand or to hold still, in the stronger sense of to hold one's own, to hold a position, to stand one's ground, thus to resist—in short, to endure and to make endure. Hence, permanence (*manere, permanere*) will be attributed, as constitutive characteristic, to everything that is insofar as it really is through itself. In fact, the permanence that endures in presence does not qualify merely the thinking thing (25, 23 and 73, 8 = 17 and 51) or the extension (30, 19–20; 30, 25 = 20; 20) of a thing stripped of its sensible qualities (*Principia Philosophiae II,* §4). It also qualifies extension as principal attribute[65] and place—"... nullum esse permanentem ullius rei locum, nisi quatenus a cogitatione nostra determinatur [Nothing has a permanent place, except as determined by our thought]" (*Principia Philosophiae II,* §13)—because it draws its permanence from the originally permanent *cogitatio.* And finally, God himself accomplishes permanence most perfectly, since, to take the concept rigorously, he alone deserves the title *substance* as a result of his complete independence: "... te creaturae tribuere perfectionem creatoris, quod nempe independenter ab alio in esse perseveret [You are attributing to a created thing the perfection of a creator, if the created thing is able to persevere in existence independently of anything else]..." (AT VII, 370, 8–10 = PW II, 255 [modi-

---

64. *To Regius,* January 1642 (AT III, 502, 11 = PW III, 207).
65. Thus in *Principia Philosophiae II,*

... mutato corpore quod spatium implet, non tamen extensio spatii mutari censeatur, sed remanere una et eadem, quamdiu ejusdem magnitudinis ac figurae, servatque eumdem situm inter externa quaedam corpora, per quae illud spatium determinamus. [When a new body comes to occupy the space, the extension of the space is reckoned not to change but to remain one and the same, so long as it retains the same size and shape and keeps the same position relative to certain external bodies which we use to determine the space in question.]

(§10.) Also, "... advertamus, nihil plane in ejus [lapis] idea remanere, praeterquam quod sit quid extensum in longum, latum et profundum [We will see that nothing remains in the idea of the stone except that it is something extended in length, breadth, and depth]" (§11). See *To More,* 5 February 1649 (AT V, 268, 22–25 = PW III, 360), where *remanere* yields to *retinere,* to retain; but *to retain* still marks insistence in the present.

fied]). Even the existence of God is understood in terms of permanence, or better, of perseverance—and what other mode of Being would God illustrate, if not the sole one Descartes recognized: *nunc esse* (44, 28 = 30)? God, in order to be, since he has to be, must remain insistently in presence; thus he must persevere in the present. This universality must also be the conclusion if one starts from another reference, one that in fact puts forth a principle: "Unamquamque rem, quatenus est simplex et indivisa, manere, quantum in se est, in eodem semper statu, nec unquam mutari nisi a causis externis [Each thing, in so far as it is simple and undivided, always remains in the same state, as far as it can, and never changes except as a result of external causes]." Formulated otherwise, the principle says: ". . . unaquaeque res, non composita, sed simplex, qualis est motus, semper esse perseveret, quamdiu a nulla causa externa destruitur [Everything that is not composite but simple, as motion is, always persists in being . . . so long as it is not destroyed by an external cause]"; or: ". . . unaquaeque res tendat, quantum in se est, ad permanendum in eodem statu in quo est [Everything tends, so far as it can, to persist in the same state]."[66] We understand this as follows: all that is is in terms of presence in the present; thus, as a consequence of the demand to be as presence, everything perseveres in Being in the mode of insistent permanence (*ständiger Verbleib*) and accordingly ends up as subsistence (*Vorhandenheit*). This understanding at once gives rise to an apparently irrefutable objection: as principle for a determination of the mode of Being of beings, we just cited some formulations of what, in other contexts, it has always been appropriate to call the "principle of inertia"; we have thus illegitimately transposed a principle of physics—one that concerns objects at rest or in motion, in any case, extension—into the domain of ontology, which exceeds extension and concerns the *res cogitans* and God. This objection is in fact susceptible to several counter-objections. First and above all, is it necessary to rule out the possibility of an ontological interpretation of the "principle of inertia"? Moreover, as a principle of physics, does it not arise from a field prior to physics—*de facto* for Descartes ever since the theses of 1630,[67] *de jure* in terms of its concept? Does not the very history of its slow emergence confirm our claim that this principle belongs less to experimental physics than to an

66. *Principia Philosophiae II*, respectively §§37, 41, and 43.
67. *To Mersenne*, 15 April 1630 (AT I, 144, 10 = PW III, 22): ". . . discover the foundations of physics . . ." and 144, 15 = 22: ". . . prove metaphysical truths. . . . " On this important point, see *supra*, chap. I, §2.

ontological meditation on the conditions for the possibility of motion and its mathematical expression?[68] There is more: it seems legitimate and even obligatory to acknowledge that for Descartes, according to the formulation of 1644, the principle—all beings, at rest and in motion, persevere in Being in the sense of an insistence in presence—falls within metaphysics, even and precisely because it determines physics. This principle actually stems from the immutability of God: "Intelligimus etiam perfectionem esse in Deo, non solum quod in se ipso sit immutabilis, sed etiam quod modo quam maxime constanti et immutabili operetur [We understand that God's perfection involves not only his being immutable in himself, but also his operating in a manner that is always utterly constant and immutable] ... ," " ... ex hâc eadem immutabilitate Dei, regulae quaedam sive leges naturae cognosci possunt [From God's immutability we can also know certain rules or laws of nature] ... ," "Demonstratur etiam pars altera ex immutabilitate operationis Dei, mundum eadem actione, quâ olim creavit, continuo jam conservantis [The second part of the law is proved from the immutability of the workings of God, by means of which the world is continually preserved through an action identical with the original act of creation]."[69] From 1643 on, the metaphysical status of what is called the "principle of inertia" will be stated expressly:

> The other principle is that whatever is or exists remains always in the state in which it is, unless some external cause changes it. ... I prove this by metaphysics; for God, who is the author of all things, is entirely perfect and unchangeable; and so it seems to me absurd that any simple thing which exists, and so has God for its author, should have in itself the principle of its destruction.[70]

This remarkable text claims not only that God alone, through his original immutability (for he alone perseveres perfectly according to AT VII, 370, 8–10), makes possible the derived permanence of created beings; it also claims more than just that this proof arises from "metaphysics." Above all, it claims that the principle thus determined concerns "all that is or exists," and not just the physical domain, namely, extension. It must

---

68. See *The World or Treatise on Light VII* (AT XI, 38, 1–21 = PW I, 93). We refer to the works of A. Koyré (Paris, 1966), particularly *La Loi de la chute des corps. Descartes et Galilée,* pp. 83–158, and *L'élimination de la pesanteur,* pp. 291–341. Koyré, too, treats the "principle of inertia" as an "ontological" principle (in a sense that, to be sure, remains undetermined).

69. *Principia Philosophiae II,* respectively §§36, 37, and 42.

70. *To Mersenne,* 26 April 1643 (AT III, 649, 12–25 = PW III, 216–17).

therefore be concluded that, for Descartes at least, the "principle of inertia" states only one of the regional, ontic applications of a metaphysical principle. This metaphysical principle declares that all beings are in terms of presence in the present, and that in consequence they can only persevere, insist, and persist in presence, thus endure in the present. These characteristics befall all beings just as substance had first of all befallen them—through a deduction that starts from the *ego*. This principle must be understood as an ontological thesis concerning the way of Being of all beings, both possible and real. The strangest confirmation of the fact that this metaphysical principle bears on all beings without exception comes from its application to the mystery of transubstantiation—and this owes nothing to chance. If, Descartes argues with Arnauld, "... docuit Ecclesia species panis et vini remanentes in Sacramento Eucharistiae esse accidentia quaedam realia, quae, sublata substantiacui inhaerebant, miraculose subsistant [The Church has ... taught that the 'forms' of the bread and wine that remain in the sacrament of the Eucharist are real accidents, which miraculously subsist on their own when the substance in which they used to inhere has been removed] ..." (AT VII, 252, 18–21 = PW II, 177), then these "real accidents" must be considered authentic substances. This is so because substance consists entirely in subsistence, seeing as "... nihil reale potest intelligi remanere, nisi quod subsistat, et, quamvis verbo vocetur accidens, concipiatur tamen ut substantia [Nothing real can be understood to remain, except as subsisting; and though the word 'accident' may be used to describe it, it must nonetheless be conceived of as a substance]" (253, 25–27 = 176 [modified]). Inversely, no confirmation of this ontological statement can arise out of the disputed question about the contradiction, or not, between continual creation, or not, and discontinuous duration, or not. In effect, it is precisely because finite beings, first of all the *ego* but also the world, are not perfectly independent substances that on the one hand, they cannot endure, persevere, and subsist in presence, and that on the other hand, they must have recourse to the continual divine creation in order to verify in themselves the insistent permanence that defines the temporality of Being.[71] Thus we have answered, at least

71. We think here of J. Laporte, *Le rationalisme de Descartes* (Paris, 1950), pp. 157*ff.*, discussed by M. Gueroult, *Descartes selon l'ordre des raisons* (Paris, 1953), vol. 1, pp. 272–85. The theses are clearly organized around a fundamental pronouncement:

Quoniam enim omne tempus vitae in partes innumeras dividi potest, quarum singulae a reliquis nullo modo dependent, ex eo quod paulo ante fuerim, non sequitur me nunc debere esse, nisi aliqua causa me quasi rursus creet ad hoc momentum, hoc est me conservet. [For a lifespan can be divided into countless parts, each completely independent

in outline, the second question: the insistent persistence, which the temporality of the *ego* puts into operation, is deployed in "all that is, or exists" according to an egological deduction of presence in the present, which duplicates the egological deduction of the substantiality of all beings. Not only is Being understood on the basis of thought in the mode of the *ego cogito*—"ego autem substantia" (AT VII, 45, 8)—but—since "percipio me nunc esse" (44, 28)—the temporality of all beings is understood in terms of the presence to itself of the *ego* persisting in the present. According to Descartes, Being and time come together in the one and only subsistence (*res subsistans, Vorhandenheit*).

A final question still remains untouched: *(c)* Are there other dimensions of time analyzed as such by Descartes? If this is the case, do the

---

of the others, so that it does not follow from the fact that I existed a little while ago that I must exist now, unless there is some cause which as it were creates me afresh at this moment—that which preserves me.]

(AT VII, 48, 28–49, 5 = PW II, 33.) This pronouncement carries with it two connected and not contradictory consequences. (1) The discontinuity of time, which does not imply that it is stretched thin into imperceptible instants, but that it admits two parts: "... attendamus ad temporis sive rerum durationis naturam; quae talis est, ut ejus partes a se mutuo non pendeant, nec unquam simul existant [We attend to the nature of time or the duration of things. For the nature of time is such that its parts are not mutually dependent, and never coexist] ..." (*Principia Philosophiae I,* §21). Along the same lines, see: "... considero temporis a se mutuo sejungi posse, atque ita ex hoc quod jam sim non sequi me mox futurum, nisi aliqua causa me quasi rursus efficiat singulis momentis [I regard the divisions of time as being separable from each other, so that the fact that I now exist does not imply that I shall continue to exist in a little while unless there is a cause which as it were creates me afresh at each moment] ..." (*Responsiones I* [AT VII, 109, 9–13 = PW I, 78–79]); or: "... quod explicui de partium temporis independentia [This can be plainly demonstrated from my explanation of the independence of the divisions of time] ..." (*Responsiones V,* 369, 26–27 = 255). (2) What follows, by conversion of the temporal insufficiency of created time into the ontic insufficiency of created substance, is the necessity for a continual creation: "Tempus praesens a proxime praecedenti non pendet, ideoque non minor causa requirur ad rem conservandam, quam ad illam primum producendam [There is no relation of dependence between the present time and the immediately preceding time, and hence no less a cause is required to preserve something than is required to create it in the first place]" (*Responsiones II,* 165, 4–6 = 116); and:

... atque ideo ex hoc quod jam simus, non sequitur nos in tempore proxime sequenti etiam futuros, nisi aliqua causa, nempe eadem quae nos primum produxit, continuo veluti reproducat, hoc est, conservet. [Thus from the fact that we now exist, it does not follow that we shall exist a moment from now, unless there is some cause—the same cause which originally produced us—which continually reproduces us, as it were, that is to say which keeps us in existence.]

(*Principia Philosophiae I,* §21.) In this sense, so long as it is applied to finite substance (the only one that Descartes really studies), we must subscribe to the opinion of J. Laporte: "The notion of substance such as it is conceived by Descartes does not imply permanence in duration, but merely a capacity for this permanence" (*Le rationalisme de Descartes,* p. 436).

past and the future confirm the primacy of presence in the interpretation of Being in terms of the present as the persistence of subsistence? But to envision this final question, we have to enter into entirely new regions of Cartesian thought.

§15. The *Ego* Outside Subsistence

Before deciding whether or not the *ego* admits any modes of Being that cannot be reduced to subsistence in presence, it is not out of place to venture an *a priori* induction. If persistence determines as subsistence nothing less than substance itself, it must be concluded that the time of the present governs not just the existence of substance, but also all possible existence. Existence already counts as the category that, according to Kant, dominates all modality: actual existence (*Dasein*). It is thus opposed to the two other categories of modality: possibility and necessity. We ask: can one establish between past and future on the one hand, and possibility and necessity on the other, a relation that corresponds to the one that Descartes established explicitly between the present and actuality (in the single subsisting presence)? If it could be shown that in its two other dimensions, Cartesian time plays itself out according to and as modality, we would confirm the claim that, with presence in the present, the way of Being of beings has been decided. In trying to envisage the temporality of the past and the future in Descartes' thought, we are trying to assess the likely exceptions to the primacy of presence in the present, therefore to persisting subsistence as the privileged way of Being of beings. But, *a contrario,* we will also ask these other temporalizations to confirm the claim that, from the outset, the question of time has decided the way of Being of beings.

An exception to the present is found first in the past and thanks to it. A difficulty must be emphasized right away: it is not easy to reach the past in a landscape as thoroughly governed by the privilege of presence as is the Cartesian. To accede to the past implies, in effect, that one undoes oneself from presence understood as the only correct epistemological attitude (present evidence) and the only completed ontological position (persisting subsistence). It therefore implies departing from presence in the present, seceding from it and heading toward an absolutely unthinkable horizon. In effect, at the start and rightfully, presence governs the *cogitatio,* which cannot not endure provided that it remain exposed to evident presence: "... ea certe est natura mentis meae ut nihilominus non possem iis non assentiri, saltem quamdiu ea clare percipio [The nature of my mind is such that I cannot but assent to these things, at least so long as I clearly perceive them]" (AT VII, 65, 7–8 = PW II, 45); or "... cum naturam trianguli considero, evidentissime quidem mihi ... apparet ejus tres angulos aequlaes esse duobus rectis, nec possum non credere id verum esse, quamdiu ad ejus demonstrationem attendo [When I consider the nature of a triangle, it appears most evident to me ... that its three angles are equal to two right angles; and so long as I attend to the proof, I cannot but believe this is true]" (69, 27–70, 1 = 48). The actuality of present evidence is therefore radically transformed into a necessity: as long as present evidence endures, the *cogitatio* cannot cease from assenting to this evidence, nor by assenting, from enduring. The actual presence of evidence does not merely posit it in actuality; it imposes it on the *cogitatio* with necessity, and the *cogitatio*, being unable to extricate itself, submits to it by enduring along with it. Even the most avowed of skeptics cannot resist assenting to present evidence: "... numquam negavi ipsos Scepticos, quamdiu veritatem clare perspiciunt, ipsi sponte assentiri [I have never denied that the sceptics themselves, as long as they clearly perceive some truth, spontaneously assent to it]...."[72] It must not be objected that this is only a matter of the temporality of knowledge, and that therefore the necessity exerted over thought by actually present evidence is circumscribed by certain limits. For, in Descartes' eyes, temporality in general is defined in terms of the *motus cogitationis*. And in fact, by following the principle that everything perseveres—inasmuch as it is in itself—in its state, whatever that state might be, it is easy to see that all actual presence perseveres in its actuality—inasmuch as it is in itself—and thus is necessarily imposed as necessary existence on the *cogitatio* that brings it to mind. Consequently, one has to admit the paradox that, if time is defined first according to the *cogitatio*, if present evidence necessarily determines the *cogitatio*, then the greatest difficulty is not to be found in achieving present evidence, but in reaching the past—in tearing oneself away from the necessity of thinking actual presence persevering incessantly. How would an exception to the actuality of presence be possible, if the thing by definition perseveres in itself, and if the *cogitatio* is necessarily submitted to present evidence? Presence in the present would thus make both the past and contingency—and therefore also the freedom of the

---

72. *To Hyperaspistes,* August 1641, n. 13 (AT III, 434, 1–3 = PW III, 196). See *Responsiones II*: "... quamdiu recordamur ipsas [conclusiones] ab evidentibus principiis fuisse deductas [when we simply recollect that they (these conclusions) were previously deduced from quite evident principles]..." (AT VII, 146, 21–22 = PW II, 104). Similarly, *To Regius,* 24 May 1640 (AT III, 64, 21–65, 15 = PW III, 147).

ego cogito—impossible. It is a question of removing the *cogitatio* from the necessity of the evidence that a persisting presence exerts over it. The possibility of the past implies the possibility of the *cogitatio* extricating itself from the necessary thought of present evidence. Possibility of the past, in fact, here states a pleonasm: if presence in the present sets forth its actuality as a necessity, possibility itself will become possible and thinkable only by breaking with necessary actuality—only by passing into the past. Possibility thus falls to the past, as it falls to the past to dissolve the persevering necessity of present actuality. If it is a matter of undoing present actuality, it need not be surprising that the past issues from what, from the perspective of the present, can appear only as some kind of impotence; for only impotence can suspend the sempiternal potency of presence:

> Etsi enim ejus sim naturae, ut quamdiu aliquid valde clare et disincte percipio, non possim non credere verum esse, quia tamen ejus etiam sum naturae ut non possim obtutum mentis in eandem rem semper defigere ad illam clare percipiendam, recurratque saepe memoria judicii ante facti. . . . [Admittedly my nature is such that so long as I perceive something very clearly and distinctly I cannot but believe it to be true. But my nature is also such that I cannot fix my mental vision continually on the same thing so as to keep perceiving it clearly; and often the memory of a previously made judgment may come back.] [69, 16–21 = 48.]

My nature implies two contrary temporal postulates: on the one hand, my mind cannot not follow a present evidence (thus undergo its necessity) as long as it remains attentive to it; on the other hand, my mind cannot always remain attentive to the same piece of present evidence. It cannot elude present evidence, but it does not remain present to the evidence. The "so long as, *quamdiu*" of present evidence is suspended by the "not always, *non semper*" of inattentiveness. The power to suspend presence characterizes the human mind at every turn: ". . . non potest [mens] semper ad illas attendere [The mind . . . cannot attend to them all the time] . . ."; ". . . mens nostra non sine aliqua difficultate ac defatigatione potest ad ullas res attendere [Our mind is not able to keep its attention on things without some degree of difficulty and fatigue] . . ." (*Principia Philosophiae I,* §§13 and 73); ". . . infirmitatem humanae naturae quae semper in iisdem cogitationibus non immoratur [the weakness of human nature . . . we do not always remain fixed on the same thoughts] . . ."; "We cannot continually pay attention to the same thing . . . however clear and evident the reasons may have been that convinced us of some truth in the past."[73] Inattentiveness suspends the necessary hold that actually present evidence exerts over thought. From here on out, evidence no longer succeeds in reaching the *cogitatio* except by the indirect mediation of a memory (*memoria judicii ante facti,* 69, 21 = 48), most often *mendax* (24, 15 = 16), which blurs the last glimmer of light shining forth from an evidence dissolved in the past.[74] It must be emphasized that here it is not the past that calls for memory and renders it possible, but rather memory that, as the dissolution of the present evidence that inattentiveness has just torn away from its actuality, opens the past. Therefore, by suspending the actuality of necessary presence, memory also opens the domain of the possible. By suspending the necessity of actual presence, inattentiveness to the present and the spurious memory of actuality give rise to the highest form of freedom, the freedom of positive indifference. The 1644 exposition of this freedom makes mention of all the elements we have just pointed out:

> ... if we see very clearly that a thing is good for us, it is very difficult—and, on my view, impossible, as long as one continues in the same thought—to stop the course of our desire. But the nature of the soul is such that it hardly attends for more than a moment to a single thing; hence as soon as our attention turns from the reasons which show us that the thing is good for us, and we merely keep in our memory the thought that it appeared desirable to us, we can call up before our mind some other reason to make us doubt it, and so suspend our judgment, and perhaps even form a contrary judgment.[75]

This text must be read according to the clues provided by time. It then supports the following claims: (1) The present evidence of a truth im-

---

73. Respectively, *Epistula ad G. Voetium* (AT VIII-2, 170, 11–13 = PW III, 223), and *To Elisabeth,* 15 September 1645 (AT IV, 295, 24–28 = PW III, 267).

74. Here, one must think of the examples in opposition to which Descartes defines and wins the *intuitus* (for which "necessaria est praesens evidentia [Present evidence is necessary]" [AT X, 370, 7–8 = PW I, 15 (modified)]): namely, the shifting testimony of the senses and "male componentis imaginationis judicium fallax [the deceptive judgment of the imagination as it botches things together]" (AT X, 368, 14–15 = 14), an imagination about which Descartes will say, farther on, that "fallit ... fere semper [It almost always is deceiving]" (424, 8 = 47 [modified]). What counts for imagination counts also for memory, since "... hanc phantasiam ... eadem est quae memoria appellatur [the phantasy ... is to be identified with what we call memory]" (AT X, 414, 19–24 = PW I, 41–42). Memory, as the temporal application of the imagination, is therefore opposed in principle to the *intuitus.* On these points, see our more precise statements in *Règles utiles et claires* ..., pp. 119–25, 201–2, 206, 224–25, and 232.

75. *To Mesland,* 2 May 1644 (AT IV, 116, 3–5 = PW III, 234).

poses its actuality on the mind with such necessity that every autonomous decision becomes impossible; in short, by its necessity, the actuality of presence in the present destroys all possibility. (2) Suspending necessity implies modifying the mode of temporalization that sets it up; inattentiveness sidesteps present evidence, cheats the hold of actuality, eludes at every turn the necessity void of possibility by weakening the present with the screens of memory, forgetfulness, and other reasons. (3) By contesting the "impossible," the suspension of present actuality ends up reestablishing "a real and positive power to determine oneself."[76] We thus have verified the claim that temporality is put into play as the temporality of the Being of beings: just as the present put actuality into play as the central category of modality, the past puts possibility into play and shows that the present, as presence persevering in subsistence, exceeded the limits of actuality and passed into necessity. This result, even if it supports our previous discussions, nonetheless gives rise to a few problems. In particular, how are we to understand that the *ego* accedes to possibility, which welcomes its freedom, only by contesting the present of the *cogitatio* with the past of memory? Isn't it self-evident that freedom is temporalized in terms of the future, and that the future is opened by the possible? Isn't it self-evident that the past concerns bygone and irreversible beings, and thus marks the necessity of the impossible?

But it is also possible that the temporalization of the Being of beings according to the categories of modality does not obey the most ordinary order of succession, and that bypassing the actuality of presence subsisting in the present requires more subtle combinations of past and futurity, necessity and possibility. Analyzing the time of the future will confirm this at once. The future comes up explicitly in the *Passions de l'âme,* when Descartes wants to mark "the order and enumeration of the passions." After wonder and the pair love/hatred, all of which concern only the present, he introduces the parameter of time: ". . . in order to put them [the other passions] in order, I shall take time into account; and seeing that they lead us to look much more to the future than to the present or the past, I begin with desire," about which "it is obvious that this passion always concerns the future."[77] What does desire desire when it bears on futurity, or rather, more in keeping with what Descartes says,

76. Ibid., 116, 17 = PW III, 234.

77. *The Passions of the Soul,* respectively title of the Second Part (AT XI, 373, 1–2; then §57, 374, 22–375, 2 and 7–8 = PW I, 350 then 350. See §80, 387, 19–20 and §86, 392, 22–24 = PW I, 356 and 358–59). [I have translated the French *futur* as "futurity," *avenir* as "future," and *à venir* as "time to come."— Trans.]

on the "time to come [*le temps à venir*]"? It sets out to acquire good and avoid evil, but it also appears "when we merely wish for the preservation of a good or the absence of an evil," for "we desire not only the presence of goods which are absent but the preservation of those which are present."[78] The future that desire opens remains so determined by subsistent presence that it repeats the very principle of subsistence literally—that is, preserving a present good corresponds exactly with every subsisting thing persevering in its state. To extricate itself from the primacy of presence persevering in the present, it is not enough for desire to invoke the future. To the contrary, the future could well serve only to perpetuate it. Futurity would open an authentic future to desire only if possibility were manifest as such—by freeing itself from the actuality of presence. The question about the future of desire is thus transformed into a question about the possibility of an object that can be desired; but for this object to be desired, it must fall within the domain of possibility, and make an exception to necessity, which would render it merely hated or loved with certainty. In short, for Descartes, does the future of desire admit the modality of possibility? The desires are arranged in three classes. Those "whose attainment depends only on us" are, in fact, reducible to the exercise of our free will, and do not imply the actuality of any exterior object. They therefore do not pose the question of possibility.[79] In contrast, the desires "which depend solely on other causes" set out "things" that "may not happen." Are we to infer from this that, for the first time, Descartes is thinking as such the modality of possibility, which the future opens par excellence? It is, however, the opposite that is the case: the possible implies uncertainty and escapes representation just as the future escapes the present. Now, all uncertainty of itself implies something harmful and a danger. It is therefore necessary to reduce the uncertainty of a still-to-come and nonrepresentable possibility. To safeguard the rights of actual presence, Descartes tries to reduce the possibility that the future opens by means of the necessity in which presence perseveres: ". . . We should reflect upon the fact that nothing can possibly happen

---

78. *The Passions of the Soul,* §57, 375, 5–6; then §86, 392, 22–24 = PW I, 350 then 358.

79. *The Passions of the Soul,* §144, 436, 13 = PW I, 379. The "things which depend on us" do not merely depend "on us—that is, on our free will" (436, 26–27 = 379); they are, in fact, reduced to it: ". . . nothing truly belongs to him but this freedom to dispose his volitions" (§153, 446, 2–3 = 384). See *To Mersenne,* 3 December 1640 (AT III, 249, 3–13 = PW III, 160), and *To Queen Christina* (20 November 1647, AT V, 82, 21–83, 19 = PW III, 324– 25). For an analysis of the ideal of wisdom, see *Sur la théologie blanche de Descartes,* §17, pp. 396–426.

other than as providence has determined from all eternity. Providence is, so to speak, a fate or immutable necessity"; ". . . We must consider everything that affects us to occur of necessity and as it were by fate, so that it would be wrong for us to desire things to happen in any other way."[80] Descartes thus explicitly outlines, in just a few lines, what will be essential to Spinoza's ethical intention: the possible implies a contingency, which appears definitive to us only because we are ignorant of the totality of causes that concur in every actual and hence necessary event: ". . . This opinion is based solely on our not knowing all the causes which contribute to each effect."[81] Necessity cannot actually be known, but it is postulated in principle so that the very possibility of a possible event

80. Respectively, *The Passions of the Soul,* §145, AT XI 437, 17, 19, 22; then §145, 438, 2–7 and §146, 439, 9–12 = PW I, 379, 379, 380; then PW I, 380 and 380. These must be read together with a pronouncement made *To Elisabeth,* 15 September 1645: "The first and chief of these is that there is a God on whom all things depend, whose perfections are infinite, whose power is immense and whose decrees are infallible. This teaches us to accept calmly all the things which happen to us as expressly sent by God" (AT IV, 291, 20–26 = PW III, 265).

81. *The Passions of the Soul,* §145 (AT XI, 438, 16–18 = PW I, 380), which anticipates Spinoza literally. See *Ethics I,* §33, *sc. I:* "At res aliqua nulla alia de causa contingens dicitur, nisi respectu defectus nostrae cognitionis [A thing is termed contingent for no other reason than the deficiency of our knowledge]." Contingency does not determine the thing really, but attests to the inadequacy in our knowledge of it: ". . . pendet a causis ignotis [dependent on causes which are unknown to us] . . ." (*Treatise on the Emendation of the Intellect,* §53, see §§92 and 96), ". . . ignari causarum, a quibus determinantur [ignorant of the causes by which they are determined]" (*Ethics II,* §35, *sc.*),

> . . . ipsa experientia non minus clare quam Ratio doceat, quod homines ea sola de causa liberos se esse credant, quia suarum actionum sunt conscii, et causarum, a quibus determinantur, ignari. [So experience tells us no less clearly than reason that it is on this account only that men believe themselves to be free, that they are conscious of their actions and ignorant of the causes by which they are determined.]

(*Ethics III,* §2 [English trans., p. 106].) One must not give in too easily to the opposition between Cartesian free choice, presupposing contingency in the world, and the necessity of *natura naturata,* which, according to Spinoza, excludes such freedom. In fact, Spinoza repeats the initial position of Descartes. From the epistemological point of view and in terms of the *cogitatio,* there is no room for contingency: the requirements of order (for the *cogitatio*) and the *dictat* of reason (*causa*) dispel on principle even the least possibility of an interruption in the *series rerum.* The difference between Descartes and Spinoza comes up only afterward, when it is a question of interpreting the observed necessity. Spinoza transposes the necessity of *natura naturata* into ethics, without distinguishing orders or domains. Descartes refuses to think physical events and the freedom of the human mind in terms of the same representation of necessity; he therefore dares to think these two literally contradictory statements—without eliminating one of them (Spinoza) and without reconciling them (Malebranche, Leibniz). It is not out of place to suggest that here Descartes directly signals Kant, as he often does in other places.

might be reduced to impossibility—futurity merely ratifies actual necessity without doing justice to the advent of the possible. Futurity without a future, possible on condition of being necessary, desire entirely renounces representing its object as yet to come. Actual presence persists to the point that it dominates, as its own necessity, futurity and the possible. To the preceding paradox—the past opens the modality of possibility—a second, parallel one is added: the future is closed according to the modality of necessity. The categories of modality are therefore temporalized according to a rigorous but strange schema: past/possibility, present/actuality, futurity/necessity.

Can we confirm and understand the paradox that we thus observe? To attempt doing so, let us ask if the two times involved in the paradox—past and futurity—proceed from something in common. The past is open to possibility insofar as it suspends, by inattentiveness and memory, the rule of actual presence. Inversely, futurity is sunk in necessity insofar as it admits being represented in terms of the actual presence that perseveres in it. Thus, in both temporalizations, the two modalities come onto the scene only by offering a common opposition to the presence of actuality. We find support for this if we return to the question of desire. It is now established that, by confining itself to the representation of an event and the knowledge of the object's causes, necessity forbids even the least bit of possibility, therefore of freedom. Does it follow that the *ego* must renounce the possibility of freedom? Not at all, on condition of acting as if necessity could not intervene, though we know with certainty that it does: ". . . Suppose that Providence decrees that if we go by the route we regard as safer we shall not avoid being robbed, whereas we may travel by the other route without any danger. Nevertheless, we should not be indifferent as to which one we choose, or rely upon the immutable fatality of this decree."[82] The ambiguity of this twofold position corresponds to the ambiguity of the third class of desires "which depend on us and on others." Seeing as we are unaware of the causes that impose necessity on the future event, we can behave as if it were still possible, and act as if the event really were yet to come, because it is undetermined for representation. That even here it is a matter of overstepping the representation of actual, present evidence is confirmed by the argument that Descartes always invoked in order to justify the assumption of

---

82. *The Passions of the Soul,* §146, 439, 26–440, 4 = PW I, 380–81. The situation in which we act as if we were free and as if the event obeyed a foreseeable rationality had already been discussed as the second maxim of the "provisional moral code" in the *Discourse on the Method* (DM, 24, 18–25, 19 = PW I, 123). See the excellent commentary by E. Gilson in *Discours de la Méthode. Texte et commentaire* (Paris, 1925), pp. 242–44.

freedom and a nonrepresentable possibility: freedom is not represented, but experienced. Better: this experience is posited no matter what rational arguments might contradict it: "Sed interim, a quocunque tandem simus, et quantumvis ille sit potens, quantumvis, fallax, hanc nihilominus in nobis libertatem esse experimur [Whoever turns out to have created us, and however powerful and however deceitful he may be, in the meantime we nonetheless experience freedom within us] . . ."; ". . . nihilominus enim hanc in nobis libertatem esse experibamur [in spite of that supposition, the freedom which we experienced within us] . . ."; and

> . . . ego certe mea libertate gaudebo, cum et illam apud me experiar, et a te nulla ratione, sed nudis tantum negationibus, impugnetur. Majoremque forte apud alios merebor fidem, quia id affirmo quod expertus sum, et quilibet apud se poterit experiri, quam tu, quae idem negas ob id tantum, quod forte non experta sis. [I am certainly very pleased with my freedom since I experience it within myself. What is more you have produced no arguments to attack it but merely bald denials. I affirm what I have experienced and what anyone else can experience for himself, whereas your denial seems to be based on your own apparent failure to have the appropriate experience.][83]

Freedom is not represented, since representation implies the presence of an object to the *cogitatio,* and since all presence tends to persist in its state, therefore to extend its actuality into necessity. Thus, freedom becomes possible—accedes to the possible as to its own proper domain—only by passing beyond the present representation. The past located the possible by suspending present evidence through inattentive memory. Here, freedom wins its own possibility only by opposing to the present evidence of the *cogitatio* the unquestionable—and therefore unrepresentable—experience of free choice. Freedom is laid bare precisely insofar as it is experienced as the possibility of the impossible—whence

83. Respectively, *Principia Philosophiae I,* §6 [modified] and §39, *Responsiones V* (AT VII, 377, 22–28 = PW II, 259–60). This "experience" is recorded as early as *Meditatio IV:* "Nec vero etiam queri possum, quod non satis amplam et perfectam voluntatem, sive arbitrii libertatem, a Deo acceperim; nam sane nullis illam limitibus circumscribi experior [I cannot complain that the will or freedom of choice which I received from God is not sufficiently extensive or perfect, since I know by experience that it is not restricted in any way]" (56, 26–30 = 39); and: "Sola est voluntas, sive arbitrii libertas, quam tantam in me experior, ut nullius majoris ideam apprehendam [It is only the will, or freedom of choice, which I experience within me to be so great that the idea of any greater faculty is beyond my grasp]" (57, 11–13 = 40). Similarly, *Responsiones III:* "Nihil autem de libertate hîc assumpsi, nisi quod omnes experimur in nobis [On the question of our freedom, I made no assumptions beyond what we all experience within ourselves]" (191, 5–6).

the aporia clearly constructed and assumed by Descartes. On the one hand, we understand that the omnipotence of God entails his foreknowledge, thus necessity: "... hanc quidem a nobis satis attingi, ut clare et distincte percipiamus ipsam in Deo esse [We may attain sufficient knowledge of this power to perceive clearly and distinctly that God possesses it]. ..." On the other hand, we understand that this necessity contradicts the freedom of which we remain inwardly conscious:

> ... non autem satis comprehendi, ut videamus quo pacto libertas hominum actiones indeterminatas relinquat; libertatis autem et indifferentiae, quae in nobis est, nos ita conscios esse, ut nihil sit quod evidentius et perfectius comprehendamus. [But we cannot get a sufficient grasp of it to see how it leaves the free actions of men undetermined. Nonetheless, we have such a close awareness of the freedom and indifference which is in us, that there is nothing we can grasp more evidently or more perfectly.]

How then do we reconcile and understand these contradictory demands? Descartes' decision must be set forth quite forcefully: he decides precisely without attempting a reconciliation that would doubtlessly be impossible for cognitive representation. He decides that he can decide (in favor of freedom), even if he cannot understand how he can do so; he is decided about making a decision that he cannot understand and whose possibility he cannot represent because he experiences it beyond the *cogitatio* present to actuality:

> Absurdum enim esset, propterea quod non comprehendimus unam rem, quam scimus ex natura sua nobis esse debere incomprehensibilem, de aliâ dubitare, quam intime comprehendimus, atque apud nosmet ipsos experimur. [It would be absurd, simply because we do not grasp one thing, which we know must by its very nature be beyond our comprehension, to doubt something else of which we have an intimate grasp and which we experience within ourselves.] [*Principia Philosophiae I,* §41.][84]

Necessity therefore does not yield before a cognitive representation of

---

84. See also:

> Etsi vero multi sint qui, cum ad praeordinationem Dei respiciunt, capere non possunt quomodo cum ipsa consistat nostra libertas, nemo tamen cum seipsum tantum respicit, non experitur unum et idem esse voluntarium et liberum. [There may indeed be many people who, when they consider the fact that God pre-ordains all things, cannot grasp how this is consistent with our freedom. But if we simply consider ourselves, we will all realize in the light of our own experience that voluntariness and freedom are one and the same thing.]

(*Responsiones V,* 191, 9–13 = PW II, 134.)

a future possibility since representation necessarily produces what is in presence. Rather, it yields before the incomprehensible experience of freedom, which opens the possibility of an event yet to come only by exiting the face-to-face encounter of presence with the present, thus by passing beyond representation. Just as inattentive memory awakens the past, and not the inverse, so too does the decision in favor of freedom open the possibility yet to come, and not the inverse. In both cases, the past and the future work to the benefit of possibility alone, even if in the second case the future at first confirmed necessity by letting itself be understood and represented. From now on, the ultimate organization of the categories of modality in terms of time should be corrected and go as follows: past/possibility without representation (inattentive memory)—present/actuality, therefore necessity by representation of present evidence persisting in the present—futurity/possibility of a future outside representation (decision in favor of experienced freedom). In a word, the *ego* accedes to other modalities of Being besides presence, or to other temporalizations besides the present, by accomplishing a single and unique feat: transgressing the *cogitatio* of present evidence, such as it presents to itself the persisting presence of subsistent beings. Because actual presence is itself begotten as the necessity of its own perseverance, one modality alone exceeds necessary presence—possibility. It opens onto the past and future only insofar as they themselves pass beyond the present of cognitive representation. Actual existence is temporalized in the present so radically, and the present is accomplished in the *cogitatio* so intimately, that in Cartesian terms only abandoning the *cogitatio* and actuality provides access to the possible and, consequently, the possibility of the past or the future. We have thus already answered the third and final question concerning the egological deduction of time: the past and the future confirm Descartes' temporal interpretation of the Being of beings, and in it the primacy of presence in the present. Indeed, the *ego* can pass beyond persisting presence and come to the possibility of the past or the freedom of the future only by at the same time renouncing the ordinary exercise of the *cogitatio*—namely, representation in and through present evidence. Temporalization in terms of presence thus distinguishes actual beings from beings that are no longer or not yet; but above all it bars the *ego* from thinking outside its presence to itself. The equivalence of Being and thought is itself temporalized in accordance with the present persisting in the present. The *ego* would not have been able to deduce subsisting substantiality from itself, if it had not first enacted presence (to self) persisting in the present. From the outset, time—in terms of the present—saw to the egological deduction of substance.

The *ego* has therefore fully accomplished its metaphysical function—not only is it set up as the being par excellence, but on the basis of its own mode of Being, it determines the universal mode of Being of all beings; on the basis of the *ego*, and because "ego autem substantia," all beings, in order to be, will be (or not) in the mode of substance; similarly, on the basis of the *ego*, and because "percipio me nunc esse," all beings, in order to be, will endure (or not) in the mode of presence persevering in the present. The *ego* therefore does not simply belong to Cartesian metaphysics; it plays a decisive, if not exclusive, role in constituting it. However, these positively metaphysical results having been won, a flaw in the *ego* is revealed: it can be accomplished as the agent of the *cogitatio* only if it confines itself to present evidence and remains fixed in its own persisting substantiality, without possibility or freedom. Inversely, the *ego* reaches possibility only by renouncing present evidence; it can practice its freedom only by renouncing any attempt at understanding it, so that it is simply experienced. Is the *ego* then split into a sovereign but limited agent of the *cogitatio* and a free possibility, obscured from itself? Here, as often, Descartes' almost unique greatness is found in his capacity to face up to an internal contradiction—because it is not a matter of incoherent reasoning, but of a duality in the things themselves. In other words, if the *ego* completely acquires a metaphysical status, is it completely exhausted in it? The possibility of passing beyond the limits of the persisting presence of the *cogitatio* and of stepping through the mirror, as it were, is attested to in the possibility of an incomprehensible freedom. When Descartes substitutes freedom and the union of body and soul for all other primary notions, by explicitly renouncing any attempt to reconcile them with the preceding ones, does he not admit a noncognitive and nonsubstantial *ego*?[85] To pose the question otherwise:

85. On the one hand, "we are as sure of our free will as of any other primary notion; for this is certainly one of them" (*To Mersenne,* December 1640 [AT III, 259, 9–11 = PW III, 161]). This means that free will does not depend on any theoretical presupposition, but presupposes its own *factum* and inaugurates an absolutely new order of reasons—"for since they are primitive notions, each of them can be understood only through itself" (*To Elisabeth,* 21 May 1643 [AT III, 666, 4–6 = PW III, 218]). On the other hand, the union of the body and soul constitutes a primitive notion: "Lastly, as regards the soul and the body together, we have only that [the primitive notion] of their union, on which depends our notion of the soul's power to move the body, and the body's power to act on the soul and cause its sensations and passions" (ibid., 665, 20–24 = 218. See 28 June 1643, 691, 26–292, 20 = PW III, 226–27). Here the union remains inaccessible to "the intellect alone

am I, as *ego,* because and insofar as I exert the *cogitatio* persisting in presence, or because and insofar as, as a free possibility, I am destined to die? To say it in Heidegger's terms:

This certainty, that "I myself am in that I will die," is *the basic certainty of Dasein itself.* It is a genuine statement of Dasein, while *cogito sum* is only the semblance of such a statement. If such pointed formulations mean anything at all, then the appropriate statement pertaining to Dasein in its being would have to be *sum moribundus* ["I am dying"], *moribundus* not as someone gravely ill or wounded, but insofar as I am, I am *moribundus. The MORIBUNDUS first gives the SUM its sense.*[86]

Is this an issue only for a meditation proper to the existential analytic of *Dasein,* for which the Cartesian *ego* would occasionally be of an ambiguous interest; or does it also bespeak an attempt to extract the *ego* of the "cogito, sum" from the metaphysical status that it just attained under our very eyes, and to make a direct attempt (too direct, certainly, to succeed) at overcoming the metaphysics of the Cartesian *ego*?

---

or even the intellect aided by the imagination" (692, 1–2 = PW III, 227). Accordingly, we must have recourse to the "senses" (692, 3 = 227) and to "the ordinary course of life and conversation" (692, 17 = 227) if we are to understand it. Thus the union of the body and soul shares with free will more than just the rank of primitive (or primary) notion. As when we try to know our free will, when we want to have any knowledge of the union of body and soul, we must have recourse not to the *cogitatio* but to a more confused experience, one that does not deliver objects to the gaze on present evidence. To this wrinkle in the *cogitatio,* both as a mode and as an object of knowledge, there corresponds the disappearance of *substance* in the definition of the *ego:* in *The Passions of the Soul,* this term is reduced to a *hapax,* which designates only the brain, never the *mens* or the *ego:* ". . . a certain very small gland situated in the middle of the brain's substance . . ." (§31, AT XI, 352, 12–13 = PW I, 340).

86. Heidegger, *Prolegomena zur Geschichte des Zeitbegriffs,* G. A., 20, pp. 437–38 [English trans., pp. 316–17]. One thinks here of Derrida: "Therefore *I am* originally means *I am mortal.* . . . The move which heads from the *I am* to the determination of my being as *res cogitans* (thus as immortality) is the move by which the origin of presence and ideality is concealed in the very presence and ideality it makes possible" (*La Voix et le phénomène* [Paris, 1967 1st ed., 1983 4th ed.], pp. 60–61 [English trans., pp. 54–55]).

FOUR

GOD

§16. The Question of the Divine Names

A great divide thus separates the ego from itself; or rather, it separates a strictly metaphysical sense of the *ego*—one in which the *ego* exists in the mode of permanent subsistence—from another, rarer and less easily thematizable sense, in which the *ego* harbors possibility and even impossibility. Before we can identify this second face of the *ego*, and in order that we might succeed in doing so, we have to confirm the reality and the legitimacy of such a separation, which claims to manifest nothing less than the limits of metaphysics. Aren't we attributing to Descartes, quite imprudently, either a damaging incoherence or anachronistic investigations? We must therefore repeat the distinction that we thought we recognized between two senses of the *ego*, with an eye toward affirming or else nullifying it. And we can in fact do so with regard to another being, God. Several observations suggest this possibility to us. *(a)* We saw that the *ego* achieves its metaphysical status, and thus eventually escapes from it, only by starting from the equivalence of thought and Being, which Hegel posited as a fundamental metaphysical thesis. And yet this equivalence, Hegel often insists, does not concern only, nor first of all, the *ego*, but rather God: ". . . the unity of thought and Being. In the form of God no other conception is thus here given than that contained in *Cogito, ergo sum,* wherein Being and thought are inseparably bound up."[1] In short, the theoretical decision that metaphysically institutes the *ego* also metaphysically enthrones God. Consequently, in the same way that they share a similar metaphysical status, they could similarly modify it and eventually transgress it, at least to some extent, which remains to be determined in both cases. *(b)* There is another reason to suspect that God enters into metaphysics equivocally: the redoubling

1. Hegel, *Vorlesungen über die Geschichte der Philosophie, Jubileum Ausgabe,* Bd. XIX, p. 350 [English trans., p. 237].

of onto-theo-logy which was made clear earlier (chapter II). In this re-doubled onto-theo-logy, God receives not one but two metaphysical positions—first as the most thinkable being, then as the being *causa sui.* This discrepancy calls for clarification all the more as it grows wider on account of a second disharmony: of these two positions, only the second affords God the rank of the being par excellence, of the *causa sui* that, through its effectivity, carries out the universal determination of all beings *ut causatum;* by contrast, in the first position, God does not carry out the universal determination of beings *ut cogitatum,* since he too is no more than a *cogitatum* submitted, despite his divinity, to the being par excellence—the *ego* as the sole *cogitatio sui.* Our inquiry can thus no longer avoid confronting this multifaceted aporia; it must inquire whether or not the two metaphysical names attributed to God can fit together without contradiction, and thus whether or not they exhaust the Cartesian thought of God and limit it strictly to the metaphysical domain marked out by the redoubled onto-theo-logy. *(c)* In fact, seeing as he claimed to have thought the attributes of God, Descartes can be said to have consciously attempted to determine the nature of God through, and also over and above, his existence: "I proved quite explicitly that God was the creator of all things, and I proved all his other attributes at the same time."[2] Admitting the idea of God necessarily implies that one admits the divine attributes. He who denies this implication contradicts himself: ". . . How could he affirm that these attributes [infinity, incomprehensibility] belong to him, and countless others which express his greatness to us, unless he had the idea of him?" Accordingly, the attributes are as inseparable from the idea of God as the idea of God is from the attributes: "It would be no good saying that we believe that God exists and that some attribute or perfection belongs to him; this would be to say nothing, because it would convey no meaning to our mind. Nothing could be more impious or impertinent."[3] Consequently, the idea of God can be known—and in point of fact we do know it, "Habemus autem ideam Dei [we have an idea of God]" (AT VII, 167, 17 = PW II, 118)—only if the attributes are set forth in the light of clear evidence. In consequence, the *Meditationes* will investigate ". . . de singulis Dei attributis, quorum aliquod in nobis vestigium agnoscimus [the individual attributes of God of which we recognize some trace in ourselves]" (137, 13–14 = 98) by starting from the presupposition that

2. *To Mersenne,* 28 January 1641 (AT III, 297, 15–17 = PW III, 172).
3. *To Mersenne,* July 1641 (AT III, 394, 1–4 then 8–13 = PW III, 185 then 185).

"... intelligamus existentiam actualem necessario et semper cum reliquis Dei attributis esse conjunctam [We understand that actual existence is necessarily and always conjoined with the other attributes of God]" (117, 6–7 = 83); thus that, inversely, the existence of God cannot be separated from the other attributes and in fact even demands that they be studied. When the existence of God is established for the first time, it provokes contemplation, but an act of contemplation whose scope is immediately enlarged to include the attributes: "... in ipsius Dei contemplatione immorari, ejus attributa apud me expendere [I should like to pause here and spend some time in the contemplation of God; to reflect on his attributes]" (52, 12–13 = 36). When God's existence is established for the second time, this time by means of a demonstration, Descartes mentions the divine attributes in advance: "Multa mihi supersunt de Dei attributis . . . investiganda [There are many matters which remain to be investigated concerning the attributes of God]" (63, 4–5 = 44). Given that the examination of God's attributes makes up an integral part of the attempt to demonstrate his existence, when Descartes studies them, he should make a decision, a clearer one than we have yet seen, about God's essence; therefore, according to the terms of our investigation, he should also make a decision about the coherence of the disparate definitions applied to God, and, eventually, about their belonging—or not—to the metaphysics designated by the redoubled onto-theo-logy of the *cogitatio* and the *causa*. *(d)* A final argument could, though it remains extrinsic, confirm our claim. Descartes once acknowledges in passing that he has "said nothing about the knowledge of God except what all the theologians say too."[4] While in context this statement concerns the possibility of a natural knowledge of God, in general it is also possible to understand this protestation as the sign of a discussion or at least a tacit confrontation with the theologians of his day—in particular a discussion concerning the determination of the divine attributes. How could Descartes have entirely ignored the celebrated theological debates of his time? We here suggest one hypothesis in particular: a Jesuit, Lessius, former student of Suarez, born in Anvers (in 1554) and died in Louvain (in 1623), after a brilliant teaching career not without its share of famous controversies, had published a treatise *De perfectionibus mori-*

---

4. *To Mersenne,* March 1642 (AT III, 544, 17–19 = PW III, 211). Perhaps it is also necessary to consider the formula *Deus est suum esse* (AT III, 433, 9–11 and VII, 383, 15 = PW III, 196 and 263), taken directly from Saint Thomas, "Deus non solum est sua essentia . . . , sed etiam suum esse [God is not only His own essence . . . but also His own existence" and ". . . sua igitur essentia est suum esse [His essence is His existence" (*Summa Theologiae,* Ia, q. 3, a. 4, *resp.* [English trans., pp. 17 and 17]).

busque divinis (Anvers, 1620; Paris, 1620), then, posthumously, at the same time as the *Meditationes* were being edited, a treatise on the *Quinquaginta nomina Dei* (Brussels, 1640). Without claiming that Descartes was directly influenced by these texts (which no argument could suggest), nor even that he read them seriously, we will not rule out the possibility that he was aware of them, at least indirectly (and experience shows, time and again, that this sort of relation is not the weakest). This rapprochement could have a twofold usefulness: first of all, it would permit a comparison, on certain delicate matters, between Descartes' decisions about the divine attributes and those of an acknowledged theologian; next and above all, it would permit reconsidering the Cartesian project—to give metaphysically rigorous names to God and to the God of the Christian revelation—within the ongoing theological debate that plays itself out in the treatise on the divine names and that, inaugurated thematically by Dionysius the Areopagite, traverses the entire Middle Ages until it finds one of its last notable representatives precisely in the person of Lessius.[5] What appears notable is Lessius' insistence on maintaining the Dionysian distinction between, on the one hand, knowledge of God "by affirmations or positive concepts," and, on the other, knowledge by "negations or negative concepts." This couple allows God to be named

> ... most sublime, best, greatest, eternal, most powerful, wisest, kindest, holiest, most just, most merciful, most beautiful, present to all things, inward creator of all, the fashioner, conserver, governor, and ordainer of all things to his glory as their first principle and their ultimate end

just as well as, inversely, he can be named

> infinite, immense, eternal, infinitely raised above all perfection, excellence and magnitude conceivable by a created mind: beyond all substance, all power, all wisdom, all understanding, all light, all beauty, all holiness, all justice, all goodness, all beatitude, all glory; in such a way that he is properly speaking none of these things, like unto none among them and infinitely more sublime and more elevated than them.[6]

5. A history of the treatise on the divine names remains to be written. In this regard, we permit ourselves the liberty of referring to the studies in our *L'idole et la distance* (Paris, 1977), chap. III, and *God without Being,* chap. III.

6. L. Lessius, *Quinquaginta nomina Dei,* respectively: "... per affirmationes seu conceptus positivos ... per negationes, seu conceptus negativos ..." (chap. I, p. 6—the prologue makes explicit reference to Dionysius, p. 5); then: "Priori modo, concipimus Deum esse spiritum sublimissimum, optimum, maximum, sempiternum, potentissimum, sapientissimum, benignissimum, sanctissimum, justissimum, misericordissimum, pulcherri-

This twofold pronouncement defines the horizon within which the Cartesian determination of God's attributes appears not only more understandable (in its innovations as well as its repetitions), but above all as a kind of treatise on the divine names. In short, we propose to try reading the Cartesian discussion of the attributes of God as a metaphysical repetition of the theological treatise on the divine names. Only on this condition will it become possible to answer the crucial question: how and within what limits does God enter, with Descartes' redoubled onto-theo-logy, into metaphysics? More than just an arbitrary appeal, the comparison with Lessius makes up an invaluable landmark. And moreover, it seems to us even less illegitimate since, among other points in common, Lessius and Descartes closely link infinity to incomprehensibility. When Descartes retorts to Gassendi that ". . . idea enim infiniti ut sit vera, nullo modo debet comprehendi, quoniam ipsa incomprehensibilitas in ratione formali infiniti continetur [The idea of infinity, if it is to be a true idea, cannot be grasped at all, since the impossibility of being grasped is contained in the formal definition of the infinite]" (368, 2–4 = 253), he seems to be citing Lessius: "Deum ratione suae infinitatis esse incomprehensibilem [God is incomprehensible by definition of his infinity]."[7] For these four reasons, the determination of God's essence be-

---

mum, rebus omnibus praesentem, omnia interius creantem, formantem, conservantem, gubernantem et ad suam gloriam ordinantem tanquam primum principium et finem rerum omnium" (chap. I, pp. 6–7); and finally:

> Posteriori modo Deus concipitur esse Spiritus infinitus, immensus, sempiternus, infinitus supra omnium perfectionem, excellentiam et magnitudinem a mente creata conceptibilem elevatus: supra omnem substantiam, supra omnem potentiam, supra omnem sanctitatem, omnem justitiam, omnem bonitatem, omnem beatitudinem, omnem gloriam; adeo ut ipse nihil horum proprie sit, nulli horum sit similis, sed infinite sublimior et praestantior.

(Chap. I, p. 8.)

7. L. Lessius, *De Perfectionibus moribusque divinis,* I, 2 (Paris, 1620), p. 11. See the subsequent development:

> Omnis hi modi incomprehensibilitatis sequuntur ex ejus infinitate: sed nos hic potissimum agimus de tertio, quo Deus dicitur *incomprehensibilis* omni intellectui creato. Hoc modo Dionysius et Damascenus Deum dicunt esse ἀκατάληπτον, ἀπερίληπτον, ἀπεριχώριστον. [All these modes of incomprehensibility follow from his infinity: but we hold this most especially concerning the third, in which God is said to be incomprehensible to every created thing. This is why Dionysius and Damascene said God is ἀκατάληπτον, ἀπερίληπτον, ἀπεριχώριστον]

(Ibid.) If Descartes' formula depended on Lessius, even from a distance, it would thus go back directly to Dionysius, and through him to the entire tradition of the Church Fathers. Permit us to let this ever so fascinating hypothesis remain open. See *infra,* n. 36.

comes a fundamental task when assessing the Cartesian constitution of metaphysics.

The *Meditationes* evoke the name or the names of God from their very beginning, the raising of universal doubt. However, no explicit definition of God is fixed at that time—for rigorous reasons that will be made more clear below. It is only with *Meditatio III* that, in order to support the proof for God's existence, developed formulations of the essence and the attributes of God appear. As a result, Descartes enters, consciously or not (it matters little), into the debate about the divine names. Let us therefore read the two formulae introduced here. Here is the first definition:

[1] . . . illa [idea] per quam summum aliquem Deum, aeternum, infinitum, omniscium, omnipotentem, rerumque omnium, quae praeter ipsum sunt creatorem intelligo [the idea that gives me my understanding of a supreme God, eternal, infinite, omniscient, omnipotent and the creator of all things that exist apart from him]. (AT VII, 40, 16–18 = 28)

Here is the second formulation:

[2] Dei nomine intelligo substantiam quandam infinitam, independentem, summe intelligentem, summe potentem, et a qua tum ego ipse, tum aliud omne, si quid aliud extat, quodcumque extat est creatum [By the word 'God' I understand a substance that is infinite, independent, supremely intelligent, supremely powerful, and which created both myself and everything else (if anything else there be) that exists]. (45, 11–14 = 31)

These two pronouncements, which we will cite from now on as [1] and [2], are framed by the so-called proof for the existence of God by effects, which opens just before [1]—"Sed alia quaedam via mihi occurrit [But it now occurs to me that there is another way] . . ." (40, 5 = 27)— and closes a little after [2], "Ideoque ex antedictis Deum necessario existere, est concluendum [So from what it has been said it must be concluded that God necessarily exists]" (45, 17–18 = 31). This quite clearly de-limited situation immediately gives rise to a difficulty, itself multifaceted: obviously [1] and [2] come up only within the second onto-theo-logy, since [1] appears on the same page in which there also arise, in a tremen-dous relaunching of the *ordo rationum, substantia* (40, 12 = 28) and the principle of universal causality (40, 21–23 = 28). What thread connects these three theses, if their textual proximity is not conceptually just by chance? Is the validity of the divine attributes advanced by [1] and [2] limited to the onto-theo-logy of the *ens ut causatum* alone, or do they exceed it in advance? For that matter, can [1] and [2], which are introduced by one and the same *intelligo,* claim to offer a real definition of God and his attributes, or must they be proposed simply as working hypotheses?[8] In this case, how are we to understand that this idea of God can at once remain hypothetical and be actually given to us—"Si detur Dei idea (ut manifestum est illam dari) [if we do have an idea of God—and it is manifest that we do] . . ." (183, 21 = 129), "Habemus autem ideam Dei [We have an idea of God] . . ." (167, 17 = 118)? Such difficulties can find neither a rapid nor an easy resolution; they call for a detailed examination of each of the attributes successively mentioned by [1] and [2]. Only once such an examination has been performed will the objection of incoherence (*inconsistency*) be able to receive something more than a formal or superficial confirmation or nullification—a carefully considered validation, historically and conceptually carefully considered.[9] Let us therefore retrace, step by step, the terms attributed to God by [1] and [2], with an eye toward testing their many coherences or incoherences and reconstituting their partial necessities.

Quaedam [*substantia*]. This announces, as the first determination of God, indetermination itself. The two formulae agree in this. *Quaedam* [2] (45, 11) in effect corresponds to *aliquis* [*Deus*] in [1] (40, 16). Though the French translation hides it behind a simple indefinite article (*un/une,* AT IX-2, 32, 5 and 35, 41), this indetermination constantly determines all the previous places where God is mentioned in the *Meditationes;* or rather, all the places where Descartes suggests a definition of what, before the first demonstration of the existence of the true God, could lay claim to this title. Two occurrences confirm this claim. The first is found at the end of *Meditatio I.* When Descartes constructs hyperbolic doubt by invoking, equally and indifferently, the two contrary hypotheses of an omnipotent God and an evil genius, he nonetheless gathers them together in the imprecise phrase "tam potentem aliquem Deum [some God so powerful]," a phrase that is not rendered in the French transla-

8. *Intelligo* introducing a definition of God: AT VII, 50, 19; 40, 18; 45, 11; 109, 7; etc. = PW II, 34; 28; 31; 78; etc. Formulas [1] and [2] are directly commented upon by, among others, E. M. Curley, *Descartes against the Skeptics* (Cambridge, Mass., 1980), pp. 127–28 ("Is this definition stipulative or reportive?").

9. H. Frankfurt, "Descartes on the consistency of reason," in M. Hooker, ed., *Descartes: Critical and Interpretive Essays* (Baltimore/London, 1978), p. 36. See also, by the same author, the study "Descartes' Validation of Reason," *American Philosophical Quarterly* II/2 (1965), particularly pp. 223–25. Whence our study "The Essential Incoherence of Descartes' Definition of Divinity," in A. O. Rorty (ed.), *Essays on Descartes' Meditations* (Berkeley–Los Angeles, 1986).

tion (21, 17–18 = 14 [modified]). Next, when *Meditatio III* in its opening
stages recalls the situation at which *Meditatio I* ended up, it again evokes
"aliquem Deum [some God]" (36, 11 = 25); "quelque Dieu" translates
the French (AT IX-1, 28, 36). The indetermination would not be marked
so consistently if it did not have an essential function. In fact, it has
several. First, during each moment of the rational proceedings that precede the first proof for the existence of a God, Descartes reasons without
yet having a precise concept of God; or to say it more precisely, he hesi-
tates between several hypotheses: a God who can do everything, thus
one who also allows me to deceive myself (21, 1–16 = 14); a *Deus fictitius*
(21, 20 = 14) who can be identified indifferently with destiny (*fatum,*
ἀναγκή) or with chance (*casus,* τύχη) or with the necessary order of nature (21, 20–21 = 14), in short with any mode of deception whatsoever
("seu quovis alio modo [or by some other means]," 21, 21–22 = 14);
and finally, an evil genius who is himself indefinite (". . . genium aliquem
malignum [some evil genius]," 22, 24 = 15 [modified], rendered in French
by "un certain mauvais génie," AT IX-1, 17, 37). This indefinite evil genius can be imagined only insofar as the concept of God invoked up until
now has itself remained fundamentally undetermined. And moreover,
the entire second *Meditatio* works within the determinate hypothesis of
a decidedly indeterminate God; the *ego* found itself certain of itself only
by struggling against an uncertain God. Whence these decidedly unde-
cided denominations: ". . . est aliquis Deus, vel quocumque nomine illum
vocem [is there not some God, or whatever I may call him]" (24, 21–22 =
16 [modified], translated in French by "quelque Dieu," AT IX-1, 19, 19);
by virtue of the same indefiniteness, this can also become "deceptor nescio quis [I know not what deceiver]" (25, 6 = 17 [modified], or "je ne
sais quel trompeur," AT IX-1, 19, 30), therefore properly *deceptor aliquis*
[some deceiver] (26, 24 = 18, or "quelqu'un qui est . . . ," AT IX-1, 21,
3–4). In fact, before the proof by effects, Descartes does not base his
reasoning on the hypothesis of God, nor on that of the evil genius,
chance, necessity, or destiny; he bases it solely on the determined hypothesis of something undetermined. The sole point that all of these
hypotheses have in common is to be found in their very indetermination.
Before the proof by effects, the *ego* confronts only an adversary hidden
by his very indetermination, one that, for each proper name, is named
only with a name so common that it is not even a name: *aliquis.* Therefore, when the definition advanced by *Meditatio III,* in [1] as much as in
[2], opens with a marker of indeterminacy, it is not saying nothing: it
sums up in a single word the only characteristic proper to the previous

hypotheses—their radical impropriety. *Aliquis* in [2] does not add indetermination to the subsequent list of qualifiers so much as it opposes the
indetermination previously established as the sole determination to the
determinations yet to come. About what he attempts for the first time
to define categorically as God (and no longer merely as anything whatsoever that can be defined, so long as it is other than the *ego*), Descartes
first says the only thing that experience has, as of now, taught him about
it: namely, that it is indeterminate. By God, I mean an undetermined
someone, *aliquis.* Here, it is not the *ego* who can say "larvatus prodeo [I
come forward masked]" (AT X, 213, 6–7 = PW I, 2), but God who, like
Voëtius later, ". . . in me non prodeat nisi personatus [does not come
forward against me except in disguise]" (AT VIII-2, 7–8 = not included
in PW). God comes to the *ego* only hidden beneath the mask of the role
(*persona*) that he has until now been playing in the theater of the previous *Meditationes*—that of an *aliquis.* In short, God appears beneath the
most dissimulating mask, that of the most total indetermination. In contrast with theology, which proffers negations of God only after having
exhausted the affirmations, here the *ego* begins by saying of God that he
is named *nescio quis* [I know not what], a *je ne sais qui:* negative philosophy, in which one must acknowledge the echo, no doubt barely conscious, of the negating moment in the divine names: "All things are denied of him because he is higher than all reason and all *species* comprehensible by a created mind," Lessius said.[10] Descartes, however, stands
apart from the more common opinion that Lessius has formulated: first
because he starts with indetermination, instead of reaching it after affirmations have been denied each in their turn; next because he practices
the denegating indetermination with penury, not with excess. That is to
say, indetermination holds the place of the affirmations provisionally; it
does not correct them after they have been uttered. The negative moment thus loses its theological originality. Far from leading to the overcoming of predicative and categorical discourse in general, the negative
moment intends such discourse and always strives for it, all the more so
when it clearly designates its absence. In this, one has the feeling that
affirmations can be established further along, that there is no negation
or indetermination that will not be alleviated—thus opening the metaphysical discourse on the essence of God to the threat of idolatry.

10. L. Lessius, *De Perfectionibus moribusque divinis*, I, 3: "Negantur de ipso omnia,
quia ipse est supra omnem rationem et speciem creatae menti conceptibilem" (op.
cit., p. 14).

However, indetermination is justified by its fulfilling a second function. Hyperbolic doubt can exert its radical *épochè* over genuine science (for it destroys Cartesian science itself)[11] only by confusing two different characteristics. There must first of all be an authority that offers enough omnipotence to disqualify all mathematical and rational logic. Next, it must be the case that this authority, itself absolutely unsurpassable, pass beyond the humanly unsurpassable conditions of science, thus that it be identified, in one way or another, with God. And yet, upon serious reflection, it is seen that these two characteristics are contradictory. In effect, as soon as their utmost consequences have been developed, they can be uttered in the untenable paradox of a deceptive omnipotence, directly (evil genius) or indirectly (omnipotent God who created the conditions of my self-deception). As soon as one poses the question of logical possibility and noncontradiction, the initial hypothesis of the *Meditationes* appears to be not only hyperbolic, but also incoherent. And Descartes does not hide this fact either: outside the strict boundaries of the provisional *ordo rationum,* he will always respond to the objections of atheism by claiming that an omnipotent God can neither deceive, nor let one deceive oneself:

> Et ineptum est quod subjungit, nempe *Deum ut deceptorem cogitari.* Et si enim, in prima mea Meditatione, de aliquo deceptore summe potenti locutus sim, nequaquam tamen ibi verus Deus concipiebatur, quia ut ipse [Voëtius] ait, fieri non potest ut verus Deus sit deceptor. Atque si ab eo petatur unde sciat id fieri non posse, debet respondere se scire ex eo quod implicet contradictionem in conceptu, hoc est, ex eo quod concipi non possit. [(He claims that in my philosophy) "God is thought of as a deceiver." This is foolish. Although in my First Meditation I did speak of a supremely powerful deceiver, the conception there was in no way of the true God, since, as he [Voëtius] himself says, it is impossible that the true God should be a deceiver. But if he is asked how he knows this is impossible, he must answer that he knows it from the fact that it implies a conceptual contradiction—that is it cannot be conceived.]

Or, according to Burman's testimony, "Loquitur hîc auctor [Descartes] contradictoria cum summa potentia malignitas consistere non potest [What the author (Descartes) says here is contradictory, since malice is

---

11. On this essential point, see F. Alquié, "Expérience ontologique et déduction systématique dans la constitution de la métaphysique de Descartes," in *Descartes. Cahiers de Royaumont* (Paris, 1957), and our work *Sur la théologie blanche de Descartes,* §14, pp. 323*ff.*

incompatible with supreme power]." Finally: ". . . *auctor contradictoria loquitur, si dicat potentissimum et malignum, quia potentia et malignitas simul consistere non possunt* [If he calls it both most powerful and malicious, the author contradicts himself since power and malice are incompatible with each other]."[12] And yet it is precisely this conceptual contradiction that is called for, at least provisionally, by the unfolding of the *Meditationes;* but to make such a notion bearable, simply as a hypothesis not yet contested, it must be toned down, indeed dissimulated. This is precisely how the indeterminacy of an *aliquis* functions. The debate about the omnipotence of God being opposed (or not) to the merely very great power of the evil genius—however much it might be highly instructive—has in the end only something very limited at stake in it; and the same is true of the general distinction between these two engines of hyperbolic doubt. For despite their being incompatible by right, a single indetermination is enough for them to be confounded in the same role, as provisional as it is unified.[13]

But there is more. The indetermination also permits, though again provisionally, another difficulty to be removed. One could and even should raise an objection to the primacy of indetermination as the first determination of what lays claim to the title *God.* In effect, the evil genius, the *Deus fictitius,* chance, necessity, and destiny come up only on account of a single common point—namely, the function of omnipotence, through which, whatever they might be, they could disqualify the evidence of order and measure. Omnipotence would thus precede inde-

---

12. Respectively, *To Voëtius* (AT VIII-2, 60, 16–24), then *Conversation with Burman* (AT V, 147, 7–8); finally, AT V, 150, 30*ff.* = PW III, 222 then 333; finally, not included in PW. When the *ordo rationum* permits, the *Meditationes* will raise this contradiction: AT VII, 53, 23–29 = PW II, 37 (see *Principia Philosophiae* I, §29); similarly, the *Letter to Buitendijck* from 1643 (AT IV, 64, 1–28 = PW III, 229–30). H. Frankfurt made this point clear: ". . . Descartes does not recognize in the *First Meditation,* that the notion of a being both omnipotent and evil is logically incoherent. And as long as the existence of the demon *seems* possible to him, it provides him with what he must take to be a reasonable ground for doubt" (*Demons, Dreamers and Madmen: The Defense of Reason in Descartes' Meditations* [Indianapolis, 1970], p. 48).

13. We are thinking of the famous debate between R. Kennington, "The Finitude of Descartes' Evil Genius," *Journal of the History of Ideas* (1971), pp. 441–46, and H. Caton, "Kennington on Descartes' Evil Genius," *Journal of the History of Ideas* (1973), pp. 639–41; then R. Kennington, "Reply to Caton," ibid., pp. 641–43, and H. Caton, "Rejoinder: The cunning of the Evil Genius," ibid., pp. 641–44. See also H. Caton, *The Origin of Subjectivity* (New Haven: Yale University Press, 1973), pp. 115–21. In fact, *summe potens* in 45, 12–13 is equivalent to *omnipotens* at least in 40, 17 [1], as well as in *Principia Philosophiae* I, §§14 and 22.

termination, and nothing would be submitted to indetermination except for the sake of coming under the sway of power. In fact, as we will soon see, omnipotence constitutes an essential qualification of the Cartesian God. But one must ask what right it has to enter—before all clear and distinct knowledge of the essence as well as the existence of God—the *ordo rationum.* Whence comes the fact that before envisaging God in the strict sense and as such, it is already possible and even permissible to mobilize the idea of an omnipotent God? Descartes' response is always the same: "Verumtamen infixa quaedam est meae menti vetus opinio, Deum esse qui potest omnia [And yet firmly rooted in my mind is the long-standing opinion that there is an omnipotent God]" (21, 1–2 = 14) says *Meditatio I,* which the parallel text in *Meditatio III* will take over: ". . . haec praeconcepta de summa Dei potentia opinio [my preconceived opinion as to the supreme power of God]" (36, 8–9 = 25 [modified]). Omnipotence qualifies something like God, but only by way of an opinion; and for that matter, it could even be demonstrated that such an equivalence finds its origin in the nominalism of William of Ockham.[14] But the only thing that is important to us here is the modality according to which a positive doctrine, thus one foreign to the *ordo rationum,* can get mixed up in this *ordo.* It enters in the mode of *opinio,* that is to say, of a confused, not rationally determined thought having neither origin nor reason—in short, it enters as an undetermined thought. Omnipotence thus only apparently precedes indetermination, since in fact only its indetermination can permit omnipotence to enter into the *ordo rationum,* as an opinion with neither genealogy nor status.

Thus, by opening the list of divine names and attributes with the reticence of an *aliquis/quaedam,* Descartes is not simply signaling the inevitably provisional character of a definition that still awaits an answer to the question *quid sit* as well as *an sit.* To understand this, one has only to compare his work to that of Suarez. To be sure, when Suarez comes up against the impossibility of defining God, he too will immediately have recourse to a *praeconceptio* in order to continue his reasoning: ". . . nevertheless, for us to be able to reason about God, it is certainly necessary to presuppose and have a preconception (*praeconcipere*) as to what this word means." But for Suarez, the *praeconceptio* has a function that is the inverse of the role it plays for Descartes: it precedes and introduces a correct and universally admissible nominal definition of God,

14. For this identification, see *Sur la théologie blanche de Descartes,* pp. 330–33 and 303–5.

far from making provisionally possible an inadmissible contradiction: "For this name signifies a certain (*quoddam*) very noble being, one who surpasses all the others, and all depend on it as on their first author, who, for that very reason, must be served and worshipped as the supreme divinity. This is in effect the ordinary and so to speak first concept that we all form when we hear the name of God."[15] No doubt Suarez's pre-comprehension, like the Cartesian *praeconcepta opinio,* introduces a vague and indeterminate concept of God. But while in Descartes this indeterminate concept is contradictory, provisional, and false, in Suarez it is already correct, thus, in this sense, definitive and established. In the context of Descartes' thought, indetermination makes up an integral part of the concept, which would collapse without it. Accordingly, the genuine concept of God, if one can be found, will have to be won by starting with an already constitutive and forever irreducible indetermination. Imprecision belongs to the concept of God, intrinsically—either for the sake of dissimulating its impossibility during hyperbolic doubt or for the sake of permitting its sudden irruption in the renewal of the *ordo rationum.* Thus a new task imposes itself on us: it is no longer a matter of interpreting the indetermination that constitutes the concept of God as the condition for the possibility of a logical and theological impossibility; rather, it is a question of interpreting this indetermination as the path to a new conceptual situation. The fact that formulas [1] and [2] show up in the same passage where the first occurrence of *substantia* appears now takes on its full meaning: indetermination, preliminary determination of God, in effect opens onto substance.

§17. Substance and Infinity

Substantia: this term characterizes not only formula [2], ". . . Dei nomine intelligo substantiam quandam . . . ," but also, indirectly, definition [1].

---

15. Suarez, *Disputationes Metaphysicae, XXIX,* s. 3, n. 4: ". . . tamen ut de illo [Deo] ratiocinari possimus, necesse est saltem praeconcipere et praesupponere, quid hac voce significetur" (op. cit., vol. 26, p. 35); then n. 5: "Significat ergo hoc nomen [Deus] quoddam nobilissimum ens, quod et reliqua omnia superat, et ab eo tanquam a primo auctore reliqua omnia pendent, quod proinde ut supremum numen colendum est ac venerandum; hic enim est vulgaris et quasi primus conceptus quem omnes de Deo formamus, audito nomine Dei" (ibid.) Like Suarez, Descartes admits a spontaneous preconception of God; on this occasion, he borrows it from the nominalist tradition (or simply from the first article of the *Credo*). However, while for Suarez this preconception maintains a certain theoretical validity, for Descartes, based on the fact of hyperbolic doubt, the preconception not only loses all solidity, it is also inverted into an argument against all correct thought, as much of God as of *reliqua omnia.* Indetermination is inverted for the same reason as the preconception.

The latter, definition [1], appears just after the first opposition between substance and accident, whose hierarchy allows Descartes to conclude that a certain idea of God "... plus profecto realitatis objectivae in se habet, quam illae [ideae] per quas finitae substantiae exhibentur [has in it more objective reality than the ideas that represent finite substances]" (40, 19–20 = 28). In other words, the still undetermined idea of God is made more precise by being opposed not only to all accidents, but also to all finite substance. In fact, shortly after this, Descartes will introduce the third term, *substantia infinita*—first in definition [2] (at 45, 11 = 31), then in the text: "... non tamen idcirco esset idea substantiae infinitae, cum sim finitus, nisi ab aliqua substantia, quae revera esset infinita procederet [This would not account for my having the idea of an infinite substance, when I am finite, unless this idea proceeded from some substance which really was infinite]" (45, 20–22 = 31). In other words: "... manifeste intelligo plus realitatis esse in substantia infinita quam in finita [I clearly understand that there is more reality in an infinite substance than in a finite one]" (45, 26–27 = 31), a formula that is repeated in the *Second Set of Replies:* "... substantia plus habet realitatis, quam accidens vel modus; et substantia infinita, quam finita [There is more objective reality in the idea of a substance than in the idea of an accident; and there is more objective reality in the idea of an infinite substance than in the idea of a finite substance]" (165, 29–31); or: "... si detur substantia infinita et independens, est magis res quam finita et dependens [If there is an infinite and independent substance, it is more of a thing than a finite and dependent substance]" (185, 25–29 = 130).

The introduction of the concept substance backs up the points we have already established and gives rise to a difficulty. Our first point was the profound coherence of formulas [1] and [2]. One, [1], introduces substance into God for the sake of opposing it to accidents and especially to *substantia finita* (40, 20). The other, [2], positively determines this substance as infinite. In this way, we reached our second point: Descartes overcomes the imprecision necessary to the definition of God, an imprecision that is imposed by the contradictory hypotheses sustaining hyperbolic doubt—in short, the inevitable indetermination of his first point of departure—only by constructing a second definition of something like God. This second definition is constructed solely on the basis of the new parameters that are imposed by the "alia quaedam adhuc via": namely, causality, the nonrepresentative status of the idea, and, above all, substantiality. The fact that [1] and [2] are constructed around and on the basis of *substantia* signifies that they belong completely to the new beginning of the *ordo rationum.* In other words, it signifies that, without this new beginning and without *substantia,* no definition of God could ever pass beyond the initial indetermination. In short, for Descartes, God will be defined according to substantiality and causality, or not at all—otherwise (and this amounts to the same thing), he will be defined by the indetermination of *aliquis Deus.* But more precisely, what is implied by the recourse, as obligatory as it is resolute, to substantiality in order to be able to define God?

In fact, consciously or not (a distinction that makes little difference), Descartes here runs up against a previous theological debate, one that forces upon him a very precise conceptual difficulty. Theologically, can God be named according to substance? For a positive answer, one can rely on the formula "quoddam pelagus infinitae substantiae [that sea of infinite substance]," which accurately translates an expression of John Damascene's, οἷόν τι πέλαγος οὐσίας ἄπειρον καὶ ἀόριστον.[16] However, this authority does not entirely remove a difficulty that finds its origin in at least three authors of the utmost theological importance. Let us consider first Saint Augustine. He holds that "it is clear that God is improperly called a substance," and proposes that οὐσία be translated by *essentia,* essence, no longer by *substantia.* The reason for this rejection is found in the very definition of substance: it implies the permanence of a substrate, which thus makes possible accidental qualifications from which, at the same time, it stands in contradistinction. Accordingly, "neither changeable nor simple things are properly called substances." Thus the body constitutes a substance because qualities, accidents, and attributes find their subsistence in it, according to the Aristotelian couple οὐσία/συμβέβηκος. But in God, properties—such as greatness, goodness, omnipotence, etc.—are not added like accidents to a different substance. All that is in God is identically God: "It is an impiety to say that God subsists and is a subject in relation to His own goodness (*ut subsistat et subsit Deus bonitati suae*) and that this goodness is not a substance, or rather essence, and that God Himself is not His own goodness, but that it is in Him as in a subject (*tanquam in subjecto*)."[17] Saint Anselm also

16. John Damascene, *De Fide Orthodoxa, I,* 9, Patrologia Graeca, vol. 94, col. 833 A-B.
17. Saint Augustine, *De Trinitate, VII,* 5, 10 [English trans., p. 111], respectively: "... manifestum est Deum abusive substantiam vocari, ut nomine usitatiore intelligatur essentia, quod vere ac proprie dicitur: ita ut fortasse solum Deum dici oporteat essentia." Then: "Res ergo mutabiles neque simplices, proprie dicuntur substantiae." And finally: "... nefas est autem dicere ut subsistat et subsit Deus bonitati suae, atque illa bonitas non substantia sit vel potius essentia, neque ipse Deus sit bonitas sua, sed in illo sit tanquam in subjecto." On the same point, see *V,* 2, 3, and *VI,* 5, 7, as well as note 33 of M. Mellet and T. Camelot, in their edition *La Trinité* (Paris, 1955), vol. 1, p. 584, and the excellent

contests the notion that substantiality befits God. That is, "Substance is principally said of individuals, which especially constitute a plurality. For it is individuals that especially stand under (i.e. underlie) accidents and therefore more properly take the name 'substance'." In short, substance implies accidents that it lies under. The inevitable plurality of accidents implies in turn the plurality of substances. And this plurality in the end contradicts the divine simplicity. Therefore, "the supreme essence (*summam essentiam*), which does not underlie any accidents, cannot properly be called a substance unless 'substance' is being used in place of 'essence'."[18] However, such a refusal of *substantia* is not limited to the Augustinian tradition—it is found in Saint Thomas as well. The first reason for this is obvious: God does not have any ontic determination because he is defined only as the pure act of Being (*actus essendi*), in which *esse* takes the place of all *essentia,* thus excluding *substantia* all the more. But the traditional reason remains operative, being presented first in the guise of an objection: "God cannot be called an individual substance since matter is the principle of individuation, while God is immaterial: nor is He the subject of accidents (*neque etiam accidentibus substat*), so as to be called a substance. Therefore the word person ought not be attributed to God." The reply concedes what is essential to the objection and claims for God the name *substance* only in a very restricted sense: "Substance can be applied to God in the sense of (*secundum quod*) signifying self-subsistence."[19] In fact, Saint Thomas will admit *substantia* into discourse about God only by first interpreting it as a quasi-synonym of

---

chapter "L'idée de Dieu chez saint Augustin," written by A. Koyré and appearing in his study of *L'idée de Dieu dans la philosophie de saint Anselme* (Paris, 1923 and 1984). In the last of these, see in particular the felicitous formula "None of the Aristotelian categories can be applied to God" (p. 172). More recently, Roland J. Teske, "Augustine's Use of 'Substantia' in Speaking about God," *Modern Schoolman* (March 1985).

18. Saint Anselm, *Monologion, LXXIX* [English trans., p. 89]: "... substantia principaliter dicitur de individuis quae maxime in pluralitate consistunt. Individua namque maxime substant, id est subjacent accidentibus, et ideo magis proprie substantiae nomen suscipiunt. Unde jam supra manifestum est summam essentiam quae nullis subjacet accidentibus proprie non posse dici substantiam, nisi substantia ponatur pro essentia."

19. Saint Thomas, *Summa Theologiae, Ia,* q. 29, a. 3, obj. 4 [English trans., p. 148]: "... Deus dici non potest individua substantia, cum principium individuationis sit materia: Deus autem immaterialis est: neque etiam accidentibus substat, ut substantia dici possit; nomen ergo personae Deo attribui non debet." Then *ad 4m* [English trans., p. 158]: "Substantia vero convenit Deo, secundum quod significat existere per se." See also *In Sententiarum libros, I,* d. XXIII, a. 2, obj. 3 (which cites Augustine) and *ad 3m* (which cites Richard of Saint-Victor's interpretation of the trinitarian *substantia* as *existentia, De Trinitate, IV,* 20, *PL* 196, col. 943–44).

the divine *esse* held to be subsistent: "God is subsisting *esse* itself."[20]
Permanent subsistence can be said of God without his having to bear
the status of substance, nor the relation to accidentality and materiality
that it implies. Subsistence dispenses with substantiality in order to directly attain the *actus essendi*. Following his own paths, Saint Thomas
thus recovers the Augustinian thesis. Hence Descartes' decision to attribute to God the name *substantia* cannot pass for a trivial repetition of
previous decisions. Moreover, the fact that echoes of this debate were
still ringing among his contemporaries forbids us to suppose the question
to be minor or resolved. Take Gassendi: on the one hand, he agrees that
". . . it is customary to exclude God from the category of substance"; on
the other hand, he contradicts this common opinion—"it is wrong to
exclude God from the category of substance"—by treating the divine
substance strictly in parallel with divine causality, just as Descartes did:
"Seeing as God is really a cause—in fact the prime cause—and therefore is rightly counted among the causes, then he is really a substance
and must be counted among the substances—and in fact even as the
prime substance; for obviously it is more reasonable to call God a prime
substance than Socrates, Bucephalus, or this stone."[21] Gassendi was
therefore perfectly conscious of opposing the regnant thesis when, like
Descartes, he attributed substantiality to God. And he is not the only
one. In 1613, Goclenius juxtaposes the two possibilities for justifying
such an attribution, either its near-univocity or its restriction to Being
per se:

> Substance is understood at first generally, so that it might also be suitable
> to God. 2. [Secondly] in a specific sense, such that it is suitable only to
> creatures. . . . Substance is understood more properly and [also] abusively.

20. Saint Thomas, *Summa Theologiae, Ia,* q. 4, a. 2, c. [English trans., p. 22]: ". . . Deus
est ipsum esse subsistens."

21. P. Gassendi, *Exercitationes Paradoxicae Adversus Aristoteleos, II,* d. 3, §6 [English
trans., p. 54 (modified)], respectively: ". . . Deus vulgo excludatur a Categoria substantiae";
then: "Immerito Deum a Substantiae Categoria excludi"; finally: "Quippe ut vere Deus
est causa et propterea inter causas (et prima quidem) merito habetur, ita vere substantia,
ut proinde inter substantias numerari valeat (et quidem tanquam prima substantia, quia
scilicet Deum potiore ratione, quam Socratem, quam Bucephalum, quam hunc lapidem
primam substantiam appelaveris)," ed. B. Rochot (Paris, 1959), pp. 325–27. As is well
known, only *Book I* of the *Exercitationes* appeared during the lifetime of Gassendi, in
1624, from the house of Verdier. The rest of the work, constantly amended, appeared only
posthumously (*Opera postuma,* Lyon, 1658). Consequently, Descartes should have been
unaware of Gassendi's arguments on this point. However, it can be seen, with H. Jones, that
Gassendi criticized the ambiguities in the Cartesian doctrine of substance: *Pierre Gassendi,
1592–1655: An Intellectual Biography* (Nieuwkoop, 1981), pp. 150*ff.*

More properly [when it is understood] in the most universal sense such that it is suitable even to God. Thus the being who really subsists *per se* is τὸ καθ᾿ ἑαυτὸ ὑφεστηκος.[22]

Only the perseity of subsistence legitimates calling God a substance. Eustache de Saint-Paul adopts the same solution: faced with the substance spoken of as *a substando*, as "subject of accidents," he attempts to introduce a substance that can be thought exclusively as "existing *per se*, or rather not existing in another, which is what it means to subsist."[23] Scipion Dupleix applies substantiality to God only in this restricted sense: "God is a true and most perfect substance, however not predicable or categorical . . . , as he is not the subject or the lackey of any accident."[24] In view of this trend, Descartes appears to be one of the supporters of a weak sense of substantiality, one that makes it acceptable when speaking of God: namely, no longer the supposed subject of attributes, but subsistence *per se;* not categorical subsistence, but self-subsistence referred to itself: ". . . substantiae, hoc est res per se subsistentes [substance, that is, things which exist on their own (*per se*)] . . ." (AT VII, 222, 18 = 157); ". . . haec est ipsa notio substantiae, quod per se, hoc est absque ope alterius ullius substantiae possit existere [The notion of a *substance* is just this—that it can exist by itself (*per se*), that is without the aid of any other substance]" (226, 3–5 = 159). "Per substantiam, nihil aliud intelligere possumus quam rem quae ita existit, ut nulla alia re indigeat ad existendum [By *substance* we can understand nothing other than a thing which exists in such a way as to depend on no other thing for its existence]" (*Principia Philosophiae, I,* §51).[25] It can thus be observed in

22. Goclenius, *Lexicon Philosophicum:* "Substantia primum accipitur generaliter, ut etiam de Deo conveniat. 2. Specialiter, ut tantum conveniat creaturis. . . . Substantia accipitur magis proprie et abusive. Magis proprie generalissime, ut Deo etiam, conveniat. Ita est ens revera per se subsistens τὸ καθ᾿ ἑαυτὸ ὑφεστηκός" (op. cit., p. 1097).

23. Eustache de Saint-Paul, *Summa Philosophiae Quadripartita, I, Logica, III,* s. 1, q. 2: "Ut autem planius intelligas, cur particulares substantiae maxime proprie substantiae dicantur, nota substantiam dici tum a substando, cum a subsistendo; proprium enim substantiae est tum substerni seu subesse accidentibus, quod est substare, cum per se seu in non alio existere, quod est subsistere" (op. cit., p. 97). Only the second sense befits God, since ". . . vero repugnat Deum accidentibus subesse, cum nulli mutationi sit obnoxius [In truth, it is contradictory to say that God lies under accidents, since he is not susceptible of any change.]" (ibid., q. 3, op. cit., p. 98).

24. Scipion Dupleix, *La Métaphysique ou science surnaturelle, V,* 2, §4, op. cit., p. 193. Whence the recourse also to the qualifier *sur-substance* (*X,* 7, §12, op. cit., p. 88).

25. Or also: *vera substantia sive res per se subsistens, To Regius,* January 1642 (AT III, 502, 11 = PW III, 207). Here *vera* is opposed to the customary definition of substance as substantial form in relation to matter: ". . . substantiam quandam materiae adjunctam [a certain substance joined to matter]" (502, 8 = 207). See *Principia Philosophiae I,* §51 and

Descartes and his contemporaries that the very concept of substance undergoes a radical modification—it is freed from all reference to attributes and is summed up by subsistence *per se*. It can therefore be said beyond any doubt that the chief objection that was holding back Saint Augustine, Saint Anselm, and Saint Thomas—among others—now disappears. But despite that, not every objection disappears, if persiety does not just qualify God alone, but also defines all the other substances. With this alone, the indisputable displacement of the meaning of substantiality is not enough to make us understand how and why Descartes can determine God properly with the name *substance*. In fact, the first precise examples of a substance "quae per se apta est existere [which is capable of existing on its own (*per se*)]" given in *Meditatio III* do not lead to God, but to a stone (44, 22–23 = 30 [modified]) or to the *ego* (44, 22; 45, 7 = 30; 31 "ego autem substantia"). If substance *can* define God, it can also correctly define every extended or thinking finite thing. The new understanding of substantiality gives access to God only to at once come to a halt before a formidable aporia: the univocity, at least the near-univocity, of the henceforth indifferent notion of substance. This danger is one that Descartes sees, since he denounces it quite vigorously:

> Atque ideo nomen substantiae non convenit Deo et illis [res omnes quae non nisi ope concursus Dei existere posse percipimus] *univoce*, ut dici solet in Scholis, hoc est, nulla ejus nominis significatio potest distincte intelligi, quae Deo et creaturis sit communis. [Hence the term "substance" does not apply *univocally*, as they say in the Schools, to God and to other things (namely, all things which we perceive cannot exist without help from the ordinary concurrence of God); that is, there is no distinctly intelligible meaning of the term which is common to God and his creatures.] [*Principia Philosophiae I*, §51.]

In Scholis, "in the Schools," substance tends to become a determination that has the same meaning when it concerns God as it does when it concerns other things—at least if one trusts Suarez, for example: "... Created substance does not agree with uncreated substance merely by definition of being, but also by definition of substance." Consequently, substantiality is attributed intrinsically to the creature in the same way as it is to God, in a finally undetermined relation: "... Even if God admits a

---

especially *Responsiones VI* (AT VII, 435, 5–8 = PW II, 293), which, with regard to the Eucharist, makes the distinction between the two senses of substantiality (see *supra*, chap. III, §13, n. 28).

certain agreement with some created beings by definition of substance, this is not spoken univocally but analogically."[26] If one keeps in mind the drift toward univocity that analogy has in Suarez and others, one can sense that this stylistic reserve in fact covers over a univocity. This is what Descartes points out in the text cited above. But it is not enough to see a danger in order to avoid it. Though challenging all univocal application of substance to God and other beings, Descartes never succeeds in conceptualizing these two different senses with distinct terms. He maintains the same concept, and merely juxtaposes two contradictory uses of it: *(a)* Substance is said of a thing that has no need of anything else in order to exist. In the strict and only real sense, this definition admits only one consequence: "Et quidem substantia quae nulla plane re indigeat, unica tantum potest intelligi, nempe Deus. Alias vero omnes, non nisi ope concursus Dei existere posse percipimus [There is only one substance which can be understood to depend on no other thing whatsoever, namely God. In the case of all other substances, we perceive that they can exist only with the help of God's concurrence]" (*Principia Philosophiae I,* §51). To put this in other terms, if the former definition of substance rules out applying it to God, the new one rules out applying it to anything but God alone. God alone is absolutely *per se;* therefore, he is the only actual substance. God is not just solely substance; he is the sole substance. Spinoza's solution is already in play. *(b)* Nonetheless, Descartes does not stick to this position, even though he never contests it explicitly. Without the least theoretical justification, he will juxtapose to the first definition of the sole substance, God, a second definition of what persists—without reason—and will again use the name *substance.* In the *Meditationes,* one finds *ratio substantiae* (common to extension and the ego, according to 44, 27 = 30 and echoing Suarez). In *Principia*

---

26. Suarez, *Disputationes Metaphysicae, XXXII,* s. 1, respectively n. 1: ". . . substantia creata non convenit cum increata solum in ratione entis, sed etiam in ratione substantiae"; then n. 9: ". . . licet [Deus] aliquo modo conveniat in ratione substantiae cum aliquibus entibus creatis, non tamen univoce, sed analogice" (vol. 26, pp. 312 and 314). On this point, we refer to our analyses in *Sur la théologie blanche de Descartes,* §7, pp. 110–20. According to the same logic and more radically than Suarez, Gassendi concludes:

> . . . dico, ut nihil recedam ex Principiis communibus, tam nomen quam definitionem substantiae vere ac formaliter convenire Deo et creaturis, quare et convenire ipsis substantiam, sive conceptum substantiae abstractum univoce. [So that I might not fall back onto ordinary principles, I say that the name as well as the definition of substance truly and formally is suitable to God and to creatures, and for that reason substance too, that is the concept of substance abstracted universally, is suitable to them.]

(*Exercitationes . . . , II,* d. 3, §9, op. cit., p. 335.)

Philosophiae I, §52, one finds a *communis conceptus,* which, however (*autem*), in contradiction with the preceding definition, names as substances "res, quae solo Dei concursu egent ad existendum [things that need only the concurrence of God in order to exist]." Here, the divine concurrence is put out of play, so to speak, with the result that not needing the concurrence of God and being totally in need of it amount to the same thing—namely, to the same denomination of substance. Here, in its lexicon if not in its intention, it is still a matter of Suarez's imperfect solution.[27] Thus, Descartes does not elaborate a definition of substantiality that is sufficiently articulated to avoid falling into an untenable alternative: either repeat Suarez or anticipate Spinoza. The simple notion of substance does not offer a sufficient criterion for him to distinguish the three terms arranged hierarchically in *Meditatio III:* substance without help from any other thing is enough to distinguish between accident and substance, but not between created and uncreated substance.

This is why Descartes will introduce a new criterion: the infinite, which, in opposition to finite substance, will determine the fully constituted substance. It is important to emphasize that the infinite appears in definition [2] in, as it were, the same move that explicitly fixes its third term, ". . . quandam substantiam infinitam. . . ." For only when the criterion of infinity appears is it possible to apply substantiality to God. God is not *first* defined as a substance and *then subsequently* qualified as infinite or an infinite substance. To the contrary, God could never be named substance if Descartes did not first understand substance—with regard to God—as thoroughly infinite. The terms *substantia infinita* form a single and indivisible phrase, and this phrase is added to the definition without having any subset in common with the two other preceding terms. According to the hierarchy of perfection: accident < substance (always finite) < infinite-substance. One must even venture to say that substance, when applied to God, becomes a simple qualification added to the infinite, the only substantive, and then speak less of an infinite substance than of a substantial infinite. No doubt the texts do not explicitly confirm this interpretation. Sometimes it seems that God can be named substance by making just a slight adjustment: "Substantia, quam summe perfectam esse intelligimus, et in qua nihil plane concipimus

27. On this point, we would like now to correct the thesis that we advanced in *Sur la théologie blanche de Descartes,* p. 113 and n. 3: Descartes does not refute the Suarezian doctrine of substance by limiting substance to created things, but by deducing it, in the case of God, from the infinite.

quod aliquem defectum sive perfectionis limitationem involvat, Deus vocatur [The substance which we understand to be supremely perfect, and in which we conceive absolutely nothing that implies any defect or limitation in that perfection, is called *God*]" (*Second Set of Replies*, AT VII, 162, 4–7 = PW II, 114). This text, drawn from a group arranged *more geometrico*, an order that, so strangely non- Cartesian, often alters the most Cartesian of conceptions, nonetheless remains an isolated example. It is counterbalanced by the commentary, from Descartes' own hand, on the phrase *substantia infinita* in *Meditatio III:*

> Per infinitam substantiam, intelligo substantiam perfectiones veras et reales actu infinitas et immensas habentem. Quod non est accidens notioni substantiae superadditum, sed ipsa essentia substantiae absolute sumptae, nullisque defectibus terminatae; qui defectus, ratione substantiae, accidentia sunt; non autem infinitas et infinitudo. [By "infinite substance" I mean a substance which has actually infinite and immense, true and real perfections. This is not an accident added to the notion of substance, but the very essence of substance taken absolutely and bounded by no defects; these defects, in respect of substance, are accidents; but infinity or infinitude is not.][28]

Thus we are clearly informed of three things: First, the perfections defining the infinite substance are themselves totally affected by infinity; accordingly, their reality becomes actually synonymous with the infinite itself (which eliminates the new definition of substantiality). Second, this substance does not admit of any accidents (which eliminates the categorical definition that former theologians had argued over). Third, the infinite and infinity, not being accidents added to substance, are identified with it. The definition of substance—in a word, the substance of substance—is therefore stated: the infinite. The infinite is not added—regarding God—to substance; it is substance that results from the infinite originally in God, and is suitable to him only in this way. Substantial infinite, less *substantia infinita* than, as here, *infinita substantia*. Thus, in sequence [2] of the attributes, *infinite* is added to *substance* lexically because, conceptually, substance itself is suitable to God only as subject to the primordial condition of infinity. Just as the lack of precision (*aliquis/ quaedam*) called for the intervention of substance, substance in turn calls

---

28. *To Clerselier*, 23 April 1649, n. 4 (AT V, 355, 22–356, 2 = PW III, 377). As this explanation follows three others, each of which comments on a formulation from *Meditatio III*, it seems possible to relate it to [2] (and perhaps also to 45, 21, 22, and 27).

for the infinite. This is what—by a simple juxtaposition in his text, but in a much longer course for his reader—Descartes teaches.

Infinita/infinitus [*Deus*]. Therefore, in the end, God is properly qualified *Deus . . . infinitus* according to [1], or *substantia infinita* according to [2]. This name in fact dominated Descartes' rational theology from 1630 onward: contrary to "the common . . . way of imagining him as a finite thing," contrary to "the majority of people who do not regard God as a being who is infinite," Descartes established "that God is infinite."[29] In 1637, the infinite already counts among "all the perfections which I could observe to be in God" (DM 35, 5–6 = PW I, 128). The *Praefatio* to the *Meditationes* recommended at the outset that we remember ". . . mentes nostras considerandas esse ut finitas, Deum autem ut . . . infinitum [Our minds must be regarded as finite, while God is infinite]" (AT VII, 9, 15–17 = PW II, 8). All the way until the *Conversation with Burman,* God is defined by *infinita perfectio.*[30] We here find an unchanging Cartesian absolute, one that remains operative in all his writings. This privilege, as we already know, rests on strict theoretical reasons: only the infinite permits attributing substantiality to God; only this substantiality permits passing beyond the inevitable indetermination, and therefore entering upon "alia quaedam adhuc via." With the infinite, it is a matter of the highest Cartesian determination of God's essence, one that overarches and gives access to all the terms of both formulations [1] and [2], but also to any other foreseeable definition. *Infinite* does not express merely one among many other characteristics proper to God (as in DM, 35, 4 = PW I, 128), nor does it express the divine essence directly (". . . Dei naturam esse . . . infinitam [the nature of God is . . . infinite]," AT VII, 55, 20–21 = PW II, 39). Rather, it defines God as such: ". . . Deum autem ita judico esse actu infinitum [God, on the other hand, I take to be actually infinite]" (47, 19 = 32); or, as an immediate corollary of [2] puts it, ". . . in me esse perceptionem infiniti . . . hoc est Dei [my perception of the infinite, that is God]" (45, 28–29 = 31). In a word, God "intelligitur enim esse infinitus [is understood to be infinite]" (365, 20 = 252 [modified]). This excellence is attested to explicitly by the infinite's anteriority to the finite; it is not the posterior negation of the finite, but indeed its *a priori* horizon: ". . . *priorem* quoddamodo in me esse perceptionem infiniti quam finiti, hoc est Dei quam mei ipsius [My perception of the infinite, that is God, is in some way prior to my perception of the finite,

---

29. *To Mersenne,* respectively, 15 April 1630 (AT I, 146, 18–19); 6 May 1630 (150, 5–7); and 27 May 1630 (152, 11; = PW III, 23; 24 [modified]; and 25).

30. AT V, 153, 30 = PW III, 338.

that is myself]" (45, 28–29 = 31); or also: "In re ipsa *prior* est Dei infinita perfectio, quam nostra imperfectio [In reality the infinite perfection of God is prior to our imperfection]."[31] Far from having used negation to constitute the infinite on the basis of the finite, it is the finite that, despite its appearance of positivity, results from a negation of the infinite, the sole positive *de facto* and *de jure:* "Nec verum est intelligi infinitum per finis sive limitationis negationem, cum e contra omnis limitatio negationem infiniti contineat [It is false that the infinite is understood through the negation of a boundary or limit; on the contrary, all limitation implies a negation of the infinite]" (365, 6–8 = 252).[32] Attested to in this way, the priority of the infinite should not be understood in a restricted sense. It does not mark merely a logical priority (negation of the negation), nor an epistemological priority (idea *maxime clara et distincta,* 46, 8); rather it marks the priority of an *a priori.* The infinite precedes the finite in that it makes experience and the objects of this experience possible. Thus doubt but also all the (finite) modalities of the *cogitatio* find their condition of possibility in the idea of God as idea of the infinite. Descartes insists on the paradoxical fact that it is "per eandem facultatem [by the same faculty]" (51, 22 = 35) and even "simul [at the same time]" (51, 27 = 35) that the *ego* both perceives itself and apperceives the infinite, thus God (51, 29 = 35). "Totaque vis argumenti [the whole force of the argument] . . ." (51, 29–30 = 35) stems from this coincidence. The infinite does not precede the finite merely as a transcendent being, but above all as a transcendental condition for the possibility of the finite. Paradoxically, the idea of the infinite can claim to be *prior,* first after a long course of thought, only insofar as it shows itself as an *a priori* of the finite. It is thus imperative that the infinite be the first proper name of God, for at least two reasons: first because it alone makes it possible to attribute substantiality to God without running the risk of univocity; next because it causes God to be conceived as the *a priori* of finite experience and of the finite objects of experience.[33] This second reason reinforces, and perhaps even lies under, the first, whose innermost truth it constitutes.

The transcendental primacy of the infinite in the qualification of God

31. *Conversation with Burman* (AT V, 153, 30–31 = PW III, 338).

32. See *Responsiones I* (AT VII, 113, 11–14) and the response, *To Hyperaspistes,* August 1641 (AT III, 426, 27–427, 20 = PW II, 81 and PW III, 192).

33. See F. Alquié, *La découverte métaphysique de l'homme chez Descartes* (Paris, 1950), pp. 236*ff.;* E. Levinas, *Totalité et infini* (The Hague, 1964), pp. 186*ff.;* and "Sur l'idée d'infini en nous," in *La passion de la raison. Hommage à Ferdinand Alquié* (Paris, 1983), as well as N. Grimaldi, *L'expérience de la pensée dans la philosophie de Descartes* (Paris, 1978), p. 283.

is immediately developed into several other determinations. They all take up the prefix, apparently negative but in fact supereminent and more than affirmative, that identifies the infinite: *in-*. Hence immensity, incomprehensibility, independence.[34] *Immensitas:* this qualifies God either directly (*Dei immensitas,* AT VII, 231, 26–232, 1 = PW II, 162) or through the mediation of his essence (*essentia immensa,* 241, 2–3 = 168) or through the mediation of his power (*immensitas potentiae,* 237, 8 = 165; *immensa potentia,* 110, 26– 27; 119, 13; 188, 23 = 79; 85; 132; *immensa potestas,* AT VIII-1, 20, 8–9 = not included in PW; ". . . the immensity of his power . . . ," AT IV, 119, 7–8 = PW III, 235) or even through the mediation of certain of his faculties (AT VII, 57, 11 = PW II, 40). In all these cases, immensity, more exactly the *absoluta immensitas* (137, 15–16), is to be understood at once in its most banal and its most rigorous meaning: what cannot be measured. Now, ever since the *Regulae,* measure determines, by means of the order that institutes and governs it, the entire field of the method. There is method solely in the realms of that objectivity ". . . in quibus aliquis ordo vel mensura examinatur [in which questions of order and measure are of concern" (AT X, 378, 1–2 = PW I, 19); in this way, the *Mathesis universalis* is carried out. In consequence, to qualify God by immensity retroactively affects all his properties; it amounts to subtracting God from the field in which the method is applied and removing him from the sciences that it elaborates. Immensity therefore does not rank with the other divine properties; it is not counted like one term among others. Rather, deduced directly from the infinite, it marks its extraterritoriality. Not measurable by infinity, God does not have a place, at least not in the method that must, in this case, admit a non-place. From the moment that measure—and thus the *Mathesis universalis*—can no longer comprehend the divine determinations within itself, it must be concluded that nothing in the definition of God, as much in [1] and [2] as in the other elaborations, will belong to the methodic science, and that therefore nothing in the definition of God can be treated in the mode of objectivity. Between the methodic science that uses all the simple natures indistinctly and the knowledge of God, immensity—immediately deduced from the infinite—cuts an unbridgeable chasm. Nothing of God can be constituted as object of a methodic science. Nothing of methodic objectivity can be attributed to God.

---

34. To this list, one should add immutability, mentioned in *Principia Philosophiae II,* §§37, 39, and 42, *To Mersenne,* 26 April 1643 (AT III, 649, 22–23 = PW III, 217), etc. See *supra,* chap. III, §14.

Hence, *incomprehensibilitas*—the second determination, which Descartes also deduces directly from the divine infinity: ". . . Deum autem, ut incomprehensibilem et infinitum [God is infinite and beyond our comprehension] . . ." (AT VII, 9, 16–17 = PW II, 8), ". . . Dei autem naturam esse immensam, incomprehensibilem, infinitam [The nature of God is immense, incomprehensible, infinite]" (55, 20–21 = 39). In fact, as early as 1630, this deduction appears in the same terms as it does in 1641. It can be found in one of the texts from 1630, which introduces the doctrine of the creation of the eternal truths: ". . . God as a being who is infinite and incomprehensible."[35] This does not happen by chance; for if the eternal truths, thus also the simple natures that the method makes operative, are created by a God, this God, obviously, passes beyond the method, thus appears as incomprehensible to it. If the infinity of God on principle passes beyond (creation of the eternal truths) the strictly objectifying method, incomprehensibility will not betray an imperfection, a deficiency, or an irrationality in the definition of God; on the contrary, it will attest to its perfection, as the sign of another rationality. God the infinite is not known despite his incomprehensibility, but through it. For in casting itself toward the divine incomprehensibility, human reason truly surpasses itself and transcends the finite that it is in the direction of the infinite that is. Hence a doctrine that is as constant as it is paradoxical: "It is possible to know that God is infinite and all powerful although our soul, being finite, cannot comprehend or conceive him" (AT I, 152, 10–13 = PW III, 25 [modified]); ". . . intellectum meum, qui est finitus, non capere infinitum [My intellect, which is finite, does not encompass the infinite]" (AT VII, 107, 1–2 = PW II, 77); ". . . infinitum, qua infinitum est, nullo quidem modo comprehendi, sed nihilominus tamen intelligi [The infinite, *qua* infinite, can in no way be comprehended. But it can still be understood]" (112, 21–23 = 81 [modified]); ". . . idea infiniti, ut sit vera, nullo modo debet comprehendi, quoniam ipsa incomprehensibilitas in ratione formali infiniti continetur [The idea of the infinite, if it is to be a true idea, cannot be comprehended at all, since incomprehensibility itself is contained in the formal definition of the infinite]" (368, 2–4 = 253 [modified]); and finally: ". . . est de ratione infiniti ut a nobis, qui sumus finiti, non comprehendatur [It is in the nature of the infinite

35. *To Mersenne,* 6 May 1630 (AT I, 150, 6–7 = PW III, 24 [modified]), confirmed by the letter to the same correspondent in July 1642: "God is infinite and incomprehensible" (AT III, 393, 29–30 = PW III, 185), completed by ". . . Deus est ineffabilis et incomprehensibilis [God is ineffable and incomprehensible]" (*To Mersenne,* 21 January 1641 [AT III, 284, 7–8 = PW III, 169 (modified)]).

not to be fully comprehended by us, who are finite] . . ." (*Principia Philo-sophiae I,* §19 [modified]).[36] With divine incomprehensibility, it is not a matter of renouncing the rational knowledge of God, but of allowing rationality to know the infinite, thus to know, beyond the objectivity that it methodically masters, the infinite as such, as incomprehensible to the finite. Incomprehensibility will even become the surest sign that it is indeed God that the *cogitatio* knows, in accordance with the rule that nothing divine can be thought except as incomprehensible, and that nothing truly incomprehensible can be offered to the *cogitatio* without it in the end concerning God. From now on, all the subsequent elements of definition [1] and [2] will verify this rule, and with incomprehensibility, they will bear the mark of the infinite that they illustrate.

Independens: The attribute of independence (in [2], 45, 12) is deduced immediately from the infinite in accordance with a fundamental equivalence: "independence, conceived distinctly, involves infinity."[37] The idea of God implies independence as necessarily as it does noncreation and substantiality par excellence: ". . . ideam claram et distinctam substantiae cogitantis increatae et independentis, id est Dei [a clear and distinct idea of uncreated and independent thinking substance, that is of God]" (*Principia Philosophiae I,* §54). Of course, in God, substance accedes to independence only by virtue of the infinite, as opposed to the finite, which will therefore be dependent: ". . . si detur substantia infinita et independens, est magis res quam finita et dependens [substantia] [If there is an infinite and independent substance, it is more of a thing than a finite and dependent substance]" (*Third Set of Replies,* AT VII, 185, 25–27 = PW II, 130). The same opposition can be deduced directly from doubt, in which the divine independence appears as the transcendental *a priori* of the experience that the *ego* has of its own incompleteness: "Cumque attendo me dubitare, sive esse rem incompletam et dependentem, adeo clara et distincta idea entis independentis et completi, hoc est Dei, mihi occurrit [When I consider the fact that I have doubts, or that I am a thing that is incomplete and dependent, then there arises in me a clear and distinct idea of a being who is independent and complete, that is, an idea of God]" (53, 9–12 = 37). Independence is directly equivalent to aseity, as the French translation of the formula ". . . si a me essem [if

36. See *To Mersenne,* 11 October 1638 (AT II, 383, 16–20) and 11 November 1640 (AT III, 234, 1–2 = PW III, 126 and 157). See *Sur la théologie blanche de Descartes,* pp. 396–402.

37. *To Mersenne,* 30 September 1640 (AT III, 191, 15–16 = PW III, 154). Independence can be combined, within certain limits, with the finitude of free will: *To Elisabeth,* 3 November 1645 (AT IV, 332, 12–333, 7 = PW III, 277).

I derived my existence from myself] . . ." (48, 7 = 33) suggests with the gloss ". . . si j'étais indépendant de tout autre et que je fusse moi-même l'auteur de mon être [if I was independent of all others and was myself the author of my Being]."[38] If independence defines the divine aseity as *a priori,* then it determines in advance all that is not God as dependent. The concept of substance is thus divided between, on the one hand, the (substantial) infinite and, on the other, (substantial) dependence. One could even venture to say that, in both cases, "substance" plays the role of a simple attribute, either of the infinite or of the dependent. Since it always characterizes the created, nothing could be more coherent than to qualify the (created) eternal truths with the title dependent: ". . . The mathematical truths which you call eternal have been laid down by God and depend on him entirely no less than the rest of his creatures. Indeed to say that these truths are independent of God is to talk of him as if he were Jupiter or Saturn and to subject him to Styx and the Fates." Or: ". . . non autem contra veras [the eternal truths] Deo cognosci quasi independenter ab illo sint verae [They (the eternal truths) are not known as true by God in any way which would imply that they are true independent of him]." This thesis of 1630 is found again unchanged in 1641:

> . . . ego non puto essentias rerum, mathematicasque veritates quae de ipsis cognisci possunt, esse independentes a Deo; sed puto nihilominus, quia Deus sic voluit, quia sic disposuit, ipsas esse immutabiles et aeternas. [I do not think that the essences of things, and the mathematical truths which we can know concerning them, are independent of God. Nevertheless I do think that they are immutable and eternal, since the will and decree of God willed and decreed that they should be so.][39]

Even the problem of man's free will will not alter the chasm between the divine independence and the dependence of the finite; man, though free,

---

38. AT IX-1, 38, 17–18, confirmed by ". . . if I had existed alone and independently of every other being . . . , then for the same reason I could have got from myself everything else I knew I lacked, and thus been myself infinite, eternal, immutable, omniscient, omnipotent . . ." (DM, AT VI, 34, 30–35, 5 = PW I, 128).

39. Respectively, *To Mersenne,* 15 April 1630 (AT I, 145, 7– 13); *To Mersenne,* 6 May 1630 (149, 23–24 [see also 150, 8 and 17]); *Responsiones* V (AT VII, 380, 8–12 [see ibid., 370, 6–12] = PW III, 23; 24 [see also 25 and 25]; PW II, 261 [see 255]). See also *To Mesland,* 2 May 1644 (AT IV, 119, 1–14) and *Conversation with Burman:* ". . . illa et omnia alia pendent a Deo [These too depend on God, like everything else] . . ." (AT V, 160, 1 = PW III, 235 and 343).

nonetheless remains dependent.[40] It must therefore be concluded first that independence is deduced directly from the infinity of God, and next that, by this peculiarity, the infinite determines *a contrario* what is not it. Accordingly, definition [2], precisely because it is anchored in the infinite as such, will from now on be inclined, in and through the transition from independence, toward the finite; or rather, it allows infinity to be declined from the point of view of the finite. And besides, how could the infinite give itself to be conceived, if not from the point of view of the finite, which the *ego* is? Consequently the subsequent attributes will only explicate the infinite, which, so to speak, oversees the relation between the infinite and the finite, either directly (creator/creatures) or indirectly (passage to the infinite from the finite perfections).

§18. Power and Perfections

The appellations attributed to God up until now all have a point in common. They are stated and justified negatively: God refuses finitude, measure, dependence. No doubt these negations are put right, first by the initial indetermination, then by the claim to the positive primacy of the infinite. But this does not stop one from hearing in them an echo of the "theological negations," and it is even more likely that one will hear this echo insofar as the latter lead directly to the "way of eminence"— which transcends negation as well as affirmation by passing to excess. Such a theological identification of the first divine attributes (and names) can be confirmed in another way, too: By beginning with infinity and adding incomprehensibility, immensity, and its possible substance, Descartes retrieves the same order that Lessius followed when he intended to set forth the names and perfections of God.[41] Consequently, shouldn't

---

40. For example, *To Elisabeth,* 3 November 1645 (AT IV, 332, 12–333, 7) or January 1646 (AT IV, 352, 28–354, 14 = PW III, 277 or 282).

41. L. Lessius, in the *Quinquaginta nomina Dei,* devotes the two first chapters to *De Deo et divinitate,* then he passes to the infinity of God (chap. III), which governs his immensity (chap. IV), his indivisibility (chap. V), his eternity and his *altitudo* (chaps. VI and VII), then *immutabilitas* (chap. VIII), *immortalitas* (chap. IX), *invisibilitas* (chap. X) and, as for Descartes, *incomprehensibilitas* (chap. XI) accompanied by *ineffabilitas* (chap. XII). Thus, at issue is a series of theological negations. *Omnipotentia* appears only next (chap. XIII), making the transition to the affirmative attributes: wisdom, beauty, goodness, holiness, mercy, justice, etc. Still more significant, at least for purposes of a comparison with Descartes, is the order followed by Lessius in the treatise *De perfectionibus moribusque divinis:* at the outset, one finds the *infinitas Dei,* which engenders *incomprehensibilitas* (chaps. 1 and 2), then immensity (chap. II, 1) and immutability. Here again it is *omnipotentia* that permits passing to the affirmative perfections (chap. V).

we seek to determine a theological status for the qualifications that will follow? They too have a point in common: they open with the index of a superlative—*summe intelligens, summe potens, summe perfectum.* The mention of the creator does not really count as an exception here, since it results directly from the *ego*'s consciousness of its own imperfection (from the inversion of *summe*). The superlative still indicates eminence, to be sure; but this time by means of affirmation and, in the end, in the mode of affirmation. Descartes thus discovers the "theological affirmations," not *before* the "theological negations"—as Dionysius the Areopagite and Saint Thomas would have it—but *after* them. This carries a twofold consequence. First of all, eminence no longer constitutes a third moment, autonomous if not equivalent to the first; rather, it simply crowns the other two ways, without really surmounting them. Next, since they do not open onto any third term, the negations (positive) and the affirmations (superlative) run the risk of being juxtaposed, indeed of contradicting each other, without there being any possibility of a final arbiter or court of appeals. This gives rise to an incurable tension in the Cartesian doctrine of the divine attributes and names—or at least these are the hypotheses that it is now time for us to test.

Summe intelligens: To this qualification of [2] (in 45, 12) there corresponds in [1] "Deum . . . omniscium [God . . . omniscient]" (40, 16–17 = 28); in the *Discourse on the Method,* "the perfect being . . . omniscient;"[42] and in *Principia Philosophiae I,* §14, *ens summe intelligens.* In itself, this attribute does not call for any particular commentary, since it seems obvious that God should have supreme intelligence attributed to him. Nonetheless, not only in [1] and [2], but in the entirety of the Cartesian corpus, the attribute of supreme intelligence never receives any noticeable elaboration. This silence is all the more noticeable since the superlative *summe* sets up the parallel with the immediately following attribute, *summe potens,* whose privilege we have already seen in the initial indetermination (*vetus opinio* 21, 1–2; *praeconcepta opinio,* 36, 8–9) and whose development we have already pointed out. From this an inescapable question arises: why is there such an imbalance between two attributes that are ordinarily put on the same level? Or: why doesn't supreme intelligence play a role comparable to omnipotence? Why is supreme intelligence not developed into a supreme *cogitatio,* which would correspond to omnipotence (however, without falling back into a distinction

42. DM, 35, 2–5 = PW I, 128. The Latin translation of P. de Courcelles reads *omniscius* (*Specimina Philosophiae* [Amsterdam, 1644], p. 32 = AT VI, 560, 4).

of faculties—understanding, will—in God)? One answer appears, at the very least, plausible, though provisional: God is not essentially determined by intelligence, and therefore Descartes mentions intelligence only briefly.

Summe potens. This title, formulated by [2] in 45, 12–13, confirms *omnipotens* in [1], 40, 17. In *Meditatio III,* its occurrences are not so numerous that they require particular commentary. However, omnipotence does not come up for the first time in [1] and [2]. In fact, it appears before the attempt at a real definition of the true essence of God; more specifically, it appears in the confused, not critical but working, definition of a "certain" God who provokes hyperbolic doubt. Descartes identifies this notion quite clearly: ". . . haec praeconcepta de summa Dei potentia opinio [my preconceived belief in the supreme power of God] . . ." (36, 8–9 = 25), ". . . infixa quaedam est meae menti vetus opinio, Deum esse qui potest omnia [Firmly rooted in my mind is the long-standing opinion that there is an omnipotent God] . . ." (21, 1–2 = 14). *Meditationes I* and *III* correspond to one another precisely: God is given to be thought as omnipotent, even before the *ordo rationum* becomes operative (*vetus/ prae*), thus by a historically transmitted conception (*infixa/opinio*). In this way, omnipotence shows up before the *ordo rationum.* It even precedes the correct definitions of God; and its status as opinion takes away nothing from this factual privilege: first of all because such a status was the sole mode in which it was possible for the *ordo rationum* to appear at that time; and, more important, because the determination of God in terms of a preconceived opinion (21, 1–2 and 36, 8–9 = PW II, 14 and 25) is then confirmed rationally by [1] and [2]. The opined omnipotence becomes concept; the modality has changed, the meaning remains. Therefore omnipotence truly qualifies God in [1] and [2], but also, by anticipation, as early as the very first *Meditatio* in which the *vetus opinio* was definitively true, though not yet certain. From even before the raising of doubt, the divine omnipotence that provokes this doubt lies beyond it and withdraws from it, being hyperbolically certain. For if omnipotence deceives me, it is certain that it is. The omnipotence of God is freed from the *ordo rationum,* since it is always effective at playing its many roles, though with a different status each time. How are we to understand this exorbitant privilege, one shared by no other term in [1] and [2], of something theoretically valid yet indifferent to the *ordo rationum*? In fact, omnipotence does not hold this privilege in 1641 alone. To what does the opinion that has been firmly rooted in *my* mind (". . . infixa quaedam . . . mea menti vetus opinio [firmly rooted in my mind is the long-standing opinion] . . ." 21, 1–2 = 14), and that befalls *me* (". . . mihi occurrit [comes to my mind] . . ." 36, 9 = 25), refer? Before searching for probable historical origins,[43] it is necessary to go back to the origin of Descartes' own properly metaphysical career. From 1630 on, following a definitive decision, he thinks God as and through "incomprehensible power."[44] This point, which is held by the *Discourse on the Method* in 1637, is thus something of an ancient and unchanging fact, traversing the texts of 1641 and, beyond *Meditationes I* and *III*, blossoming in the *Responsiones*, which resume to the letter the phrase from 1630: ". . . attendentesque ad immensam et incomprehensibilem potentiam, quae in ejus idea continetur [We attend to the immense and incomprehensible power that is contained in the idea of God] . . ." (AT VII, 110, 26–27 = 79). This revival of the theme allows for its overabundant orchestration: *infinita potestas* (220, 20 = 155), *immensitas potentiae* (111, 4 and 237, 8–9 = 80 and 165), *immensa potentia* (119, 13 and 188, 23 = 85 and 132), *potentia exuperans* (110, 27 = 79), *exuperantia potestatis* (112, 10 = 80). When it defines God as *summe potens*, definition [2] does not only anticipate *Responsiones I* (119, 6; 19; 22 = 85; 85; 85) by retrospectively justifying the hypothesis of *Meditatio I* (22, 25); it also designates the concept that Descartes will privilege, from 1630 until the end, whenever he wants to define the essence of God. Until the end: in the chronological sense to be sure, but also because everything, in God, can be deduced from omnipotence; for God alone can ". . . sibi dare omnipotentiam totam simul, aliasve perfectiones divinas collective sumptas [give himself omnipotence and the other divine perfections all together]."[45] As a constant, omnipotence determines the divine essence, be it epistemologically (1630) or hypothetically (*Meditatio I*) or as merely one of the divine attributes (*Meditatio III*, [1] and [2], *Discourse on the Method*, and *Principia Philosophiae*) or as the very essence of God as in the *Responsiones*—". . . immensitatem potentiae, sive essentiae [the immensity of his power or essence] . . ." (AT VII, 237, 1 = PW II, 165). Permanent, unchanging, indifferent to the *ordo rationum*, omnipotence rejects every parallel with other attributes, like supreme intel-

43. See *supra*, n. 14.

44. *To Mersenne*, 15 April 1630 (AT I, 146, 4–5) and again 6 May 1630 (AT I, 150, 22 = PW III, 23 and 25). The *Principia Philosophiae I* read *summe potens* (§14) or *omnipotens* (§22).

45. *To Arnauld*, 4 June 1648 (AT V, 194, 1–3 = PW III, 355 [modified]). See *To Mersenne*, March 1642: ". . . [This] is known by natural reason—that he is all good, all powerful, all truthful, etc." (AT III, 544, 20–21 = PW III, 211).

ligence. Etienne Gilson saw in it nothing less than "a new idea of God," and we detect in it the oldest and most abiding Cartesian idea of God.[46] However, are we not thus contradicting ourselves massively? On the one hand, we are here positing omnipotence as the primordial definition of God; but on the other hand, we had established the infinite as the proper name of God. No doubt the contradiction cannot be hidden. What is still to be asked is the following: First, could this contradiction be eased by interpreting the infinite itself as the infinity of an omnipotence? Next, doesn't this contradiction, be it provisional or definitive, betray a tension that is constitutive of Descartes' discourse on God—in other words, don't definitions [1] and [2], indisputably built on the primacy of the infinite as the proper name of God, harbor the possibility, already operative, of their displacement, replacement, indeed subversion by omnipotence, pregnant with another definition? Finally, does this contradiction stigmatize the fallibility of the interpreter or an incoherence that characterizes the rational theology of Cartesian metaphysics? As omnipotence, instead of being inscribed harmoniously in the *ordo rationum* like the infinite is, is deployed with total indifference to it and is also authorized by an unjustified anteriority, it could indeed, precisely by the contradiction that it effects, put us on the trail of an architectural incoherence.

. . . *et a qua tum ego ipse, tum aliud omne, si quid aliud extat, quodcumque extat, est creatum* [and which created both myself and everything else (if anything else there be) that exists]. This formulation from [2], at 45, 13–14 = 31, confirms [1] ". . . rerumque omnium, quae praeter ipsum sunt, creatorem [creator of all things that exist apart from him] . . ." (40, 17–18 = 28). Even though ". . . [he had] proved quite explicitly that God was the creator of all things,"[47] Descartes in the metaphysical texts does not grant the title *Deus creator omnium* (AT VII, 255, 10) a frequency proportionate to its dogmatic importance. It does, however serve, two functions: Either (1) that of a God who creates the *ego* in such a way that even the most evident things might in fact deceive it: "Deum esse qui potest omnia, a quo talis qualis existo, creatus sum [an omnipotent God who made me the kind of creature that I am]" (21, 2–3 = 14); ". . . talem me creasse, ut semper fallar [created me such that I am deceived all the time]" (21, 13–14 = 14); "Nec dubium est quin potuerit Deus me talem creare ut numquam fallerer [There is, moreover, no

46. E. Gilson, *Etudes sur le rôle de la pensée médiévale dans la formation du système cartésien* (Paris, 1930), chap. V, pp. 224–33.

47. *To Mersenne,* 28 January 1641 (AT III, 297, 15–16 = PW III, 172).

doubt that God could have given me a nature such that I was never mistaken]" (55, 10–11 = 38). Or (2), that of a God who is creator of, among all things, the theoretical truths ("eternal truths"); thus, in 1630: "You ask me *in quo genere causae Deus disposuit aeternas veritates.* I reply: *in eodem genere causae* as he created all things, that is to say, *ut efficiens et totalis causa.* For it is certain that he is the author of the essence of created things no less than of their existence; and this essence is nothing other than the eternal truths."[48] In 1644, the *Principia* again state this doctrine by mobilizing the concept of creation: ". . . omnipotentem, omnis veritatis bonitatisque fontem, rerum omnium creatorem [omnipotent, the source of all goodness and truth, the creator of all things] . . ." (*I*, §22),

> . . . quia Deus solus omnium quae sunt aut esse possunt vera est causa, perspicuum est optimam philosophandi viam nos sequuturos, si ex ipsius Dei cognitione rerum ab eo creatarum explicationem deducere conemur, ut ita scientiam perfectissimam, quae est effectuum per causas, acquiramus. [Since God alone is the true cause of everything which is or can be, it is very clear that the best path to follow when we philosophize will be to start from the knowledge of God himself and try to deduce an explanation of things created by him. This is the way to acquire the most perfect scientific knowledge, that is knowledge of effects through their causes.] [*I*, §24.]

Of these two functions of creation, apparently only the first appears in 1641. Without being able to demonstrate it at length here, we believe that, in fact, in the *Meditationes* the first plays the role that the second has in the other texts. For God (or his provisional placeholder) could not overdetermine an evidence that my consciousness regards as perfect if he did not exceed this same evidence, and thus the truths and the essences in general; and he can exceed them only insofar as he creates them and thus is distinct from them. In this way, the two metaphysical functions of the attribute *creator* count as just one.[49] But at the same time, it becomes clear that, in all cases, creation is understood in terms of efficient causality (mentioned in 1630 and 1644), which is itself deduced directly from divine omnipotence (mentioned in 1630, 1641, and 1644). Descartes does not add any new qualification to his definition of God when he mentions that he is creator, since, for him, creation becomes

48. *To Mersenne,* 27 May 1630 (AT I, 151, 1–152, 5 = PW III, 25).
49. See the demonstration in *Sur la théologie blanche de Descartes,* §13, pp. 267*ff.*

intelligible only on the basis of omnipotence being carried out as *ultima causa* (50, 6). In contrast to the nominalists, who justified the (metaphysical) omnipotence of God by reference to (theological) creation, Descartes renders creation intelligible by reducing it to omnipotence, which is itself rationalized as efficient cause. This then is why definitions [1] and [2] do not begin with the creative function, conceived as an *explicans* drawn from theology, but instead are completed by it—as an *explicandum* rationally reduced to the preceding determinations, and, first of all, to omnipotence. Thus the attempt at two definitions of God in *Meditatio III* should be closed here. This however is not the case, despite appearances. A final name, strangely absent here, must still appear.

Ens summe perfectum. This phrase has to come up, since formulae [1] and [2] suffer not only from the incoherence that they introduce between the infinite and omnipotence, but also from a quite obvious incompleteness: they omit a number of qualifications that the theologians—but also the philosophers and, among them, Descartes himself—mention elsewhere: namely unity, eternity, truthfulness, goodness, beauty, justice, etc. That on its first try the *ordo rationum* cannot include them in its inventory is acceptable; but it cannot eliminate them without saying anything more. Descartes, no doubt well aware of the difficulty, therefore introduces, at the very heart of *Meditatio III,* something like a complementary definition, which, later, will be of use to *Meditatio V* when it tries to restate the *a priori* proof. Let us take this to be the third pronouncement:

> [3] . . . unitas, simplicitas, sive inseparabilitas eorum omnium [rerum] quae in Deo sunt, una ex praecipuis perfectionibus quas in eo esse intelligo [The unity, the simplicity, or the inseparability of all the attributes of God is one of the most important of the perfections which I understand him to have]. (50, 16–19 = 34)

This pronouncement must be completed by the formulations surrounding it: ". . . omnesque perfectiones quas Deo tribuo [all the perfections which I attribute to God]" (46, 30 = 33) ". . . reliquas omnes Dei perfectiones [all the other perfections of God]" (47, 5 = 32), ". . . nihil enim ipso perfectius [nothing more perfect than God] . . ." (48, 5 = 33), ". . . omnium perfectionum, quas Deo tribuo, ideam [the idea of all the perfections which I attribute to God] . . ." (49, 28–29 = 34), ". . . omnes [perfectiones] quas in Deo esse concipio [all the perfections which I conceive to be in God]" (50, 3–4 = 34), and finally ". . . Deus, inquam, ille idem cujus idea in me est, hoc est habens omnes illas perfectiones quas ego ... quocumque modo attingere cogitatione possum [By 'God' I mean that of which the idea is in me, that is, the possessor of all the perfections which I ... can somehow reach in my thought]" (52, 2–6 = 35 [modified]). God thus becomes accessible to thought in a new way: his idea, thus also his existence, is not imposed right away, as previously the idea of infinity was, but can be constructed by the human understanding that counts up the perfections, reconciles them with each other, then attributes them to God. We must follow, quickly, these three operations in a new definition of God. First, the counting up or the inventory: after unity, simplicity, and inseparability (50, 16–17), Descartes mentions goodness (85, 25; 87, 28; 88, 20), truth ("... cum enim Deus sit summum ens, non potest non esse etiam summum bonum et verum [Since God is the supreme being, he must also be supremely good and true]" (144, 3–4 = 103), beauty (52, 14), etc. Among the perfections, even *summum ens* must be counted,[50] and especially *existentia* (66, 13–14; 67, 14–15, 26–27). In fact, the list of perfections to be counted up for the new notion of God can never be closed, since "all the perfections which I could observe to be in God" (DM, AT VI, 35, 5–6 = PW I, 128) include nothing less than "... omnes omnino perfectiones [absolutely all the perfections]": "... Deus tale quid dicat quod omnes omnino perfectiones in se comprehendit [God is spoken of as the one who includes absolutely all the perfections in himself]."[51] Quantitatively, God accumulates perfections indefinitely; their inventory will thus always remain, on principle, incomplete. But God can receive these perfections legitimately by marking them with the infinite, which characterizes him in the first place. To the practice of a (quantitative) inventory, the human mind must therefore add that of a (qualitative) amplification. Descartes describes this by reference to "... facultas omnes perfectiones creatas ampliandi, hoc est aliquid ipsis majus sive amplius concipiendi [a faculty for amplifying all created perfections (i.e., conceiving of something greater or more ample than they are)]," or "... vis perfectiones humanas eousque ampliandi ut plusquam humanae esse cognoscantur [the power of amplifying all hu-

50. *Summum ens* (AT VII, 54, 18 = PW II, 38); *ens primum et summum* (67, 21 = 47); "... cum animadverto existentiam esse perfectionem, recte concludam ens primum et summum existere [When I later realize that existence is a perfection, I am correct in concluding that the first and supreme being exists]," 67, 26–28 = 47; *summum ens sive Deum*, 69, 8 = 47; "cum enim Deus sit summum ens [since God is the supreme being] ...," 144, 3 = 103; "... Dei sive entis summi ideam [the idea of God, or a supreme being] ...," *Principia Philosophiae I*, §18. See *supra*, chap. II, §8, n. 40.
51. *Conversation with Burman* (AT V, 161, 8–9 and 3, 4 = not included in PW).

man perfections up to the point where they are recognized as more than human]."[52] For it is clear that the perfections, such as they are apprehended by the *ego* while it counts them up, still belong to the finite and the created human. It must therefore be the case that the idea of the infinite that inhabits the *ego* "stretches" each of them to the infinite, by means of an operation that renders them incomprehensible but only thus appropriate to the infinite. Only then can the perfections quantitatively and qualitatively carried to infinity be attributed to God, conceived as *cumulum perfectionum* and *omnium perfectionum complementum.*[53] God therefore does not accomplish merely the summation of perfections, but most important, their elevation to an infinite power: from an infinity of perfections to the infinity of the perfections. Thus the highest perfection of God consists in the utterance of perfection itself, carried to the superlative—the ". . . idea entis perfectissimi hoc est Dei [idea of a most perfect being, that is, God]" (51, 3–4 = 35), says *Meditatio III,* along with other names. In what follows, this phrase constantly reappears: ". . . Dei, sive entis summe perfecti [God, or a being who is supremely perfect]" (54, 13–14 = 38), ". . . Deum (hoc est ens summe perfectum) [God, that is a supremely perfect being]" (66, 12–13 = 46), ". . . Deum . . . (hoc est ens summe perfectum) . . . [God . . . (that is, a supremely perfect being) . . ." (67, 9–10 = 46), "Substantia, quam summe perfectam esse intelligimus . . . *Deus* vocatur [The substance which we understand to be supremely perfect . . . is called *God*]" (162, 4–7 = 114). The superlative of perfection, in other words the perfection of perfection, fills the role of dominant qualification of God, as much by its frequency in 1641 as by its enduring unchanged in 1637 and 1644.[54] The

52. *Fifth Set of Replies* (AT VII, 365, 15–17 and 370, 25– 371, 2 = PW II, 252 and 255). At issue here is the transformation of the finite attributes (human perfections) into infinite attributes (divine), as is suggested quite explicitly by a text from the *First Set of Replies* (AT VII, 137, 15–138, 10 = PW II, 98–99). See *To Regius,* 24 May 1640 (AT III, 64, 5–20 = PW III, 147). The perfections thus become superlatives: ". . . summarum Dei perfectionum ideam [an idea of the supreme perfections of God] . . . ," *Principia Philosophiae I,* §20; ". . . summas perfectiones . . . in Deo [the supreme perfections . . . in God]," *I,* §18 [modified].

53. Respectively, *Comments on a Certain Broadsheet* (AT VIII- 2, 362, 12 = PW I, 306) ("le comble et l'accomplissement des perfections," translates F. Alquié, in Descartes, *Œuvres philosophiques,* vol. 3, p. 812) then *Principia Philosophiae I,* §18 [modified], which goes on to define God as "Archetypus aliquis, omnes ejus perfectiones reipsa continens [some archetype which contains in reality all the perfections]" [modified].

54. See, among other occurrences: ". . . nihil enim ipso perfectius [nothing more perfect than God] . . ." (AT VII, 48, 5 = PW II, 33); ". . . Deum . . . summe perfectum [God, who is supremely perfect] . . ." (62, 17–18 = 43); ". . . illis omnes perfectiones tribuere

definition of God [3] by superlative perfection proves its primordial role by sustaining the *a priori* proof for the existence of God; but it offers especially strong proof of playing this role by its limitless capacity to integrate any perfection whatsoever into a single determination of God—provided only that this perfection pass into the superlative (or have the adverb *summe* attached). Definition [3] furnishes, far more than *a* definition of the divine essence, the matrix for an infinite number of possible definitions of the divine essence by means of any perfection whatsoever being taken to the infinite. The infinite is concretely accomplished in the summation of perfections, as Descartes indicates at least once: "... nomen *infiniti,* quod rectius vocari posset *ens amplissimum* [I kept the term infinite, when the 'greatest being' would be more correct]."[55] The sum of the perfections designates God as *ens perfectissimum*—as a sort of divine name, and not merely like a concept of being in general.[56] The determination of God by perfection thus takes up, through summation, an infinity of other perfections borne to the infinite in each case. God as *ens summe perfectum* should therefore appear at the forefront of the definitions. This is not the case, however, seeing as this divine name, directly implied by the last attributes stated in [1] and [2], is explicitly thematized only with formula [3]. The tension between the two divine names in each of the first two formulations is now compli-

---

[attribute all perfections to him] ..." (67, 23–24 = 47); "... in causa illa contineri omnes perfectiones, ac proinde illam Deum esse [that this cause contains every perfection, and hence that it is God] ..." (108, 5–6 = PW II, 78); "... ista idea Dei ... naturam entis summe perfecti [the idea of God ... the nature of a supremely perfect being] ..." (138, 10–13 = PW II, 99); "... natura Dei, sive entis summe perfecti [the nature of God, or the supremely perfect being] ..." (163, 12 = 115); DM, 34, 20–24 = PW I, 128: "... a nature truly more perfect than I was and even possessing in itself all the perfections of which I could have any idea, that is—to explain myself in one word—by God; 'a perfect being'" (38, 20 = 130); "... God, who is all-perfect .." (40, 10–11 = 130); "... the infinite perfections of God ..." (43, 7–8 = 132).

55. *To Hyperaspistes,* August 1641 (AT III, 427, 12–13 = PW III, 192).

56. We therefore cannot subscribe to Heidegger's thesis:

> Gott ist einfach der Titel für das jenige Seiende, in dem sich die Idee von Sein überhaupt im echten Sinne realisiert. "Gott" ist hier einfach ein rein ontologischer Begriff, und daher wird er auch das *ens perfectissimum* genannt. [God is the name for that entity in which the idea of being as such is realized in its genuine sense. Here "God" is but a purely ontological concept and is therefore also called the *ens perfectissimum*] [most perfect entity].

(*Prolegomena zur Geschichte des Zeitbegriffs,* G. A., 20, p. 233, see p. 239 [English trans., p. 173, see 177].) This interpretation, put forth explicitly with regard to Descartes, is found again in *Sein und Zeit,* §20, op. cit., pp. 92, 19 [English trans., p. 125].

cated by a new tension between, on the one hand, these two formulae, and, on the other, a third—since it alone clearly states the third divine name, presupposed by but not made explicit in the first two. If one inventories the attributes that define God in *Meditatio III,* it then becomes possible to refer each of them to a precise divine name: Falling under the jurisdiction of the divine name *infinitum* are the attributes (cited by [1] and [2]) *substantia,* infinity, independence, immensity, and incomprehensibility, all within the domain of the *via negativa.* Falling under the jurisdiction of the divine name *potentia* are the attributes (also cited in [1] and [2]) creation and supreme power, each within the domain of eminence, since power remains at once incomprehensible (negation) and productive (affirmation). Finally, falling under the jurisdiction of the divine name *ens summe perfectum* is the attribute (cited by [1] and [2]) of supreme intelligence, but also all the thinkable perfections (cited in [3]), each within the domain of the *via affirmativa.* Descartes thus recognizes three principal divine names, and following the three moments of the theology of divine names such as it has unfolded since Dionysius the Areopagite, he attaches to them three series of God's attributes. If this classification is correct, a question immediately forces itself upon us. Descartes simply juxtaposes three names, three modes of utterance, and three series of attributes, without giving any cause to suspect that a rigorous organization of them might be possible. Meanwhile, the theologians—the ancient ones, at least—arrange these terms in the coherent itinerary of a mystical theology. The rhapsody that Descartes substitutes for this coherence certainly does not totally eliminate it; it merely masks it, since we have been able to reconstitute it. However, isn't it exposed to a disorder that reaches the point of incoherence? Can the three divine names here juxtaposed without a theologically justified organization be deployed without contradicting each other? Doesn't the absence of all hierarchy condemn them to unveil their incompatibility in the field of metaphysical pronouncements? In short, doesn't the metaphysical revival of the divine names outside of their theological situation lead to tensions that are so strong that, in the end, they appear contradictory? The hesitations and the imprecisions stigmatized in [1], [2], and [3] would thus offer only the signs of a more essential conceptual distortion.

§19. The System of Contradictions

The task before us now is to test, with an eye toward proving or disproving, the irreducible plurality of divine names implied by the attributes enumerated in formulae [1], [2], and [3]. The three divine names, designated approximately as *infinitum, potentia,* and *ens summe perfectum,* oppose each other for a reason: each of them takes up one of the ways of mystical theology; but instead of being organized into a single anabasis, they are simply juxtaposed without any conceptual links. Everything happens as if Descartes deployed successively, but without any conceptual connection, a *via negativa* (God the infinite), a *via affirmitiva* (God as *ens summe perfectum*), and finally a passage unto eminence (*potentia*). This verdict could be tested by two procedures, one internal and one external. The internal procedure: which body of concepts issued from Descartes' texts emphasizes the irreducibility of each of the three terms just distinguished? We propose the following hypothesis: each of the three divine names is discussed in one of the three principal proofs for the existence of God constructed by Descartes: *infinitum* names God in *Meditatio III; ens summe perfectum* names God in *Meditatio V; potentia* names God in *Responsiones I* and *IV,* by way of the proof by *causa sui.* The compatibility, or lack thereof, of the three divine names would thus be decided by reference to the compossibility, or lack thereof, of the three principal Cartesian proofs for the existence of God. The organization of the proofs would display the arrangement of the divine names that they put into operation and presuppose.[57] This procedure, that is, this internal examination, should also be followed up by an external examination. The divine names that Descartes privileged, like the corresponding proofs, have a history. By identifying their respective genealogies, be it only summarily, it would perhaps become possible to point out conceptual decisions that are more precise than their Cartesian consequences. In a word, the tensions between the divine names would appear all the more visible if they were seen diachronically, and no longer just synchronically. For each of the three divine names Descartes kept, we will therefore attempt to identify a historically probable and conceptually significant origin, so as to widen the debate about the Cartesian divine names to include the debate about the history of the divine names in general. Subject to this twofold condition, it will perhaps becomes possible to situate the Cartesian decisions about the essence of God

57. We thus again come across the difficulty at which the earlier analysis of *Sur la théologie blanche de Descartes* ended up, particularly §19, pp. 444*ff.,* and are obliged to oppose our position, at least methodologically, to F. Alquié: "The distinction of the different proofs employed by Descartes cannot be essential, and their nature will be better revealed to him who, on the contrary, will consider their unity" (*La découverte métaphysique de l'homme chez Descartes,* op. cit., p. 219).

within the ranks of the theological treatise on the divine names. That is
to say, it will become possible to really broach the most basic question—
does God, for and through Descartes, enter into metaphysics, and, if so,
with what names?

The first determination of the essence of God—which, for the sake
of convenience, we will designate [A]—apprehends him as infinite. In
formulations [1] and [2], the infinite governs substantiality, independence, immensity, and incomprehensibility. It also makes possible the so-
called proof by effects in *Meditatio III*. Can we pinpoint its historical
origin? Caterus' conviction was this: discussing the derived and pedagogical form of the proof by the idea of infinity, a proof that is set out as a
search for the productive cause of this idea in me, he concludes:

> Illa demum ipsa via est, quam et S. Thomas ingreditur, quam vocat viam
> *a causalitate causae efficientis,* eamque desumpsit ex Philosopho; nisi quod
> isti de causis idearum non sint solliciti. [This is exactly the same approach
> as that taken by St. Thomas: he called this "the way based on the causality
> of the efficient cause." He took the argument from Aristotle, though nei-
> ther he nor Aristotle was bothered about the causes of ideas.] [AT VII,
> 94, 15–18 = PW II, 68.]

No doubt one can make a favorable comparison between the proof by
effects, arriving at God as a *causa ultima* ". . . quae erit Deus [and this
will be God]" (50, 6 = 34), and the second of the five *viae* constructed
by St. Thomas: "It is necessary to admit a first efficient cause, to which
everyone gives the name God."[58] But the limits of this rapprochement
appear at once, and even Caterus himself sees them: causality is exerted
not over beings, according to an Aristotelian and trivial ἀνάγκη στῆναι,
but over the *idea* of the infinite, and this infinite is understood positively,
such that it never need come to a stop anywhere. This is why Descartes
declines, discreetly but firmly, the improperly attributed support of Thomistic authority: ". . . sed permittat, quaeso, de aliis me tacere, atque
eorum tantum, quae ipse scripsi, reddere rationem [However, I hope he
will allow me to avoid commenting on what others have said, and simply
give an account of what I have written myself]" (106, 11–13 = PW II,

---

58. *Summa Theologiae, Ia,* q. 2, a. 3, *resp.* [English trans., p. 13]: ". . . ergo est necesse
ponere aliquam causam efficientem primam, quam omnes Deum nominant." Caterus
makes such a comparison, noting all the while that ". . . isti [Thomas and Aristotle] de
causis idearum non sint solliciti [Neither he nor Aristotle was bothered about the causes
of ideas]" (AT VII, 94, 15–18 = PW II, 68). This comparison is supported by AT VII, 383,
15 = PW II, 263 and by F. Alquié in *Descartes. Œuvres philosophiques,* op. cit., vol. 2,
p. 254.

77). The reference to Saint Thomas, in fact inaccurate, also seems perfectly useless, since Descartes could have direct access to two denominations of God by the infinite: first Lessius, who, as we have seen, makes it the first of the divine names; then Suarez, who establishes that "... the first and most essential division of being is into finite and infinite,"[59] such that God's way of Being consists in the infinite itself. By this twofold intermediacy, Descartes can be seen to be affiliated with Duns Scotus, who—more clearly than anyone, if not perhaps before anyone—had thought God as infinite:

> The most perfect and at the same time the most simple concept possible for us is the concept of infinite being. For this is simpler than the concept of good being, true being or other similar concepts since infinite is not something like an attribute or an affection of being or of that to which it is predicated. Rather it signifies an intrinsic mode of that entity so that when I say "infinite being," I do not have a concept composed accidentally, as it were, of a subject and its affection, but a single concept of the subject with a certain degree of perfection, namely infinity.

In other words, "this most perfect concept which we have formed about God is the concept of infinite being; for it is the most simple, the most proper and the most perfect of the concepts we conceive of God." That is, it is the most simple because every other concept is extended to beings other than God (for instance the true, the good, etc.); it is the most proper because it is not counted among the other attributes of God, but on the contrary, overdetermines them: "Infinity is formally included in any [divine] attribute whatsoever as a certain degree of perfection"; finally, it is the most perfect "because it contains virtually all the other concepts which are spoken of God."[60] Like Descartes after him, Duns

59. Suarez, *Disputationes Metaphysicae, XXVIII,* prol.: "Diximus autem in superioribus, disp. 4, sect. 4, primam et maxime essentialem divisionem entis esse in finitum et infinitum secundum essentiam seu in ratione entis, quod solum est proprie et simpliciter infinitum" (op. cit., vol. 26, p. 1).

60. Duns Scotus, respectively *Ordinatio,* d. 3, p. 1, q. 1– 2, n. 58 [English trans., p. 30 (modified)]:

> ... conceptus perfectior simul et simplicior, nobis possibilis, est conceptus entis infiniti. Iste enim est simplicior quam conceptus entis boni, entis veri, vel aliorum similium, quia "infinitum" non est quasi attributum vel passio entis, sive ejus de quo dicitur, sed dicit modum intrinsecum illius entitatis, ita quod cum dico "infinitum ens" non habeo conceptum quasi per accidens, ex subjecto et passione, sed conceptum per se subjecti in certo gradu perfectionis, scilicet infinitatis.

Opera omnia, ed. C. Balič (Rome, 1950), vol. 3, p. 40; then *Lectura, I,* d. 3, p. 1, q. 1–2, nn. 50–52: "... ille conceptus perfectissimus quem nos concipimus de Deo, est conceptus entis

Scotus privileges the infinite as concept. From the perspective of conceiving him, thus of knowledge and its particular demands, God is said with the infinite—most simple, most proper, and most perfect to be known. With this presupposition, both Scotus and Descartes break with Saint Thomas, who, all the while acknowledging infinity in God, subordinates it to *esse,* to the detriment of the epistemological privilege of conceptualization: "Since therefore the divine being is not a being received in anything [other than itself], but He is His own subsisting being . . . , it is clear that God Himself is infinite and perfect."[61] Here the infinite is deduced from subsisting *esse,* and therefore remains an attribute that is secondary from the perspective of subsisting beingness. Thus Descartes adopts a second position from Duns Scotus (one from which the first point of agreement derives directly)—the concept's primacy over beingness. It is inasmuch as he is conceivable that God must first be spoken of as the infinite. In concluding "Deum autem ita judico esse actu infinitum [God, on the other hand, I take to be actually infinite]" (47, 19 = 32), Descartes is, as it were, citing Duns Scotus: ". . . ergo aliquod infinitum ens existit in actu [Therefore some infinite being actually exists]."[62] Of course, the infinite is understood not negatively, but positively. Besides the authority of Duns Scotus, Descartes could invoke that of Suarez: "Though the term *infinite* is negative, by this negation we are defin-

---

infiniti; est enim simplicior et magis proprius, et perfectior conceptus quem nos concipimus de Deo. . . . infinitum formaliter includitur in quolibet attributo tanquam gradus perfectionis cujuslibet. . . . Item, est perfectior conceptus quem de Deo concipimus, quia virtualiter continet alios conceptus dictos de Deo" (op. cit. [Rome, 1960], vol. 16, p. 244). See also *Quodlibet V,* n. 4, and *V,* n. 17: "Divinitas est formaliter infinita [Divinity is formally infinite]." On this point, in addition to the classic works of E. Gilson, one should consult P. Vignaux, "Etre et infini selon Duns Scot et Jean de Ripa," in *De doctrina Ioannis Scoti.* Acta congressus scotistici internationalis, Oxonii et Edimburghi, 11–17 Sept. celebrati (Rome, 1966), vol. 4, as well as "Infini, liberté et histoire du salut," in *Deus et homo ad mentem I. Duns Scoti.* Acta tertii congressus scotistici internationalis, Vindobonae, 28 Sept.–2 Oct. 1970 (Rome, 1972). Both these articles are reprinted in *De saint Anselm à Luther* (Paris, 1976), pp. 353*ff.* and 495*ff.* See also C. Berubé, "Pour une histoire des preuves de l'existence de Dieu chez Duns Scot," in *Deus et homo ad mentem I. Duns Scoti,* op. cit.

61. Saint Thomas, *Summa Theologiae, Ia.,* q. 7, a. 1, *resp.:* ". . . cum autem esse divinum non sit esse receptum in aliquo, sed ipse sit suum esse subsistens, ut supra ostensum est (q. 3, a. 4), manifestum est, quod ipse Deus sit infinitus et perfectus" [English trans., p. 31]. On this text and the opposition between Thomas and Scotus on matters concerning the infinite in God, see E. Gilson, *Jean Duns Scot. Introduction à ses positions fondamentales* (Paris, 1952), pp. 149–215 (particularly pp. 208– 10).

62. Duns Scotus, *Ordinatio I,* d. 2, p. 1, q. 1–2, n. 147 (op. cit., vol. 2, pp. 214*ff.* [English trans., p. 80]).

ing a certain supreme being or excellence."[63] Confronted with the same paradox, Descartes will say: ". . . priorem quodammodo in me esse perceptionem infiniti quam finiti [My perception of the infinite . . . is in some way prior to my perception of the finite]" (45, 28–29 = 31). This is to say that he will invert the verbal negation with a semantic affirmation: "Nec verum est intelligi infinitum per finis sive limitationis negationem, cum e contra omnis limitatio negationem infiniti contineat [It is false that the infinite is understood through the negation of a boundary or limit; on the contrary, all limitation implies a negation of the infinite]."[64] An objection of the Hegelian sort—the infinite, remaining without determination or delimitation, does not offer any actually thinkable rational content—would here ring false: the infinite is determined as first, most simple, most proper, most perfect, most intelligible, condition for the possibility of the finite, etc. With the choice of the infinite as first divine name, Descartes does not make a solitary departure into some uncharted territory, but is inscribed in an ongoing tradition that comes to him from Duns Scotus through Suarez in philosophy and Lessius in theology. The fact that he is not the first to so distinguish the infinite provides even more support for our claim that the infinite can count as the first of all the divine names. We have thus identified, in what is essential, the status and the origin of determination [A] of God as infinite. It remains for us to determine how the *via negativa,* from which [A] unquestionably arises, does not weaken its theoretical rigor. Or, in other words, how can a denomination obtained negatively (even if it claims to be semantically positive), a denomination that is the origin of a series of negations (independence, immensity, ineffability, etc.), perform the function of ". . . praecipuum argumentum ad probandum Dei existentiam [principal argument for proving the existence of God]" (AT VII, 14, 18–19 = PW II, 10), or of *praecipua ratio* (101, 17)? It, [A], does not hold this incomparable primacy on account of its anteriority in the *ordo rationum* (which depends on it), but on account of its intrinsic excellence. This excellence follows from its characteristic property: incomprehensibility. And we have seen that incomprehensibility results directly from the infinite: ". . . idea enim infiniti, ut sit vera, nullo modo debet comprehendi, quoniam ipsa incomprehensibilitas in ratione formali infiniti continetur [For

63. Suarez, *Disputationes Metaphysicae, XXVIII,* respectively s. 2, n. 12: "Nam licet vox *infinitum* negativa sit, per illam negationem nos circonscribimus summam quamdam entitatem seu excellentiam" (op. cit., vol. 26, p. 11).

64. *Responsiones V,* 365, 6–8 = PW II, 252. See *Responsiones I,* 113, 9–14 = PW II, 81.

the idea of the infinite, if it is to be regarded as a true idea, cannot be comprehended at all, since the impossibility of being comprehended is contained in the formal definition of the infinite]."[65] The incomprehensibility of the infinite is not the same as the impossibility of knowing it (*incognoscibilitas*); it designates precisely the particular mode of its knowability: the infinite is known without being comprehended—that is to say, without admitting a construction according to the rules and the parameters of the method as a measurable and ordered object, one made evident and available to the mind. Without resuming here a line of inquiry that we have taken up elsewhere,[66] we will recall a weighty argument: definition [A], thus the proof by the infinite, comes up in a passage between the end of *Meditatio I* and the ultimate conclusion of *Meditatio III* (52, 6–9); it thus shows up when the evidence of objects of the method is suspended and disqualified. If God must be known nevertheless, he has to be known in another mode besides that of the evidence of objects of the method. Whence a knowledge of God that, by virtue of hyperbolic doubt, also hyperbolically passes beyond the evidence (now out of play) of the material simple natures, which is to say, beyond the evidence of, among other things, the mathematical truths. But, it will be asked, what do we really know of the infinite if it is interchangeable with the incomprehensible? What reality will its idea have if we absolutely cannot apprehend it as an object? The answer to this question had already been formulated by Descartes in 1630: ". . . The greatness of God, on the other hand, is something which we cannot comprehend even though we know it. But the very fact that we judge it incomprehensible makes us esteem it the more greatly . . . his power is incomprehensible."[67]

---

65. *Responsiones V,* 368, 2–4 = PW II, 253 [modified]. Without here reviving the debate about "the ontological, and not purely representational, character" of the idea of infinity (F. Alquié, *La découverte métaphysique de l'homme chez Descartes,* p. 219) or, on the contrary, "its representative character" (M. Gueroult, *Descartes selon l'ordre des raisons,* vol. 1, pp. 161*ff.*), two points will simply be noted: *(a)* Non-comprehension does not mean non-knowledge, but a knowledge that does not construct its object according to the parameters of the *Mathesis Universalis.* Thus God can and must be known as infinite without the clarity of a methodic object and, at the same time, with an evidence greater than it. *(b)* This deduction of incomprehensibility from the infinite does not prevent Descartes from speaking—on the very same page—of a representation of the infinite: ". . . repraesentare . . . totum infinitum, eo modo quo debet repraesentari per humanam ideam [represent the infinite in its entirety in a manner which is appropriate to a human idea]" (368, 6–8 = 253 [modified]). See *Sur la théologie blanche de Descartes,* pp. 404–6.

66. References in *Sur la théologie blanche de Descartes,* p. 399, n. 6.

67. *To Mersenne,* 15 April 1630 (AT I, 145, 21–24 and 146, 4–5 = PW III, 23 and 23 [modified]). See: "But they should rather take the opposite view, that since God is a cause

With its incomprehensibility, the infinite transgresses the truths commensurate with our mind by assuming the figure of a power that is itself incomprehensible. Descartes' position in 1641, in formulae [1] and [2] of *Meditatio III,* thus remains in line with the creation of the eternal truths first promulgated in 1630. From this, one must draw a decisive consequence concerning the first determination of God [A]: it is incompatible with any determination of God that would maintain that his essence is accessible to the same evidence as the mathematical truths and the essences of finite objects. If such a determination comes to light in Descartes' texts, it will be inconsistent with [A]. There is yet another consequence: [A] applies to God the determination 'cause' in 1641 (*causa ultima,* AT VII, 50, 6), and also already in 1630 ("... a cause whose power surpasses the bounds of human understanding...," *efficiens et totalis causa*).[68] However, this causality is here limited to defining the action of God exterior to himself, with regard to creatures and to them alone. Now, ever since the *Regulae,* cause has belonged to the simple natures. Therefore, it presents an evidence that is perfectly comprehensible, and exemplarily so; better, it produces methodic evidence, in excess of and well before any other simple nature. Therefore it renders intelligible, among other things, God's relation to the world. But precisely because it arises from comprehensible evidence and always produces it, cause cannot be applied intrinsically to God. In short, comprehensible causality is an extrinsic determination of the infinite and incomprehensible (*ad extra*) God. From this, we must conclude by observing a second incompatibility: determination [A] of God as incomprehensible infinite will be inconsistent with any determination of God's essence in terms of intrinsic causality. This double incompatibility of [A], first with the methodic objectivity and evidence of the created truths, then with causality as one of the simple natures, thus characterizes God inasmuch as he is infinite; but more important, it decides, in advance, his relations with two other essential determinations of God.

---

whose power surpasses the bounds of human understanding, and since the necessity of these truths does not exceed our knowledge, these truths are therefore something less than, and subject to, the incomprehensible power of God" (*To Mersenne,* 6 May 1630 [AT I, 150, 17–22 = PW III, 25]). It should also be noted that the *res cogitans,* which bears in it the likeness of the divine infinite (51, 15–29 = 35), will in the end be described more specifically as a will, and thus that it also experiences the infinite within the perspective of power (57, 11–21 = 40).

68. Respectively AT I, 150, 18–19 and 152, 2 = PW III, 25 and 25. In short, *cause,* in 1630 as much as in formula [1], has no further meaning in God than *creator.*

Determination [B] is announced in *Meditatio III* by formula [3]—
"... una est ex praecipius perfectionibus quas in eo [Deo] esse intelligo
[one of the most important of the perfections which I understand him to
have]" (50, 18–19 = 34)—but also in formulae [1] and [2], when they
mobilize the superlative (*summe potens, summe intelligens, omnisciens,
omnipotens*). However, it is fully developed only in *Meditatio V,* where
it allows first for defining the essence of God and then for proving his
existence, which was understood previously as one of the perfections.
From this, there follows the complete determination of God as *ens
summe perfectum* (54, 13–14; 66, 12–13; 67, 9–10; etc. = 38; 46; 46; etc.).
Subject to certain conditions, it seems possible to refer this determination to the fourth of Saint Thomas's *viae,* which also claims to reach
God by means of the superlative: "There is something which is truest,
something best, something noblest, and, consequently, something which
is uttermost being, *maxime ens.*"[69] To stick more precisely to perfection,
it will be observed that, if Saint Thomas posits in principle that "... everything that is perfect must be attributed to God," he does not however
think perfection on its own terms. Just as previously he had deduced the
divine infinite from *esse subsistens,* far from illuminating the former by
means of the latter as Descartes does, here too he derives divine perfection from the *esse* of God. Several texts indicate this reduction: "God is
pure act, simply and in all ways perfect." Even better: "The first being
which is God must needs be most perfect and consequently supremely
good." Or: "The first being must therefore be most perfect. But we have
shown that God is the first being. He is therefore the most perfect."[70]
Here, perfection results— immediately to be sure, but all the more as a
consequence—from the more fundamental determination of God as the
ens whose essence consists in *esse* itself. Saint Thomas thinks divine perfection on the basis of the *esse* of the divine being, while Descartes first
thinks the divine perfection in order to then, eventually, qualify God
with the name *ens.* Saint Thomas never stopped until he had led perfec-

69. Saint Thomas, *Summa Theologiae, Ia,* q. 2, a. 3, *resp.* [English trans., p. 14]: "Est
igitur aliquid quod est verissimum, et optimum, et nobilissimum, et per consequens maxime ens."

70. Saint Thomas, respectively *Summa Theologiae, Ia,* q. 29, a. 3, *resp.* [English trans.,
p. 158]: "... omne illud, quod est perfectionis, Deo sit attribuendum ... ," q. 25, a. 1, *resp.*
[English trans., p. 136]: "... Deus est purus actus, et simpliciter et universaliter perfectus,
neque in eo aliqua imperfectio locum habet"; *De potentia,* q. 7, a. 1, *resp.* [English trans.,
vol. 3, p. 4]: "... portet primum ens, quod Deus est, esse perfectissimum, et per consequens
optimum"; and finally, *Contra Gentes,* I, 28 [English trans., p. 136]: "... primum ens debet
esse perfectissimum. Ostensum est autem Deum esse primum ens; est ergo perfectissimus."

tion (as well as all the other attributes) back to the more fundamental determination of the *actus purus essendi,* while Descartes, who in no way privileged the divine *esse,* reaches God directly through the thought of supreme perfection. From here on out, when it is a question of historically situating Cartesian denomination [B], it is clear that Saint Thomas does not provide the best point of reference. Another reference immediately presents itself in support of Descartes' choice, Suarez: ". . . God is the first being . . . ; therefore he is also essentially the greatest and the most perfect; therefore it is the case that his essence in some way includes all possible perfection in the total range of beings."[71] Through Suarez, there is no doubt but that Descartes rejoins a prior tradition. Just which one is the question that must be addressed more precisely. At first glance, it seems evident—even to the most educated critics—that one must turn to Saint Anselm, as much because of his presumed and real "Augustinianism" as because of his renowned argument for proving the existence of God, an argument revived precisely in *Meditatio V.* And yet, if the continuity between Descartes and Anselm cannot be contested on this point, it seems that one should be cautious in admitting the hypothesis of Descartes' debt to Saint Anselm for determination [B]. For in fact, the texts of the *Monologion*—remote and presumed source of *Meditatio V*—mention perfection only rarely, and when they do, they always subordinate it to beingness. For example: "He alone [God] will be seen to exist in an unqualified sense and perfectly and absolutely, whereas all other things nearly do not exist at all"; or: "each of them [the persons of the trinity] is perfectly the supreme essence."[72] That is, the force of the *Monologion* bears on more than perfection in particular; it is directed toward making every property pass into the superlative, with the intention of thereby making it attributable to God. In short, it is less an issue of perfection, even supreme, than of each quality passing to the limit, heading toward a common superlative that juxtaposes them all in God. Hence, one finds enumerations of qualities that enact the

71. Suarez, *Disputationes Metaphysicae, XXX,* s. 1, n. 5: "Deus est primum ens, ut ostensum est; ergo est etiam summum et perfectissimum essentialiter; ergo de essentia ejus est, ut includat aliquo modo omnem perfectionem possibilem in tota latitudine entis" (op. cit., vol. 26, p. 61). In s. 2, n. 21 (ibid., p. 71), among other texts, perfection is directly deduced from the superlative (*summum*).

72. Saint Anselm, *Monologion,* respectively *XXVIII* [English trans., p. 47]: ". . . ille solus videbitur simpliciter et perfecte et absolute esse, alia vero omnia fere non esse et vix esse," then *LIX* [English trans., p. 72]: ". . . uniusquisque illorum sic est perfecte summa essentia . . ." (S. Anselmi, *Opera Omnia,* ed. F. S. Schmidt [Edinburgh, 1946], vol. 1, respectively, p. 46 and p. 70).

affirmative way: "And so he is the supreme essence, supreme life, supreme reason, supreme salvation, supreme justice, supreme truth, supreme immortality, supreme incorruptibility, supreme immutability, supreme beatitude, supreme eternity, supreme power, supreme unity, which is none other than supremely being (*summe ens*) supremely living and other similar things."[73] No doubt we can here recognize certain Cartesian determinations cited in [1] and [2]: *summa potestas* is equivalent to *summe potens*, *summa veritas* announces *summe intelligens*, *summa aeternitas* is found again in *aeternum*, *summa essentia* and *summe ens* correspond in advance with *substantia*. The case is similar, with certain qualifications, in [3]: *unitas* corresponds to the Cartesian *unitas*, *summa incorruptibilitas* is related to *inseparabilitas*, etc. Nonetheless, in the *Monologion*, these qualities, even when carried to their maximum intensity, remain merely juxtaposed; they lack a deduction or an organization that would consolidate them in a final, unique, and infinite perfection. There where Descartes puts forth an essential determination—[B], God as the most perfect being—Saint Anselm employs the superlative (and not perfection as such) only so that each quality might be borne to its maximum, but in its own genus only. For him, perfection does not put forth a name of God so much as for each quality, it effects the passage to the limit. In this precise sense, Descartes could not have found any anteced-

---

73. Saint Anselm, *Monologion XVI* [English trans., p. 31]: "Illa igitur est summa essentia, summa vita, summa ratio, summa salus, summa justitia, summa sapientia, summa veritas, summa bonitas, summa magnitudo, summa pulchritudo, summa immortalitas, summa incorruptibilitas, summa immutabilitas, summa beatitudo, summa aeternitas, summa potestas, summa unitas, quod non est aliud quam summe ens, summe vivens, et alia similiter" (op. cit., p. 31). In the same vein, see *IV* and *VI*. A more coherent and radical formulation is approached in *III*: ". . . aliquid quod, sive essentia, sive substantia, sive natura dicetur, optimum et maxime est et summum omnium quae sunt [There is something (whether he is called essence or a substance or a nature) that is best and greatest and supreme among all existing things]" (op. cit., p. 16 [English trans., p. 13]). But in this case too, it is only a matter of a maximum, thus more of quantification than of perfection. On this tendency in Anselm, see C. Viola, "La dialectique de la grandeur. Une interprétation du *Proslogion*," in *Recherches de théologie ancienne et médiévale*, 37, 1970, pp. 23– 55. Significant in this regard is the gap between the formula *ens perfectissimum*, constantly used by A. Koyré, and the absence of any text from Anselm that would confirm its legitimacy (*L'idée de Dieu dans la philosophie de saint Anselme*, pp. 41, 43, 44, 47, etc.). The same strangeness appears in D. Heinrich, *Der ontologische Gottesbeweis* (Tübingen, 1960), pp. 3, 11, 19, and E. Jüngel, *Gott als Geheimnis der Welt* (Tübingen, 1977), p. 147 (who, by the way, depend quite closely on Koyré, like the student of D. Heinrich, X. Tilliette, "L'argument ontologique et l'histoire de l'ontothéologie," *Archives de Philosophie* 25/1 [1962]). A good collection of texts can be found in R. Payot, "L'argument ontologique et le fondement de la métaphysique," *Archives de Philosophie* 39/2, 39/3, 39/4 (1975).

ent nor any assistance for his own denomination of God as *ens summe perfectum* in the Anselmian conceptualization. Moreover, he always rejected the rapprochement that his correspondents suggested to him: "I shall look at St. Anselm at the first opportunity," he declares in December 1640, without ever giving, afterward, the least indication of having done so.[74] Now, which author could have preceded Descartes and was likely to have influenced him? Without making a decisive argument, but taking account of other probable rapprochements (such as AT VII, 21, 1–2 and 36, 8–9 = PW II, 14 and 25), we risk making the hypothesis of Descartes' affinity with William of Ockham. The latter explicitly defines God by perfection taken to the superlative and considered as unique: "... God is the most perfect being. This is why, since he is in a certain way knowable to us ... , he will be the most perfectly intelligible." Here particular perfections do not precede perfection understood as such, but rather are deduced from it as from *illa perfectio simpliciter quae est Deus* [that perfection which quite simply is God].[75] This perfection taken simply as such can be understood in two quite distinct, though convergent, senses: in its proper sense, perfection befits only God; in its wider and thus improper sense, the attributed perfections are said first with respect to creatures so that then, by passing to the limit, they might be applied to God; in this case, these common concepts remain purely nominal and do not attain the divine essence as such.[76] The identification of this nominalist antecedent to Cartesian definition [B] of God at once gives rise to a difficulty. Specifically, when Ockham privileges the *ens perfectissimum* as the first divine name, he clearly knows that he is opposed—on this point as on so many others—to Duns Scotus. There where Scotus concludes that "... the most perfect concept that we can conceive of God is the concept infinity," thus reducing perfection to infinity, Ockham says in opposition that "... the concept of infinite being is not formally in and of itself a concept that is more perfect than any possible concept concerning God because any negative concept is formally less perfect than a positive concept; but the concept of infinite being includes, be-

74. *To Mersenne,* December 1640 (AT III, 261, 9 = PW III, 161).

75. William of Ockham, *In Sententiarum, I,* d. 3, respectively q. 1: "Tertium patet, quia Deus est ens perfectissimum; igitur cum sit aliquo modo cognoscibilis a nobis, sicut in sequenti quaestione patebit, erit intelligibile perfectissimum"; and q. 2, *In Opera philosophica et theologica,* ed. S. Brown (New York, 1970), vol. 2, pp. 390 and 413. On the possibility of an indirect line of descent, see G. Rodis-Lewis, "Descartes aurait-il eu un professeur nominaliste?" *Archives de Philosophie* 34/1 (1971): 37–46.

76. See William of Ockham, *In Sententiarum, I,* d. 2, q. 2 and q. 3, op. cit., pp. 62 and 98.

yond the concept of being, something negative."[77] This clear-cut opposition indirectly confirms that Cartesian determination [A] of God by the infinite arises at once from Duns Scotus and the *via negativa,* while Cartesian determination [B] of God by perfection belongs—according to its champion, Ockham—to the *via affirmativa.* This fully justifies our initial effort to situate Descartes' proofs within the ranks of a problematic of divine names. But it gives rise to an unavoidable difficulty: Descartes at once and successively holds two determinations of God, [A] and [B], which, historically, were posited as adversaries, and irreconcilable ones at that. Can the antagonism between Duns Scotus and Ockham disappear simply because the same author claims in the same text to use both their theses? Mustn't we rather admit that in all likelihood, the antagonism between Duns Scotus, championing the primacy of the infinite, and Ockham, championing the priority of perfection, is to be rediscovered, just barely veiled, within *Meditationes III* and *V?* This hypothesis seems even more difficult to avoid in that the majority of critics have noted, as an "unexpected occurrence" (Hamelin), that on the threshold of *Meditatio V,* indeed at the end of *Meditatio III,* ". . . *perfect* replaces *infinite*" (Beyssade).[78] For that matter, it suffices to recall the famous polemic that this difficulty provoked: either the proof stemming from [B] depends on the *idea infiniti* guaranteed by [A] in *Meditatio III* (Alquié, Gouhier, Kenny), or the proof stemming from [B] remains perfectly independent (Gueroult, Beck, etc.). In one case, subordination implies (without explaining why) that a first divine name, *ens summe perfectum,* become a simple derived name. In the other, it suggests a rupture in the *ordo rationum,* thus the irreducibility of [A] and [B]—which could be deepened into an antagonism and contradiction. In both cases, the question arises, one that we will have to take up again (§20): is not the divine name *infinity* incompatible with the divine name *perfection* for reasons that are not only historical, but also intrinsically and conceptually Cartesian?

There remains a third and final fundamental determination of the es-

---

77. William of Ockham, *In Sententiarum, I,* d. 3, q. 3: ". . . quod conceptus entis infiniti non sit formaliter in se perfectior conceptus omni conceptu possibili haberi de Deo, quia nullus conceptus negativus est formaliter perfectior conceptu positivo; sed conceptus infiniti est includens ultra conceptum entis aliquid negativum" (op. cit., p. 422), against Duns Scotus, *Lectura I,* d. 3, p. 1, q. 1–2, n. 50: ". . . ille conceptus perfectissimus quem nos concipimus de Deo est conceptus entis infiniti" (op. cit., vol. 16, p. 224).

78. O. Hamelin, *Le Système de Descartes* (Paris, 1911), p. 202, n. 1, and J.-M. Beyssade, *La philosophie première de Descartes,* p. 311.

sence (therefore of the existence) of God—we will designate it [C]. It appears, almost in the same terms, in *Responsiones I* and *IV*. During his discussion with Caterus, Descartes defines God as existing through himself, *a se*, positively—that is to say as exercising a cause over himself—and no longer negatively, as subtracted from the sway of causality. In short, God ". . . quodammodo idem . . . respectu suî ipsius quod causa efficiens respectu sui [stands in the same relation to himself as an efficient cause does to itself]" (AT VII, 111, 5–7 = PW II, 80). What holds the place of a cause internal to God is nothing less than the very essence of God interpreted as an *immensa et incomprehensibilis potentia* such that it might be "causa, cur île [Deus] esse perseveret [the cause of (God's) continuing existence]" (110, 28–29 = 79). This interpretation of the divine essence as power therefore defines it as "ens summe potens [a supremely powerful being]" (119, 22 = 85) and recovers the very terms of [1] and [2]: *omnipotens, summe potens* (40, 17 and 45, 12–13 = 28 and 31). But this interpretation [C] would be neither useful nor necessary if God himself did not have to satisfy a principle that is stated as a *dictat* of reason:

> Dictat autem profecto lumen naturae nullam rem existere, de qua non liceat petere cur existat, sive in ejus causam efficientem inquirere, aut si non habet, cur illa non indigeat, postulare. [However, the light of nature does establish (Dictat autem profecto lumen naturae) that if anything exists we may always ask why it exists; that is, we may inquire into its efficient cause, or, if it does not have one, we may demand why it does not need one.] [108, 18–22 = 78.]

The discussion with Arnauld then posits that the divine essence exerts a formal causality, which ". . . magnam habet analogiam cum [causa] efficiente, ideoque quasi causa efficiens vocari potest [will be strongly analogous to an efficient cause, and hence can be called something close to an efficient cause]" (243, 25–26 = 170). Here again the *immensitas potentiae sive essentiae* (237, 1 = 165) assimilates the divine essence to a power, which then holds the place of a positive cause: ". . . inexhausta Dei potentia sit causa sive ratio propter quam causa non indiget [The inexhaustible power of God is the cause or reason for his not needing a cause]" (236, 9–10 = 165). If God becomes something like the efficient cause of himself, by letting his essence be interpreted as power, this is because he must do so; and he must do so, in the eyes of Descartes, because ". . . considerationem causae efficientis esse primum et praecipuum medium, ne dicam unicum, quod habeamus ad existentiam Dei probandam [A consideration of efficient causes is the primary and principal way, if not the only way, that we have of proving the existence of God]" (238, 11–13 = 166). The two expositions are thus organized into two parallel sequences: the absolute principle of causality (and, already, of reason) compels one to seek a cause even in God—"de ipso Deo [even concerning God himself]" (164, 29 = 116 [modified]). This cause will be his own essence, which can play the role, since it admits of being interpreted as inexhaustible, immense, and incomprehensible power. Therefore God will be spoken *a se* positively—that is to say, *causa sui.*[79] Before taking a look at the relation of [C], just now defined quickly, with [A] and [B], one must also briefly determine its historical position. It is precisely because Etienne Gilson was right when he declared Descartes to be "without any known predecessor"[80] that we have to seek out historically the reason for this (almost) total absence of genealogy. If we again consider the five Thomistic *viae,* we observe almost immediately in the course of the *secunda via* the explicit refusal of the hypothesis, which is nonetheless clearly seen, of a *causa efficiens sui:* ". . . There is no case known (neither is it indeed possible) in which a thing is found to be the efficient cause of itself; for so it would be prior to itself, which is impossible." Such a rebuke presupposes, it is true, that the efficient cause be exclusively transitive (and not immanent), so that either a being can exert it only over a being other than itself, or else by exerting it over itself, it has to become other than itself. Two of the other *viae* that could potentially have ended up at *causa sui* corroborate this condemnation: the first *via* in effect leads to ". . . a first mover, put in motion by no other"; the third to ". . . some being having of itself its own necessity, and not receiving it from another, but rather causing in others their necessity."[81] In contrast to things in motion, God is determined as the first mover, therefore as himself not in motion. In contrast with contingent things, he is determined as the cause of their necessity, therefore as himself free from external necessity. Thus, in contrast with what needs a cause in order to be, God is defined as the cause of beings, a cause that

79. On this collection of texts, see *supra,* chap. II, §9, and *Sur la théologie blanche de Descartes,* §18.

80. E. Gilson, *Etudes sur le rôle de la pensée médiévale dans la formation du système cartésien,* p. 226.

81. Saint Thomas, *Summa Theologiae, Ia,* q. 2, a. 3, *resp.,* respectively ". . . nec tamen invenitur, nec est possibile, quod aliquis sit causa efficiens sui ipsius, quia sic esset prius seipso, quod est impossibile"; then ". . . ergo necesse est devenire ad aliquod primum movens, quod a nullo moveatur" and ". . . ergo necesse est ponere aliquid, quod sit per se necessarium, non habens causam necessitatis aliunde, sed quod est causa necessitatis aliis" [English trans., p. 13].

is itself free of all cause. Absolute, God appears free of the motion, the necessity, and the efficiency that nonetheless—better: for that very reason—he provokes and guarantees. If God exerts efficiency and is manifest by it, he therefore does not depend on it. Causality touches on God because it comes from him, not because it would include him; it remains contiguous with him, but neither co-extensive nor connected. When Saint Thomas admits an acceptation of *causa sui*—"the free is that which is its own cause (*causa sui*)"—it is in no way a matter of causality (cause/effect), still less of efficient causality (transitive), but solely of a translation of the classic Aristotelian formula: ἐλεύθερος ὁ αὑτοῦ ἕνεκα καὶ μὴ ἄλλου [The man is free, we say, who exists for himself and not for another].[82] Saint Thomas does not stand alone on this point, either, given that even his adversaries reason as he does. For example, Saint Anselm: "The supreme nature could not come about either by his own agency or by that of some other thing." Also, Duns Scotus: "The totality of essentially ordered effects is caused consequently by some cause which is nothing of that totality; for then it would be *causa sui*."[83] Suarez alone hints at some ambiguity. No doubt he maintains that "God . . . is without principle or cause," and that *a se*, ". . . though appearing to be positive, adds only a single negation to being itself, for being cannot be *a se* by a positive origin and an emanation. . . . And it is in this sense that it is fit to explain what certain saints mean when they say that God is by himself cause of his Being, his substance, or his wisdom."[84] Nevertheless, Suarez

82. When reading the formula "Liberum quod sui causa est" (*Contra Gentes, II,* 48 [English trans., vol. 2, p. 144]), one has to think of *Metaphysics A,* 2, 982 *b,* 25–26 [English trans., p. 1555]. The same prudence is forced upon us when confronted with its uses by Plotinus (*Enneads, VI,* 8, 14 or 20) and Proclus (*Elements,* §46). The question does not reside so much in the formula *causa sui* as in its Cartesian interpretation in terms of efficiency, if not entirely as efficient (which relativizes the pertinence of the Spinozist revival of this term). On the opposition between the Thomist and Cartesian theses, see the recent clarification by J. de Finance, "La formule 'Deus causa sui' et l'oubli de l'être," in *Pela Filosofia.* Homenagem a Tarcisio Meireles Padilha (Rio de Janeiro, 1984). And, within a broader frame, S. Breton, "Origine et principe de raison," *Revue des Sciences philosophiques et théologiques* 58/1 (1974).

83. Duns Scotus, *De Primo Principio, III,* 2: "Universalitas causatorum essentialiter ordinatorum est causata; igitur ab aliqua causa quae nihil est universitatis; tunc enim esset causa sui" (*Ioanni Duns Scoti Tractatus de Primo Principio,* ed. M. Müller [Freiburg im Breisgau, 1941], pp. 41–42 [English trans., p. 45]). See also *Ordinatio, I,* d. 2, p. 1, q. 1–2, nn. 57 and 59, op. cit., vol. 2, pp. 162–63 and 165. Likewise, Saint Anselm, *Monologion, VI,* op. cit., pp. 18–20 [English trans., p. 16].

84. Suarez, *Disputationes Metaphysicae,* respectively *I,* s. 1, n. 27: ". . . Deum qui est sine principio et sine causa . . ." (op. cit., vol. 25, p. 11), *XXVIII,* s. 1, n. 7: "Nam quod dicitur ex se vel a se esse, licet positivum hoc esse videatur, tamen solam negationem addit ipsi enti, nam ens non potest esse a se per positivam originem et emanationem; . . . et hunc

also envisages the possibility of a *causa sui* when he invokes it only to at once restrict its scope: ". . . and God does not have a *causa sui*, through which it would be *a priori* demonstrated that he is. And, if he had one, God is not known exactly or perfectly enough that we could reach him on the basis of his own principles."[85] Does God have a *causa sui* or does he not? Why does Suarez put forth both positions? How is this ambivalence to be explained? It seems to us that its origin should be located in the interpretation—which Descartes will push to its conclusion—of the divine essence as holding the place of a cause, and thus before offering reasons for his necessary existence: "Though we suppose that being as being does not have causes properly speaking nor in the most rigorous sense . . . , there is however a certain reason for its properties, and reasons of this sort or of this type can be found even in God (*etiam in Deo*), for starting from the infinite perfection of God, we can give a cause stating why he is one only, and thus for the rest."[86] Suarez anticipates Descartes' daring formula, *de ipso Deo* (AT VII, 164, 29 = PW II, 116), because, like him, he begins by submitting God to what will become the principle of reason, and, in order to succeed in this, to an interpretation of the divine essence as a *ratio*: "Hoc enim de ipso Deo quaeri potest, non quod indigeat ulla causa ut existat, sed quia ipsa ejus naturae immensitas sit causa sive ratio, propter quam nulla causa indiget ad existendum [This question may even be asked concerning God, not because he needs any cause in order to exist, but because the immensity of his nature is the cause or reason why he needs no cause in order to exist]" (164, 29–165, 3 = 116). Suarez already assimilates, tangentially, the divine essence to a *ratio* for its infinity, indeed to a cause. It will fall to Descartes to take the decisive step: directly interpreting the divine essence as power, so that it can then be built into an efficient cause of itself. Despite this considerable gap, it is therefore necessary to modify Gilson's opinion, which was cited previously: Descartes no doubt finds a

---

modum exponendi sunt aliquid Sancti, cum dicunt Deum esse sibi causam sui esse, vel substantiae suae aut sapientiae" (op. cit., vol. 26, p. 3).

85. Suarez, *Disputationes Metaphysicae, XXIX,* s. 3, n. 1: ". . . supponendum est simpliciter loquendo, non posse demonstrari a priori Deum esse, quia neque Deus habet causam sui esse, per quam a priori demonstretur, neque si haberet, ita exacte et perfecte nobis cognoscitur Deus, ut ex propriis principiis (ut sic dicam) illum assequamur" (op. cit., vol. 26, p. 47). See the similar ambiguity in *XXIX,* s. 1, n. 20, op. cit., vol. 26, p. 27.

86. Suarez, *Disputationes Metaphysicae, I,* s. 1, n. 29: "Quamvis ergo demus ens, in quantum ens, non habere causas proprie et in rigore sumptas priori modo, habet tamen rationem aliquam suarum proprietatum; et hoc modo etiam in Deo possunt hujusmodi rationes reperiri, nam ex Dei perfectione infinita reddimus causam, cur unus tantum sit, et sic de aliis" (op. cit., vol. 25, p. 12).

partial predecessor in Suarez. But the question takes a new turn: if even Suarez is hesitant to think God as *causa sui,* because he is hesitant to submit his essence to the *causa sive ratio,* and thus to return, for his fundamental position, to the traditional thesis, how can Descartes reconcile the categorical affirmation of the *causa sui* [C] with two other divine names [A] and [B], which are supposed to take up the traditional theses? Posed otherwise: Can Descartes at one and the same time submit God to the *causa sive ratio* by defining him as a *causa sui* that exercises the general requirement of a *causa* over itself, and also accord to him supreme, absolutely unconditional names such as infinite and *ens summe perfectum*? In short, doesn't the conditioned name *causa sui,* in which *potentia* [C] is accomplished, contradict *in fine* the first two names, infinity [A] and supreme perfection [B], without making any prior judgments as to the compatibility of these last two terms? On the contrary, shouldn't it be seen that once Descartes admits the difficulty raised by the *causa sui,* a difficulty that had caused even Suarez (a virtuoso in daring reconciliations) to reel, a new contradiction in the corpus of divine names arises and the incompatibility between [A] and [B] is doubled by another incompatibility, one between [A] and [B], on the one hand, and [C], on the other? About this latent conflict, the critics never fail to differ: while one side thinks that "here the real unity of the new theodicy is perceived" (H. Gouhier), another believes that Descartes "subordinates God himself to causality" (F. Alquié), and a third welcomes in Descartes, who ". . . reconciles by overcoming Saint Anselm and Duns Scotus," ". . . the reconciliation of God the efficient cause and God the archetype" (M. Gueroult).[87] Be it only for the sake of resolving—or at least not avoiding—a difficulty in the Cartesian corpus, we should ask about the compatibility, or lack thereof, of [C] with [A] as well as with [B].

Can the contradictions be reduced, or do they form a system? Availing ourselves of these elements, we must now attempt to bring them together in the unity of a system, for the sake of either reconciling them or opposing them.

§20. The Exceptional Name

Descartes thus uses successively, but in a single *ordo rationum,* three determinations of the essence of God, and these determinations hold the

---

87. Respectively, H. Gouhier, *La pensée métaphysique de Descartes,* p. 175; F. Alquié, note in *Descartes. Œuvres philosophiques,* vol. 2, p. 682; M. Gueroult, *Descartes selon l'ordre des raisons,* vol. 1, pp. 204 and 207—where, obviously, the mention of Saint Anselm is to be criticized.

place of three divine names. It is now time for us to assess their relation-ships with each other, that is, their compatabilities and their contradic-tions, two by two. Only then will it eventually become possible to attempt a hierarchization of the divine names such as Descartes elaborates them.

The first task focuses on the relations between determination [A] of God as infinite and his determination [B] as the most perfect being. The criterion that distinguishes them seems to be connected to the possibility, or lack thereof, of comprehending the idea of God exactly. We have established that the idea of infinity in 1641 is as incomprehensible as was the creator of the eternal truths in 1630. This incomprehensibility transposed the ontic transcendence at play between infinite being and finite being into an epistemological gap between the objects comprehen-sible to the human mind and the divine non-object, incomprehensible though known all the more certainly. And yet in *Meditatio V* it seems that this gap vanishes, so that the idea of a supremely perfect God can, in the end, be reduced to the level of the ideas of finite objects. Three arguments can establish this. *(a)* It will be observed, first of all, that just as all the innate ideas are drawn from thought (". . . alicujus rei ideam possim ex cogitatione mea depromere [I can produce from my thought the idea of something] . . . ," 65, 16–17 = 45), so too is the idea of God drawn from the warehouse in which it was stored among other ideas, as it were: ". . . quoties de ente primo et summo libet cogitare, atque ejus ideam tanquam ex mentis meae thesauro depromere [whenever I do choose to think of the first and supreme being, and bring forth the idea of God from the treasure house of mind] . . ." (67, 21–23 = 46). No doubt, in [1], the idea of infinity is given before all experience; neverthe-less, arising with the act of the *cogito* (51, 21–23 = 35), and by opening the horizon of possibility, it did not remain, permanently and subsist-ently, "in" thought as in a receptacle for extension. Here, on the contrary, the idea of a supreme being is not actually enacted—it remains stored in the treasure house (*thesaurus mentis meae*) of ideas that the *cogito* keeps available to itself. The idea of God, innate to be sure, is only one innate idea among others, though the first. The difference is found not between it and the innate ideas, but between the innate ideas—thus that of God—and the forged ideas: ". . . magna differentia est inter ejusmodi falsas positiones et ideas veras mihi innatas, quarum prima et praecipua est idea Dei [There is a great difference between this kind of false suppo-sition and the true ideas which are innate in me, of which the first and most important is the idea of God]" (68, 7–10). *(b)* A second contradiction with incomprehensibility will then be observed: the idea of God, as an innate idea, is inevitably compared to other innate ideas. Which ones? All those that offer ". . . suas . . . veras et immutabiles naturas [their own true and immutable natures]" (64, 11 = 44), and thus attest to ". . . determinata quaedam ejus natura, sive essentia, sive forma, immutabilis et aeterna [a determinate nature, or essence, or form . . . which is immutable and eternal]" (64, 14–16 = 45). This refers, obviously if not explicitly, to two previous themes. At the outset, let us consider only the first: that of the simple natures. The innate ideas of *Meditatio V* define as true natures and forms the following: quantity, extension, shape, sizes, position in space, motion, and duration (63, 16–21 = 44). That is to say, they define something like the mathematical truths enumerated by *Meditatio I* before they are cast into doubt (20, 15–19 = 14). As we have tried to show elsewhere, both cases are concerned with the *naturae simplicissimae,* whose theory is worked out definitively in 1628 by the *Regulae.*[88] And in fact here it is a matter of the pure and abstract *Mathesis* (65, 13–14 = 45), echoing the *Mathesis Universalis* of 1628. From this, it follows that the idea of God and the idea of a simple mathematical nature will be put on an equal footing: "Certe ejus ideam, nempe entis summe perfecti, non minus apud me invenio, quam ideam cujusvis figurae aut numeri [Certainly, the idea of God, or a supremely perfect being, is one which I find within me just as surely as the idea of any shape or number]" (65, 21–23 = 45). This pronouncement is as clear as it is stupefying: the idea of God is not found in me any less than—that is to say, it is found in me at least as much as—the idea of a triangle and thus the simple natures extension, shape, number, etc. God thus comes to his idea in the same way as the simple natures do. When related to the *ordo rationum* of the *Meditationes,* this takes on a very clear meaning: the simple natures can intervene validly only before or after hyperbolic doubt, not during it (and in fact only the beginnings of *Meditatio I* and *Meditatio V* invoke them). The idea of God constructed in [B] therefore could be homogeneous with the simple natures only if it belongs to the domain that is not, or is not any longer, affected by hyperbolic doubt: namely, the science of corporeal things, of simple material natures, and thus of the method. One must not shrink back before this consequence: the fundamental determination of the essence of God in [B] is still grasped [*comprise*]—and therefore is still comprehensible [*compréhensible*]—

---

88. In particular, *Regula XII* (AT X, 419, 18–20 = PW I, 44–45). See *Sur la théologie blanche de Descartes,* pp. 351–56.

within the field and in the mode of the method. Consequently, it cannot, by definition, coincide with the fundamental definition of God's essence given in [A], seeing as this latter definition, belonging like all of *Meditatio III* to the moment of hyperbolic doubt, transgresses the domain of the method. Determinations [A] and [B] do not differ merely in the sense in which the idea of the infinite differs from the idea of a supremely perfect being; they contradict each other, as a thought within hyperbolic doubt contradicts a thought outside this same hyperbolic doubt. What is more, inasmuch as determination [B] shares precisely, neither more nor less, the status of the simple natures revoked by hyperbolic doubt, it must be said that it too would be revoked by the determination of God as the infinite [A] if by chance [B] had been mentioned *before* hyperbolic doubt (as would have been possible, from a strictly theoretical point of view). And besides, hadn't it been revoked, *de facto,* by hyperbolic doubt as early as *Meditatio I*? This doubt mobilizes an all-powerful God, who renders caducous the perfection goodness (*summe bonus,* 21, 12) and who remains indifferent to the thinkable degrees of perfection, to the point that it can be named chance, destiny, or the necessity of things—indeed, this God can even be replaced by the fiction of the evil genius. In any case, the God who disqualifies evidence anticipates determination [A], as was seen above. As for the equivalent names, they are situated within the horizon of perfection; they thus anticipate determination [B] (*imperfectio,* 21, 23 = 14; *imperfectum,* 21, 25 = 14).

(c) We can now broach the final argument, the one that appears first, since simple nature is also defined as *vera, immutabilis et aeterna* nature (64, 11 and 16 = PW II, 44 and 45). We believe that it is possible to see in this the immutable, true, and eternal mathematical truths whose created character Descartes proclaimed in 1630. But, it will immediately be objected, this rapprochement is insane: the idea of God is caused in me by the infinite, and therefore cannot be a created truth. However, this objection holds only to the extent that the idea of God considered in [B] can be identified with the infinite, that is to say, with determination [A]. And yet this is obviously not the case, since, on the contrary, the following paradox must be maintained: if one juxtaposes the position from 1630—in which God, by his "incomprehensible power," creates the mathematical truths that we can comprehend—with the position in *Meditatio V,* one notices that determination [B] of God as supremely perfect is not confused with divine omnipotence; rather, it assumes a place among the created mathematical truths. This is proven by the following observation: in 1630, those who work with the simple natures "perfectly comprehend

mathematical truths and do not perfectly comprehend the truth of God's existence" precisely because this existence is demonstrated "in a manner which is more evident than the proofs of geometry" and that "makes me know that God exists with more certainty than I know the truth of any proposition of geometry."[89] In this way, the idea of God—in fact, as we have shown, the fundamental determination [A]—stands beyond the mathematical truths, and for that matter the created truths, in terms both of evidence and of certainty. In *Meditatio V,* the situation is inverted radically: the existence of God is concluded from his perfect essence—according to determination [B]—with neither more (*non magis,* 66, 8 and 12 = 46 and 46) nor less (*non minus,* 65, 21–22, 23 = 45; 45) certainty and evidence than those with which the sum of the angles is deduced from the essence of a triangle. The existence of God is neither more nor less evident than mathematical truths (". . . ad minimum eodem gradu [having at least the same level] . . . ," 65, 28–29 = 45)—which contradicts the greater evidence that it provided in 1630. Is the existence of God more evident than or only as evident as the mathematical truths? Is it a created truth or not? Confronted with this question, there are only two answers.[90] Either Descartes is grossly contradicting himself, or *Meditatio V* concerns another idea of God besides that of 1630—which, referred to our problematic, amounts to saying two things. First, determination [B] of the divine essence as the supremely perfect being, implying a rational construction of comprehensible perfections, remains within the domain of the simple natures, the mathematical truths, and the method; therefore, determination [B] is still to be counted among the creations of the incomprehensible and infinite power of God. Second, determination [A] of God as infinite, implying his incomprehensibility as well as his immensity, causes him to surpass (by means of creation) the measure and order of the method; therefore, determination [A] surpasses even the supreme perfection that [B] applies to God. Thus, from these three arguments, we conclude that the first two fundamental determinations of God's essence are incompatible with each other, as are the two corresponding proofs for his existence. The one, [A], thinks him as infinite,

89. *To Mersenne,* 6 May 1630 (AT I, 150, 14–17); then 15 April 1630 (AT I, 144, 15–17); and 25 November 1630 (AT I, 182, 2–4 = PW III, 25; then 22; and 29).

90. *The Discourse on the Method* vacillates between the two positions. On the one hand, it follows [B]: ". . . I found that this included existence in the same way as . . . the idea of a triangle includes the equality of its three angles to two right angles . . ." (DM, 36, 22–26 = PW I, 129). On the other hand, it seems to want to follow [A] by amending this with ". . . or even more evidently than."

creator of the truths and surpassing the method, therefore incomprehensible. The other, [B], thinks him as the supreme perfection constructed from the created truths and the simple natures, therefore comprehensible. In one case, the evidence for God transgresses the ordinary schema of methodic evidence; in the other, it is officially inscribed within it. In order to avoid having the incompatibility between [A] and [B] degraded into a pure contradiction, it is certainly permissible to see it as just a subordination. It will be said that, as the "incomprehensible power" creates the eternal truths, so does determination [A] of God as incomprehensible infinite hyperbolically surpass determination [B] of God as the sum of comprehensible perfections. But this hierarchy of two determinations of the divine essence marks, more than it masks, their irreducible *inconsistency*. It must be admitted that [A] and [B] contradict each other in terms of the parameter incomprehensibility—definitively.[91]

A second task now stands before us. To determinations [A] and [B], a final determination [C] is added. It is put forth in formula [4] from the *Responsiones* and is stated in terms of divine omnipotence:

> ... plane admitto aliquid esse posse, in quo sit tanta et tam inexhausta potentia, ut nullius unquam ope eguerit ut existeret, neque etiam nunc egeat ut conservetur, atque adeo sit quodammodo sui causa; Deumque talem esse intelligo. [I do readily admit that there can exist something which possesses such great and inexhaustible power that it never required the assistance of anything else in order to exist in the first place, and does not now require any assistance for its preservation, so that it is, in a sense, its own cause (*sui causa*); and I understand God to be such a being.] [AT VII, 109, 3–7 = PW II, 78.]

What relationship does this have with the two preceding determinations? To come to some decision about this, it must be recalled that the

---

91. In a way, this conclusion does nothing more than take a position within a now classic debate concerning the subordination or the independence of the two proofs *a priori* and *a posteriori*. Holding positions that defend their independence are F. Alquié, *La découverte métaphysique de l'homme chez Descartes,* pp. 225–26 (who holds, against all appearances, that "... Descartes does not say that the idea of God is similar to the ideas of mathematics ..."); H. Gouhier, "La preuve ontologique de Descartes (A propos d'un livre récent)," in *Revue internationale de Philosophie* 29 (1954), and *La pensée métaphysique de Descartes,* chaps. VI–IX; and J. Brunschwig, "La preuve ontologique interprétée par M. Gueroult," in *Revue philosophique* 1960/2. Supporting their subordination are M. Gueroult, *Descartes selon l'ordre des raisons,* vol. 1, chap. VIII, then *Nouvelles réflexions sur la preuve ontologique* (Paris, 1955), followed by L. Beck, *The Metaphysics of Descartes: A Study of the Meditations* (Oxford, 1965), pp. 231–37. We are content with radicalizing this second interpretation, by taking into account the *Letters* of 1630.

parameter incomprehensibility does not permit making a distinction between [A] and [C] in the way that it distinguished [A] from [B]. Actually,
the determination of God by cause [C], pushed to the point of assuming
the figure *causa sui,* interprets the incomprehensible divine essence (according to formulae [1] and [2]) as a cause, eventually an efficient cause,
of itself by way of its tangential status of power—in turn incomprehensible. If God can be assimilated to a *causa sui,* this is because his incomprehensible essence begets, as its derivative, a power, still incomprehensible—*incomprehensibilis potentia* (AT VII, 110, 26–27)—that
corresponds to the "incomprehensible power" of 1630 (AT I, 146, 4–5
and 150, 22). The transition from infinite essence to the power of this
essence and then to *causa sui* is unfolded within the incomprehensibility
proper to God. Consequently, in terms of the criteria that oppose [A]
and [B], [A] will always agree with [C]. We must therefore pursue our
analysis in terms of a new criterion of differentiation. In order to identify
it, a consideration of the *causa sui* itself will suffice. Among the numerous objections to which *causa sui* gives rise—is it self-contradictory, logically or temporally; must it be understood *quodammodo* and analogically, or directly as *causa efficiens sui ipsius* (111, 1)?—the most serious
does not receive the most attention. Descartes establishes on principle
that nothing escapes from the requirement of having to have a reason
for existing—". . . nihil possumus fingere ita esse a se, ut nulla danda sit
ratio cur potius existat quam non existat [It is impossible for us to imagine anything deriving existence from itself without there being some reason why it should exist rather than not exist]" (112, 7–8 = 80)— and,
reciprocally, that for every thing, no matter what it might be, an efficient
cause can be sought: ". . . nisi putarent cujusque rei causam efficientem
posse inquiri [unless they thought it possible to inquire into the efficient
cause of anything whatsoever] . . ." (244, 24–25 = 170). This requirement, which admits no exception, results from a *dictat* (108, 18 = 78) of
the natural light, which itself admits of no exception. To this law pertaining to all, God belongs like every other being: "Hoc enim de ipso
Deo quaeri potest [For this question may even be asked concerning
God] . . ." (164, 29–165, 1 = 116), ". . . licentiam . . . in rerum omnium,
etiam ipsius Dei, causas efficientes inquirendi: quo enim jure Deum inde
exciperemus, priusquam illum existere sit probatum? [We cannot develop this proof with precision unless we grant our minds the freedom
to inquire into the efficient causes of all things, even God himself. For
what right do we have to make God an exception, if we have not yet
proved that he exists?]" (238, 15–18 = 166). No doubt, once the proof
has been made, certain allowances will be made for God: efficiency is,

for him, analogical; cause is always equivalent to the power of his essence; the *ratio* for his existence is not totally confused with a *causa;* etc. But these allowances, which Descartes concedes only reluctantly when pressed by his critics, would not have a place to occur, if, precisely, there did not still stand the *dictat* stating that all existence must be justified with an efficient cause—or with some *ratio,* which takes its place: the more latitude God is granted in satisfying the *dictat* (and in fact Descartes will grant it to him broadly), the more he officially recognizes this same *dictat,* and therefore is submitted to it. The characteristic peculiar to [C] can now be identified. This characteristic opposes [C] to determination [A] in terms of a new criterion—causality. According to [A], God exerts causality, while according to [C] God is exerted by causality. More particularly, according to [A], "God is a cause whose power surpasses the bounds of human understanding" (AT I, 150, 18–19 = PW III, 25), because as *efficiens et totalis causa* (AT I, 152, 2; AT VII, 40, 22–23 = PW III, 25; PW II, 28), this cause creates, transcends, and produces all at once the totality of its effectively finite effects. The effects alone are effective; effectivity characterizes finite effects. In short, efficiency is relevant only to creation, as an act and as a region. Consequently, it is possible to go back from the effects—finite, created, and submitted to effectivity—all the way to God, as their efficient cause, which itself is exempt from causality and efficiency—". . . ad causam ultimam deveniatur, quae erit Deus [until eventually the ultimate cause is reached, and this will be God]" (50, 6 = 34). Here, God escapes from efficient causality because he exerts it. In determination [A] of God's essence, Descartes respects the dominant medieval interpretation of divine causality—namely, that it remains strictly external to him. According to [C], the matter is quite different: God is a function of causality because with regard to him, the human mind functions by seeking out a cause, one that justifies his existence. God satisfies a causality that he first undergoes; ". . . si prius de causa cur sit, sive cur esse perseveret, inquisivimus . . . [if we have previously inquired into the cause of God's existing or continuing to exist]" (AT VII, 110, 24–25 = PW II, 79). We, that is to say, the light of reason announcing its *dictat,* inquire (*inquirere*) into the reason that authorizes God to exist and to continue existing. It is then always the same *dictat* that is satisfied, when the power of the divine essence is understood (*intelligi*) as the reason for his existence, standing in the place of a cause (eventually an efficient cause): ". . . verbum, *sui causa,* nullo modo de efficiente potest intelligi, sed tantum quod inexhausta Dei potentia sit causa sive ratio propter quam causa non indiget

[The phrase 'his own cause' cannot possibly be taken to mean an efficient cause; it simply means that the inexhaustible power of God is the cause or reason for his not needing a cause]" (236, 7–10 = 165). If God is not submitted to efficiency, this is precisely because he is submitted, already and even without it, to the demand for a *causa sive ratio*. He is submitted to it all the more radically as he *is* himself, directly and by his essence, such a cause and reason: ". . . quia ipsa ejus naturae immensitas est causa sive ratio, propter quam nulla causa indiget ad existendum [because the immensity of his nature is the cause or reason why he needs no cause in order to exist]" (165, 2–3 = 116). Essentially, God is submitted to the requirements of the inquiry in search of a *causa sive ratio* that justifies existence. Determination [C] of God's essence anticipates the Leibnizian formulation of the principle of reason and submits the divine existence to it in advance—more specifically, causality, as the reason for his existence, becomes internal to God, and even identical with his essence. Thus, according to the criterion of causality, a second contradiction between the determinations of God's essence comes up in Descartes' thought: in determination [A], as in previous medieval metaphysics, God transcends all causality, because he exerts it and thereby remains free in the face of that which cannot be presented as the principle of reason; by contrast, in determination [C], which in fact is decisive for the development of all subsequent metaphysics, the principle of reason transcends God because it is raised to the point of proving and legitimating his very existence and can thereby suggest in advance a definitive formulation of God. The contradiction between [A] and [C] thus does not merely mark a new tension in the Cartesian revival of the thematic of the divine names. More important, it decides the future direction of the history of metaphysics, a history that could therefore be played out not between Descartes and some other "adversary," but, more originally, between Descartes and himself.

Having succeeded in reaching this result, it is now possible for us to compare the three Cartesian determinations of the essence of God. This multiple comparison is clearly organized around the two consequences of determination [A]: God is incomprehensible; God exerts, without undergoing, causality. *(a)* Determination [A] is opposed to determination [B] in terms of incomprehensibility, since in [B] the divine essence has regressed to the level of the objects of the method; but [A] is also opposed to [B] in terms of the second criterion, since the idea of the supremely perfect being admits a cause that constructs it or that produces it for us. *(b)* Determination [A] is opposed to determination [C] in terms of cause and principle of reason; but, according to the criterion of incomprehensibility, [A] agrees with [C], which clearly determines the divine essence as "incomprehensible power." *(c)* Determination [B] is opposed to determination [C] according to the criterion of incomprehensibility: the essence methodically constructed of the perfections contradicts the "incomprehensible power," maintained from 1630 until 1641. But [B] agrees with [C] in terms of causality: the *causa sive ratio,* which exerts its *dictat* over the God *causa sui,* also exerts it over the eternal truths that it, as their *causa efficiens et totalis,* creates; thus the *causa sive ratio* is in the end exerted over the sum of comprehensible perfections that culminate in the *ens summe perfectum.* These term-by-term comparisons can be summarized in a table:

Determination	[A]	[B]	[C]
		IDENTIFICATION	
Divine Name	*idea infiniti*	*ens summe perfectum*	*causa sui*
Formula	*Meditatio III* [1] and [2]	*Meditatio V* [3]	*Responsiones I and IV* [4]
Antecedent	Duns Scotus	William of Ockham	Suarez?
		(IN-)COHERENCE	
Incomprehensibility	yes	no	yes
Not causable	yes	no	no
Not methodic	yes	no	yes

From this table, several lessons follow directly. Concerning identification, it appears evident from now on that one cannot avoid the simple question of the plurality of divine names in Cartesian metaphysics. The use, surprising to be sure, of the phrase *divine names* in metaphysics is justified by the same reasons that cause their plurality to be admitted: Descartes employs several determinations that can no longer be used interchangeably as soon as their origins are identified (even in a cursory fashion, as here); and these historical origins all refer to theological debates in which these determinations earned an irreducible singularity. As a general rule, Descartes' discourse depends quite closely on its predecessors, and all the more so when it is a matter of his discourse on God. Without considering these genealogies, the interpretation of Descartes' discourse becomes almost impossible. Thus the theological origins of this discourse compel us to speak of a debate about the divine names; but the characteristics peculiar to the Cartesian new beginning also demand that we assess the displacement and the transmutation of these divine names into metaphysics. Descartes translates, no doubt for the first time, some of the divine names elaborated by medieval Christian theology into the field of the chiefly systematic metaphysics of modernity. Today, reflection on this historic translation constitutes the stakes of the history of philosophy as it is applied to Descartes. We hope to have established this. Concerning the coherence, or rather the incoherence, of the three Cartesian determinations, it must first be said (according to a horizontal reading of the table) that they never agree in such a way that the three criteria are satisfied unanimously: incomprehensibility, satisfied by [A] and [C], is in contradiction with [B]; transcendence with respect to cause is annulled by [B] and [C], but satisfied by [A]; as for the transgression of the methodic horizon (which does not coincide with being submitted to causality), it is confirmed in [A] and [C], but annulled by [B]. Thus this tension, going so far as to become a complex web of contradictions, leaves out no determination, nor any of the criteria, but cuts across the depths in the ultimate strata of Descartes' thought about God. Such is the risk run by the daring of a new beginning, one that nonetheless claims to be taking up several distinct theological legacies. It must next be said (according to a vertical reading of the table) that each of the three determinations of the divine essence does not contradict the three criteria of differentiation equally. Without minimizing the arbitrariness with which they were chosen, certainly limited but still likely, and without in the least underestimating the fact that these criteria are borrowed from particular moments of the *ordo rationum,* it seems clear that a hierarchy of determinations is set up. More particularly, [B] contradicts the three criteria retained; in conformity with its being the divine name belonging to the *via affirmativa,* as we already noted, the *ens summe perfectum* can do nothing but reject the three negative (at least grammatically negative) criteria retained here. *Causa sui,* [C], satisfies two of the three criteria because the *potentia incomprehensibilis* on which it rests safeguards its incomprehensibility, and is excluded from the horizon of the method, in an equilibrium that could offer at least a formal echo of eminence. There remains the idea of infinity, [A], which is the only one to respond to all three distinctive criteria of the idea of God being opposed to every other knowable object. These three criteria define it negatively to be sure: neither comprehensible, nor submitted to the exercise of causality in it, nor held within the horizon of the method.

We thus find confirmation of its belonging, at least formally, to the *via negativa*. However, it is not limited strictly to it, seeing as Descartes never stops emphasizing that the infinite, seen from all angles and with all its implications, states positive properties negatively. The affirmative and negative ways are here grounded in a tension where the authentic eminence should be recognized, more so than in the *causa sui*. In fact, beneath the negative appearances, *causa sui* accomplishes affirmations: incomprehensibility does not pose any obstacle to giving a *ratio* for the divine existence that would be formally univocal with the *ratio* for all other existences; its transcendence with respect to the method does not stop it from deferring, like the objects of the *Mathesis universalis*, to the privilege of *causa*, itself one of the first simple natures. Consequently, if *causa sui* [C] and *ens summe perfectum* [B] tend to privilege the *via affirmativa* conceptually if not in their formulation, only the idea of infinity [C] would hold not simply the role of the *via negativa*, but also that of eminence. Therefore, on the basis of an internal examination of the network of interlaced contradictions among the three Cartesian determinations of the divine essence, we posit the primacy—as more operative, more complete, and alone unconditioned—of the idea of infinity.

There is, however, a much more compelling reason to admit the primacy of the idea of infinity (determination [A]) over the two other determinations of God, [B] by *ens summe perfectum* and [C] by *causa sui*. More specifically, if we look back over the previous results (chapter II, §10), which concluded with a redoubling of the onto-theo-logy of *cogitatio* by an onto-theo-logy of *causa*, we can certainly risk a rapprochement that is itself redoubled. On the one hand, the onto-theo-logy of *cogitatio* would correspond with determination [B] of God as *ens summe perfectum*: the summation of perfections would offer to the *cogitatio* an (infinite) sum of perfect objects to be thought; and God would manifest his excellence all the more in that all thinkable perfections are actually found to be completed in him in such a way that the supreme perfection of God also brings to completion the search for the most perfect of the *cogitata*. On the other hand, the onto-theo-logy of *causa* would correspond with determination [C] of God as *causa sui*: the third proof ends up directly at the divine name that corresponds to the second onto-theology; God accomplishes, exemplarily, as his own essence the causality that he exerts over the other beings, as their reason and, above all, as their way of Being. This would confirm two separate analyses with a remarkable consistency: the redoubling of onto-theo-logy (chapter II) displayed a tension in Cartesian thought that is even less open to debate since it was detected a second time in the plurality of determinations of God's essence, thus of the divine names (chapter IV). But an objection immediately arises: the redoubling of onto-theo-logy can take up only two of the three divine names, and therefore leaves the idea of infinity undetermined; doesn't such an aberration disqualify the reconstitutions and remodelings that we just attempted (chapters II and IV)? It could be, on the contrary, that with this we have attained a fundamental result. What, really, does the Cartesian redoubling of onto-theo-logy signify? Answer: the most rigorous and most operative (in the present state of thought) conceptual determination of the fact and the limits of Descartes' belonging to metaphysics. Therefore, if the idea of infinity, as one of the divine names according to Descartes (and in fact the first), does not find shelter in any of the Cartesian figures of onto-theo-logy, it must inevitably be concluded that it does not arise from the Cartesian constitution of metaphysics. As surprising as this conclusion appears, it perhaps states only something obvious. In bearing the names *ens summe perfectum* and *causa sui,* God puts into operation the way of Being of all other beings—and, in fact, Descartes elaborates regional ontologies, in the guise of a physics, a theory of the soul, a cosmology, etc., which deal with the simple natures, thus the intelligible perfections, by recourse to efficient causality. But when God bears the name infinity, he does not put into operation any science of beings or of their ways of Being. The pair infinite/finite does not allow one to think the Being of finite beings, nor to elaborate any particular science of beings. It authorizes only the irreparable and inconfusible distinction between God and creatures—which for Descartes is no minor point. This distinction is of no use to the elaboration of the sciences, since it ends up at the incomprehensibility of the infinite by the finite and at the strict delimitation of the sciences practiced by the finite understanding. This distinction is likewise of no use in the elaboration of a general ontology because the very thinkers who privilege it (Duns Scotus and Suarez) suspend it just as quickly when it is a matter of establishing a univocal concept of being. The metaphysical extraterritoriality of the divine name drawn from the idea of infinity could also be confirmed from outside the thought and texts of Descartes. That is, those who inherit the themes put into play by Descartes reproduce diachronically the point that we have established synchronically in a strictly Cartesian field. Without yielding too much to simplification, and without anticipating a study still to be done concerning their respective doctrines of divine names, Malebranche and Leibniz here cast a powerful light on these matters. Of the three Cartesian determinations, which ones do they privilege? Malebranche certainly knows determination [A] of God by the idea of infinity; however, he makes use of it only by integrating it with determination [B], *ens summe perfectum,* according to a clear and precise transition: "By 'Deity' we all understand the Infinite, Being without restriction, infinitely perfect Being." And in fact, the most frequent and most functional name is said "infinitely perfect Being,"[92] where *infini* is absorbed into a mere indication of perfection, and amounts to saying *summe,* while losing all its own, proper, signification. No doubt it can be presumed that this evolution toward the massive privileging of the divine name drawn from the perfections maintains a close relationship, though one still to be clarified, with the interpretation of God as the very place where truth is known and the sciences are practiced—in opposition to the doctrine of the creation of the eternal truths. We therefore suggest a hypothesis: Malebranche develops a single one of the two figures of the onto-theo-logy Descartes redoubled, that of the *ens* as *cogitatum;* and consequently, from among the three Cartesian determinations of God's essence, he privileges the one that best corresponds to it: namely, *ens summe perfectum* become, by incorporating the infinite, "the infinitely perfect Being." Leibniz obviously was aware of Cartesian determinations [A] and [B], and, sometimes, grants them certain rights; but it cannot be contested that he privileges determination [C] when he evokes the *final reason of things:* "Thus the sufficient reason, which needs no further reason, must be outside this series of contingent things, and must lie in a substance which is the cause of this series, or which is a necessary being, bearing the reason of its existence within itself; otherwise we should still not have a sufficient reason, with which we could stop. And this final reason of things is called *God.*" Or else: "This is why the ultimate reason of things must lie in a necessary substance, in which the differentiation of the changes only exists eminently as in their source; and this is what we call *God.*" Or finally: "Est scilicet Ens illud ultima ratio Rerum, et uno vocabulo solet appellari Deus [This entity is the ultimate reason for things, and is usually called by the one word 'God.']"[93] *Ratio* of the world and of himself, God thus

92. Malebranche, *Entretiens sur la métaphysique et sur la religion, VIII,* 1, *Œuvres complètes,* vols. XII–XIII (Paris, 1965), p. 174. Then *VIII,* 2, p. 175 [English trans., p. 171 then 173]. The formula *l'Etre infiniment parfait* is so frequent that it seems as useless as it is difficult to give a list of references for it.
93. Leibniz, respectively, *Principes de la Nature et de la Grâce,* §8, then *Monadology,* §38; and finally *Résumé de philosophie, Opuscules et Fragments inédits,* ed. L. Couturat, p. 534 [English trans., p. 198, then 185; and finally 145]. On the fate of the most original

fulfills, as an echo of the *causa sui* and no doubt more radically than it, the role of making the Being of each being manifest according to the measure of cause, *ut causatum*. The Leibnizian privilege thus accorded to Cartesian determination [C] of God as *causa sui,* by privileging the divine name *final reason of things,* answers to the parallel choice of taking up the onto-theo-logy of the *ens ut causatum.* In this way, Malebranche and Leibniz could each be seen to deploy one of the two figures of the redoubled onto-theo-logy in Descartes; and in each of these efforts at metaphysical simplification, they privilege the only one of the three determinations of the divine essence that corresponds to the figure of metaphysics previously retained. Whence this consequence, which is at the very least probable and would deserve to be tested in the details of the texts: the divine name drawn from the idea of infinity does not assume a place in any figure of post-Cartesian onto-theo-logy. Therefore it ought to be understood as a nonmetaphysical utterance of Descartes' thought about God, belonging more to the previous theology of the divine names than to the subsequent onto-theo-logies, where the conceptual idol excludes God from the horizon of metaphysics by pretending to sequester him within onto-theo-logical functions. Descartes here, as elsewhere, reaches beyond his successors, as the incomprehensible complex of contradictions that the secret of the thing itself imposes surpasses and also allows for the simplicity of multiple rival intelligibilities, each a widow of the incomprehensible itself. By drawing out and maintaining the primacy of the idea of the infinite, Descartes does not merely accomplish, for the last time, the itinerary of a treatise on the divine names, expired fragment of a silent disappearance. Most important, in the very moment in which he fixes the onto-theo-logical figures that are going to govern all modern metaphysics, Descartes marks their limits: the *ego,* which rules the first onto-theo-logy, can itself transgress metaphysics when it is temporalized by means of possibility (chapter III, §15); but the *ego* would not succeed in doing so if God, who rules the second onto-theo-logy, did not himself first transgress metaphysics when he is spoken with the most divine name, infinity. Instituting the possible figures of modern metaphysics, Descartes, with an unsurpassable authority, redoubled his own institution, by establishing, in advance and before anyone else, the limits of metaphysics. We have not finished contemplating the

---

and decisive of the Cartesian theses, see our sketch, "De la création des vérités éternelles au principe de raison. Remarques sur l'anti-cartésianisme de Spinoza, Malebranche, Leibniz," *XVIIeme siècle* 1985/2: 147.

import of this magnificent acknowledgment: "...I have never written about the infinite except to submit myself to it."[94] And if the Cartesian names of God are organized in a confused complex of contradictions, this is not because Descartes lacked conceptual power or conceptual rigor; on the contrary, it is because he dared face up to the contradiction that is necessarily imposed on the finite by the infinite advancing upon it—and to which, perhaps, only a certain conceptual madness can testify without being unworthy of it. Before God, reverentially, and as a rarity among the metaphysicians, Descartes stands hidden—he does not keep secrets, nor does he sneak away, but hides his face before that of the infinite—*larvatus pro Deo*.[95]

94. *To Mersenne,* 28 January 1641 (AT III, 293, 24–25 = PW III, 172).

95. Descartes, of course, writes "Larvatus prodeo [I come forward masked]" (AT X, 213, 6–7 = PW I, 2). We transform this *j'avance masqué* into an abusive *masqué devant la face de Dieu* only because this modification gives cause for thought, and also because others before us have ventured to put it forth, of course with a wholly other meaning (J.-L. Nancy, in *Ego sum* [Paris, 1979], and especially L. Brunschvicg, "Métaphysique et mathématiques chez Descartes," *Revue de métaphysique et de morale* [1927], p. 323).

FIVE

Overcoming

§21. Pascal within Cartesian Metaphysics

In reconstructing the metaphysics of Descartes, we end up at a re-doubled onto-theo-logy. If it serves all the better to confirm the claim that Cartesian thought belongs to metaphysics in general, it is no less striking for leaving out a twofold remainder. That is, two doctrinal elements remain irreducible to the constitution of Cartesian metaphysics. When the *ego* is thought, it is defined in the first onto-theo-logy as a *cogitatio sui,* and in the second as an *ens causatum,* that is to say, a *substantia creata.* But its ultimate determination—namely, the freedom that, in morality, reestablishes possibility as the first modality of beings (chapter III, §15)—does not find a place in either of the two figures of onto-theo-logy. Nonetheless, the freely acting *ego* mobilizes each of their respective concepts: *cogitatio* and cause permit it to exert a causality through representation (according to the Kantian formula); thus the third determination of the *ego* again has an impact on metaphysics, even though it does not belong to the redoubled onto-theo-logy. What status can be granted to it? This line of questioning is even more unavoidable in that isolating a second doctrinal element validates the question: among the concurrent determinations of the divine essence, if one— *ens perfectissimum*—agrees exactly with the onto-theo-logy of the *ens cogitatum,* and if the other—*causa sui*—corresponds literally with the onto-theo-logy of the *ens ut causatum,* the first and most fundamental— *infinitum*—is not justified by any figure of metaphysics; it could even be that it explicitly contradicts the two figures of the redoubled onto-theo-logy (chapter IV, §20). What status can then be granted to the determination of God as infinite? The excellence of these two exceptions to the onto-theo-logical constitution of Cartesian metaphysics bars one from seeing them as merely negligible and insignificant residues. On the contrary, fundamental concepts are at issue: it belongs as radically to the *ego* to act freely as it does to God to be deployed infinitely. The fact that 277 these two properties do not find ample development among Descartes' heirs, until Kant revives them, does not nullify, but on the contrary confirms, how interesting and how difficult they are. How are we to understand them? The dilemma is stated easily: either determining Cartesian metaphysics through a redoubled onto-theo-logy remains insufficient (be it because a third figure must be mobilized, or because the very notion of onto-theo-logy is not pertinent, or be it finally for these two reasons combined), and runs up against essential theses that it cannot interpret; or these theses resist the redoubled onto-theo-logy because, more radically, they simply do not belong to metaphysics. There are no quick and easy adjustments that can mitigate the strangeness of this harsh affirmation. Let us remark nonetheless that, in fact, post-Cartesian metaphysics privileges neither the determination of God as infinite, nor the determination of the ego as acting freely; to the contrary, it develops in the directions opened up by the *ens ut cogitatum* and the *ens ut causatum.* In the end, the two irreducible theses can be joined in a single formula—*ego, ut ad imaginem Dei:* the freedom found in the *ego* follows from the infinity of its will, which itself depends on its likeness to God. Descartes even uses formulations that resemble this theme.[1] The interpretive difficulty thus resides less in recognizing the particular status these theses hold in relation to the redoubled onto-theo-logy than it does in identifying their status. In supposing that they transgress metaphysics, can one expect Descartes to think clearly such a transgression of the transgression already accomplished by metaphysics (chapter I, §2)? When he thinks his first concept of metaphysics so unexplicitly, how can one expect him to think its transgression with any clarity? Moreover, wouldn't the suspected willfulness of the interpreter become insufferable, if it went so far as to introduce, after the redoubling of onto-theo-logy, yet

---

1. Our formulation merely synthesizes classic Cartesian texts: ". . . me quodammodo ad imaginem et similitudinem ejus [Dei] factum esse [I am somehow made in his image and likeness] . . ." (AT VII, 51, 19–21 = PW II, 35); or: ". . . imaginem quamdam et similitudinem Dei me referre [I understand myself to bear in some way the image and likeness of God] . . ." (57, 14–15 = 40). When Descartes sets up a direct relationship between the love of God (*To Chanut,* 1 February 1647 [AT IV, 608, 10–16 = PW III, 309]), or the desire for perfections (*To Mersenne,* 25 December 1639 [AT II, 628, 3–9 = PW III, 142]), and our infinite will or our spiritual nature, which bears the *image* (AT II, 628, 9 = PW III, 142) or *some resemblance* of God (AT IV, 608, 13 = PW III, 309), does he still reside strictly in the field of the redoubled onto-theo-logy? No doubt yes, if one believes that he can see here only the *cogitatio;* but, to be more precise, doesn't the *cogitatio* change status when it is taken up in the *imago Dei*—the biblical formulation of the determination of the finite by the infinite?

another duplication within Cartesian thought? For, like beings and hypotheses, distinctions must not be multiplied needlessly. If therefore a
metaphysical extraterritoriality of the *ego* as free and of God as infinite
can be sustained, it would have to be established and confirmed through
other arguments. These arguments will be all the more powerful as they
come from an authority that is more and more exterior. We therefore
are searching for a point of reference, on the basis of which it becomes
possible to consider Cartesian thought as metaphysics—that is to say,
eventually and in part as nonmetaphysical. This reference point could
not itself be defined metaphysically, but would have to be identified in
terms of some other authority. The more this authority will try to think
and to be thought outside metaphysics, the more it will permit us to
test *a contrario* the metaphysical character (partial or total) of Cartesian
thought. It is of course necessary that it be posited in the course of taking
a position vis-à-vis Descartes—without doing so, it would not offer any
reference and would not measure any distance. In a word, we are searching for an explicitly nonphilosophical (and thus, most probably, nonmetaphysical) thought, one that knows Cartesian thought, recognizes it
as metaphysics, and criticizes it in terms that, perhaps, permit us to conceive of an overcoming of metaphysics in the Cartesian epoch of its historical destiny.

Such a thought can be found only in Pascal, who takes up and general-
izes the Cartesian pronouncement of the *ego ad imaginem Dei*—"There
are perfections in nature to show that she is the image of God and imper-
fections to show that she is no more than his image" (§934/580).[2] He
devotes himself to understanding this pronouncement in opposition to
philosophy, in particular to the philosophy of "Descartes useless and uncertain" (§887/78), and outside of all metaphysics—at least this is what
we shall attempt to establish.[3] Pascal measures Descartes' inclusion in

2. In every case, we cite Pascal according to the *Œuvres complètes,* ed. L. Lafuma
(Paris, 1963) (see *supra,* chap. II, §6, n. 20), hereinafter *OC.* For the *Pensées,* we give the
Lafuma and Brunschvicg numeration successively. [Note that all English citations of works
taken from the *Œuvres complètes* refer to *Great Short Works of Pascal.*—Trans.]

3. Attributing a philosophy to Pascal (as in, for example, F. Rauh, "La philosophie de
Pascal," *Annales de la Faculté de Bordeaux* [1892], reprinted in *Revue de métaphysique et
de morale* 1923/1, or E. Baudin, *Etudes historiques et critiques sur la philosophie de Pascal*
[Neuchâtel, 1946–47]) rests on an insufficient concept of philosophy itself. The precept
"To have no time for philosophy is to be a true philosopher" (§513/4) must be understood
with all its force, however banal it might have become. As for evoking a *Métaphysique de
Pascal* (as does E. Morot-Sir [Paris, 1973]), this can be only an abuse of language, or a
rhetorical effect (". . . a new broadening of the meaning of the word 'rhetoric': it becomes

metaphysics only by starting from his own theological exile from philosophy.

An understanding and a discussion of Descartes by Pascal is as important to Descartes—so that we can measure how far and in what way he falls within metaphysics—as it is to Pascal, who was obliged to contest philosophy—thus the philosophy of Descartes—in order to achieve his theological position. In this way, Pascal and Descartes measure each other reciprocally; or rather, by confronting each other, they measure the limits between metaphysics and theology. Not that Descartes holds solely the part of metaphysics—the contrary was established and constitutes what is at stake in this debate as a whole—nor that Pascal plays exclusively the role of theologian—we will see this soon enough. It must rather be said that Descartes and Pascal show or trace the limits between metaphysics and theology insofar as they uphold them, but also overcome and transgress them. At least this will be the theoretical result that we now aim to win. Put otherwise: to what authority do the freedom of the *ego* and the infinity of God answer?

Examining this question presupposes that one first establish the theoretical relationship between Pascal and Descartes. Pascal can revoke Descartes, for the sake of eventually overcoming what is metaphysical in him, only insofar as he reaches an authentic understanding of him; this implies that he explicitly recognize in Cartesian thought a figure of metaphysics. In short, the sought-after debate will take place only if one demonstrates that Pascal read Descartes before he criticized him and precisely in order to do so—in a word, it will happen only if Pascal is confirmed as a Cartesian. The relations between Pascal and Descartes do not cause any trouble, even if they were sometimes troubled: a public encounter in September 1647, the discussion about the experience that establishes the physical reality of the void and about its interpretation— the concerned parties have themselves related these tales.[4] But what is essential seems to lie elsewhere: Pascal read and approved of Descartes.

---

a synonym of metaphysics," op. cit., p. 13). On this point, Heidegger's rash use of Pascal (for example in *Sein und Zeit*, §1, p. 4, and §29, p. 139) would deserve a critical discussion.

4. See Descartes, *To Mersenne*, 13 December 1647 (AT V, 98, 1–100, 21), and *To Carcavi*, 11 June 1649 (366, 6–10 = PW III, 327–28; not included in PW; and not included in PW), and the story reported by Jacqueline Pascal to Gilberte Perier, her sister, dated 25 September 1647 (*Œuvres de Blaise Pascal,* ed. L. Brunschvicg and P. Boutroux, vol. II [Paris, 1923], pp. 42–48; and reproduced in AT V, 71–73). The intermediary who made this encounter possible was Jacques Habert of Saint-Léonard, as J. Mesnard has established: "Entre Pascal et Descartes: Jacques Habert de Saint-Léonard," *Mélanges de littérature française offerts à Monsieur René Pintard* (Strasbourg, 1975).

Without a doubt, when he cites him explicitly, it is often in order to criticize him (§§84/79; 553/76; 887/78; 1001); without a doubt the celebrated reproach of uselessness and uncertainty will dominate the entire interpretation, to the point that Malebranche will soon be obliged to emphasize that if "it is true that the majority of sciences are very uncertain and quite useless," nonetheless it is "established that there are purely human sciences [that are] quite certain and quite useful," and that in particular "it is very necessary to know certain truths of metaphysics."[5] This does not prevent Pascal from also being able to pass for a Cartesian in the eyes of certain acquaintances, even enlightened ones, like Méré: ". . . Descartes, whom you esteem so much. . . ."[6] That is, Pascal read Descartes and retained what he had read there, with a precision that must be emphasized more clearly. *(a)* In the opuscule *De l'esprit géométrique,* dating from 1657–58, Pascal resumes, in clearly Cartesian terms, the search for "the true method in which to conduct one's reasoning in all things." No doubt this is a reference to "the true method of attaining the knowledge of everything within my mental capacities," which was established in the *Discourse on the Method* (AT VI, 17, 8–10 = PW I, 119). This "true method" includes, Pascal says, "two principal matters": ". . . not employing any term whose meaning one has not previously explained clearly," and next ". . . never putting forth any proposition that one has not demonstrated by truths already known." Joined together, these two precepts define the "true order which consists . . . in defining and proving all." In such a result, one surely recognizes the Cartesian definition of the method in terms of the order: "Tota methodus consistit in ordine et dispositione eorum ad quae mentis acies est convertanda [The whole method consists entirely in the ordering and arranging of the

5. Malebranche, *Recherche de la Vérité,* IV, 6, §2, *Œuvres complètes,* ed. G. Rodis-Lewis, vol. 2 (Paris, 1974), pp. 52–53 [English trans., p. 291]. The fact that this text constitutes a response to Pascal's criticism of Descartes was established by H. Gouhier, "Note historique sur Pascal et Malebranche," *Bulletin de la Société française de philosophie* 1938/3.

6. *Letter from Méré to Pascal,* 1658?, 1659? The imprecision of the date, the no doubt composite character of the text that has come down to us, and the ridiculously fatuous quality of the character are not enough to disqualify the witness (*Œuvres de Blaise Pascal,* ed. Brunschvicg, Boutroux, and Gazier [Paris, 1923], pp. 222–23). Against R. Jolivet, who admits only "superficial analogies" between Pascal and Descartes ("L'anticartésianisme de Pascal," *Archives de Philosophie* 1923/3: 251), we, along with J. Pucelle, must insist upon "a historical complex, a *constellation* . . . a common cultural atmosphere" ("La 'lumière naturelle' et le cartésianisme dans l'*Esprit géométrique* et l'*Art de Persuader*," *Chroniques de Port-Royal* 11–14 [1963], p. 51). With regard to this "atmosphere," Pascal, at the chateau of Vaumurier, made the acquaintance of no one less than the Duc de Luynes and A. Ar-

objects on which we must concentrate our mind's eye]" (*Regula V,* AT X, 379, 15–16 = PW I, 20). Similarly, the "true method" repeated the Cartesian reduction of truth to the method: "Necessaria est Methodus ad rerum veritatem investigandam [We need a method if we are to investigate the truth of things]" (371, 2–3 = 15). As for the two precepts, the second corresponds to the *deductio/inductio* and the first to the *intuitus.* As for the requirement of a definition, it too is connected with Cartesian theses. For definition, according to Pascal, obeys two limitations. At times, definition must come to a halt because of an excess of evidence: "... as we carry our search farther and farther, we necessarily arrive at primitive words which permit of no further definition, and at principles which are so clear that no clearer ones can be discovered to aid in proving them." This echoes the most simple natures, which, apprehended before all others, can no longer be divided into anything simpler, except, paradoxically, by appearing more complicated (*Regula XII,* 418, 1–419, 5 = PW I, 44). Other times, definition will come to a halt because of a lack, as when the explanation is more confused than the notion to be explained. Pascal gives two examples, both taken from Descartes. First:

> What need is there of explaining what we mean by the word *man*? Do we not know well enough what the thing is that we want to designate by that term? What advantage did Plato think it would be to us for him to say that man is a two-legged animal without feathers? As if the idea which I naturally have of man and which I cannot express were not clearer and more certain than the one that he gives by his useless and even ridiculous explanation.

It is easy to recognize a Cartesian denegation in this:

> Quidnam igitur antehac me esse putavi? Hominum scilicet. Sed quid est homo? Dicamne animal rationale? Non, quia postea quaerendum foret, quidnam animale sit, et quid rationale, atque ita ex una quaestione in plures difficilioresque delaberer. [What then did I formerly think I was? A man. But what is a man? Shall I say "a rational animal"? No; for then I should have to inquire what an animal is, what rationality is, and in this

---

nauld (a balanced consideration of the issue can be found in H. Gouhier, *Blaise Pascal. Commentaires* [Paris, 1971], pp. 82*ff.*). The most convincing demonstration that Pascal read precise Cartesian texts was given by M. Le Guern, *Pascal et Descartes* (Paris, 1971), which counterbalances Julien-Aymard d'Angers, *Pascal et ses précurseurs* (Paris, 1954), and dispenses with J. Pucelle, "Malentendus sur 'Descartes et Pascal': Pascal et les philosophes," *Chroniques de Port-Royal* 20–21 (1972).

way one question would lead me down the slope to other harder ones.]
[AT VII, 25, 25–29 = PW II, 17.]

Second: "How many there are likewise who think they have defined motion when they say: *Motus nec simpliciter actus nec mera potentia est, sed actus entis in potentia.*" In this, one hears *Regula XII:*

> At vero nonne videntur illi verba magica proferre, quae vim habeant occultam et supra captum humani ingenii, qui dicunt *motum,* rem unicuique notissimam, *esse actum entis in potentia, prout est in potentia?* Quis enim intelligit haec verba? Quis ignorat quid sit motus? [When people say that motion, something perfectly familiar to everyone, is "the actuality of a potential being, in so far as it is potential (*esse actum entis in potentia, prout est in potentia*)," do they not give the impression of uttering magic words which have a hidden meaning beyond the grasp of the human? For who can understand these expressions? Who does not know what motion is?] [AT X, 426, 16–21 = PW I, 49.][7]

Additionally, Pascal acknowledges the Cartesian intention quite clearly in *De l'art de persuader:* ". . . prove the distinction between material and spiritual natures, and make of it a firm principle supporting an entire physics, as Descartes claimed he was doing"[8]—which obviously echoes *Meditatio II:*

> Nihil nisi punctum petebat Archimedes, quod sit firmum et immobile, ut integram terram loco dimoveret; magna quoque speranda sunt, si vel minimum quid invenero quod certum sit et inconcussum. [Archimedes used to demand just one firm and immovable point in order to shift the entire earth; so I too can hope for great things if I manage to find just one thing, however slight, that is certain and unshakable.] [AT VII, 24, 9–13 = PW II, 16.]

Without bringing up other correspondences, which no doubt belong as much to the atmosphere of the time as to precise readings, one can already conclude that Pascal revives the Cartesian doctrine of the method, without anything suggesting that he later contested it in its own domain. *(b)* The correspondences between certain of the *Pensées* and several Cartesian texts do not seem to be any less precise. For example, the

---

7. *De l'esprit géométrique, OC,* respectively, pp. 349, 350, and 351 [English trans., pp. 191, 192, and 194]. On the Cartesian criticism, see *Règles utiles et claires pour la direction de l'esprit en la recherche de la vérité,* pp. 248–49.

8. *De l'art de persuader, OC,* p. 358 [English trans., p. 209 (modified)].

Preface to the French translation of the *Principles* (1647) governs §§532–33/373–81, as is suggested by the abbreviated title *"Princ."* (and not "Pyrr.," a faulty rendering). When Pascal declares, "I will write down my thoughts here without any order and in a perhaps not aimless fashion. This is the true order and it will always show my aim by its very disorder [modified]," he is reversing the aim confessed by Descartes: "Now in all ages there have been great men who have tried to find a fifth way of reaching wisdom. . . . This consists in the search for the first causes and the true principles which enable us to deduce the reasons for everything we are capable of knowing."[9] Consequently, there where Descartes dogmatically discusses the principles of Plato and Aristotle and discusses what "gave them such great authority,"[10] Pascal ironically mimics the at least apparent respect of Descartes: "We always picture Plato and Aristotle wearing long academic gowns, but they were ordinary decent people like anyone else, who enjoyed a laugh with their friends." The continuity of the allusions confirms how precise they are. Moreover, the same *Preface* to the *Principles* also inspires §698/119. In the text "a seed cast on good ground bears fruit, a principle cast into a good mind bears fruit. . . . Roots, branches, fruit: principles, consequences," Pascal does not merely revive the platitude the "seeds of truth" (DM, 64, 4 = PW I, 144) that give their fruit to us (". . . prima cogitationum utilium semina ita jacta sunt, ut . . . spontaneam frugem producant [The first seeds of useful ways of thinking are sown . . . (such that they) often bear fruit of their own accord]," AT X, 373, 8–11 = PW I, 17). More important, this text corresponds with the parallel that the *Preface* set up between the results of the sciences and the fertility of a tree: the *Preface* says not only that "the whole of philosophy is like a tree. The roots are metaphysics, the trunk is physics, and the branches emerging from the trunk are all the other sciences, which may be reduced to three principal ones, namely medicine, mechanics, and morals . . ."; it also says, ". . . just as it is not the roots or the trunk of a tree from which one gathers the fruit, but only the ends of the branches, so the principal benefit of philosophy depends on those parts of it which can only be learnt last of all."[11] This confirms that §698/119 is just a note taken while reading the *Principles.* Similarly, §699/382, describing rela-

9. AT IX-2, 5, 18–24 = PW I, 181; see 8, 10; 8, 16–25; 9, 13–18; 10, 12–18, etc. = 183; 183; 183; 184; etc.

10. AT IX-2, 5, 26–6, 16 (in particular 6, 13–14) = PW I, 181.

11. AT IX-2, 14, 24–28 and 15, 1–5 = PW I, 186 and 186. We here follow the results of M. Le Guern, op. cit., 1st part.

tive motion and immobility according to the example of a ship, reproduces *Principes II,* §13. Other precise examples could easily be called to mind.[12]

Pascal's Cartesianism is not limited merely to reading notes and methodological precepts. It concerns first philosophy. *(c)* Not only must it be remembered that, in 1655 (?), during *Pascal's Conversation with Monsieur de Saci,* the role of philosopher falls to Pascal—"thus these two men ... met on common ground which, however, they had reached by different routes, Monsieur de Saci having arrived there at once thanks to the clarity of his Christian insight, and Monsieur Pascal only on a circuitous course by following the reasoning of these two philosophers" (OC, 297 *b* = 133)—but it must be emphasized that among these philosophers, the most present is in fact never cited by name, Descartes, even though he intervenes constantly, seeing as *Meditatio I* provides food for *Conversation,* at least twice. First, *Meditatio I* appears in the hypothesis of a divine deception: "Since we know only by faith alone that a thoroughly good Being has given these [principles] to us as true, by creating us to know the truth, who can know without the light of faith whether they are not uncertain because they may have come into being by chance, or whether they were not fashioned by a false, evil being which gave them to us to lead us astray" (OC, 294 *b* = 126). This hypothesis reappears, moreover, in the *Pensées,* in §131/434: "There is no certainty apart from faith as to whether man was created by a good God, an evil demon, or just by chance...." This is to say that in one and the same line Pascal revives not only the *genius aliquis malignius* of *Meditatio I* (AT VII, 22, 23), but also the similar hypotheses, which amount to a God who would let us deceive ourselves:

> Sed ... totumque hoc de Deo demus esse fictitium; at seu fato, seu casu, seu continuata rerum serie, seu quovis alio modo me ad id quod sum pervenisse supponant. [Let us ... grant them that everything said about God is a fiction. According to their supposition, then, I have arrived at my pres-

---

12. Among other correspondences, let us mention the allusion to the debate between Descartes and Harvey (citations from *De motu cordis et sanguinis in animalibus* in DM, 46, 27–56, 9 = PW I, 134–40) in §736/96—perhaps also in §737/10 and §740/340, which corresponds with DM, 50, 6–18 = 136. Similarly, §957/512 should be read as a refutation of Descartes' Eucharistic doctrine, as it is expressed in particular in the *Letter to Mesland,* 9 February 1645 (AT IV, 163, 24*ff.* = PW III, 241). Pascal's "The same river flowing over there is *numerically identical* to that flowing at the same time in China" corresponds with "... the Loire is the same river as it was ten years ago, although it is no longer the same water" (AT IV, 165, 3–4 = PW III, 242).

ent state by fate or chance or a continuous chain of events, or by some other means. . . .] [21, 19–22 = 14.]

Perfectly consistent with this first implicit citation is what Pascal describes as the effect of such a deceptiveness in the principles: namely, error with regard to the most evident truths: "[Would the soul] know when it is in error, since the essence of error consists in not being aware of error; amid all this obscurity [would it] not believe as firmly that two and three make six as it subsequently knows that they make five?" (OC, 294 *a* = 125–26). This cannot not be seen as one of the examples of the undetectable error that would be provoked by the Cartesian hypothesis of a God "qui potest omnia" (21, 2 = 14):

> Imo etiam, quemadmodum judico interdum alios errare circa ea quae se perfectissime scire arbitrantur, ita ego ut fallar quoties duo et tria simul addo, vel numero quadrati latera, vel si quid aliud facilius fingi potest? [What is more, since I sometimes believe that others go astray in cases where they think they have the most perfect knowledge, may I not similarly go wrong every time I add two and three or count the sides of a square, or in even some simpler matter, if that is imaginable?] [21, 7–11 = 14.]

The insistent presence of *Meditatio I* is all the more noteworthy here as Pascal ascribes this text to the patronage of Montaigne alone (OC, 294 *a* = 125). Such a rebuke of Descartes renders, *a contrario,* his sway over Pascal's argumentation all the more decisive and incontestable.[13] *(d)* There is more: Descartes does not provide merely a reserve of concepts to be used for the purpose of eventually strengthening the arguments borrowed from Montaigne; he gives Pascal some of his fundamental concepts, by means of a direct and radical influence. This is clearly the case with *Meditatio II.* In contrast to "nearly all philosophers [who] confuse their ideas of things, and speak spiritually of corporeal things and corporeally of spiritual ones" (§199/72), Descartes actually distinguished thought from extension, and defined man as *res cogitans:* "Sum autem res vera et vere existens; sed qualis res? Dixi, cogitans [I am a thing

---

13. This rapprochement has already been noted by P. Courcelle, *L'entretien de Pascal et Sacy. Ses sources et ses énigmes* (Paris, 1960 and 1981), pp. 28–29. For a more fully developed examination, see the studies by G. Rodis-Lewis, "Pascal devant le doute hyperbolique de Descartes," *Chroniques de Port- Royal* 20–21 (1972); "Doute et certitude chez Pascal et Descartes," *Europe* 594 (1978) (as well as the suggestions made in *L'oeuvre de Descartes,* pp. 230 and 521).

which is real and which truly exists. But what kind of a thing? As I have just said—a thinking thing" (AT VII, 27, 15–17 = 18). Pascal repeats this fundamental position exactly, and will never put it into question: "I can certainly imagine a man without hands, feet, or head, for it is only experience that teaches us that the head is more necessary than the feet. But I cannot imagine a man without thought; he would be a stone or an animal" (§111/339); "... it is not in space that I must seek my human dignity, but in the ordering of my thoughts" (§113/348); "... my self consists in my thought ..." (§135/469); "... all our dignity consists in thought. It is on thought that we must depend for our recovery, not on space and time, which we could never fill. Let us then strive to think well; that is the basic principle of morality" (§200/347). As a logical consequence of this perfectly Cartesian decision, Pascal will also take up as his own two of its corollaries. First, the knowledge of extension and of the sensible is reducible to the *solius mentis inspectio* (AT VII, 31, 25 = 21). When he asks, for example, "What part of us is it that feels pleasure? Is it our hand, our arm, our flesh, or our blood? It must obviously be something immaterial" (§108/339), Pascal is repeating the Cartesian reduction of the piece of wax first to *extensum quid,* then, and more importantly, to what renders the latter possible, that is to say thinkable—namely, thought itself; for "We know for certain that it is the soul which has sensory perceptions and not the body."[14] Thus Pascal maintains, in several lines, the entire Cartesian doctrine of perception as representation by the *cogitatio*. The second corollary also depends on *Meditatio II*. That is, the celebrated and difficult fragment that seems to conclude with an I that cannot be located—"Where then is this self, if it is in neither the body nor the soul?"—opens with a famous experience: "A man goes to the window to see the people passing by; if I pass by, can I say that he went there to see me? No, for he is not thinking of me in particular ..." (§688/323). Now, this experience appears first of all in *Meditatio II*:

> ... nisi jam forte respexissem ex fenestra homines in platea transeuntes, quos etiam ipsos non minus usitate quam ceram dico me videre. Quid autem video praeter pilos et vestes, sub quibus latere possent automata? Sed judico homines esse. [If I look out of the window and see men crossing the square, as I just happen to have done, I normally say that I see the

14. *Optics IV* (AT VI, 109, 7–8 = PW I, 164). (See *Optics VI,* [141, 7]; *Responsiones II* [AT VII, 160, 14–161, 3]; and *Principia Philosophiae IV,* §196: "Animam non sentire nisi quatenus est in cerebro [The soul has sensory awareness only in so far as it is in the brain]" = PW I, 172; PW II, 113; PW I, 283–84.)

men themselves, just as I say that I see the wax. Yet do I see any more than hats and coats which could conceal automatons? I *judge* that they are men.] [AT VII, 32, 6–10 = 21.]

No doubt, in its new, Pascalian usage, this passage undergoes a complete reversal: it is no longer a matter of seeing other *egos* beneath the clothed automata that walk about beneath the window, but of being seen as a loved or lovable self by an *ego,* loving spectator. It nonetheless remains the case that the problem Pascal posed gets its meaning from the phenomenological situation imported from Cartesian doctrine, including the *res cogitans* as much as the *inspectio mentis.*[15] Consequently, it must be concluded that Pascal remains faithful to *Meditatio II,* and thus to the Cartesian egology.

But couldn't one hold a more restrained position? Pascal would adopt Cartesian theses in the profane domains—methodology, definition of the sciences and of philosophy, theory of knowledge, essence of the soul, etc.—without however following Descartes when it is a matter of theological questions, and in the first place of the very definition of God. The counter-proof would be furnished by examining the implicit citations of *Meditatio III.* In the case of such a restrained Cartesianism, *Meditatio III* would be either passed over in silence or contradicted. The attempt must be made. What does *Meditatio III* say about God? It thinks God quite particularly as infinite: *substantia quaedam infinita* (AT VII, 45, 11 = PW II, 31), *summus aliquis Deus, aeternus, infinitus* (40, 16–17 = 28), ". . . Deum . . . esse actu infinitum . . ." (47, 19 = 32, see chapter IV, determination [A]). Now it seems according to the evidence that Pascal adopts and privileges this definition of the divine essence, first in the *Conversation:* "the sovereign being that is infinite by his own definition" (OC, 294 *a* = 125), then in several places in the *Pensées:* ". . . There is in nature a being who is necessary, eternal, and infinite" (§135/469), ". . . an infinite and immutable object; in other words . . . God himself" (§148/425), ". . . to pray this infinite and indivisible being . . ." (§418/233), ". . . that God might be infinite and indivisible . . ." (§420/231), ". . . an infinite good . . ." (§917/540). And like Descartes, Pascal at once deduces from the infinity of God his incomprehensibility: ". . . If there is a God, he is infinitely beyond our comprehension" (§418/233). According to Descartes, the infinite characterizes God only by manifesting to man that he is finite and thus bears in himself the mark of the infinite (idea of

15. See the study by H. Birault, "Pascal et le problème du moi introuvable," in *La passion de la raison. Hommage à Ferdinand Alquié* (Paris, 1983).

infinity, free choice, will).[16] Consequently, he acknowledges in man a *participation in perfect being* (DM, 35, 1–2 = PW I, 128) as well as a *participation in nothingness* (DM, 37, 28 = 219). Pascal, in response, posits that ". . . man infinitely transcends man," because ". . . in the state of his creation, or in the state of grace, [he] is exalted above the whole of nature, made like unto God and sharing in his divinity . . . ," and, inversely, ". . . in the state of corruption and sin he has fallen from that first state and has become like the beasts" (§131/434). Despite the difference in the registers, in both cases the twofold postulation is articulated in terms of the ambivalence of the infinity in man. Even when Pascal implicitly but clearly takes aim at Descartes for having exhibited, simply by the title *The Principles of Philosophy,* ". . . a presumption as infinite as [its] object" (§199/72), he does nothing more than turn against its author a warning first put forth by Descartes himself: "I have read M. Morin's book [*Quod Deus sit Mundusque ab ipso creatus fuerit in tempore, ejusque providentia gubernetur*]. Its main fault is that he always discusses the infinite as if he had completely mastered it and comprehended its properties. This is an almost universal fault which I have tried carefully to avoid. I have never written about the infinite except to submit myself to it, and not to determine what it is or is not."[17] Pascal's reproach reproduces that of Descartes, who, even if he did not always succeed in "carefully avoiding" the pretension of comprehending the infinite, at least always denounced it. Accordingly, this criterion is not enough for opposing Pascal to Descartes. On the contrary, we must not hesitate to conclude that *Meditatio III* determines Pascal's definition of God as radically as *Meditationes I* and *II* decided his notions of doubt and thought. In a word, Pascal's thought starts from Descartes and maintains metaphysical theses that are strictly in conformity with the Cartesian orthodoxy, at least in what is essential. What brings Pascal close to Descartes, conceptually, has been easier to establish—up until this point—than that which opposes them.

§22. Descartes Useless and Uncertain

By keeping the determination of God as infinite, Pascal seems to assume the Cartesian legacy. And in fact he does indeed bring it to its highest

16. On this doctrine, some suggestive passages can be found in *Sur la théologie blanche de Descartes,* §17, pp. 396–414.

17. *To Mersenne,* 28 January 1641 (AT III, 293, 20–27 = PW III, 171–72). The work of J.-B. Morin appeared in Paris in 1635. See also *To Mersenne,* 11 October 1638 (AT II, 383, 16–20 = PW III, 126), in which a similar reproach is made against Galileo. Pascal here

point of accomplishment. However, this very same treatment of the infinite could also mark an inversion of Pascal's relation to Descartes: the infinite, which does the best job of showing how close they are, also marks their first point of divergence. For Descartes, not only does God admit the qualification infinite, but he alone is worthy of it; every other being, even if it does not offer any limit to our (finite) knowledge, deserves to be qualified only as indefinite:

> Et hîc quidem distinguo inter *indefinitum* et *infinitum*, illudque tantum proprie *infinitum* appello, in quo nullâ ex parte limites inveniuntur: quo sensu solus Deus est infinitus; illa autem, in quibus sub aliqua tantum ratione finem non agnosco, ut extensio spatii imaginarii, multitudo numerorum, divisibilitas partium quantitatis, et similia, *indefinita* quidem appello, non autem *infinita*, quia non omni ex parte fine carent. [Now I make a distinction here between the *indefinite* and the *infinite*. I apply the term "infinite," in the strict sense, only to that in which no limits of any kind can be found; and in this sense God alone is infinite. But in cases like the extension of imaginary space, or the set of numbers, or the divisibility of the parts of a quantity, there is merely some respect in which I do not recognize a limit; so here I use the term "indefinite" rather than "infinite," because these items are not limitless in every respect.]

The infinite requires an absence of limits in an infinity of parameters, and not simply in just a single one of them. In the latter case, nonfinitude results directly from the conditions for the exercise of our finite mind, which privileges this or that parameter, in such a way as to produce this or that finitude, or, more exactly, this or that indefinite. The infinite appears, by contrast, when the absence of limits results from the positive self-affirmation of the infinite, transgressing every limit but also every parameter and every measure. But then ". . . nomen infiniti soli Deo reserv[a]mus [(We) reserve the term infinite for God alone]."[18] The distinction between the infinite (positive, in itself) and the indefinite (relative to knowledge, determined) furnished Descartes with three different determinations that could be used to compose an unconfused and undivided system of the three privileged beings of special metaphysics: infinite God, the finite *ego*, the indefinite world. In this system, the

---

follows Descartes exactly. H. Gouhier, *Blaise Pascal. Commentaires* (Paris, 1966, 1971), pp. 288*ff.*

18. *Responsiones I* (AT VII, 113, 1–8); then *Principia Philosophiae I*, §27 (= PW II, 81; then PW I, 202).

mediation of the infinite and indefinite (God and the world) can be guaranteed by the finite, since the *ego* on the one hand governs and produces the indefinite by representing it according to the *Mathesis universalis,* and on the other, knows—without comprehending it and by a reversal—the infinite whose idea it bears within it. Far from leading the finite *ego* into confusion, the question of the infinite/indefinite manifests its self-assurance. It is here that Pascal takes his leave of Descartes: he maintains the determination of God as infinite only while annulling the indispensable distinction between the infinite and the indefinite. That is, he constantly qualifies as infinite the very thing that Descartes would never have wanted to name otherwise than indefinite: "infinite immensity of spaces" (§68/205); "infinite spaces" (§201/206); "infinite sphere" (§199/72); "infinite . . . numbers" (§110/282; §663/121); "infinite speed" (§420/231); "infinite movement" (§682/232); etc. The infinite thus qualifies extension and the mathematical idealities in precisely the same way as it does God. This upheaval carries with it several consequences. *(a)* As the same title—infinite—refers to two terms as distinct as the world and God, it no longer counts as the name proper to God, nor as the first of divine names. What is the most decisive point according to Descartes thus finds itself reduced to playing the role of an index of the incommensurability between the finite *ego* and something else. God thus no longer has any proper name in the discourse of philosophy. To name him infinite says nearly nothing about him, or rather, it describes his relation to the *ego:* God cannot be measured by the *ego,* any more than an infinity of other notions could be. The crisis of the divine names is opened once again. *(b)* For the three privileged beings of special metaphysics, Pascal will avail himself of just two (and not three) determinations. It therefore becomes impossible to articulate them in a system, since each of the three could stake a claim to the infinite: God "by his own definition" (OC, 294 *a* = 125); the world and the mathematical idealities through (almost) infinitesimal calculus; and finally the *ego,* because, though properly finite, "man infinitely transcends man" (§131/434). The multiplied infinite annuls the system of the three privileged beings by rendering all possible mediations uniform and substituting for it only a "chaos and [a] monstrous confusion" (§208/435). We can anticipate and understand that nothing will ever be able to remedy this annulment of the three Cartesian mediations (finite/indefinite/infinite) between the three privileged beings of special metaphysics—except the acknowledgment of three orders, which are distinct to the point of being heterogeneous (flesh/mind/charity), but which will mediate nothing less than beings,

within nothing less than special metaphysics (*infra*, §23). Pascal's trivial-
izing the Cartesian infinite will thus summon forth, in turn, the distinction of several orders in the very place where the Cartesian method admitted just one. *(c)* The inflation in the occurrences of *infini* in the
Pensées attests to a weakening, not a deepening, of the concept of infinity. By an inversion of strict Cartesian usage, it will now be enough if the
end remains unknowable "sub aliquâ tantum ratione" for one to be able
to speak legitimately of infinity. At the same time as it marks a decisive
triumph in mathematics, the mathematical treatment of the infinite also
suggests a blatant regression in the thought of the positive and absolute
infinite such as Descartes understands it. In other words—to avoid all
misunderstanding—what can be apprehended in and through a calculus
does not, by definition, deserve the appellation infinite. Pascal passes
from the strong to the weak meaning of infinite. Must it be concluded
from this that his is a weak thought of the essence of the infinite? Perhaps, to be more precise, Pascal perceived the infinite as deprived of
essence: the infinite, or rather the infinity of infinites, is not given as a
concept to be thought, but as the index, constantly reformed, deformed,
and reformulated, of the absence of mediation between the *ego* and every other possible object. The infinite becomes a category of relation
between the *ego* and being, indeed of modality—the *ego* in the actual
situation of an impossibility of measuring the possible. That being the
case, infinite can be applied to an infinity of beings so long as they enter
into a nonmediated relation with the *ego*. The infinite is multiplied infinitely, not as an equivocal or weak concept, but as the metaphor for
the immeasurable situation of the *ego,* exiled in the incommensurable—
through which Pascal's opposition to Descartes is confirmed. With the
Mathesis universalis, the Cartesian *ego* has at hand a means of ordering
that guarantees that the beings reduced to the rank of objects can be
measured, with the sole exception of the *ego* itself and God (chapter IV,
§19). The Pascalian *self (moi)* is found universally and perpetually to be
situated in the midst of incommensurability (surrounded by an infinity
of infinites): the method of calculus can extend its sway over new domains (for example, the mathematical infinite itself), but it does not for
all that guarantee the least mediation between these infinites.[19] The infi-

19. The polysemy of the henceforth aporetic infinite was clearly analyzed by P. Magnard: "The double infinity has not only effaced every referent, confused all evaluation,
ruined all certitude, and broken all analogy, it has also introduced a discontinuity amidst
the rubble of a world which vainly is referred to their image without being able to totalize
it" ("L'infini pascalien," *Revue de l'enseignement philosophique* 31/1 [1981], p. [10], but

nite, sliding toward its weak sense, escapes all concepts—even and especially the concept in which Descartes wanted to establish it: namely, the being that the *Mathesis universalis* does not comprehend. God is said by the infinite, for Pascal as for Descartes; but for Pascal, infinite no longer says anything, while for Descartes it utters a privileged concept. From now on, as the infinite is dissolved, God, drawing back in the same degree, fades away. His nameless silence abandons the discourse—grown idle, gregarious, and vain—of the sciences, and first of all of metaphysics.

This break is clearly marked in an almost automatic refusal on the part of Pascal: that of the proofs for the existence of God, whichever one might be at issue. It is not so much a question of refusing natural theology as it is of disqualifying the metaphysical discourse applied to God. This at least is how contemporary witnesses understood it: "He claimed to show that the Christian religion had as many marks of certainty as the things which are accepted in the world as being the most indubitable. For that reason, he did not make use of metaphysical proofs..." (Gilberte Périer); "After he has explained to them what he thought about the proofs which were customarily used, and showed how ... men's minds are barely fit for metaphysical reasonings, he will show clearly that there are only moral and historical proofs..., which are within men's capability" (Filleau de la Chaise).[20] There is a still more

---

also *Nature et histoire dans l'apologétique de Pascal* [Paris, 1975 1st ed., 1980 2d ed.], pp. 13*ff*., 47–58, 98–110, etc.).

20. Respectively G. Périer, *La Vie de Monsieur Pascal* (Paris, 1686, and *OC*, p. 24 *b*); then Filleau de la Chaise, *Discours sur les pensées de M. Pascal* (Paris, 1672), in *Blaise Pascal, Pensées sur la religion et sur quelques autres sujets. Introduction de Louis Lafuma* (Paris, 1952), vol. 3, p. 92. These texts can also be compared favorably with this one from E. Périer:

It is quite to the point, it seems to me, for the sake of disabusing those persons who perhaps are expecting to find in this work proofs and geometrical demonstrations for the existence of God, the immortality of the soul and several other articles of the Christian faith, to warn them that this was not the plan of M. Pascal. He did not pretend to prove all these truths of religion by those sorts of demonstrations, founded on evident principles, capable of convincing the stubbornness of even the most hardened, nor by metaphysical reasonings ... but by moral proofs which go more to the heart than to the mind.

(*Préface* to the Port-Royal edition, 1670, and in *Blaise Pascal. Pensées sur la religion...*, op. cit., vol. 3, p. 142.) Following P. Magnard, it must be emphasized that, in refusing proofs, "never had an apologist gone so far...; Pascal's entourage tried to limit the scandal to which such intransigence could not fail to give rise: Gilberte Périer in the *Vie* of his brother, Etienne Périer in his preface to the Port-Royal edition and in the corrections made to the text of the *Pensées*, Pierre Nicole in several engagements, all try to pass off as an omission what must in fact be seen as an exclusion" (*Nature et histoire dans l'apologétique de Pascal,*

remarkable point to note: in all the *Pensées,* the term *métaphysique* remains a *hapax,* but a *hapax* that qualifies precisely the (metaphysical) proofs for the existence of God and that, moreover, is found in a "Preface," and therefore has the authority of a declaration of principles: "*Preface.* The metaphysical proofs for the existence of God are so remote from human reasoning and so involved that they make little impact, and, even if they did help some people, it would only be for the moment during which they watched the demonstration, because an hour later they would be afraid they had made a mistake" (§190/543). The allusion to Descartes seems clear to us: it is a question of remembering evidences and, eventually, of the objection of the circle (raised by Arnauld, as Pascal knew). In this way, Pascal radically casts into question the Cartesian goal not just of demonstrating the existence of God, but also of *adorare* (AT VII, 52, 16 = PW II, 36), of worshiping him, by following the metaphysical paths of the demonstration. After having shattered the pretense that the infinite had to determining a first divine name in metaphysics, Pascal contests the legitimacy of any metaphysical attempt in general to win access to God. In short, metaphysics cannot know God because it does not have to know about him. We will therefore not be concerned with Pascal's critique of the physical proofs for the existence of God, by which the Thomists are perhaps intended.[21] We will, however, examine the critique of the metaphysical proofs with the intention of deciding if and to what degree it finally touches on Descartes' special metaphysics such as we have reconstructed it in relation to God. We will pose two questions: *(a)* Do the reproaches made against the metaphysical proofs correspond to the reproaches addressed to Descartes in particular? *(b)* Is there a Cartesian proof that is cited literally and contested as such? Let us consider the first question *(a).* A first reproach is made, futility: "The metaphysical proofs for the existence of God are so remote from

---

op. cit., p. 304). See also the carefully considered explanation by P. Cahné, *Pascal ou le risque de l'espérance* (Paris, 1981), pp. 54–58.

21. On the refusal of the physical proofs, see §781/242 and §463/243: "It is a remarkable fact that no canonical author has ever used nature to prove God. They all try to make people believe in him. David, Solomon, etc., never said: 'There is no such thing as a vacuum, therefore God exists.' They must have been cleverer than the cleverest of their successors, all of whom have used proofs from nature. This is very noteworthy." It happens to be the case, however, that at least two canonical authors have in fact constructed a physical line of reasoning, if not a physical proof: Wisdom 13:5, ἐκ γὰρ μεγέθους καὶ καλλονῆς κτισμάτων ἀναλόγως ὁ γενεσιουργός αὐτῶν θεωρεῖται and Romans 1:20. Pascal is perhaps targeting the Thomistic *viae* (*Summa Theologiae, Ia,* q. 2. a. 3, *c*), but especially the apologists of Mersenne's stripe (see *Sur la théologie blanche de Descartes,* §9, pp. 161–78).

human reasoning and so involved that they make little impact . . ." (§190/ 543); and: "All those who have claimed to know God and prove his existence without Jesus Christ have only had futile proofs to offer" (§189/ 547). But often, a second lament is added to the theoretical futility, uselessness: "It is not only impossible, but useless to know God without Christ" (§191/549), and: "Knowing God without knowing our own wretchedness makes for pride" (§192/527); and especially: "That is why I shall not undertake here to prove by reasons from nature either the existence of God, or the Trinity or the immortality of the soul, or anything of that kind: not just because I should not feel competent to find in nature arguments which would convince hardened atheists, but also because such knowledge, without Christ, is useless and sterile" (§449/ 556). The "metaphysical proofs of God" by "reasons from nature" are thus susceptible to two objections: on the one hand, their difficulty and their imperfection make them hardly convincing, that is to say "futile," therefore uncertain; on the other hand, they do not make one enter into the mystery of Jesus Christ, God, and God who saves us from sin—that is to say, they are "useless" (§191/549; §449/556). Therefore, it will at once be asked: are they all *de facto* uncertain? Pascal admits the contrary at least once, since he does seem to put forth a proof: "I feel that it is possible that I might never have existed, for my self consists in my thought; therefore I who think would never have been if my mother had been killed before I had come to life; therefore I am not a necessary being. I am not eternal or infinite either, but I can see that there is in nature a being who is necessary, eternal, and infinite" (§135/469). Here one can easily recognize the "popular" version of the *a posteriori* proof in *Meditatio III*. As in this proof, Pascal repeats the argument based on the fact that the idea of infinity is inherent to the *ego* in that it acknowledges itself "a parentibus productus [produced . . . by my parents]" (AT VII, 49, 21–50, 6 = 34). Certain readers will even recognize in this argument an Augustinian line of argument—a reading that does not contradict the first suspected source.[22] For these two reasons, shouldn't this proof be accepted as convincing? But looking more closely, even if one supposes that its evidence lasts more "than an hour," this proof would not make Jesus Christ known, and would thus deploy a useless certainty. Pascal himself perfectly illustrates this twofold requirement in the fragment "Infinity—nothing," the so-called "argument of the wager." It is

---

22. We here follow P. Sellier, *Pascal et saint Augustin* (Paris, 1970), pp. 57–58, and refer to E. Gilson, *Introduction à l'étude de saint Augustin* (Paris, 1928), pp. 11–30.

composed of three moments: first, the metaphysical argument, which, sketched in outline, starts from the finite and concludes with the infinite (in the Cartesian manner of §135/469): "We know that the infinite exists without knowing its nature ... Therefore we may well know that God exists without knowing what he is"; second, for the perhaps certain proof not to founder in uselessness, it is repeated in a way that makes a greater impact, and ends with success: "This is conclusive and if men are capable of any truth this is it"; however, the "conclusive" success does not do away with a third moment, the sole fundamental one: "... Pray this infinite and indivisible being ... that he might bring your being also to submit to him for your own good and for his glory" (§418/233). Pascal therefore admits at least one certain metaphysical demonstration, and the ever so trivial reproach of irrationality or fideism counts for naught. But to this proof he appends a second attempt, one that is all the more indispensable insofar as the rational attempt succeeded: namely, to double the compulsion imposed by evidence with the move of faith, or, more precisely, with God's assistance in believing in him. The uselessness would be all the more glaring if, at the end of a compelling and rigorous metaphysical proof, the interlocutor refused to engage his faith in God. Even though convinced, if he does not abandon himself, "I should not consider that he made much progress towards his salvation" (§449/556). The metaphysical proofs pose an even greater danger (thus uselessness) as they are held to be certain. We are now in a position to clarify the significance of the suspected uselessness: the goal and the stakes of a discourse on God are not summed up in the knowledge of God; knowing God even exposes one to a fearful danger: pride. It is not a matter of either first or only knowing God, but of loving him. Loving him implies recognizing his glory and admitting that the sin of men hides him; thus it implies having recourse to Christ, who, at one and the same time, reveals God, that he is, and frees us from the sin that we are. The pride of knowing God (deism) does not draw any closer to God than does ignorance of him (atheism), for the knowledge of God is made worthy only by loving him: "... at the same time [as we know Jesus Christ our true God] we know our own wretchedness, because this God is nothing less than our redeemer from wretchedness. Thus we can know God properly only by knowing our own iniquities. Those who have known God without knowing their own wretchedness have not glorified him but themselves" (§189/547); or: "*Quod curiositate cognoverunt, superbia amiserunt* (What they gained by curiosity they lost through pride) [Augustine, *Sermo* 141]. That is the result of knowing God without Christ, in other words of communicating without a mediator with the God known without a mediator. Whereas those who have known God through a mediator know their own wretchedness" (§190/543); and finally:

> ... It is equally dangerous for man to know God without knowing his own wretchedness as to know his own wretchedness without knowing the Redeemer who can cure him. Knowing only one of these points leads either to the arrogance of the philosophers, who have known God but not their own wretchedness, or to the despair of the atheists who know their own wretchedness without knowing their Redeemer. . . . All those who seek God apart from Christ, and who go no further than nature . . . fall into either atheism or deism, two things almost equally abhorrent to Christianity. [§449/556.]

Thus, in place of the metaphysical stakes of the proofs for the existence of God—Does God exist or not? Which name defines his essence?—Pascal puts at stake something entirely different, something of which metaphysics cannot not be unaware, since it mobilizes a parameter that is a stranger to the question of the Being of beings: do I love God, to the point of renouncing my pride and my sin (which are the same) for the sake of approaching him? The ultimate question is no longer pursued in view of grasping the relation between God, the being par excellence, and existence in general, but in view of the relation between man and his own pride (or sin), thus between man and charity (Jesus Christ). The irruption of the parameter instituted by charity or pride disqualifies the pretense that metaphysical discourse has to posing the highest question about God. With respect to God, it is not a matter of knowing if he exists or not, as if *to be/to exist* would benefit, vis-à-vis God, from an unconditioned and unquestionable precedence and a similar excellence. In contrast, faced with God, *to be/to exist* are seen as one idol among others, though no doubt the most radical, since it permits the metaphysician to dodge, by dissimulating, the reversal of the interrogation. With Pascal, this interrogation, far from setting out from the metaphysician and heading toward God (who will be charged with the task of establishing his rights to existence), is now deployed from God to man, who has been despoiled of the ontological idol and charged with the task of deciding if he loves God—or not. God no longer has to prove his existence before the metaphysician so much as the latter, unveiled in his humanity, has to decide if he can say "'Lord, I give you all'" (§919/553). In this way, a metaphysical proof can indeed be called useless, even if, extraordinarily, it offers all the certainty in the world. It is enough that it provoke pride

and forbid salvation: ". . . salvation or something of no use . . ." (§859/
852), ". . . useless for salvation . . ." (§110/282). For it remains "useless to
know God without Jesus Christ" (§191/549); ". . . such knowledge without Christ is useless and sterile" (§449/556). In this context, the rejection
"Descartes useless and uncertain" (§887/78) becomes understandable.
Though illustrated more broadly with regard to his physical theory—
"*Descartes.* In general terms one must say: 'That is the result of figure
and motion,' because it is true, but to name them and assemble the machine is quite ridiculous. It is pointless, uncertain, and arduous" (§84/
79)—in this case as in the majority of its other occurrences, uselessness
refers to the love of God, the sole thing that is necessary. Pascal does
not reproach Descartes for ignoring God, but for knowing him only for
the purpose of using him to regulate the machine of the world, far from
submitting to him. "I cannot forgive Descartes: he really did want, in all
his philosophy, to be able to pass over God; but he was unable to stop
himself from assigning to him the brief role of putting the world into
motion; after that, he no longer has anything to do with God" (§1001).
What makes Descartes useless—for salvation—is that he puts God at
the service of knowing, instead of knowing God in order to put himself
at his service. In this way, he furnishes the paradigm of the "useless curiosity" (§744/18 [modified]) of the other sciences.[23] Descartes misses the
question of God, not just because his metaphysical proofs remain uncertain, but above all because they remain useless for salvation—in short,
because they simply do not see that with God, it is less an issue of his
existence than of our decision concerning him. In this way, we have established that Pascal's objections to the "metaphysical proofs of God"
take aim at Descartes' metaphysics, paradigmatically.

This demonstration will remain insufficient, however, as long as we
have not answered the second question: *(b)* Is there a Cartesian proof
that Pascal cites literally and criticizes? In the absence of such verifica-

23. For example, *To Fermat,* 10 August 1660: "For to speak to you frankly about geometry, I consider it to be the highest exercise of the mind, but at the same time I know it to
be so unprofitable that I make little distinction between a man who is merely a geometrician and a skillful artisan" (*OC,* 282 *b* = 216). And "No human science can keep it [the
order]. St. Thomas did not keep it. Mathematics keeps it, but it goes so far as to be useless"
(§694/61). The complaint addressed to Descartes pertains first to his uselessness for salvation, not to his theoretical uncertainty: "Descartes. . . . Even if it were true we do not think
that the whole of philosophy would be worth an hour's effort" (§89/74). And for that
matter, the first, subsequently erased, version of §887/297 reads: "*decarde inutile et cer-
tenne,*" which is to say "Descartes useless and certain" (see *Blaise Pascal. Pensées sur la
religion . . . ,* op. cit., vol. 1, p. 472).

tion, the complaint of uselessness could be applied to Cartesian thought only in a very general way, without affecting the special metaphysics of *Meditatio III*—as we want to claim it does. Now, it seems to us that such a citation does indeed appear, preceded and followed by a decisive critique, in a fragment of the utmost importance, §449/556. In it, Pascal shows that "the Christian religion consists of two points," and not just one: ". . . There is a God of whom men are capable . . . , there is a corruption in nature which makes them unworthy." Consequently, simply the knowledge of the existence of a God does not make one Christian; to the contrary, it makes one deist. Thus, men ". . . imagine that it [the Christian religion] consists simply in worshipping a God considered to be great and mighty and eternal, which is properly speaking deism. . . ." Among men, it is the philosophers who, par excellence, commit this error: "Knowing only one of these points leads either to the arrogance of the philosophers, who have known God but not their own wretchedness, or to the despair of the atheists, who know their own wretchedness without knowing their Redeemer." Thus Pascal cites the project of special metaphysics explicitly, in order to contest it. As Pascal presents it, this project includes that which the title of Descartes' *Meditationes* announces: ". . . I shall not undertake here to prove by reasons from nature either the existence of God, or the Trinity or the immortality of the soul, or anything of that kind. . . ." This text from Pascal is opposed word for word—or almost so, making an exception of the Trinity—to the Cartesian project, a project that Descartes specifies in two points, both equally unacceptable to Pascal: *Meditationes de prima Philosophia in qua Dei existentia et animae immortalitas demonstrantur* [*Meditations on first philosophy in which are demonstrated the existence of God and the immortality of the soul*]. First: ". . . I deal not just with God and the soul, but in general with all the first things that can be known by philosophizing according to the order"—which anticipates "anything of that kind."[24] Especially to the point here is the opening of Descartes' address to the Sorbonne: "Semper existimavi duas quaestiones, de Deo et de anima, praecipuas esse ex iis quae Philosophiae potius quam Theologiae ope sunt demonstrandae [I have always thought that two topics—namely God and the soul—are prime examples of subjects where demonstrative proofs ought to be given with the aid of philosophy rather than theology]" (AT VII, 1, 7–9 = PW II, 3). This is precisely what Pascal will not hesitate to

---

24. *To Mersenne,* 11 November 1640 (AT III, 239, 5–7 = PW III, 158 [modified]). See *supra,* chap. I, §3.

qualify as "blasphemy": to claim to deal in a strictly philosophical rigor with what belongs first of all to charity, thus to theology. The Cartesian project mentioned here once again falls under the accusation of constructing a ". . . knowledge, without Christ, [that] is useless and sterile." To radically disqualify the metaphysical project concerning God, Pascal will cite Descartes directly, and, what is most remarkable, he will cite Descartes' most original thesis, the thesis that was the least well received by his successors and that was no doubt the most powerful: namely, the doctrine of the creation of the eternal truths advanced in the three *Letters to Mersenne* of 15 April, 6 May, and 27 May 1630. Let us follow the central line of argument in §449/556. *(a)* As soon as the "useless" knowledge has been stigmatized, Pascal adds: "Even if someone were convinced that the proportions between numbers are immaterial, *eternal truths, depending* on a *first truth* in which they subsist, called *God,* I should not consider that he has made much progress towards his salvation." He is citing Descartes literally (we have emphasized the common words): "The mathematical *truths* which you call *eternal* have been laid down by *God* and *depend* on him entirely no less than the rest of his creatures . . ." (AT I, 145, 7–10 = PW III, 23); and also: ". . . the existence of *God* is the *first* and the most *eternal* of all possible *truths* and the one from which alone all others proceed" (AT I, 150, 2–4 = PW III, 24). One will also grant, in addition, the equivalence of "the proportions between numbers" and the "mathematical truths." *(b)* Pascal continues: "The Christian's *God* does not consist merely of a *God* who is the *author* of the mathematical *truths* and the order of the elements. That is the portion of the heathens and Epicureans." Descartes wrote: "It is certain that he is the *author* of the essence of things no less than of their existence; and this essence is nothing other than the eternal *truths*" (AT I, 152, 2–5 = PW III, 25). Moreover, by the very definition of God in which Pascal sees a "blasphemy" and "the portion of the heathens and Epicureans," Descartes means to avoid a "blasphemy" (AT I, 149, 26 = PW III, 24) that is characteristic of pagan philosophers: "Indeed to say that these truths are independent of God is to talk of him as if he were Jupiter or Saturn and to subject him to the Styx and the Fates" (AT I, 145, 10–13 = PW III, 23). The effort through which Descartes attempts to extricate himself from a pagan definition of God thus appears to Pascal as the pagan blasphemy par excellence. *(c)* There is more. In the end, Pascal mentions as the "portion of the Jews" a second notion: "He [God] does not consist merely of a God who extends his *providence* over the life and property of men so as to grant a happy span of years to those who worship him." Here again, there is perhaps an allusion to Descartes, who, in the final travail of his own thought, acknowledged another determination of God, no longer theoretical but practical, one that he names providence: "... We should reflect upon the fact that nothing can possibly happen other than as *Providence* has determined from all eternity. *Providence* is, so to speak, a fate or immutable necessity"; or: "... There is a God on whom all things *depend,* whose perfections are infinite, whose power is immense and whose decrees are infallible. This teaches us to accept calmly all the things which happen to us as expressly sent by God."[25] This conception of God is still governed by the preceding one, whose founding omnipotence it maintains and modulates. Thus, Pascal does cite Descartes, and does so in a way that is all the more significant as he chooses his most original, least well known, and strongest line of argumentation.[26] Thus, once again the obviously Cartesian enterprise of constructing "metaphysical proofs of God" (§190/543) loses all legitimacy before the sole God to be known. "But the God of Abraham, the God of Isaac, the God of Jacob, the God of the Christians is a God of love and consolation: he is a God who fills the soul and the heart of those whom he possesses." And, not in metaphysics but in Jesus Christ, "... everything blazes with proofs. ..." At the very moment when metaphysics reaches the God who is creator of eternal truths and thereby completes its greatest attempt at abolishing the conceptual idol, it becomes lost and goes astray—before "the presence of a hidden God" (§449/556).

Through an examination of the texts, we have established that the antagonism between Descartes and Pascal concerns the legitimacy of a metaphysical proof (and thus of a metaphysical name) for God. We have

25. Respectively, *The Passions of the Soul,* §145 (AT XI, 438, 2–7), and *To Elisabeth,* 15 September 1645 (AT IV, 291, 20– 26 = PW I, 380 and PW III, 265).

26. Two reasons give cause to suppose that the *Letters to Mersenne* could have been accessible to Pascal. Indirectly, for Descartes recommended that Mersenne make his feelings known widely: "Please do not hesitate to assert and proclaim everywhere that it is God who has laid down these laws in nature just as a king lays down laws in his kingdom" (AT I, 145, 13–16 = PW III, 23); and we know that if Mersenne knew how "to proclaim everywhere" the opinions of his correspondents, this thesis would hit the critics in no time (Spinoza, Malebranche, before Leibniz)—Pascal making no exception. Beginning in 1635, wasn't he a frequent attendee at the circle that Mersenne gathered and for which Descartes wrote? Also, he could have had direct access to these *Letters* through the edition of the *Correspondance* from Clerselier. The first volume—*Lettres de M. Descartes où sont traitées les plus belles questions de la Morale, Physique, Médicine et des Mathématiques* (Paris, 1657)—contains the *Letters* of 6 and 27 May, while the second volume—*Lettres de M. Descartes où sont expliquées plusieurs difficultés touchant ses autres ouvrages ...* (Paris,

also identified the theoretical reason for this refusal: according to Pascal "the Christian's God" can be known only in Jesus Christ, inseparably God and redeemer, precisely because man remains at the same time capable of God by nature and incapable of God by sin; accordingly, for man to pretend to know God without Jesus Christ amounts to denying his sin—and there is no sin greater than this. To construct a metaphysical proof for God thus amounts to "blaspheming." This twofold result, how-ever, does not yet allow us to understand why Pascal chooses to cite and refute precisely the Cartesian doctrine of God the creator of the eternal truths. This choice is surprising because it concerns texts that are less accessible and less well known than those of the *Meditationes,* and it is especially surprising because it seems possible (and this was our own position) that the "evident proof" (AT I, 181, 29 = PW III, 29) given in 1630 sacrifices less to metaphysics than the two other proofs and divine names, which operate strictly within an onto-theo-logy: God as *ens per-fectissimum* in the onto-theo-logy of the *ens ut cogitatum,* God as *causa sui* in an onto-theo-logy of the *ens ut causatum.* It used to seem (and still can) that the "incomprehensible power" of 1630 (AT I, 146, 4–5 and 150, 22 = PW III, 23 and 25), just like the *idea infiniti* of 1641 that it foreshad-ows, stands at a remarkable distance from all metaphysical interpretation of God—and in both cases, Descartes emphasizes as much as he possibly can that he is opposed to the "blasphemy" of the pagans and that his

---

1659)—includes the *Letter* of 15 April. One must neither rule out nor abuse the hypothesis, verified in the case of the *Regulae,* that copies of the letters circulated among the interested and the curious.

That Pascal had at least an indirect acquaintance with the Cartesian doctrine of a God who created the eternal truths found abundant confirmation in the manuscript (BN ms. 43333, new acquisitions) published by E. Griselle (in *Pascal et les pascalins d'après de documents contemporains,* extracts from the *Revue de Fribourg,* 1908). It comprises a col-lection of reflections having diverse origin but put forth in a circle of Pascal's friends or acquaintances—in short, of ". . . the opinion of a certain intellectual circle contemporane-ous with Pascal and concerned with his work" (op. cit., p. 2). The allusions and discussions of the thesis of 1630 are not absent. "Descartes has a dry and stoic morality. He says that God established the eternal truths and the propositions of eternal truth, and that he could make a thing not be, that the parts be greater than the whole, that a square be a triangle. According to him, one could say that God, having clear knowledge of God, could even make it that he would not be himself" (fol. 70–71, op. cit., p. 21). "What is good in the philosophy of Des Cartes is that one can barely go farther. Beyond, there are only abysses. Des Cartes shows where the mind can go, and we can confine ourselves there and add new experiences to it" (fol. 79 verso, op. cit., p. 79). "Des Cartes. He grants to the mind the knowledge of God by a mode which God gives to life. He believed that God could create us with ideas contrary to those that we have. M. Paschal called him the Doctor of reason" (fol. 182, op. cit., p. 61, text already noted by L. Lafuma in *Blaise Pascal. Pensées . . . ,*

knowledge is for purposes of *admirari, adorare* (AT VII, 52, 15–16 = PW II, 36). Far from Pascal seeing this already somewhat heroic effort as an overcoming of the metaphysical interpretation of God, or at least the suggestion of such an overcoming, he directs the brunt of his critique against it, without any concessions or reservations. Why then does Descartes remain "useless"? Why does he not succeed, like Plato, to whom Pascal does concede as much (§612/219), in "disposing people towards Christianity"? Confronted with this difficulty, a considerable one at that, all anecdotal answers—ignorance, misunderstanding—would be unacceptable. We will risk two arguments, in the expectation of a more fundamental reflection. *(a)* The Cartesian thesis of an omnipotent God who passes beyond every creature and all rationality can seem even less Christian to Pascal as he perhaps read it in the writings of Montaigne, who attributed it to the pagans. That is, the *Apology for Raimon Sebond* anticipates Descartes: "Of all the ancient human opinions concerning religion, that one, it seems to me, was most probable and most excusable which recognized God as an incomprehensible power, origin and preserver of all things, all goodness, all perfection." According to Montaigne, Saint Paul on the Areopagus would have welcomed this conception by evoking the "hidden God," and "Pythagoras adumbrated truth more closely in judging that the knowledge of this first cause, and being of beings, must be undefined, unprescribed, undeclared."[27] And from this Montaigne concludes, in the style of Descartes, the impossibility of confining God within the limits of our understanding: "What! Has God placed in our hands the keys and ultimate springs of his power? Has he pledged himself not to overstep the bounds of our knowledge?"; "I do not think it is good to confine the divine power thus under the laws of our speech"; "How rashly have they [the Stoics] bound God to destiny (I would that none bearing the surname of Christian would still do it!), and Thales, Plato, and Pythagoras have made him a slave to necessity!";

---

op. cit., vol. 2, p. 168). L. Brunschvicg had precisely, though allusively, indicated Pascal's opposition to the creation of the eternal truths (*Descartes et Pascal lecteurs de Montaigne* [Neuchâtel, 1940], pp. 188*ff.*). The same rapprochement we are making here had been put forth and then retracted by H. Gouhier, "Le refus de la philosophie dans la nouvelle apologétique de Pascal," *Chroniques de Port-Royal* 20–21 (1972), p. 30, n. 35.

27. Montaigne, *Essais II,* 12, in *Œuvres complètes,* ed. R. Barral and P. Michel (Paris, 1967), p. 213 *a* and *b* [English trans., pp. 380 and 381]. It is all the more likely that Pascal did indeed read this page, as it quite certainly contains the source of §513/4: "An ancient who was reproached for professing philosophy, of which nevertheless in his mind he took no great account, replied that this was being a true philosopher" (*OC,* p. 212 *b* [English trans., p. 379]).

or: "this fancy, that human reason is controller-general of all that is outside and inside the heavenly vault, embracing everything, capable of
everything, by means of which everything is known and understood."[28]
If Montaigne had thus held, oftentimes to the benefit of the pagans
(Pythagoras, Epicurus), the very doctrine that Descartes took up to the
benefit of the Christians, Pascal can reasonably doubt that this doctrine
establishes a clear boundary between the idols and the "Christian's
God"—whence his refusal to read it as a privileged metaphysical proof,
even though Descartes had used it to overcome the more essentially
metaphysical proofs and divine names. *(b)* This external criticism is not
sufficient to our purposes, however; for Pascal could have read Descartes
without thinking about Montaigne. But it seems possible to make a second argument, internal to the reasoning Pascal has put at play here. The
very text that uses the *hapax "métaphysique"* (§190/543) also calls attention to the *curiositas* that "is the result of knowing God without Christ"
and thereby imagining that one knows God all too clearly, by having
dispensed with also admitting the wretchedness owed to sin. The text
that criticizes the Cartesian doctrine of the God who is creator of the
eternal truths (§449/556) also takes up this reproach and puts it more
precisely. Knowing God requires, in truth, knowing not one but "two
truths alike: that there is a God, of whom men are capable, and that there
is a corruption in nature which makes them unworthy." Consequently, to
reach God amounts to progressing toward a "God who does not manifest himself to men with as much evidence as he might [modified]" precisely on account of man's sin. At issue is a knowledge that knows not
according to evidence, but according to the half-light of a "presence of
a hidden God." In short, "one must see and not see." By contrast, the
goal of all metaphysics concerned with God, and of Cartesian metaphysics more so than any other, consists in knowing with all the evidence
in, knowing without remainder, without confusion, without any appeal
elsewhere. In each of his proofs, Descartes aims for and lays claim to the
evident knowledge of God. In 1630 first of all, it is a matter of "proving
metaphysical truths in a manner which is more evident than the proofs
of geometry" (AT I, 144, 15–17 = PW III, 22). During the proof by the

---

28. *Essais II*, 12, op. cit., respectively pp. 217 *b*, 219 *a* and *b*, and 225 *a* [English trans.,
pp. 389, 392, 393, and 404]. See also *I*, 27, *OC*, pp. 85 *b* and 86 *b*. The necessity of taking
a detour through Descartes caused B. Croquette to omit these observations. His work
nonetheless is exemplary in calling to mind the direct correspondences between the two.
See *Pascal et Montaigne. Etude des réminiscences des Essais dans l'oeuvre de Pascal*
(Paris, 1974).

idea infiniti, this idea (and the knowledge that it allows) is given as *maxime clara et distincta* (AT VII, 46, 8 = PW II, 31). During the *a priori* proof, the *ens summe perfectum* appears as the most clear of all beings: "... Nihil illo prius aut facilius agnoscerem; nam quid est apertius? [I would certainly acknowledge [God] sooner and more easily than anything else. For what is more self-evident?] ..." (AT VII, 69, 6–7 = PW II, 47). During the proof of the *causa sui,* Descartes relies on a *dictat* ("Dictat autem profecto lumen naturae [However the light of nature does dictate] ..." AT VII, 108, 18–19= PW II, 78) that anticipates the principle of reason, a *dictat* that the natural light decrees as a common notion that is indisputable (AT VII, 164, 27 = PW II, 116) and manifest to all (AT VII, 238, 13–14 = PW II, 166). For Descartes, the knowledge of God is accomplished in the evidence because first of all it accomplishes the evidence itself: in order to know God, one must first, always, and only know; and if it is then fitting to worship him, indeed to love him, this will be possible and justified only on the basis of a knowledge that is certain because it is clear and distinct. Here resides the blasphemy and the idolatry in the eyes of Pascal, for whom the love of God precedes and renders knowledge of him possible, since whoever reasons with regard to God thinks, whether he knows it or not, in a theoretical situation affected by the "wretchedness" of sin. "Truth is so obscured ... that unless we love the truth we shall never be able to know it" (§739/864 [modified]). The very fact that knowledge is directed from the objects of the world toward God imposes upon it a sort of epistemological conversion—renouncing the horizon of evidence for that of love. Not that love dispenses with knowing or requires some sacrifice of intelligibility, but love becomes, instead of and in the place of *intuitus,* the keeper of evidence, the royal road to knowledge: "When speaking of things human, we say that we should know them before loving them—a saying which has become proverbial. Yet the saints, on the contrary, when speaking of things divine, say that we should love them in order to know them, and that we enter into truth only through charity" (OC, p. 355 *a* = 203 [modified]). Metaphysics is widowed of the thought of God—less on account of the insufficiency of its procedures and the unadaptability of its concepts (it incessantly refines and amends them—Descartes has shown as much) than by its epistemological and methodological failing: it still claims to base itself on a method of evidence when it aims to elevate itself, as if by a theoretical Jacob's ladder, to God. But from the moment the question of God is opened, the method and, more radically, the gaze on evidence lose all efficacy. Better, the "Christian's God" would not become accessible to charity alone, if he were not exhausted in it. To have the pretense of knowing him without loving him amounts to missing, from the outset and on principle, both the destination and the road. Metaphysics is closed to God precisely because it wants to reach him with full certainty and total evidence. Between evidence and charity, one must choose. What separates Pascal and Descartes is nothing less than this choice. And this choice separates them infinitely, for "What a long way it is between knowing God and loving him!" (§377/280).[29]

§23. The Distance between the Orders

Confronted with metaphysics, such as Descartes represents it for him, Pascal takes a step back, the very step that separates knowledge (of God) from love (of God). This step back clears the way, for the first time, for a "distance" (§308/793). But naming this "distance" is not enough for conceiving it, and especially not for justifying it. Before Pascal had crossed, in reverse, the gap that separates him from Cartesian metaphysics, we had no notion of it, nor did we even suspect its possibility: the evidence of evidence still seemed unsurpassable and unalterable; the "metaphysical proofs for the existence of God" (§190/543) always provided the ultimate goal. Therefore, to understand Pascal's critique, we must not only give a name to his endeavor, but—without falling back on the foolish things commonly said about his excited nature, his fideism, and his irrationalism—we must repeat it step by step. In other words, it is a question of laying bare the fundamental operation that allows Pascal to leave metaphysics destitute—that is to say, either to drive its concepts to madness, or to contest them. Drive its concepts to madness: as when the infinite passed from the status of divine name and privileged determination of God to being the endlessly multiplied index of the incommensurability between the shattered elements of what can no longer be named a cosmos; from concept, it finds itself lowered to the rank of a metaphor used to undo other concepts. Contest its concepts: "evidence," "metaphysical proofs," "author of the mathematical proofs," "providence," "principles," "philosophy," etc., are disqualified at one fell swoop,

---

29. It must be noted, however, that Pascal passes over in silence the distinction between evidence obtained by the method ("to comprehend") and evidence seen without the method ("to understand"), a distinction that, however, is essential according to Descartes (see *supra,* chap. IV, §§19–20). On the conflict between evidence and charity, see our essay "De connaître à aimer: l'éblouissement," *Revue catholique internationale. Communio* III/4 (1978).

without any conceptual refutation ever justifying this disqualification; everything happens as if, for the rational discussion, Pascal substitutes a blunt refusal that annuls the thesis without paying it the least bit of attention. In either case, the debate did not take place: metaphysics was disqualified, not really destroyed. How then are we not to conclude that the critique is merely an ideological or fanatic violence? Precisely by trying to accomplish the step back from metaphysics that alone freed Pascal from having to debate with metaphysics, because from now on he *saw* it from a place that was decidedly foreign to it. As long as this place is not identified and—at least in its nascent stages—reached, as long as we have not really succeeded in completing the backward movement to whose terminal point Pascal precedes us, we will be able to see it only as a senseless violence. Step back [*Pas en retrait*]: one could even say a retreat [*une retraite*], for Pascal's step back from metaphysics (in its Cartesian guise) borrows its status at once from a religious retreat—to divert one's attention from the world so as to no longer be diverted from God—and from a military retreat—to refuse to fight an all too frightening adversary. Here the step back from metaphysics does not go back to the nonmetaphysical origin of metaphysics; it attempts to reach a land other than metaphysics itself. Whence the difficulty of Pascal's enterprise—a continual turning from one authority to another—but also that of his interpreter, who must again and again put back into relation, so as to understand their "distance," two terms that all Pascal's effort was directed at separating. The ambivalence of "distance," inseparably a gap and a common station, here becomes what is at stake in the debate and also its condition.[30] The question thus would be announced in these terms: does Pascal know that he leaves metaphysics destitute of its status as primordial science? And if he knows it, does he risk an open confrontation with it, be it only once? We hold that this is indeed the case in fragment §308/793, the one devoted to the three orders. Before any examination, it is wise to emphasize a massive, though disguised, fact: the three orders take up the three objects of special metaphysics. The first order assembles "the bodies," that is to say the world, by which one understands the cosmos of powers, goods, and "things," or that one interprets as the extension found in physics. The second order concerns the

---

30. Let us be permitted to make use of the essential ambivalence of "distance" such as we elaborated it in *L'idole et la distance* (Paris, 1977). H. Urs von Balthasar also insists on it, but with the obvious sense of a separation (*Abstand*), *Herrlichkeit*. Bd. II, *Fächer der Style* (Einsiedeln, 1962), pp. 561 and 579.

soul, as most probably an immortal understanding: Archimedes, the "great geniuses," ". . . outward shows of knowledge," "the curious and the scholars [whose] interest is in the mind" (§933/460). The third order concerns God, either in the person of Jesus Christ, ". . . humble, patient, thrice holy to God, terrible to devils and without sin," or directly: "[The saints] are seen by God and the angels, and not by bodies or by curious minds. God is enough for them." This confrontation cannot be underestimated; for not only does it testify that, in fact, Pascal brought together the three objects of special metaphysics as Descartes treated them in the *Meditationes,* but more important, it also establishes that he took them into account only to pull them apart. That is, far from constituting a system, in which the existence of each refers to that of the others by the lines of efficient causality or logical implication, here, in their revival by Pascal, a "distance" separates them definitively. The entire text orchestrates this irreparable fragmentation; and it even opens with a proclamation of this catastrophe: "The infinite distance between body and mind symbolizes the infinitely more infinite distance between mind and charity, for charity is supernatural" (§308/793). It is certainly the case that the elements of special metaphysics are revived and taken into account, but it falls to "infinite distance" to mediate them. Infinite here stands for the incommensurability. The "infinite distance," which is then "infinitely infinite," abolishes from the outset every commensurable relation, indeed all organization, among the three terms. Neither *ordo* nor *mensura* guarantees, in a systematic sequence, the evidence of the objects of special metaphysics. The three elements—the world, the soul, and God— are juxtaposed for the sake of showing that they do not make a system, and that no common parameter gathers them into a univocal intelligibility. In contrast, metaphysics submits the privileged beings to the common measure of a single, univocal—at least rightfully if not always expressly—parameter: the concept "being." Descartes does not make an exception to this rule, attempting as he does to think the objects of his special metaphysics sometimes in terms of *ens ut cogitatum,* sometimes in terms of *ens ut causatum.* In both cases, the same parameter, whatever adjustments might be made to it, concerns God, the soul, and the world: God is known as *(ens) cogitatum* or as *(ens) causa sui,* according to concepts that form a system with all the other concepts admissible within the corresponding onto-theo-logies. By contrast, the heterogeneity implied by the "infinite distance," then by the "infinitely infinite distance," excludes even the least univocal parameter or concept, which would make the three objects accessible according to a single logic. What is more, it even seems legitimate to infer from the heterogeneity provoked by the distances the unacceptability of all onto-theo-logy in general, if the latter implies, at the very least, a common (indeed univocal) concept for all the terms (beings) that it includes. The argumentation, missing until now, is therefore suggested by the architecture that juxtaposes, in distance and perfect heterogeneity, the very terms that special metaphysics uses to build the system and whose univocal knowledge and foundation all onto-theo-logy tries to provide. This observation gives rise to a second: between each of the three terms, Pascal institutes the incommensurable gap of an "[infinitely] infinite distance" that can be crossed only by a transgression. Now, metaphysics is defined precisely by a transgression (chapter I, §2). This transgression is at play between natural things and immaterial things (the separate intelligences of the *ens in quantum ens*), and the first Pascalian distance is also at play between the material sensible (world, "flesh") and the immaterial insensible ("minds"). Wouldn't the two transgressions coincide, Pascal repeating between the two first orders the transgression that already characterizes metaphysics proper? Without a doubt. But then doesn't Pascal *acknowledge* the legitimacy of metaphysics, far from disqualifying it? To the contrary. It is precisely here that he most decisively leaves metaphysics destitute: for supposing that the "infinite distance" between bodies and minds repeats the metaphysical transgression, it must immediately be added that this first transgression itself undergoes a second transgression—and, moreover, a transgression that raises the first incommensurability to the next level— "infinitely infinite distance." If by chance metaphysics found a legitimate place in the second order, it would just as quickly be convicted of illegitimacy—of "injustice," Pascal will say—by the second transgression, which opens onto the third order. This is the decisive paradox: if metaphysics is established at the center of the hierarchy of the three orders— a possibility that, literally, can be conceived—it must just as quickly be left destitute of all authority in light of a transgression of the transgression; in short, of a metabasis out of metaphysics. It is not a question of a "metaphysics of metaphysics,"[31] but of a crossing beyond metaphysics. The step back from metaphysics can be detected in the very transgression of the "infinite distance," mimicking the metaphysical transgression, by the "infinitely infinite distance." For a second time, then, Pascal's still

---

31. Kant, *To Markus Herz,* 1 May 1781: "Schwer wird dieser Art Nachforschung bleiben, denn sie enthält die Metaphysik von der Metaphysik" (*Kants Werke,* op. cit., vol. X, p. 269 [English trans., p. 95]).

hidden argument is detected in the architecture of the three orders and
their distances: even if metaphysics holds a place there, it undergoes an
infinite transgression. We now have enough signs indicating a formal
correspondence between the question of the status of (Cartesian) metaphysics and the Pascalian doctrine of the three orders to study the latter
with an eye to determining the former. In short, we can now read §308/
793 as a structure of the overcoming of Cartesian metaphysics.

"They are three orders differing in kind." Three things must be determined: *(a)* the meaning of "order," *(b)* which three terms are retained,
(c) why they remain different in kind. *(a)* The two possible meanings
of "order" appear in the group numbered XXIII and entitled "Proofs of
Jesus Christ." Order is understood first as an organized arrangement of
demonstrations and discourse. Thus, "against the objection that there is
no order in Scripture," it must be seen that "the heart has its order, the
mind has its own, which uses principles and demonstrations. The heart
has a different one" (§298/283). In evoking two ways of arranging in
order, Pascal obviously is thinking of Descartes: ". . . to demonstrate it
with an ordered proof as in geometry . . ." (§512/1), but he is free from
Descartes as well, since he claims to institute an order other than that of
evidence: "I will write down my thoughts here as they come and in a
perhaps not aimless confusion. This is the true order and it will always
show my aim by its very disorder" (§532/373). The order of evidence is
not always appropriate, especially when it is a question of treating what
excludes evidence: "I should be honoring my subject too much if I
treated it in order, since I am trying to show that it is incapable of it"
(ibid.) Thus is broken the equivalence between order as the arrangement
of a series and the production of evidence, an equivalence that sums up
the entire Cartesian method. In short, Pascal has broken the identity
between making evident and putting in order.[32] Order, as the ordering
of matters or reasons, is again free, according to Pascal, for an end other
than evidence. The "intuitive mind [*esprit de finesse*]" serves first of all
to name a use of order and an authentic reasoning that owe nothing to
the method taken as an arrangement according to the order that aims at
evidence. The order can be exercised beyond its Cartesian definition,
and can convince without demonstrating—it transgresses evidence. The

32. For the Cartesian doctrine of the order, see Equipe Descartes, "Contribution à la
sémantèse d'*ordo-ordre* chez Descartes," in *Ordo. Atti del II Colloquio Internazionale [du
Lessico Intellettuale Europeo], Roma, 7–9 gennaio 1977* (Rome, 1979), pp. 279–328, along
with *Sur l'ontologie grise de Descartes,* §§12–15, and *Règles utiles et claires pour la direction
de l'esprit en la recherche de la vérité,* pp. 159–60, 165–66, 169–72, etc.

second meaning of order, a class, makes a comparable distinction. And this is so precisely because it is necessary to distinguish several orders or classes among beings: "Different kinds of right thinking, some in a particular order of things but not in others where they go quite astray" (§511/2). In particular, the distinction between thought and extension implies nothing less than a distinction between two orders: "Our intelligence occupies the same rank in the order of intellect as our body in the whole range of nature" (§199/72). Likewise, the preceding distinction between two modes of arranging thoughts (aiming at evidence or not) rests on the distinction of two classes: "Jesus Christ and St. Paul possess the order of charity, not of the mind, for they wished to humble, not to teach" (§298/283). Let the mind, namely the agent of this rationality, which is organized exclusively toward evidence, have to admit ". . . an other order" (§308/793), and Pascal has demolished the universal privilege that Descartes accorded to "common sense" and the *bona mens.* No doubt Descartes admitted the irreducible domain of faith and revelation; but he attributed it only to the will, without doing harm to the understanding: ". . . fides, quaecumque est de obscuris, non ingenii actio sit, sed voluntatis [Faith in these matters (what has been revealed by God), as in anything obscure, is an act of the will rather than an act of the understanding]."[33] Pascal, in contrast, defines a new order, which, while also privileging "the will" (§933/460), exerts its sway and makes a criticism over and against the evidence that it drives mad, the truth whose idolatry it can stigmatize, the very science that it condemns to vanity (see *infra,* §25). Like "the order of Melchisedek" (§609/736), the order that redoubles evidence owes nothing to the world or to the spirit—having neither genealogy nor condition, it could therefore accuse all the other orders. In this way, the two meanings of *order,* though semantically distinct, bring about the same subversion of the Cartesian concept of order: they bypass the uniform and homogeneous arrangement of the *series* where universal evidence is produced. Now, it seems appropriate *(b)* to identify the three terms that mobilize the three orders. It can be considered established that, in the first place, Pascal revived a biblical enumeration of the three concupiscences: ". . . omne, quod est in mundo, concupiscentia carnis est, et concupiscentia oculorum, et superbia vitae [All that is in the world is concupiscence of the flesh and concupiscence

33. AT X, 370, 21–22 = PW I, 14 (see *Règles utiles et claires pour la direction de l'esprit en la recherche de la vérité,* pp. 129–30 and pp. 245–46), confirmed by AT VII, 147, 12–148, 13 = PW II, 105.

of the eyes, and the pride of life]" (1 John 2:16). A very clear and precise interpretation of this had already been given by Saint Augustine: "Three classes . . . are thus identified; for lust of the flesh means those who love the lower pleasures, lust of the eyes means the curious, and ambition of this world denotes the proud."[34] This thematic of the three temptations directly inspires an apparent parallel to §308/793:

> Concupiscence of the flesh, concupiscence of the eyes, pride, etc./ There are three orders of things: flesh, mind and will./ The carnal are rich men and kings. Their interest is in the body./ The curious and scholars; their interest is in the mind./ The wise; their interest is in what is right./ God should govern everything and everything should be related to him./ Things of the flesh are properly governed by concupiscence./ Things of the mind by curiosity./ Wisdom by pride. [§933/460.]

The orders do indeed appear, but they are deduced strictly from the concupiscences. This is why the third order cannot yet receive the rank of charity: it is still defined by pride (which the will exercises). In consequence, God comes up only outside the three orders, since all three are still reduced to the three Johannine concupiscences and must be combated equally. Pascal's ingenious and characteristic innovation consists in transforming the triple danger into a triple inspection of things (§308/793). Concupiscence of the flesh no longer includes just the temptation of pleasurable things, but designates first of all everything insofar as it is bodily; that is to say, all that the eyes of flesh allow to be seen: a first world is thus disclosed. The concupiscence of the eyes is no longer limited to the *libido sciendi,* understood as a mere distracted curiosity ("divertissement"), but covers everything insofar as it is intelligible, that is to say, all that which the *intuitus mentis* or the gaze of the mind alone succeeds in seeing: "Mentis enim oculi, quibus res videt observatque, sunt ipsae demonstrationes [Logical proofs are the eyes of the mind, whereby it sees and observes things]," as Spinoza says[35] for once in a highly Pascalian style—offering the definition of the second world that is disclosed: namely, that of the sciences and of knowing, which only the

---

34. Saint Augustine: "Hoc modo tria illa sunt notata: nam concupiscentia carnis, voluptatis infimae amatores significat; concupiscentia oculorum, curiosos; ambitio saeculi, superbos" *De Vera Religione,* XXXVIII, 70 [English trans., p. 261]. The Augustinian sources of this doctrine were studied in a remarkable way by P. Sellier, *Pascal et saint Augustin,* pp. 169–96 (who speaks perhaps imprudently of a "system of concupiscences," p. 190: at the very least, it is certain that the orders do not form a system).

35. Spinoza, *Ethics V,* §23, *sch.* [English trans. p. 214].

respublica litteraria and the "scientific community" reach. The concupiscence of pride disappears, giving way to its inverse, the order of charity,
which becomes visible only to a third mode of vision—the "eyes of the
heart, which see wisdom" (§308/793 [modified]), "to see with the eyes of
faith" (§500/700), ". . . it is good to see with the eyes of faith . . ." (§317/
701 [modified]). Charity no longer intervenes as the pious and superfluous auxiliary to the passion of love; it opens a distinct world by opening
other eyes in man: "For my part, I confess that as soon as the Christian
religion reveals the principle that men are by nature corrupt and have
fallen away from God, this opens one's eyes so that the mark of this
truth is everywhere apparent" (§471/441). From being a secondary and
ambiguous passion, charity achieves the rank of hermeneutic principle:
once its point of view is admitted—that is to say, once the mind succeeds
in reaching it, another world, or other dimensions of the old world, is
disclosed to the gaze. Charity interprets because it reveals [*parce qu'elle
révèle*], as photographic developer [*comme un révélateur*] causes the un-
foreseeable burst of colors to appear on the obscurity of the paper. Thus,
charity provokes the world, seen first in its two natural orders, to be
soaked, tinted, and redrawn in the unthinkable and unexpectedly visible
colors of its glory or its abandon. Beneath the bright and iridescent light
of charity, the world appears in all its dimensions, according to all its
parameters, with all its contrasts—in short, in truth. Pascal's decisive
innovation is thus not contained in his having introduced the phrase *order of charity*, nor even in his having instituted three orders rather than
three concupiscences,[36] but in his having established a third order. Pascal's daring is accentuated as soon as one notices which contradictory
traits define the "order of charity." On the one hand, it dominates the
two other orders, whose "principle" (§471/441) it brings to light and in
which it is recognized only as "the truth was recognized from the figure"
(§826/673). Charity regulates the first and the second orders by theoretical necessity. On the other hand, however, it transcends them by "an

36. This originality was seen by G. Rodis-Lewis, especially in regard to the second
concupiscence, but without placing an emphasis on the transition from *libidines* to the
orders. See "Les trois concupiscences," *Chroniques de Port-Royal* 11–14 (1963). As for
determining if the phrase "order of charity" appears before Pascal, in for instance Louis
de Lesclache, Antoine Sirmond, Léonard de Marandé, or Louis Bail (E. Joly, "L'ordre de
la charité et le pari," *Etudes pascaliennes*, vol. 8 [Paris, 1932], pp. 121–51, reappearing in
Etudes pascaliennes. Recueil de notes sur les Pensées, with a foreword by J.-R. Armogathe
[Paris, 1981]), this project is as interesting as it is unessential to the strictly metaphysical
stakes of the debate that Pascal here undertakes against Descartes.

infinitely more infinite distance" than the "distance between body and mind." The second gap does not merely repeat the first as in an analogy; it raises its incommensurability to the next level. The entirety of fragment §308/793 is framed between the two mentions of this incommensurability and the reasons for it—". . . it is supernatural," concludes the first paragraph; ". . . of a different, supernatural, order," the final paragraph concludes. The same "order of charity" thus passes itself off as both necessary and supernatural. The contradiction appears insurmountable: either the third order is necessary to the understanding of the first two and it remains natural; or else, revealed by the gracious gift of God, it no longer belongs to the natural field, nor necessarily defines its logic.

This contradiction shows up only because we have not yet correctly considered the third characteristic of the orders: *(c)* "They are three orders differing in kind." This heterogeneity does not stop them from relating to each other, but rather defines these relations precisely, and does so in such a way that the third order can, without any contradiction, be a theoretical requirement necessary to the first two and still remain supernatural. Thus, "carnal greatness . . . has no relationship" with the "great geniuses," and "the saints," in turn, ". . . have no relationship . . ." with inferior greatness. In this sense also, under the light of charity, the concupiscences show that they are incommensurable with each other: "I see the depths of my pride, curiosity, concupiscence. There is no link between me and God or Jesus Christ the righteous" (§919/553). Doesn't such incommensurability, which prevents one from measuring any relationship between the orders, call for an absolute heterogeneity, to the point that the orders themselves would give rise to an interpretive difficulty, far from securing a hermeneutic function? This is not the case, however: a relation, incommensurable to be sure, reconnects the orders by fixing them in a hierarchy—the gaze. The orders differ "in kind" because the inferior order cannot see the "greatness" of the superior order, because the "greatness" of each order becomes visible only to a gaze appropriate to this order, and because finally the superior order always also judges the "greatness" of the inferior order. In contrast with sensible or mundane experience, which teaches that the more one is exalted, the more one becomes visible and the less one sees that from which one is distant, in Pascal's terms, the more one progresses in the hierarchy of the orders, the less visible one becomes—". . . the greatness of intellectual people is not visible to kings, rich men, captains, who are all great in a carnal sense./ The greatness of wisdom, which is nothing if it does not come from God, is not visible to carnal or intellectual people" (§308/

793). The more "greatness" at work in an order, the more excellent will be the gaze that can see it. All are carnal, thus the first order makes itself visible to all. All are not capable of thinking intellectually, therefore the second order remains invisible to the first: the legionnaire kills Archimedes, to be sure because he does not know him, but above all because he does not see in the marks that Archimedes makes in the sand lines, circles, and polygons; to spare Archimedes, one would have to have been a geometer first. Finally, few accede to charity, thus the third order remains invisible to the first two: Jesus Christ was put to death by the legionnaires (first order), but also by the "intellectual people" (scribes and pharisees, judges: second order), because no one saw the Word of God in him. In order not to kill Christ, one would have to have seen him as he was "seen by God and the angels, and not by bodies or by curious minds" (§308/793 [modified]). But the superior order still sees the inferior order or orders: "The least of minds . . . knows them all [bodies, firmament, stars, the earth and its kingdoms] and itself too, while bodies know nothing" (§308/793). The second order judges, in terms of its value, the first. Likewise, the third order judges, in terms of its value, the second: "All bodies together and all minds together . . . are not worth the least impulse of charity" (§308/793). "Thought, then, is admirable and incomparable by its very nature. It must have had strange faults to have become worthy of contempt, but it does have such faults that nothing is more ridiculous" (§756/365). Consequently, the "invisible holiness" (§275/643) knows and serves as the standard for what is ignorant of it and does not see it, exactly as, aside from their sensible effects, which everyone sees, ". . . causes can only be seen by the mind" (§577/234 [modified]). The heterogeneity of the orders is verified in the course of ascending their hierarchy; the superior order remains invisible to the inferior order. In this way, the system of special metaphysics becomes disjointed. But in the course of descending the hierarchy, a continuity is reestablished, since the superior order evaluates and judges the inferior orders. Thus is opened the possibility that charity might judge each and every thing. Each order suffices unto itself—at least it appears to in its own eyes—governs the inferior, and dispenses with any superior. It is bound necessarily to the first, and optionally (supernaturally) to the other. Only the third order sees the two others, in such a way that, paradoxically, it must remain invisible to them. Therefore, the fact that we do not easily—naturally—accede to the "order of charity" does not cast its reality or its efficacy into doubt, but to the contrary confirms that charity is given to be seen only by the "eyes of the heart" and not by the "curious minds." To see the "order of charity," one has not so much to know a new object, as to know according to a new condition, loving: "We enter into truth only through charity" (OC, p. 355 *a* = 203 [modified]). The second order, which does not have to love in order to produce evidence, therefore does not reach the third order, and does not even see that it does not reach it; it does not see the invisible, nor that it does not see it.

We have laid out, briefly, the three principal characteristics of the doctrine of the orders. What still remains to be established is that this is indeed a structure of the overcoming of Cartesian metaphysics—in other words, that Descartes' metaphysics fits perfectly into the structure of the orders in such a way that its overcoming is carried out. This attempt, however enormous it might appear, does not require an endless presentation. Two arguments are enough for what is essential to satisfy its demands. *(a)* The second order has Descartes for its paradigm. Descartes was engaged in "pursuits of the mind" (seeing as two of his works bear this expression [*recherches de l'esprit*] in their title). Descartes can be seen in "Archimedes" (whom he takes as a model in *Meditatio II:* "Nihil nisi punctum petebat Archimedes [Archimedes used to demand just one firm and immovable point] . . .").[37] Like Archimedes, Descartes "fought no battles visible to the eyes, but enriched every mind with his discoveries" (§308/793), for ". . . attempting to overcome all the difficulties and errors that prevent our arriving at knowledge of the truth is indeed a manner of fighting battles . . ." (DM 67, 10–13 = PW I, 145). More important, the second order is instituted by transgressing "all bodies together" by means of the thought that the mind has of them: "For it knows them all and itself too, while bodies know nothing" (§308/793). Obviously, this concerns the distinction between *res extensa* and *res cogitans;* it is also obvious that it concerns self- consciousness (*cogito, cogitatio sui ipsius*) as the condition for the possibility of consciousness of any other thing. Parallel texts are not absent either: "It is not in space that I must seek my human dignity, but in the ordering of my thought. . . . Through space the universe grasps me and swallows me up like a speck; through thought I grasp it" (§113/348); "Man is only a reed, the weakest in nature, but he is a thinking reed. . . . Even if the universe were to crush

---

37. AT VII, 24, 9–10 = PW II, 16. M. Serres has shown how Pascal put back into question the very legitimacy of the search for an absolutely fixed Archimedean point, *Le système de Leibniz et ses modèles mathématiques,* III, 1, "Le paradigme pascalien" (Paris, 1968 and 1982), pp. 647*ff.*

him, man would still be nobler than his slayer, because he knows that he is dying and the advantage the universe has over him. The universe knows nothing of this. Thus all our dignity consists in thought. It is on thought that we must depend for our recovery, not on space . . ." (§200/347).[38] The second order stems from thought, but thought adopts the figure of the *ego*, ". . . for my self consists in my thought . . ." (§135/469). An additional characteristically Cartesian trait confirms the preceding: thought operates by representing extension and by thus affirming the anteriority of the *ego*. Not only does the second order repeat the determinations of the *cogitatio*, operated by an *ego*, but it succeeds in establishing its transcendence vis-à-vis the first order ("Out of all bodies together we could not succeed in creating one little thought" [§308/793]) only by virtue of the Cartesian privilege of the *cogitatio* over every possible *cogitatum:* the former does not result from the world, but precedes it as its *a priori*. In this way, Descartes does indeed enter into the structure of the three orders, at the transition between the first two. From now on, nothing will touch the second order without also affecting the metaphysical figure of Descartes. *(b)* Whence the second argument: just as the transition from the first to the second order is carried out thanks to the metaphysical operation of the *ego cogito*, so too will the transition from the second to the third order be accomplished to the detriment of the Cartesian figure of the *ego cogito*, thus confirming that the Cartesian *ego cogito* is indeed what is at stake in the entire structure of the three orders. From the second to the third orders, the discontinuity is self-evident: ". . . All minds together and all their products are not worth the least impulse of charity. This is of an infinitely superior order. . . . Out of all bodies and minds we could not extract one impulse of true charity. It is impossible, and of a different, supernatural, order" (§308/793). But the explanation of this discontinuity is not self-evident. The discontinuity between the two first orders becomes intelligible first on the basis of the common experience of thought and corporeality, then from the doctrine, also Cartesian, of perception: the subjectively perceived sensible can be

38. See also §620/146: "Man is obviously made for thinking. Therein lies all his dignity and his merit; and his whole duty is to think as he ought"; §756/365: "Thought. All man's dignity consists in thought"; §759/346: "Thought constitutes man's greatness." The criticism ". . . nearly all philosophers confuse their ideas of things, and speak spiritually of corporeal things and corporeally of spiritual ones" (§199/72) introduces its restriction (*nearly*) through an allusion to the Cartesian distinction. Descartes already addressed this reproach to Gassendi. J. Laporte had insisted on the fact that here Pascal proceeds ". . . according to the Cartesian theory of the *Cogito* . . . ," *Le cœur et la raison selon Pascal* (Paris, 1950), p. 27.

figured in intelligible models—invisible to sensation, visible to the mind—that Nature is supposed to have instituted.[39] But between the last two orders, the heterogeneity, indeed the transition, offers an imposing difficulty: we cannot naturally claim to know the "order of charity," for "it is supernatural" and "of a supernatural order"; moreover, it is no longer even a matter of knowing, since knowledge results from thought and thus falls under the second order; and, in any case, Pascal eliminates all "thought" concerning charity and substitutes for it the "impulse of charity." Charity is not represented, nor does it represent; it acts, as love is made more than known. How, now, can the "order of charity" be reached? Strictly speaking, Pascal admits only one direct way, holiness. Let us confess that it will discourage and rebuff the vast majority of the "educated bunch"; and let us acknowledge also that it will no longer allow one to conceive the transition between the last two orders, nor how the truth of the *ego cogito* could not "be worth" an "impulse of charity." Paradoxically, the solution of the aporia can come to us, in part, through reference to Descartes. The transition between the first order (extension) and the second (thought) is described in Cartesian doctrine by the theory of the code: sensations are only the sensible effect of intelligible figures (mathematical models) effectively instituted by nature; between the effects and the causes, an encoding is at play; the sensible effects decode (disfigure) intelligible and actual figures. Now, Descartes had put this (two-termed) coding in doubt in *Meditatio I* when he entertained the hypothesis of an overencoding: just as the blue of the sky in fact results from strictly rational causes and figures (models) that do not resemble them in any way whatsoever, couldn't one imagine that these initial rational models also obey a system of axioms totally different from those which we know and of which they would be only the effects— effects of unknown principles?

> Imo etiam, quemadmodum judico interdum alios errare circa ea quae se perfectissime scire arbitrantur, ita ego ut fallar quoties duo et tria simul addo, vel numero quadrati latera, vel si quid aliud facilius fingi potest? [Since I sometimes believe that others go astray in cases where they think they have the most perfect knowledge, may I not similarly go wrong every time I add two and three or count the sides of a square, or in even some simpler matter, if that is imaginable?][40]

39. At least, this is what we have tried to establish in *Sur la théologie blanche de Descartes,* §12, pp. 232–63.

40. AT VII, 21, 7–11 = PW II, 14. Another text confirms the claim that Descartes did indeed entertain the hypothesis of an overencoding (AT VII, 144, 28–145, 9 = PW II, 103).

By the end, Descartes had abandoned the hypothesis of an overencoding because it supposed a lie in God, and he reestablished the simple coding between extension and thought. We suggest that the Pascalian structure of the three orders could be constituted along the lines of the Cartesian hypotheses of coding and overencoding. The major objection against an overencoding in effect disappears here, since Pascal has recourse to it for the purpose of thematizing not a divine deception, but on the contrary, the very charity of God. Let us review the three stages. The first order (extension, sensible) is done away with in the second (thought, models, figures) by means of the factors that articulate the heterogeneity between them (representation, coding, figuration, disfiguration, etc.); the parameter of the second order is still Cartesian evidence. Pascal follows Descartes exactly, up until this point. They diverge at the border of the second order: for Descartes, this order has no precise limit except that of the human understanding, and it is not exposed to any overencoding, since evidence remains unsurpassable. Pascal, in contrast, takes up the Cartesian hypothesis of an overencoding and manages to confirm it. Why? Because he isolates a new parameter. In contrast to Descartes, who envisaged only a second evidence, or an evidence doubled over and against its first status, thus over and against itself, and who thus ended up with an untenable contradiction, Pascal tries to overencode thought (already the code for extension) only by submitting it to another parameter than its own. He will do this by no longer exposing it to the natural light of evidence, but to the invisible radiance of charity. The third order will thus be revealed indirectly, by the distorting effects that its radiance—the luminosity of charity—will have on the elements of the second order. The first and principal term of the second order—the first *being* that it defines—bears the name *ego*. In the light of evidence, Pascal admits and welcomes the primacy of the *ego* within the order of thought: "Man is obviously made for thinking. . . . Now the order of thought is to begin with the self, and with its author and its end" (§620/146 [modified]). As for Descartes, the *immortalitas animae* (second order) or its *distinctio a corpore* (first order) precedes and commands *Dei existentia* (third order). What becomes of this primacy in terms of evidence and in

---

We have discussed these points in *Sur la théologie blanche de Descartes,* §14, particularly pp. 319–33. Within this framework, one would have to investigate Spinoza's intent in his (ever-changing) doctrine of the kinds of knowledge. Everything happens as if the ambiguity surrounding intuitive knowledge resulted from a perpetual hesitation between the Cartesian overencoding (redoubling of evidence) and the Pascalian overencoding (passage out of evidence by recourse to a new parameter). See the studies by F. Alquié, *Le rationalisme de Spinoza* (Paris, 1981), III, "Raison connaissante et raison salvatrice," pp. 181–262.

thought once it is exposed in the light of charity? What becomes of this primacy, required by the demand to make evident and incontestable in the second order, when it pretends to transpose itself into the third order? In other words, can the *ego's* anteriority in terms of evidence—". . . primus enim sum [For I am the first] . . ."[41]—be maintained identically in the third order? Between the second and the third order, "the infinitely infinite distance" is found in the gap between the parameters: evidence on the one hand, charity on the other. Now, "we should worship only in its order" (§926/582), and not pretend to displace the parameter of one order to the other—which is the definition of "tyranny."[42] When the *ego,* under the pretext that primacy in terms of evidence necessarily defines the second order, demands the same primacy in the third, and thus that other men love it first because it, as *ego,* is the first to know, it is confusing the orders. It thus exerts a "tyranny," since the recognized center of the second order contradicts the third. Moreover, because "the wise men have justice for their object," this "tyranny" shows that the *ego* is unjust: ". . . I hate it [the self] because it is unjust that it should make itself the centre of everything. . . . It is unjust in itself for making itself the centre of everything" (§597/455).

> The nature of self-love and of this human *self* is to love only self and consider only self. But what is it to do? It cannot prevent the object of its love

41. Descartes, *Comments on a Certain Broadsheet* (AT VIII-2, 348, 15 = PW I, 297); see *supra,* chap. II, §6.

42. "Tyranny./ Tyranny is wanting to have by one means what can only be had by another. We pay different dues to different kinds of merit; we must love charm, fear strength, believe in knowledge./ These dues must be paid. It is wrong to refuse them and wrong to demand any others. So these arguments are false and tyrannical: 'I am handsome, so you must fear me. I am strong, so you must love me, I am . . .'" (§58/332). Descartes therefore would be true in his own order and tyrannical when he has the pretense to overstep it. But, more to the point, does Descartes ever apply the *ego cogito* outside the theoretical field? No doubt, yes—by maintaining it as the paradigm of morality. *(a)* The sovereign good is defined by the "contentment of the self" (*To Elisabeth,* May–June 1645 [AT IV 221, 9–10]; 4 August 1645 [AT IV, 264, 7–9 and 265, 7]; 18 August 1645 [AT IV, 275, 4–7]; *The Passions of the Soul,* §§63, 153, 190 = PW III, 251; 257 and 257; 261; PW I, 351–52; 384; 396). *(b)* What follows then is an "injustice," the injustice of making oneself the center, like God: ". . . it [human free will] renders us in a certain way like God by making us masters of ourselves" (*The Passions of the Soul,* §152 = PW I, 384); ". . . free will is in itself the noblest thing we can have, since it makes us in a way equal to God and seems to exempt us from being his subjects" (*To Christina,* 20 November 1647 [AT V, 85, 12–16 = PW III, 326]). In this sense, we pointed out ". . . the self-grounding of the human will . . . in its function of mimicking the self-grounding of the ground (God)" (*Sur la théologie blanche de Descartes,* p. 414).

from being full of faults and wretchedness: . . . it wants to be the object of men's love and esteem and sees that its faults deserve only their dislike and contempt. This predicament in which it thus finds itself arouses in it the most unjust and criminal passion that could possibly be imagined, for it conceives a deadly hatred for the truth which rebukes it and convinces it of its faults. [§978/100.]

"Who can fail to see that there is nothing so contrary to justice and truth [than to make himself into a God]? For it is false that we deserve this position and unjust and impossible to attain it, because everyone demands the same thing" (§617/492). Origin of evidence, the *ego*, though first term in the arrangement according to the order, cannot, with any justice, stake a claim to the position of center loved by all in charity: "It is untrue that we are worthy to be loved by others. It is unjust that we should want such a thing. . . . / For everything tends towards itself: this is contrary to all order. . . . / Thus we are born unjust and depraved" (§421/ 477). The Cartesian *ego* lacks as much justice, when related to charity as a center, as it lacked appropriateness when related to evidence as a first principle. The same *ego* becomes, from one order to the other, "a strange monster" (§477/406), not through an internal alteration, but through its relation to a situation. It is appropriate to know oneself (*cogitatio sui*), not to love oneself (*amour-propre*). For self- knowledge enables the *ego* to know other beings, while the love of self blocks the *self* from loving other beings. Moreover, self- knowledge attests to the anteriority of the *ego,* which can in fact get by without any other certainty, while self-love betrays its "tyranny" up front—in order to be carried out, destroy every other object. The *ego* now shows itself to be "unjust" in the eyes of the third order, thus also "useless" to charity, in the sense that "it would have been useless or pointless for Our Lord Jesus Christ to come as a king . . . , but he truly came with the splendour of his own order" (§308/ 793 [modified]).

Passing from the second order to the third implies subverting the *ego,* or, more exactly, disqualifying in the order of charity the legitimate primacy that Descartes accorded to it in the order of the mind: the *ego* must be known before all else; thus it cannot be loved to the exclusion of all else. Overcoming the Cartesian figure of metaphysics consists in not loving oneself as one thinks oneself. As it is necessary to see the *ego*'s "dignity" in the realm of thought, it is necessary to "hate" the *ego* in the realm of charity, such that only God remains to be loved. "We must love God alone and hate ourselves alone" (§373/476). In the first order, the universe is moved according to the body (extension). In the second, the *ego* thinks [itself] according to thought (Descartes). In the third, God is given to be loved according to charity. Cartesian metaphysics occupies the center of the structure of the orders—this is why it cannot constitute what the third order means by "center." Intrinsically linked to the *ego cogito,* Cartesian metaphysics shares in its subversion by charity.

§24. The *Ego* Undone and the Decentering of the Self

Overcoming metaphysics in its Cartesian figure—if this is indeed the goal set by the doctrine of the three orders in §308/793, "the heart of the *Pensées,* the fragment that draws the whole work together" (H. U. von Balthasar),[43] it immediately calls for overcoming its "first principle" (AT IX-1, 10, 5–6): the originary and autonomous existence of the *ego cogito.* Pascal is even more obliged to attempt such an overcoming, given that the *ego* marks and identifies the metaphysical enterprise not only in Descartes, but also as early as Montaigne, who is often read in terms of Descartes (or inversely). In effect, Montaigne, who employs the term "métaphysique" only parsimoniously, identifies the *ego*—"this experience we have of ourselves, which is more familiar to us, and certainly more sufficient to inform us of what we need"—precisely with metaphysics: "I study myself more than any other subject. That is my metaphysics."[44] Two reasons, and not insignificant ones at that, seeing as they concern the two privileged interlocutors of the *Pensées,* set up something like an obligation to overcome, along with metaphysics, its privileged vehicle, the *ego,* such as it is "studied" or cognized by itself. Against the *ego,* Pascal will therefore object that its autonomy in the second order becomes illusory, in the third, and prevents it from making any claim to the status of an origin or a center.

More so than anywhere else, the undoing of the *ego* is accomplished

---

43. H. U. von Balthasar, *Herrlichkeit,* vol. 2: *Fächer der Style* (1962), p. 543 [English trans., p. 180].

44. Montaigne, *Essais III,* 13, "De l'expérience," *OC,* p. 431 *b* [English trans., p. 821]. There it is a matter of the real departure made by metaphysics, in contrast with the more usual way of proceeding: "The metaphysicians take as their foundation the conjectures of physics" (II, 12, "Apology for Raimond Sebond," *OC,* p. 224 *b* [English trans., p. 404]). Pascal is perhaps reminded of another occurrence of "métaphysique" when he takes as the source of §533/331 (an anti-Cartesian paragraph if ever there was one; see *supra,* §21, n. 10) the following reflection: "Chrysippus said that what Plato and Aristotle had written about logic they had written as a game and for exercises and could not believe that they had spoken seriously of such an empty matter. Plutarch says the same of metaphysics" (*II,*

in fragment §688/323, which asks precisely: "What is my self? [*Qu'est-ce que le moi*] (modified)]." First question: why does Pascal substitute self or me [*moi*] for *I/ego*? This is not simply a question of style, as is proved by the quite numerous occurrences of *I*.[45] It is a conceptual decision: *I* governs the verb (nominative), while *my self* or *me* [*moi*] complements it directly (accusative). *I* think, see, say; the *me* is thought, said, seen. And what is more, this fragment revives, by inverting, a famous analysis found in Descartes. In *Meditatio II*, *I* stand by the window in order to see the appearances of men who perhaps are not: "... respexissem ex fenestra homines ..., quos ... dico me videre [If I look out the window ..., I normally say that I see the men themselves]" (AT VII, 32, 6–8 = PW II, 21). In §688/323, by contrast, the speaker no longer stands in the window and has a commanding view of the passing appearances; he walks among them and sees the gaze of an *I* that is cast over the street, falls upon him, and reduces him to the posture of a *me:* "A man goes to the window to see the people passing by; if I pass by, can I say he went there to see me?" (§688/323). But there is more: not only does the *I* become a *me* by no longer exerting the gaze but suffering it (below from above), but from this gaze, the *me* no longer expects any evidence or clear and distinct knowledge. There where the Cartesian analysis ends

---

12, *OC*, p. 211 *b* [English trans., p. 376]. More broadly, Montaigne constantly claims to ground morality (and no longer just the second order) on the *self:* "Certainly a man of understanding has lost nothing, if he has himself" (*I*, 39, "De la solitude," *OC*, p. 111 *b* [English trans., p. 177]); "The greatest thing in the world is to know how to belong to oneself" (ibid., *OC*, p. 112 *b* [English trans., p. 178]); "It is not my deeds that I write down; it is myself; it is my essence" (*II*, 6, "De l'exercitation," *OC*, p. 160 *b* [English trans., p. 274]); "And then finding myself entirely destitute and void of any other matter, I presented myself to myself for argument and subject. It is the only book in the world of its kind, a book with a wild and eccentric plan" (*II*, 8, "De l'affection des pères aux enfants," *OC*, p. 162 *b* [English trans., p. 278]). In Pascal's terms, this "void of any other matter" proves "How hollow and foul is the heart of man!" (§139/143). It must be emphasized that the Cartesian morality of "self-contentment" (*supra*, n. 42) achieves Montaigne's aim exactly.

45. The *Pensées* include 173 occurrences of *j'*, 580 of *je*, 99 of *moi*, and 10 of *moi-même*, according to Hugh M. Davidson and Pierre H. Dubé, *A Concordance to Pascal's Pensées* (Ithaca and London: Cornell University Press, 1975), ad loc. The passage from the *je* to the *moi* was outlined by J. Nédoncelle, "Le *moi* d'après les *Pensées*," in *Chroniques de Port-Royal* (1963). On fragment §688/323, one is referred to H. Birault, "Pascal et le problème du moi introuvable" (loc. cit., *supra*, n. 15). By comparison, see the statistics for the *Discourse on the Method*, an interpretation of which is suggested in our study "A propos d'une sémantique de la méthode," *Revue internationale de Philosophie* 103/1 (1973). [Note that the French *moi* has no exact English equivalent. We have rendered it as "self," "my self," or, when Marion stresses its status as the object of a verb, "me." This has at times necessitated that the existing English translation of Pascal be modified.—Trans.]

up confirming that all that *I* believe I see with my sensible eyes, *I* see with the eyes of the mind—"... sola judicandi facultate, quae in mente mea est, comprehendo [Something which I thought I was seeing with my eyes is in fact grasped solely by the faculty of judgment which is in my mind]" (AT VII, 32, 11–12 = PW II, 21)—the counter-experience of Pascal discovers "the eyes of the heart" (§308/793): "No, for he is not thinking of me in particular. But what about someone who loves someone for the sake of her beauty; does he love *her*?" (§688/323). Of the inverted gaze, *I* become *me* ask neither to know nor even to be known, but to be recognized, that is to say, loved. The *ego* attempts to exhaust the *mens humana*, first by knowing through *intuitus,* then by redirecting the *intuitus* onto itself; in short, by practicing the *intuitus mentis* in accord with the ambiguity of the genitive. This operation maintains all its legitimacy in the second order, where it is a question of evidence. But in the light of the third, it falls to pieces: *I* is doubled into this *I,* which I no longer am, and a *me,* which awaits being seen in order to be; the gaze goes deeper, from evidence to love. To become a self, I need to be neither seen, nor thought, nor known, but nothing less than loved. For the Cartesian question about the conditions for exercising my *cogitatio,* Pascal has substituted an investigation into the possibility that someone loves *me, my self,* as such: "And if someone loves me for my judgment or my memory, do they love me? *me,* myself? No, for I could lose these qualities without losing my self. Where then is this self [*moi*], if it is neither in the body nor the soul?" (§688/323). For the me or my self to be, it must be loved, and not merely known; from this moment on, all that can be known about it without love is no longer important. *I* is what it necessarily knows about itself, *mens, res cogitans, substantia;* but the me cannot be confined to its most likely substance, "... for would we love the substance of a person's soul, in the abstract, whatever qualities might be in it?" (§688/323). The gap between substance and its principal attribute, a gap that Descartes had discerned without ever filling,[46] can now no longer be reduced. Descartes avoided the difficulty, first because the *ego,* redirecting the *cogitatio* onto itself, was experienced directly in thought (*cogito me cogitare*); next and above all because, residing in the second order, it did not have to take persons into account—which would mean pushing the gaze all the way to the unsubstitutable and irreducible individuality of *haecceitas.* By contrast, Pascal, transcending the order of

---

46. *Principia Philosophiae I,* §§52–53. On what is difficult about these paragraphs, see *supra,* chap. III, §13, *(b).*

evidence by that of love, imposes on the *ego,* become *me,* infinitely more infinite demands: the *me* can be loved only as such, as ". . . a person's soul"; and yet neither the mind and its qualities nor *a fortiori* the body and its modalities include the person fully. Whence it follows that if loving is at issue, the *ego* become the *me* is still insufficient, rudimentary, untenable. Consequence: "We never love any person" (§688/323). This point must be understood: the *ego,* to be loved as a *me,* not only cannot remain autonomous, since another gaze that loves it is necessary to it, but also does not suffice for defining the only possible addressee of a love, the unsubstitutable person. In this context, one begins to understand a passage from §427/194: "I do not know who put me into the world, nor what the world is, nor what I am myself. I am terribly ignorant about everything. I do not know what my body is, or my senses, or my soul, or even that part of me which thinks what I am saying, which reflects about everything and about itself, and does not know itself any better than it knows anything else." On a first reading, this confession of ignorance could be surprising: in the second order, Cartesian and admitted as such, I know that I think, I grasp extension through thought, and I know myself. Has it not already been established that "my self [*moi*] consists in my thought" (§135/469)? Must these sorts of questions be attributed to an interlocutor who is an "atheist" and called upon from the "infinite spaces," or to the rhetorical gifts of Pascal himself? Another explanation remains: this line of questioning does not concern thinking (oneself) within the calm serenity of the second order, but becoming acknowledged as such (as a "person") "in the eyes of the heart"—and of the heart of an other besides *me.* For, just beneath the surface of the text, this fragment crosses the gap from the initial *I* to the final *me:* "*I* do not know . . . what it is . . . nor myself; . . . or even that part of *me* which thinks what I am. . . ." From now on, the *ego/I* no longer occupies the center, no longer holds the office of the center, is found decentered from itself. Anticipating Nietzsche's critique of the autonomy of the *ego cogito,* Pascal stigmatizes it as the effect, unconscious of its own origin, of a more essential cause; better, he pushes the critique deeper, since, far from simply showing the representation to contradict itself, Pascal puts it into question on the basis of a superior order: the sufficiency of the *ego* to fix the center is admissible only in the second order, where in fact it can think itself perfectly; but in the third order, where the *ego/I* cannot, by itself, love itself perfectly, it can no longer occupy nor define a center. Central in thought, the *ego* is shown to be peripheral in charity. *I* could no longer be but a *me,* decentered from *I* to the point that, already, *I* is an other—not another *me*, nor an other besides *me*, but an other than *I*. *I* am alienated, or, literally, *I* is other than *I*, namely (a) *me*. I am not (an) *I*, because *I* am (is) a *me* [*moi*].

The claim that a decentering transforms the *I* into a *me* is immediately met with an objection: Pascal reproaches the *me* for making the pretense of being an absolute center and for loving itself and itself alone. The texts leave no room for any ambiguity on this point: "He wanted to make his self his own centre and do without my [the wisdom of God] help . . . in his desire to find happiness in himself" (§149/430); or ". . . It believes it is a whole, and, seeing no body on which it depends, believes it depends only on itself and tries to make itself its own centre and body" (§372/483); and finally: ". . . It is unjust that it should make itself centre of everything" (§597/455). But to be precise, this is only an observation, not an approbation. It is accompanied by a quite clear diagnosis of the confusion of orders—of the "tyranny"—that sustains *my self*'s pretense to being a center. In the second order, it is self-evident that ". . . the order of thought is to begin with oneself . . ." (§620/146); but in the order of charity, ". . . I am no one's goal nor have I the means of satisfying anyone" (§396/471). Such a pretense to occupying the center results, before any moral fault, from a logical fault: misrepresenting the heterogeneity and the hierarchy of the orders. When the Cartesian *ego* claims to be "independent" in morality[47] because it is so in thought, it sins against right reasoning, even before sinning against God. For it is not enough to lay claim to the center, even in the third order; one must be able to reach it, and the *ego* does not allow the *self* to succeed in doing so. That is, the *ego* verifies its primacy as "first principle" by subtraction (hyperbolic doubt, an almost phenomenological reduction), and thus wins its independence by the elimination of all *cogitata*, whose very absence makes room for the absolute anteriority of the *ego cogito*. The *ego* is affirmed precisely because it appears *solus in mundo* (AT VII, 42, 22 = PW II, 29). In the third order, what is at stake demands love—that the *self* serve as addressee and receive the love of the others, who are thus defined as subject. And it is precisely this which calls for the inversion of the subject *ego/I* into the object *me*. Consequently, the *me* must operate in the opposite way of the *ego/I*, no longer by subtraction but by summation, not by

---

47. On the Cartesian ego's pretense to an "independence," even in morality (the third order), see the *Letter to Elisabeth*, 3 November 1645 (AT IV, 332, 12–333, 7 = PW III, 277) (and our discussion in *Sur la théologie blanche de Descartes*, pp. 411*ff*, as well as "L'exactitude de l'ego," in *Destins et enjeux du XVIIeme siècle* [Paris, 1985]).

abstraction but by accumulation. It no longer aims at solitude, but at gathering all around it, to the exclusion of every other center or beneficiary. "Each self is the enemy of all the others and would like to tyrannize them" (§597/455). On the pretext that "each man is everything to himself, for with his death everything is dead for him. That is why each of us thinks he is everything to everyone" (§668/457), the *ego,* so much the prisoner of its own illusions that it builds itself up as the ". . . center of idolatry . . ." (§609/736), infers that the *me* not only must, but indeed can by its own means, establish itself as center of the love of all: "The nature of self-love and of this human self is to love only self and consider only self" (§978/100). If ". . . everything tends towards itself, this is contrary to all order./ The tendency should be towards the general" (§421/ 477). Even if the *me* could, without injustice, make itself loved as a center toward which everything tends without "injustice" (§396/471; §421/477) or "incommodity" (§597/455), it quite simply would not have the means to succeed in doing so. Its independence would depend on the loving dependence of the others, its centrality on the periphery, and its self-love on the love of non-selves. The *ego* neither ought nor can transpose its dignified rank of principle from the second order into the third. The *ego* remains "first principle" in thought, but in the case of love, the *me* cannot, by any means, become first loved. If therefore the *me* cannot be set up as lovable, it must be concluded that it remains "hateful." Whence the thesis that serves to consecrate the decentering of the *me* and the undoing of the *ego*: "The self [*moi*] is hateful" (§597/455). Accordingly, "the true and only virtue is therefore to hate ourselves, for our concupiscence makes us hateful, and to seek for a being really worthy of love in order to love him" (§564/485). What does it mean to hate my self? Certainly not, despite certain locutions, to hate oneself with an all too modern hatred of oneself: first because, in a nearly perfect inversion, self-hatred amounts to the idolatrous love of oneself; next because at issue is a positive renunciation of love for the *ego,* when it has the tyrannical pretense of imposing itself in the last order—in short, it is an issue of denying that the Cartesian *ego* can preside over love as it presides over thought. One must not hate the self, but the figure that my soul borrows from the *ego,* a figure that hides the autonomous logic of charity from it. In charity, the center is not identified in terms of the model that, in thought, the "first principle" provides. The hatred of the self therefore would have no meaning, except a perverse one, if by contrast the love of a real center was not revealed in it—the only one that is not "unjust" or "incommodious," and the only one that is effective, the love for God:

"They want to love only God, they want to hate only themselves. . . . They hear it said in our religion that we must love only God and hate only ourselves . . ." (§381/286); and also: "We must love God alone and hate ourselves alone" (§373/476); finally: "If God exists we must love him alone and not transitory creatures. . . . We ought to hate ourselves, and everything which drives us to become attached to anything but God alone" (§618/479). Obviously, Pascal is here retrieving one of Saint Augustine's fundamental doctrines:

> Two cities were created by two kinds of love: the earthly city was created by self-love reaching the point of contempt for God, the Heavenly City by the love of God carried as far as contempt of self. In fact, the earthly city glories in itself, the Heavenly City glories in the Lord. The former looks for glory from men, the latter finds its highest glory in God, the witness of a good conscience. The earthly city lifts up its head in its own glory, the Heavenly City says to its God: "My glory, you lift up my head." In the former, the lust for domination lords it over its princes as over the nations it subjugates; in the other both those put in authority and those subject to them serve one another in love, the rulers by their counsel, the subjects by obedience. The one city loves its own strength shown in its powerful leaders; the other says to its God, "I will love you, my Lord, my strength."[48]

But in conformity with other Augustinian tendencies, Pascal unambiguously situates this thematic within the field of the individual soul and passes from universal history to individual history. The reinterpretation leaves no room for doubt: "I shall be compelled to tell you in general the source of all vices and of all sins. . . . The truth which opens up this mystery is that God has created man with two loves, the love of God and the love of self; yet with this law that the love of God shall be infinite, that is to say, with no end other than God Himself, and that the love

---

48. Saint Augustine:

Fecerunt itaque civitates duae amores duo, terrenam scilicet amor sui usque ad contemptum Dei, caelestem vero amor Dei usque ad contemptum sui. Denique illa in se ipsa, haec in Domino gloriatur. Illa enim quaerit ab hominibus gloriam; huic autem Deus conscientiae testis maxima est gloria. Illa in gloria sua exaltat caput suum; haec dicit Deo suo: *Gloria mea et exaltans caput meum.* Illi in principibus ejus vel in eis quas subjugat nationibus dominandi libido dominatur; in hac serviunt invicem in caritate et praepositi consulendo et subditi obtemperando. Illa in suis potentibus diligit virtutem suam; haec diliget Deo suo: *Diligam te, Domine, virtus mea.*

(*De Civitate Dei XIV,* 28 [English trans., p. 593].) See other texts in P. Sellier, *Pascal et saint Augustin,* op. cit., pp. 140–44.

of self shall be finite and leading back to God." After original sin, this prelapsarian situation gives way to the disappearance of the infinite love for God, with the result that, "since love of self has remained alone in this great soul which is capable of infinite love, this self-love has spread and overflowed into the vacuum which the love of God has left. And thus he has loved himself and all things for himself, that is to say, infinitely."[49] The duality of the orders is all the more susceptible of confusion, thus to the "tyranny" of the *I/ego* become *me*, as it is deployed against the background of a duality already inscribed in the third order itself. According to the parameter of charity, and originally, two loves must be practiced, in accordance with two precise propositions: one finite, for the finite *me*, the other infinite, for the infinite *me*. When metaphysics deploys, in its own order, the primacy of the *ego*, it is all the more susceptible of committing the injustice of an infinite love of self by the *me* as it runs into an already confused conflict between two postulations of the third order. The metaphysical *ego* does not provoke self-love so much as it lends it new weapons and the appearance of a rationality. Only the order of charity could incite its own perversion, since an inferior order cannot see (or act on) a superior order. Charity alone can lead charity astray, because it alone practices it and performs it. The *ego* of metaphysics becomes idolatrous only when taken up by charity become self-love, to the exclusion of the love of God. The authentic status reserved for the metaphysical *ego* in the order of charity can ultimately be determined only in terms of the requirements proper to this order and to charity. Such a determination would consist in two moments: *(a)* Identifying the *self* who justly deserves to play the role of the center before which the finite *self,* and with it the *ego* of the second order, must be decentered; *(b)* Pinpointing the precise status of the finite *me,* and with it that of the metaphysical *ego,* in the order of charity.

Identifying *(a)* the *self* that is just in terms of charity— this task presupposes that it is still a question of loving a *self.* Now, the antagonist of the unjust *self* that self-love privileges does not bear the title *self.* To hate the *self* in oneself, one must "have the good will to fall in with the universal soul" (§360/482), ". . . [to] tend towards the general . . ." (§421/477 [modified]), toward ". . . universal being . . ." (§564/485). But universality does not at all suggest the abstraction of being, which would forbid the

49. *To Monsieur and Madame Périer,* 17 October 1651, *OC,* p. 277 *b* [English trans., pp. 87 and 88]. The same original ambivalence of love can be seen in §423/277 and (if its authenticity is admitted) in the *Discours sur les passions de l'amour, OC,* p. 286 *a.*

irreducibility of a person. It designates the sign contrary to that of self-love, so particular as to be "tyrannical," without excluding the possibility that a person might correspond to it. Universality determines the requirements that must be met by any *self* who would not be unjust: perfectly lovable because transcending all particularity. Whence the naming of this universal again as a center, Jesus Christ: "Jesus Christ is the object of all, the center towards which all tend" (§449/556 [modified]). No doubt the proof for the claim that Christ fixes in himself the only just center is based first in the interpretation of the Scriptures: "Jesus Christ with whom both Testaments are concerned . . . , both as their centre" (§388/740); and "The two oldest books in the world . . . both regard Jesus Christ as their common center and object" (§811/741 [modified]). But on the one hand, the Scriptures serve as a perfect memory of history and of anthropology; on the other hand, the first of the formulae here cited comes from the fragment that had refuted the God of the metaphysical proofs—particularly the God of the creation of the eternal truths.[50] Accordingly, the process of identifying the center as Christ has recourse to Scripture only insofar as philosophical discourse no longer succeeds in drawing out ". . . the object and centre towards which all things tend."[51] If Christ alone deserves the function of center, this is because he alone respects the requirements of the third order: he can be loved universally because he ". . . has his own order of holiness. He made no discoveries; he did not reign, but he was humble, patient, thrice holy to God, terrible to devils, and without sin. With what great pomp and marvelously magnificent array he came in the eyes of the heart, which perceive wisdom" (§308/793). The "center" is identified in and with Jesus Christ, whose holiness achieves the order of charity in a perfectly just fashion: he is universally lovable, because he himself never loves aught but God, and not himself. He can say: "May mine be the glory, not thine, worm and

50. §449/556. There is nothing surprising in the fact that the disqualification of the strongest of the Cartesian (and consequently metaphysical) proofs should be preceded (and not followed) by the doctrine of the new "center" (of its obscurity, of the incapacitated capacity of men, etc.). In effect, it is from the superior point of view that the weakness of the inferior can appear, far from the criticism of the inferior permitting one, after the fact, to accede to the superior. Consequently, it should not be surprising to see that the *ego* gives way to a new "center" only through revelation. That is to say, the *ego* discovers it not through reasoning, but through the Scriptures. The fact that the doctrine of the Christic "center" comes from the Scriptures does not weaken its pertinence in matters concerning the *ego* of thought—the contrary is true.

51. §449/556 [modified], which repeats the formula by saying: ". . . Jesus Christ is the object of all things, the centre towards which all things tend."

clay," claiming for his *self* the love of what is mine, precisely because he can say in truth: "The Father loves all I do."[52] That the "center" remains, in Jesus Christ, a *self* is confirmed again by its function as "object." "Object" suggests obviously the objective or goal of a desire and a tension, which it fulfills only by maintaining some inward analogy with them: "Happiness is neither outside nor inside us: it is in God, both outside and inside us" (§407/465); ". . . As we cannot love what is outside us, we must love a being who is within us but is not our own self. . . . The kingdom of God is within us, universal good is within us, and is both ourselves and not ourselves" (§564/485). How could the Augustinian theme *interior intimo meo, superior summo meo*[53] be applied to a *self,* whose objective it designates well enough, if it did not indicate the actuality of a *self* at work chiefly in the finite *self*? If Jesus Christ offers himself as universal "object" for the love of all, he discloses the universal *self* for the sake of all men, and does so as a consequence of his playing the role of a *self* "thrice holy to God" and "in the eyes of the heart." In the Christ, charity can recognize a *self*—no longer "unjust," "incommodious," and "tyrannical," but holy. Therefore it must love him.

The attempt *(b)* to pinpoint the precise status of the self can now be made, first because Christ establishes the legitimacy of this concept by carrying it out without yielding to self-love, next and above all because Christ also assumes the function of the *I/ego.* It is remarkable that, in its second part, *The Mystery of Jesus* (which must be treated as an essential *theoretical* text in Pascal's project, precisely because it belongs to the most sober of spiritualities) lets Christ speak directly. That is to say, it lets him perform the function of uttering the *I;* and, in contrast with the "Word" that Malebranche blasphemes by lending it all too human doctrines—his own—Christ speaks his own words, directly from the Bible. Indeed, Christ speaks of Christ: "*I* thought of you . . . ," "*I* will do it in you . . . ," ". . . all *I* do . . . ," ". . . *I* guided . . . ," "*I* am present with you . . . ," "*I* am delivering you . . . ," "*I* am a better friend to you . . . ," "*I* love you. . . ." And the one who meditates can in turn venture to say *I* only in response to the word and the gaze that, transfixing him, permit

---

52. *The Mystery of Jesus,* §919/553, *OC,* respectively, 621 *a* and 620 *b.*

53. Saint Augustine, *Confessiones,* III, 6, 11. See *De Trinitate,* VIII, 7, 11. God knows us better than we know ourselves in and through the *cogito* because, in the depths of our selves, we have not first to be known, but loved. If in the second order we have at our disposal the means to be equal to ourselves (the *cogito*), we cannot actually succeed in loving ourselves in the third order—because we know not, or know no longer, how to love, and because loving always amounts to loving another besides the lover himself.

him to do so: "In that case, I shall lose heart, Lord . . . ," "Lord, I give you all," "I see the depths of my pride, curiosity, concupiscence" (§919/553). Because Christ becomes "center" and therefore *self,* man can invoke him as a *self;* but he becomes "center" only insofar as he can, in the first place, utter *I.* In this *I,* which is confused neither with the *I/ego* of the second order, nor with the "unjust" *self* of the third, one has to see, according to the evidence, the ἐγώ εἰμι that Christ assumes, according to John 8:24 and 8:58, from the Name revealed in Exodus 3:14. But such a divine ἐγώ εἰμι cannot not evoke the metaphysical *Ego sum, ego existo* won by Descartes (AT VII, 25, 12 = PW II, 17). This rapprochement should not be surprising; what should be surprising, rather, is the silence that, ordinarily, surrounds so exceptional an encounter: the same name—ἐγώ εἰμι, *ego sum*—is applied to God or to the human *ego,* depending on whether the second or the third order has been opened. To avoid the confusion of the orders, which here would double the "tyranny" with blasphemy, the following difficulty must be cleared up: on what condition can man maintain in the third order the title that falls to him in the second? In short, do the *I/ego* and the (finite) *self* maintain some legitimacy within charity, where the *I* of Christ ". . . shines forth in his reign of holiness"? To come to a decision on this matter, we must reinterpret what will eventually become an *ego* no longer in terms of the *cogitatio* that it masters, but on the basis of the "center" that it loves. The question is then put more precisely as follows: can the "center" and the loved "object" define, in return, he who loves them and intends them? Can he who loves be known by this other whom he loves (according to the logic of the third order, where it is only a matter of loving), rather than by he himself who thinks (according to the logic of the second order, where it is a matter of thinking)? Pascal is decisive on this point: "Not only do we know God through Jesus Christ, but we only know ourselves through Jesus Christ. . . . Apart from Jesus Christ we cannot know . . . ourselves" (§417/548). Does Jesus Christ know us better than we know ourselves because, concerning our soul, he would have at his disposal a clear and distinct idea refused to us, as in Malebranche? In short, does he know us better than we know ourselves because he would think us and represent us better than we ourselves can succeed in doing? This weak interpretation confuses the orders absolutely: in the third, God's excellence stems not from thought, but from charity. What remains then is for us to interpret the knowledge that Christ has of us— a knowledge that is better than our own—in terms of charity. And, in fact, Pascal dares to do so when he defines the "duty" of men as "consenting to the guidance of the whole soul to which they belong, which loves them better than they love themselves" (§360/482). This proclamation finds precise echoes in *The Mystery of Jesus*, where Christ performs them in the person of his *I:* "Your conversion is my concern," "I am a better friend to you than this man or that . . . ," "I love you more ardently than you have loved your foulness" (§919/553). If it is still legitimate for finite and sinful man to say *I* here in the third order, he owes this prerogative to Christ, who recognizes him as a *self.* This *self* is not suspected of having committed the "injustice" of an abusive *self,* since it is no longer affirmed by itself as the *ego* of the second order, but is received from an authority that is more original than itself. For Christ goes back "more deeply" into the origin of this *self,* by loving it "more deeply" than any self-love could idolize itself ("I love you more ardently than you have loved your foulness"), "more deeply" than any *cogito* could think itself ("I thought of you in my agony"), because he institutes this *self* in charity ("I am a better friend than this man or that, for I have done more for you than they") and thus legitimates it in the final order. By a strange substitution, one that manifests the *admirable commercium,* the *I/ego,* which is lost in passing from the second to the third order, is in return received from Christ as an infinitely loved *self*—on the sole condition that it infinitely abandon its thought *I/ego,* for the sake of acknowledging, thus loving, only the *I* of Christ as the sole "center." In this exchange, man loses an *I/ego,* finite in the second order and unjust in the third, so as to win a *self* infinitely loved in the third. He abandons a finite sufficiency or else a "tyranny" in order to receive a just and infinite *self* through grace. It is of this economy of grace that it must be said: ". . . Our argument carries infinite weight, when the finite is wagered in a game where there are even chances of winning and losing and an infinite prize to be won" (§418/233 [modified])—with the considerable emendation that here there is no wagering, since charity has given all in advance. The *ego,* in which metaphysics is secured, must lose itself—or better, give itself up—for the sake of receiving itself in the third order. Metaphysics reaches charity only by being absolutely decentered; if not, it is frozen in a "center of idolatry" (§609/736). Against the *Meditationes* in their order, the only thing that can stand, in the order of charity, is *The Mystery of Jesus.*

§25. The Destitution of Metaphysics

We have shown that Pascal conducts a two-pronged polemic against Descartes: first against his determination of God (§22), then against the *ego*'s being set up as first principle by means of the *cogitatio* (§24). What remains is for us to determine the scope of this polemic. Several hypotheses offer themselves for interpretation. Either (1) one sticks to the theses explicitly criticized and infers that, in what is left of the conceptual field, Pascal remains, consciously or not, a strict Cartesian; or (2) radicalizing this influence, one will emphasize the idea that a discussion can refute only by first confirming its dependence on its adversary, and that in this way, Pascal, precisely because he criticizes Cartesian metaphysics, admits it as the unsurpassable horizon of his thought. These two hypotheses agree in restricting the scope of Pascal's charge against Descartes: his accusation concerns only specific disagreements about the demands of the "heart" in the face of rationalism, and in no way concerns a step back from metaphysics; the metaphysical horizon stays intact and remains Cartesian.[54] Or else (3), the last hypothesis: by contesting certain Cartesian theses, Pascal accuses not only the entire metaphysics of Descartes, but also all thought, Cartesian or not, that would like to be constituted as metaphysics. In a word, Pascal would anticipate what we have learned to call the end of metaphysics.[55] Of them all, the last hypothesis seems the most doubtful, because it appears to be the most bold. Upon reflection, however, the most bold could show itself to be the most correct. That is, Pascal does not criticize merely certain Cartesian theses, as if he meant to correct them or replace them with others—that is a matter for post-Cartesian metaphysicians. Pascal does not even contest Descartes' decisions concerning the two most privileged beings of a special

54. On this point, paradoxically, the following authors are in agreement: L. Brunschvicg, "Descartes et Pascal" (*Ecrits* [Paris, 1951], vol. 1, p. 92), and L. Laberthonnière, "L'apologétique et la méthode de Pascal" (*Essais de philosophie religieuse* [Paris, 1903], reedited by C. Tresmontant following *Le réalisme chrétien* [Paris, 1966]. See the study by V. Carraud, "Laberthonnière et Descartes," *Revue de l'Institut catholique* 8 [Paris, 1983] or Heidegger, *Nietzsche II*, p. 187, and G. Sebba, "Descartes and Pascal: A Retrospect" (*Modern Language Notes* 87/6 [1972]). This restrained interpretation found its clearest and most arguable expression in the presentation of Kierkegaard by J. Beaufret, in the introduction to the first public lecture of *La fin de la philosophie et la tâche de la pensée*, 23 April 1964: "The fact that Kierkegaard is not properly speaking a philosopher is something that he himself said—without any false modesty whatsoever. A religious writer and even a 'poet of the religious,' he wants only to describe the religious situation of man in so far as it is implicit in the theology of Christianity. . . . But more original than Christianity itself is the onto-theo-logical structure of metaphysics" (*Questions IV* [Paris, 1976], pp. 109–10). In his courses, Beaufret assimilated Pascal and Kierkegaard, each to the other, under the single title "religious writer." It is self-evident that the primacy of onto-theo-logy over Christian theology would have appeared to Pascal as, par excellence, the "tyranny" and "idolatry" exercised by the second order over the third.

55. In this sense, H. Birault does not hesitate to speak of an ". . . abandon of philosophy . . ." ("Pascal et le problème du moi introuvable," op. cit., p. 165, here more radically than in "Science et métaphysique chez Pascal et Descartes," *Archives de Philoso-*

metaphysics—the soul and God; for that falls to other metaphysicians, not Cartesian but still within onto-theo-logy. What is characteristically Pascalian consists in disqualifying the very legitimacy of all metaphysics as such, by reference to the two essential theses of Descartes' special metaphysics—God as creator of the eternal truths, the *ego* as first principle inasmuch as *ego cogito*. Or rather, Pascal contests neither the justice nor the rigor of a metaphysics, but only its unconditioned character. A metaphysics is valid only in its own order—the mind, evidence, knowing. Beyond this, a superior order is disclosed, already infinitely distant from that in which metaphysics can be constituted. From the perspective of this order, metaphysics becomes secondary and cannot exert its sway over the order. Metaphysics suffers neither refutation nor denial nor contempt from the fact of a third order; charity abandons the evidence of the mind to its own logic. To put it simply—but this concerns what is decisive if one considers metaphysics' ascent to power from Descartes to Hegel—metaphysics must from now on recognize the irreducibility of an order that it does not see, but which sees it, grasps it, and judges it, "the order of charity." According to the letter of the text, Pascal proclaims neither the end of metaphysics nor the death of philosophy. In observing that "the great Pan is dead" (§343/695), he is simply noting the already old demise of paganism. Thus, after Pascal, and apparently as if nothing had changed, philosophy will be able to pursue its metaphysical course and accomplish the destiny of onto-theo-logy on the basis of what Descartes instituted, a guiding force all the way until Husserl. But after Pascal, one point will have been gained definitively: the order of the mind and evidence where metaphysics is deployed absolutely does not in any way include "the order of charity." In other words, the personal revelation of the "God of Abraham, God of Isaac, God of Jacob,/

---

phie 27/2–3 [1964]), and to ask, "How, in the first place and in a general way, could the *same* name of God ever be suitable to the God of the *causa sui* and the God of Abraham . . . ?" (*Nietzsche et Pascal,* unpublished thesis, 1970, p. 244, cited by H. Gouhier, "Le refus de la philosophie dans la nouvelle apologétique de Pascal," *Chroniques de Port-Royal* 20–31 [1972], p. 30). In this sense also G. Granel demands that we "take seriously Pascal's idea of an idolatry of philosophy" (referring, quite aptly, to the idolatrous "god" challenged by *Identität und Differenz,* op. cit., p. 64 [English trans., p. 72]), for ". . . the metaphysical idea attained by Pascal is in effect nothing less than *the very idea of metaphysics itself* (though *for him* it is not clearly and thematically such)" ("Le tricentenaire de la mort de Pascal," *Critique* 203 [April 1964], respectively p. 299 and p. 301). This last qualification, unless it is limited to saying only something trivial, points out the limits of Granel's judgment, a judgment that is in other respects so illuminating. What is still to be established is the organic relationship of Pascal to the metaphysics that he transgresses. This could not be possible without mediation from Descartes, which itself is impracticable so long as Descartes is not read according to onto-theo-logy (*supra,* chap. II).

not of philosophers and scholars" (§913) is orchestrated, according to a certain logic and a rigorous set of concepts, in a nonmetaphysical doctrine of man, God, and the world. From now on, metaphysics will be reduced to its own assumptions—onto-theo-logy in all its variations—without ever being able to claim to comprehend the God who is revealed in Jesus Christ, nor any of the words that follow. And in fact, this is never seen more clearly than when metaphysics intends in a final, supposedly religious, effort to confuse the orders (Spinoza, Leibniz, and especially Malebranche) and go so far as to use evidence to reason about the economy of grace. The magnitude of this disaster will mark well enough that, from this point forward, charity is neither to be shown nor to be spoken of except in its own order. With Pascal, metaphysics enters into a long, and no doubt definitive, widowhood of the "order of charity." Its path will pass through the absolute concept, mind, and knowing, all the way until it endures its own twilight, but it will never touch charity, not even from afar. The Pascalian precept, organizing all his hermeneutics of the Scriptures—"Everything which does not lead to charity is figurative" (§270/670), "Charity is not a figurative precept" (§849/665)—could be applied to metaphysics with just as much relevance: metaphysics does not lead to charity, it is therefore a figure; but charity is not figurative, therefore metaphysics is, once again, a figure. A figure, but of what? The Old Testament bears the mark of Christ because it announces him without knowing him and without having seen him. Perhaps metaphysics bears the mark of Christ because it keeps the scars of his words and the hollowed-out spaces of the places that he occupied in it. Metaphysics does not suffer, from Pascal, any refutation in its own order, any more than Descartes endures a criticism in terms of the order of his own reasons; it suffers far more and not less. The Heideggerian way of dodging Kierkegaard, and thus also Pascal, by designating them mere "religious writers" who do not broach the serious onto-theo-logy of metaphysics, overlooks a simple question: if they do not practice onto-theo-logy (which will be granted willingly), do they think on its hither side or beyond it? We will suggest that Pascal at least does not ignore metaphysics, but deserts it and leaves it destitute. By destitution, one must understand a disqualification that does not criticize metaphysics in its own order, but takes precautions against its unjust crossings into "the order of charity" by reducing it from the point of view of this very same charity. Just as phenomenology performs reductions, but unto consciousness, just as Descartes performs reductions to evidence, then to the *ego,* just as Hei-

degger performs a reduction of beings to the Being of beings,[56] so too
does Pascal accomplish a reduction of all that happens to charity. The
unconditional reduction to charity is called destitution. To leave metaphysics destitute means: to show that a superior order remains infinitely
distant from it, and that, from this point of view, the evidences of the
mind "are not worth the least impulse of charity" (§308/793) and thus
can be judged in terms of charity. For if the inferior orders cannot regulate the superior order without being guilty of some "injustice," "the
order of charity" sees everything, including the inferior orders, in terms
of whether or not they keep the light of charity. And if Pascal is at once
informed by and set apart from Descartes, this is not because of some
unavowed dependence on an epoch-making metaphysics; it is because
destitution exerts a "constant swing from pro to con" (§93/328), since it
retrieves metaphysical theses in order to repeat them—thus to dislodge
and judge them—from the point of view of charity. Reason for the effects: metaphysics could be the development in the second order of effects of a reason—in fact, charity—that it is ignorant of and does not
see, since this reason inhabits the inaccessible light of the third order.
Would metaphysics for Pascal deal with inadequate ideas, according to
the sense that, in the same era, Spinoza gave to them—a knowledge of
effects whose causes we are ignorant of? No doubt yes—on condition
of making a slight correction: while for Spinoza the causes of the effects
remain ideas, in Pascalian terms, metaphysics deals in the second order
with the senseless effects of a reason that is in no way ideal or representable because it plays, at an infinite distance, in the "order of charity."
Effect of an invisible reason, figure of a lost charity, metaphysics appears
as such—destitute of charity.

One cannot, on principle, prove that charity has left metaphysics destitute: like all the other reductions, this destitution must be accomplished, step by step, every man for himself, in an ordeal that is all the
more rigorous as charity leaves even less room for approximation and
solipsism. But this destitution can be confirmed by following some of the
things it makes operative. We will bring forth three, suggested by Pascal
himself and chosen here because they concern the fixtures common to

56. On this complicated point, see the contrasting essays of J.-F. Courtine, "L'idée de
la phénoménologie et la problématique de la réduction," and J.-L. Marion, "L'étant et le
phénomène" (especially section IV, "Une double réduction phénoménologique re-
doublée"), in *Phénoménologie et métaphysique* (Paris, 1984).

all metaphysics (thus, to be sure, also that of Descartes): namely, the destitution of *(a)* truth, *(b)* Being, and *(c)* philosophy itself. We will outline the three. *(a)* Truth is never defined by *adaequatio* or by the method as in the second order, but, seen from the third, it obeys a new parameter: loving it or not. To be sure, "When speaking of things human, we say that we should know them before loving them" (and in his scientific work, Pascal provides a good illustration of this precept); but in "things divine . . . , we should love them in order to know them" (OC, 355 *a* = 203). Now, in the course of everyday life, we are much more often among "divine things" than before "human things," given that self-love invades every domain, including the flesh and the mind. As a result, most of the time, "truth is so obscured nowadays, and lies so well established that unless we love the truth we shall never recognize it" (§739/864). In effect, the *self* claims to be loved by all, while realizing over and over again that it does not deserve the love to which it lays claim. What follows is "the most unjust and criminal passion that could possibly be imagined . . . a deadly hatred for the truth." The truth, empirical as well as rational, does not remain neutral, but always depends on the reinterpretations or preconceptions that our interests impose on it (Nietzsche and the Frankfurt School, among others, have confirmed this since then). Accordingly, when the truth contradicts our interests, which it almost always does, we hate it: ". . . We hate the truth and those who tell it to us. . . . we hate the truth and it is kept from us" (§978/100). The truth, which claims to belong to the second (indeed the first) order with a perfect disinterestedness, in fact obeys the iron-fisted rules of self-love; it thus falls ultimately within the third order. Men can be divided not so much into those who know the truth and those who don't, but into those who ". . . are against the truth . . ." (§843/836) by hatred and those who love it *de facto,* according to "the greatest of the Christian virtues, which is love of the truth."[57] The truth, at least when understood in its full scope, falls first in the province of love, before it is produced methodically as a certainty. The proof for this paradox is found in the always possible and often actual refusal of scientific evidence itself when it poses a danger to self-love. Consequently, the truth can sometimes become perfectly synonymous with charity: "Those who do not love truth dispute it on the

---

57. *Fragment d'une XIXeme lettre à un provincial, OC,* p. 469 *b.* We do not privilege fragment §110/282, which speaks about the "heart" that knows the first principles, out of respect for the recent caution put forth by H. Gouhier ("Le cœur qui sent les trois dimensions," in *La passion de la raison. Hommage à F. Alquié*), who concludes that there is just a simple "analogy" (op. cit., p. 212).

grounds that it is disputed and that very many people deny it. Thus their error is solely due to the fact that they love neither truth nor charity" (§176/261); or: ". . . Anything offensive to truth and charity is wrong" (§962/902). Charity does not intervene here as a "value judgment," which would come up after the fact and overdetermine an already certain evidence; it plays *a priori* the role of something like a quasi-epistemological condition for the manifestation of evidence, which, without it, can always be misrepresented. However, Pascal seems to venture dangerously forward when he claims that one ". . . makes an idol of truth itself, for truth apart from charity is not God, but his image and an idol that we must not love or worship. . . ." How can one not sense in this the violence of ideology's noonday sun? On the one hand, there is the truth established by its own proofs, and on the other, charity, which forms its judgments according to an exterior criterion (in the present case, God) and runs the risk of rejecting the truth in order to serve the needs of an uncontested cause. It is in a similar fashion that the influence of ideology is exercised, in our time better than in the theological-political debates of the seventeenth century. Such an interpretation of fragment §926/582 would be a misreading, however, reflecting how much the ideological mode of thought infects us, since it easily leads us to condemn ideology in its opposite and to better tolerate it in what is left. The text in fact continues: "Still less must we love or worship its opposite, which is falsehood"; and it specifies that, just as with truth, "I [make] an idol of darkness, separated from God's order" (§926/582). Error is no less exposed to idolatry than is the truth, and the (Nietzschean?) reversal of the one into the other does not do away with charity. Pascal thus does not confuse truth and charity, as if he were anticipating the ideology of completed nihilism; he dislodges the sufficiency of the two values of truth, for the purpose of substituting a thematic in three parts: falsity, inadmissible in all cases; truth without charity, refused out of self-love or accepted with self-love, thus truth falsified "in the eyes of the heart, which see wisdom" (§308/793 [modified]); truth loved, thus accepted as such.[58]

---

58. See also §949/930, especially: "It is false piety to preserve peace at the expense of truth. It is also false zeal to preserve truth at the expense of charity." Descartes, by contrast, seems to pervert the opposition truth/falsity when he troubles it through the direct introduction of interest: "Even a false joy is often more valuable than a sadness whose cause is true" (*The Passions of the Soul*, §142 [AT XI, 435, 13–14 = PW I, 378]). Pascal distinguishes the orders and introduces three terms; Descartes confuses the orders by maintaining only two terms. Here again he leaves out the question of the truth (see *To Mersenne,* 16 October 1639 [AT II, 596, 25–597, 27 = not included in PW]).

Such a thematic calls for a duplication of truth, in which, to the falsified
truth, there corresponds a truth redoubled because loved—one of Pascal's drafts will go so far as to risk saying a ". . . true truth. . . ."[59] In this
way, metaphysics is shown to be destitute of the truth, not because a
higher instance would disqualify the truth (Pascal expressly contests obscurity), but because the truth requires, more than the method, the practice of charity in response to the self-love that tyrannizes it with a silent
and violent rule. Metaphysics claims to accede to the truth by the
method alone, as if to an object to be constructed; it deceives and is
deceived, since truth must be loved in order to be attained. Destituting
metaphysics of the truth permits being open to it, not despite but indeed
thanks to ". . . the defects of a rigid method" (§780/62). The truth passes
from metaphysics, which is missing its most determinative instance, to
charity, which sees it because it loves it enough not to obfuscate it.

The destitution *(b)* of Being presents a particular difficulty, paradoxically because Pascal seems to accomplish it right away and all too easily.
Two famous statements go as follows: "Who can even know what Being
is, which cannot be defined since there is nothing more general, and since
to explain it one would have to use the same word by saying: It is . . . ,"
and "We cannot undertake to define Being without involving ourselves
in this absurdity, for we cannot define a word without beginning with the
words *it is,* whether expressed or understood. Therefore, to define Being
we should have to say *it is,* and thus should use the word to be defined
in the definition."[60] The aporia resides paradoxically in the ease with
which Pascal infers, from the impossibility of defining the use of the verb
to be as a copula, the uselessness of a radical investigation of the Being
of beings. It thus appears to go without saying that Pascal repeats the

59. §826/673, ". . . the resemblance . . . of the *(true)* truth of the Messiah . . . ," according
to *Pensées sur la religion . . . ,* ed. L. Lafuma, op. cit., vol. 1, p. 442.
60. Respectively, *Entretien avec M. de Saci, OC,* p. 294 *b,* then *De l'esprit géométrique,*
OC, p. 350 *a–b* [English trans., p. 126, then 192]. Heidegger's citation of the second text in
Sein und Zeit, §1, op. cit., p. 4, n. 1, presupposes precisely what must be examined: whether
or not *in this case* the noninterrogation of *Being* is a result of metaphysics. As for the use
Heidegger made of the text furnished by *De l'art de persuader,* ". . . we enter into truth
only through charity" (*OC,* 355 *a* [English trans., p. 203 (modified)], cited in *Sein und Zeit,*
§29; p. 139, n. 1 [English trans., p. 492]), it is totally illegitimate: Heidegger invokes charity,
appropriate to "divine things," in order to illustrate the *Befindlichkeit* of a *Dasein,* previously defined by its radical divorce from "the anthropology of Christianity and the ancient world" (§10; p. 48 [English trans., p. 74]). Without insisting on the misreading involved in seeing "interested affects" here (in a mode close to Scheler), we have to
denounce a surreptitious confusion of the orders, which leads the instances of the third
back to the second, and thus at once contests them and recovers them.

decision of the metaphysicians: Being is *notissimum* (contradiction of a definition) or *per se notum* (metaphysical abandon of Being). From this, shouldn't it be concluded that Pascal belongs precisely to metaphysics, thus to the second order? Another interpretation is still possible, however. First because, in the incriminating texts, Pascal is noting only the undemonstrable and forever incomplete evidence of *Being* as copula, without making any other decision about it—in particular without reducing it to the rank of *conceptus objectivus entis.* If the question of Being remains in suspense, at the very least no metaphysical decision has closed it. Next and above all, Pascal introduces a new sense of *Being:* "... our Being unintelligible to us ..." (§131/434 [modified]). How is this to be understood? From the Cartesian point of view, our Being (and way of Being) attains a perfect intelligibility: I am inasmuch as I think, or I am inasmuch as I am caused. However, Pascal maintains that there is an unintelligibility that is itself unintelligible for the second order. It must then be that *unintelligibility* here refers to the third order; and in fact, it is a question of the man who "infinitely transcends man," because man is not what he is, but is what he is no longer or not yet, "... like unto God and sharing in his divinity" (§131/434). Being, which here signifies a way of Being and beingness, must not be referred to the order of metaphysics (the second order), but to that of charity (the third). On account of this displacement, Being will have to submit to other requirements besides those of the question of Being. As with truth, Being will fall under the jurisdiction of charity. It will be a question, for the soul (and not for the mind), of constantly choosing between two dispositions: either "... hatred of our Being ..." (§123/157 [modified]), which issues necessarily from the consecration of self-love; or else conversion to "... the universal Being ... ," which allows for it to be loved: "... a Being who is really worthy of love ..." (§220/468), "... it is natural for the heart to love the universal Being ..." (§423/277). The Aristotelian theme ὄν (. . .) ἀεὶ ζητούμενον[61] will from now on be declined according to the standard of charity: "... Seek for a Being really worthy of love in order to love him" (§564/485). It is important not to overlook the force of this transposition by arguing about a confusion—wholly metaphysical— between Being and beings. The concept "universal Being" is not reduced, in terms already taken from Malebranche, to the universality of

61. Aristotle, *Metaphysics Z,* 1, 1028 *b* 2–4 [English trans., p. 1624]—a formula whose Cartesian equivalent is applied to the *I think, therefore I am,* taken "... as the first principle of the philosophy I was seeking" (DM, 32, 22–23 = PW I, 127).

Being, abstract and nonetheless erected as a divine name. At issue is a way of Being of the being that I am, since I can love either according to the Being that is reduced to the sole being proper to me, or according to the Being that passes beyond my being unto the infinite. It is not an issue of loving an object that is more or less universal, but of loving universally, which implies a sense of Being that is freed from the tyrannical reduction that a being—the *self* of self-love—is constantly accomplishing. Beyond the ontological difference, another difference struggles to come to light. Under what ontic, but also ontological, conditions could a being privileged by metaphysics—the *ego cogito* as *cogitatio sui*—manage to love? Answer: on condition that the Being revealed by and to this being passes beyond it infinitely, by an opening that disappropriates this being of itself. The non-ontological difference exerts its sway over Being through "the infinitely infinite distance" of the second order from the third. Metaphysics attempts to be done with Being by knowing the privileged beings with certainty. Nonmetaphysical thought attempts to think Being as such, without beings. The "order of charity" endeavors to convert the privileged being by submitting Being itself to the ordeal of love: "Know that [these words] came from a man who went down on his knees before and after to pray this infinite and indivisible [B]eing to whom he submits his own, that he might bring yours too to submit to him for your own good and for his glory" (§418/233). And it might be asked whether or not this is indeed the long-awaited antagonist of the god before whom "man can neither pray nor ... fall to his knees in awe."[62] At the very least, we think we have the right to conclude that, for Pascal, the question of Being is not exhausted simply within the horizon of metaphysics, because, beyond the second order, the third stakes a claim not just to all the beings but to Being—in terms of whether it is offered to be loved or held back for hatred. Love and hate do not belong to metaphysics; thus metaphysics suffers a second destitution—that of Being. One must not rule out the possibility that the nonmetaphysical thought of Being as such is also exposed to this requirement, and it is all the more pressing that this be emphasized, as this thought never stops pretending to subtract itself from it.

There remains one last destitution, the one that is the most radical, because it is exerted over *(c)* philosophy itself: Pascal leaves metaphysics destitute of philosophy. This operation is accomplished by doubling the θαυμάζειν proper to philosophy: "Philosophers:/ They surprise the ordinary run of men./ Christians: they surprise the philosophers" (§613/

62. Heidegger, *Identität und Differenz*, op. cit., p. 64 [English trans., p. 72].

443).[63] Already there is a discrepancy: it is no longer a matter of the astonishment that the philosophers feel before the fact that the world is, but of the astonishment that their astonishment incites in the view of the "ordinary run of men"; instead of seeing, philosophers are seen. Seen from the outside by "ordinary men," they are seen by those who do not comprehend them, thus as invisible. The inferior order (ordinary men: flesh, the first order) sees without seeing the superior order (here, the mind). This astonishment before the invisible, superior order can be duplicated; philosophers then see Christians without understanding them, thus see them as invisible within the third order. θαυμάζειν no longer just characterizes the philosophical gaze; it phenomenologically defines the impossibility of crossing the distance from an inferior to a superior order. It can be applied to the philosophers' incomprehension as well as to that of the ordinary man. From now on, philosophers will be seen by "Christians" from the perspective of the third order. In this hazy light, how do they appear? They offer the spectacle of a twofold foolishness— that of their object and that of their gaze. The foolishness of their object stems from its "vanity"—"Vanity of science," because the sciences know only ". . . exterior things" (§23/67 [modified]); vanity of untenable doctrines: "What the Stoics propose is so difficult and vain" (§144/360); vanity of attempts at wisdom: ". . . show the vanity of ordinary lives, and then the vanity of philosophers' lives" (§694/61). Whence comes this vanity? From ". . . the vanity of the world . . . ;" ". . . so obvious . . ." and yet ". . . so little recognized . . ." (§16/161). The vanity of the world stems from its not perceiving itself in the light of the third order and from its not seeing which economy of charity embraces it. Philosophers, practicing their knowledge and their wisdom only in the second order, do not see the vanity of the world; thus they share in it: "Anyone who does not see the vanity of the world is very vain himself" (§36/164). Whence the "folly" of philosophy (§408/74) and its uselessness (§84/79, §887/78, etc.). The foolishness of the philosophers' object results, more originally, from the foolishness of their gaze, which ignores the last order to the point of being ignorant that it is so ignorant. This failing also attests to the fact that they are governed, without acknowledging it, by the refusal of charity. In effect, rational doctrines can be read as so many effects, in the second order, of a reason—self-love—that belongs to the third order. A

63. See Plato's *Theatetus*, 155 *d*, and Aristotle, *Metaphysics A*, 2, 982 *b* 12. Descartes maintains this tradition, *The Passions of the Soul*, §125. Here one should consult the study by P. Magnard, "Utilité et inutilité de la philosophie selon Pascal," in *Philosophie* 7 (Summer 1985), alongside that of H. Gouhier, *Blaise Pascal. Conversion et apologetique* (Paris, 1986), chaps. VIII–X.

philosophy can then, indeed can in the first place, be interpreted as the rational symptom of a decision for (non-)charity: "The three forms of concupiscence have created three sects, and all that philosophers have done is to follow one of these three sorts of concupiscence" (§145/461). This can be explained as follows: pride, the concupiscence of the third order (*libido dominandi*), designates the stoics and, in general, ". . . the arrogance of the philosophers, who have known God but not their own wretchedness" (§449/556). Pleasure, the concupiscence of the first order (*libido sentiendi*), refers to the Epicureans. As for knowledge, concupiscence of the second order (*libido sciendi*), it could concern the skeptics or the Pyrrhonists, since by doubting, they confirm the ideal of knowing. In fact, in these three sects, philosophy is first inclined not to the love of wisdom, but to making the men who philosophize be loved by those who do not. "They believe that God alone is worthy of love and admiration"—this is the avowed plan in the second order. "They too wanted to be loved and admired by men and do not realize their own corruption"—this is the latent intention that "the order of charity" detects in them. The discrepancy between the avowed plan and the intention is enacted in the "unjust" ideal of the man of wisdom; and ". . . such perfection is horrible" (§142/463). The philosophers do not make an exception to this uniform and universal vanity: "Vanity is so firmly anchored in man's heart that a soldier, a rough, a cook, or a porter will boast and expect admirers, and even philosophers want them" (§627/150). Pascal does not simply revive the polemic against the theoretical incoherence of the philosophers—though he cites the Ciceronian adage, "Nihil tam absurde dici potest quod non dicatur ab aliquo philosophorum [Nothing is too absurd for some philosopher not to have said it]" (*De Divinatione,* II, 58) and remarks "divine!" (§507/363). Pascal disqualifies philosophy's claim to be its own norm, to regulate itself exclusively according to the requirements of the second order, without also, indeed first of all, seeing itself, *in via,* to be among the phantasmagoria produced by self-love and the hazy light of charity. A man, in order to be according to philosophy, indeed in order to be a philosopher, is no less a sinner (or a saint) in the first place. And if philosophy has no time for charity, charity judges it, and it happens that "to have no time for philosophy is to be a true philosopher" (§513/4). Philosophy should therefore be destitute of itself, or rather let itself be instituted in charity, no longer simply in the second order. If philosophy truly *loves* wisdom, it should fearlessly endure the gaze cast upon it by ". . . the eyes of the heart which see wisdom" (§308/793). In short, it should love Wisdom, and at once, philosophy passes out of the domain and the range of the second order; it is already an issue of "the order of charity."

These three destitutions of metaphysics do not exclude others. They are, however, sufficient to confirm the situation of metaphysics. To speak more precisely, because metaphysics occupies *a* place according to *an* order, it can be overcome, bypassed, indeed confirmed. The doctrine of the three orders carries out, before and no doubt with more sobriety than the modern attempts, a questioning of the sufficiency and pertinence of metaphysics, simply because it puts metaphysics in its proper place. Pascal gives notice to metaphysics that it must notice its proper place: it is legitimate only in the second order; it cannot pretend to regulate the third order; it cannot remove itself from the judgment that the third order exerts over it. Pascal gives notice to metaphysics that it must admit its decentering when confronted with the sole "center and object," with the single "universal Being," with the only "eyes which see wisdom"—charity, incommensurable with and lacking any analogy to the greatness belonging to the inferior orders.

In his confrontation with Descartes, Pascal has not conducted a polemic of one metaphysician against another; nor has he simply refuted Descartes, as apologists and "religious writers" would have done (and in fact have done). He has compelled Cartesian metaphysics—and, through it, all figures of onto-theo-logy yet to come—to admit that it dwells, ultimately and obscurely, in charity, just as the second order is exposed to the gaze of the third, which nonetheless remains invisible to it. In this way, metaphysics suffers its last destitution: far from seeing without being seen, it is seen without seeing and without seeing that it is seen. Pascal's greatness is found in this destitution of metaphysics by charity. But among the things that are great about Descartes, not the least was to have offered up his redoubled onto-theo-logy to the ordeal of these destitutions.

THE QUESTION OF AN OPENING

Before posing the question of an opening, and so that we might do so correctly, it seems wise to complete the closure of a question that from the very beginning we have outlined as our program.[1] In fact, these two operations can be accomplished by taking stock of four principal conclusions. These conclusions echo those which summed up the points obtained by our previous studies *Sur l'ontologie grise de Descartes* and *Sur la théologie blanche de Descartes.* In reconsidering them and confirming what is essential in them, we will also be obliged to displace and rectify them from time to time—which simply goes to show that it was a matter of real questions and tried-and-true results. And moreover, precisely because we have ended up with such points, new problems arise at every turn, with the expectation of new research into territories still not well enough known.

Descartes takes up the title *Metaphysica,* but radically modifies its conceptual articulations. In particular, he substitutes for *metaphysica generalis* (and soon enough *ontologia*) the primacy, unheard of before that time, of all the things that can possibly be known first, thus the *ego;* as a result, the *prima philosophia* of the *Meditationes* no longer concerns first, (despite the title) God and the soul, but doubles, without contesting, this classic part of *Metaphysica* with another primacy. Two primacies in search of a universality: does this still constitute a metaphysics? If one sticks solely to the study of the nomenclature of the conflicting sciences, one must no doubt answer negatively. But if one refers, for a working hypothesis, to the onto-theo-logical constitution of metaphysics such as it was set out by Heidegger, a positive—though more complex—answer seems plausible. In effect, the new primacy, exerted by the *ego,* interprets all beings universally as *cogitata*—which means that the gray ontology of the *Regulae* not only is confirmed in a precise ontology of the *ens ut cogitatum,* but finally attains its ground in the *ego* as *cogitatio*

1. See *supra,* "The Closure of a Question."

sui. The *Regulae*'s hesitation between epistemological and ontic inter-pretations of the object thought is decided definitively by the conquest, in the *Meditationes*, of a ground, the *ego*, which bends the *cogitatio* back over itself to the point that it reaches itself as *ens*, ". . . primus enim sum [for I am the first]. . . ."[2] The new primacy therefore institutes not merely an epistemological "order of reasons," nor even a new being par excel-lence, but universally an ontology of the *ens* in general as *cogitatum*. In short, it accomplishes a completed onto-theo-logy. Descartes, however, does not just revive the goal of completing a metaphysics—he is not limited to making possible the simple position of a Berkeley or a Male-branche. The first onto-theo-logy of the *ens ut cogitatum* is in fact dou-bled, in the middle of the *Meditationes*, by a second, in which the inter-pretation of the *ens* in general as *causatum* is founded on the being par excellence thought as *causa sui*. Hence, *conclusion 1: the difficulty of assigning a metaphysical status to Cartesian thought comes far less from a disappearance of the doctrine of the* ens *in general than it does from the ambivalence of a redoubled onto-theo-logy*. This conclusion immediately gives rise to a corollary and a task. Corollary: Descartes belongs offi-cially to the history of metaphysics, whose destiny he shares and orients radically. To the line of questioning that has guided us for a decade—does Descartes, who challenges ". . . omnia Platonis et Aristotelis argu-menta [all the arguments of Plato and Aristotle] . . ." (AT X, 367, 20 = PW I, 13), confront the question of the Being of beings?—we can offer an affirmative answer. This definitively established point nonetheless im-mediately imposes a new task: since we now recognize a continuity between Suarez and Kant *through* Descartes, and not just through the *Schulmetaphysik* despite Descartes, how are we to explain the fact that this same Descartes totally ignored the elaboration by his contem-poraries (Calov, Goclenius, et al.), indeed by his most faithful dis-ciples (Clauberg), of the concept "*ontologia*"? A history of the birth of *ontologia* remains to be written; it would have to clarify this paradox: the science of being as such finds its name and its standing in the epoch of Descartes and, according to Clauberg, its inventor, thanks to Des-cartes; nevertheless, it does so without Descartes' ever busying himself with it. In other words, why does the double ontology clearly offered by Descartes' redoubled onto-theo-logy remain anonymous at the very moment when, for the first time in the history of metaphysics and un-

---

2. *Comments on a Certain Broadsheet* (AT VIII-2, 348, 15 = PW I, 297); see *supra*, chap. II, §6.

der the influence of Descartes, it wins its emblematic name—*ontologia*?

If the metaphysical relevance of Cartesian thought stems from the fact that a figure of the onto-theo-logical constitution is deployed in it—if therefore the onto-theo-logical constitution helps explain Descartes—the relationship must also be reversed: Descartes complicates the onto-theo-logical constitution by doubling it. This added complexity demands that one choose between two hypotheses concerning the essence of onto-theo-logical constitution. First hypothesis: this onto-theo-logical constitution admits only the dual unity of a the*i*ology and an ontology, as Heidegger has explained in the famous seminar of 1957. According to this hypothesis, the doubling would attest either to an error of the interpreter, or to an aberration on the part of Descartes himself. But in that case, it would be necessary to explain either the fecundity of an error in interpretation or the ever-so-perfect rigor of an aberration. A second hypothesis remains, however: the Cartesian initiative of a redoubling reveals and probes deeper into the essence of the onto-theo-logical constitution of metaphysics, for which Heidegger would have formulated only an elementary blueprint, and whose hermeneutic fecundity would increase in direct proportion to its eventual complexity. From this other hypothesis, *conclusion 2* would follow: *Descartes can be interpreted by the onto-theo-logical constitution only inasmuch as he confirms it by redoubling it, in such a way that it is once again put forth as a hermeneutic hypothesis.* Corollary: never was the onto-theo-logical constitution so visible as in its Cartesian redoubling—precisely because it is duplicated in it; but never before had it shown the fragility of metaphysics so well, precisely because the game is played out in daylight; a game between two articulated modalities, a game played by the daylight that filters between their ill-adjusted joints; a game between two beings par excellence, each privileged in turn, where the interpreter is less obliged to stand astonished before the *ego* assuming the rank of first being as he is to investigate the attribution of *causa sui* to God, as a divine name—while it is only a matter of one function of an onto-theo-logy among other possible ones. From the very fact that he illustrates to perfection the onto-theo-logical essence of metaphysics, Descartes quite obviously flushes out its fundamental inconsistency. Hence, he could shed some light on the essence of onto-theo-logy as such, even more than the latter sheds light on the metaphysical status of Cartesian thought. This paradoxical result calls forth a new question: Descartes' successors, whether they claim to be his disciples or his adversaries, depend on him, and in particular they depend on him for their metaphysical status, which they all, except Leibniz, have left undetermined, or, at least, implicit. Couldn't one attempt to reconstitute each of their respective statuses on the basis of one or the other of the Cartesian postulations? Who is attached to the onto-theo-logy of the *ens ut cogitatum,* and according to what modifications? Who depends on the onto-theo-logy of the *ens ut causatum,* and according to what variations? Who is not connected to any of them and therefore does not accede to metaphysical standing? In the prism of Descartes' redoubled onto-theo-logy there could thus be revealed the true metaphysical posterity of Cartesianism, a posterity that no doubt would only partially coincide with the critical and doxographic influences that the history of ideas legitimately calls for. On this view, a metaphysical history of the *causa sui* would become possible. At the very least, it would have the merit of not attributing its paternity to Spinoza, and would face the more arduous task of weighing its relationship to the Leibnizian formulation of the *principium reddendae rationis.*

Confirmed as an authentic metaphysician by the onto-theo-logical constitution whose essence he best discloses by making it more complex, Descartes nonetheless escapes it in part. By a paradox that surprised us along the way, Descartes puts onto-theo-logy into play only to transgress it, by dint of manifesting what is at stake in it. We saw that the *ego* dispenses with its role as privileged substance after having won it by a hard-fought struggle, so as to pass from actuality to the related conflict between necessity and possibility—and there to win freedom (chapter III, §15). We observed that among the three determinations of the divine essence, only two were integrated into the redoubled onto-theo-logy (*ens perfectissimum* and *causa sui*), leaving the third—in fact the first—without a metaphysical site: the infinite remains outside the play of metaphysics (chapter IV, §20). We thus rediscovered the ultimate conclusion of a previous study: ". . . The the[i]ology of all metaphysics leaves behind it, like a fortress bypassed but not conquered, the question of a mediated relation of the finite to the infinite."[3] Along with the determination of God as infinite, what is also at issue is the incomprehensibility of God the creator of the eternal truths; thus, from 1630 until 1649, this incomprehensibility governs Descartes' thought. Hence, *conclusion 3: Descartes belongs to metaphysics all the more as he onto-theo-logically establishes its exact limits and sometimes succeeds, under certain conditions, in transgressing them.* Only a thesis that can be refuted deserves to be

3. *Sur la théologie blanche de Descartes,* op. cit., p. 454.

proved: the redoubled onto-theo-logical constitution of Cartesian metaphysics can be confirmed over and over, given that it admits exceptions.
The Cartesian metaphysics has limits, seeing as Descartes sometimes
crosses them. Whence a question: is that enterprise meaningful and rigorous which would like to distinguish at the heart of a single corpus
between metaphysical and nonmetaphysical statements? Don't the latter
always belong, whether we know it or not, to metaphysics? The extreme
difficulty of the question strengthens the objection, and it does so all the
more in that our own work offers an argument against making such a
distinction: the creation of the eternal truths, just like the determination
of God as infinite, is in fact not integrated into any of the figures of the
redoubled onto-theo-logy. From this, we have concluded that it does not
belong to metaphysics closed in its constitution. And yet Pascal, when
he criticizes Descartes as a metaphysician, stigmatizes the very doctrine
that we claimed made an exception to metaphysics (the creation of the
eternal truths) precisely as a metaphysical doctrine (chapter V, §22). Is
it necessary then to conclude with the impossibility or inconsistency of
a delimitation of metaphysics? We suggest, on the contrary, that with
each occurrence of *metaphysics* or a metaphysical statement, it would be
necessary to determine exactly which onto-theo-logy sustains and justifies it. In the case at hand, a double response removes the difficulty; for
Descartes, the "metaphysical truths" (AT I, 144, 15) being created, the
creative instance remains "incomprehensible" (AT I, 146, 4) and trans-
metaphysical; in this sense, it does not belong to the redoubled onto-
theo-logy. For Pascal, this creative instance is deployed first as a "first
truth" (§449/556 = AT I, 150, 2–3) and a cause ("Author," §449/556 =
AT I, 152, 3); in this sense, the creation of the eternal truths concentrates
within it the two pronouncements of the redoubled onto-theo-logy. The
conflict between Pascal and Descartes could therefore suggest that establishing the limits of a metaphysics makes up an integral part of its
constitution. It falls to the interpreters to elaborate an onto-theo-logical
hermeneutic detailed enough to detect the signs of such a limit, and to
become the patient denizens of these borderlands.

As for Pascal, he does not come up as just a marginal figure in a study
of the Cartesian constitution of metaphysics. He plays an absolutely essential role in it because he challenges Descartes on just one point—at
least this is what we have tried to show: Descartes, in the role of metaphysician, claims to have integrated the question of God into onto-theo-
logy. In this way, Pascal powerfully confirms the fact that Descartes thoroughly assumes the function of a metaphysician, since he reproaches

him only for this function. In refuting certain metaphysical doctrines of Descartes, Pascal guarantees his metaphysical authenticity in general. This first role obviously implies a second one: posing, through the discussion of Cartesian metaphysics, the question of the limits of all metaphysics. But positing limits can happen, at least in principle, only if they are transgressed. Hence, a third role for Pascal: crossing the limits of onto-theo-logy there where Descartes has only a dim sense of them. We thus reach *conclusion 4: Descartes redoubles onto-theo-logy in such a way as to provide Pascal a complete metaphysics to overcome.* "Overcoming metaphysics"—without sinking to the rank of an appalling buzzword, this formula can signify only: *(a)* inverting Platonism (Nietzsche), *(b)* destroying the history of ontology (Heidegger), and *(c)* deconstructing meaning (Derrida). However diverse these three projects might be, they have two characteristics in common: first, they overcome metaphysics only diachronically, at the terminal point of its unfolding. Accordingly, not a single one of them could have been practiced or could have appeared before the historic or historiological closure of metaphysics. Consequently, each of them makes it impossible for there ever to be a new arising of metaphysics, whose terrain they at once occupy and forbid. They are therefore carried out with an invisible violence, since they overcome metaphysics only by completing it and substituting themselves for it. Pascal, in contrast, introduces a new mode of overcoming: *(d)* destitution. Destitution can be carried out synchronically, contemporaneously with each of the epochs of metaphysics. It succeeds in doing so without destruction, without interdiction, and without putting forth its own claims, because it alone abandons metaphysics to itself. Destitution passes through metaphysics and surpasses its limits (which it thus discerns better than metaphysics itself does) because it passes to another instance besides metaphysics, which it therefore has no need to combat. Another instance—in Pascal's terms, another order. Pascal does not refute Descartes' redoubled onto-theo-logy; he simply sees it. But he *sees* it from the point of view of a more powerful order, charity, which, simply by considering metaphysics as an inferior order, judges it and leaves it destitute. Metaphysics undergoes neither refutation nor recuperation, nor even delimitation: it appears as such—vain in the gaze of charity. The metaphysics left destitute still remains, but in its order and its place, which from now on has lost primacy. We were able only to suggest in regard to a particular case the characteristics of such a destitution of metaphysics (chapter V, §25). In order to clarify them more precisely and to confirm them in the analysis of comparable conflicts in the history of metaphysics, it would behoove us to undertake a twofold task: on the one hand, to once again win the fundamental elements of a doctrine of charity considered in its own rigor; on the other hand, to point out the guiding axes for a history of charity. Facing up to these tasks would serve the purpose first of testing charity's irreducibility to onto-theo-logy in its diverse figures, then of drawing out the different occurrences of the destitution of metaphysics by charity. This twofold task suffices to open our final question. It is, to be sure, the most fragile of affairs, seeing as it calls for something better than the mind and resolution; but "it is right that so pure a God should disclose himself only to those whose hearts are purified."[4]

In this way, Descartes remains one of our closest contemporaries. To the reasons that our forerunners have already given for this, we will add two: Descartes teaches us what is at stake in the onto-theo-logical constitution of all metaphysics, and Descartes recognizes limits to onto-theological constitution to the point of exposing it to its eventual destitution.

4. Pascal, *Pensées,* §793/737.

English-Language Editions Cited

Aristotle. *The Complete Works of Aristotle*. Ed. Jonathan Barnes. Princeton: Bollingen, 1984.

Anselm. *Monologion and Proslogion*. Trans. Thomas Williams. Indianapolis: Hackett, 1995.

Augustine. *De Civitate Dei. The City of God*. Trans. Henry Bettenson. New York: Penguin Books, 1972.

———. *De Trinitate. On the Holy Trinity*. In *The Nicene and Post-Nicene Fathers of the Christian Church*, vol. 3. Ed. Philip Schaff. Grand Rapids, Mich.: Wm. B. Eerdmans, 1980.

———. *De Vera Religione*. "Of True Religion." In *Augustine: Earlier Writings*. Trans. and ed. John H. S. Burleigh. Philadelphia: Westminster Press, 1953.

Balthasar, Hans Urs von. *Herrlichkeit. The Glory of the Lord: A Theological Aesthetics*. New York: Crossroads, vol. 3, 1984; vol. 5, 1986.

Derrida, Jacques. *La Voix et le phénomène. Speech and Phenomena and Other Essays on Husserl's Theory of Signs*. Trans. David E. Allison. Evanston: Northwestern University Press, 1973.

Descartes, René. *The Philosophical Writings of Descartes*. Vols. 1 and 2, ed. and trans. John Cottingham, Robert Stoothof, and Dugald Murdoch. Vol. 3, ed. and trans. John Cottingham, Robert Stoothof, Dugald Murdoch, and Anthony Kenny. Cambridge: Cambridge University Press, 1984–91.

———. *Discours de la Méthode. Discourse on the Method*. In *The Philosophical Writings of Descartes*, vol. 1.

———. *Entretien avec Burman. Conversation with Burman*. In *The Philosophical Writings of Descartes*, vol. 3.

———. *Lettres. Letters*. In *The Philosophical Writings of Descartes*, vol. 3.

———. *Meditationes, Objectiones et Responsiones. Meditations* and *Objections and Replies*. In *The Philosophical Writings of Descartes*, vol. 2.

———. *Notae in Programma quoddam. Comments on a Certain Broadsheet*. In *The Philosophical Writings of Descartes*, vol. 1.

———. *Les Passions de l'Ame. The Passions of the Soul*. In *The Philosophical Writings of Descartes*, vol. 1.

———. *Principia Philosophiae. Principles of Philosophy*. In *The Philosophical Writings of Descartes*, vol. 1.

———. *La recherche de la Vérité par la lumière naturelle. The Search for Truth*. In *The Philosophical Writings of Descartes*, vol. 2.

————. *Regulae ad Directionem Ingenii. Rules for the Direction of the Mind.* In *The Philosophical Writings of Descartes,* vol. 1.

Duns Scotus, John. *Ordinatio.* In *Philosophical Writings: John Duns Scotus.* Trans. Allan Wolter, O.F.M. Indianapolis: Bobbs-Merrill, 1962.

————. *De Primo Principio. The De Primo Principio of John Duns Scotus.* Trans. Evan Roche. St. Bonaventure, N.Y.: Franciscan Institute, 1949.

Gassendi, Pierre. *Exercitationes Paradoxicae Adversus Aristoteleos. The Selected Works of Pierre Gassendi.* Trans. and ed. Craig B. Brush. New York: Johnson Reprint Corp., 1972.

Gilson, Etienne. *Le Thomisme. The Philosophy of Saint Thomas Aquinas.* Trans. Edward Bullough. Freeport, N.Y.: Books for Libraries Press, 1979.

Guéroult, Martial. *Descartes selon l'ordre des raisons. Descartes' Philosophy Interpreted According to the Order of Reasons.* Minneapolis: University of Minnesota Press, 1984–85.

Hegel, G. W. F. *Phänomenologie des Geistes. The Phenomenology of Spirit.* Trans. A. V. Miller. Oxford: Oxford University Press, 1977.

————. *Vorlesungen über die Geschichte der Philosophie. Hegel's Lectures on the History of Philosophy,* vol. 3. Trans. E. S. Haldane and Frances H. Simson. New York: Humanities Press, 1974.

Heidegger, Martin. *Die Grundbegriffe der Metaphysik. The Fundamental Concepts of Metaphysics: World, Finitude, Solitude.* Trans. William H. McNeill and Nicholas Walker. Bloomington: Indiana University Press, 1995.

————. *Identität und Differenz. Identity and Difference.* Trans. Joan Stambaugh. New York: Harper and Row, 1969.

————. *Nietzsche II. Nietzsche,* vol. 4. Trans. Frank Capuzzi. In *Nietzsche.* Ed. David Farrell Krell. San Francisco: HarperCollins, 1982.

————. *Prolegomena zur Geschichte des Zeitbegriffs. History of the Concept of Time, Prolegomena.* Trans. Theodore Kisiel. Bloomington: Indiana University Press, 1985.

————. *Der Satz vom Grunde. The Principle of Reason.* Trans. Reginald Lilly. Bloomington: Indiana University Press, 1991.

————. *Sein und Zeit. Being and Time.* Trans. John Macquarrie and Edward Robinson. San Francisco: Harper and Row, 1962.

————. "The Word of Nietzsche, 'God is Dead'." In *The Question Concerning Technology and Other Essays.* Trans. William Lovett. New York: Harper and Row, 1977.

Husserl, Edmund. *Cartesianische Meditationen. Cartesian Meditations.* Trans. Dorion Cairns. Dordrecht: Kluwer Academic Publishers, 1993.

————. *Ideen . . . I. Ideas,* vol. 1. Trans. F. Kersten. The Hague: Martinus Nijhoff, 1983.

Kant, Immanuel. *Kritik der reinen Vernunft. Critique of Pure Reason.* Trans. Norman Kemp Smith. New York: St. Martin's, 1965.

————. *Letter to Markus Herz,* 1 May 1781. In *Kant: Philosophical Correspondence, 1755–99.* Trans. and ed. Arnulf Zweig. Chicago: University of Chicago Press, 1986.

————. *De Mundi sensibilis atque intelligibilis forma et principiis.* "On the Form and Principles of the Sensible and Intelligible World (Inaugural Dissertation)." In *Kant's Latin Writings.* Ed. Lewis White Beck. New York: Peter Lang, 1986.

Leibniz, G. W. *24 Propositions.* "A Résumé of Metaphysics." In *Leibniz: Philosophical Writings.* Ed. G. H. R. Parkinson. London: J. M. Dent and Sons, 1973.

————. "Correspondence with Arnauld." In *Leibniz: Philosophical Writings.*

————. "Discourse on Metaphysics." In *Leibniz: Philosophical Writings.*

————. "Letter to de Volder, 20 June 1703." In *Philosophical Papers and Letters.* Trans. and ed. Leroy E. Loemker. Dordrecht: D. Reidel, 1969.

————. *Monadology.* In *Leibniz: Philosophical Writings.*

————. "New System, and Explanation of the New System." In *Leibniz: Philosophical Writings.*

————. "Principles of Nature and of Grace." In *Leibniz: Philosophical Writings.*

————. *Theodicy.* Trans. E. M. Huggard. London: Routledge and Kegan Paul, 1951.

Malebranche, Nicolas. *Entretiens sur la métaphysique et sur la religion. Dialogues on Metaphysics.* Trans. Willis Doney. New York: Arabis Books, 1980.

————. *Recherche de la Vérité. The Search after Truth.* Trans. Thomas M. Lennon and Paul J. Olscamp. Columbus: Ohio State University Press, 1980.

Maritain, Jacques. *Le songe de Descartes et autres essais. The Dream of Descartes.* Trans. Mabelle L. Andison. New York: Philosophical Library, 1944.

Merleau-Ponty, Maurice. *Le visible et l'invisible. The Visible and the Invisible.* Trans. Alphonso Lingis. Evanston: Northwestern University Press, 1968.

Montaigne, Michel. *The Complete Works of Montaigne.* Trans. Donald Frame. Stanford: Stanford University Press, 1957.

Nietzsche, Friedrich. *Wille zur Macht. Will to Power.* Trans. Walter Kaufmann. New York: Random House, 1967.

Pascal, Blaise. *De l'art de persuader.* "The Art of Persuasion." In *Great Shorter Works of Pascal.* Trans. Emile Cailliet and John C. Blankenagel. Philadelphia: Westminster Press, 1948.

————. *Entretien avec M. de Saci.* "Pascal's Conversation with Monsieur de Saci . . ." In *Great Shorter Works of Pascal.*

————. *De l'esprit géométrique.* "The Mind of the Geometrician." In *Great Shorter Works of Pascal.*

————. *Pensées.* Trans. A. J. Krailsheimer. New York: Penguin, 1966.

————. "Selected Letters." In *Great Shorter Works of Pascal.*

Schelling, F. W. J. *Zur Geschichte der neueren Philosophie. On the History of Modern Philosophy.* Trans. Andrew Bourne. Cambridge: Cambridge University Press, 1994.

Schopenhauer, Arthur. *Ueber die vierface Wurzel des Satzes vom Zureichenden Grunde. On the Fourfold Root of the Principle of Sufficient Reason.* Trans. E. F. J. Payne. LaSalle, Ill.: Open Court, 1974.

Spinoza, Baruch. *Ethics, Treatise on the Emendation of the Intellect, and Selected Letters.* Trans. Samuel Shirley. Indianapolis: Hackett, 1992.

Thomas Aquinas. *Contra Gentes. Summa Contra Gentiles.* Trans. Vernon Bourke. Notre Dame: University of Notre Dame Press, 1956.

————. *In XII Libros Metaphysicorum Expositio. Commentary on the Metaphysics of Aristotle.* Trans. John P. Rowan. Chicago: H. Regnery Co., 1961.

————. *In Libros Physicorum. Commentary on Aristotle's Physics.* Trans. Richard J. Blackwell, Richard J. Spath, and W. Edmund Thirlkel. New Haven: Yale University Press, 1963.

————. *De potentia. On the Power of God.* Trans. English Dominican Fathers. Westminster, Md.: Newman Press, 1952.

————. *Summa Theologica.* Trans. Fathers of the English Dominican Province. New York: Benziger Brothers, 1947.

INDEX

abducere mentis a sensibus, 27–28,
  28n. 29, 31
Abra de Raconis, 23, 51
  on abstraction, 26
  definition of metaphysics, 43
  God as object of metaphysics, 51
  metaphysics and *prima Philo-*
    sophia, 23
  model for Descartes' *Principia,*
    12n. 4
abstraction
  Cartesian, 27–31
  scholastic, 25–27
adorare, 294, 303
all beings as caused, 105–9
all that exists (*omne id quod est,* AT
  VII, 112), 114–15
Alquié, F., 1, 5n. 9, 32, 82n. 20, 123n.
  68, 215n. 11, 229n. 33,
  245, 250n. 65, 261, 319n.
  40
Alsted, J. H., 73n. 8
Anselm, Saint
  on *causa sui,* 259
  on *ens summe perfectum,* 253–55
  on God as substance, 220–21
argument of the wager (Pascal),
  295–96
Aristotle
  acceptation of ὄν, 77–78
  and *cogito sum,* 133–36
  definition of time, 183–87
  first philosophy as universal and
    first science, 59
  hierarchy of the sciences, 18–22

meaning of Being, 70
  unity of philosophy, 41
Armogathe, J.-R., 154
as if, 200, 200n. 82
atheism, 296, 299
Augustine, Saint, 328
  and *cogito sum,* 129–32
  on God as substance, 220
  love of God and love of self,
    328

Balthasar, H. U. von, 137n. 14, 307n.
  30, 322
Baudin, E., 279n. 3
Baumgarten, A. G., 2
Beaufret, J., 334n. 54
Becco, A., 123n. 66
Beck, L., 2n. 1
Being, 38
  as *causa sui,* 88
  destitution of, 340–42
  as *ego/sum,* 69–71, 150, 171
  equivalent to thought, 138–41,
    142–50
  as existence, 78–81, 149
  history of, 171
  objective concept of, 49–50
  in onto-theo-logy, 86
  question of, 41, 69–71, 78, 85
    outside metaphysics, 342
    transgressed by love of God,
      297
  representation, 80
  See also *ens;* onto-theo-logical
    constitution; onto-theo-logy   *357*